D1765086

Irish English

English has been spoken in Ireland for over 800 years, making Irish English the oldest variety of the language outside Britain. This book traces the development of English in Ireland, both north and south, from the late Middle Ages to the present day. Drawing on authentic data ranging from medieval literature to contemporary examples, it reveals how Irish English arose, how it has developed and how it continues to change. A variety of central issues are considered in detail, such as the nature of language contact and the shift from Irish to English, the sociolinguistically motivated changes in present-day Dublin English, the special features of Ulster Scots, and the transportation of Irish English to overseas locations as diverse as Canada, the United States and Australia. Presenting a comprehensive survey of Irish English at all levels of language, this book will be invaluable to historical linguists, sociolinguists, syntacticians and phonologists alike.

RAYMOND HICKEY is Professor of Linguistics in the Department of English, Essen University, Germany. His previous books include *Motives for Language Change* (Cambridge University Press, 2003) and *Legacies of Colonial English* (Cambridge University Press, 2004).

STUDIES IN ENGLISH LANGUAGE

General editor
Merja Kytö (Uppsala University)

Editorial Board
Bas Aarts (University College London), John Algeo (University of Georgia), Susan
Fitzmaurice (Northern Arizona University), Richard Hogg (University of Manchester),
Charles F. Meyer (University of Massachusetts)

The aim of this series is to provide a framework for original studies of English, both
present-day and past. All books are based securely on empirical research, and represent
theoretical and descriptive contributions to our knowledge of national and international
varieties of English, both written and spoken. The series covers a broad range of topics
and approaches, including syntax, phonology, grammar, vocabulary, discourse,
pragmatics and sociolinguistics, and is aimed at an international readership.

Already published in this series:

Christian Mair   *Infinitival Complement Clauses in English: a Study of Syntax in Discourse*

Charles F. Meyer   *Apposition on Contemporary English*

Jan Firbas   *Functional Sentence Perspective in Written and Spoken Communication*

Izchak M. Schlesinger   *Cognitive Space and Linguistic Case*

Katie Wales   *Personal Pronouns in Present-day English*

Laura Wright   *The Development of Standard English, 1300–1800: Theories, Descriptions,
    Conflicts*

Charles F. Meyer   *English Corpus Linguistics: Theory and Practice*

Stephen J. Nagle and Sara L. Sanders (eds.)   *English in the Southern United States*

Anne Curzan   *Gender Shifts in the History of English*

Kingsley Bolton   *Chinese Englishes*

Irma Taavitsainen and Päivi Pahta (eds.)   *Medical and Scientific Writing in Late
    Medieval English*

Elizabeth Gordon, Lyle Campbell, Jennifer Hay, Margaret Maclagan, Andrea Sudbury
    and Peter Trudgill   *New Zealand English: Its Origins and Evolution*

Raymond Hickey (ed.)   *Legacies of Colonial English*

Merja Kytö, Mats Rydén and Erik Smitterberg (eds)   *Nineteenth-Century English:
    Stability and Change*

John Algeo   *British or American English? A Handbook of Word and Grammar Patterns*

Christian Mair   *Twentieth-century English: History, Variation and Standardization*

Evelien Keizer   *The English Noun Phrase: the Nature of Linguistic Categorization*

Irish English

History and present-day forms

RAYMOND HICKEY
Essen University

CAMBRIDGE
UNIVERSITY PRESS

CAMBRIDGE UNIVERSITY PRESS
Cambridge, New York, Melbourne, Madrid, Cape Town,
Singapore, São Paulo, Delhi, Tokyo, Mexico City

Cambridge University Press
The Edinburgh Building, Cambridge CB2 8RU, UK

Published in the United States of America by Cambridge University Press, New York

www.cambridge.org
Information on this title: www.cambridge.org/9780521174152

First published 2007
First paperback edition 2011

A catalogue record for this publication is available from the British Library

ISBN 978-0-521-85299-9 Hardback
ISBN 978-0-521-17415-2 Paperback

Cambridge University Press has no responsibility for the persistence or
accuracy of URLs for external or third-party internet websites referred to in
this publication, and does not guarantee that any content on such websites is,
or will remain, accurate or appropriate.

Contents

Detailed contents

Maps

Tables

Preface

This book offers an overview of Irish English, both of its history and its present-day forms. English has existed in Ireland for over 800 years and so is the oldest form of the language outside the island of Britain. It has furthermore developed internally in many ways, for instance, through the early establishment of urban varieties, particularly in the cities of the east coast, most notably in Dublin. The language has also been under the continuing influence of Irish, which was the first language of the majority of the population until the beginning of the nineteenth century. This makes Irish English a language-shift variety and so offers a scenario for the development of English which it shares with countries as far apart as Scotland and South Africa.

The question of language contact is considered in detail in the present book (see section 4.2). Recently, there has been much linguistic discussion of the relative weight to be accorded to contact or to the retention of inherited features of British English and the treatment here is intended to reflect prevailing concerns and standpoints in variety studies.

The development of English in Ireland has seen several periods characterised by waves of settlement. Perhaps the most significant of these for present-day Irish English was the large-scale settlement of the north of the country from the west of Scotland and the Lowlands in the seventeenth century, yielding Ulster Scots, a unique variety of English which has increased in topicality in recent years. The interaction of Scots settlers with both Irish speakers and other settlers, chiefly from the north of England, has led to a complex linguistic landscape in Ulster which is given special treatment here (see chapter 3).

From a sociolinguistic point of view the study of Irish English is a rewarding enterprise. The two major cities of Ireland, Belfast and Dublin, are important because of the varieties of English found there (see section 5.5). Studies of these offer perspectives on sociolinguistic developments which are undoubtedly of interest to scholars in the field. The investigations of Belfast English have provided insights into the linguistic nature of social networks. These are available in the many studies by James and Lesley Milroy and are summarised here. For Dublin English the investigations carried out by the author in the past decade

(Hickey 2005) are presented to show what change has taken place recently and in what direction contemporary supraregional Irish English is moving.

The transportation of English from the British Isles to overseas locations began in the early seventeenth century. The precise nature of the transported varieties is of importance to the genesis of overseas forms of English (see the contributions in Raymond Hickey (ed.), *Legacies of Colonial English*, Cambridge University Press, 2004). For scholars working in this area it is essential to have first-hand descriptions of the source varieties. A primary aim of this book is to provide this kind of description, seeing as how Irish English has fed into varieties of English at such diverse locations as Canada, the United States, the Caribbean, Australia and New Zealand in the course of three centuries.

The field of Irish English is served well by many studies in article form and a few monographs (see Hickey 2002a for details). In recent years a more data-driven approach has become obvious (see Filppula 1999). The present study is to be understood in this light. For the historical sections (in sections 2.3 and 2.4) the author has used his *Corpus of Irish English* (available in Hickey 2003a). For the discussion of present-day varieties (see chapter 5) several sets of data were employed, above all *A Sound Atlas of Irish English* and *A Survey of Irish English Usage* (Hickey 2004a), as well as data collected specifically for the present book. These sources offer a new basis on which to both test traditional views and reach new conclusions about the exact nature of Irish English.

To conclude, I would like to thank the three anonymous reviewers for Cambridge University Press who went to considerable lengths to offer constructive criticism from which the book has benefitted appreciably. In addition, my thanks go to various colleagues who have helped me with their expertise in areas which interface with Irish English (acknowledgements are given at the appropriate points in the book). Lastly, I would like to thank the staff at Cambridge University Press, especially Helen Barton, the linguistics editor, for her encouragement and professionalism, as well as Kay McKechnie for her help and patience during the production process.

Raymond Hickey
October 2006

1   Introduction

1.1   The aim of the present book

The English language has existed in Ireland since the late Middle Ages and has experienced phases of prosperity and decline during some 800 years. Even a cursory glance reveals that English in Ireland involves many subtypes, traceable to the origin of those settlers who carried English to the country. This is most obvious in the linguistic and political division between the north and south. However, the linguistic diversity within Ireland is much more subtle than this basic split suggests. Ulster shows major differences in varieties, above all that between Ulster Scots and Ulster English (see chapter 3). The south of the country has a long-standing distinction between forms of English spoken on the east coast (the oldest in the country) and those found to the south and west, which show greater evidence of the shift from Irish to English which largely took place in the last 300 years or so.

For the development of English at locations outside Europe, varieties spoken in Ireland are of importance as many of England's former colonies were populated by deportees and settlers from Ireland who provided input to incipient forms of English at overseas locations. This lasted from the early seventeenth century in the Caribbean to the nineteenth century in the United States, Canada and the southern hemisphere. This diffusion of Irish English has been considered by many linguists as relevant to the genesis of overseas varieties (see Rickford 1986 as a typical example) and is given separate treatment in chapter 6.

The synchronic parts of this book attempt to give an overview of English in Ireland at the beginning of the twenty-first century. The various forms of the language are by no means static; all show changes which are linguistically interesting in their own right. In Ulster the vernacular norms, so extensively investigated by James and Lesley Milroy in the 1970s and early 1980s, continue to evolve in Belfast. On a more conscious level, the question of what will happen to Ulster Scots is increasing in political and social relevance. In the south of Ireland, major changes have taken place in Dublin English recently (see section 5.5.4) and are indicative of the rapid expansion in size and wealth of the capital of the Republic of Ireland (Hickey 2005).

1.1.1 SCOPE OF THIS STUDY

In writing the present book the author has tried to strike a balance between forms of English in the north and south of the island. The political division of Ireland has a linguistic equivalent and many of the subareas, e.g. phonology, are defined by this split within the country. Because of the formal partition of Ireland with the Government of Ireland Act of 1920, Northern Ireland and the Republic of Ireland have diverged politically and socially, rendering even more distinct the differences between varieties of English in each part of the island. The two groups are independent of each other although there is a transition zone between north and south, and although English in Co. Donegal – a part of the Republic – is of a broadly northern type. There is also no significant tendency for southern Irish English and northern Irish English to become more similar (Barry 1982: 127).

English in Northern Ireland – on various linguistic levels – has been described quite exhaustively (see the bibliographical references in Adams 1964a: 193ff.; Harris 1984a: 133f.; 1985: 352ff.; A. Henry 1997: 107f.; Hickey 2002a: 229–98; Kirk 1997b; Rahilly 1997: 130ff.). With southern Irish English the matter is slightly different. There have always been studies of English in the Republic of Ireland, usually in the form of lists of words and expressions (see the references in Aldus 1976, 1997 and Hickey 2002a), many of which are not of a scholarly nature (e.g. O'Farrell 1993 [1980]). Early linguistic investigations of southern Irish English are less numerous, though there are examples such as Hayden and Hartog (1909) and Hogan (1927). The situation improved quite considerably in the latter half of the twentieth century, initially in a traditional vein with studies by P. L. Henry and Alan Bliss and more recently with the work of Markku Filppula, Jeffrey Kallen and the present author. A significant feature of this work is that it does not claim to investigate southern Irish English, although this is what in effect it does. There is a sense in which southern Irish English is the default case and so studies of Ulster Scots (by Michael Montgomery, Philip Robinson and Rona Kingsmore), Ulster English, English in Belfast (by James and Lesley Milroy), Derry (by Kevin McCafferty) or Armagh (by Karen Corrigan) are labelled as such.

1.1.2 THE OLD AND THE NEW

In terms of time depth and speaker background, there are two types of language described in this book. On the one hand there is that of the elderly rural population and on the other that of the younger urban population.

The speech of older rural inhabitants is of interest because it reflects usage which is closer to forms of Irish English spoken when the Irish shifted from their previous native language to that which the vast majority of them speak today. Such forms are of interest to linguists concerned with language contact and language shift (see chapter 4) as well as with the transportation of English overseas in the past few centuries (see chapter 6). The role of language contact in the rise of early varieties of Irish English has always been a concern for scholars in the field. P. L. Henry (1957) is an early monograph on English in a region in which Irish used to be spoken and highlights the influence of the latter language on English in this area. Later work, such as that of Harris (1984a), sought to give the input varieties to Ireland their rightful place in the genesis of Irish English. A further facet is that of possible creolisation in the early period of development (Hickey 1997a). While this model does not apply in the same manner as, for example, with established creoles of the Caribbean, nonetheless the consideration of restructuring and universal features of young languages offers new interpretative possibilities for traits of Irish English.

The speech of young urban inhabitants is interesting in that it reflects recent sociolinguistic developments in southern Irish English. The changes which have taken place illustrate a scenario in which non-local speakers dissociate themselves from vernacular varieties spoken around them (see chapter 5) and thus represents a type of language change which is also of relevance to linguists working outside Ireland. In this context the focus is on English in Dublin. Despite the central position of the city, both in history and at present, English in the metropolis has never been investigated fully before. The section on Dublin English, derived from Hickey (2005), represents an attempt to redress this imbalance.

1.2   Questions of terminology

1.2.1 ANGLO-IRISH, HIBERNO-ENGLISH AND IRISH ENGLISH

Any treatment of English in Ireland must begin with a consideration of terminology as there are various labels to be found in the relevant literature, some linguistic, some general and some both. The terminological confusion associated with the linguistic treatment of Irish English stems from the fact that scholars have, as yet, not been able to agree on a single term for the English language in Ireland. The longest established, but also the most problematical, is the label *Anglo-Irish*. It is attested as a term for the English settlers of Ireland as early as 1626 (P. L. Henry 1958: 56) and this use as a term for a section of the Irish population has remained. Linguistically, it is unacceptable for at least two reasons. First of all, the term *Anglo-Irish* literally means an English variety of Irish, as the element 'Anglo-' functions as a modifier to the head 'Irish'. Secondly, this term has many inappropriate connotations in the present context. It is by no means a uniquely linguistic term; on the contrary, it is used in literature, in politics, etc. Given the loaded nature of the term it is scarcely appropriate as a linguistic label. These remarks hold for Ireland. Abroad, the term is seen as less problematical. Hence *Anglo-Irish* is used by Canadian authors, e.g. Kirwin (1993). Related to this usage is the label *Anglo-Celtic*, sometimes used in Australia (McArthur 1992: 66) but not in Ireland, to refer to the section of the community which is either of English or Irish descent.

The second term for Irish English is *Hiberno-English* in which the first element derives from Latin *Hibernia* 'Ireland'. T. F. O'Rahilly (1932: 234) is one of the first to have used it when referring to a specifically Irish form of English, though he himself did not think it necessary to comment on the term. Hutson (1947: 23) is another early author with whom the term is found. The label *Hiberno-English* gained currency in the 1970s as an alternative to *Anglo-Irish*; for instance, Bliss (1972a) uses *Anglo-Irish*, but for another article, published in the same year (Bliss 1972b), he switched to *Hiberno-English*.[1] Filppula is a scholar who has clung to the use of *Hiberno-English* (1993: 202 and also 2006) as has Dolan (2004). The label has also been used by non-Irish authors. Rickford (1986: 246, fn) maintains that *Hiberno-English* is a collective term for all varieties of English in Ireland and that *Irish English* is restricted to the language of those for whom Irish is their first language.

Some authors (like P. L. Henry 1977 or Todd 1992, for example) attempt to draw an artificial distinction between *Hiberno-English* and *Anglo-Irish*. Todd maintains that *Anglo-Irish* is a mainly middle-class variety spoken over most of Ireland and deriving from input forms of English in the seventeenth century and that *Hiberno-English* is a mainly working-class variety used by communities whose ancestral language was Irish (Gaelic). There are a number of difficulties here. The first is that there is no smooth dialect continuum across the whole of Ireland. Hence to hold the view that *Anglo-Irish* is spoken over most of the country is erroneous. Although certain features are shared by most varieties throughout Ireland (Hickey 1999b) there is no identifiable common variety between the north and south, irrespective of who is supposed to speak it.

Within present-day Ireland only some varieties can be clearly identified on the basis of source. This really only applies to Ulster Scots and to contact English in the small Gaeltachtaí, the remaining Irish-speaking districts (see section 4.2). It would be a distortion to speak now of 'Gaelic-based English' in a general sense. Nor can one identify anything like 'planter-based English' today. However, although the groups who supplied input to Ireland in the early modern period are difficult to make out, there are features from the earliest forms of English which were taken to Ireland and which can be discerned in vernacular varieties on the east coast.

The distinction between *Hiberno-English* and *Anglo-Irish*, drawn by P. L. Henry (1977), is diametrically opposed to that made by Todd. He explains that *Anglo-Irish* is a label used by the English for the people of Ireland and by extension for their literature and language and pleads for a use of the term to refer to that kind of English which has been most heavily influenced by Irish.

---

[1] This term has also been used for English in the north: 'Northern Hiberno-English' is a label used by Corrigan (1993a).

Leaving aside such attempts to establish a distinction between the two terms, one can evaluate their usefulness for linguistic studies. The first, *Anglo-Irish*, is unsuitable because of its non-linguistic connotations and its imprecise reference. In the opinion of the author, the second, *Hiberno-English*, suffers from two drawbacks. On the one hand, it is too technical: the use of the term demands that it be explained in studies intended for a general readership outside Ireland. On the other hand, the use of the term within Ireland may imply a somewhat popular, if not sentimental, attitude towards English in Ireland which is often not regarded as a topic worthy of academic research.

In the present study, the simpler, more neutral label *Irish English* is used. There is no substantial objection to the term.[2] It refers to varieties of English in Ireland (internal distinctions can be made additionally) and is parallel to labels like *Canadian English* or *Australian English*. Of recent date, many authors, such as Kallen (1997) and the present author, favour the term as do some non-Irish scholars such as Thomason and Kaufman (1988).

Given that all present-day speakers of Irish also speak English and are in contact with English speakers from outside their immediate community, there exist contact varieties spoken by these people. Sometimes labels are used to refer to these forms in a certain region, e.g. *Contact Ulster English* denoting English spoken within or adjacent to Irish-speaking areas in Co. Donegal and which is assumed to have been influenced by Irish in its development. Such labels can be used to differentiate between specific forms of English within Ireland.

A much wider term which has found favour with many scholars working on language contact and shift with English in the Celtic regions is *Celtic Englishes*. The popularity of this label as a cover term has been boosted by the significant series of volumes, entitled *Celtic Englishes I–IV*, edited by Hildegard Tristram as proceedings of a number of conferences on this topic held in Potsdam between 1995 and 2004.

1.2.2 NORTHERN IRISH ENGLISH

In studies on northern Irish English the question of labels is not any less topical. Some are straightforward as there are not usually any alternatives. For instance, *Ulster Scots* refers to Scots as brought to Ulster primarily during the plantations of the first half of the seventeenth century (Adams 1964b; Montgomery 1997). *Ulster Scotch* is not a common means of labelling the English of Scottish descendants, just as *Scotch* in Scotland is no longer used in a linguistic sense. The label *Scotch-Irish* – or *Scots Irish* – is sometimes found in politics to refer to the Scottish-derived population of Northern Ireland and has been used by Robert Gregg in various articles (see references section). The term is also found in the

---

[2] The objection to 'Irish English' which Harris (1985: 12) raises, namely that it sometimes refers to the English of native speakers of Irish, is based on a potential use of the term which, however, is not encountered in the literature.

United States to refer to people descending from the eighteenth century emigrants from Ulster to the east of North America.

The artificial label *Ullans*[3] is now used by a section of the Protestant population in Northern Ireland (Görlach 2000) to refer to Ulster Scots, especially in written form. Its status is at the centre of much political and linguistic debate (see section 3.3.2).

Ulster English designates English brought to Ulster from England, particularly from the north-west Midlands of England (Adams 1958: 61ff.) and is separate from the Scots element in the province. Because Ulster Scots is found in the peripheral parts of counties of Ulster (north Down, Antrim, Derry and to a lesser extent in Donegal) the label *mid Ulster English* (Harris 1984b) is sometimes used to refer to general forms of English in Northern Ireland which are not derived from Scots. *Ulster Anglo-Irish* is also found as a term for the language of English descendants (J. Milroy 1981: 22). James Milroy briefly suggested the use of *Anglo-English* (1981: xiii) 'English as used in England, as distinct from Irish English (Hiberno-English), Scots English, etc.'. This usage is echoed by Harris in his treatment of English in the north of Ireland (Harris 1984b: 115) but has not established itself.

The label *Urban Vernacular* refers to a group of varieties spoken chiefly by inhabitants of large urban centres on a lower social level, chiefly Belfast (as examined by James and Lesley Milroy in many publications). The urban vernacular of Belfast is distinctive because it reflects a merger of traditional and essentially rural varieties, as a result of migration into Belfast for employment in industry during the nineteenth century, but which is now spreading to other urban centres within Northern Ireland.

Of the three remaining areas in Ireland where Irish is still spoken (see map A6.3 in appendix 6) Ulster is the most northerly: the variety spoken there is known as *Ulster Irish*. In terms of geographical distribution this Irish-speaking region does not extend outside Co. Donegal,[4] hence the alternative designation *Donegal Irish*. In some instances *Ulster Irish* is taken to have a historical reference, in which case it would include Irish spoken in north Antrim, Rathlin Island, central Tyrone and south Armagh, areas where the language died out early in the twentieth century.[5] Without this historical dimension, Ulster Irish can still be taken to include second-language varieties of Irish spoken in urban centres like Belfast and Derry by members of the nationalist community for reasons of cultural identification.

---

[3] The name was formed as a parallel to the term *Lallans* for Lowland Scots.

[4] The occasional reference to a 'West Belfast Gaeltacht' is more political than linguistic and reflects the attempts of nationalist sections of the population to establish an Irish-speaking base in the city.

[5] A few studies have been concerned with the influence of Irish on English within Northern Ireland. As the subtitle of Todd (1971) suggests – *Tyrone English: the Influence of Gaelic on Tyrone English* – the author is concerned with tracing those words which she regards as stemming from Irish. After discussing about twenty instances in some detail, she concludes the article by mentioning syntactic features (verb forms and the supposed over-use of *would*) and morphology (distinctions among second-person personal pronouns, singular and plural).

1.2.3 NON-LINGUISTIC TERMS

Apart from the more or less linguistic terms discussed above there are a number of popular labels for Irish English. First and foremost of these is *brogue*. The term was already used in the seventeenth century and became quite established in the eighteenth century (used by Swift, for instance, in his 'On barbarous denominations in Ireland'). The first mention of the term *brogue* would appear to be by John Skelton (?1460–1529) in *Speke, Parrot*, in which a parrot imitates various languages and dialects, including that of Ireland. The text probably dates from 1525 (Hogan 1927: 55f.). The use of *brogue* as a reference to a non-standard accent became common in later centuries among British commentators on the Irish use of English, as the following remarks by B. H. Smart in the early nineteenth century show.

> *Hints for softening a Hibernian Brogue*
> The first point our Western friend must attend to for this purpose is, to avoid hurling out his words with a superfluous quantity of breath. It is not 'broadher' and 'loudher' that he must say, but the 'd' and every other consonant in the language must be neatly delivered by the tongue, with as little riot, cluttering, or breathing as possible. (Smart 1836: xli)

The contemporary use of the label *brogue* is rather vague. It implies a low-status accent of English in Ireland, typically a rural dialect. The term is not used by the Irish to refer to their general form of English because of its negative connotations. *Brogue* is found in non-Irish contexts, for instance, with reference to traditional, non-urban dialects in coastal North Carolina (see remarks on Ocracoke Brogue in Wolfram and Schilling-Estes 1997).

The common assumption is that *brogue* stems from Irish *bróg* 'shoe' (this meaning is also found in early modern English, and was known to Shakespeare). Bergin (1943) rightly points out that the word cannot have been originally Irish as the final /-g/ would have been lenited to /-ɣ/ had it been inherited from Old Irish. Old Norse *brók* meaning 'trousers' (a Germanic word related to English *breeches*) may be the source. If this is so, the meaning of the Irish loan *bróg* must have been wider with a later semantic narrowing to an item of footwear. Another investigation, by coincidence from the same year, is Murphy (1943), who comes to the conclusion that the use of *brogue* meaning 'Irish accent' is a purely English development. This is because the nearest equivalent is *barróg* 'grip', which can be used with 'tongue' with the approximate meaning 'to have a lump in one's throat' (Irish *barróg teangan* 'grip tongue-GEN'). In a more positive sense the word *lilt* is occasionally found to refer to an Irish accent, typically by the non-Irish favourably disposed to it.

Blarney is a general term for eloquence which is both flattering and deceptive and which is often associated with the Irish. The origin of the term is well known. In 1602 Queen Elizabeth I demanded of one Cormac McCarthy that he surrender Blarney Castle not far from the city of Cork. McCarthy procrastinated, repeatedly promising to do so but not fulfilling his commitment, which led Elizabeth to exclaim in exasperation 'This is all Blarney – he never does what he says, he never does what he promises', establishing the phrase in English.[6]

The figure of the stage Irishman has a long pedigree in English literature. It goes back at least to the end of the sixteenth century, for example to the anonymous play *The Life and Death of Captain Stukeley* (1596/1605), which contains unflattering portrayals of Irish characters. Throughout the following century a tradition arose of using Irish characters as stock figures for parody and ridicule. In essence, this was a typically colonial attitude to the colonised who lacked power and prestige. The image stuck and the figure survived well into the twentieth century, at least to George Bernard Shaw.

In linguistic terms there are no established features which are diagnostic of *Stage Irish*. Rather the salient features of (largely rural) Irish English are emphasised: the fortition of /θ, ð/ to alveolar stops, the use of monophthongs for /eɪ/ and /əʊ/, a mid vowel in the MEAT lexical set and perhaps epenthesis in words like *arm* ['aːɹəm] and *form* ['foːɹəm]. The characteristics depend largely on traditions of representing Irish pronunciations. Hence the spelling *Oirish* is often used by fictional authors for stage Irish characters. This can be taken to indicate [əɪrɪʃ] which is actually the pronunciation typical of local Dublin English and the east coast and not of rural dialects in the west which would tend to have [aɪ] for /ai/.

In connection with translations into Irish English, mention should be made of work done in translation studies. This is of relevance to research into Irish English as it is directly concerned with the features and structures of this form of English which can be employed to achieve equivalents to local flavouring and ambience in the work of source authors. The potential of Irish English for this purpose was recognised in the nineteenth century by creative writers of the Irish Literary Revival and used in many translations, e.g. by Douglas Hyde and Lady Gregory, the latter translating Molière into 'Kiltartanese', as her form of western rural Irish English was somewhat belittlingly called. But for her it was an 'act of cultural self-confidence' which implied that 'Hiberno-English is a fit vehicle for one of the greatest playwrights of the European literary tradition' (Cronin 1996: 140). The issues around translation are still topical in Ireland today; see Cronin (2006) for an analysis of poetry translation and many of the contributions in Cronin and Ó Cuilleanáin (2003).

1.2.4 IRELAND AND BRITAIN

Another area of sensitive terminology is that of geographical references in an Irish/English context. In geographical terms, the British Isles refer to the island

---

[6] The castle of Blarney still stands and a stone on its battlement is reputed to impart the ability to beguile others with *blarney* if kissed. Rickford (1986: 282) notes that there is a parallel between Irish *blarney* – the use of verbal eloquence to outsmart a more powerful opponent – and a speech event known as *coppin' a plea* 'bargaining' though as he rightly points out this may very well be a universal strategy for coping with the more powerful who surround one.

of Britain (comprising England, Wales and Scotland) and that of Ireland. The label *British Isles* is not always welcome in the Republic of Ireland or in nationalist quarters of Northern Ireland. Instead the vague label *these islands* is common to refer to both Britain and Ireland. Analogously, the label *this island* refers to the entire island of Ireland.

Again from a political standpoint, the label *north of Ireland* can be found rather than Northern Ireland, the name given to that part of Ireland which remained within the United Kingdom under the provisions of the Government of Ireland Act of 1920. It consists of six of the nine counties in the province of Ulster. Despite the fact that Northern Ireland only contains two-thirds of these counties, in the south the term *Ulster* is often used synonymously with the state. Again the vague labels *north* and *south* refer to Northern Ireland and the Republic of Ireland respectively. Two more precise terms are also found currently in Ireland.

The six counties is a reference to the state of Northern Ireland without actually using its name (the counties in question are Antrim, Down, Tyrone, Derry, Armagh and Fermanagh). Correspondingly, *the twenty-six counties* is an unofficial reference to the Republic of Ireland deriving from the number of counties it embraces. Both of these terms have, however, fallen out of official use, though their Irish translations are still used in the Donegal Gaeltacht.

According to the 1937 Constitution of Ireland, Irish is the first language of the country, with English – in theory – enjoying a supplementary function. As might be expected, the official designation for Ireland is the Irish form of the country's name *Éire* (this replaced the label *Irish Free State* (Irish: *Saorstát na hÉireann*) which had been used from 1922 to 1937). The label *Republic of Ireland* (Irish: *Poblacht na hÉireann*) is in use since 1949 when the country was declared a republic.

1.2.5 EXTERNAL REFERENCES

Within Ireland there are various means of referring to Britain and its inhabitants. The most neutral term is *England* and the *English*. To refer to the entire island and the people as *Britain* and the *British* can often carry negative connotations of a political establishment unsympathetic to Ireland. In abbreviated form, the term *Brit* is definitely pejorative when used by the Irish. The label *West Brit* is scarcely less negative and is applied to those Irish, frequently Protestant urbanites, who orient themselves towards middle-class Britain and identify themselves less with distinctively Irish culture.

1.2.6 THE TERM *IRISH*

The name of the Celtic language, brought to Ireland in the first centuries BC and still spoken in pockets on the north-western, western and south-western seaboard, is *Irish*. The term *Gaelic* /ˈgeːlɪk/ is not frequent in Ireland. The designation *Scottish Gaelic* is used for the Celtic language spoken on parts of the west coast of Scotland (historically derived from northern forms of Irish). The

Scots themselves refer to their variety of Gaelic by their pronunciation of the word, i.e. /galɪk/, written *Gaidhlig* in Scottish Gaelic and anglicised as *Gallick*. The word for the language is feminine in Irish (and Scottish Gaelic) so that the initial sound changes to a velar fricative on using the article before it: *An Ghaeilge* /ən ɣeːlʲgʲə/ 'the Irish language'.

The term *Erse*, an earlier Scots form of *Irish*, is all but unknown in the Republic of Ireland. It was used in previous centuries as a term for both Irish and Scottish Gaelic but fell into disuse. The term *Scoti* was used at least until the late Middle English period as a label covering both the Irish and Scots and not just in English; cf. the *Schottenklöster* 'Scottish monasteries' founded by Irish monks in southern Germany (Fowkes 1997).

In a wider context one should note that *Celtic* is pronounced [kɛltɪk], and not [sɛltɪk]. The spelling *Keltic* is quite unusual in English and definitely not used by Irish scholars. In literature of a philological nature, Irish and Scottish Gaelic are referred to collectively as *Q-Celtic*; this includes the extinct variety of the Isle of Man, Manx Gaelic, which died out in the twentieth century. The term *Q-Celtic* derives from the fact that Indo-European *k^w remained unchanged in this section of Insular Celtic, having shifted to *p* in Welsh, Cornish and Breton, hence the designation *P-Celtic* for the latter three; cf. Irish *ceann*, Welsh *pen*, both meaning 'head'.

The label *Irish* can equally refer to the native people of Ireland. Throughout history various qualifiers have been added to *Irish*. For instance, the phrase *the wild Irish* was at first derogatory, referring to a supposedly barbarous people; later it became complimentary with the implication of natural, untamed, unspoiled by civilisation. This sense is reflected in the novel *The Wild Irish Girl* (1806) by Lady Morgan. This phrase is already recorded from the mid sixteenth century for those who lived 'beyond the Pale': Andrew Boorde's *The Breviary of Healthe* (c. 1547, published 1552) contains the following reference: 'Irland is deuyded in ii. partes, one is the Engly[sh] pale, & the other, the wyld Irish' (Crowley 2000: 24). The term was later extended to those descendants of the original English settlers who had adopted Irish habits, spoke Irish and of course were still Roman Catholics and hence not unduly loyal to post-Reformation England (Palmer 2000: 74–107). Another early reference is found in Philemon Holland's *Camden's Britain* (1610): 'They that refuse to be under lawes are termed the Irishry, and commonly the Wilde Irish.'

The adjective *wild* has also been used in Irish history to refer to Irish adventurers, particularly in the phrase *Wild Geese*, used as a label for the Irish mercenaries and soldiers of fortune in the seventeenth and eighteenth centuries.

Some older terms have become more or less obsolete and are only properly recorded in history. An instance is *Teigue* or *Tague*, derived from the Irish first name *Tadhg* /taɪg/, which was used as a generic reference for a Catholic Irishman for centuries and is found occasionally in the north of the country.

Another case is *Old English* which was employed as a label for English settlers in pre-Reformation Ireland (Byrne 2004: 211f.). As they were Catholic in religion and remained so, their implicit allegiance to the Gaelic Irish was reinforced after the adoption of Protestantism as the state religion of England by Henry VIII.

The opposite label, *New English*, referred to those largely Anglican settlers (Church of England Protestants) who came during the plantations in the seventeenth century. They distinguished themselves from both the native Catholics (Irish and Old English) and the Presbyterian dissenters in Ulster.

Internally in Ireland derogative terms may be found which refer to sections of the population. Often the group being derided can be identified along the rural–urban axis. For instance, the term *Jackeen* is used unflatteringly of a Dubliner, while *culchie* (either derived from 'agriculture' or from the town of Kiltimagh in Co. Mayo, Dolan 2004: 70) is a label for someone lacking in urban experience and sophistication.

1.3   The identity of Irish English

Recognising an accent is easier than describing one. There are salient traits in varieties which one can point to, but the acoustic impression of a variety is composed of many features, only some of which are sufficiently discrete for them to be described satisfactorily. Many aspects have to do with the general setting for a variety. For instance, there is a degree of indistinctiveness about southern Irish English, probably due to the amount of elision and assimilation found in the variety. In addition, the lenition of alveolar stops to fricatives adds to the impression of slurred speech which is often conveyed. In this section attention will be paid to those features which are amenable to phonetic description as these are sufficient to delimit this variety from others.

For this characterisation only features of pronunciation are discussed (Hickey 1996b). Syntactic features do not occur as frequently as phonological ones and hence syntactic variation is more likely to be conditioned by linguistic factors which depend on situation and style rather than social factors. Because syntactic structures are repeated less often than phonological ones they are less available for social assessment. On the other hand, phonological features have a strong identification function, given their frequent occurrence, and offer clear clues as to the linguistic affiliation of the speaker. Typical grammatical features of Irish English are described in chapter 4.

Plosivisation of dental fricatives. A fricative realisation of the initial sounds in the THIN and THIS lexical sets is very much an exception in southern Irish English. Instead the sounds are manifested as dental stops, i.e. [t̪] and [d̪] respectively. This applies to all but a few varieties of the south which may have alveolar stops at the beginning of such words as *thin* and *this*.

This alveolar realisation is quite stigmatised and rural speakers are frequently ridiculed by having their speech imitated using alveolar rather than dental stops, e.g. [tɪŋk] and [dɪs] for [t̪ɪŋk] and [d̪ɪs]. The ability of speakers to imitate this shows that they are aware of the distinction between a dental and an alveolar place of articulation.

The dental stop realisation of /θ/ and /ð/ may well be a contact phenomenon going back to Irish (Bliss 1972a, 1976, 1977a) where the two coronal plosives are realised dentally, i.e. /t/ and /d/ are phonetically [t̪] and [d̪] as in *tá* [t̪ɑː] 'is' and *dún* [d̪uːn] 'castle', for example.

The obvious plosivisation of English dental fricatives leads to the frequently found but erroneous statement that Irish English is characterised by dentalisation (Todd 1992: 530). This observation shows underdifferentiation on the part of external observers. There is a clearly audible difference between [t̪] and [t] for speakers of Irish English, i.e. pairs like *thank* and *tank*, *thinker* and *tinker* are not homophones for the majority of the Irish.

It goes without saying that because (southern) Irish English does not have fricatives in the THIN and THIS lexical sets, then the TH-fronting of /θ/ to /f/ and /ð/ to /v/, seen in *three* [friː] and *brother* [brʌvə], for example (Kerswill 2003: 321–38), and which is found increasingly in urban British English, is not found in Ireland.

Lenition of /t/. The normal alveolar stops of English have a further characteristic which is particularly Irish. In weak positions they are reduced to fricatives. The sound thus produced is an apico-alveolar fricative which can, following a convention introduced in Hickey (1984a), be transcribed by placing a caret below the relevant stop symbol, giving, for instance, [t̬] as in *put* [put̬]. The fricativisation of alveolar stops does not apply to dental stops in the THIN and THIS lexical sets so that the contrast of word final, pre-pausal (and intervocalic) /θ/ versus /t/ in standard English is realised in Irish English as [t̪] # [t̬] as in *both* [boːt̪] versus *boat* [boːt̬].

The apico-alveolar fricative is formed by using the tip of the tongue as active articulator and is thus clearly distinguished from the fricative /s/ (or /z/) which has the tongue blade as active articulator; consider the minimal pair: *kiss* [kɪs] versus *kit* [kɪt̬].

The [t̬] sound occurs in intervocalic position or between a vowel and pause, i.e. word finally. These are weak positions as the consonant is not flanked by a further consonant on either side. Hence a preceding or following consonant blocks this lenition, *fact* [fækt], *hitlist* [hɪtlɪst], where the [t] is both released and non-released respectively and in both cases is still a stop.

The situation in Northern Ireland is somewhat different. In Ulster Scots areas along the north coast, the fricative [t̬] is not found. Kingsmore in her detailed treatment of Coleraine speech does not even mention it as a possibility (Kingsmore 1995: 138–85). In general Ulster English, an unreleased stop is found where the fricative would occur in the south, e.g. *put* [put˺] as opposed to [put̬] in the south.

t-lenition would appear to be confined to southern Irish English and not to be found in either mainland English (with the exception of local Liverpool speech) or in overseas varieties of English with the exception of Irish-derived Newfoundland English (Kirwin 1993: 74; Clarke 1986: 68); see chapter 6.

Another allophone of /t/ is the intervocalic flap as in *city* ['sɪɾi] which is becoming increasingly common in this position in Dublin English and with young supraregional speakers (Hickey 2005: 77f.). This is established usage in Northern Ireland. The new realisation in the south is probably unrelated to that in the north.

Unique delimiting characteristics for a variety are difficult to find individually, but the combination of plosivisation in the THIN and THIS lexical sets and *t*-lenition is certainly strongly indicative of southern Irish English.

Realisation of <wh>. A conservative feature of Irish English is the use of a voiceless approximant [ʍ] in words spelt with *wh* (Hickey 1984b). This feature, however, has little identification value as it is also found among other varieties of English, e.g. in Scottish English or forms of American English, and was still found in older varieties of RP according to phoneticians active early in the twentieth century, such as Daniel Jones. In addition, in more recent varieties of English based on non-local Dublin usage, the voiced approximant [w] is increasingly common, rendering *which* and *witch* homophones.

Realisation of /l/. A less obvious characteristic of conservative Irish English is the lack of a velarised /l/ [ɫ] in syllable-final position. Here Irish English has the same alveolar allophone as in syllable-initial position. A possible exception to this is found with truly bilingual speakers (with Irish and English) who may have a velarised [ɫ] as a transfer phenomenon from Irish, e.g. in *like* [ɫaɪk] as /l/ before the diphthong /ai/ is generally velar in Irish (Hickey 1986a).

Although the use of clear /l/ [l] has long been a feature of Irish English, recent changes in Dublin English (Hickey 1999a, 2005) have led to velarised [ɫ] occurring in non-local Dublin speech. This pronunciation spread very rapidly during the 1990s so that velarisation is typical of younger non-local speakers throughout the Republic of Ireland and is presently one of the chief distinguishing features between younger and older speakers.

In Northern Ireland velarised [ɫ] shows a different distribution from the south. It is frequently found in working-class urban vernaculars so that the clear [l] has enjoyed favour with the middle classes, despite its absence word-finally in RP, as Rona Kingsmore has documented in detail in her study of English in Coleraine (Kingsmore 1995: 111–37).

Phonological processes. Apart from the realisation of individual segments, there are a number of phonological processes which could be used to identify speakers of Irish English.

1. EPENTHESIS. This consists of the insertion of an unstressed centralised vowel in so-called heavy syllable-final clusters, i.e. those which consist of two sonorants. Examples of such clusters are /lm/ and /rm/. A condition on epenthesis, which may apply, is that the sonorants in question not be homorganic. Thus one has pronunciations like ['fɪlɪm], ['ærəm] and possibly ['aɪɹən] if the prohibition on epenthesis in homorganic clusters does not apply.

The epenthesis in clusters where /l/ is the first element is found in the south and the north of Ireland and is clearly attested in the recordings for both parts of the country contained in Hickey (2004a). Where /r/ is the first element, the epenthesis is not usually present in supraregional varieties of the south or north, but is to be found in rural forms of southern Irish English.

2. METATHESIS. This involves switching around the linear sequence of two sounds. Historically, the motivation for this may have been the avoidance of heavy clusters, as with epenthesis. Examples of commonly metathesised forms are *pattern* ['pætɹən], *modern* ['mɒdɹən], *lantern* ['læntɹən]. The syllables of metathesised segments are never stressed (but may have been historically; see section 5.1.5) and contain short vowels, preferably in combination with /r/ as in *secretary* ['sɛkərtri].

The appearance of metathesis in Irish English is something which can in the main be traced back to Irish where it is abundantly attested both in the history of the language and today. The metathesis of /sk/ clusters, as in *ask* [aːks], which is attested in varieties outside Ireland such as African American English, was previously present in Irish English but has since disappeared (no instances were recorded for *A Sound Atlas of Irish English*, though it was commented on by some older speakers in the south who recollected hearing it in their youth).

New cases of metathesis in contemporary Irish English do not seem to occur and many non-local speakers tend to limit the use of such forms, e.g. having ['mɒdəɹn] for *modern*.

Preference for pronunciation variants. An example of this is the preferred use of a pattern such as initial stress in *harass* and *harassment* as opposed to [hə'ræs] and [hə'ræsmənt]. There are also variants which can be attributed to a general preference in Irish English. For example /s/ is sometimes preferred to /ʃ/ in those words where this variation is tolerated, e.g. *appreciate*. Where voiced and voiceless sibilants can vary there is a preference for voiceless variants. This results in pronunciations like *version* ['vəːɹʃən] and *parse* [paːɹs], although proper names tend to be lexicalised so that one has *Asia* ['eːʒə] for ['eɪʃə].

Vowel quality in Irish English. An aspect of Irish English which is intuitively recognised by the non-Irish is vowel quality. Two general statements can be made about Irish English vowels. Where expected, they are rhotic, i.e. /r/ is pronounced where it occurs in writing, e.g. in words like *bird, where, torn*. Irish vowels have a more monophthongal quality than those of RP-like varieties of British English.

In traditional varieties, rhotic vowels show a velarised /r/, i.e. [ɹˠ]. However, because of the changes emanating from non-local Dublin English in the 1990s, the velarisation of /r/ has been largely replaced by retroflexion among younger speakers. Furthermore, the vowel in the GOAT lexical set for non-local southern speakers now has a diphthong like [əʊ] (Hickey 2005: 88–92), heard most clearly with young female speakers.

1.3.1 ENGLISH IN NORTHERN IRELAND

The prosody of northern Irish English is quite distinctive. This manifests itself most clearly in the fall in pitch on stressed syllables (Jarman and Cruttenden 1976), the highlighting of which is realised in the south, as in most varieties

Table 1.1. *Prominent features of northern Irish accents of English*

1. fronting of /u/ to [ʉ]
2. retroflexion of /r/
3. lowering of short front vowels
4. lack of distinctive length differences between vowels (Ulster Scots)
5. different intonational patterns from south

of English, by a slight lengthening of the stressed syllable. This fall may have been responsible for the lowering of short high front vowels as in: *He was hi*[ɛ]*t by a car*. General features, typical of northern speech, are shown in table 1.1.

Retroflexion of /r/. Northern Irish English is clearly rhotic and speakers who attempt to approach something like RP retain rhoticity longest. Syllable-final /r/ is different in both parts of the country, so that one can tell where speakers come from by their pronunciation of a word like *north*. While in the south /r/ is traditionally velarised in post-vocalic position, it is retroflex in the north, so that one has [nɒːɹˠt̪] in the south as opposed to [nɔːɻθ]. As with velarised [ɫ] mentioned above, a retroflex [ɻ] has become very common in the south in recent years (Hickey 2005: 45f.) as a result of the spread of new Dublin English; see section 5.5.4.

Vowel length. A feature shared with varieties of Scottish English is the lack of contrastive vowel length. This naturally applies in particular to Ulster Scots. Although the latter is largely a rural form of English, the lack of distinctive vowel length can be found in urban varieties and those outside the core Ulster Scots areas. The distinction between vowels is reduced to one of quality so that a pair of words like *bid* and *bead* are distinguished by a more central versus a more peripheral vowel articulation, if at all. In those cases where quality differences are not available homophony often arises, as in *cot* and *caught*, both [kɔt].

The vowel shortening only applies to high and mid vowels. All short low vowels are lengthened in accordance with the phonetically open nature of such segments. This results in pronunciations like [baːn] for *ban*, [baːg] for *bag* with a long central low vowel (vowel height and frontness can vary here as well, e.g. [bɑːn] and [bɛːg] are possible pronunciations).

Fronting of /u/. A further feature of northern Irish English which it shares with Scotland[7] is the fronting of /u/ to a mid high vowel [ʉ]. In the case of /uː/ one often has shortening leading to homophones like *fool* and *full*, both [fʉl].

---

[7] The high mid [ʉ] is also found in both Ulster Irish (now only attested on the coast of Donegal) and in Scottish Gaelic. It is this fact which reinforces the areal argument (Hickey 1999b), especially when one considers that Scottish Gaelic is an offshoot of Ulster Irish dating back to before the Middle Ages.

There is a transition area between the north and south of Ireland (cf. the recordings for this region in Hickey 2004a). Some features, like non-distinctive vowel length, are confined to Ulster, whereas others, such as fronted [ʉ], reach quite far down into the south (Hickey 2004a: 74f.). The transition area stretches approximately from Co. Sligo in the north-west to Co. Louth in north Leinster.

The status of southern accents in the north deserves mention here. For many Catholics, particularly in Derry, south Armagh and city areas like west Belfast, southern accents are quite acceptable. However, the nationalist community in Northern Ireland does not appear to have adopted features of southern speech.

In both the north and south of Ireland, RP-like accents are not regarded as worthy of emulation. They are associated with people with an English orientation and are generally interpreted as a sign of snobbishness. In fact there is a common ridiculing of RP-like accents as *grand* with a retracted /ɑː/ vowel as opposed to the normal centralised /aː/ of Irish English [graːnd] (Hickey 1986a).

Features can be listed which could serve as negative diagnostics of Irish English, that is features which are common in many varieties of British English but not in Irish English. The following is a list of the most prominent of these.

1. *Glottalisation of /t/*. The realisation of /t/ as a glottal stop [ʔ] is a long-recognised feature of popular London speech but it is also found widely in other parts of Britain (including Scotland) as a realisation of intervocalic and/or word-final /t/. This does not hold for supraregional varieties of Irish English, either in the north or south. The south has a fricative [t̞] in these positions while the north frequently has a flap, cf. *butter* [bʌt̞əɹ] versus [bʌɾəɻ]. As a manifestation of lenition, glottalisation occurs in local Dublin English, e.g. *butter* [bʊʔɐ], *right* [ɹəɪʔ] (see section 5.5.4). This fact may explain its absence in non-local Dublin English, despite the change in this variety in recent years. Glottalisation does not occur in southern rural forms of English either. Nor is it found in Irish, so that transfer from the substrate, either historically or in the remaining Irish-speaking areas, does not represent a source.

    In the north, glottalisation is found, especially in Ulster Scots areas, as documented by Kingsmore in her detailed study (1995: 144–85). In her investigation she distinguishes between different forms of glottalisation, such as pre-glottalised stops and glottal stops in intervocalic position. She also notes the perceptual difficulty of distinguishing between glottal stops and unreleased voiceless stops (1995: 153). In her study she found that, intervocalically, a glottal stop was the preferred vernacular realisation of /t/, especially among female speakers (1995: 184).

2. *H-dropping.* This is regarded as endemic in urban British English nowadays. It is lacking in Irish English both in the north and the south, the two areas maintaining all instances of historical /h/. Consequently, hypercorrection,[8] as in *obviously* [hɒbviəsli], is not found in Irish English.

   The position of *h* in Irish English is very stable, particularly as it is present medially in many anglicised Irish words such as *Haughey* ['hɒːhi] (surname), *Drogheda* ['drɒhədə] (town name). Furthermore, /h/ is linked structurally with [ʍ] which can be analysed phonologically as /h/ + /w/ (see section 5.4.2).

3. *Linking and intrusive /r/.* These two features are typical of non-rhotic varieties of English. The first is a sandhi phenomenon where a final /r/ is treated as intervocalic if followed by a vowel-initial word, as in *far* [-r-] *away*. Intrusive /r/ is unexpected in non-rhotic English as it contradicts just this quality. It is often quasi-lexicalised, as in words like *idea* and *China*. It is not to be found in Irish English, northern or southern, where the only instances of /r/ are those which are historically justified.

4. *Individual pronunciation differences.* These are usually pronunciations which arose in English at some date after the anglicisation of Ireland, not infrequently as spelling pronunciations, and which did not manifest themselves in Irish English, for instance, *often*/ɒftn̩/ (general Irish English:/ɒfn̩/, though the pronunciation with /t/ is becoming more common) and *again* /ə'geɪn/ (Irish English: /ə'gɛn/).

5. *Morphological and lexical features.* There are further negative diagnostics from other linguistic levels. The form *ain't* is not Irish, nor is *do* with *use* in the past, e.g. *He didn't use to live in London* would be *He usen't to live in London.* There are of course corresponding positive diagnostics on the morphological level, such as the use of epistemic *must* in the negative (*He mustn't be Scottish*), though these are not exclusively Irish (this feature also occurs in Australian English; see section 6.5). The auxiliary *shall* is virtually never found: *will* is the emphatic form, otherwise the contracted form *'ll* is usual.

On the lexical level, various markers of British usage are absent or very rare in Irish English, e.g. *ta* for *thanks*, *mate* for *friend* or the use of *folk* in the sense of 'people'. Phrases may also be regarded by the Irish as significantly English and hence avoided, for instance, the augmentative *ever so (nice)*.

1.3.4 MISCONCEPTIONS ABOUT IRISH ENGLISH

Knowledge of Irish English, even among linguist colleagues, can often be imprecise, not least because of a lack of sources with accurate descriptions.

---

[8] The distribution of /u/ and /ʌ / does not present difficulties for the Irish (as it often does for speakers of northern English) because /ʌ/ is present in all those instances in which it occurs in standard English (except in local Dublin English).

Misconceptions have a tendency to perpetuate themselves and are very rarely rectified. Some of these concern pronunciation, for instance the notion that alveolar plosives are dentalised in Irish English. Like many misconceptions, it consists of a half-truth (see description above). Others are indeed true, but only for a sub-variety of Irish English. For instance, the notion that short high /ʊ/ is typical of Irish English is inaccurate: this realisation is only found in vernacular Dublin English, most probably deriving from English before 1600, and is definitely not found in the supraregional variety of the south today.

On the levels of morphology and syntax there are also misconceptions about Irish English. For instance, the use of *youse* as a second-person-plural pronoun is often taken as indicative of Irish English. However, this is typical of vernacular varieties, for instance on the east coast, but also the north. The normal form for the second-person-plural pronoun in the supraregional variety of the south is *ye* [ji] (Hickey 1983a).

The area of verbal aspect also needs to be considered in this context as the various types are represented to differing degrees in vernacular and supraregional varieties. The main aspectual distinctions in Irish English are (i) perfective (two forms) and (ii) habitual. The resultative perfective is expressed by placing the object before the past participle, e.g. *She has the meal prepared*, i.e. 'the meal is now ready'. The immediate perfective is expressed using *after* followed by a continuous form of the verb, e.g. *He's after breaking the glass*, and is only found with non-stative verbs. Both these constructions are common across all varieties of Irish English. Awareness of the resultative perfective is very low indeed, if the acceptance rate of 94 per cent in *A Survey of Irish English Usage* can be taken as any indication. The same would seem to apply to the immediate perfective, which had a mean acceptance rate of 88 per cent.

The use of *do* for the habitual, as in *He does be working in the evening*, is definitely stigmatised. Prescriptive remarks by Irish people attest to this. For instance, one local teacher in Co. Limerick commented during a survey that linguistically 'things have changed in recent years. All that boreen[9] business, for example, *do be* and *does be* is gone. Television and good reading has helped to make this change.' Needless to say, such attitudes mean that this feature is not present in the supraregional variety of the south: the *do(es) be* habitual had a mean acceptance rate in the survey of just over 25 per cent.

The relative acceptance rates for the three main aspectual structures can be interpreted in terms of an implicational scale, that is those speakers who have the structure with the lowest acceptance rate are likely to also have those with higher rates. This gives the distribution shown in table 1.2.

1.3.5 MALAPROPISMS AND SHIBBOLETHS

It is no coincidence that the term 'malapropism' stems from a character, Mrs Malaprop, in the play *The Rivals* (1775) by the Irish writer Richard Brinsley

---

[9] 'Boreen' < Irish *bóirín*, 'little road', i.e. 'rural and backward' – RH.

Table 1.2. *Implicational scale for syntactic features of (southern) Irish English*

1. habitual (*do(es) be*) >
2. immediate perfective (*after* V-*ing*) >
3. resultative perfective (O + PP word order)

Sheridan. Such phonological near-hits are typical of colloquial Irish English, as with the common case of *ulster* for *ulcer* or *deduct* for *deduce*. Confusing semantic neighbours can be seen in instances like *breastplate* for *nameplate*.

Most varieties of English have shibboleths which rest on the external perception of salient features, such as [ʊ] in *but* in northern English. The use of a central starting point for the diphthong in *Irish* [əɪɹɪʃ] or the use of /eː, ɛː/ in the MEAT lexical class could be quoted as instances in Irish English, at least for outsiders who would associate such pronunciations with traditional Irish accents of the south.

For present-day supraregional Irish English in the south, *t*-lenition would be a clear shibboleth. But this feature does not enjoy high awareness among lay speakers. It is not stigmatised and hence is not deliberately avoided by speakers in situations of careful or monitored speech. There may be a case in the north of the country for the pronunciation of the letter *h* as [heːtʃ], i.e. with an initial [h-], acting as a shibboleth and distinguishing the Catholic and Protestant populations. But this is not agreed upon by all scholars working in the field (many west Ulster Protestants also have /h-/ in the name of the letter according to Macafee (1996: 160). For the south, this is not an issue as the name of the letter always has the sound it indicates.

In handwriting, some Irish have a specific habit, that of using the same shape for uppercase *R* and for lowercase *r*, i.e. <R> for <r>, a practice which stems from Irish orthography which does not have a separate form for the lowercase version of the letter.

1.4 An outline of attitudes

1.4.1 THE HISTORICAL BACKGROUND

A brief glance at the historical relationship of England and Ireland shows that from the beginning the English held the view that the Irish were uncivilised and generally inferior. This attitude was adopted officially not least to legitimise the conquest of Ireland in the first place. Somewhat later Giraldus Cambrensis, 'Gerald of Wales', wrote two famous works, *Topographia Hiberniae*, a historical and geographical description of Ireland, and *Expugnatio Hibernica*, an account of the Norman conquest. Giraldus distinguished between the uncivilised Irish and the enlightened conquerors and such a stance remained true of English officialdom with regard to Ireland for centuries (Byrne 2004: 116; Palmer 2000).

Within Ireland this attitude waned somewhat in the immediate aftermath of the invasion with the increasing assimilation of the Normans to the native Irish. It really only came to the fore again with the rise of the House of Tudor (1485–1603). Under Henry VIII Protestant doctrine became received wisdom and the political and theological break with Rome was complete. This left the Old English (the original settlers in Ireland) out on a limb vis-à-vis the English establishment, and the desire of the latter to subjugate unruly Ireland led to a revival of the two-dimensional view of the inherently barbarous Gaels and the civilised English (Palmer 2000: 74–107). This distortion of reality was adhered to by many authors. The English poet Edmund Spenser (*c.* 1552–1599), who served in Munster from 1580 to the end of his life, had no difficulty in accepting and propagating this attitude. The Irish historian Richard Stanihurst (1547–1604) wrote *The Description of Ireland* (1577), included in Holinshed's *Chronicles*. He was from Dublin and regarded the penetration of the Irish language into the Pale as something to be resisted at all costs (Lennon 1981: 81).

> . . . this canker took such deep root, as the body that before was whole and sound was by little and little festered and in a manner wholly putrified . . . it is not expedient that the Irish tongue shall be so universally gaggled in the English Pale: because that by proof and experience we see, that the Pale was never in more flourishing estate than when it was wholly English, and never in worse plight than since it hath enfranchised the Irish.

This attitude was, if anything, reinforced in the violent seventeenth century which saw the hopes of the Catholic Irish grow at the sign of a Catholic English monarch (James II) and evaporate under the reality of Protestant power after 1690.

Now, while the negative view of the native Irish was diluted somewhat in the eighteenth century, particularly among the Protestant Ascendancy, who recognised that their own position within the English-speaking community of the British Isles was peripheral, there was no reversal of position until at least the beginning of the nineteenth century. Curiously enough, a more sympathetic view of the specifically Irish background did not come from the political leaders of the time but from romantic literature which saw in the non-industrialised, rural Irish an unspoiled and natural people, at least at the safe distance of fictional literature (see comments in section 1.2.6).

From this time onwards, the attitutude to the Irish language was to change among the native Irish. The major Catholic leader of the first half of the nineteenth century, Daniel O'Connell, was decidedly against the Irish language (as was the writer William Carleton in his later life). In a statement, attributed to O'Connell by someone recollecting him, he maintained:

> I am sufficiently utilitarian not to regret its gradual abandonment. A diversity of tongues is no benefit; it was first imposed upon mankind as a curse, at the building of Babel. It would be of great advantage to mankind if all the

inhabitants of the Earth spoke the same language. Therefore though the Irish language is connected with many recollections that twine around the hearts of Irishmen, yet the superior utility of the English tongue, as the medium of all modern communication, is so great that I can witness without a sigh the gradual disuse of Irish. (Crowley 2000: 153)

As Eagleton (1995: 12) reports, after the Famine there were still many areas of rural Ireland where Irish was spoken but where the language was avoided because it was supposed to bring bad luck. This attitude is understandable given that the use of Irish did not do much to improve the lot of the native population. The ultimate consequence was of course the shift from Irish to English which by the second half of the nineteenth century had taken place for the majority of the Irish population.

The shift to English led to varieties of the language arising in Ireland, all of which were quite distinct in pronunciation and grammar from more standard varieties in Britain. There was no continuation of planter English comparable to settler English in the southern hemisphere, which led from the late eighteenth century onwards to South African, Australian and New Zealand English. Hence there is no historically continuous variety of English in Ireland which is anywhere close to south-eastern British English. Given this fact, the attitude in Ireland to the latter type of English plays a role which is quite different from that in other colonies whose English is much closer to standard forms of British English.

1.4.2 BRITISH ENGLISH AND IRISH ENGLISH

The difference between varieties of Irish and British English has meant that the Irish see the latter as quite distinct from their own forms of the language. Standard British English pronunciation is closely associated with the English establishment and because of this the Irish do not in general approve of those of their compatriots who emulate this kind of pronunciation.

Supraregional Irish English derives from non-local Dublin usage and provides an orientation for the southern middle-class Irish. Certain characteristics of this speech, such as rhoticity, monophthongisation in the FACE and GOAT lexical sets, central realisation of /a/ and retraction of /ʌ/, plosives in the THIN and THIS lexical sets, are so obvious that no possibility of confusion with the British standard is possible. And yet it is obvious to any observer of Irish English in the south that there are speakers, however few, with accents close to RP. The following are some generalisations which would appear to hold in such cases.

Those who show accents similar to RP are middle-class urban individuals. Particularly in Dublin, there are cases of people with such accents who have leanings towards and connections with England and who would be generally classified as 'West Brit' (a rather derogatory term in the Irish context; see section 1.2.5). Whether or not this epithet is used, the attitude is clear: those who use RP, or anything like it, are regarded as un-Irish, at least linguistically.

RP-like accents cover a wide spectrum in Ireland. There is a definite cline that has at one end supraregional varieties with some of the more prominent features (like rhoticity or monophthongisation) removed or at least toned down and at the another end an accent which is not recognisably Irish.

Speakers who gravitate towards RP usually maintain some traits of Irish English in their speech. If any feature remains as a trace of Irish origin then it is *t*-lenition. One can observe speakers with something very close to RP (non-rhotic speech, diphthongs for mid vowels, /ʌ/ as [ä], /aː/ as [ɑː], etc.) but with /t/ as [t̞] where the phonotactic environment demands it. In the opposite direction there are many southern British English who for whatever reason – business, retirement, etc. – live in Ireland. It is *t*-lenition which such individuals pick up as the most 'infectious' Irish feature.

If there are users of RP-like accents in Ireland, then why are their numbers so small and why did not more features of RP enter supraregional varieties of Irish English? The answer is implicit from the above remarks. RP is often associated with a kind of old-fashioned genteelness which is not regarded as particularly desirable by the present-day population. For many it is connected with the practice of elocution where schoolchildren were taught apparently clear diction and delivery which in effect meant trying to speak some more or less garbled version of RP (see Millar 1987a on this practice in Belfast). Furthermore, as said above, it would not befit any independently minded Irish person to emulate an English accent. Although the vast majority of Irish speak English as their native language, using an English accent is seen as pretentious and likely to evoke derision.

Finally, it should be remarked that Irish people do not in general have a clear perception of different accents within England. For instance, in an informal test involving thirty-seven individuals from Dublin, Waterford and Limerick it was found that only four could identify the pronunciations *but* [bʊt] and *cast* [kast] as indicative of northern English.

1.4.3 ATTITUDES, CONSCIOUSNESS AND RECOGNITION

Many Irish have an ambivalent attitude to English. On the one hand the language is undoubtedly the native language of the vast majority of the population. On the other hand there is a reluctance to give open recognition to this fact because national feelings demand that one views the Irish language as the carrier of native culture, although the language has receded greatly over the past 150 years and continues to do so (Ó Riagáin 1997).

Attitudes to Irish have consequences for English in Ireland. To accord English equal status with Irish in the consciousness of the people would be somehow to openly acknowledge the language of the former colonisers. Hence there is no strong awareness of a supraregional form of English (in the south) although unconsciously this does exist and is adhered to by educated speakers. Another consequence is that there is no general name for Irish English, nothing like

Cockney, Scouse or Geordie in England, terms like *brogue* being somewhat negative in their connotation (see section 1.2.3). Furthermore, there is no established popular description of Irish English like H. L. Mencken's *The American Language* or S. J. Baker's *The Australian Language*. The nearest equivalent is P. W. Joyce's *English as we Speak it in Ireland* (first published in 1910) but this work did not achieve anything like the degree of popularity of, say, Mencken and is largely unknown outside academic circles in Ireland today.

Compared to other anglophone countries, Ireland shows little if any recognition of its own varieties of English (with the exception of Ulster Scots in Northern Ireland; see section 3.3). Dictionaries and popular treatments of Irish English deal with rural vocabulary and put an emphasis on colloquial and slightly farcical items. A view is often found that Irish English is a substandard form of language not to be taken seriously.[10] Many publications serve, intentionally or not, to support this. Often the impression conveyed is that Irish English is a bemusing form of language confined to colloquial usage. Irish publishers seem prepared to support and further this view; see Beecher (1991), Ó Muirithe (2004) and Share (2006), or in a vulgar vein, Murphy and O'Dea (2004).

The denial of a role for vernacular Irish English in modern Irish society also lies behind the dissociation from colloquial Dublin English which was the motor behind the major changes in metropolitan Irish English during the 1990s (see section 5.4.1). This dismissive attitude is not necessarily found in other countries where a non-standard variety of an extranational language is spoken. In Switzerland, for instance, local forms of German are used preferentially by the native population. The same is true of Austria, though there the distance from standard German is slighter.

The question remains as to why the Irish do not hold the specific features of their own variety of English in higher regard. Any answer here must refer to several factors. The rise of a native middle class in the late nineteenth century brought with it a large amount of linguistic prejudice against prominent features of Irish English. These were removed by supraregionalisation (see section 5.3.) with the effect that they were then confined to vernacular varieties, e.g. the habitual with *do*, *them* as a demonstrative, *went* as a past participle or *learn* in the sense of *teach*, to mention just a few examples.

Two further factors may well play a role here. The first is a post-colonial attitude that anything homegrown is inferior, an attitude which still lingers on and which is often seen in the lack of support the Irish give to each other. The second is that endorsing English in Ireland is tantamount to disloyalty to Irish. From an external perspective this notion might seem strange. But recall that in previous centuries Irish was the native language of the majority of the population.

---

[10] Outside Ireland, especially in Britain, the view of the country can often betray remnants of colonial attitudes and this may find linguistic expression as well. Previously, expressions like *that's a bit Irish* for anything which smacks of eccentricity or disorganisation were found and an *Irish bull* was a statement which was inherently illogical. The latter phrase, reduced to *bull*, is still found in Ireland and outside in the general sense of 'nonsense'.

The Irish shifted to English and a legacy of this shift is a certain uneasiness on the part of the Irish towards their present-day native language English. It may seem a little far-fetched, but there could well be an unconscious trauma among English-speaking Irish today over having abandoned the Irish language in the recent past.

1.4.4 IRISH UNIVERSITIES AND THE ENGLISH LANGUAGE

A glance at the websites of Irish universities reveals a remarkable fact: none of the Irish universities – Trinity College Dublin, the University of Limerick and the component universities of the National University of Ireland (in Dublin, Maynooth, Cork and Galway) – has a chair for English language[11] and certainly not for the English language in Ireland. Departments of English are first and foremost concerned with literature, including medieval English literature. Earlier forms of English are taught, in the tradition of philology, as a means of accessing this literature.

In the past few decades there have been a few individuals, working within English departments, who out of personal interest concerned themselves with Irish English. Foremost among these were Alan Bliss (former Professor of Anglo-Saxon at University College Dublin) and P. L. Henry (former Professor of Old and Medieval English, University of Galway) whose work is quoted widely in the present book. But neither of these scholars had PhD students[12] working on English in Ireland who continued to work in Irish universities so that a following generation of scholars did not arise and no continuity in Irish English studies was established.

The situation in Irish universities contrasts starkly with that in England where there is an obvious representation of the English language on the level of university chairs and research centres. This fact is all the more surprising as history is represented in all Irish universities, indeed it is given special prominence, for instance in University College Galway and University College Dublin. In Galway there is a Centre for the Study of Human Settlement and Historical Change. In Dublin there is the Humanities Institute of Ireland. Such centres would be suitable frameworks in which to embed research into the English language in

---

[11] Queen's University in Belfast is, however, an exception. It is not coincidental that this is in Northern Ireland. The chair at Queen's is not specifically dedicated to Irish English.

[12] One exception is Séamus Ó Maoláin who worked with P. L. Henry at the University of Galway, collecting lexical data around Ireland for the project *A Linguistic Survey of Ireland* which did not get beyond a set of vocabulary notebooks with some grammatical information, despite the promising start published as Henry (1958). The notebooks are now housed in the Special Collections section of the library at the University of Galway. Ó Maoláin's PhD was on the vocabulary of Co. Kilkenny (Ó Maoláin 1973), part of the envisaged survey. This was later published as Moylan (1996). Ó Maoláin worked as a lecturer in the English department of the University of Galway. The notebooks of the projected survey have been consulted for the section of this book on the grammar of Irish English; see section 4.4.

Ireland, indeed the former would be suited to the study of the transportation of Irish English during the colonial period.

In Northern Ireland there are at least two comparable research centres, the Academy for Irish Cultural Heritages (University of Ulster) and the Institute of Irish Studies (Queen's University Belfast). The emphasis here would seem, as in the south, to be on history, society and literature but not on the English language in Ireland. Curiously, the institution which is primarily concerned with language in Northern Ireland is The Ulster-Scots Agency / Tha Boord o Ulstèr-Scotch. Its formal counterpart in the south is Foras na Gaeilge 'the Irish language foundation' (see section 3.3.2 below) which has nothing to do with the English language.[13]

Given the lack of chairs for language in English departments, one might imagine that research into English in Ireland is done in departments of linguistics, as in the United States and Canada, for instance. But there are no departments of linguistics in Ireland with the exception of University College Dublin, which has a small department where the English language is not a focus of research.[14]

The remarkable absence of departments of linguistics in Irish universities is directly related to the following fact. There are departments of Irish in Maynooth, Cork, Limerick, Galway, Derry, Coleraine and Belfast, i.e. in all universities, north and south. The firm position which Irish holds means that colleagues and administrators outside the field of language studies would see no necessity for linguistics to exist as a separate department in an arts faculty or college. The reaction to any such demand would be that linguistics is done in Irish departments. This is only partly true as Irish departments are traditional and do not normally absorb linguistic ideas from outside Ireland. They are not generally open to new directions in language research, such as treating the development of Irish and English together, for instance in the context of research paradigms like language contact, language shift or language variation and change. It is thus not surprising that the scholars working in such areas are located outside Ireland, e.g. Karen Corrigan, Nancy Stenson, Markku Filppula, Kevin McCafferty, Michael Montgomery and the present author, or are not Irish themselves, e.g. Jeffrey Kallen (Dublin) and John Kirk (Belfast).

---

[13] When discussing this situation with an Irish colleague, the author mentioned universities like London, Manchester, Leeds, Sheffield, Lancaster, which all have chairs of English language. The reaction of the Irish colleague was to say 'of course they [the English] would, it's their language, isn't it?' Such throw-away comments betray much about the underlying and unarticulated attitudes of the Irish to English. However, the fact is that in the not-too-distant past the Irish switched to English, rendering later generations as much native speakers of English as those elsewhere in the anglophone world. Today, English is the native language of 99 per cent of the native population of Ireland.

[14] Linguistics is also done in centres which service foreign language departments or teach these languages themselves, e.g. the Centre for Language and Communication Studies at Trinity College Dublin and the Department of European Languages at the University of Limerick where individual scholars carry out research into English in Ireland.

Table 1.3. *Haugen's criteria for standard languages*

	Form	*Function*
Society	Selection	Acceptance
Language	Codification	Elaboration

Source: Haugen (2003 [1964]: 421)

In general one can say that the standing of the English language in Irish universities, and of Irish English in particular, reflects broader views in Irish society as a whole. The lack of recognition is not the result of conscious neglect but is an unintended legacy of the historical language shift mixed together with attitudes in Ireland resulting both from its post-colonial status and from native ideas about what is worthy of academic study which derives from wider notions of social class and 'correct language'.

1.4.5 IS THERE 'STANDARD IRISH ENGLISH'?

The discussion of recognition for English in Ireland is closely bound to the question of whether one can speak of 'Standard Irish English' and just how this would be delimited both from vernacular varieties of English in Ireland and from extranational norms of the language, particularly in Britain.

If it is legitimate to speak of 'Standard Irish English' then this entity arose from the suppression of vernacular features in non-local Irish English which set in during the late nineteenth century with the establishment of a Catholic middle class in Ireland. However, such a variety did not and does not enjoy the consciousness of standard languages in other countries. In this context one can consider the features which Einar Haugen listed as typical of standard languages, as given in table 1.3.

Irish society certainly selected and accepted supraregional Irish English of the early twentieth century as the standard of English in independent Ireland. But this was a largely unconscious process and defined more by what vernacular features were excluded from this non-local form of Irish English. Specifically, the variety did not undergo any codification or elaboration. Haugen's codification refers in the main to an orthographical and grammatical standard used for writing. In Ireland this was, and still is, standard British English. A particularly Irish elaboration[15] of supraregional Irish English did not take place either. Any lexical

---

[15] Haugen's notion of elaboration might imply that a standard is somehow 'more' than a vernacular. This can only be true on a lexical level, where a standard is likely to have vocabulary for a larger range of contexts than a vernacular. However, vernaculars clearly show greater differentiation on a phonological level. This holds both for general distinctions, such as that between short vowels before /r/ in vernacular Irish English (see discussion of NURSE and TERM lexical sets in section

or stylistic elaboration of English found in Ireland is again derived from standard British English.

Explicit investigations of 'Standard Irish English' have been few so far. The concern of linguists to date has been to determine what vernacular features exist and then consider their possible origin and/or their continuation in overseas varieties of English. With the compilation of the Irish section of the *International Corpus of English* the focus was directed explicitly at the speech of speakers who had been educated through the medium of English at least to the end of secondary school (S. Mac Mathúna 2006: 114). The value of investigating the speech of this group of educated speakers remains to be seen and detailed analyses of *ICE-Ireland* (the Irish section of the much larger corpus) have yet to be written. One aspect of the *ICE-Ireland* corpus which looks promising concerns specific discourse features contained in the data.

In a programmatic article, written just after the completion of *ICE-Ireland*, Kirk and Kallen (2006) attempt to identify how much of the data is standard (British) English and how much can be traced back to 'Celticity', which, in their words, 'amounts to those features of lexis, grammar, and discourse which appear in ICE-corpora and for which there exists a plausible case of transfer or reinforcing influence from Irish' (Kirk and Kallen 2006: 88). The term 'Celticity', on first encounter, would seem to encompass all Celtic languages and/or linguistic features which are found in the varieties of English spoken in the Celtic regions. Such features are quite heterogenous and differ in source and scope (see sections 4.4.1.4.1 and 4.4.1.4.3 for a discussion of Scottish English grammar in the context of Irish English).[16]

In order to determine the nature of standard English it would seem appropriate to devise scales of standardness by means of which the speech of various individuals could be classified as showing greater vernacularity or standardness. These two qualities would represent opposite ends of the scales (according to levels of language). Hence individuals with a low index for vernacularity would be automatically classified as more standard and vice versa. Furthermore, scales of standardness would have cut-off points beyond which individuals could no longer be classified as speakers of Irish English (from the north or south) at all. Certainly on the level of phonology, there are identifiable features whose presence would be required in speech for a classification as Irish English. For instance, if an individual has neither epenthesis in *film* nor fricative *t* nor dental stops for ambidental fricatives, then there is a very real sense in which that individual is not a speaker of (southern) Irish English. Table 1.4 attempts to specify roughly what

5.4.6), and for the lexical occurrence of certain sounds which cannot be predicted from phonetic environment (see discussion of /ʊ/ and /ʌ/ in vernacular forms of Belfast English in section 5.5.1).

[16] A term which appears to apply to all the Celtic regions would seem inappropriate, particularly for a discussion of standard Irish English as both Scottish English and, even more so, Welsh English are heteronymous with respect to southern British English.

Table 1.4. *Approximate scales of standardness for Irish English*

Syntax	
standard	resultative perfective (O + PP word order)
↓	inversion with embedded questions
	lack of *do* in *have*-questions
	punctual use of *never*
	lack of *to* with infinitives after *ask, help, allow, use*
	use of present in present perfect contexts
	moderate fronting for topicalisation purposes
	mustn't as negative epistemic modal
	be as auxiliary with verbs like *go, finish*
	immediate perfective (*after* V-*ing*)
	generic use of article
vernacular	*for to* with infinitives of purpose
↓	subordinating *and*
	unmarked plurals after numerals
	zero subject relative pronoun
	non-standard subject concord
	habitual (*do(es) be*)
	negative concord
	failure of negative attraction
Morphology	
standard	*ye* as second-person-plural pronoun
vernacular	*them* as demonstrative
↓	*youse, yeez* (rather than *ye*)
	unbound reflexives
	seen and *done* as preterites
	learn for *teach*
	went as past participle
Phonology	
standard	*t*-lenition to apico-alveolar fricative [t̬]
↓	dental stops for ambidental fricatives
	central [aː] in BATH lexical set
	vowel epenthesis in *film, helm*
	monophthongs in FACE and GOAT lexical sets
vernacular	alveolar stops for ambidental fricatives
↓	*t*-lenition beyond [t̬], to [ʔ, h] or zero

features would be typical of standard and vernacular Irish English. All these features are discussed in detail at other points in the relevant sections of this book.

Table 1.5. *Recessive features in mainstream Irish English*

1. syllable-final alveolar /l/ (now velarised [ɫ])
2. syllable-final velarised /r/ (now retroflex [ɻ])
3. monophthong or slight diphthong in GOAT ([goːt̪] ~ [gout̪], now [gəʊt̪])
4. open back vowel in THOUGHT ([t̪ɒːt̪], now [t̪ɔːt̪])
5. low starting point for diphthong in CHOICE ([tʃɒɪs], now [tʃɔɪs])
6. central starting point for diphthong in MOUTH ([maʊt̪], now fronted [mæʊt̪])

1.4.6 POSSIBLE FUTURE DEVELOPMENTS

It is a truism to say that Irish society has undergone major change in the past decade or two and that this change is ongoing. The economic boom which set in during the 1990s shows no signs of abating at the time of writing (2006). These developments have had, and still have, considerable implications for the development of the English language in Ireland. The most obvious of these is that supraregional Irish English will cease to show features of twentieth century Irish English because of the rapid spread of new Dublin English pronunciation among young people throughout the Republic of Ireland (Hickey 2005). For non-local speakers under twenty-five it is already the case that they do not generally show the features in table 1.5. This means that features traditionally associated with (southern) Irish English will become increasingly rare and eventually disappear as speakers with the conservative mainstream pronunciation become fewer and fewer.

Another development which will have consequences for varieties of Irish English in the near future is the large-scale immigration into Ireland which has accompanied the economic boom. Estimates for the number of non-Irish now living in the country vary, but it could be over half a million, more than 10 per cent of the population. Among the foreigners, immigrants from eastern European countries predominate, especially since the accession of these countries to the European Union in 2004. The Poles are the most numerous with something between 100,000 and 150,000, or maybe more, currently living in Ireland. For a relatively small country this is a significant proportion of the population. Consider that Poles in Ireland now outnumber native speakers of Irish by at least three to one. Even if a large proportion of the Poles return to their native country or re-emigrate, a significant number are likely to stay and it is this sector of Irish society which will speak the main non-native variety of Irish English (see chapter 5, epilogue 1). The Poles furthermore show strong social cohesion which means that their variety of Irish English may well establish itself in the coming years and be passed on to the following generation, interacting with native forms of Irish English in the process.

2   History I: The coming of the English

2.1   External developments

The history of Ireland since the late Middle Ages is the unending story of its relationship with England. This is taken to have begun in the late twelfth century. But just as there had been contacts with the Germanic tribes of the continent before the actual invasion of England in 449, trade had been carried on between Ireland and England before the invasion of the country by a collective force of Anglo-Normans, English, Welsh and some Flemish in 1169.[1]

According to the (forged) Donation of Constantine, the Pope ruled over all islands which of course included Ireland and England. For this reason Henry II (1154–89) sought papal permission to invade Ireland from Pope Adrian IV (Nicholas Breakspear, the only English pope, who held office from 1154 to 1159). It is probable that the latter issued a bull *Laudabiliter* in 1155 authorising Henry to carry out the task, which he then did fourteen years later on the grounds that the church had fallen into a state of disarray there.

The external circumstances of the invasion were roughly as follows. One Dermot MacMurrough, King of Leinster, was attacked in 1166 by one Tiernán O'Rourke (Martin 1967: 123f.) from Breifny (in the north-west midlands), whose wife had been abducted by MacMurrough; the king fled to Wales. In an effort to reassert his power in Leinster, MacMurrough returned a year later with a force consisting of Normans and Welsh from Pembrokeshire. MacMurrough had little success and returned the following year, this time establishing a base in Wexford. He promised his daughter Eve in marriage to the Norman warlord Strongbow (Richard Fitz Gilbert de Clare, Earl of Pembroke) and made the latter his heir to the kingdom of Leinster (something which he was not entitled to do according to Irish law). Another Welsh force, more determined and better equipped than the previous ones, landed in the early summer of 1169 at Bannow Bay in south Co.

---

[1] The date of 1169 has been agreed upon by a historiographical tradition. This was established by Gerard of Wales (Giraldus Cambrensis, 1146–1223) who wrote two works based on two journeys to Ireland in the 1180s, *Topographia Hiberniae* and *Expugnatio Hibernica* 'The conquest of Ireland' (see translation by John J. O'Meara 1982).

Wexford and established a bridgehead in that part of the country. The following year Strongbow landed with MacMurrough and married the latter's daughter in Waterford, more or less immediately in the Viking stronghold, Reginald's Castle. Strongbow advanced on Dublin and captured it but it was besieged by Rory O'Connor, the leader of the Irish forces of the time. However, the Irish were no match for the Normans and after MacMurrough's death in 1171 Strongbow assumed his titles and was granted the eastern towns of Dublin, Wexford and Waterford by O'Connor, effectively cementing the Norman presence in Ireland. In the same year Henry II visited Ireland to affirm his authority in a country which offered the opportunity for vassals of the king to exercise power outside the reach of the English monarch. There were subsequent visits with a similar purpose such as that by Henry's son John in 1210.

The first adventurers to arrive on Irish soil appear to have been quite a motley bunch. They came from Pembrokeshire in west Wales (Moody and Martin 1967: 127ff.). It is known from historical records that there were at least three languages represented in this early group. Anglo-Norman, a variety of medieval English, Welsh and perhaps, to some degree, Flemish (Cahill 1938: 160). Much as the presence of the latter may serve to spice the demographic picture of medieval Ireland, for the further linguistic development of both Irish and English, Flemish is of no relevance. A few loanwords survived in the archaic dialect of Forth and Bargy (see section 2.4) but that is about all. No traces of a Flemish influence are to be seen in Irish. Welsh was in all probability also among the languages of the first invaders. However, traces of Welsh are not to be seen anywhere in Irish English.

2.1.1 THE SPREAD OF ENGLISH

The development of English in Ireland since the twelfth century has not been continuous. This is due both to the settlement of the island by the English and to the political conditions in England itself.

Only the east and south-east coast of Ireland were settled to any appreciable extent in the late Middle Ages, above all the cities of Wexford, Waterford, Kilkenny and Dublin, though there were outposts of the Anglo-Normans, such as Carrickfergus immediately north of present-day Belfast. At this time Dublin had already gained the status of capital of the country. Like other cities in Ireland, Dublin largely owes its origins to a Viking settlement before the turn of the millennium (Moore 1965: 10). Because of its favourable position in the middle of the east coast and with the central plain as its hinterland, Dublin was able to assert itself over other urban settlements on river estuaries in Ireland. This fact is of some importance for the English language. The city was quickly occupied by the English after its conquest. Henry II issued the Charter of Dublin in 1172 (Dolley 1972: 68ff.). From this time onwards, English has existed continuously in Dublin, indeed within an area along the east and south-east coast known as the 'Pale'. This term comes from Latin *palus* 'stake', via French, and refers to a stake in a fence. In the post-invasion period it denoted the part of Ireland which was firmly under English (and Anglo-Norman) control beyond which the native Irish lived. Its actual size varied, reaching a maximum in the fourteenth century when it covered an area from Drogheda north of Dublin to at least Waterford in the south south-east and included some of the midlands (Meath) and south midlands (parts of Tipperary). With the resurgence of Gaelic influence in Ireland in the late fourteenth and fifteenth centuries the Pale shrank (Palmer 2000: 41). However, with the settlements (plantations, Andrews 2000) in the sixteenth and seventeenth centuries, the English presence spread gradually throughout the entire countryside and the term 'Pale' lost its relevance. The phrase *beyond the pale* 'socially unacceptable' suggests that those inside the Pale in the late medieval period regarded the natives outside as unruly and uncivilised.

Within the boundaries of the Pale the political influence of England never ceased to exist. This is basically the reason for the continuous existence of English in Dublin: in the history of Ireland the English language has maintained the strongest influence in those areas where English political influence has been mostly keenly felt.

After the twelfth century settlements spread to other cities, e.g. in the south (Cork) and in the west (Limerick and Galway). The impact on rural Ireland (T. Barry 2000a) was slight. This is of importance when considering the linguistic status of English vis-à-vis Irish in the late Middle Ages. English was not a dominant language at this stage (as it was to become in the early modern period). Indeed English competed with Anglo-Norman in medieval Ireland and both of these definitely interacted with the quantitatively more significant Irish language.

An ever increasing assimilation of the original settlers by the native Irish occurred in the post-invasion period. This assimilation had two main reasons. For one thing the English settlers of this early, pre-Reformation time were of course Catholic and for another the connections with England were in fact quite loose. Those adventurers who had sought land and political influence in Ireland evinced only nominal allegiance to the English crown. They had become to a large extent independent in Ireland (Moody and Martin 1967: 133ff.). Indeed one can interpret the visits of English kings in Ireland, such as that of Henry in Dublin in the late twelfth century, as a scarcely concealed attempt to assert the influence of the English court in a colony which did not lay undue emphasis on crown loyalty. In later centuries other monarchs were to follow suit. Thus John came to Ireland in 1210 and Richard II twice, in 1394 and 1399. Each of these visits was intended to serve the purpose of constraining the power of the ostensibly English nobility. With the severing of ties with England the original English naturally drew closer to the native Irish.

This development explains the decline of English in Ireland in the late fourteenth and fifteenth centuries. Especially after the adoption of Protestantism by the English government, initiated by the 'Reformation Parliament' (1529–36) of Henry VIII, the English settlers in Ireland, 'Old English' as they are often termed, felt cut off and identified themselves increasingly with the native Catholic population. The fortunes of the English language were at their lowest in the first half of the sixteenth century (Moody and Martin 1967: 158ff.).

2.1.2 THE SITUATION IN LATE MEDIEVAL IRELAND

The history of English in Ireland is not that of a simple substitution of Irish by English. When the Anglo-Normans and English arrived in Ireland the linguistic situation in Ireland was quite homogeneous. In the ninth century Ireland had been ravaged by Scandinavians just like most of northern Britain. The latter, however, settled down in the following three centuries. The decisive battle against the Scandinavians (Clontarf, 1014) is taken to represent on the one hand the final break with Denmark and Norway, and on the other to have resulted in the complete assimilation of the remaining Scandinavians with the native Irish population, much as happened in other countries, such as large parts of northern Britain and northern France. At the time of the English invasion one can assume, in contradistinction to various older authors such as Curtis (1919: 234), that the heterogeneity which existed was more demographic than linguistic. Old Norse had indeed an effect on Irish, particularly in the field of lexis (see Sommerfelt in Ó Cuív 1975; Geipel 1971: 56ff.), but there is no evidence that a bilingual situation obtained any longer in late twelfth-century Ireland.

As one would expect from the status of the Anglo-Normans in England and from the attested names of the warlords who came to Ireland in the late twelfth century, these Anglo-Normans were the leaders among the new settlers. The English were mainly their servants, a fact which points to the relatively low status of the language at this time. As in England, the ruling classes and the higher positions in the clergy were occupied by Normans soon after the invasion. Their language was introduced with them and established itself in the towns. Evidence for this is offered by such works as *The Song of Dermot and the Earl* and *The Entrenchment of New Ross* in Anglo-Norman as well as contemporary references to spoken Anglo-Norman in court proceedings from Kilkenny (Cahill 1938: 160f.). Anglo-Norman seems to have been maintained in the cities well into the fourteenth century as the famous Statutes of Kilkenny (1366) attest (Lydon 1973: 94ff.; Crowley 2000: 14–16). These were composed in Anglo-Norman and admonished both the French-speaking lords and the native Irish population to speak English. The statutes were not repealed until the end of the fifteenth century but they were never effective. The large number of Anglo-Norman loanwords in Irish (Risk 1971: 586ff.), which entered the language in the period after the invasion, testifies to the existence of Anglo-Norman and the robustness of its position from the late twelfth to the fourteenth century (Hickey 1997b). In fact as a language of law it was used up to the fifteenth century, as evidenced by the Acts of Parliament of 1472 which were in Anglo-Norman.

The strength of the Irish language can be recognised from various comments and descriptions of the early period. For instance, Irish was allowed in court proceedings according to the municipal archives of Waterford (1492–3) in those cases where one of the litigants was Irish. This would be unthinkable from the seventeenth century onwards when Irish was banned from public life.

Still more indicative of the vitality of Irish is the account from the sixteenth century of the proclamation of a bill in the Dublin parliament (1541) which officially declared the assumption of the title of King of Ireland by Henry VIII (Dolan 1991: 143).[2] The parliament was attended by the representatives of the major Norman families of Ireland, but of these only the Earl of Ormond was able to understand the English text and apparently translated it into Irish for the rest of the attending Norman nobility (Hayes-McCoy 1967). Needless to say, the English viewed this situation with deep suspicion and the lord chancellor William Gerrard commented unfavourably in 1578 on the use of Irish by the English 'even in Dublin', and regarded the habits and the customs of the Irish as detrimental to the character of the English. Furthermore, since the Reformation, Irishness was directly linked to popery. Accordingly, the Irish and the (Catholic) Old English were viewed with growing concern.

2.1.3 IRELAND UNDER THE TUDORS

The view of Ireland which prevailed in the Tudor period (1485–1603) was one of a country peopled by primitive tribes, permanently involved in internecine strife. There is undoubtedly some truth in this view: family and neighbourhood hostilities have always been characteristic of Irish life. The English stance was clear from the beginning: the salvation of the Irish lay in the imposition of English government and public order. Only this could guarantee a stable state of affairs. Added to this was the desire to impose Protestantism as the state religion of England on the popish Irish. The self-righteousness of the English attitude in this period is perhaps difficult to appreciate for present-day observers with an awareness of ethnic individuality and claims to independence. But the unquestioned conviction that English rule was divinely inspired, and the only option for the 'wild Irish', is one which permeates English writings on matters Irish from this period. One of the more representative authors and major poets of the time, Edmund Spenser (c. 1552–99), is no exception in this respect.[3]

Historians vary in their interpretation of Tudor and later Elizabethan attitudes towards the Irish. In her discussion of the matter, Palmer (2000: 15f.) notes

---

[2] Henry VIII became King of Ireland in 1541. Before that Ireland had technically been a 'lordship' of the English crown (Foster 1988: 3), though various laws severely curtailed the parliamentary freedom of the Irish. The most notorious of these was Poynings' Law, introduced by Sir Edward Poynings in 1494, which specified that meetings of the Irish parliament had to be sanctioned by the Council in Ireland (headed by the king's deputy) and by the king with the Council in England. This was later regarded as one of the main fetters in the Irish struggle for independence.

[3] Spenser's views are to be found in *A View of the Present State of Ireland* (Canny 2001: 42–55), a dialogue between proponents of strict and of liberal policies in Ireland which was written in the 1590s. There is disagreement among historians in their assessment of Spenser, some seeing him as a proponent of English colonial policy and others regarding him as an advocate of an ideal and liberal pastoral society (Rankin 2005).

that some believe the early modern English stance towards Ireland was part of a 'Renaissance anthropology' which saw the Irish as inherently inferior because they were outside the realm of civilisation and ordered government. Other historians see the attitude towards the Irish as more pragmatic, determined by Protestantism, the state religion of England by then, and by the need to tame the unruly neighbours to the west who were a constant source of rebellion.

Given the Reformation, the Tudors were particularly concerned with the anglicisation of the inhabitants of Ireland (of whatever origin). Henry VIII's daughter Elizabeth I inherited this concern from her father. Initially, her attitude to the Irish would appear to have been reasonably conciliatory: it is even reported that she expressed the wish to understand Irish. In keeping with the aims of the Reformation, Elizabeth decided to have the Bible translated; she provided a press with an Irish font to print it and commissioned Irish bishops to organise the work (though these were later chided for not moving this project forward speedily enough).

The press supplied by Elizabeth was first used for poetry in 1571 but it was not until almost thirty years later in 1602–3 that the New Testament was printed in Dublin by one Seán Francke. The task of translation would not have presented insuperable difficulties given the presence of Irish scholars in Dublin and the favour or at least tolerance many of them enjoyed at the hands of the English. Indeed the vibrancy of intellectual life in Dublin is attested by the founding of Trinity College Dublin as a university in 1592 by Elizabeth I, albeit solely for the benefit of the Protestant classes.

2.1.3.1 The Munster plantation

Of all the events which affected Ireland in the Tudor era, it is the organised settlement of the Irish landscape which was to have the greatest consequence in terms of anglicisation. These settlements are known collectively as 'plantations' and were carefully planned (Foster 1988: 59–78; MacCurtain 1972: 89ff.; see Dudley Edwards with Hourican 2005: 158 for maps). The practical success of plantations depended on a number of factors and there were many setbacks. But in the long run they were responsible for the establishment of a large-scale English presence throughout the country. The first plantations originated in the period from 1549 to 1557 (Moody and Martin 1967: 189ff.) when the two counties Offaly and Laois (read: [liː ʃ])[4] in the centre of the country were settled (Duffy et al. 1997: 58f.).

Apart from a few cases of private initiatives, the plantations in Ireland were affairs devised and sanctioned by the English government. In terms of size and scope, two can be highlighted. The first is the Munster plantation and the second is the Ulster plantation, which will be dealt with below (see section 3.1.2).

---

[4] These counties were formerly called King's and Queen's County respectively (Lalor 2003: 815f. and 609f.).

The prerequisites for the plantations were provided by Henry VIII who was the first English king to lay a practical claim to all of Ireland (Bardon 1996: 45). The old distinction between the English within the Pale and the Irish beyond was to be abolished and English rule was to apply to the entire island.

The trigger for the plantations was the confiscation of lands after the defeat of the Earl of Desmond in north Munster (McCarthy-Morrogh 1986: 16ff.). With this defeat a large amount of land (some 300,000 acres, Duffy et al. 1997: 58) fell to the government and it was decided to settle English on the escheated land (McCarthy-Morrogh 1986: 29f.). The system provided for the establishment of seignories, land units allotted to Englishmen who were to assume a leading role in recruiting further English settlers on the land. These people came to be termed 'undertakers' and the number of settlers was stipulated for each unit of land (McCarthy-Morrogh 1986: 30f.). In 1586 land in Munster was divided into seignories of 12,000, 8,000, 6,000 and 4,000 acres. On the largest seignory an undertaker had to plant ninety-one families including his own. The tenants were also subdivided: freeholders obtained 300 acres each, farmers 400 acres, copyholders 100 acres, the rest being at the discretion of the undertaker. A seven-year time schedule was assumed for the realisation of a seignory; in the case of the Munster plantation of 1586 the task was to have been completed by 1593 (McCarthy-Morrogh 1986: 30f.). Certain other provisions were made, for instance for the defence of the lands. By and large the native Irish were excluded from tenancy on seignories, but the Old English were not, as land could be granted to 'such as be descended from Englishmen'.

Among the English who came to Ireland at this time was the poet Edmund Spenser who was appointed secretary in 1580 to the then governor of Ireland, Lord Grey de Wilton. Spenser was allotted land in Munster (north Co. Cork). However, his efforts did not bear fruit; his own castle being burnt down in 1598 a year before his death.

The Munster plantation was beset by certain difficulties from the start. Many of the English who moved to the province in 1586–92 (Moody and Martin 1967: 190) assimilated to the local Irish. Furthermore, many of the undertakers failed to carry out their commitments so that the plantation finally failed in 1598 (McCarthy-Morrogh 1986: 119). Historians mention that there may have been other extenuating reasons, which McCarthy-Morrogh attempts to identify, but the net result is that the English population in Munster did not increase appreciably in the late 1580s and the 1590s. The estimated 4,000 newcomers – spread across four counties: north Kerry, Limerick, north and north-east Cork, west Waterford (McCarthy-Morrogh 1986: 130) – would not have had a significant effect on the nature of English in the province.

Of course, the major reason for the failure of the plantation of Munster was the rebellion of 1598 (Canny 2001: 162). This uprising, along with the Spanish intervention on the side of the Irish under Hugh O'Neill, was a cause of serious concern to the Elizabethan administration which saw the real likelihood of a collapse of the English presence in Ireland (Canny 2001: 165).

Despite the immediate negative outcome of the Munster plantation, it was shown that plantation could be made to work and that a society within a society was possible if enough precautions against attack and disruption were taken. With the defeat of the Irish in 1601, the framework for later plantations was laid, a much firmer one in which military threat from the Irish was less.

2.1.4 THE SEVENTEENTH CENTURY

For the history of English in Ireland, the sixteenth century represents a break in its development. Politically, it was marked by increasing separatist activities on the part of the Irish (of native and/or original English/Norman stock) which ended in the final victory over the Irish by English forces at the Battle of Kinsale (Co. Cork) in 1601. The subsequent departure from (the north of) Ireland by native leaders in 1607 – known somewhat romantically as the Flight of the Earls (Byrne 2004: 123) – left a political vacuum which was filled energetically by the English.[5]

Plantations were undertaken in the first years of the seventeenth century throughout the country. The early decades saw further settlements of English people in Munster, for instance in south-west Cork (McCarthy-Morrogh 1986: 151). But the largest and most successful settlements were in Ulster (Canny 2001: 165–242). These will be dealt with below in section 3.1.2. With regard to the south of the country, further developments were to have a negative effect on the Irish presence in the countryside and to increase the number of English there. Cromwell's transplantation policy (see section 2.1.4.2 below) was to push the Irish further west and the reallocation of freed lands to those loyal to the crown – overwhelmingly English settlers – led to increasing anglicisation.

2.1.4.1 Language of the planters

The language of the planters in the seventeenth century came under the influence of the native Irish quite quickly, if representations such as Swift's *Dialogue in the Hipernian Stile* (Bliss 1976: 557, 1977b) can be regarded as genuine. But the linguistic group which would have been responsible for the transfer characteristics of Irish into English is the large section of the Irish-speaking community which switched from Irish to English between the seventeenth and the nineteenth centuries. There were different reasons for this language shift. On the one hand the Penal Laws (Byrne 2004: 230f.) imposed draconian punishment on the use and practice of Irish. But on the other hand large sections of the native population

---

[5] The Flight of the Earls in 1607 has a parallel in the exile of Sarsfield, a military leader in Limerick, and the Wild Geese in 1691 because the treaty of Limerick, which he had negotiated with William III, was not respected by the English parliament. More than 10,000 soldiers are reputed to have emigrated to the continent, mainly to Catholic France, rather than face their uncertain fate in Ireland after military defeat.

changed over to English of their own accord because of the social advantages to be gained from a knowledge of the language.

The role of the planters in the genesis of Irish English can be considered minimal, not least because they were numerically much less significant in this context than the native Irish.[6] Of course, the English which the Irish switched to was that which was available in their environment and for some this was the language of planters. But for many the varieties of English they were exposed to were those which had existed since the early period of settlement on the east coast and in towns around the country.

Even if the planters, by virtue of their social standing, 'imposed' (Guy 1990) features of their English onto that of the Irish engaged in the language shift, there is no way of showing this. Today, it is not possible in southern Ireland to distinguish between a group descended from original Irish speakers and a group which stems from early English settlers. In the north of the country, however, there is this distinction given the clear profile of Ulster Scots which derives from the speech of the seventeenth century settlers from Scotland (see section 3.3).

In their remarks on the Irish language shift, Thomason and Kaufman (1988: 43) assume that descendants of settlers did not emulate the English used by Irish speakers but, given that the latter group was much more numerous, their 'speech habits prevailed anyway'. They furthermore note the large amount of phonological and morphosyntactic interference from Irish into Irish English and the comparative lack of lexical transfer (Thomason and Kaufman 1988: 129); indeed they postulate that the few items there are may well have been introduced by English speakers confronted with Irish rather than by speakers of Irish English themselves.

The cumulative effect of the English presence in the south of the country from the late sixteenth century onwards would have meant that the native Irish were increasingly exposed to the English language. What cannot be determined in retrospect is whether the accents represented by the English settlers were homogeneous enough to have represented a recognisable model for the Irish switching to English. The phonology of Irish English, certainly in the rural south-west where settlements took place in the late sixteenth century (see above), is determined by the sound system of Irish, as one might expect of a language acquired in a non-prescriptive environment by adults, so that a linguistic influence of English settlers on the shape of later southern Irish English is not discernible.

2.1.4.2   *Transplantation and transportation*

In 1642 the English parliament decided that 2,500,000 acres of profitable Irish land should be 'taken out of the four Provinces of that Kingdom' and given

---

[6] This view is also held by scholars working on language contact who have considered the Irish situation, e.g. Sarah Thomason who maintains that 'the shifters' variety of English was able to influence the English of Ireland as a whole because the shifters were numerous relative to the original native speakers of English in Ireland' (Thomason 2001: 79).

as security to those who would invest money – so-called 'adventurers' (Foster 1988: 110) – in the attempt to establish orderly government in Ireland (Canny 2001: 553). This scheme continued to influence English thinking under Oliver Cromwell (1599–1658) who after attaining military victory in Ireland – over both Catholic and royalist Protestant segments of society in the late 1640s (Bardon 1996: 79f.) – proceeded to implement a land settlement in the 1650s. After the military subjugation of the Irish, Cromwell was in the position of having to remunerate his army and the donation of land was in a number of cases a preferred solution as the state finances in England at the time did not permit direct payment for services rendered (Foster 1988: 112).

An essential part of the Cromwellian land settlement was *transplantation*: in general, those landowners who had not shown continued allegiance – 'constant good affection' – to the Cromwellian parliamentary cause were banished to the poorest province of Connaught in the west,[7] and forcibly moved from north to south: to the counties of Roscommon, Mayo, Galway and Clare.[8] The scheme was carried out between 1654 and 1658 and although plans to shift the entire Catholic population to the west were abandoned, it may be that several hundred thousand in all were actually transplanted. After 1660 and the restoration of the English crown under Charles II, loyalist Catholics were not regranted their lands as the king did not dare upturn the Cromwellian land settlement (Bardon 1996: 80). The land vacated during this period was re-allocated to English settlers (Barnard 2000 [1975]: 11), this group providing fresh linguistic input to the island. Scholars like Alan Bliss viewed this input as the seed of modern Irish English.

The second policy implemented by Cromwell in the 1650s was one of *transportation* which involved the dispatchment overseas of several thousand persons regarded by the regime at the time as undesirable (Hickey 2004c). These variously included prisoners, members of the Catholic clergy and general vagrants. But it should be noted that not all the Irish emigrants of this period were deported persons. For instance, for some Galway families, movement to the Caribbean can be traced back to the 1630s (Cullen 1994: 126).

Irish migration was to the eastern Caribbean – to Barbados and later to Montserrat – where a certain degree of intermingling with the native population led to an Afro-Irish community arising, known as the Black Irish. Given the migration within the Caribbean which started from Barbados, the language of these transported Irish may have affected the embryonic forms of English in this area and provided models for structures, above all in the

---

[7] Foster (1988: 101–16, 'Cromwellian Ireland') details the confiscation and resettlement to the west (except the coastal areas).

[8] The people transplanted from Ulster cannot be traced in Connaught today on the basis of an accent of English (there are no enclaves of Ulster English in the south). But the Irish, which is still spoken in small pockets on Achill Island and on the adjoining mainland and slightly north of this, does show clear Ulster features. What this would imply is that the Ulster people maintained northern traits in their Irish but shifted then to the more general western form of English which was being spoken around them in Connaught.

area of verbal aspect, which later appear in creolised Caribbean English and African American Vernacular English; see the discussion of this and related matters in Rickford (1986) and the critical assessment in Hickey (2004b). See also chapter 6.

2.1.4.3   The later seventeenth century

Settlement policy from the late sixteenth to the mid seventeenth century was aimed at reorganising the demographic and property structure of Ireland by making it decidedly English, i.e. loyal to the crown and Protestant in character. But the picture of a harmonious society overrun by a more powerful neighbour is, however, a simplistic view of native Ireland at that time. Many elements of Irish society were already quite anachronistic (see chapter 'The end of the old order' in Lydon 1998: 129–62). The leaders were out of touch with reality in many respects, certainly the literary sectors of Irish society were (Canny 2001: 426). There were attempts to defend Irish culture against what was perceived as English dominance. The most notable example was by Geoffrey Keating (Seathrún Céitinn, c. 1580–1644, a member of an Old English family) in his native narrative of Irish history *Foras Feasa ar Éirinn* 'Store of knowledge about Ireland' (Byrne 2004: 123), which did much to enhance the cultural assessment of pre-Norman Ireland and so throw a better light on native Irish culture (Canny 2001: 414).

Whether native Irish society was robust and adaptive enough to have counterbalanced English influence in the seventeenth century is a matter of debate amongst historians. However, the survival of Irish society was not decided by its internal organisation but by military events. After the victory over the Catholic forces under James II by William III and his forces at the Battle of the Boyne (1690) and after the militarily decisive Battle of Aughrim under his Dutch general Ginkel (Bardon 1996: 88–92) in the following year, Catholics were excluded from political power and from higher positions in society. After this the spread of English throughout the entire country could advance unhindered.

The linguistic legacy of the seventeenth century is somewhat paradoxical. The only group, introduced into Ireland in this period, which changed the linguistic landscape was the one least loyal to the crown and non-conformist in religion. Because of the perceived and practised otherness of the Ulster Scots, it is their speech which has maintained itself longest and most distinctively (see section 3.3). Indeed in Ulster, the English planters, if anything, adopted features of the Scots probably by diffusion throughout the province. Other planters do not appear to have had an appreciable effect on the speech of the majority Irish, or if they did, then this effect was not lasting and has not been recorded. This may have been the case because in many instances the English settlements on the agriculturally more profitable land were interspersed with native Irish who remained as tenants rather than moving to less arable land (H. Clarke 1994 [1967]: 154).

2.1.5 THE EIGHTEENTH CENTURY

The next two centuries were to see a gradual transition on the part of the native population to English with the attending demise of Irish. The eighteenth century was the period of the Penal Laws (Byrne 2004: 230f.), a set of legislative measures which had the effect of excluding the Catholic Irish from political and social life. These were relaxed towards the end of the century but without any substantial improvement in the lot of the Catholics. No general education was available for Catholics in this period but there was a loosely organised system of so-called 'hedge schools' where migrant teachers offered tuition to individuals or small groups in largely rural areas (see section 2.1.5.3).

In Ireland the eighteenth century is at once a period of blossoming and decline, of liberty and of oppression. There was a long-lasting relative peace: between William's suppression of the Jacobites in Ireland (1689–91) and the United Irishmen uprising of 1798 there were no significant military campaigns against English rule. This is the age of the writer Jonathan Swift (1667–1745), of the philosopher Bishop Berkeley (1685–1753), of the political thinker Edmund Burke (1729–97), of the elocutionist and grammarian Thomas Sheridan (1719–88) and of his more famous son, the dramatist Richard Brinsley Sheridan (1751–1816). It is the period in which Dublin was almost on a par with London and could vie with it as a cultural centre with such events as the first performance of Händel's *Messiah* in 1741 and the founding of the Royal Dublin Society in 1731 and of the Royal Irish Academy in 1785. Dublin Protestants prospered as burghers and landlords and their self-confidence is amply documented by the impressive Georgian buildings in the city, a living testimony to this period of relative wealth.

The sector which benefited most in this century was of course the Protestant middle and upper class which was assessed positively by later writers such as Yeats. There are, however, many critical voices which rightly point to the darker sides of this era with its ostracisation of the indigenous population; see Ó Tuama and Kinsella (1981) for neglected Irish poetry of this period. The story of the Gaelic subculture of the time is recounted in a light much less favourable to the Protestants, and with an ideological slant of its own, in Daniel Corkery's *The Hidden Ireland* (1967 [1924]).

During the eighteenth century the rural population was particularly disadvantaged. Not only did it not partake in the prosperity of the Protestant sector but it was subject to the ravages of famine, for instance in 1740–1 when it struck very severely. However, despite the exclusion from urban prosperity, there was nonetheless a flourishing of Irish literature, particularly of poetry in Munster. This period produced such lasting literary works as *Cúirt an Mheán-Oíche* ('The midnight court', *c.* 1780; see dual language translation in Power 1977) by Brian Merriman (?1745–1805) and the *Lament for Art O'Leary* written by the widow of the individual in the poem's title. It was also the period of Turlogh Carolan (1670–1738), the blind harpist who travelled in Connaught and Ulster and who has almost mythical status as a wandering bard, maintaining something of the old Gaelic order which had flourished before the final defeat of the Irish at the beginning of the seventeenth century.[9]

In the (early) eighteenth century there was still a survival of Irish literary culture, in this case in Dublin, at a time when Jonathan Swift was the major literary figure of English in Ireland. Writers in Irish were present in the city and with Seán Ó Neachtain's *Stair Éamuinn Uí Chléire* 'The story of Eamonn O'Cleary', written about 1715, one has an amusing story with linguistic jokes for a bilingual audience. For example, Ó Neachtain ridicules the efforts of the Irish to speak English and gives examples which show the strong influence of Irish syntax (Ó Cuív 1986). This work offers support for the notion that both Irish and English literary cultures existed side by side in the capital at the beginning of the eighteenth century (Ó Háinle 1986).

2.1.5.1   The consolidation of the ascendancy class

Any discussion of language development in eighteenth-century Ireland must deal with the question of the ascendancy, if only at the end to dismiss its relevance for the current subject matter. The term is a fixed quantity in Irish cultural discourse and one, which in its very vagueness, has emotional connotations. It is interpreted as a broad reference to the dominant Protestant section of Irish society with strong leanings towards England and with wealth which was ultimately based on the misappropriation of Catholic land and the implementation of the Penal Laws. As such it is a mythologised concept which is viewed with distrust and resentment by the native population of (southern) Ireland to this day (see chapter 8 'The ascendancy mind' in Foster 1988).

Strictly speaking, the term 'ascendancy' refers to the Anglican Protestant ruling classes of the eighteenth century. As a label it implies a unity which may not have been present in reality. Clearly, it refers to the Protestants of the established church and hence does not include religious non-conformists such as the Presbyterians, chiefly in the north of Ireland. Equally, Protestants in (southern) Ireland in the eighteenth century must be divided at least into a rural and an urban group. The former was a landed elite which lived on considerable estates with large residences. It is this section which was at the centre of later idealisation, seen in the poetry of Yeats, who regarded this group as the bearers of high culture in Ireland (later writers like Louis MacNiece offer a much more realistic evaluation of the landed Protestant gentry). The physical presence of their residences in the Irish landscape led to the notion of the 'Big House' (Genet 1991), an important concept in Irish literature where the life within such houses and the

---

[9] From a literary point of view, the Irish poetry of this former period, which was written in praise of aristocratic patrons, had become very archaic and virtually incomprehensible to the persons whose patronage was being sought. Hence the reasons for the demise of this system were as much internal as external.

Table 2.1. *Features shared by middle-class Protestants and Catholics in southern Ireland*

1. *t*-lenition	2. centralisation of /ɑː/
3. fortition of /θ, ð/ to [t̪, d̪]	4. rhoticity
5. monophthongal mid vowels	

relationship with the surrounding, much poorer native population is a common theme.

The ascendancy declined in importance in the course of the nineteenth century with the general emancipation of the Catholics. The landed class was dealt a final death blow in the upheavals following the 1916 uprising which, during the struggle for independence, led to most of the big houses being ransacked and burnt down.

It is not possible to reconstruct any historical accent of specifically Protestant Irish English in the eighteenth century. The question of a linguistic legacy of the ascendancy must therefore be seen in a wider context, namely whether there exists, or has existed, a discernible Protestant accent of (southern) Irish English (Barry 1982: 128). The answer involves a redefinition of Protestant in terms of social class. For the Protestants as a religious group there are certainly no recognisable linguistic features which are not shared by others. But seen in terms of class affiliation one can say that the Protestants share those features which are typical of middle-class speakers in (southern) Ireland with leanings towards England. In terms of pronunciation one can note a number of features which Protestant middle-class southern Irish still maintain despite any emulation of southern British accent models (see table 2.1).

The ascendancy showed no signs of maintaining a specific dialectal tradition, in distinct contrast to the Scottish settlers in rural Ulster who have maintained Ulster Scots to this day (see section 3.3 below). Their relatively small numbers would also have militated against the formation of a specific ascendancy accent. It is more likely that they partook in the general development of middle-class Irish English, including those features noted by Sheridan (1781) for Dublin English (see section 5.5.4 below), and that they were also involved in the supraregionalisation of (southern) Irish English which took place in the nineteenth and early twentieth centuries (see section 5.3 below).

The above remarks apply to the Protestants as a group in southern Irish society. It does not mean that every member of this group, particularly with country estates, spoke general Irish English. Many of these people spent much time in England, often receiving their education there and thus adopting English accents. For instance, the novelist Elizabeth Bowen (1899–1973) was born into an ascendancy family with an estate and big house at Bowen's Court in Co. Cork. Because of her position as a writer, there exist recordings of her speech which is indistinguishable from that of standard English speakers from southern Britain who grew up at the beginning of the twentieth century.

2.1.5.2   Prescriptivism and elocution

The latter half of the eighteenth century saw a steep rise in prescriptivism in Britain (Beal 2004a: 89–123) which was not without effect in Ireland. Indeed there is a curious connection here: the English prescriptive grammarian Bishop Robert Lowth (1710–87) considered Swift as a paragon of English style (Tieken-Boon van Ostade 1990). During this century the concern with standards in language led to the Irishman Thomas Sheridan – father of the playwright Richard Brinsley Sheridan (Kelly 1997) and son-in-law of Swift – travelling widely in the British Isles. He advised others on what was correct English usage and how to attain it (Sheridan 1970 [1762], 1781; for assessments, see Beal 1996 and the contributions in Howell 1971). Sheridan had a considerable influence on other writers in the prescriptivist tradition, notably John Walker (see Walker 1791).

The practice of elocution – the cultivation of a standard accent by non-standard speakers for the purpose of public speaking – gained much impetus from Sheridan's activities and writings. In particular one should mention his *Rhetorical Grammar of the English Language* (1781), which contains an appendix in which a series of rules to be observed by the Irish in order to speak English 'properly' are outlined. These features are diagnostic of Dublin English in the late eighteenth century (see section 5.5.4 below).

2.1.5.3   Hedge schools

Because there was no general public education for the Catholics before the early nineteenth century,[10] a system of so-called 'hedge schools' (Dowling 1968 [1935], 1971) arose where the native population were instructed in various subjects, including English, by wandering schoolmasters who taught privately, sometimes in the open air (hence the designation) to avoid being caught by the authorities. The figure of the hedge schoolmaster has been mythologised, like much in Irish history, and it is difficult to obtain a clear picture here. The northern Irish writer William Carleton (1794–1869) portrayed him as a mixture of real learning and pedantry. The figure also appears in Brian Friel's play *Translations* (1980). Originally, the hedge schoolmasters were often poets and scholars who had lost patronage when the native Irish aristocracy declined after the sixteenth century.

Assessing the numbers of hedge schools presents considerable difficulties. For instance, the figure of 300,000 to 400,000 pupils being serviced by hedge schools by the early nineteenth century (Byrne 2004: 147) is unconfirmed. Official quarters in Ireland did not want to accord too much weight to them. Hence in

---

[10] An act of 1695 forbade Catholics to visit or teach in schools. It was not until after Catholic emancipation in 1829 and the founding of the system of National Schools (primary schools) in 1831 that basic education was possible for the broad masses in Ireland.

his report the 'State of popery in Ireland' (1731) the bishop of Derry does not give any recognition to informal Catholic instruction in the countryside and only grudgingly mentions that there were some straggling schoolmasters. In his study of the hedge schools, Dowling (1968 [1935]) mentions that the number increased significantly in the second half of the eighteenth century (Dowling 1968 [1935]: 41f.). Especially in the south-west of the country, in Kerry, there was a strong presence of hedge schools, as attested by remarks by various travellers to that part of the country in the mid eighteenth century. It is not perhaps a coincidence that the tradition of Irish poetry was strongest in Munster in the early modern period.

A survey of schools was conducted in 1824, returning a figure of more than 11,000 schools which showed a daily attendance of over half a million pupils. By the beginning of the nineteenth century there were so-called 'Pay Schools' with Catholic lay teachers. These were independent, privately organised schools for the native population who could afford to send their children there. Of the 11,000 schools registered by the 1824 report, between 7,500 and 8,000 were Pay Schools (Dowling 1968 [1935]: 41f.).

The subjects taught reflected the concerns of those who paid the fees for these schools. Classical languages were common subjects as many pupils intended to enter the priesthood. But basic literacy in English would seem to have been an essential part of instruction, especially as the native population had grasped the necessity of a good knowledge of English for social advancement. Naturally there has been speculation about the role of these schools in the development of later forms of Irish English.

One of the features traced to the influence of the hedge schools is the differing stress patterns in Irish English, with verbs of several syllables compared to southern British English, e.g. *exaggerate, distribute, realise*, which frequently have final stress, particularly in vernacular varieties. Bliss (1977a: 18) maintained that because the Irish learned English from people for whom this was not their native language these non-standard patterns arose. But irregular accentuation is more or less confined to such verbs in Irish English and variation in these patterns is known from British English as well, so that hedge schools need not be appealed to in this context.

There is, however, a certain tendency in Irish English towards spelling pronunciations with certain words. This may well have its origin in the mediators of the target language, i.e. in the speech of second-language users of English, a practice which has to some extent continued to the present day. For instance, words with <a> are often found with [aː] rather than English [eɪ] as in *data* ['daːtə] or *status* ['staːtəs].

2.1.6 THE NINETEENTH CENTURY

The nineteenth century opened with the political union of Ireland and England in 1801, which in itself had no linguistic effect on the country. Paradoxically, it was the efforts of the Catholic community for emancipation, under their leader

Table 2.2. *Illiteracy in mid to late nineteenth century Ireland*

Illiteracy (over five years of age)
1841   over 70% for Galway, Mayo and Kerry; 60–70% for Cork, Roscommon, Sligo and Donegal; there is a general gradient from West to East in this respect
1861   60–70% only for Galway/Mayo
under 50% for Kerry, Cork, Waterford, Donegal
1891   under 40% for Galway, Mayo, Kerry, Cork, Waterford, Donegal; under 30% for the rest of the country

Daniel O'Connell, which had by far the greater effect. O'Connell's championing of the Catholic cause led to the Catholic Emancipation Act of 1829. He himself urged his fellow countrymen to abandon Irish as he saw English as the necessary pre-condition for social advancement (see section 1.4.1).

One linguistically far-reaching consequence of the emancipation was the formation of a system of National Schools (for primary education) in 1831 in which instruction was in English. This led to a marked decline in illiteracy in Ireland (see table 2.2), but also added considerable momentum to the language shift which was already fully under way.

The second major factor in language shift in the first half of the nineteenth century was the blow which was dealt to the Irish language by the Great Famine of the late 1840s. There had been many previous cases of famine, some of which were confined locally (de Fréine 1965: 30f.), but the event at the middle of the nineteenth century overshadowed all that went before. The famine was triggered by a failure in the potato crop due to blight, a fungus (*phytophthera infectans*) which spread rapidly in the damp and crowded conditions of the Irish countryside. Because the pre-famine economy was heavily reliant on potatoes as the staple diet of the great majority of the rural population (Duffy et al. 1997: 88f.) the failure of the crop, above all in the three years following 1845, had particularly serious consequences. This decimated the native population, approximately 1 million dying of starvation or malnutrition (Duffy et al. 1997: 88f.). Of those who died, some 40% were from Connaught, 30% from Munster, 21% from Ulster and 9% from Leinster. This breakdown shows clearly that it was the exclusively rural regions far from the more prosperous east coast that suffered most. The famine also provoked waves of emigration, mostly to North America. In 1847 this was anxious flight (Neal 1997) but in 1848 it was more organised. Many established farmers left, draining vital human resources from the countryside (Woodham-Smith 1991 [1962]: 371). The poverty triggered by the famine also affected the commercial life of the country in the towns and in general weakened the structure of Irish life (Woodham-Smith 1991 [1962]: 378). Needless to say, this was not a scenario in which the Irish language could flourish. Given the prospect of emigration to less distressed parts of the anglophone world, knowledge of English became an even greater priority.

Table 2.3. *Population and land holdings in mid to late nineteenth century*

Growth in population
1841–51   Dublin 9%
1891–1926   Dublin 20% or more

Decline in population
1841–51   20–29%, Roscommon 30–39%
1851–1891   20–50% in all counties bar Dublin
             greatest decline in midlands and mid south (Tipperary, Kilkenny) along
             with Clare
1891–1926   20–29% for all Connaught
             10–19% for Munster (bar Waterford with 20–29%) and Leinster

Holdings in number of acres
1841   1–5 acres for over 60% of Connaught and 30–49% of Ulster
1911   over 15 acres applied to 50–60% for all Munster, most of Connaught and
             Leinster

2.1.6.1   Population changes

The nineteenth century is the period of greatest change in population density
and agricultural holdings (Guinnane 1996; Kennedy and Clarkson 1993). Most
of the south of Ireland was reduced between 1841 and 1891 from 200–400 to
100–200 inhabitants per square mile (Dudley Edwards with Hourican 2005:
214–20). The figures given in table 2.3 attempt to indicate changes in population and farm holdings (Gray 1999). The rural decline was due to the twin
effects of famine and emigration (largely to Britain and the United States). With
the reduction in population, the size of holdings increased as the vicious circle of dividing and subdividing land with each generation lost its grip on the
countryside.

2.1.6.2   The decline of Irish

The nineteenth century, more than any previously, experienced the decline of
the Irish language (Duffy et al. 1997: 94f.; Hindley 1990: 13–20; Ó Cuív 1969:
137–40). Because of the Great Famine (1845–8) Ireland may have lost anything
up to two million native speakers of Irish (about a quarter of the population in the
mid nineteenth century), either through starvation or emigration. Those Irish
who sought work in North America or England were for the most part rural
inhabitants from the west and south of the country, i.e. they were in the main
native speakers of Irish.

There is little statistical documentation of the decline of Irish in the eighteenth
century. Any estimates there are rely on figures for individual baronies, some of

which have been assessed by scholars concerned with the matter (Fitzgerald 1984). By the nineteenth century a clearer picture emerges, particularly after the census of 1851 which was the first to return figures for language use. Unfortunately, this census is after the Great Famine and a considerable reduction in the number of speakers had already taken place. Furthermore, the extent to which the Irish themselves favoured the move to English should not be underestimated. The 1851 census shows a widespread denial of Irish. The returns maintain that only 300,000 people knew no English. But later censuses show a larger number of monolinguals and there was no increase in this group in the nineteenth century, but rather a severe decline. The conclusion is that the census figures show gross over-reporting of a knowledge of English by the native Irish (de Fréine 1965: 73f.).

The decline of the language proceeded rapidly during the latter half of the nineteenth century. According to the 1851 census (if anything, conservative in its figures), the entire region from Donegal in the north-west down the western seaboard and across to Waterford in the south-east was a contiguous area with about 50 per cent of the population Irish-speaking. There were also pockets of Irish in Ulster, for instance in mid Tyrone and north Antrim. By 1891 the large western area had been broken into three subareas which continued to shrink during the first half of the twentieth century, ultimately yielding the situation today where there are only three remaining Irish-speaking regions on the western seaboard, in the south-west, the mid-west and the north-west, with not significantly more than 30,000–40,000 native speakers of Irish left.[11] The three areas furthermore speak divergent dialects, none of which is automatically accepted as a standard for Modern Irish.

2.2   Languages in medieval Ireland

A reliable assessment of the languages of medieval Ireland must take into account the ethnic composition of the newcomers, their internal relations and their relative social position. As stated above, the Normans were the military leaders with the English occupying a lower rank. However, the English had a greater status vis-à-vis the Welsh and Flemish as they were the representatives of the majority language of England. The latter groups may have continued to use their native languages for a time but without any influence on the remaining languages in Ireland.[12]

---

[11] It is difficult to give exact figures here because government statistics today exaggerate in favour of Irish. In addition, the issue of just who is a native speaker is not easy to determine, especially because virtually all speakers of Irish are fluent in English.

[12] There is a certain amount of influence of Welsh on Irish from the Old Irish period. This was due to previous contacts between both sides of the Irish Sea during the period of early Christianisation (see C. O'Rahilly 1924 in which there are two sections on loans: 'British loanwords in Irish', pp. 137–41, and 'Irish loanwords in British', pp. 142–6). This led to a moderate amount of linguistic influence either directly or to be seen in the British form of Latin borrowings.

The linguistic traces of Middle English and Anglo-Norman[13] allow certain conclusions regarding their development in the centuries after the invasion. Because the Normans settled in rural Ireland and hived themselves off from their related rulers in England, they quickly assimilated to the local Irish, adopting the language of the latter and influencing it considerably in the process (Risk 1971, 1974). English was represented by different varieties due to the diverse regional origins of the early English settlers. This fact may have led to an intermediate variety[14] arising in the fourteenth century, a compromise between the varieties of different speakers. It is this language which is incorporated in the major literary document of medieval Irish English, the *Kildare Poems* (see section 2.3).

2.2.1 ENGLISH AND ANGLO-NORMAN

Almost the entire records of medieval Irish English are represented by the poems in the collection to be found in the British Library Harley 913 manuscript (Lucas and Lucas 1990). The sixteen English poems are known at the latest since Heuser (1904) as the *Kildare Poems*. Apart from this, there are a few smaller pieces which illustrate Irish English before the early modern period. Among these are an English version of the *Expugnatio Hibernica* by Giraldus Cambrensis, 'Gerald of Wales', from some time between the first quarter of the fifteenth and the second half of the sixteenth century (Hogan 1927: 26f.), and an English translation by James Yonge (a Dublin notary of the early fifteenth century) of *Secreta Secretorum*, a treatise on moral questions and duties (see Steele 1898). What is called the *Book of Howth* is a sixteenth-century compilation containing several pieces in English. In addition to these there are a few literary pieces in Anglo-Norman (Risk 1971: 589), notably *The Song of Dermot and the Earl* (Orpen 1892; Long 1975) and *The Entrenchment of New Ross* (Shields 1975–6). The former piece is about the relationship between Dermot MacMurrough and Strongbow and the second deals with the building of a fortification for the medieval town of New Ross in the south-east of the country (see the annotated excerpts of these works by Terence Dolan in Deane 1991: 141–51).

If the language of the *Kildare Poems* is a genuine representation of medieval Irish English, then it would seem that an amalgam of the different varieties which were spoken by English settlers had arisen by the thirteenth century. As there is no mention of the Bruce invasion of 1315 (Lydon 1967: 153), one can be

---

[13] This term is taken to refer to the variety of northern French which was transported to England immediately after the Norman conquest and which was spoken by the Norman inhabitants in south-west Wales from where the original settlers of Ireland originated. The later, more central variety of French which is important in the development of English played no role in the linguistic changes in Ireland after the twelfth century. On the literature of the period, see Legge (1963) and Vising (1923); specifically on Anglo-Norman in Celtic countries, see Trotter (1994).

[14] The notion of a compromise dialect arising in Ireland has been aired before by McIntosh and Samuels (1968) but not followed any further; see discussion below.

reasonably confident in dating the *Kildare Poems* to before this event or at least not long after it.[15]

2.2.2 THE STATUS OF ANGLO-NORMAN

Anglo-Norman remained the language of the ruling landlords for at least two centuries after the initial invasion in 1169. The English rulers of the time were themselves French-speaking: Henry II, who came to Ireland in 1171 and issued the Charter of Dublin in the same year, could not speak English according to Giraldus Cambrensis (Cahill 1938: 164). There would appear to have been a certain tension between French and English in Ireland and not just between Irish and English. This is later attested quite clearly by the Statutes of Kilkenny (1366, Lydon 1967: 155), a set of regulatory laws which prohibited, among other things, Irish in public dealings and recommended English (see section 2.1.2).[16]

The Normans also exerted a considerable ecclesiastical influence in Ireland. Before their arrival, the religious focus of the country was Clonmacnoise on the River Shannon in the centre of the country. This waned in status after the introduction to Ireland of new continental religious orders (Watt 1972: 41ff.) such as the Cistercians (founded in 1098 in Cîteaux near Dijon) and the Franciscans.

The extent of the Norman impact on Ireland can be recognised in surnames which became established. Such names as Butler, Power, Wallace, Durand, Nugent and all those beginning in Fitz-,[17] e.g. Fitzpatrick, Fitzgibbon, testify to the strength of the Normans in Ireland long after such events as the loss of Normandy to England in 1204. Anglo-Norman influence on Irish is considerable in the field of loanwords but the reverse influence is not attested, although official documents exist to almost the end of the fifteenth century which were written in Anglo-Norman or Latin (Cahill 1938: 160). The high number of everyday loans (see below) would suggest close contact between Anglo-Norman speakers and the local Irish.

The Anglo-Norman landlords established bases in the countryside, as clearly attested by the castles they built. These Normans were granted land by the English king and in principle had to render service or pay scutage. These in their turn had others on their land who would also have been of Norman or

---

[15] This invasion was carried out from Scotland at the invitation of some of the Irish and led to large parts of Ulster and north Leinster falling into the hands of Edward Bruce, the brother of Robert Bruce of Scotland, and his gallowglasses (Scottish mercenaries). Edward was crowned king on 1 May 1316 in Dundalk. His reign was brief, however, as he died in battle at Faughart near Dundalk in 1318 (Dudley Edwards with Hourican 2005: 38–41).

[16] According to Cahill (1938: 164), Anglo-Norman began to cease as a vernacular in the mid fourteenth century and was replaced by Irish. Compare this with the position in England where the demise was more rapid (Rothwell 1975–6).

[17] This derives from the Norman pronunciation of *fils, fiz* 'son' (Rothwell 1992: 306) and matched the prefixes *Ó* '(grand)son' and *Mac* 'son' already present in Irish.

English stock, while the native Irish were on the level of serfs.[18] Because of this organisation there were clear lines of contact between the natives and the new settlers which account for the linguistic influence of Anglo-Norman on Irish.

The high number of everyday loanwords from Anglo-Norman in Irish (Risk 1971, 1974; Hickey 1997b), e.g. *páiste* 'child' (< *page*), *garsún* 'boy' (< *garçon*), suggests that the new settlers used Anglo-Norman words in their Irish and that these then diffused into Irish by this variety being 'imposed' on the native Irish (see Guy 1990 for a discussion of this type of language contact). A similar model has been suggested for the appearance of a large number of Old Norse words in Scottish Gaelic with initial /s/ + stop clusters. Here the Old Norse settlers are assumed to have imposed their variety of Gaelic – which would have included many Old Norse words, identifiable by characteristic initial clusters – on the general Scottish Gaelic-speaking population around them (Stewart 2004).

The quantity of loans from Anglo-Norman into Irish and their phonological adaptation to the sound system of Irish (see Hickey 1997b for details) speaks for both a socially important donor group (the Anglo-Normans) and at the same time for a large and stable group of substrate speakers. This latter fact would explain why the loans from Anglo-Norman were completely adapted to the sound system of Irish, e.g. the word *páiste* /ˈpɑːsʲtʲə/ 'child' shows obligatory metathesis and devoicing of the /dʒ/ in *page* to make it conform to Irish phonotactics. This adaption is evidence of the robust position of Irish at the time and contrasts with that today where English loans are entering the language in large numbers (Hickey 1982; Stenson 1990) and are not necessarily adapted phonologically, e.g. *seaicéad* /ˈsʲakʲeːd/ 'jacket', an older loan which has a modern equivalent /ˈdʒakɪt/, where the voiced affricate is not devoiced and simplified as in the earlier case.

The strong position of Irish in the post-invasion period led to extensive bilingualism among the Anglo-Normans. It is known that they assimilated rapidly to the Irish, intermarrying and, from the point of view of the mainland English, eventually becoming linguistically indistinguishable from them. Indeed two members of the Anglo-Norman nobility became noted Irish poets, the first Earl of Kildare (died 1316) and Gerald, the third Earl of Desmond (died 1398), 'Gerald the Rhymer'. This situation lasted throughout the fifteenth and sixteenth centuries and led commentators on the state of Ireland like Richard Stanihurst (1586) to bemoan the weak position of English with respect to Irish even in the towns of the east coast.

It was a practical step for the Anglo-Normans to change over to Irish and one which facilitated their domination of Ireland. The retention of Irish for such a long period after the initial invasion (Cosgrove 1967) helped to cement their independence from English-speaking mainland Britain, something that was not

---

[18] See the chapter 'The structure of Norman-Irish society', pp. 102–25, in Otway-Ruthven (1968) and Flanagan (1989). Works which deal specifically with urban development in the history of Ireland are Butlin (1977) and Harkness and O'Dowd (1981).

seriously threatened until the advent of the Tudors (Dudley Edwards 1977); see section 2.1.3.

2.2.3 THE POSITION OF ENGLISH

The English settlers in medieval Ireland[19] came from different parts of the west and the south-west of England. The speakers of these different varieties were later to be found in greatest numbers in the east of the country, i.e. in the area of initial settlement. They did not always spread out into the west as the Normans did or, if so, then frequently as servants of the latter. Many of the English and Welsh settlers left after pressure from the local Irish of equal standing. Apart from a few towns like Galway and Limerick, it was the eastern coast with its urban centres, from somewhat north of Dublin down to Waterford in the south-east, that formed the main area of English settlement from the late twelfth and thirteenth centuries onwards.

The historian Edward Cahill saw the position of English in the post-invasion period as relatively weak (Cahill 1938), giving way to Irish by the end of the fourteenth century in rural areas. Edmund Curtis, writing somewhat earlier, saw the towns (the east coast with Galway and Limerick on the west) as the strongholds of English, places from where it spread again during the Tudor period (Curtis 1919: 242).

Both authors agree that, however weak English was in terms of the whole country, it was relatively strong on the east coast. Within this region, English was widespread not only in the towns but also in some rural areas, as testified by the two language enclaves, the baronies of Forth and Bargy in the extreme south-east corner in county Wexford and the area named Fingal, immediately north of Dublin. These areas retained their features well into the early modern period. The major towns of this eastern area are Waterford, Wexford, New Ross, Kilkenny, Kildare and of course Dublin.

The east coast variety of English, which developed out of an amalgam of varieties in the course of the thirteenth century, came under increasing pressure from Irish. By 1500 one can safely say (Bliss 1976: 559; 1977a) that Anglo-Norman and English in rural Ireland had largely succumbed to Irish. In the towns, the position of Irish was also strong but it did not succeed in supplanting English in the east of the country.

The linguistic features of early Irish English fall into two groups. The first are those which can be reasonably regarded as characteristic of the medieval variety of Irish English and the second are those which can be traced back to influence from Irish.

When dealing with medieval Irish English, McIntosh and Samuels (1968: 9) refer to a 'phonetic compromise' of forms in a community of speakers with mixed

---

[19] See the overview chapter by Lydon (1967) for an outline of the English colony in Ireland in the fourteenth century. On language in particular, see Bliss (1984a) and Bliss and Long (1987). Irish English literature of this period has been dealt with by Seymour (1970 [1929]).

Table 2.4. *Features of medieval Irish English after McIntosh and Samuels (1968)*

1. Initial /θ/ in the third-person-plural pronouns for the nominative (*þay, þai, thay*)
2. The inflected and possessive forms *ham, har* 'them, their'
3. A high vowel in *sill, syll(e)* 'sell' and *hir(e), hyr(e)* 'hear'
4. *I, y* as a prefix for past participles and as a suffix for the infinitive
5. Initial *h-* in *hit, hyt* 'it'

dialect backgrounds. To substantiate their arguments they quote the form *euch(e)* 'each' which is the preferred form in medieval Irish texts. This they see as an intersection of the form *each(e)* to the south of Herefordshire and south-west Worcestershire and *uch(e)* to the north of this area in England. It is compromise of this type which they see as relevant for the 'evolution of new colonial dialects'. Other features which one could enumerate are listed in table 2.4. With regard to the last feature, one can note that initial *h-* was lost in many words which have retained it to the present-day: *ad* 'had', *is* 'his' (Heuser 1904: 31f.) and is found at the beginning of words where there is no etymological justification for it: *hoke* 'oak', *hold* 'old' (P. L. Henry 1958: 67). This could be uncertainty on the part of Irish English speakers as /h-/ occurs only as a morphologically determined prefix in Irish and the triggering environment for it would, of course, not have been present in English.

Possible transfer in medieval Irish English could be responsible for the confusion of *t* and *th* in writing, the use of *w* for /v/ – possibly due to Irish where the non-palatal /v/ is often realised without any friction as [ß, w] – the devoicing of stops in unstressed final syllables and gemination (in writing at least) after short vowels (Hickey 1993: 228) and some long vowels as well such as *botte* 'boat', *plessyd* 'pleased'.

2.2.3.1 Phonological evidence of early Irish English and Irish

The pronunciation of early Irish English can be partially confirmed by various loanwords which appear in Irish after the twelfth century. Because the Great Vowel Shift had not yet occurred the vowels written as <a, i, u> were pronounced as /aː, iː, uː/, as can be seen in the loans *bácús* /baːkuːs/ 'bakehouse' and *slísín* /sʲlʲiːsʲiːnʲ/ 'little slice, rasher'. In some cases, the rendering of English loans in Irish offers confirmation of a suspected pronunciation in the latter language. For instance, the vowel written <ao> is taken to have been pronounced /iː/ in the north and west of Ireland and /eː/ in the south. The word *whiting* [ʍiːtɪŋ] (pre-vowel shift) gave *faoitín* in Irish which in its orthography confirms that *ao* was definitely /iː/ in many forms of Irish. In addition, one sees here that English [ʍ] was rendered by Irish /f/ (phonetically [ɸ] in western and northern dialects). The equivalence of these sounds is also attested in the opposite direction with the rendering of the Irish surname *Ó Faoláin* as *Pheelan* or *Wheelan*.

2.3   A singular document: the *Kildare Poems*

Irish English of the late Middle Ages (Benskin 1980) is recorded in two sources. The first is the *Kildare Poems* and the second is the so-called *Loscombe Manuscript*. The designation *Kildare Poems* is used as a cover term for sixteen poems which are scattered among Latin and Old French items of poetry in the Harley 913 manuscript in the British Library.[20] The *Loscombe Manuscript* is so-called because it came into the possession of one C. W. Loscombe. This volume probably dates from the end of the fourteenth century and contains two poems of interest, 'On blood-letting' and 'The virtue of herbs', which, according to the analyses of Heuser (1904: 71–5), Irwin (1933b) and Zettersten (1967), are to be considered without a doubt as Irish. In discussing both sets of poems, Heuser mentions a variety of features which point to the south-west of England (the assumed source of English in medieval Ireland) and to Ireland in particular. These poems also betray the influence of the Irish language (Heuser's *Keltischer Einfluß* 'Celtic influence'). The poems were known in the early nineteenth century to Thomas Wright and Joseph Halliwell who published the first in its entirety and a fragment of the second in their *Reliquiae Antiquae I* (1841). The poem 'The virtues of herbs' is contained in MS 406 of the Wellcome Historical Medical Library (in its possession since 1914).

The history of the manuscript containing the *Kildare Poems* is outlined in T. Crofton Croker's *Popular Songs of Ireland* (1939). The Irish provenance of the *Kildare Poems* is not doubted, although whether Kildare is the town of origin is disputed. The case for Kildare is based on the explicit mention of one Michael of Kildare as author of a poem. Waterford is just as likely a candidate (McIntosh and Samuels 1968: 2). Benskin (1989) maintains that the *Kildare Poems* were composed in Kildare but copied in Waterford as they show in-line spellings like *cherch* (and often *church*), a specifically Waterford form (found in the municipal records of that city), for the more general *chirch*.

It is a matter of debate whether the manuscript in the British Library is the work of one or more hands. Two studies – Benskin (1989 and 1990) – regard the pieces as the work of a single scribe (Benskin 1990: 163) as do Lucas and Lucas (1990: 288). Furthermore, Benskin maintains that the compiler of the manuscript copied the texts in the dialectal form in which they were available to him, i.e. he did not 'translate' them into his own variety of English (Benskin 1990: 189). The *Kildare Poems* were critically edited by Wilhelm Heuser in 1904 in the *Bonner*

---

[20] Both Heuser (1904) and Hogan (1927) refer to the Harley 913 manuscript as being in the British Museum and the empty page opposite the opening of *Land of Cockaygne* has a stamp reading *Museum Britannicum*. But later authors, such as Benskin (1990) and Lucas (1995), refer to it as being in the British Library where it is currently located.

Beiträge zur Anglistik [Bonn Contributions to English Studies]. Lucas (1995) is a more recent edition.[21]

Irish English of the fourteenth century is recorded briefly in two other sources. The first is an account book of the Priory of Holy Trinity Chapel in Dublin, where the poem 'The pride of life' was discovered. The manuscript was prepared around 1340 (Heuser 1904: 66). The second source is the Acts and Statutes of the City of Waterford from 1365. Although there is no critical edition of these, there are remarks on their language in P. L. Henry (1958: 66). There are a few further manuscripts which are either positively Irish or which can be assumed with reasonable certainty to be so. These are listed in McIntosh and Samuels (1968). Additional treatments of medieval Irish English material are to be found in Holthausen (1916), Irwin (1933a, 1933b, 1935) and Zettersten (1967).

Mention should be made here of the Slates of Smarmore, a number of inscriptions found near the ruins of a church at Smarmore, a small village near Ardee in Co. Louth. The slates contain medical recipes and some musical and religious material (Bliss 1965; Britton and Fletcher 1990). The provenance of the slates is clearly Irish and their language is medieval Irish English.

From the sixteenth century there is the motley *Book of Howth* (Kosok 1990: 28), which is not, however, particularly interesting linguistically. Despite the relatively long period for which there are documents, their actual number is small, very small, if one compares it with the number for mainland England or Scotland in the same period: the remnants of medieval Irish English can be counted on the fingers of one hand.

2.3.1 SOUND SEGMENTS

It is difficult to say to what extent the remains of Irish English can be viewed as a true representation of this variety in the fourteenth century. They appear to be fairly close to many orthographic practices of the period. Nonetheless, there are recurring deviations from Middle English, particularly from the dialects of west and south-west England, which formed the initial input to Ireland. As noted above (see section 2.2.3), some of the unexpected forms may derive from compromises which occurred between various dialects of English in Ireland at the time. A further issue which has not always been discussed in the scholarly literature – but see Hickey (1993) for an assessment – is the extent to which the idiosyncrasies of medieval Irish English can be traced to substrate influence from Irish.

---

[21] For the following investigation the electronic versions of the *Kildare Poems* and the *Loscombe Manuscript*, containing 'On blood-letting' and 'The virtue of herbs', were used. These are contained in *A Corpus of Irish English* (on the CD-ROM accompanying Hickey 2003a). The attestations were determined by the present author, using the retrieval software *Corpus Presenter*, which is contained and discussed in Hickey (2003a). For up-to-date information on this software, please consult the website at the following address: www.uni-due.de/CP.

In the following sections mention is made of the possibility rather than the fact of interference from Irish. This caution is required in the case of the *Kildare Poems* and the *Loscombe Manuscript* as nearly all unexpected features have at least one possible explanation.

The morphology of these documents has been commented on in the relevant literature; see Heuser (1904: 35ff.) on the *Kildare Poems* and Zettersten (1967: 36) on the *Loscombe Manuscript*.

Coronal fricatives and plosives. In the *Kildare Poems* written forms are attested in which instead of *th* a single *t* occurs in the ending of the third person singular of the present with verbs: *fallyt* (= *fallyþ*) 'falls', *growit* (= *growiþ*) 'grows', *sayt* (= *sayþ*) 'says'. These forms are normally just registered but not commented on (see Zettersten 1967: 15; Heuser 1904: 31). It is, however, probable that the written *t* was intended to indicate the fortition of /θ/ to a dental or alveolar stop, i.e. to [t̪] or [t].

There are also cases of English *t* written as *th* in medieval Irish English: *lythe* 'lit', *sith* 'sit', *nogth* 'nought'.[22] The digraph *th* may have been used for the alveolar fricative [ṱ] which still is the realisation of the stop in the post-vocalic, word-final position shown here (Hickey 1984a). If this is the case, then the lenition of alveolar stops to fricatives is an archaic feature of Irish English. Support for this vintage is given by many apparent instances in the glossaries of Forth and Bargy (see section 2.4).

Labial fricatives and approximants. This area is more complex than in modern Irish English. Two factors play a role here: (i) the varieties of English which were imported into Ireland initially and (ii) the contact with Irish and the phonetic substitutions which resulted from this.

The language of the *Kildare Poems* in its English base resembles that of the west and south-west of England in the Middle English period. Many of the original immigrants to Ireland came not just from west Wales but also from the south-west of England (Hogan 1927: 15; Curtis 1919: 234ff.). In this area the initial voicing of fricatives is a prominent feature. Due to the orthographic distinction of voiced and voiceless labial and alveolar fricatives in English, the initial voicing is quite evident in medieval Irish English texts: *uadir* (= *father*), *uoxe* (= *fox*), *velle* (= *fell*). As the grapheme *u* in Middle English could represent both the vowel /u/ and the consonant /v/, one can assume the initial segment /v/ for the first two words just quoted.

The etymological comparison of the forms *uadir, uoxe, velle* suggests that the initial forms for these words in east Middle English had /f/. Looking at forms which have /v/ etymologically, one finds that a substitution took place. Consider *wysage* (= *visage*) and *trawalle* (= *travail*). To explain the substitution one must

---

[22] These forms which occur in the poem 'The virtue of herbs' are only briefly commented on by Zettersten (1967: 15). He maintains that they perhaps represent an 'aspirated consonant due to the influence of Irish'. By the term 'aspirated consonant' he probably means a lenited consonant. Zettersten's terminology stems from Pedersen (1897) where the (Danish) term 'aspiration' stands for 'lenition'. This is, however, more of a guess than an explanation.

interpret the orthography. In English the grapheme *w* indicates the labio-velar approximant /w/. On the basis of present-day contact English one can suspect that the *w* in the words just given does not represent this approximant but the bilabial fricative [β]. This sound in Irish is the realisation of the non-palatal phoneme /v/ in front of vowels (but not before sonorants). The sound has been assumed for the Old Irish period as well (Thurneysen 1946: 76), so that the same assumption for the late Middle Ages (around 1300) would seem justified. The conclusion here is that Irish English had a bilabial realisation of /w/ due to substrate influence from Irish. Thus the representation of these fricatives in the *Kildare Poems* with *w* is not surprising. This can also be found in word-final position, e.g. *abowe, hawe, fywe*.

Loss of nasals. A general Middle English development which can also be observed in the language of the *Kildare Poems* and the *Loscombe Manuscript* is the loss of a final nasal with verb forms: *haue* 'have', *come* 'come' (Zettersten 1967: 15f.). Possessive pronoun forms are also normally realised without a nasal in medieval Irish English, a nasal only appearing in an intervocalic position (as a hiatus nasal) in order to avoid the contact of two vowels and to provide a consonantal onset for a stressed syllable, e.g. *min, þin* (Heuser 1904: 33).

What is characteristic of medieval Irish English is the loss of nasals in the position immediately before coronal stops: *fowden* (= *founden*) 'found', *powde* (= *pounde*) 'pound', *mouthes* (= *months*) 'months' (Zettersten 1967: 15f.). It is furthermore to be found in a few pre-velar instances: *fowge* (= *fong*) 'catch', *зowge* (= *yong*) 'young'. If one regards this case of nasal loss as parallel to the more frequent loss before coronal plosives, then one can establish a connection with a process in Irish. Here the word-final sequence /nd/ does not occur. Already by the Old Irish period, clusters of dental nasal plus homorganic voiced stop were simplified to a single nasal: *clann* < *cland* 'children', *linn* < *lind* 'liquid, pool' (Thurneysen 1946: 93). The phonotactics of Middle Irish thus prohibited a final, post-nasal /d/. It would seem legitimate to view the loss of post-nasal stops in medieval Irish English in connection with this phonotactic restriction in the Irish of the time: *stowne* 'stand' (Heuser 1904: 74). Stop insertion, in instances like *ferdful* 'fearful' (Heuser 1904: 74; Zettersten 1967: 15), does not contradict the substrate hypothesis being put forward here because the cluster /-rd/ is very common in Irish.

Loss of /h/. With the neutral pronoun *hit, hyt*, the dropping of /h/ and with *jiſ*, that of /j/, are general Middle English developments. However, in both the *Kildare Poems* and the *Loscombe Manuscript* one finds further instances of etymologically justified /h/ being dropped: *is* (= *his*) 'his', *abbiþ* (= *habbiþ*) 'has', *ad* (= *had*) 'had' (Heuser 1904: 31f.). It is uncertain whether there was a general deletion of initial /h/ in medieval Irish English, much as there is in present-day urban British English (Wells 1982: 322). Irish influence might have been operative here. In Irish initial /h-/ only occurs under certain morphological conditions, before a vowel-initial noun when preceded by either the possessive pronoun 'her' or the plural of the article, e.g. *a hanam* /ə 'hanəm/ 'her soul' (from *anam* 'soul'), *na heaglaisí* / nə 'haɡləsʲiː / 'the churches' (from *eaglaisí* 'churches'). Because of the marked nature of initial /h-/ in Irish, it might have been avoided by the scribes of medieval Irish English.

For the *Kildare Poems* this would be a possible explanation. Such a situation would have led to uncertainty about where initial /h-/ occurs in English and there may well have been instances of hypercorrection, such as those in the *Dublin Book* from the second half of the fifteenth century, where a number of words show an additional /h/: *hable* (= *able*), *hoke* (= *oak*), *hold* (= *old*) (P. L. Henry 1958: 67). Even the later *Early Merchant Guild* documents have an unetymological /h/ as in: *hour* (= *our*), *hall* (= *all*), *hat* (= *at*) (P. L. Henry 1958: 67).

It should be mentioned that Anglo-Norman scribal tradition is responsible for spellings like *hour* and *honour* in Modern English. However, scribal practice of this kind is insufficient as an explanation of the variation in written *h-* in medieval Irish English which is found with verbs, pronouns and prepositions (the Anglo-Norman examples are confined to nouns).

Consonant doubling. Both the *Kildare Poems* and the *Loscombe Manuscript* show an unexpected doubling of consonants in word-internal position. This doubling is assumed in the relevant literature to be a sign of vowel shortness – *delle* (= *deal*), *hoppe* (= *hope*), *nosse* (= *nose*), *hotte* (= *hot*), *bitte* (= *bit*), *didde* (= *did*) (Zettersten 1967: 15f.; Heuser 1904: 34; P. L. Henry 1958: 65) – and may well indicate that the words in question did not undergo open syllable lengthening (see section 2.3.3 below for a discussion).

The interpretation of <sch> *and* <ss>. In Middle English texts there are different orthographical devices for representing the sound /ʃ/. Those which were used at the beginning of the Middle English period are *s* and *ss* (Mossé 1952: 39–43). Later *sch* was used (Scragg 1974: 46) as were *sh* and *ssh* (Berndt 1960: 10). In the *Kildare Poems*, the final two options are not attested (Heuser 1904: 29f.), but the sequences *sch* and *ss* occur alongside simple *s*.

The interpretation of *sch* as a palatal-alveolar fricative /ʃ/ receives support from both the orthographic practice in other dialect areas on mainland England in the Middle English period and from the etymological comparison with modern forms which show /ʃ/: *scholder* 'shoulder', *schame* 'shame', *schores* 'shores' (Heuser 1904: 29).

The digraph *ss* also points to the /ʃ/ sound. It does not occur in all the poems and excludes the option of *sch*: *flesse* (= *flesh*), *uerisse* (= *fresh*) (Heuser 1904: 30). Due to the distribution of *sch* and *ss* in the poems, one can assume that both spellings represent the same /ʃ/ sound.

A degree of confusion is caused in some forms by simple *s*. Normally, it represents /s/, but in some cases one is forced on etymological grounds to assume that it stands for /ʃ/: *sal* (= *shall*), *sul* (= *should*) (Heuser 1904: 29). Both these words are irrelevant with regard to the question of an Irish influence as, etymologically, they already contain /ʃ/.

There are, however, cases in which the orthography would seem to suggest a /ʃ/ sound rather than inherited /s/: *grasshe* (= *grass*), *hasshe* (= *has*) (Heuser 1904: 74; Zettersten 1967: 15). In the *Loscombe Manuscript*, from which these

Table 2.5. *Consonantal features in the language of the* Kildare Poems

1.	dental fricatives to stops	/ð/ > [t̪], /θ/ > [d̪]
2.	voicing of initial fricatives	*uadir* (= *father*), *uoxe* (= *fox*)
3.	fricative to approximant	*wysage* (= *visage*), *trawalle* (= *travail*)
4.	loss of nasals	*fowden* (= *founden*), *mouthes* (= *months*)
5.	loss of /h/	*is* (= *his*), *abbiþ* (= *habbiþ*)
6.	consonant doubling	*delle* (= *deal*), *hoppe* (= *hope*)
7.	possibly /ʃ/ for /s/	*grasshe* (= *grass*), *hasshe* (= *has*)

forms are taken, the sequence *ssh* is used to represent /ʃ/. These forms are interesting in connection with the substitution of /s/ by /ʃ/ in present-day contact English. The above examples show /ʃ/ after a low vowel and before a pause. In this position, however, /ʃ/ is not attested for /s/ in contact English. The substitution in the latter variety occurs immediately preceding or following plosives and after /r/, e.g. *west* [wɛʃt], *curse* [kəɹʃ]. But in this position one does not find it in the medieval manuscripts, although there are ample attestations of this position which triggers the substitution in present-day contact English: *speche, mystere, forst* (Zettersten 1967: 16).

2.3.2 SOUND PROCESSES

Vowel raising. Many words in the *Kildare Poems* and the *Loscombe Manuscript* show a raising of short vowels, of /a/ *a* to /ɔ/ *o*, but more commonly of the front vowel /ɛ/ *e* to /ɪ/ *i*. This is found most frequently in unstressed syllables (though *silf* 'self' shows this in a stressed syllable) and would appear to be conditioned as it only occurs before alveolars. The sounds which trigger this raising are usually /t/ and /s/ as well as nasals, the latter causing a more general type of raising. In post-stress position, the raising is most common with plural endings: *namis, herbis, synnis, enemys* (Zettersten 1967: 14). The letters *i* and *y* probably represented the same sound as there are no grounds for assuming that a front high rounded vowel /y/ existed at any time in Irish English. This assumption seems correct, although the vowel /y/ had maintained itself longest in south-western varieties of Middle English. In the latter, /y/ was indicated orthographically by *u* (Fisiak 1968: 39) and largely confined to stressed syllables. In the *Kildare Poems* and the *Loscombe Manuscript*, *i* and *y* are free orthographic variants of each other. For instance, with the present-tense ending of the third person singular, *-iþ/t* and *-yþ/t* are attested without any apparent conditioning: *falliþ, commiþ, semyþ* (Zettersten 1967: 14f.). Even if a /y/ sound had existed in the speech of the first settlers, it would not have received any support through Irish as there are no front rounded vowels in the latter language (nor were there in Middle Irish).

In the *Kildare Poems* the two most common plural endings of Middle English, *-s* and *-n*, are represented. Although the nasal plural was recessive in later Middle English (Fisiak 1968: 79), there are sufficient examples in both the *Kildare Poems* and the *Loscombe Manuscript*: *wortyn* 'warts', *wykyn* 'weeks', *kine* 'cows', *been* 'bees' (Zettersten 1967: 16). These instances provided further sites for the raising of short front vowels, here in the plural endings. Further examples of raising before nasals in the form of high offglides are found in the texts under consideration, e.g. *streinþ, leinþ* (Heuser 1904: 35). These words additionally show the shift of /ŋ/ to /n/ and the loss of /k/ in the final cluster, /leŋkθ/ > /leınθ/, a feature still found in Irish English.

Parallel to the vowel raising in unstressed position, there is in the *Kildare Poems*, and above all in the *Loscombe Manuscript*, a vowel shift in post-stress position before /r/. This would seem to be a contact phenomenon. The shift is to a high back vowel /u/, as attested in the words *wondur* and *sommur* (Zettersten 1967: 15).

The orthography here coincides with the Old and Middle Irish practice of indicating a velar sound by a preceding /u/ (Greene 1973: 127). What is interesting in this connection is the fact that the velarisation with /r/ would appear to have been particularly marked; cf. Thurneysen (1946: 97) who speaks of 'r-quality' (= velarisation – RH), e.g. with Old Irish *fiur* 'man' (dative singular) from *fer* (nominative singular). The velarisation of /r/ in *wondur*, *sommur* was probably strengthened by the /u/ of the first, stressed syllable in these forms, this leading to the particular orthography found here.

Metathesis. In the history of Irish, metathesis is well attested. It is already to be seen in the many orthographic variants of words in Old Irish (Thurneysen 1946: 113). In the Middle Irish period metathesis is frequent with loanwords from Anglo-Norman and Latin. Different types of metathesis occur in Irish: (i) metathesis of /s/ and a plosive; (ii) metathesis of two sonorants; and (iii) metathesis in which an /r/ and a (short) vowel change in sequence (Hickey in press). The first type is to be seen with loanwords, but is not attested in medieval Irish English: *coláiste* /-ʃtʲ-/ < *college* /-dʒ-/. The second type does not occur either but the third is to be found in the *Kildare Poems* and in the *Loscombe Manuscript*: a short vowel and /r/ switch sequence: *fryst* < *first, forst* < *frost*, *Gradener* < *Gardener, þroʒ* < *þorʒ* (Zettersten 1967: 16). This metathesis only takes place with short vowels, a restriction which still applies to present-day Irish English.

Undue importance should not be attached to /r/ ~ short vowel metathesis as it is common in dialects of mainland Britain and occurred quite commonly in Old English (Campbell 1959: 184f.). It continued in the Middle English period and indeed reverses many instances of earlier metathesis: *gærs* > *grass, cerse* > *cress, brinnen* > *burn* (Luick 1940: 917). It may well be the case that metathesised forms were imported with the original settlers rather than arising on Irish soil.

The continuation of /r/ ~ short vowel metathesis in Irish English could be interpreted not so much as a transfer phenomenon, but rather as a type of linguistic behaviour which gained support due to similar phenomena in Irish.

Epenthesis. This is a phonological process which is quite extensive in Irish (as is metathesis). It is not just quantitatively common, the number of cluster types which are susceptible to epenthesis in Irish is quite high (Hickey in press). The difficulty with determining whether epenthesis occurs in a variety only available in written form is that it is not usually represented orthographically. In the documents under consideration here, a number of cases of epenthesis can nonetheless be recognised in writing. The *Kildare Poems* show epenthesis in different positions, e.g. in medial and initial clusters: *Auerill* (= *April*), *uerisse* (= *fresh*) (Heuser 1904: 29). The form *uerisse* is a *hapax legomenon* in the *Kildare Poems* and the *Loscombe Manuscript*. *Auerill* is recorded several times, once in the poem 'Pers of Birmingham' (one of the *Kildare Poems*) and twice in the poem 'The virtue of herbs' in the *Loscombe Manuscript*. There is a possibility that *Auerill* was imported with epenthesis as it is also recorded in other Middle English dialects, e.g. in Scottish English (Onions 1966: 46).

For the existence of epenthesis in the *Kildare Poems* and the *Loscombe Manuscript* two further facts can be cited. The first is that epenthesis is recorded extensively in the dialect of Forth and Bargy which is closely connected with the language of the *Kildare Poems* (Heuser 1904: 56ff.; Zettersten 1967: 13f.; P. L. Henry 1958: 75ff.). The second fact concerns language-internal arguments, the main one being that syncope is not attested in the *Kildare Poems*. Unstressed vowels between segments which together would represent a legal syllable onset do not trigger syncope, thus one finds *wonderis*, not *wondris*, *breþeren*, not *breþren*, *norþeren*, not *norþren*, etc. There is a causal connection between epenthesis and syncope. In those languages in which epenthesis is extensively recorded, syncope is hardly known (for instance in Dutch; see Hickey 1986b). Thus the lack of syncope in the language of the *Kildare Poems* would offer support for the view that it also had epenthesis.

Final devoicing and fortition after sonorants. Apart from changes in place of articulation (dental fricative to plosive) there are other alterations in the area of coronal obstruents. Here one finds that final devoicing is well attested in the language of the *Kildare Poems*: *callit* 'called', *ihelpyt* 'helped', *purget* 'purged', *delet* 'dealed' (Heuser 1904: 31; Zettersten 1967: 15). Despite these forms one cannot speak here of general final devoicing. There is no such devoicing for labials and velars; it would appear to be restricted to alveolars and dentals and only occurs in unstressed syllables. As there are no attestations of voiced final labial or velar stops in unstressed syllables in the *Kildare Poems*, alveolar stops remain the only sounds which are affected by this process.

There is a phonetic motivation for final devoicing: in anticipation of the pause after a word, a stop becomes voiceless when it is also in an unstressed syllable, i.e. when the decline in phonation within the word has already begun in the unstressed syllable.

A further process, when viewed phonetically, can have the same effect as final devoicing, but shows a different phonotactic environment. In a position immediately after a sonorant, above all after /n/, a plosive in medieval Irish English shows a tendency to be voiceless. A condition on this process is that the stop in question is homorganic with the preceding sonorant: *fent* 'fend', *spent*

Table 2.6. *Phonological processes in the language of the* Kildare Poems

1.	unstressed vowel raising	*namis, herbis; falliþ, wondur, sommur*
2.	metathesis	*fryst < first, forst < frost*
3.	epenthesis	*Auerill* (= *April*), *uerisse* (= *fresh*)
4.	final devoicing	*ihelpyt* 'helped', *purget* 'purged'
5.	fortition after sonorants	*fent* 'fend', *spent* 'spend'

'spend', *trent* 'separated' (Heuser 1904: 31). In order to distinguish between the two kinds of voiceless final stops the terms 'final devoicing' and 'fortition after sonorants' are used here. Although fortition after sonorants is quite well attested for present-day contact English and in general Irish English, the significance of *fent, spent, trent* in terms of interference is slight as fortition after /n/ is common in mainland varieties of Middle English as well. Especially in late Middle English many instances of a preterite in /d/ after /n/ changing to /t/ with simultaneous loss of the preterite ending are recorded.

2.3.3 OPEN SYLLABLE LENGTHENING

At the end of the nineteenth century Karl Luick devised the term 'open syllable lengthening' for the phenomenon in the early Middle English period in which inherited short vowels which occurred in open syllable position were lengthened, this accounting for the long vowels in words like *nose* and *meat* in Modern English.

The original analysis whereby the open nature of the stressed syllable was responsible for the lengthening has been questioned in the past few decades. This discussion was triggered by Donka Minkova's 1982 analysis of the phenomenon in which she saw the loss of post-stress short /-ə/ as the trigger for the lengthening of the stressed vowel, i.e. the change was a kind of quantity adjustment on the loss of the short final vowel. More recent analyses, such as that by Nikolaus Ritt, see the lengthening as deriving from a variety of contributing factors. Ritt (1994) notes that the high vowels, /i/ and /u/, do not undergo lengthening, or hardly at all, so that words like *pity* and *city* retain a short stressed vowel although they represent a possible input to rule. Contrariwise, he notes that words with the low vowel /a/ always partake in the lengthening process, i.e. there would appear to be no words of the *tale* type which do not experience lengthening of their stressed vowel. The reason Ritt puts forward is that low vowels have greater sonority (openness, lack of constriction) than high vowels and this favours the tendency to lengthening which was present when the phenomenon known as 'open syllable lengthening' was active. Evidence from other languages supports the contention that low vowels tend to lengthen more than high ones, for instance in western Irish there is a lengthening of short /a/ to [aː] but not of /i/ or /u/ (Hickey 1986c).

Bearing the above situation in mind, one can turn to the *Kildare Poems* to see whether they offer evidence either for or against open syllable lengthening, given that they fall broadly into the period when this phenomenon was taking place in mainland Britain.

Final -e in medieval Irish English. Before attempting an analysis one must note that written final *e*, which according to many linguists (Jespersen 1909–49: I, 186f.; Prins 1974: 176) was pronounced until the fourteenth century, was apparently silent in the language of the *Kildare Poems*. Evidence for this is found in spellings without the final *e* in the *Loscombe Manuscript*, for example: *thos, tak, mak* (Zettersten 1967: 15). For the last two verbs the short forms, i.e. imperative and infinitive, have the following distribution in the *Kildare Poems*: *make* (7 instances), *mak* (3 instances); *take* (5 instances), *tak* (11 instances). If the *-e* in these forms was phonetic then it is most unlikely to be dropped in repeated occurrences of the same word in the same short text. Furthermore, the form *mak* rhymes with the form *sake* in 'Pers of Birmingham', which is another indication of a purely orthographic *-e*.

Reverse spellings are also attested in which a non-etymological *e* appears finally: *welle, grasshe, schalle*. These spellings are just as firm evidence as are late Middle English written forms with *-igh* for /iː/ in forms without an etymological /x/, this then showing the loss of /x/: *wright* for *write* (Wyld 1956 [1936]: 305).

Consonant doubling. As noted above, both the *Kildare Poems* and the *Loscombe Manuscript* show a doubling of consonants in a word-internal position, probably indicating a preceding short vowel, cf. *hoppe* (= *hope*), *nosse* (= *nose*), *botte* (= *but*), *bidde* (= *bid*), *didde* (= *did*). The doubling appears in words which have a short vowel in Middle English in general (last three instances just quoted). But in forms such as the first two this consonant doubling might suggest that – in the language of the *Kildare Poems* and the *Loscombe Manuscript* – there was probably no lengthening of vowels in open syllables.

A question which arises with the orthography is whether there was a phonetic basis for this consonant doubling, i.e. whether geminates still existed in this variety of Middle English. It is safe to assume that at this period – early fourteenth century – consonant quantity differences had already been lost (Jespersen 1909–49: I, 146; Jordan/Crook 1974: 152; Kurath 1956: 441). But in Irish the phonological distinction between long and short consonants in this position existed at this time and indeed is still retained in Donegal Irish (Wagner 1979: 16; Ó Baoill 1979: 88). While the possibility that the length difference was maintained in medieval Irish English because of the preservative influence of Irish cannot be dismissed entirely, the orthographic evidence suggests that the consonant doubling had the purpose of indicating vowel shortness. This is because the forms which exhibit such doubling do not necessarily have to be reflexes of older forms with geminates in Old English. In the non-literary texts of Irish English in the fourteenth and above all in the fifteenth century, such consonant doubling is frequent with words where the only interpretation is as an indicator of vowel shortness: *lyff* (= *life*), *wrytt* (= *write*), *gottes* (= *goats*), *strettes* (= *streets*) (P. L. Henry 1958: 65).

Differential lengthening. A differential application of open syllable lengthening may have occurred such that primarily the low vowel /a/ was lengthened. This rests on the assumption that a single consonant after a stressed vowel indicates that the latter was long; cf. forms of the verb *make* such as *makid* 'made'. Two difficulties arise here, however. Firstly, the assumption that single consonants indicate preceding long stressed vowels implies a very consistent use of orthography which simply may not have held. This is particularly true if one bears in mind that the *Kildare Poems* may have been composed by more than one author. The second difficulty concerns the nature of open syllable lengthening. If it is the case, as Minkova (1982) has demonstrated with conviction, that the vowel lengthening was due to the loss of schwa in disyllabic words, then a form like *makid* should at best only show lengthening by analogy with the uninflected form of the infinitive as there is no alteration in the quantity of the preterite form until the internal /k/ is deleted.

Variant spellings in the *Kildare Poems* may be of assistance in deciding the matter. The poem 'Pers of Birmingham' has monosyllabic words with reflexes of Old English /a/ (or /a/ from Scandinavian) and a final *-e*, e.g. *make*, *take*. If Minkova's thesis that the loss of schwa led to vowel lengthening as quantity compensation is valid, then one can assume a long /aː/ in *nam* 'name' and indeed in *make* as this has the variant *mak*. Consider that with the 26 instances of the verb *take* and the 34 of *make* in the *Kildare Poems* all have the spelling *-ak(-)*, i.e. there is no indication of a short vowel before the final consonant. In fact, of all the 11 instances of *-kk-* none occur in words with long vowels in later standard English, cf. the etymologically short vowels as in *sakke*, *blakke*, *lakke*, etc. These spellings would furthermore show that the final *-e* is not phonetic.

Length and number of syllables. Words of one syllable in English tend to have a longer vowel phonetically than those with more than one vowel where this vowel is the same phonologically. Hence the vowel in *mad* is longer than that in *madder*. Applying this knowledge to Middle English would lead one to expect a similar distribution of phonetic vowel quality.

The *Kildare Poems* offer evidence of just such a distribution. If one considers the forms of the verb *have* in this collection, then one sees that there are 9 instances of *habbeþ* / *habbiþ* with double-consonant spelling but only one instance of *habiþ*. The bare form of the verb, infinitive or imperative, is always written *hab* (31 instances). Remarkably, there is no instance of *habb(e)*, i.e. with the exception of the one form *habiþ* there is a complementary distribution between the double spelling in words of two syllables and the single spelling in monosyllables. If one interprets the double consonants as an indication of shortness of the preceding vowel, then one has for the *Kildare Poems* a distribution of vowel length in forms of the verb *have* such that a long vowel occurs in monosyllabic and a short vowel in disyllabic forms. The reading of double consonants as indicators

Table 2.7. *Open syllable lengthening in the* Kildare Poems

		Monosyllabic forms	Disyllabic forms
High vowels	back/u/	no	no
	front/i/	no	no
Mid vowels	back/o/	no	no
		nosse	(no attestation)
	front/e/	yes	yes
		speke	*weniþ*
Low vowel	/a/	yes	yes/no
		mak, hab, nam(e)	*makid, habbeþ*

of vowel shortness is again supported in the *Kildare Poems* by such verbs as *libbe* (= *live*) of which there are 6 instances and only one instance of *lib* with a single consonant.

Of the various vowel types above, the high vowels are not subject at all to lengthening. There are no instances of high back vowels which are lengthened and lowered in the *Kildare Poems*. The two occurrences of *wode* are not from Old English *wudu* 'wood', but the word for 'mad'. Old English *duru* 'door' which would provide a possible case of lengthening is not attested and, as Wełna (1978: 81) points out, there are no other clear cases of lengthening of late Old English /u/ in open syllables.

Front high vowels are not subject to lengthening either. Original short high front vowels are retained, again going on the interpretation of double consonants assumed here. The verb *witan* appears with the expected short vowel as in *ye witte* (= *you know*). The adjectival form derived from this is also attested with a short vowel: *witti*.

There is an important issue of chronology which should be addressed here. It is generally assumed that the *Kildare Poems* were composed in the first quarter of the fourteenth century (Lucas 1995). Open syllable lengthening is taken to have first affected the mid and low vowels /e, o, a/ and later the high vowels /i, u/, starting in the north of England in the latter half of the thirteenth century and spreading southwards in the course of the fourteenth century. This could well have meant that the lack of lengthening for high vowels in the *Kildare Poems* could be due to the separation of speakers of English in Ireland from mainland Britain before the change had been generalised throughout England. But even if this were the case, it does not invalidate the linguistic suggestion that the high vowels did not lengthen in medieval Irish English because of their slight sonority compared with lower vowels. If open syllable lengthening was present for low and some mid vowels, then forces of analogy could have been enough to act towards lengthening of high vowels. That this did not take place can be attributed to the low sonority and close articulation of high vowels.

The examination presented here is of general relevance to the phonology of Middle English. The quantitative analysis of the attestations of medieval Irish English lends credibility to the view that open syllable lengthening did not apply across the board but was sensitive to at least three factors: (i) loss of final schwa; (ii) relative height of the vowels, where high vowels were least likely and low vowels most likely to undergo the shift; and (iii) the number of syllables in a word. This would seem to have played a role, with monosyllables being most likely to experience vowel lengthening.

2.4   The antiquarian temptation: Forth and Bargy

The dialect considered here was once spoken in the south-east corner of Ireland, in the baronies of Forth and Bargy (read: [bargi]). After a period of decline, it was replaced entirely in the early nineteenth century by general Irish English of the region. The earliest record may well be contained in a late sixteenth-century drama: the seventh scene of the play *The Famous Historye of the Life and Death of Captain Thomas Stukeley* (from the 1590s, printed in 1605) has been handed down in two versions, the second of which was probably in the Forth and Bargy dialect. But for all practical purposes, the knowledge we have of this dialect is due to the work of a few scholars who at the end of the eighteenth and the beginning of the nineteenth century recorded it in the form of glossaries. These glossaries are available in database and text form in *A Corpus of Irish English* by the author, on the CD-ROM accompanying Hickey (2003a), and have been used for the present analysis.

The main sources of information on Forth and Bargy are two studies: the first is a 22-page essay with a glossary and some text by Charles Vallancey[23] which was published as a 'Proceeding of the Royal Irish Academy' in 1788. The second study is somewhat more substantial (70 pages in all) and consists again of a glossary with some texts which were collected at the end of the eighteenth century by a Protestant farmer, Jacob Poole,[24] though not published until 1867 by an Anglican

---

[23] Charles Vallancey (1721–1812) was an English army general and Irish antiquarian. Born in Windsor to a Huguenot family, Vallancey came to Ireland in 1762 as a member of the army and by 1803 had attained the rank of general. In keeping with the antiquarian fashions of his age, he founded a journal, *Collectanea de Rebus Hibernicis* (1770–1804), which dealt with all aspects of Irish culture. He speculated on the origin of the Celtic languages, seeing their origins in Asia Minor. Although Vallancey did not know Irish well, he published a *Grammar of the Hiberno-Celtic or Irish Language* in 1773, in which he praised the genius of Irish and characterised the language as 'masculine'. He was also one of the founders of the Royal Irish Academy (1785) after he had established the Hibernian Antiquarian Society in 1779. Although his own scholarship is scarcely acceptable by present-day standards, Vallancey did pave the way for later more objective research, particularly on the Irish language. His relevance for Irish English studies lies in the publication in 1788 (as one of the first proceedings of the Royal Irish Academy) of a glossary of the dialect of Forth and Bargy in Co. Wexford.

[24] Jacob Poole (died 1827) was a Protestant minister, born in Growtown, Co. Wexford, of a Quaker family. He is known in Irish English studies for his glossary of the Forth and Bargy dialect which he compiled in the first years of the nineteenth century. This glossary is much more comprehensive

clergyman, Rev. William Barnes[25] (see the foreword in the reprint by Dolan and
Ó Muirithe 1996: 33). A report by the Englishman J. A. Picton, also dating from
1867, is of secondary interest, although it contains an ostensibly original address
in the dialect. Two further studies from the nineteenth century, which, however,
hardly add to the decipherment of the dialect, are Hore (1862–3) and Russell
(1892 [1857]).

At the beginning of the twentieth century this variety of English aroused a
degree of linguistic interest. The anglicist philologists Edmund Curtis and James
Jeremiah Hogan comment on the dialect in two works of a general nature on the
history of Irish English (Curtis 1919: 248; Hogan 1927: 37ff.). The Celtologist
T. F. O'Rahilly compared the stress system of this dialect with that of surrounding
varieties of Irish (1932: 94f.). Since then no further analyses of this variety of Irish
English have appeared. Dolan and Ó Muirithe (1996 [1979]) is a reprint of Barnes
(1867) which, while it offers some etymological information, does not present
a linguistic analysis of the material. Ó Muirithe (1977a, 1990) do not contain
anything new and consist almost entirely of quotations. It is characteristic of
these works that the authors reject any attempt at phonological analysis, though
Ó Muirithe does offer guidelines to the pronunciation of modern Irish English
in the area of Forth and Bargy (Dolan and Ó Muirithe 1996: 17–20).

The only scholar who tried to evaluate the material of Forth and Bargy linguistically is Heuser. He relies on Barnes' edition of Poole (Heuser 1904: 56ff.)
and sees the dialect as a continuation of the language of the *Kildare Poems* despite
the relatively long period of time which lies between the attestations of the two
varieties of diachronic Irish English. This view is shared by the present author,
hence arguments are offered in support of regarding this archaic dialect as a relic
of Middle English rather than a form of Modern Irish English.

2.4.1 ORIGIN

The south-east of Ireland is the area in which the first English settlers arrived, so
that the Forth and Bargy dialect can be assumed to reach back to the initial phase of
settlement in the late Middle Ages. Furthermore, the baronies of Forth and Bargy
were – and still are – quite isolated. Located to the south of Wexford, without
any towns and no passage to any other part of the country, the baronies were
geographically separate from the areas to the west and north. Their position as
an enclave is shared with one region whose speech is even less attested and which
has been still less the object of scholarly interest, namely the dialect of Fingal,

---

than that of Vallancey and contains a few text pieces (songs) in an appendix. It was later edited by
William Barnes in 1867.
[25] William Barnes (1801–86) received limited school education (up to the age of fifteen) but then
studied privately, becoming a schoolmaster and later a country parson. His oeuvre consists of poetry
in his native Dorset dialect and a number of philological works (Barnes 1970 [1886]), including
many which are regarded as linguistic curiosities, such as *An Outline of English Speech-craft* (1878),
in which he aired his anti-classical views on the English lexicon.

an area immediately north of the city of Dublin (see map A6.2 in appendix 6 for locations). Knowledge of this variety of Irish English is due to historical references and to three small texts which are, however, corrupt (Bliss 1979: 194ff.; for a relatively detailed analysis, see Hogan 1927: 39ff.). Initial voicing, final stressed vowels and a number of Irish loanwords as well as syntactic constructions link Fingal linguistically with Forth and Bargy. After the seventeenth century there are no more extant texts in the Fingal dialect and – as opposed to the situation with Forth and Bargy in the south-east corner – there are no records of speakers of the dialect. As the texts in the Fingal dialect are of a satiric nature, and as they were probably composed by non-native speakers of the dialect, they are of correspondingly less value for linguistic analysis than the glossaries of Forth and Bargy, but see remarks in section 2.4.5.

The origin of the enclaves of Fingal and of Forth and Bargy can be accounted for by considering the geopolitical developments in Ireland in the fifteenth and sixteenth centuries. After the extensive cultural and political assimilation of the Old English, Ireland became more and more Irish-speaking. The wave of gaelicisation continued into the fifteenth century and was mentioned frequently by contemporary historians such as Richard Stanihurst in his 'Description of Ireland' in Raphael Holinshed's *Chronicles* (Stanihurst 1965 [1577]: 3ff.). He maintains that English was only spoken in the area of the Pale (then encompassing Co. Dublin and north Co. Kildare) and some adjoining counties such as Meath and Louth to the north and Wicklow, Carlow, Kilkenny, Wexford and Waterford to the south. Stanihurst also mentions a certain county 'Fingal', probably to him the area around Dublin city. A pocket in north county Dublin is the only area where the Fingal dialect survived in the seventeenth century.

Stanihurst also refers to the second region in which English succeeded in maintaining itself: Forth and Bargy. From this it is evident that the two areas, Fingal and Forth and Bargy, are relic areas in which the English of the pre-Elizabethan period continued to be spoken beyond 1600. The varieties of English which were introduced into Ireland in the course of the seventeenth century, in the period of general colonisation of the south of the country, formed the basis for general southern Irish English today and were clearly distinguished from the varieties of the older period, i.e. those of Fingal and Forth and Bargy. These later varieties were themselves also influenced by Irish. However, certain prominent features of the English of the older period, such as initial voicing, are no longer to be found.

In Forth and Bargy quite a number of loanwords are attested. Most of these are from Irish, but some may be due to the influence of Flemish settlers from Pembrokeshire in south-west Wales who came to Wexford in the wake of the Norman invasion (their presence is also confirmed by the surname *Fleming* found in the south-east of Ireland). The number of words which are of Flemish origin is small, something which may be due to the fact that the glossaries of Forth and Bargy stem from a period 600 years after the first immigrants from Wales. Other Flemish words, had they existed, could have been replaced by English or

Table 2.8. *Possible Flemish loanwords in Forth and Bargy*

Forth/Bargy	Mid Eng	Flemish	
1. *grate*	*groat*	*groot*	'small coin'
2. *hamas*	*hame*	*hame*	'wooden frame on horse collar'
3. *prate*	*prate*	*praten*	'talk'

Irish words given the prolonged contact with Irish and competing varieties of English in the area over the centuries. Of the words in the Poole glossary only one is definitely Flemish (and Dutch) and not simultaneously attested in Middle English: *bebber* ~ *bibber* 'shiver'. This is doubtlessly the Flemish/Dutch word *bibberen* (van Wijk 1949 [1912]: 62), which is also found colloquially in north German. Certain other words are less firm signs of Flemish influence as they are also to be found generally in Middle English (see table 2.8).

Even if one considers the evidence for Flemish influence as conclusive, it is still not certain. Many scholars maintain (Curtis 1919: 235; Hogan 1927: 15; Cahill 1938: 159) that Flemish settlers were to be found in Wexford, but the loanwords listed in table 2.8 could simply have come indirectly into the dialect via English settlers from south-west Wales. For a phonological analysis of Forth and Bargy the question of Flemish influence is of interest with respect to one particular phenomenon, initial voicing.[26] As this is widespread in Flemish, at least for alveolar fricatives (Hermkens 1969: 64f.), it is also probable that it was a feature of the speech of the first settlers in this area of Ireland. However, because initial voicing is so widespread in the south and south-west of England (Wakelin 1977 [1972]: 91ff.), Flemish influence does not necessarily have to be postulated for its appearance in Forth and Bargy.

2.4.2 HANDLING THE ORTHOGRAPHY

For the present analysis certain points must be clarified in advance. It is essential to reach as unambiguous an interpretation of the orthography as possible. The authors concerned with this material always quote the written forms of words. These derive either from Vallancey or from Poole. In two recent works (Dolan and Ó Muirithe 1996: 7; Ó Muirithe 1977a: 50) doubts are raised about the originality of Vallancey's sketches of the dialect. The glossary in Vallancey (1788) is supposed to have been taken (without acknowledgement) from Poole's collections which at that time had not been published. Whether Vallancey's notes on the dialect are original or not cannot be determined anymore. What is more important, however,

---

[26] This feature is amply attested in the glossaries for Forth and Bargy (Hickey 1988: 236). Bliss (1979: 45ff.) has comments on the similarly archaic dialect of Fingal, north of Dublin, which also had initial voicing.

is to determine according to what principles (if any) he wrote down the words he noted.

Some words can be interpreted phonologically without much difficulty. For instance, it is safe to assume that *aany* 'any' had /aː/ and not /ɛ/ in this dialect. Phonetic detail cannot usually be captured in writing so that one cannot say in the above example whether the low vowel was central [aː] or back [ɑː]. For phonological analysis this detail is not significant.

In many cases standard English orthography is used and can usually be interpreted clearly. For example, the spelling *runt* for mainland English *rent* in all probability stood for /rʊnt/. Problems arise, however, when English orthography is ambiguous anyway. For instance, one cannot say whether the *ea* in *ear* 'before' was meant to indicate /iː/ (as in *fear*) or /eː/ (as in *great*).

With loanwords, above all from Irish, it is easier to conclude the pronunciation. The spelling *sleeveen* 'rogue, sly person' was obviously intended to represent the pronunciation [sliːviːn] or [ʃliːviːn] as the form is an Irish loanword, *slíbhín*, the vowels of which are definitely /iː/ in each case. When analysing Forth and Bargy forms Irish loanwords are important as the phonological form of the Irish source words is in almost all cases clearly established.

The greatest obstacle to unambiguous phonological identification is presented by those words which show an orthography which corresponds neither to that of English nor of Irish. These forms represent the attempt of the authors (Poole and/or Vallancey) to indicate a sound value which did not occur in more general forms of English. Within this group of words those which have an initial consonant followed by *h* present the greatest difficulty, e.g. *mhyne* 'much', *lhose* 'less', *khoal* 'coal', *rhin* 'run', *fhyne* 'fine', *dhew* 'dew'. It is uncertain who introduced this orthographical convention. Vallancey (1788: 28ff.) does not have such spellings although similar forms are also to be found in his glossary, for example the doubling of initial sonorants: *llean* 'grief, affliction' (Vallancey (1788: 31), from Irish *léan* where the double *ll* probably represents the palatal /lʲ/ found at the beginning of the word in Irish.

The few scholars who have commented on such spellings trace them back to Irish influence (Heuser 1904: 59) and speak of post-aspirated or aspirated consonants. It is true that there is lenition in Irish in which stops change to fricatives but this does not affect sonorants and the process is only to be seen word-initially under specific morphological conditions. In Forth and Bargy a post-consonantal *h* can appear at the beginning of a word and after a sonorant, so the simple interpretation of C+*h* as the fricative corresponding to a particular stop (for example *kh* = /x/, given *k* = /k/) is hardly correct in these instances.

2.4.3 FORTH AND BARGY AND THE *KILDARE POEMS*

To make the ties between Forth and Bargy and the *Kildare Poems* more credible, two facts must be borne in mind. The first is that Forth and Bargy, through contact with Irish over the centuries, obviously adopted a large number of loanwords

Table 2.9. *Comparison of features in the* Kildare
Poems *and Forth and Bargy*

	Kildare Poems	Forth and Bargy	
1.	*siþ*	*zeeth*	'since'
2.	*seue*	*zeven*	'seven'
3.	*for*	*vor*	'for'
4.	*fram*	*vrem*	'from'

which do not occur in the *Kildare Poems*. The second is that the language of the *Kildare Poems* is relatively standardised. For example, the initial voicing which is so characteristic of Forth and Bargy (Russell 1892 [1857]: 590) is only occasionally indicated orthographically in the *Kildare Poems*. Consider the selection of forms from both sources in table 2.9.

The initial voicing in Forth and Bargy cannot be traced to Irish. Here initial voicing is only found with the shift of /f/ to /v/ (an initial mutation, Hickey in press). In addition, the fricatives /z/ and /ʒ/ do not exist in Irish. Furthermore, if one is to believe Vallancey, no Irish was spoken in the baronies of Forth and Bargy and their dialect did not extend as far as the town of Wexford, so that the population was probably isolated from the Irish language (Browne 1927: 127f.; Russell 1892 [1857]: 589f.; Vallancey (1788: 19ff.) at the time the glossaries were being prepared, though many loanwords had entered the dialect before this.

The dialect of Forth and Bargy is clearly conservative, in vocabulary, grammar and pronunciation. One can still recognise in the glossaries features which disappeared from English centuries before, e.g. the retention of affricates with the first-person-singular pronoun and with verbs (Heuser 1904: 57): *ich* 'I', *bidge* 'buy' (OE *bycʒan*), *lidge* 'lie' (OE *licʒan*). With other forms it is necessary to assume a few phonological processes of the dialect and, by reversing them, one can arrive at an older English form.

(1)   *zitchel*   'such'
       sitchel   (i) initial voicing
       siltch   (ii) /l/ ~ /tʃ/ metathesis
       swylc   (iii) simplification of syllable onset (OE form)

Many of the archaic forms are attestations of different stages of English. Some of these are essentially Middle English (ME), others show forms which were still found in early Modern English in England, e.g. *zeeth*, cf. ME *siþe* 'since', *ligt* /lɪçt/ 'light', *nickht* /nɪçt/ 'night'. The first form just quoted was already replaced in the fourteenth century by *sittenes*, later by *since* (Onions 1966: 828). The second and third forms show a palatal fricative in the syllable coda which was not lost until the Early Modern English period, at different points in time in the different dialects of English (Wełna 1978: 202).

2.4.4 A POSTULATED SOUND SYSTEM

In the following an attempt is made at reconstructing the sound system of Forth and Bargy. To do this the spellings in the glossaries are interpreted against the background of late Middle English. For the attempted reconstruction below the issue of internal variation is not addressed. The number of spelling variants of words, above all in the glossary of Poole, would suggest that there was indeed variation within Forth and Bargy (and/or that Poole was uncertain about how to represent the dialect in writing). However, nothing can be undertaken to clarify this matter for lack of precise information on variation.

The greatest difficulties in reconstructing the sound system of Forth and Bargy lie in the area of vowels and there is little in the way of help from the compilers of the glossaries. The only comments on the vowel system of the dialect are to be found on two pages in Barnes (1867). These statements themselves require phonological interpretation. To a limited extent one can look to Irish loanwords in Forth and Bargy for clues on vowel values as the phonology of early modern Irish has been established with a fair degree of certainty.

Long vowels

The system of long vowels in late Middle English (Jordan/Crook 1974: 43ff.) had seven members as follows: /iː, uː, eː, oː, ɛː, ɔː, aː/. Each of these is taken in turn and the evidence for presence or absence in Forth and Bargy is considered.

Long high front vowel /iː/. This is clearly identified by Barnes: 'double *ee* sounds like *e* in *me*'. It is confirmed by the representation of Irish loanwords in Forth and Bargy: *comree* < Irish *coimrí* 'protection, patronage'. The spelling *ee* is also used for unshifted ME /iː/ which implies that, for many forms, Forth and Bargy had not undergone the Great Vowel Shift (henceforth: GVS): *heeve* /hiːv/ 'hive', *dreeve* /driːv/ 'drive', *dee* /diː/ 'die'. There are examples of vowel raising which is not found in English because of prior shortening: *deed* /diːd/ 'dead' where the original /ɛː/ was shortened in Middle English and thus not lengthened because of the GVS. Not all instances of this vowel show raising. Indeed one frequently has vowel lowering instead, as with *haade* /haːd/ 'head'.

Long closed front vowel /eː/. This was indicated first and foremost by the digraph *ea*: *eal* 'eel', *hearth* 'heart', *lear* (= ME *lere*) 'empty'. Evidence for this interpretation is offered by Irish loanwords. The number of loans with /eː/ is small, but they are all written with *ea*: *llean* < Irish *léan* 'grief, anguish'. Apart from spellings with *ea* there are some with *e*. However, it is uncertain whether these represent a short vowel or not: *mell* (< French *meler*) 'interfere', *met* (= ME *mete*) 'food', *whet* 'wheat'.

Long open front vowel /ɛː/. The development of ME /ɛː/ in this dialect shows two directions. The first is the lowering just mentioned, as in *haade* /haːd/ 'head'. The second is the same as that in many other varieties of English, i.e. the raising of the vowel via /eː/ to /iː/. There are many words in the glossaries written with *ee* (= /iː/): *leech* (= ME *leche*) 'leech', *keen* (= ME *kene*) 'keen'. The later shortening of /ɛː/ (Prins 1974: 141f.) for some words like 'dead' is not attested in this dialect: *leed* 'lead (metal)', *deed* 'dead'. Although the lowering of mid vowels to low vowels as a rule only affected /ɛː/, there are isolated examples where a lowering of /ɔː/ to /aː/ is to be seen, e.g. *dhraat* 'throat'.

Long low vowel /aː/. This vowel has various sources in Forth and Bargy. Generally ME /aː/ was retained in Forth and Bargy without essential change, e.g. *laady* 'lady', *kaake* 'cake', *faace* 'face', *aake* 'ache', *glaade* 'glad'. ME /aː/ was also raised to a back vowel /ɔː/ as a result of the influence of the following nasal in words like *naume* 'name' and *gaume* 'game'. ME /ɛː/ was lowered to /aː/ in many instances, cf. *laafe* 'leaf', *laave* 'leave', *maate* (= *mete*) 'food'. Another source of /aː/ in Forth and Bargy is where early ME /aː/ was not shifted to /ɔː/, and later to /oː/ as part of the GVS, as with *bane* 'bone'. The last source of /aː/ is the lowering and lengthening of /ɛ/ and some back vowels before /r/: *saareth* 'served', *garr* 'anger', *aar* 'their', *vargee* 'forgive', *varreet* 'forget', *avar* 'afore', *hardhel* 'hurdle'.

Long open back vowel /ɔː/. The spelling *oa* probably had the value /oː/. There are a number of arguments in favour of this. Firstly, those words which showed /ɔː/ in Middle English have a spelling which represents /oː/ in Modern English, e.g. *oke* 'oak'. Secondly, there is a certain variability in the orthography. One and the same word can be spelt with *oa* or the discontinuous sequence *oCe*. This would suggest the same pronunciation as those words which only have the spelling *oCe*, namely /oː/. Variation in spelling is to be found above all with those words which had lost a post-nasal voiced stop and which show subsequent nasal raising: *hone* ~ *hoan* 'hand', *brone* ~ *broan* 'brand', *lone* ~ *lloan* 'land', *sthrone* ~ *sthroan* 'strand'.

The vowel /ɔː/ nonetheless existed in Irish loanwords. These were spelled with *aw* or *au* by Vallancey and Poole: *puckawne* < Irish *pocán* 'buck', *arnaauneen* < Irish *airneánín* 'a little night work', *caubaun* < Irish *cábán* 'country cabin'. From this one can conclude that those English words which showed /au/ in Middle English had already been monophthongised to /ɔː/ by the time of the recording of the glossaries: *sau* /sɔː/ 'saw', *draugh* /drɔː/ 'throw'. This spelling was also used in order to indicate unexpected vowel values, for example, the raising of /a, ɒ/ to /ɔː/ before nasals: *llawm* 'lamb', *lhaung* 'long'. Occasionally, the raising is found in other environments: *kaudes* 'cats', *scaules* 'scales', *baush* < Irish *bos* 'palm of hand'.

Long closed back vowel /oː/ This vowel is indicated by the sequence *oCe*. There are in addition some spellings with *ow* or *ou* which perhaps point to /oː/, e.g. *yowe* 'ewe', *yullou* 'yellow', *zoween* 'sowing'.

Long high back vowel /uː/. The glossarists used the digraph *oo* for /uː/. With Irish loanwords this spelling is also to be found: *stuggoone* < Irish *stagún* 'stubborn person', *coolaan* < Irish *cúlán* 'nook, secluded spot', *cooloor* < Irish *colúr* 'pigeon'. This offers confirmation of the interpretation of *oo* as /uː/ with English words such as the following: *wazcoot* 'waistcoat', *zoon* 'soon', *zoot* 'soot', *woode* 'would', *woork* 'work'.

As Forth and Bargy shows nasal raising it is plausible that *ou*, as in *knouth* 'knows', represented /u:/, given the spelling of the related noun: *knoouledge* 'knowledge'. In those cases where, etymologically, the particular form has a short /u/, the interpretation of *ou* as /u:/ is justified not least because Forth and Bargy is characterised by having general vowel lengthening: *chourch* 'church', *goun*, *joudge* 'judge'. Although not very precise with regard to this point, Barnes (Dolan and Ó Muirithe 1996: 33) suggested that with the words discussed here – but only with these – *ou* had the value /u:/.

Diphthongs

The diphthongs which one can readily assume for Forth and Bargy are /ai/ and /au/. In Modern English these are of course not found with the same words as in Middle English. For this reason one has two sets of words in Forth and Bargy: (i) those words which had a monophthong in Middle English but which have a diphthong in Modern English as a consequence of vowel shift, e.g. *deemes* 'times', *keene* 'kine', *leen* 'line', *theezil* 'thyself', all with unshifted ME /i:/; (ii) those which had the diphthongs /ai/ or /au/ in Middle English and which in Modern English have /ei/ and /ɔ:/ respectively.

Diphthong /ai/. Those words which had /ai/ in Middle English present a complicated picture. Some of them are written with *y* in Vallancey and Poole: *agyne* 'again', *gryne* 'grain', *pyle* 'pail', *ryne* 'rain'. Barnes' sole comment on these spellings is 'our double letters *ai* are often *y*'. There are two possibilities here: *y* represented either /i:/ or /ai/. It is used in medial position, so if the value /i:/ was intended, then the glossarists could have chosen *ee* to maintain consistency in their spelling. In medial position *y* rarely occurs in Modern English if one disregards surnames like *Lyle*, *Lyons*, *Pyles* and a few loanwords like *rhyme*, *thyme*. However, in Early Modern English *y* was a normal representation of /ai/ (or still /əi/, ʌi/) in medial position, e.g. *tyde* 'tide', *ryde* 'ride', *mynde* 'mind'. In all these cases it indicates /ai/. This points to *y* as /ai/ in Forth and Bargy. In some instances the first element of the diphthong seemed to have been drawn out, in keeping with the general tendency to lengthen vowels here: *daaily* 'daily', *faaighe* 'faith', *haail* 'hail', *waaite* 'wait'. Barnes remarks (Dolan and Ó Muirithe 1996: 33) that the vowel in these forms corresponds to the *äi* (his spelling) of the Dorset dialect. From descriptions of this dialect (see Widén 1949) it is known that the eye-dialect spelling *äi* indicates not the diphthong /ai/ but a sequence of /a:/ and /i/.

Diphthong /au/. This is indicated nowadays by the digraphs *ow* or *ou*. It was also found in Forth and Bargy and is remarked upon by Barnes (Dolan and Ó Muirithe 1996: 34). It was apparently realised with a fronted first element, i.e. as [ɛu] instead of [au] and is parallel to that found in present-day east coast dialects: *greound* 'ground', *keow* 'cow', *steout* 'stout', *meouth* 'mouth'. Where /o:/ occurs before velarised [ɬ] a diphthongisation to /au/ can be assumed: *houle* 'hold'. The deletion of the post-sonorant stop and the subsequent diphthongisation is paralleled by a similar process which can still be seen in colloquial Irish English today: *old* /oːld/ ~ /aul/, *bold* /boːld/ ~ /baul/.

Diphthongs /ɔi/ *and* /iu/. There are two words in the glossaries which had, and have, /ɔi/ in English: *joee* 'joy', *pint* ~ *peint* 'point'. In the first case the spelling *oee* implies that the diphthong is to be understood as a sequence of /ɔ/ and /iː/ (somewhat similar to /aːi/). The second case probably shows the diphthong /ɛi/ for /ɔi/. Without any further attestations, this realisation cannot be generalised for the dialect as a whole. The diphthong /iu/ seems to have been realised as /juː/, perhaps as /iuː/. The spelling *ew*, which is used for ME /iu/ in this dialect, would suggest this, e.g. *dhew* 'dew', *vew* 'few', *vleeu* 'flew'.

Short vowels

For southern Middle English, a system of five short vowels is generally assumed (Fisiak 1968: 41). The difference between the short and the long vowel system is that the former only has one element on the mid level, front and back, i.e. /e/ and /o/ as opposed to /eː, ɛː/ and /oː, ɔː/ in the long vowel system. One may also posit a central vowel /ə/ in unstressed positions. This results in the following system: /i, u, e, o, a/ along with schwa, /ə/.

High front short vowel /ɪ/. This vowel has been remarkably stable in the history of English, undergoing no major sound change since Old English. This is true for Forth and Bargy as well where is it represented by *i*, in some cases corresponding to /u/, later /ʌ/, in mainland British English: *gimlie* 'chimney', *grip* 'sharp pain', *hint* 'hunt', *piff* 'puff'.

Short mid front vowel /ɛ/. There are many words in the glossaries which have *e* which suggests a realisation as a short mid front vowel: *dhen* 'ten', *leth* 'let', *fest* (cf. ME *fest*) 'fist', *bellee* 'belly'.

Low short vowel /a/. There are a number of forms which point to a short /a/ vowel and which are written with *a*: *sankt* 'saint', *marreet* 'married', *knapp* 'cloth button', *dab* 'stroke of hand'. With grammatical words there are a few isolated instances where ME /a/ is raised to /ɛ/, e.g. *thet* 'that'. For a variety of further forms, lengthening of ME /a/ is in evidence: *waant* 'want', *waafur* 'not easy', *vaat* 'fat'.

Short mid back vowel /ɔ/. Words with etymological /ɔ/ in Forth and Bargy are written with *o*: *sorry* 'sorrow', *rothed* 'rotten', *vorreat* 'forehead'.

Short high back vowel /ʊ/. The lowered and unrounded /ʊ/, which developed in Early Modern English to /ʌ/, cannot be shown conclusively to have existed in Forth and Bargy. In English orthography this vowel is represented by *u* or by *o* in those words in which adjacent letters consisted of vertical strokes in handwriting (Scragg 1974: 43f.). As one cannot decide, either from the orthography or from remarks by the commentators, e.g. by Barnes, whether the lowering and unrounding of ME /ʊ/ had taken place or not, one must look for evidence that the vowel remained as /ʊ/ in this dialect, e.g. *rub* 'rib', *pit* 'put', *zin* 'sun', *vurst* 'first'. It would seem that there was an alternation between /ɪ/ and /ʊ/ in Forth and Bargy which implies that /ʊ/ was indeed a high vowel. A further argument is to be found in the raising of /ɔ/. Certain forms in the glossaries of Vallancey and Poole have *u* where one would expect *o* from mainland English: *cuck* 'cock', *kruck* 'crock'. There are also words which show a lengthened vowel corresponding to ME /ʊ/, e.g. *coome* 'come'. The alternation of front and back vowels affected /ɛ/ occasionally: *melk* ~ *mulke* 'milk', *runt* 'rent'.

Central short vowel /ə/. Unstressed schwa does not have any particular orthographic representation in Forth and Bargy. Its existence can be assumed for those words where it is to be found in other forms of English, e.g. *aboo* 'above', with initial /ə/, or *dhunder* 'thunder', with a final rhotacised schwa, /ɚ/.

The /ə/ vowel also occurs in what appears to be an epenthetic syllable in the plural of nouns. Here the glossarists have written a left-slanting accent over an *e* to indicate that the letter had phonetic value: *gaudès* 'fine clothes', *nollès* 'awls', *oathès* 'oats'.

Nasal raising. Vowels before nasal consonants tend to be raised in this dialect. The raising affected low and front vowels particularly. An obvious case is the raising of /a/ to /ɔː/ or possibly /oː/, as in *lone* 'land', *eeloan* 'island', *errone* 'errand'. This raising is a well-established feature in English (already found in Old English and known as Anglian raising; Pyles and Algeo 1993 [1964]: 102). The raising is also found with mid front vowels which moved to a high position (e.g. *England, think* < *þencan*). This shift together with lengthening and cluster reduction can result in forms which are quite distinct from later, more standard ones, e.g. *speen* 'spend', which shows all three processes of (i) stop deletion, (ii) vowel raising and (iii) vowel lengthening.

Consonants

Sibilants. There is a general substitution of /s/ by /ʃ/ in Forth and Bargy – much as in Irish English historically and in present-day contact varieties. This occurs particularly after high vowels, /ɪ/ or /ɛ/, as in *twish* 'betwixt', *treesh* 'trace', *treshpass* 'trespass'. The source for this may well be the same as for contact Irish English where the sibilant in the environment of a high vowel is interpreted as phonologically palatal – seen in the context of the Irish sound system – and hence realised as [ʃ]. There are occasional examples of [ʃ] occurring after a low or back vowel as in *lash* 'last'. Other spellings are not clear phonetically. With the cluster /st/, both word-initially and finally, one finds the spelling *sth* which might well be an indication of [ʃt]: *stheel* 'steel', *sthil* 'still', *sthoan* 'stone', *sthrone* 'strand'; *vrosth* 'frost', *priesth* 'priest'. Because the *h* occurs here after the *t* it could be an indication of a dental [t̪] after /s/. For want of further evidence and of comments from the glossarists the matter must remain unresolved.

Approximants and labial fricatives. The speech of Forth and Bargy would seem to have been affected by that of Irish speakers around the area in which it was spoken. The sibilant realisations just mentioned are one of several substitutions which are found in the dialect. Another indication of Irish influence is the use of /f/ as an equivalent to /ʍ/ in English. The reason for this is probably that the realisation of /f/ in Irish is often a bilabial fricative [ɸ] which is phonetically quite closely to [ʍ]. Examples of this shift are *fade* ~ *faade* 'what', *fen* 'when', *fidi* 'whither' and *farthoo* 'whereto'. Sometimes this fricative was then subject to initial voicing, e.g. *vidie* < *fidi* 'whither'.

Dental to labial shift. A shift which Forth and Bargy shares with popular London (Wells 1982: 328f.) and African American English (Green 2002: 117–19) is the shift of dental to labial fricative. It applies to the voiced fricative and can be seen in *brover* ~ *brower* 'brother' and *aulaveer* 'altogether'. The shift must be quite archaic as the normal realisation of /ð/ in Irish English is a stop, [d̪] or [d]. This would not have shifted to a labial fricative, so that the shift must have taken place at the initial stages of Forth and Bargy before the specifically Irish fortition of dental fricatives had set in. There is no evidence that this feature was inherited from input forms of south-western English (the shift of ambidental to labiodental fricative is indicative of London and the home counties; Wakelin 1984: 79). The south-west is noted, if anything, for a stop realisation (Upton and Widdowson 1996: 42f.).

Dentalisation before /r/. In the glossaries an alveolar plosive before or after /r/ is consistently written with a following *h*, i.e. as *th* or *dh*. These spellings are, however, used both for an etymological /t/ in the environment of /r/ and for an inherited dental fricative, e.g. *threesh* 'trace', *dhrout* 'drowned', *threeve* 'thrive', *dhurteen* 'thirteen', *dhree* 'three' (the last two with initial voicing). The assumption here is that the *h* after the stop indicates a dental pronunciation rather than an alveolar one. This shift from alveolar to dental for stops followed by /r/ is widely attested for vernacular varieties of Irish English to the present day (Hickey 2004a: 38). For Forth and Bargy there are a few instances of the shift forwards when the stop is preceded by /r/ as in *hurdhel* 'hurdle', *shoorth* 'shirt', *angarth* 'angered', *returnth* 'returned'. The last two cases additionally show the devoicing of final stops after a sonorant, again a common feature in later Irish English.

Alveolar lenition. The allophony of alveolars includes a reduction of stops to fricatives in environments of high sonority (see Hickey 1996a and section 5.4.3 below). This feature can certainly be traced to the first period of Irish English, i.e. to before the seventeenth century, and would appear to have held for the dialect of Forth and Bargy. The segments which result from lenition are [t̞] and [d̞] from /t/ and /d/ respectively. The lenition appears when the alveolars occur either intervocalically or post-vocalically/pre-pausally. The realisations share all features with the stops, bar closure. In the glossaries the sounds in question are written with a *h* following the stop symbol. This means that an orthographic ambiguity exists between the representation of [t̞r-, d̞r- / r̥t̞#, rd̞#] and [-t̞-, -d̞- / -t̞#, -d̞#]. However, the absence of /r/ renders the context unambiguous, e.g. *bothom* 'bottom', *muthon* 'mutton', *nitheen* 'knitting'.

The velar fricative /x/. Apart from conservative varieties of Ulster Scots and occasionally mid Ulster English, the sound /x/ is not to be found in present-day English in Ireland. In Irish this sound is well established and in Forth and Bargy loanwords with /x/ have any of three different spellings: *g*: *lug* < Irish *loch* 'lake', *gh*: *saaughe* < Irish *sách* 'sated, satisfied', *ch*: *boochelawn* < Irish *buachalán (buí)* 'ragwort'. These three spellings also appear with words which are not loans from Irish: *g*: *ligt* 'light', *gh*: *draugh* 'through', *ch*: *reicht* 'right'. In addition to these, there is the spelling *gk* which is used with English words which had /x/ formerly: *thaugkt* < ME *thought* 'thought', *bougkt* < ME *boght* 'bought'. The conclusion to be drawn from these different spellings is that Forth and Bargy still had the velar fricative and the glossarists were uncertain about how to indicate this in writing.

Exchange of sonorants. In Irish the exchange of sonorants is attested, above all post-consonantally as in these (western) Irish examples (de Bhaldraithe 1945: 106f.): *mná* /mraː/ 'women', *feirm* /fʲelʲimʲ/ 'farm'; *Luimneach* > English *Limerick*. In Forth and Bargy there are a few instances of this phenomenon where /r/ and /n/ shift to /l/, e.g. *gandel* 'gander'. However, these may have been input forms as in the case of *gimlie* 'chimney', which is attested in dialectal English (*Oxford English Dictionary* 2002, version 3.0 on CD-ROM), especially for the south-west (Upton and Widdowson 1996: 146f.).

Cluster simplification. A significant feature of Forth and Bargy is the simplification of consonant clusters. This would seem to conform to a hierarchy of sonority. Glides and approximants are those elements with highest sonority and thus most likely to be deleted and/or absorbed into the nucleus of the syllable containing them, e.g. *co* (< *quoth* /kwɔθ/), *zitchel* (< *swylc* /swyltʃ/), *curthere* (< *quarter* /kwartər/).

An alternative to simplification is the resyllabification of the elements of a cluster by introducing an epenthetic vowel and adding a syllable, seen in *knife* /kn-/ > *kunnife* /kən-/ and finally in *elles* 'else'.

In medial position the simplification appears as assimilation. Here the least sonorant segment assimilates to the most sonorant one, e.g. *harrest* 'harvest' (/r/ < /rv/), *varreet* 'forget' (/r/ < /rg/), *varreat* 'forehead' (/r/ < /rh/), *baarich* < ME *barlic* 'barley' (/r/ < /rl/), *arich* < ME *earlich* 'early' (/r/ < /rl/). In those cases where the second segment is a stop this is always deleted, e.g. *shuller* 'shoulder' (/l/ < /ld/), *chaamer* 'chamber' (/m/ < /mb/).

If there is only one segment intervocalically then this can be lost entirely. Forms of the verb *get* (here with initial /j-/), together with a pronoun, provide instances: *yaate* 'gave it', *yeeit* 'give it', *yeeoure* 'give our'. There are other words which are evidence of this same deletion, involving voiced fricatives, typically /ð/ or /v/, e.g. *anoor* 'another', *shoule* 'shovel', *deel* 'devil'.

Cluster simplification in final position is particularly frequent, as one would expect given the general tendency for syllables to show strong onsets and weak codas (Fallows 1981: 310). Again with a simple coda the only segment may be lost, e.g. *lee* 'leave', *aboo* 'above'. With complex codas, it is the least sonorant element which is deleted, e.g. *heal* 'health', *del* 'delve', *zil* 'self'. This type of simplification may combine with other features of Forth and Bargy to yield forms which are quite removed from more standard varieties of English. But by

unravelling the different steps, which one can assume to have occurred historically, it is possible to establish the equivalence of such forms as in the following
cases.

(2)   a. *ishe* 'ask' /ask/
               /ɪsk/   (i)   vowel raising
               /ɪʃk/   (ii) palatalisation after high vowel
               /ɪʃ/   (iii) final cluster simplification
      b. *zar* 'serve' /serv/
               /sarv/   (i)˙ vowel lowering before /r/
               /zarv/   (ii) initial fricative voicing
               /zar/   (iii) final cluster simplification

Initial voicing. This is a feature which is no longer found anywhere in Ireland
and occasionally applies to stops as well. There are two possible sources for this,
the first being the input dialects of English from the south-west (Wakelin 1977
[1972]: 91ff.) which would have had this initial voicing anyway. The second is
the (small) Flemish input to this dialect where a similar voicing is found in initial
position (see remarks above).

(3)   a. Initial voicing of fricatives
          /f/ → /v/   *vour* 'four', *vorty* 'forty'
          /s/ → /z/   *zouth* 'south', *zound* 'sound'
      b. Initial voicing of stops
          /p/ → /b/   *blenty* 'plenty', *boor* 'poor'
          /t/ → /d/   *detch* 'thatch', *dap* 'tap', *drue* 'true'
          /t̪/ → /d̪/   *dhraat* 'throat', *dhree* 'three'

Final devoicing. There are two kinds of final devoicing exemplified in the
glossaries. The first is conditioned and involves voiced stops after sonorants as
in *ee-tolth* 'told', *arent* 'around'. The second type is an unconditional devoicing
of alveolar stops. This is not as widespread as the first type but is nonetheless
amply attested, e.g. *vorreat* 'forehead', *maareet* 'married'. Of these types the first
is still a feature of colloquial Irish English and is found in words like *beyond*
[bi'jɑnt].

Epenthesis. This is a phonological process which is present in all varieties of
Irish English to varying degrees It is historically well attested and thus not unexpected in Forth and Bargy. Epenthesis occurs between two sonorants and has
the function of breaking up heavy clusters by inserting a vowel which leads
to the elements of the former cluster then occupying the codas of separate
syllables, e.g. /.fɪlm./ > [.fɪl.ɪm.] *film*. The vowel used in these cases is an
unstressed central vowel, perhaps with a front and central variant. Examples
from the glossaries are: *alomes* 'alms', *brimeles* 'brambles', *eren* /ɛrən/ 'iron'.
There are occasions where the epenthesis involves a sonorant and a fricative.
Epenthesis is a low-level phenomenon and the source of the cluster is irrelevant

to its operation; for instance, it is found with lexical stems and as a result of plural formation: *callef* 'calf', *hallaf* 'half', *elles* 'else'; and in certain plurals, e.g. *caroles* 'carols', *knuckeles* 'knuckles'.

Epenthesis may have been present in the input varieties of English to Forth and Bargy. But more significant is its occurrence in Irish where it is similarly motivated, i.e. it breaks up heavy clusters by resyllabification. Epenthesis can clearly be viewed as an areal phenomenon (Hickey 1986b, 1999b) which spread from Irish into the forms of English spoken in its vicinity.

Metathesis. A further attested process is metathesis. It is restricted in this dialect to sequences of /r/ and a short vowel. This type of metathesis is recorded in the history of English and is also found in present-day Irish English; see section 5.2. Instances from the glossaries are the following: *burgs* 'bridge', *aferth* 'afraid', *dhrives* (plural) 'turf'.

Accent

From a cursory glance at the glossaries of Vallancey and Poole it is obvious that the prosody of Forth and Bargy must have been quite different from that of later varieties of Irish English. All authors who have concerned themselves with Forth and Bargy refer to two aspects of the dialect (see remarks in Hogan 1927: 44 and those of Barnes in Dolan and Ó Muirithe 1996: 33ff.): firstly, the slow tempo of speech and secondly, the fact that the stress with most polysyllables fell on the final syllable. The slow tempo would seem to have contributed to the unexpected lengthening of vowels which is suggested by many spellings in the glossaries.

The stress on the final syllable of polysyllabic forms also led to lengthening. This would seem to have been conditioned, i.e. it occurred when the final syllable ended in a sonorant: *za'moon* 'salmon', *smadde'reen* 'smattering', *lic'keen* 'looking', *chi'sool* 'chisel', *fa'shoon* 'fashion'. Before /r/ the lengthening is also to be found: *wur'gheere* 'bellows', *wy'ddeer* 'furze'. With Irish loanwords a long vowel in the second syllable of a word is represented by a long vowel in Forth and Bargy: *knau'ghaan* < Irish *cnocán* 'small hill, heap'.

The source of final stress in Forth and Bargy can be twofold. On the one hand there may well have been an influence of Anglo-Norman on this early form of Irish English, leading to heavy syllables in non-initial position attracting stress. On the other hand the dialects of Irish spoken in south-east Ireland would also have had stress on non-initial heavy syllables, i.e. on those with long vowels. Indeed, the Irish situation may have partly been the result of earlier Anglo-Norman influence (see the discussion in Hickey 1997b and the earlier comments by T. F. O'Rahilly 1932: 94–8).

Final stress in this dialect led not only to vowel lengthening but to many cases of procope as well. Normally, other phonological processes are also at work, so that one can only understand the historical derivations when they are unravelled.

Four cases are given below to convey an impression of how an equivalence with more standard forms of English could be established.

(4)   a.   *garr* 'anger'/ˈaŋgər/

/aŋˈgər/	(i)	stress shift
/gər/	(ii)	procope and cluster reduction
/gar/	(iii)	vowel lowering before /r/

       b.   *pa* 'upon'/uˈpɔn/

/pɔn/	(i)	procope
/pɔ/	(ii)	nasal deletion
/pa/	(iii)	vowel lowering and unrounding

       c.   *mawen* 'woman' /ˈwumən/

/wuˈmaːn/	(i)	stress shift and vowel lengthening
/maːn/	(ii)	procope
/mawən/	(iii)	medial glide formation

       d.   *meyen* 'women' /ˈwɪmɪn/

/wɪˈmiːn/	(i)	stress shift and vowel lengthening
/miːn/	(ii)	procope
/mɪjɪn/	(iii)	medial glide formation

The medial glide formation in the third and fourth forms above often occurs in monosyllables with a long vowel (this still a feature of local Dublin English; see below). The correlation between vowels and glides results in /w/ appearing after a low or back vowel with /j/ after a front vowel. Procope is a conditioned process and only occurs in Forth and Bargy when the first syllable of a word is open and starts with either a vowel or glide.

Morphology

The glossaries offer little morphological information. However, what is available along with evidence in a few pieces of verse (contained as an appendix to Poole's glossary and included in Dolan and Ó Muirithe's 1996 [1979] edition) conveys a picture of a dialect which was very conservative in its grammatical structure. At the beginning of the nineteenth century the vowel prefix /iː-/, deriving from the past participle marker of Old English *ge-* /jə/, was still present, e.g. *ee-brougkt* 'brought', *ee-felt* 'felt', *ee-tolth* 'told'. The Old English first-person-singular pronoun *ic* /ɪtʃ/ still survived as a /tʃ/ prefix on auxiliary verbs, e.g. *'Chas* 'I was', *'Cham* 'I am', *'Chull* 'I will'. There are remnants of old plural types as with *been* 'bees' with a nasal plural. Case distinctions are no longer visible but occasionally the syntax seems to imply the use of a dative, which by that time in English had long since been reanalysed as a prepositional object, e.g. *Faade ee-happen'd mee lauthest Gooude Vreedie* 'What happened to me last Good Friday'. In vernacular varieties to this day, *happen* occurs without the preposition *to* (see section 4.4.1 below).

Table 2.10. *Summary of the main reconstructed features of Forth and Bargy*

long vowels	/iː, uː, eː, oː, ɛː, ɔː, aː/
diphthongs	/ai/, /au/, /ɔi/, /iu/
short vowels	/ɪ, ɛ, a, ɔ, ʊ, ə/
/s/ to /ʃ/ in high vowel environments	*twish* 'betwixt', *treesh* 'trace'
bilabial fricative [ɸ] for [ʍ]	*fade* ~ *faade* 'what', *fen* 'when'
dental to labial shift	*brover* 'brother', *aulaveer* 'altogether'
dentalisation before/after /r/	*threesh* 'trace'; *shoorth* 'shirt'
velar fricative /x/	*saaughe* < Irish *sách* 'sated'; *bougkt* < ME *boght* 'bought'
voicing of initial fricatives	*vour* 'four', *vorty* 'forty'; *zouth* 'south', *zound* 'sound'
voicing of initial stops	*blenty* 'plenty', *boor* 'poor'; *dap* 'tap', *drue* 'true'
final devoicing	*ee-tolth* 'told', *arent* 'around', *vorreat* 'forehead'
vowel epenthesis	initially: *knife* /kn-/ > *kunnife* /kən-/
	finally: *elles* 'else', *callef* 'calf', *hallaf* 'half'
metathesis	*burgs* 'bridge', *aferth* 'afraid', *dhrives* (plural) 'turf'
cluster simplification	medial: *harrest* 'harvest', *varreet* 'forget'
	final: *lee* 'leave', *aboo* 'above'; *heal* 'health', *zil* 'self'
lowering of /e/ to /a/ before /r/	*zar* 'serve', *garr* 'anger'
non-standard final stress	*za'moon* 'salmon', *lic'keen* 'looking', *chi'sool* 'chisel', *fa'shoon* 'fashion'
retention of archaic morphology	prefix-/i/ with past participles: *ee-brougkt* 'brought', *ee-felt* 'felt';
	/tʃ/ for *I* in compound forms: *'Chas* 'I was', *'Cham* 'I am', *'Chull* 'I will'
	nasal plurals: *been* 'bees'

2.4.5 THE DIALECT OF FINGAL

Although Ireland had been colonised in the late Middle Ages by English speakers, the gaelicisation which flourished in the fourteenth and fifteenth centuries led to the demise of many original varieties of English in the east of the country. Along with Forth and Bargy, English in a relic area north of Dublin on the border with Co. Westmeath survived beyond 1600. The area is known as 'Fingal', a term which is an anglicisation of Irish *Fine Gall*, literally 'group, tribe of foreigners'. This name suggests a Norse settlement north of Dublin where there was mixing with the local Irish population. This view is supported by both Jackson (1962: 4) and Sommerfelt (1962: 74). There is even a name for them, the *Gall-Ghoídhil*, i.e. the Norse-Irish, if one bears in mind that the term *Gall* 'foreigners' was applied to the Norse in the period of invasion and settlement which began at the start of the ninth century.

There is a strong Irish lexical element in the English of Fingal. It is this element which many commentators stress as being the defining difference between the

Fingal dialect on the one hand and that of Forth and Bargy on the other (Bliss 1979: 28f.). But, like the latter, the variety of language spoken in Fingal was a form of older English, whatever the Norse-Irish background had been formerly. It is to be expected that many loans from Irish would appear, given the surrounding Irish population, and similar borrowings are also attested in Forth and Bargy, indeed more might have existed in the latter than those the Englishmen Vallancey and Poole picked up when compiling their glossaries.

Early observers of the special position of Fingal, such as Richard Stanihurst in the late sixteenth century and Sir William Petty in the late seventeenth century, do not offer any linguistic evidence of the dialect and so one must rely on fragments obtained from other sources, the three most important of which are the following (these texts are available in electronic form in *A Corpus of Irish English*; see Hickey 2003a).

1. *The Fingallian Dance* (1650–60). This text is one of two short poems which are contained in a manuscript catalogued as MS Sloane 900 in the British Library. The texts have remained unedited, though the second one was printed in a book on Howth (a small town on the north side of Dublin bay) by F. E. Ball in 1917. As Bliss (1979: 45) rightly points out, the modernised text is of little linguistic interest because most of the dialect features have been ironed out. Going on the persons named in the text, who were identified by Ball, one can assume that the text was written sometime before 1660.

2. *Purgatorium Hibernicum* (1670–75). This text, like *The Fingallian Dance*, is available in the manuscript MS Sloane 900 under the title *The Fingallian Travesty: or the Sixt Book of Virgills Æneid a la mode de Fingaule*. This version is to be found in MS 470 in the National Library of Ireland under the title *Purgatorium Hibernicum: or, the Sixt Booke of Virgills Æneid; Travestie Burlesque a la mode de Fingaule*. The text consists of a humorous adaptation of book VI of the *Æneid*, placed in the setting of Stuart Ireland. The section concerns the meeting of Æneas with his former mistress Dido. No author can safely be named for this text. The copier of the extant text mentions one Francis Taubman, but as Bliss (1979: 48) points out, no independent corroboration of this can be found, nor is the character of Francis Taubman ascertainable from other sources. Bliss dates the text as not later than 1675.

3. *The Irish Hudibras* (1689). This is the latest of three adaptations of book VI of Vergil's *Æneid* to which Bliss gave the general title *The Fingallian Burlesque* (Bliss 1979: 47). The text was adapted to suit English tastes and the Irish characters depicted were referred to as *Dear-Joys*, which in the 1680s became a popular term for an Irishman just as *Teague* (a then common first-name) had done (Bliss 1979: 56). The Irishness of the text has been toned down, as seen in the relative paucity of Irish words and turns of phrase. The author of this text is not known. The speculation that it was one James Farewell seems unfounded as this author would have been far too young at the time, although he may have edited the work at a later date (Bliss 1979: 57).

The text can be dated accurately as it contains a reference to a banner (*Now or never, Now and forever*) which was hoisted over Dublin Castle when James II entered the city in March 1689.

Linguistic features. Various traits can be noted for the dialect of Fingal. Accent appears to have been word-final (in common with Forth and Bargy). This is indicated by a dash separating the first and second syllable in words with end stress: *par-doon* /par'duːn/, *far-deer* /far'diːr/, *quar-teer* /kwar'tiːr/ 'quarter', *clam-peer* /klæm'piːr/ < Irish *clampar* 'noise, racket'.

Many other traits confirm the similarity with Forth and Bargy, for instance, unshifted ME /iː/ vowel (*leef* = *life*, *dee* = *thy*, *cheeld* = *child*, etc.), unshifted ME /aː/ (*fash* = *face* with /s/ > /ʃ/), unshifted ME /uː/ (*ground* rhyming with *wound*), a shift of /w/ to /v/ (*vid* = *with*, *vill* = *will*, *vell* = *well*, etc.), as well as archaic morphological features such as the *y* prefix on the past participle (*ycome*, *ygo*, etc.); see Bliss (1979: 126–9) and Bliss (1979: 194ff.) for remarks on the accentual system. See Hogan (1927: 39ff.) for comments on *The Irish Hudibras*.

3   History II: The settlement of Ulster

3.1   Background

Any treatment of English in Ireland must take special account of the situation in Ulster. The reason for this lies in the settlement history of this province which led to the introduction of Scots and forms of northern English which were, and still are, distinct from all varieties of English in the south of the country. There has also been, as in the south, interaction between forms of English and Irish which has added a further dimension to the linguistic complexity in the north.

The northern part of Ireland is usually referred to as 'Ulster', the most northerly of the four present-day provinces. It literally means the country of the Ulaidh, the people who historically inhabited this area. The word *Ulster* consists of *Ulaidh* + *s* + *tír*, a Norse-Irish formation, similar to *Munster* and *Leinster*, provinces to the south and east respectively. The now opaque compound contains the Irish name of the people, *Ulaidh*, followed by a Norse genitival /s/ and a phonetically reduced form of /tiːr/, the word for 'country' in Irish.[1]

The label 'Ulster' is also used loosely today to refer to Northern Ireland, a part of the United Kingdom, which came into existence when Ireland was partitioned in 1921. Northern Ireland consists of six counties – Antrim, Down, Armagh, Derry, Tyrone and Fermanagh – but the province of Ulster actually consists of nine counties: the three additional ones are Donegal (north-west Ulster), Monaghan and Cavan (south Ulster) which are within the Republic, although they are linguistically northern.

The early political history of the province can be traced back at least to the various kingdoms which existed before the Middle Ages (see map of these at around 800 in Bardon 1996: 17). A prominent kingdom was that of the Dál Riata in the Glens of Antrim (in the north-east) which in the fifth century extended its

---

* My thanks go to the following colleagues who have been very helpful with comments and advice on the structure and contents of this chapter: Karen Corrigan, Kevin McCafferty and Michael Montgomery. Needless to say, they are not to be associated with any shortcomings.
[1] There is, however, another view, namely that the second syllable in each of these words derives from Old Norse *staðr* 'place' (Geipel 1971: 151).

range across the North Channel into Scotland (Bardon 1996: 14). The Scottish colony was so successful that the Latin term for Ireland, *Scotia*, came to be applied to the overseas lands of the Dál Riata, yielding the later name 'Scotland' (Duffy 2000: 40). The early period of Irish involvement in Scotland was also the beginning of the Christian era and the settlement of Scotland was connected with religious conversion.

The people who moved up north-eastwards to Scotland took the Irish language of the time with them and thus initiated the development of Q-Celtic in the north of Britain. The forms of Irish spoken in Scotland remained indistinguishable from those in Ulster for several hundred years. It is not until the thirteenth century that the first signs of an independent form of Q-Celtic in Scotland begin to appear in writing. With the demise of a classical language in Ireland and Scotland (based on older inherited forms of the language), Scottish Gaelic emerged as a form of Gaelic distinct from Irish (Thomson 1977). The two forms are no longer mutually comprehensible despite the dialect continuum which Ulster, west and north-west Scotland form to this day.[2]

The spread of Irish into Scotland and the early monastic ties were the beginning of a long association of Ulster with its north-eastern neighbour. Political and broader ecclesiastical links followed. Later on there were also military bonds, especially in the early fourteenth century when Edward Bruce invaded Ulster with his defeat in 1318 at the hands of the Gaelic lords of the time. Scottish mercenaries, called 'gallowglasses' (from Irish *gall-óglach* 'foreigner warrior'), were recruited from western Scotland to serve in Ulster armies. There were also clan connections among the great Gaelic-speaking families, such as the Macdonnells who in 1399 acquired Rathlin Island (off the north Antrim coast) and the Glens of Antrim (Montgomery and Gregg 1997: 572). These links (Adamson 1994) were of importance linguistically as they led to an importation of Scottish Gaelic into Ulster and strengthened Ulster and Scotland as a linguistic area.[3]

Events in the south of Ireland also had an effect on Ulster. After the Anglo-Norman conquest, several prominent Norman families established bases in Ulster. Of these, two were particularly successful in their domination of the region: the de Lacy and de Burgh families who held the earldom of Ulster throughout the thirteenth and into the fourteenth century (Bardon 1996: 24–41). Here, as elsewhere in Ireland, a gradual resurgence of Gaelic power set in. In the south, many of the new lords were themselves Anglo-Norman in origin, but in Ulster the Gaelic element was particularly strong.

The Tudor conquest of Ireland (see section 2.1.3) applied equally to Ulster. The determined attitude of the English during the late fifteenth and sixteenth centuries (Bardon 1996: 43–65) meant that there were continuous battles with major Gaelic clans, such as the O'Neills and O'Donnells. This was the time of

---

[2] See T. F. O'Rahilly (1932: 122–60 and 176) for examples of features common to Ulster and Scotland but not found in southern varieties of Irish.

[3] See T. F. O'Rahilly (1932: 166) where he discusses the negator *cha* which is an import to Ulster from Scottish Gaelic.

the Tudor policy of 'surrender and regrant' where the strategy was to force the native lords to relinquish their territories which would then be restored to them under conditions dictated by the English.

By the late sixteenth century, the O'Neill clan had reasserted its leading position in Ulster. Strong Gaelic resistance to English rule developed in the province and this led to more or less open rebellion, peaking with Hugh O'Neill (c. 1540–1616) and his followers in Ulster engaging in what is known as the Nine Years War from 1594 to 1603. The Gaelic forces were concentrated in Ulster and there were significant successes such as that at Yellow Ford in 1598. This convinced the Spanish to agree to O'Neill's plea for their engagement in Ireland. They intervened with an army of over 3,000 which landed in September 1601. They were besieged by English forces under Mountjoy and, despite O'Neill arriving to help, both the Irish and the Spanish were defeated in a decisive battle at Kinsale (south Co. Cork) on Christmas Eve 1601. In Ulster the rebellions ultimately led to failure with the subsequent repression of the Irish. By the time of Elizabeth's death in 1603 the dominance of the Gaelic lords of Ulster was broken, depriving the province of effective native leadership.

In the ensuing years the political situation of the Gaelic leaders became less and less tenable and on 3 September 1607 a number of these left Ireland for France without the permission of the English crown. This action has entered history as the Flight of the Earls (Bardon 1996: 68) and had far-reaching consequences for the power structure of Ireland. It paved the way for more successful and long-lasting plantations.

3.1.1 PLANTATION IN ULSTER

The succession of James VI of Scotland (1566–1625) as James I (1603–25) to the English throne led to the establishment of the Stuart monarchy. It lasted until 1688 with an interruption during the Interregnum of 1649–60, which included the Commonwealth and two Protectorates of Cromwell. The latter ended with the restoration of the English monarchy under Charles II.

After the Irish lords left Ulster in 1607, James I moved quickly and their lands were escheated. The government decided to initiate the plantation of Ulster along the lines of the Munster plantation in the late sixteenth century. This time, however, the land was reserved for Scots settlers, encouraged by their compatriot James I, together with Englishmen, mostly from the north Midlands and north of England (Adams 1958: 61ff.; 1967: 69ff.). Because of the union of the crowns in 1603 the Scottish were allowed to settle in Ireland without difficulty. Settlers were a mixture of private individuals along with royal officials (servitors) and some 'deserving' Irish, i.e. those loyal to the crown during the Nine Years War. The plantation settlements were to form the basis for the demographic split of the country (Heslinga 1962). Due to the Scottish and English background of these immigrants the division of Ireland came to be as much linguistic as political and confessional.

The plantation of Ulster (Robinson 1989a) was initiated in 1609 and encompassed the counties of Armagh, Derry, Tyrone, Donegal and Fermanagh.[4] It also included most of Co. Cavan in south Ulster (now in the Republic of Ireland). Co. Monaghan, also in the Republic, was not part of this plantation, partly because it had been unofficially planted by 'regrants' before (Robinson 1994 [1984]: 67). The position of the eastern counties of Antrim and Down was special at this period. Officially, these counties were outside the plantation scheme, but most Scots settled there (as these were nearest to Scotland). The properties they eventually came to possess were not escheated but acquired from native owners who could not survive under the new plantation dispensation with its emphasis on a more market-style economy.

There was some disagreement in the English camp about how to proceed vis-à-vis the native Irish. Some, like Lord Deputy Chichester, favoured a cautious settlement, while others, including James I and his advisor Sir Francis Bacon, were inclined towards a more radical approach which was embodied in the 'orders and conditions' issued in 1609 which offered the framework for the plantation. The allocations of land were smaller than they had been in Munster: 2,000, 1,500 and 1,000 acres were the proportions of 'profitable land' with a certain amount of waste land and bog (Canny 2001: 200). The recipients were to be of three types. English and Scottish 'undertakers' who were 'to build defensible buildings, to remove the existing occupiers from their estates by a designated date, and to populate their lands exclusively with English or Scottish Protestant tenants'. The second type consisted of servitors, civil or military servants of the crown in Ireland. The third type comprised 'individuals who could lay claim to previous landowner or freehold status in Ulster and who were considered deserving either by the king or the Dublin government' (Canny 2001: 200). The twenty-eight baronies, into which the counties of Armagh, Cavan, Donegal, Fermanagh, Derry and Tyrone were divided, had eight reserved for English and eight for Scottish undertakers. The remaining twelve baronies were for servitors and native Irish.

The Scottish undertakers tended to have smaller estates than the English, probably because they were not in as financially a robust a position as the latter (Robinson 1994 [1984]: 79). In fact, the Scottish undertakers had just slightly more acreage in plantation grants (81,500 acres) compared to the English (81,000) although they were more numerous (Robinson 1994 [1984]: 86). The settlers from lowland Scotland received the slightly less profitable lands because their average incomes were somewhat below that of the corresponding English undertakers. Furthermore, their estates were scattered across the escheated land. Additional factors for the demographic development of Ulster are important here: in 1610 many landless Irish, who were supposed to move to estates administered by the church or by officials, were given a stay of eviction. Initially, this was because

---

[4] See Foster (1988: 62) and Dudley Edwards with Hourican (2005: 160) for maps showing the plantation of 1609–13.

undertakers had not yet arrived in Ulster. But when they did, tenancies were granted to the Irish because these were willing to pay higher rents. Indeed by 1628 this situation was given official recognition by a ruling which allowed undertakers to keep native tenants on maximally a quarter of their portions at double the normal rent. There was much competition between Irish, English and Scottish settlers with the Irish generally having to be content with poorer, more marginal land, such as the Sperrin Mountains of central Tyrone, while others, for whatever reason, remained to work under Scottish/English owners.

In the context of the plantation, one can mention that James I convinced merchants from London to participate. The Irish Society was set up by twelve London-based companies and was instrumental to the plantation of Co. Derry, then renamed 'Londonderry' to reflect the engagement of these companies. However, this involvement was not continuous and the momentum waned. There were also Scots settlers in the city, forming a sizeable proportion, indeed the majority, by the 1630s.

The success of the Ulster plantation was relative: the numbers envisaged by the English administration did not always reach the targets set, nor did the landlords always have the capital to carry through the agricultural and urban projects which the government had envisaged. Many of the companies retained Irish tenants (against the wishes of the English crown) and there were conspiracies against the English, notably in 1615. Furthermore, for lack of funds or because of debt, many English and Scots withdrew from the scheme. Their land was taken over by others who extended their own estates. However, because of the Scottish credit networks, those settlements run by Scots tended to remain in Scottish hands (Canny 2001: 234), so that success or failure of the settlements did not necessarily lead to a demographic shift.

The plantation of Ulster is regarded in works on Irish history, e.g. Canny (2001) and Foster (1988), as the major event at the beginning of the early modern period. There are differences in the assessment of both its significance and value. The major grievance which it triggered stemmed from the banishment of local Irish to poorer, more marginal lands in Ulster with the fertile lowlands left in English or Scottish hands. Scholars such as Philip Robinson are grounded within a Protestant tradition and stress, in their treatment of the plantation, the achievements it brought with it in terms of improved infrastructure and economy for the province. Others scholars largely in this tradition are T. W. Moody (1939) and Raymond Gillespie (1985), both of whom have written widely on Ulster history. Such authors tend to highlight the amalgam of cultures which has occurred in the province (Robinson 1994 [1984]: 186–94), despite claims to the contrary.

Many southern historians, such as Nicholas Canny, are less keen to see Protestant settlement in a positive light. They point to the loss of native culture and the marginalisation of the Catholics in the province, both geographically and socially, from which the nationalist community was essentially never to recover (A. Clarke 1994 [1967]: 154).

3.1.2 MID-SEVENTEENTH-CENTURY ULSTER

By the third decade of the seventeenth century, the pattern of emigration had begun to change. After several thousand English and Scottish had been recruited as settlers by undertakers from their home regions, many more went to Ulster on their own initiative. From the port of entry they spread to the hinterland into areas already planted by fellow countrymen. This led to a reinforcement of the Scottish and English areas. With further internal migration the ethnic regions within the province were consolidated. The result of this on a linguistic level was that distinct areas of Scots, English and Irish speech developed. These remained recognisable well into the twentieth century (Gregg 1972). The greatest concentration of Scottish settlers was in Antrim and Down, followed by north-east Derry with further settlement areas in Donegal, Tyrone, Fermanagh and Armagh.

As the seventeenth century proceeded, the developments in Ulster were inextricably linked to those in England, especially during the reign of Charles I. It is beyond the scope of the present book to consider events in England as this time, but it is appropriate to mention the most significant English official active in Ireland. This is Viscount Thomas Wentworth who was appointed lord deputy in 1632. He was a loyal supporter of Charles I and was determined to rein in both native Irish and independently minded Protestants (Lydon 1998: 175). His aim was to organise Ireland as an effective source of income for the English crown and thus render the latter's dependence on parliament unnecessary. His disregard for the Old English, especially in his attempts to plant Connaught, was a grave error of judgement (Duffy 2000: 111). With his ruthless administration in Ireland, Wentworth also succeeded in alienating the New English whom he saw as too liberal in their attitude to the English crown. For his efforts he was made Earl of Strafford in 1640 and promoted to lord lieutenant in Ireland. But after the parliament assumed authority in England his fortunes waned and he was executed in May 1641. The turbulence during Wentworth's tenure (Canny 2001: 300–401), and the uncertainty of who held political power in England, led to leaders in Ireland such as Phelim O'Neill and Rory O'More attacking centres of English sovereignty, notably Charlemont Fort in Tyrone and Dublin Castle in October 1641 (Duffy 2000: 112). The rising was initially quite successful in Ulster where there were two major issues for the Catholics, (i) the restoration of property misappropriated by Protestants and (ii) the unhindered practice of their religion (Canny 2001: 469ff.). The strategy seems to have been to take several bastions of Protestant power in Ulster and then negotiate from a position of strength. During the ensuing fighting indiscriminate violence abounded, for instance, the attack on Protestants at Portadown or that on Catholics at Islandmagee. These and similar atrocities of the 1641 uprising – both alleged and factual – entered the folk memory of Ulster Protestants and Catholics alike, much as did the defeat of the Jacobite forces at the Battle of the Boyne in 1690. In the course of the 1640s the uprising was lost by the Catholics and finally the English were victorious over

Table 3.1. *Demographic percentages for seven counties in Ulster, c. 1660*
(after Robinson 1994 [1984]: 105)

Country	English / Scots	Irish	Country	English / Scots	Irish
Antrim	45%	55%	Donegal	28%	72%
Derry	45%	55%	Fermanagh	25%	75%
Down	43%	57%	Monaghan	11%	89%
Armagh	35%	65%			

the Gaelic Ulster forces under a Parliamentarian army at the Battle of Scarifhollis in 1650 (Canny 2001: 570).

3.1.3 ETHNIC DISTRIBUTION IN SEVENTEENTH-CENTURY ULSTER

There are no population censuses in the seventeenth century, but an estimate of the British and Irish segments of Ulster society was made by Robinson on the bases of poll-tax returns from c. 1659 (Robinson 1994 [1984]: 104f.). These show that for Antrim, Down and Derry the combined English and Scots sectors were over 40 per cent of the entire population, the remainder being Irish (see table 3.1).

Robinson (1994 [1984]: 94) also has a map of English and Scottish settlement on the basis of surnames in the muster rolls of 1630. Typical areas with Scottish settlement are (1) the Ards (north Co. Down), Carrickfergus (Co. Antrim, north of Belfast), (2) Coleraine (north-east Co. Derry) and adjacent north-west Antrim, (3) the Laggan area, west, south-west of Derry, (4) the Lifford-Strabane area between Tyrone and Donegal, south Tyrone, as well as (5) parts of Fermanagh and Down with mixed English and Scottish settlement in various areas such as north Armagh. Robinson (1994[1984]: 127) also offers a schematic representation of colonial processes in seventeenth-century Ulster, identifies internal migration and confirms that consolidation through clustering of ethnic groups played a role.

Although the bulk of Scottish emigrants to Ulster came in the early seventeenth century, giving rise to the patterns just discussed, settlement from Scotland did not cease completely. In the last decade of the seventeenth century there was an increase in emigration, not because of Protestant hegemony in Ulster but, significantly, because of the recurrent crop failures and famine in Scotland in this decade (Bardon 1996: 93).

The figures given in table 3.1 do not distinguish between English and Scottish, and it is assumed on the basis of later assessments that in the seventeenth century the number of Scottish settlers outnumbered those from England by some 6 to 1 and that in all there were some 150,000 Scots settlers and approximately 25,000 English (Adams 1977: 57; Harris 1984b: 115).

3.1.4 PRESBYTERIANISM IN ULSTER

The Presbyterian Church rests on a particular theological tradition that resulted from the Protestant Reformation of the sixteenth century. The tenets of Presbyterianism can be traced to the thinking of the Swiss Reformationist John Calvin (1509–64) from Geneva. Calvin wished to establish a church which would be governed by elders much as indicated in the New Testament. The term Presbyterian derives from Greek *presbuteros* 'elder', the comparative of *presbus* 'old'.

Calvinist ideas were quick to spread throughout Europe, first to France, Germany and Holland as well as eastern Europe and later to Britain and North America. The label 'Reformed' was used for Calvinists who organised their church with a presbyterian form of government. In the English-speaking world such churches came to be known as 'Presbyterian'. They established a particular foothold in Scotland where this form of religion was conceived of as parallel to other forms of Scottish resistance to English hegemony, as it was separate from the established Anglican Church. However, the tension between Presbyterianism and Anglicanism always receded in the face of the much greater antithesis between Catholicism and Protestantism.

In general the Presbyterians were anti-Catholic but they were excluded from public office by the so-called 'sacramental test'. This was first introduced in England in 1673 and required that those holding offices under the crown should show their eligibility by taking communion in the Anglican Church. Such an act was anathema to religious dissenters like the Presbyterians and when it was extended to Ireland by a clause added to the anti-Catholic act of 1704 (one of the Penal Laws) it caused great consternation among the Ulster Scots.

Emigration of Scottish Presbyterians to Ulster continued throughout the eighteenth century. Two groups in particular sought refuge in Ulster. The Seceders were dissenters who seceded from the Church of Scotland in 1733 because of general dissatisfaction with the Williamite church settlement of 1690 and the general liberal trends within the church in Scotland. The Covenanters were a group of Presbyterians who adhered to the Solemn League and Covenant of 1643, which was a religious–political pact between Scottish and English opponents of Charles I. Their goal in Scotland was the suppression of Catholicism and their discontent grew when the Williamite settlement failed to be fully implemented and when the church became somewhat more liberal in the early decades of the eighteenth century, leading to immigration to Ulster by many Covenanters.

Within Ulster there were two conflicting factions of Presbyterianism: the Old Lights were conservative Calvinists and the New Lights were slightly more liberal and disagreed with the requirement of subscription which demanded that ministers and ordinands subscribe to an orthodox confession of faith drawn up by the Westminster Assembly in the seventeenth century (Byrne 2004: 207). In general the Seceders joined forces with the Old Lights in Ulster and the split in the Synod of Ulster was not resolved until 1840 with the formation

Table 3.2. *Types of English in Ulster (see map A6.5 in appendix 6)*

1. *Ulster Scots.* Most of Co. Antrim (except the extreme north-east). North Co. Down, upper half of the Ards peninsula. North Co. Derry, centred around Coleraine. North-west Donegal, the lowland area immediately west and south-west of Derry city (the Laggan).
2. *Mid Ulster English.* South Co. Derry. Co. Tyrone. The north of Co. Fermanagh, Co. Monaghan and Co. Armagh. South and central Co. Down.
3. *South Ulster English.* South-west Fermanagh. South of Co. Monaghan and Co. Armagh.
4. *Contact Ulster English.* West Donegal Gaeltacht, approximately from Falcarragh down to Dunglow (An Clochán Liath) and in the less robust south-west Gaeltacht from about Glencolmcille to Kilcar.

of the General Assembly of the Presbyterian Church which unified the vying factions. The Ulster Covenanters on the other hand remained outside the Irish Presbyterian Church. Both Seceders and Covenanters were major sections of the Ulster population immigrating to the New World in the course of the eighteenth century.

Among those who remained in Ulster a sense of grievance at having been slighted by the English establishment led, at the end of the eighteenth century, to an unusual alliance with the Catholics as United Irishmen, active in the 1790s in both Belfast and Dublin and embracing northern Presbyterians as well as southern Protestants and Catholics. They joined forces briefly in the uprising of 1798 in the Ulster Scots core areas of Antrim and Down. But the sympathies between the two groups were shallow and after the Act of Union (1801) the sectarian divide between Catholic and Protestant became as sharp as ever (Bardon 1996: 112–14).

3.2 English in Ulster[5]

The north of Ireland (Adams 1965) can be divided linguistically into three main areas (see table 3.2): (1) *Ulster Scots*, stemming from seventeenth-century Scottish immigrants; (2) *mid Ulster English*, deriving from immigrants, largely from the north of England, who arrived at roughly the same period (Adams 1965, 1967); and (3) *south Ulster English* consisting of transitional varieties between the north and south of Ireland.[6] In Co. Donegal, the most westerly county of the

[5] For a general overview of scholarship on this subject, see Corrigan (1990, forthcoming), Kirk (1997b) and the relevant sections of Hickey (2002a). See also Kallen (1999). Lunney (1994, 1999) offers information on questions of community and attitude. Robinson (2003) gives the perspective of a historian.
[6] There is some debate about whether south Ulster English is an independent variety. Certainly, it does not show the clarity of profile of the first two (see section 3.4.2). English in Belfast is both an amalgam of different strands and an area *sui generis* (see section 5.5.1).

province, there are Irish speakers in the Gaeltachtaí (Irish-speaking areas, see map A6.3 in appendix 6) all of whom are bilingual. The English of this small group justifies a further subtype (4), *contact Ulster English*, which can show an influence from native-speaker Irish. Although the latter group is not of great relevance today,[7] transfer from Irish to English in Ulster in its formative period in the seventeenth and eighteenth centuries is taken by some authors to have been significant.

Adams (1966a) is concerned with the influence of Irish on English in Ulster, as are the later linguistic studies by Corrigan (1993b, 2000b).[8] The influence of Irish may well be responsible for the maintenance of distinctions and of segments lost in other varieties of English, such as [ʍ] and /x/ (Adams 1981b) and the non-existence of *h*-dropping (in all forms of Irish English). Adams also sees the existence of palatalisation on a systemic level in Irish as supporting the palatalisation of velars found, albeit recessively today, in different forms of English in Ulster, e.g. *cap* [kjæp], *gap* [gjæp].

For discussions of grammatical features, see sections 3.4.4 and 4.4. See also the various articles presented in the posthumous collection of studies by Adams in Barry and Tilling (1986).

3.2.1 IRISH IN ULSTER

The story of Irish in Ulster, as elsewhere in Ireland, is one of decline in speaker numbers and of reduction in geographical extension. Before the seventeenth century it was the native language of the overwhelming majority in Ulster. The Scottish and English immigration into the province led to alterations in Irish-speaking areas as many native Irish were shifted off their land into sections of the province which were not settled by immigrants from Britain (see discussion above). Since this time the language has withdrawn rapidly and the only points in Ulster outside Donegal where it could still be found when Heinrich Wagner published his monumental *Linguistic Atlas and Survey of Irish Dialects* (1958) were (1) west Ulster in Co. Fermanagh (his point 64 with one speaker, 1958: xix), (2) south-east Ulster in north Co. Louth (his point 65 with one speaker, 1958: xix), (3) mid Ulster in north Co. Tyrone (his point 66 with approx. 12 speakers, 1958: xix), (4) north-east Ulster on Rathlin Island (his point 67 with two speakers, 1958: xix). This last pocket is of significance because the distribution of Ulster Scots

---

[7] Traynor (1953) is a very comprehensive dictionary (over 300 pages) of English from Co. Donegal. There is a brief introduction of a few pages in which a little history is offered but no discussion of the English of Donegal as a subvariety of (northern) Irish English. Traynor drew heavily on literature from Donegal authors and from a collection of dialect words made by one Henry Chichester Hart (1847–1908), whose family came from Donegal. Traynor also used material from Joseph Wright's *English Dialect Dictionary*.

[8] Corrigan (1993b) notes traces of Irish phonology, e.g. epenthesis, and of Irish grammar, e.g. clefting and various aspectual constructions. Corrigan is careful to distinguish non-standard features which most likely stem from the English input of planters.

(see map A6.4 in appendix 6) does not traditionally cover the north-east corner of Antrim and Rathlin. These parts of north-east Ulster were Irish-speaking well into the nineteenth, indeed into the early twentieth century, and the shift to English was not to Ulster Scots but to general Ulster English (Adams 1977: 58).[9]

When collecting his data Wagner was dealing with bilinguals, the last Irish speakers in their respective areas. By the late twentieth century, Irish – as a historically continuous language – had disappeared completely in the areas just mentioned. Outside Northern Ireland, in Co. Donegal, the situation was and still is much better, with several thousand native speakers of the Irish language who use it in everyday situations.

The Irish of Ulster has continually been the subject of investigation by Celtic scholars. An early seminal work on Irish dialects is T. F. O'Rahilly (1932) which contains a chapter entitled 'Ulster Irish' (1932: 161–91). The issues involved are generally of interest to scholars concerned with the historical development of Irish. One should mention here that until the early eighteenth century no dialect differences between Ulster and southern Irish were visible in the written language (Ó Dochartaigh 1987: 1).

The fact that Irish was spoken throughout the province at the time of the initial immigration from Scotland carries with it the implication that there was considerable contact, if not bilingualism, between Scots settlers and Irish speakers in the seventeenth century and for as long a time as Irish was still spoken in English-dominated parts of the province (Gregg 1959). Historically, there was contact between Irish speakers and the Ulster Scots in north-east Co. Donegal, in the low-lying area known as the Laggan,[10] though whether this is a contemporary scenario today is not certain (*pace* Montgomery and Gregg 1997: 583). What is true, however, is that up to the beginning of the twentieth century there was seasonal migration by Donegal Irish speakers to the lowlands of Scotland in search of work (Adams 1977: 59); see section 6.2.3.

One prominent syntactic feature of English in Ulster – formerly, as it is now quite recessive – is what is termed 'positive *anymore*' by which is meant a use of the temporal adverb in positive declarative sentences in which it has the approximate meaning of 'nowadays' (Montgomery and Kirk 2001).

(1)   a. *This is the way they do the work anymore.*
       b. *Something which is true anymore.*

This usage is probably a transfer phenomenon from Irish (J. Milroy 1981: 4; Crozier 1984: 318), arising as a calque on the Irish adverb *riamh* which can co-occur in positive contexts with verbs in Irish.

---

[9] By the mid twentieth century there were no speakers left in south Armagh although this area has been and still is populated by a majority Catholic, i.e. former Irish-speaking, population. See Corrigan (1993b) for a discussion of the interaction of Irish and English there.

[10] This toponym derives from the Irish word *lag/log* 'hollow' and occurs commonly in names in Ulster such as *Leggamaddy* (Co. Down) 'hollow of the dog'. It may well be the source for the name of the River Lagan at the estuary of which Belfast is situated (Flanagan and Flanagan 1994: 103).

(2)   a. *Sin an tslí a ndéanaidís an obair riamh.*
       [this the way that did-HABITUAL-they the work always, i.e.
       'anymore']
       b. *Rud a bhí fíor riamh.*
       [something which was true always, i.e. 'anymore']

The construction has travelled well: 'positive *anymore*' is found in the Midland
area of the United States (Labov 1991). It must have been an established feature
of English in Ulster (including Ulster Scots) at the latest by the early eighteenth
century as it was carried by Ulster Scots emigrants to the New World (see section
6.3.1) and became a regular feature of Scots-derived English there.

Contact with Irish can probably be invoked, if not as a sole explanation, then
at least as a convergent source of three further syntactic features of English in
Ulster. The first is the resultative perfective of Irish English which is expressed by
using the word-order object + past participle (see discussion in section 4.4.1.4.2).
The second is habitual aspect. This shows different realisations in Irish English
but the category is widespread throughout the country (see discussion in section
4.4.1.4.3). The third feature is so-called 'subordinating *and*' (see discussion in
section 4.4.6.2).

Apart from possible contact phenomena (Adams 1980), there are areal features
in Ulster which are remarkable in that they straddle the divide between Irish and
English which are structurally so different (Hickey 1999b). Examples of such
features are discussed in section 4.6.

3.3   Ulster Scots

Of all the varieties of English taken to Ireland since the seventeenth century,
Ulster Scots (see Montgomery 2007 for a book-length treatment) is the one
which has retained a very distinct profile and which can be unambiguously linked
to related present-day varieties in western and lowland Scotland. Undoubtedly,
Ulster Scots – especially in its rural forms – is quite separate from other varieties
of English in the north of Ireland, let alone in the south. Its divergent nature has
meant that much debate has taken place concerning its status as a language or
'simply' a dialect (Kallen 1999; Montgomery 1999; Görlach 2000).

This issue is not of great linguistic relevance but does have broader external significance. In 1992 Ulster Scots achieved recognition under the European
Charter for Regional or Minority Languages (see the assessment of the latter
in Nic Craith 2003 and the general discussion in Phillipson 2003, especially
pp. 152–7). This charter was adopted by the government of the United Kingdom
in 2001. The articles of the European Charter oblige the British government,
among other things, to realise the following:

- The facilitation and/or encouragement of the use of the Ulster-Scots language, in speech and writing, in public and private life;

Table 3.3. *Main areas of Scots settlement in Ulster*

1. A broad band including most of Co. Antrim (except the south approaching Belfast and the north-east corner) and the north-east corner of Co. Derry
2. North Co. Down, most of the Ards peninsula and a section of the mainland on the west bank of Strangford Lough
3. An area flanked on the east by the River Foyle and extending in the north central part of Co. Donegal (the Laggan area)

- The provision of appropriate forms and means for the teaching and study of the Ulster-Scots language at all appropriate stages;
- The provision of facilites enabling non-speakers of the Ulster-Scots language living in the area where it is used to learn if they so desire;
- The promotion of study and research on the Ulster-Scots language at universities or equivalent institutions.

There are practical consequences resulting from these formal commitments, such as financial aid for groups concerned with the maintenance and promotion of Ulster Scots. Another consequence is the production of government documents in English and Ulster Scots (see the analysis in Kirk 2000) alongside Irish, which also has official status in Northern Ireland. A spin-off of this is that vocabulary has had to be developed which can handle the contents of official documents (see further discussion in section 3.3.2).

Ulster Scots shares official status as a regional or minority language with some thirty languages in the European Union, including Lowland Scots, Irish, Scottish Gaelic, Welsh and Cornish, with which it forms the group of six lesser-used languages of the British Isles which have achieved official recognition.

The regions where Ulster Scots is spoken are nowadays no longer contiguous because of a reduction of its geographical spread. The remaining areas are, however, regions of historical settlement. Three are located on the northern periphery from the north-west through the north-east to the south-east of Ulster, hence the term 'Coastal Crescent' or 'Northern Crescent' (see table 3.3).

Area 1 and most of 2 listed in table 3.3 were established by private plantation schemes which preceded the official efforts under James I (see section 3.1.2). The north-east of Co. Derry was part of this early seventeenth-century plantation and linked up with the already existing Antrim Scots area. A British settlement of both the city and county of Derry was attempted by various London-based companies with varying success.

In Donegal, Scots from Ayrshire – families like the Cunninghams and the Stewarts – settled from 1610 onwards (Montgomery and Gregg 1997: 572). This is the historical source of the Laggan settlement to the west, south-west of Derry

city and reflected in town names like Manorcunningham and Newtowncunning-
ham in Co. Donegal.

Of the three areas listed in table 3.3, that of Antrim is often considered the
heartland, perhaps because it is closest to Scotland. The Donegal area is, and has
been, a contact area with both Irish and other forms of Irish English; the Down
area is smaller and is bordered on the south by varieties of Ulster English which
merge fairly quickly into the transitional area with the south.

The areas just mentioned were confirmed dialectally by Robert Gregg, who,
in a number of articles and a monograph, published the results of his field work
(Gregg 1964, 1972, 1985). Research by other scholars has largely confirmed the
findings of Gregg. For instance, in Robinson's 1984 study of British settlement
in the seventeenth century (reprinted in 1994) the density of Scottish surnames
based on muster calls from the first half of that century is greatest in north
Down, Antrim and north-east Donegal (see table 3.1 above for combined English
and Scots figures). Robinson has also asserted that 'the population distribution
of English and Scottish settlers had been established into a coherent pattern
circa 1622' (Robinson 1994 [1984]: 97). Gregg was rather pessimistic about the
continuing existence of Ulster Scots, but the research of Margaret Skea (1982)
concluded that Ulster Scots had not declined to anything like the extent which
Gregg had predicted in earlier investigations.

Just as Ulster Irish and Scottish Gaelic share features which are of an areal
nature, a case can be made for regarding Ulster Scots and Scots in Galloway
in south-west Scotland as forming a dialect continuum. James Milroy (1982)
considered this question and weighed up the arguments in favour of mutual
influence of Ulster Scots speech on that of Galloway and vice versa. As the
original settlement of parts of Ulster, such as Co. Antrim and Co. Down, derives
from Galloway, the historical line is probably from Scotland to Ireland through
emigration, though there was some settlement in the nineteenth century from
Ulster back to Scotland and there were seasonal migrants who travelled from
west Ulster (Co. Donegal) to Scotland for work. Milroy lists many common
linguistic features between Ulster and south-west Scotland such as allophonic
vowel length, the lowering of short front vowels, along with various specific verb
forms (frequently modals). In his conclusion he seems to favour the view that
the similarity of Ulster Scots and Galloway Scots is largely due to their shared
conservative nature as dialects of English.

The number of speakers of Ulster Scots is difficult to estimate, especially
because there is no clear demarcation between Ulster Scots and English-based
varieties. In the late 1960s, Brendan Adams suggested that the population of the
three Ulster Scots areas amounted to about 170,000. That figure is now larger
due to a general increase in population (particularly in the towns contained
in these areas like Ballymena and Coleraine), but the number of Ulster Scots
speakers is difficult to determine, not least because the difference between it and
more general forms of English in Ulster is not always easy to perceive and this
difference has been overlain by the strong antithesis of urban and rural speech

in contemporary Ulster.[11] The optimistic figure of 100,000 which is offered, not uncritically, by Montgomery and Gregg (1997: 213) may serve as a general orientation but nothing more precise is available at the present. The use of Ulster Scots has not been registered by censuses in Northern Ireland, so that there is no way of gaining any official figures on the matter. Indeed, there has been a general negative attitude to Ulster Scots throughout its history, e.g. in the *Ordnance Survey Memoirs*, compiled in the 1830s by army officers and civil servants (Montgomery and Gregg 1997: 581f.; Lunney 1999), the suggestion is that it is merely the dialect of a section of the population and is regarded as rustic and coarse. In addition, the major linguistic dichotomy in Ireland is that of Irish versus English, so that many have been blind to the division of English in Ulster into an English- and a Scots-derived component.

The lexicography of Ulster Scots has been served by a large number of academic articles dealing with specific lexical items or word fields, as found in the work of John Braidwood and Brendan Adams (Braidwood 1965, 1969, 1972; Adams 1966b, 1978b, 1981a). A dictionary in popular style is available in James Fenton's *The Hamely Tongue: A Personal Record of Ulster-Scots in County Antrim* (2000 [1995]). Loreto Todd's *Words Apart: A Dictionary of Northern Irish English* (1990) is medium in size and coverage. A more academic work – with a broader brief – is the *Concise Ulster Dictionary* (1996), edited by Caroline Macafee. This book contains a 25-page historical introduction providing background information on Ulster English. Most of the items concern farming and rural life in general, but regional vocabulary for parts of the body, clothing and terms for individuals is also recorded. Where etymologies are known they are given, in particular the link with Scottish forms of English is highlighted.

3.3.1 ATTESTATIONS OF ULSTER SCOTS

The first documents which show Ulster Scots being used in writing are from the second and third decades of the seventeenth century (Montgomery 1997: 216) and are mostly legal texts and family letters (though there is a letter to Elizabeth I which dates from 1571, Montgomery and Gregg 1997: 586). The force operating against Ulster Scots was the ever-increasing anglicisation which was progressing steadily in both Ulster and Scotland. As a spoken medium, however, Ulster Scots was if anything reinforced in the course of the seventeenth century (Robinson 1989b) with continuing emigration of settlers from the west of Scotland, long after the official plantation (1610–25), initiated by James I, had ceased. Indeed it is estimated that as many as 80,000 Scots (a generous figure by Macafee, quoted in Montgomery and Gregg 1997: 573) left for Ulster after the Williamite victory

---

[11] See Kingsmore (1995) who offers a detailed investigation of vernacular variants of working-class speech in Coleraine in northern Ulster (an original Ulster Scots area) and who looks at the speech of three generations in four families. One of the variables looked at is intervocalic (t) and the findings suggest that the tap [ɾ] is the incoming male-led variant from Belfast, whereas a glottal stop [ʔ] is preferred by females (a generally rural variant).

in Ireland in 1690. The reason for this is that in England this victory led to the
official eradication of rebellious elements in Scotland, not just among Catholics
but among religious dissenters as well, notably the Presbyterians.

Although written attestations of Ulster Scots declined in the seventeenth century, the core areas in Ulster continued to exist. There is also evidence of Ulster
Scots features found in such documents as church records and emigrant letters[12]
and from research into neglected ephemeral publications (Montgomery 1997:
217–19). These show that Ulster Scots continued as an unofficial medium for a
large section of the population.

A modest literature[13] in Ulster Scots flourished for about fifty years from the
1780s to the mid nineteenth century, produced by a group of writers who have
come to be known as the Rhyming Weavers (Hewitt 1974) because they were
engaged in the traditional industry of linen weaving. This popular verse is by
writers, without great education, who claimed to be representing the speech of
the people in a movement similar in nature and intention to that of Robert Burns
in Scotland (Montgomery 1997: 221). Perhaps the best known of the rhyming
weavers was James Orr of Ballycarry, north-east of Belfast. This notion of Ulster
Scots as 'the voice of the people' was continued in the nineteenth century in
prose documents which described and commented on local issues. There does
not, however, seem to have been a coherent concept of an Ulster Scots tradition,
as much of this writing was not in a conventionalised spelling and does not appear
to have drawn consciously on the work of previous writers.

3.3.2 THE ULSTER SCOTS REVIVAL

No treatment of Ulster Scots at the outset of the twenty-first century would be
complete without considering the efforts being made by sections of Northern
Ireland society to revive this variety and have it widely recognised as a separate language. The Good Friday Agreement of April 1998 sees Ulster Scots
as part of the cultural heritage of the island of Ireland (north and south). As
part of the agreement an official body, The Ulster-Scots Agency/Tha Boord o
Ulstèr-Scotch, was formed. Strictly speaking, it is a cross-border[14] body with

---

[12] Montgomery (1995) stresses the value of emigrant letters for historical linguistics because they
represent first-person accounts from members of different social strata. His interest is concentrated
on a number of key features such as habitual *be*, second-person pronouns and the use of double
modals. He stresses the value of this evidence as it can offer a window on the process of diffusion of
Old World linguistic features into New World English in the formative period of its development.

[13] The remarks here refer to literature written entirely in Ulster Scots. There are many instances
where dialect is used for characterisation and effect, most notably in William Carleton's (1794–
1869) *Traits and Stories of the Irish Peasantry* which appeared between 1830 and 1833. Sections of
these tales are contained in *A Corpus of Irish English*, see Hickey (2003a). Carleton was from mid
Ulster and appears to have objected to Ulster Scots as not truly Irish; see the Preface to the 1830
edition of *Traits and Stories*.

[14] Officially, the bodies involved in the promotion of Ulster Scots and Irish apply across the island of
Ireland. In practical terms this is not always the case and there is a real danger that the highlighting
of differences between cultural groups might be divisive and serve inadvertently to strengthen the
border between north and south; see the discussion in Nic Craith (1999).

a counterpart in Foras na Gaeilge 'the Irish language foundation', which was formed at the same time and which is located in Dublin with an office in Belfast.

In practical terms the activities of The Ulster-Scots Agency are confined to the north of Ireland, but this does include (east) Donegal where the agency is active and plans to open an office. The Ulster-Scots Agency is jointly funded by the Department of Culture, Arts and Leisure in Northern Ireland and the Department of Community, Rural Affairs and the Gaeltacht in the Republic of Ireland. It maintains a comprehensive website for Ulster Scots affairs and publishes *The Ulster-Scot*, an e-newsletter.

There are a few other bodies concerned officially with Ulster Scots in Northern Ireland. The Ulster-Scots Language Society was founded in 1992 'to promote the status and re-establish the dignity of Ulster-Scots as a language' and issues a journal *Ullans, The Magazine for Ulster Scots* which offers a public forum for discussing matters, linguistic and otherwise (e.g. creative writing), of relevance to Ulster Scots. Another body is The Ulster Scots Heritage Council founded in 1994 and concerned too with the promotion of Ulster Scots culture. An Ulster Scots Academy is planned but has not been established yet (mid 2006).

However, the University of Ulster has an Institute of Ulster Scots Studies (established in 2001), located at the Jordanstown campus in Newtownabbey, just north of Belfast. There is also the Academy for Irish Cultural Heritages (initiated in 2000) within the University of Ulster and located at the Magee campus in Derry. The remit of the latter body is much broader and covers research into all cultures and languages represented in Ireland, including Ulster Scots as the academy explicitly states.

Library and archive services relating to Ulster Scots are provided by the Linen Hall Library in Belfast and the Ulster Folk and Transport Museum located in Cultra on the south side of Belfast Lough. The latter houses the Ulster Dialect and Linguistic Diversity Archive with collections of materials which relate to Ulster Scots, such as those gathered by Robert Gregg and Brendan Adams.

A grammar of Ulster Scots is available which offers a concise description of its chief traits (Robinson 1997). A regulated orthography, which would facilitate the understanding and analysis of Ulster Scots writing, has not been agreed upon yet.

Linguistic status of Ulster Scots

In the following discussion the word 'language' is used. This does not imply that the author considers Ulster Scots a fully fledged independent language, as its supporters would maintain. But he does readily concede that the label 'variety' is too weak in this context as Ulster Scots is much further removed from standard English than other varieties of English throughout Britain and Ireland, with the exception of Scots in Scotland, of course. A detailed discussion of the criteria for regarding a variety as a language is to be found in Görlach (2000: 14–17), Kallen (1999: 80f.) and Montgomery (1999: 89–99). The last of these authors tends toward the designation 'language' for Ulster Scots, if only for 'symbolic' reasons (Montgomery 1999: 99).

Before starting the present discussion a few points need to be made. The present revival is a programmatic urban phenomenon, whereas traditional Ulster Scots is largely rural. Furthermore, rural inhabitants do not perceive of themselves as speakers of Ulster Scots, let alone of 'Ullans'. In the fieldwork for *A Sound Atlas of Irish English* (Hickey 2004a), during which the present author interviewed and recorded several hundred individuals in rural Northern Ireland, not a single one identified himself or herself as a speaker of Ulster Scots – a situation very different from that with native speakers of Irish.

As one might expect, many of the individuals supporting Ulster Scots are language activists and enthusiasts rather than speakers who acquired rural Ulster Scots in their childhood. The cultural basis for scholarly work on written Ulster Scots, notably Robinson (1997), is formed by the (largely rural) poets from the late eighteenth and early nineteenth century (see above). The motivation for the current revival may derive from linguistic identity with a past which individuals wish to conserve. But the desire to establish Ulster Scots as an equivalent to Irish, but on the Protestant side of the ethnic divide, is difficult to deny.

The perception of Ulster Scots by other sections of the Northern Ireland population varies. It is viewed with suspicion by the Catholic community as it is assumed to be promoted by Protestants as a deliberate counterweight to Irish. It is often regarded with amusement and benevolent tolerance by Protestants who are not of Ulster Scots stock. Certainly, the many lexical coinages, which have been undertaken by language enthusiasts in the years since official recognition was granted, border more often than not on the ridiculous. As might be expected in a situation like that of current Ulster Scots, much effort is expended on stressing its otherness. Nowhere is this more obvious than in vocabulary where mechanisms of word formation are deliberately exploited to render new compounds which sound as different from standard English as possible. A much discussed example (Görlach 2000: 23) is *heich heid yin*, lit. 'high head one' for *director*, which is a classic case of creating a term which is maximally different from that in the language one sees oneself as struggling with for independence, in this instance, standard English. Established languages on the other hand, e.g. German, Swedish, Russian, all use a derivative of the Romance word *director(e)/directeur* (with a local pronunciation of course).

There are considerable linguistic problems with such behaviour. If vocabulary is invented randomly where the need is thought to exist, then no consistency in style can be maintained in a language. Without clearly contoured styles in a language it cannot be the vehicle of literature, for example. It may be, of course, that the present situation is one of transition and that the lexical dust, so to speak, will settle in a generation or two when all areas of modern society have been more or less furnished with appropriate vocabulary.

Another difficulty with attempts to establish Ulster Scots officially is that words and expressions have been co-opted which are not confined to Ulster Scots alone. For instance, Robinson (1997: 222) gives *houl yer wheesht* as an Ulster Scots translation for 'keep quiet'. This expression is found throughout the entire island of Ireland and cannot be claimed to be just Ulster Scots (except perhaps for the long vowel in *wheesht* which is Scottish in origin). This situation could be illustrated with many other instances, e.g. *middlin* for 'mediocre' which may be Scots in origin but is again found throughout Ireland. Other terms, like *shanks* for 'legs', are Old English and not Scots in origin.

Much is made in Ulster Scots of non-standard orthography. In fact in many cases, if one rewrites a word without the Ulster Scots spelling, then it is a straightforward English word, e.g. *leuk* for 'look', *slakken* for 'slacken'. A difference in vowel realisation does not make a word a different lexical item. For instance, the southern Irish vernacular pronunciation of *boat* as [boːt̬] does not make it a different word from RP [bəʊt].

Stressing differences between Ulster Scots and other languages in Northern Ireland has to do with establishing importance and, in keeping with this goal, Ulster Scots scholars have tended to maximise the geographical distribution of Ulster Scots speaking areas. Philip Robinson, for instance, speaks of an 'Ulster-Scots Cultural Zone' (Robinson 1997: 17, capitals his) which he sees as encompassing three quarters of Derry and half of Donegal, including the Irish-speaking districts of the north-west coast, something which is patently false.[15]

The ultimate fate of the Ulster Scots revival depends on social acceptance and whether it will be used to construct future identities (Stapleton and Wilson 2003). If the younger generation regards the enterprise as pointless or out of step with modern society, then, somewhat like the revival of the Irish language, it will not be successful. Unless a language is adopted and used consistently by a generation in their childhood, there can be no question of native speakers arising and hence there will be no community to carry the language forward. One could, however, maintain, as many activists do, that only by increasing public presence and awareness can the status of Ulster Scots increase socially and hence be favourably positioned for acceptance by following generations.

3.3.3 DELIMITING ULSTER SCOTS

A linguistic treatment of Ulster Scots must start by differentiating between conservative Ulster Scots – 'braid', i.e. broad, Ulster Scots – which has its base in rural areas of Ulster and more 'standard' forms which are spoken chiefly in urban centres, parallel to the established distinction in Scotland between Lowland Scots and Scottish Standard English (Harris 1984b: 119). An essential feature of 'standard' Ulster Scots is that most words with non-standard Scots vowel values have reallocated values which are nearer to those in English throughout Ulster. The list in table 3.4 illustrates vowel values and some consonantal features which are indicative of conservative Ulster Scots. The yardstick of reference is

---

[15] Such exaggeration also occurs in other comparable situations. For instance, the government census returns for the Irish language in the Republic of Ireland are much exaggerated, claiming several hundred thousand native speakers of the language.

Table 3.4. *Features of Older Scots and conservative Ulster Scots*

1. Retention of OS ū (not shifted to /au/): *cow* /kuː/, *hoos* /hus/
2. A low, unrounded back vowel before labials for OS *o*: *soft* /saːft/, *top* /taːp/
3. OS *ei* merges with /i/ and not /ai/ [əi, ae]: *die* /diː/
4. OS ō has a fronted, unrounded reflex: *blood* /blɪd/
5. Fronting and raising of Old English ā: *home* /heːm/
6. Little raising of above vowel after labio-velars: *two* /twɔː/
7. Lowering of /ɪ/ to /ɛ/: *thick* /θɛk/
8. No raising of Middle English /eː/ to /iː/: *beat* /bet/, *meat* /met/
9. Raising of OS /a/ especially before /r/: *farm* /feːrm/
10. Distinct open and close mid back vowels: *horse* /hɔːrs/, *hoarse* /hoːrs/
11. Distinction between short vowels before /r/: *term* /tɛrm/, *burn* /bʌrn/
12. No rounding of /a/ after /w/: *swan* /swan/
13. Retention of distinction between /ʍ/ and /w/: *whale* /ʍeː(l)/, *wale* /weː(l)/
14. Retention of syllable-final /x/: *bought* /boːxt/
15. Vocalisation of word-final velarised /l/ [ɫ]: *full* /fu/, *still* /stɛ/

Older Scots (OS in table 3.4), up to 1700 (Aitken 1977), i.e. before large-scale emigration to Ulster began.

When compared to southern British English the shifts of vowel values in Scots constitute a realignment of vowel space. A prominent shift is that of Middle English /oː/ to a front vowel, with or without rounding, i.e. Older Scots /ɪ, ø/.[16] In Ulster Scots this vowel appears as /ɪ/: /oː/ → /ɪ/ *loom* /lɪm/. Other vowel changes are seen in the following forms: /ɪ/ → /æ/ *limb* /læm/, /æ/ → /aː/ *lamb* /laːm/.

In more standardised forms of Ulster Scots the vowel deriving from Older Scots *ei* is diphthongised so that a word like *die* is realised as [dəi]; the former vowel *ai* is realised as /e/ as in *stay* /ste/ (Harris 1984b: 122). These realisations can be regarded as instances of standardisation because /əi/ and /e/ are, in the Ulster context, the equivalents of RP /ai/ and /ei/ respectively.

With consonants in standardised Ulster Scots, the reinstatement of word-final /l/ and the relative absence of /-x/ are salient. Among the vowels, one finds a general reallocation. For instance, many items from the FOOT lexical class, traditionally with /ɪ/, are reallocated to values which are derived from more standard forms of English, with /u/ corresponding to /uː/. The attestations of /ʌ, ɪ/ are considerably more numerous in Ulster Scots than in English throughout Ulster and hence reallocation may take place here as well:

---

[16] There is a general consequence of this: if the Great Vowel Shift is taken to have been a push shift with mid vowels causing the diphthongisation of high vowels, i.e. if one assumes that /oː/ → /uː/ triggered /uː/ → /au/, then the absence of the Great Vowel Shift for /uː/ in Scots can be accounted for by the fronting of /oː/ to /ɪ, ø/ which meant that the /uː/ was not pushed out of its original position (Lass 1987: 226f.).

foot /fɪt/ → /fʉt/, *blood* /blɪd/ → /blʌd/, *door* /dɪr/ → /dor/; *steady* /stʌdɪ/ → /stɛdɪ/, *winter* /wʌntər/ → /wɪntər/, *dog* /dʌg/ → /dɒg/.

When one considers the cline between conservative Ulster Scots and more standard forms of English in Ulster[17] one can see a difference in principle between phonetic realisation and affiliation to a lexical class. The reason is probably that with a change of lexical class a binary decision is made, i.e. a speaker altering his/her pronunciation from /fɪt/ to /fʉt/ makes a discrete choice in vowel type. But the phonetic realisation of English /uː/ involves degrees of movement to a high, rounded central vowel [ʉ]. An example from consonants would be the realisation of /r/: this can vary from retroflex [ɻ] to a post-alveolar frictionless continuant [ɹ]. It is remarkable that both these features are found in Ulster Scots, mid Ulster English and southern Ulster English, to varying degrees.

Vowel length. One of the features used to distinguish Ulster Scots is vowel length. Probably in the fifteenth to sixteenth century, phonemic vowel length was lost in Scots and the occurrence of long versus short vowels became a matter predictable by the nature of the following segment. Because of this, Scots departed from the organisational principle of the remaining Germanic languages, all of which retain phonemic vowel length and many of which (all the north Germanic languages, bar Danish) have phonemic consonant length as well. The innovation in Scots was to create a system where length depended on what followed the vowels. The factors determining the occurrence of phonetically long vowels are treated as a single complex, termed the *Scottish Vowel Length Rule*, or alternatively *Aitken's Law*, after the Scottish linguist Adam J. Aitken who was the first to describe the phenomenon explicitly (Aitken 1981).

In stressed syllables, before /r/, /v/, /ð/, /z/ and /ʒ/, before another vowel and before a morpheme boundary vowels are long. In all other environments they are short. Hence one has /iː/ in *here, leave, see, sees*, in *idea*, in *agreed* (= agree#d), but /i/ *beat, bead, feel, leaf, cease, greed*. The Scottish Vowel Length Rule can lead to distinctions arising which do not exist elsewhere in English, for instance, the verb *use* has a long vowel, [juːz], whereas the noun *use* has a short one [jʉs]. The matter of the morpheme boundary is important and has led to minimal pairs such as *brewed* [bruːd] (= brew#ed) and *brood* [brʉd]).

The vowels which are most subject to this regulation are the high vowels /i/ and /ʉ/ (= English /uː/). Many varieties also apply the rule to the mid vowels /e/ and /o/. For some conservative varieties of Scots, which have the vowel /ø/ (often unrounded to /ɪ/) – a front vowel deriving from Middle English /oː/ – there is a distinction between a long and short version, the words *do, floor* showing

---

[17] Montgomery (1991) has examined the anglicisation of Scots from a diachronic perspective (in the early seventeenth century as evidenced in letters written by Ulster Scots). His paper is concerned with the penetration of standard forms into Ulster Scots in this formative period. Montgomery looks at a series of features, such as negative elements like *nocht*, the indefinite article *ane*, the patterning of relative elements in *quh-*, the use of verbal *-s* with plural noun subjects and the distribution of demonstratives, to show how the language became increasingly more standard.

Table 3.5. *Reflexes of Middle English /o/ before /l/, [l]*

	Ulster Scots	Ulster English	Colloquial southern
1.	*old* [əul]	[old]	[aul]
2.	*bold* [bəul]	[bold]	[baul]

the long vowel with the words *boot, fool* having the short one. In addition, the vowel before /r/ is lowered: *poor* [peːr].

The operation of the vowel length rule has meant that many words which are distinguished primarily by vowel length (often with attendant quality differences) have homophonous counterparts in Ulster Scots, as with *cot* /kɒt/ and *caught* /kɔːt/ both of which are [kot]. A more tenuous merger can be found where the effect of lowering and lengthening of /e/ and the raising of /æ/ before velars yields the same phonetic value, as in *neck* [nɛːk] and *knack* [nɛːk].

Diphthongs are also affected by the vowel length rule. For Modern English /ai/, deriving from Middle English /iː/, there are two main realisations. The first occurs in a short environment and is characterised by a raised onset, hence *life, tide* are [ləif] and [təid] respectively. The second realisation is found in the long environment and shows a much lower onset and is phonetically long, e.g. *alive, tie, tied* are [ə'laev], [tae], [taed] respectively.

Modern English /ei/, which stems from Middle English /ai/, has a realisation [əi], as in *hay* [həi] (conservative). This can lead to homophony or near homophony in some cases, as with the word pair *tail* and *tile* which both can be [təil]. Equally, contrast can arise when /əi/ stands in opposition to /ae/. In word-final position this is particularly obvious with word pairs like *bay* [bəi], *pay* [pəi] and *buy* [bae], *pie* [pae].

Two further diphthongs also exist in Ulster Scots. The first is that inherited with French loanwords and which is fairly similar to more standard forms of English, e.g. *boy* [bɔe], *point* [pɔent]; it is also found in words deriving from Irish, e.g. *moiley* [mɔele] 'hornless cow' (based on Irish *maol* 'bare, bald'). The second is a reflex of Middle English /oː/ before /l/. Recall that this vowel was fronted in Scots and frequently unrounded so that it appears as /ø/ or /ɪ/. But before velarised /l/, phonetically [ɫ], a diphthong arose which in Ulster Scots is [əu] and which in other forms of Irish English, including east coast varieties in the south of the country, appeared as /au/[18] and is still attested in colloquial pronunciations. The situation can be summarised as in table 3.5.

The low vowels of Ulster Scots are not affected by the vowel length rule as there is a general lengthening of low vowels. This applies to those deriving from Early Modern English /ɒ/ – *stop* /staːp/, *soft* /saːft/ – and to other vowels, which

---

[18] Previously there were more attestations in the south as well, e.g. *cold* [kaul(d)], Sheridan (1781: 145).

Table 3.6. *Historical vowel quantity changes and Ulster Scots*

1a.	ME /a/	→	/aː/ before voiceless fricatives /f, s, θ/ (SBE /ɑː/) *staff* [staːf], *gas* [gaːs], *bath* [baːθ]
b.		→	/a/ before /n/ + voiceless stop (SBE /ɑː/) *grant* [grant]
2.	ME /o/	→	/ɑː/ before voiceless fricatives /f, s, θ/ *loss* [lɑːs], *soft* [sɑːft]

have arisen due to specific Scots developments, such as lowering and retraction after /w/: *wet* /wɑːt/, *twelfth* /twɑːlfθ/.

Those vowels which were short in Old English, i.e. in the north Anglian dialect which was the precursor of Lowland Scots, are generally not affected by the vowel length rule; hence words like *bit* and *fir* with /ɪ/ and *but* and *fur* with /ʌ/ show short vowels although the second of each word pair has an environment (before /r/) which would normally demand vowel lengthening.

Lastly, it should be observed that the vowel length rule can be suspended by the force of analogy. Many noun paradigms which, due to the alternation of voiceless and voiced fricatives in stem-final position, would trigger vowel lengthening in the plural, do not in fact have this due to analogy with the singular which does not form an input to the vowel length rule: *knife* [nəɪf]: *knives* [nəɪvz] (and not [naevz]) (Montgomery and Gregg 1997: 614).

When considering Ulster Scots vowels one must also bear in mind two major vowel lengthening processes which have led here to different reflexes from those in more standard varieties of British English (see table 3.6). The first lengthening (1a) is present, if permitted by the environment (vowel length rule, see above) but its second subtype (1b) is not. The second lengthening (2) is found, although it has been generally lost in standard forms of British English (SBE in table 3.6). Significantly, this vowel lengthening is still found in present-day Dublin English (see section 5.4.1).

In addition to the above, one should mention that some vowel shortenings, common in mainland English, are not found in Ulster Scots because of the Scots input, e.g. the absence of shortening of Middle English /ɛː/ before /d/, hence *dead* is pronounced [diːd].

Regional differences. There are no large-scale differences between regionally diverse forms of Ulster Scots. The major division, as mentioned above, is between rural and urban speech. Nonetheless, the main area of Ulster Scots in north Co. Antrim and stretching across to north-east Co. Derry shows one difference in front vowel realisation compared to the remaining areas in Co. Down and Co. Donegal respectively. An /e/ in the former region corresponds to an /i/ in the latter areas so that there is a contrast, for instance, between Antrim/Derry [ʃen] 'soon', [əˈben] 'above' and Down/Donegal [ʃin] 'soon', [əˈbin] 'above' (Montgomery and Gregg 1997: 616).

Consonants. As opposed to the situation with vowels, consonant realisations are not useful in distinguishing Ulster Scots from Ulster English. Indeed, there are no consonants which occur in the one group of varieties and not in the other. A good indicator of affiliation is the velar fricative /x/. While it is true that this occurs throughout Ulster, the lexical incidence in Ulster Scots is much higher than in English elsewhere in Ulster.[19] In the latter, /x/ occurs in words which are definitely of Scottish origin, e.g. [pɛːx] 'pant', [sprɑːx] 'sprawl' (Montgomery and Gregg 1997: 615). It is also found in Gaelic loanwords which have gained general currency, such as *loch* 'lake'. This applies of course to Ulster Scots as well, but /x/ is furthermore present as an inherited feature from Scots. It corresponds to the same sound in Middle English and is indicated orthographically by *gh*, e.g. *bought* [bɔːxt], *enough* [ɪˈnʌx].

3.3.4 GRAMMAR

The grammatical features of Ulster Scots bear a close resemblance to those found in Lowland Scots as well. For instance, contraction of pronoun and auxiliary (with *no* as negator), rather than that of auxiliary and negator, is a prominent feature, e.g. *She'll no be in time at this rate* and the clitic form *-nae/ny* as in *Ae didnae come home last night, He canny leave now* are also common in Scotland. This latter usage in Ulster Scots has been highlighted by Montgomery and Gregg (1997: 616) as one of the most salient grammatical aspects. Perhaps because of this, it has spread somewhat to mid Ulster English.

The principal parts of verbs show considerable deviation from those in general Ulster English. There are two reasons for this. The first concerns the vowel values found in Ulster Scots: [de] 'do', [heː] 'have' show fronted /o:/ and raised (and lengthened) /a/ respectively. The deletion of final /-v/, with lengthening of the nucleus vowel, can also be seen in /giː/ 'give'. The second reason is the fact that in Ulster Scots two forms of verbs are often found where mid Ulster English has three. Hence [din] is both 'did' and 'done' (compare the Early Modern English [dʊn], without the Scots fronting of course). Similarly, [gin] is both 'gave' and 'given'. In these cases, the past participle functions as a preterite form.

Modal verbs also have distinct forms in Ulster Scots: there is also a special form of the modal verb *must, maun* [mɑːn] (Corrigan 2000a) and *can* appears as an infinitive in phrases like [ˈɑːl ˈnoː kən ˈstəi] *I'll no can stay* for the more standard *I'll not be able to stay* (Montgomery and Gregg 1997: 616).

Noun morphology has a distinct profile in Ulster Scots as remnants of nasal and umlaut plurals are still to be found, e.g. [in] *eyes* and [ʃin] *shoes* show an /n/ as plural marker where in other forms of English the general /s/ has long since been established. [kɑe] *cows* shows a vowel which is the long variant of the

---

[19] Adams (1981b) investigates the retention of an earlier /x/ in English in Ulster and finds that widespread use is confined to certain keywords such as *laughter, lough* or *trough*.

diphthong arising from a much older /i/ which in its turn is the unrounded version of /y/, the original umlaut used in the plural of *cow*.

Further features are found among deictic elements: the demonstratives *thon* 'yon' and *thonder* 'yonder'[20] are found as equivalents to the now obsolete distal deictic pronouns of English: *D'ye mind [remember] thon man from Galway?* (MLSI, M65+, Cardonagh, Co. Donegal); *Did ever he write thon stuff?* (MLSI, M65+, Cardonagh, Co. Donegal).

Some of the grammatical structures are definitely recessive while others have, if anything, spread beyond the traditional Ulster Scots areas (Montgomery and Gregg 1997: 611). A recessive feature would be the use of two modals in a single verb phrase as in *She might could come this evening*. Such double modal structures are an established feature of Appalachian English (Montgomery and Nagle 1994; Montgomery 2001: 148) which implies that they were to be found in Ulster Scots before the emigration to the New World in the eighteenth century and are also a feature of Lowland Scots (Miller 1993: 120f.).

A diffused feature in Ulster is what is termed 'punctual *whenever*' (Montgomery 1997: 219; Montgomery and Kirk 2001), a use of the iterative adverb in situations which imply a single point in time. Again this is a feature which is found in some rural forms of English in the eastern United States (Montgomery 2001).

(3)   a. *What was the scene like whenever you arrived?* (Belfast English)
       b. *Whenever I was about eight years, when I got old enough to know where I was at, I left.* (Smoky Mountains in Tennessee)

A grammatical trait of Ulster Scots which has received considerable attention from linguists in recent years is verb–subject concord in the present tense (Montgomery 1994; McCafferty 2003). This is a complex issue with the precise nature of the subject as well as the person and number of the verb determining whether an -*s* inflection is used on the verb in question. In general one can say that a personal pronoun as subject is least likely to trigger *s*-inflection as the pronoun has the function of a verbal clitic (Börjars and Chapman 1998). The more independent the subject and the greater the distance between it and the verb form, the more probable the occurrence of *s*-inflection becomes. Here are two examples from emigrant letters of Ulster Scots which have been analysed in detail by Montgomery (1995).

(4)   *All the young men that* has *come here lately would be glad they had not come. Your letters* comes *on without delay.*

The first of these sentences shows a relative clause with a plural antecedent triggering *s*-inflection (*has* is interpreted as an *s*-inflected form here). The second

---

[20] These are contracted forms from *the yon* and *the yonder* respectively and have long been noted as features of English in Ulster (see Joyce 1979 [1910]: 82).

sentence is similar in type but in this case a single noun qualified by a possessive pronoun functions as subject.

Verbal concord is another example of a diffused feature. It is found not only in Ulster Scots. In Belfast English the phenomenon is also common, as James Milroy (1981: 7) noted with examples like *Them eggs is cracked so they are*, a finding confirmed by Alison Henry in sentences like *The glasses is broken*, *The books goes down well* (1995: 95). More recent treatments of verbal concord, especially with reference to its origin in northern dialects of English, are to be found in studies by Lukas Pietsch (2005a, 2005b).

3.3.5 VOCABULARY

Any consideration of the vocabulary of Ulster Scots must rest on the rural forms of the dialect as it is here that the most distinctive lexical items are to be found. There are some words which are now apparently confined to Ulster Scots such as *clootie* 'left-handed' (Braidwood 1972; Todd 1990: 48), *lap* 'small heap of hay', *(hay)pike* 'haystack', *crew* 'pigsty' (Montgomery and Gregg 1997: 606). Some of the items suspected of being Ulster Scots, like *mitch* 'play truant' (Todd 1990: 116) or *cog* 'cheat in school', are general in Irish English of the south and may simply be part of archaic/regional vocabulary which has survived in Ireland,[21] not solely retentions of Scots input in the north.

Furthermore, there are semantic extensions of original English words which are found in the north and the south, for example the use of *ditch* to mean 'hedge' or 'embankment' (Braidwood 1969; Todd 1990: 61).

Occurrence in the south is not, however, a sufficient criterion for a non–Scots origin: *thole* 'tolerate' (from OE *tholian*, Todd 1990: 157) is not found in the south and is not Scots either, but a Middle English retention in Ulster (Adams 1977: 64).

The clearest Scots examples are those which are attested in Lowland Scots and also found in Ulster, e.g. *brae* 'hill, slope', *firnest* 'in front of', *greet* 'to cry', *ken* 'to know', *lum* 'chimney', *oxther* 'armpit', *tae* 'to', *glar* 'mud'. Ulster Scots words/usages have sometimes diffused into general Ulster English as with *hogo* 'bad smell' (Todd 1990: 93), *drouth* 'thirst'; the word *wean* for 'child' is more common than Scots *bairn* (Adams 1977: 64, 1978b; Todd 1990: 26). Southern Irish English may show these items on occasions, e.g. *gawk* 'stare' (Todd 1990: 80).

3.4 Ulster English

In the list of main varieties of English above (see table 3.2) the term 'mid Ulster English' was used for forms of the language characteristic of areas settled in

---

[21] These retentions have led authors, both academic and popular, to liken Ulster English to 'Elizabethan' or 'Shakespearean' English; see Braidwood (1964) as an example, though such vague references carry little informational value (Montgomery and Gregg 1997: 619).

the main by people from the north of England. In a way, 'mid Ulster English' is a blanket term for English in the province which is not (i) Ulster Scots, (ii) English in contact with Irish (now outside Northern Ireland) or (iii) English in the transition area to the south. For the present section, the simpler phrase 'Ulster English' is used, bearing in mind that this refers to non-Scots and non-Irish varieties and that English in Belfast represents a special amalgam of Scots and English input along with independent developments (see section 5.5.1).

The areas of Ulster settled by the English are characterised by very heterogeneous origins. It is known that people from Devonshire and west Somerset settled in the region of Belfast, south Antrim and south-east Tyrone. Even more settlers came from the southern section of the west Midlands area (Warwickshire, Staffordshire, Shropshire) and settled again in south Antrim as well as in north-west Down, north Armagh, central and south Tyrone and east Fermanagh. The north-west Midlands area (Lancashire, Cheshire, south-west Yorkshire) was the source for many settlers in the Lagan valley, the hinterland of Belfast, and other areas across Ulster (Adams 1977: 62f.). Such settlement should also not be understood as exclusively English by any means. The English undertakers allowed Scottish settlers in the areas they were responsible for and there was internal movement in Ulster with Scots moving into areas which were outside their core areas in Down, Antrim and Derry.

The outcome of this diversity of background, and of the fact that the English were far outnumbered by the Scots, was that general Ulster English does not show the salient characteristics of the dialect regions of England which provided input. There is no trace, for instance, of the initial voicing which is common – and was then even more so – in the south-west of England. Whether this was also the case in the early period of settlement cannot be said. What is certain, however, is that a process of koinéisation must have set in quickly, most of all in areas of urban settlement.[22]

Ulster English is largely aligned with mainland varieties in England, but also retains some of the more salient features of Ulster Scots. Among the latter would be areal features like high central /ʉ/ and retroflex /ɻ/. Other Ulster Scots features may occur in diluted form, for instance, the /æ/ reflex of English /ɪ/ is found as a slightly lowered vowel, *pick* /pëk/.

The situation today is different from that which obtained previously. Not all descendants of original Scots settlers continued Ulster Scots. Both the English settlers and the native Irish population, which had shifted to English, came to use a supraregional form of English in the province which is distinct from Ulster Scots. This general form of English in Ulster is now the majority variety with Ulster Scots a minority form.

---

[22] In this connection one should mention the attempt by Loreto Todd (1989, 1992) to distinguish linguistically between (i) (her) Anglo-Irish, the language of those Ulster people descended from English settlers, (ii) Ulster Scots and (iii) (her) Hiberno-English which she sees as the language of those people descended from original Irish speakers. The difficulty lies in substantiating the distinction between group (i) and (iii).

Furthermore, Ulster Scots is now related to general Ulster English as a super-ordinate variety and not to Scots. While in its most conservative form it has many phonological and lexical[23] connections with Scots, it occupies a position on a scale whose other end is formed by general Ulster English. The present-day relationship of Ulster Scots to Ulster English is a cline from conservative rural to non-local urban speech.

3.4.1 DENOMINATIONAL DIFFERENCES

A frequently raised question is whether there are speech differences between Catholics and Protestants in Ulster. In Todd (1984) an attempt was made to document differences in the speech of the Protestant and Catholic community, the one deriving from Gaelic speakers and the other from lowland Scottish or English settlers. Todd's main thesis is that because of the separate linguistic backgrounds of the Catholic and Protestant communities in Northern Ireland and because of the segregation of the two social groups today, there are identifiable differences in their use of English, such as the use of an alveolar [l] by Catholics and a velar [ɫ] by Protestants, perhaps true of some Protestants in Belfast (see Owens 1977).[24]

Key phonological features of Ulster which Todd mentions – such as variation with /a/ or deletion of intervocalic /ð/ – cannot be classified solely along lines of ethnic and/or religious affiliation. The presence of a velar glide after /k, g/ before /a/ may be an exception as it is a recessive feature and found among older Catholic speakers. However, even this is not entirely clear (Todd builds hedges into her statements referring to 'many Catholics' and 'many Protestants'). In her refutation of Todd's stance, Millar (1987b) accepts Todd's observation that the two communities live segregated social lives, but that it is too soon to determine what linguistic effects, if any, this will have (a finding confirmed by Millar 1990). Gunn (1994) is somewhat vague and inconclusive in his consideration of the language of public figures from both sides of the ethnic divide. Kirk (1997c) also considers the question of ethnolinguistic differences in Northern Ireland and concludes that, if there are differences, then these are a matter of degree and not of kind. Zwickl (2002) provides a unique investigation into dialect use and ethnic identity in the sensitive border region between northern and southern Ireland.

By and large other scholars regard the issue as strictly non-linguistic (J. Milroy 1981). It is not possible to pinpoint differences in phonology, syntax or lexis which are exclusive indicators of affiliation to one or other of the two communities. Macafee (1996: 160) maintains that /h-/ is a shibboleth of Catholic/Protestant

---

[23] One of the main obstacles to understanding Ulster Scots is the density of specific lexical items (Montgomery and Gregg 1997: 570).

[24] Owens shows that in Belfast – as opposed to the rest of Ulster – both an alveolar [l] and a velar [ɫ] are found with approximately the distribution which one would expect from RP (syllable-initially and syllable-finally respectively). Furthermore, Owens concludes that there is no significant sociolinguistic variation in the use of /l/-allophones in initial position. However, syllable-finally there was variation with older speakers moving away from the vernacular [ɫ].

pronunciation, although many west Ulster Protestants pronounce initial /h-/.
In the name of the letter *h*, it may be true that Catholics tend to pronounce /h-/
more. But this may equally be a regional difference. The west of Ulster is closer
to Donegal, which, apart from the Laggan district, is dialectally an area closer
to southern forms of Irish English than to those in east Ulster. Additionally, the
position of initial /h-/ in Irish is firmly established because of its role in the
morphology of the language. The retention of /h-/ in the west of Ulster may
well be an areal feature resulting from a combination of Irish and southern Irish
English influence. And it is a demographic fact that, apart from west Belfast, the
greatest concentration of Catholics is in the west of the province and along the
border with the Republic of Ireland, particularly in south Armagh.

These remarks concern strictly linguistic indicators of denomination. There
are, of course, many other cues as to the religious and/or ethnic affiliation of
a speaker in Northern Ireland: discourse features are significant as are many
non-linguistic cues which people use unconsciously in trying to place someone
denominationally.

A somewhat different question is the relevance of denomination to attention
and recall in speech. Cairns and Duriez (1976) tried to determine if there was
a correlation between ethnic–religious affiliation and recall. The results showed
that Protestant children listening to both RP and other Protestant accents scored
better that their Catholic peers and that the latter showed better recall when the
speaker was southern Irish (middle-class Dublin), implying that cultural factors
play a role in speaker–hearer interaction. Cowie et al. (1984) on the other hand
think that the 'north versus south' difference, and not ethnic–religious affiliation,
is the most important factor in accent assessment.

For further discussions of possible ethnic differences, see section 5.5.2 on
English in Derry.

3.4.2 THE NORTH–SOUTH TRANSITION

The separation of the north of Ireland from the south has a long history which
reaches back much further in time than the political partition of Ireland in the
early twentieth century. It has been seen as a general cultural divide at least since
the seventeenth-century plantations. Furthermore, the contacts with Scotland go
back to the early centuries AD with the spread of Irish up to Scotland (see section
3.1). The linguistic and religious bonds which existed justify the assumption that
Ulster–Scotland formed a cultural area to which the remainder of Ireland did
not belong.

The border between Ulster and the south is a less tangible matter. References
to the Black Pig's Dyke, a series of Iron Age earthwork fortifications along the
southern rim of Ulster from *c.* 500 BC, smack of an ahistorical attempt to retro-
spectively find justification for the 'otherness' of Ulster vis-à-vis the rest of the
country.

Linguists concerned with the border between north and south (Kallen 2000;
Nic Craith 1999) assume that there is a band stretching roughly from Bundoran

(north-west) to Dundalk (east) and one between Sligo (north-west, south of Bundoran) and Drogheda (east, south of Dundalk) (Adams 1977: 56). North of this border the distinction between dental fricatives and alveolar stops as in *thin/tin* and *then/den* is maintained. For the varieties south of this transitional band there is a stop realisation for /θ, ð/, so that the distinction is one of dental versus alveolar place of articulation (Ó Baoill 1991). This distinction can be reasonably traced to the presence of /θ, ð/ in the input forms of both Scots and regional English in Ulster, whereas the plosivisation of /θ, ð/ is long attested in the south (Hickey 1993). Accepting this reason for the phonological differences between north and south implies that the major differences in varieties of English are not older than the seventeenth century.[25]

For dialects of Irish the view that the north–south distinction goes back further than 1600 is widely supported (T. F. O'Rahilly 1932: 123f.; Ó Baoill 1990), given the influence of Scottish Gaelic on Ulster Irish and the many instances of convergence in phonology and morphology between the two languages.

3.4.3 PHONOLOGY

In the following sections those features in which varieties in Ulster (U, both Ulster Scots and general Ulster English) differ from those in the south are discussed. In a number of instances it is necessary to distinguish the two main groups within Ulster. The yardstick for the south is the supraregional southern (SS) variety which ultimately is derived from non-local Dublin English of the early to mid twentieth century. This section should be read in conjunction with section 5.4 which deals with English in the south in detail.

3.4.3.1 *Consonants*

Equivalents of dental fricatives. In Ulster /θ, ð/ are generally realised as fricatives. In contact areas of Co. Donegal, the dental stops [t̪] and [d̪] are found, probably because of transfer from Irish:[26] *thick* [θɛk] (U), [t̪ɪk] (SS), *that* [ðat] (U), [d̪æt̪] (SS), *lather* [lɑː(ð)əɹ] (U), [laːd̪əɹ] (SS). Voiced dental fricatives in intervocalic position tend to be lost, e.g. *brother* [brʌəɹ] (U), [brʌd̪əɹ] (SS).

---

[25] Barry (1981a) offers a general introduction in which he discusses the spread of English in the early modern period and mentions features listed by P. L. Henry (1958) as diagnostic of the north–south divide. He then adduces further evidence on the basis of the *Tape-Recorded Survey of Hiberno-English Speech*. He lists the following as typical features: the fronting of /u/ to [ʉ] in the north and the unrounding of /ɔ/ to /ɑ/ in the south, the occurrence of /θ, ð/ in the north and the fricativisation of /-t/ in the south. He provides maps with keywords and their pronunciations in an appendix to the article.

[26] Ó Baoill (1990) rightly notes that a collapse of the distinction between dentals and alveolars to alveolar stops is common in Munster and south Leinster (particularly in rural forms, although he does not specify this). This collapse corresponds to the realisation of /t/ and /d/ in the forms of Irish previously spoken in these areas (still ascertainable for the Dingle peninsula) as alveolar stops [t, d] as opposed to the dental realisations [t̪, d̪] further north in Connemara and Donegal.

Dentalisation of alveolar stops before /r/. This is a low-level phonetic process whereby an alveolar stop – typically /t/ – is shifted forward to a dental point of articulation, most often when it is followed by an unstressed rhoticised schwa. The /r/ is realised as a tap or slight trill due to the fact that the tongue is parallel to the escaping airstream (Bernoulli effect). It is frequently voiceless by asssimilation to the [t̪] *water* [wɑːt̪ər], *better* [bɛt̪ər] (both Ulster and conservative southern vernacular).

Within Ulster, some authors (such as Kirk 1998) regard this feature as an indication of a speaker's religion because is it putatively typical of Catholic speech. This is debatable, but what is certain is that the dentalisation of alveolars has a long history in the entire island. It is one of the features chosen for stereotypical caricature with Restoration comedians of the late seventeenth century. It is now quite stigmatised in supraregional varieties of southern Irish English.

Allophones of alveolar plosives. The fricativisation of /t/ (and often /d/) inter-vocalically and word-finally before a pause is not normally found in the north: *bat* [bat] (U), [bæt̪] (SS), *bead* [bid] (U), [bid̪] (SS). For further details, see the discussion in section 5.4.3.

Palatalisation of velar plosives. A conspicuous feature of vernacular Ulster English is the palatalisation of /g/ and /k/ to /kj/ and /gj/ respectively. This palatalisation is only to be found before low vowels. It would appear to be an English and not a Scots feature and is attested in eighteenth-century mainland English (and possibly transferred to the Caribbean from there; see Harris 1987 and Holm 1994: 370): *cat* [kjæt] (U), [kæt̪] (SS), *gap* [gjæp] (U), [gæp] (SS). It was later lost in England, but not before being transported to the United States where it is found occasionally in southern varieties (Montgomery 2001: 131). In the south of Ulster the area with this palatalisation reaches into the Republic of Ireland and is seen in vernacular pronunciations of the name of Co. Cavan, i.e. [kjævən].

The 'tapping' of alveolar plosives. In intervocalic position /t/ is realised as an alveolar tap [ɾ] – much as in many varieties of North American English – and may lead to the merger of /t/ and /d/. Tapping is particularly frequent after /r/: *party* [pɑɻɾi] (U), [pɑɹt̪i] (SS), *hardy* [hɑɻɾi] (U), [hɑɹdi] (SS). In new Dublin English, this tapping has become common (Hickey 2003c, 2005: 77–9) though the source for this is hardly Ulster English; see below.

Quality of /r/. This sound is realised as a retroflex continuant without the vclarisation typical of conservative varieties in the Republic. The retroflex [ɻ] is an areal feature of the whole of Ulster. In more recent forms of Dublin English this [ɻ] has become prevalent and is quickly spreading among young speakers (as an independent development): *bar* [bɑːɻ] (U), [bɑɹˠ] (SS, conservative), *hard* [hɑːɻd] (U), [hɑɹˠd] (SS, conservative).

Loss of final /-l/. The loss of post-vocalic /l/ is an Ulster Scots (US) feature which resulted from the vocalisation of a velarised [ɫ]: *fall* [fɒː] (US), [fɒːl] (SS), *full* [fʉ] (US), [fʊl] (SS). In her study of Coleraine (a large town in a core Ulster Scots area) Rona Kingsmore (1995: 111–37) found velarised [ɫ] to be typical of working-class urban vernacular speech while an alveolar [l] was preferred by other social groups.

Retention of /x/. The voiceless velar fricative is retained sometimes, mostly with Scottish and Gaelic loans. Words which in Middle English had final /-x/, like *trough*, *laugh*, can be pronounced with a final /-x/ in Ulster Scots: *trough* [tɹɔːx] (US), [tɹɒf] (SS), *laugh* [lɑːx] (US), [laːf] (SS).

Alveolarisation of velar nasals. This is one of the most general features of English dialects. The reason it is worthy of comment in the current context is that /n/ for /ŋ/ is not as stigmatised in the north as it is in the south. The shift is found both with verbs in final /-ɪŋ/ and with nouns with a similar ending, e.g. *walking* ['wɒːkn̩], *morning* ['mɒːɲɪn]. Alveolarisation of velar nasals is probably an archaic feature in English. Wyld (1956 [1936]: 289) points to spelling evidence which suggests the alveolar [n̩] for [ŋ] occurred in England from the fourteenth century onwards. Kingsmore (1995: 100–10) offers a detailed examination of this variable in the context of her Coleraine investigation.[27] She notes [ɪn] as an intermediary form between the syllable nasal [n̩] and the standard [ŋ]. Kingsmore also notes that young females have the highest incidence of [n] with the (ng) variable, for instance 83 per cent for males and 89 per cent for females with verbal forms in final *-ing*. The linguistic conditioning shows that the verbal forms, e.g. *talking*, *waking*, have the highest incidence of [n] for (ng), as is the case in other varieties of English.

Glottalisation. In Ulster Scots glottalisation of voiceless stops is common. This can take the form of a pre-consonantal glottal stop with the consonant gesture being retained. In final position the stop, especially [t], may disappear entirely: *flop* [flɔʔp], *lot* [lɔʔ]. At one or more removes from Ulster Scots, glottalisation may only apply to [t] as in *bottle* [bɒʔl̩]. In vernacular Belfast English, where the influence of Ulster Scots is greatest (in east Belfast), glottalisation of [t] also occurs.

In southern Irish English pre-glottalisation or glottal replacement of voiceless stops is unknown with the significant exception of local Dublin English (Hickey 2005: 41–3) which is, however, quite unconnected with its occurrence in Ulster (see section 5.5.4).

Epenthesis. The insertion of a schwa in clusters of two sonorants is found in Ulster English just as in southern Irish English, e.g. *film* ['fɪləm]. However, some speakers have a greater range for this feature, including consonantal epenthesis, e.g. *Onst* [wʌ nst] *in a month or onst* [wʌ nst] *in two months* (TRS-D, U18-2).

3.4.3.2   Vowels

Fronting of high back vowels. The high back vowels /ʊ/ and /uː/ have high centralised realisations in Ulster – /ʉ/ – much as is typical for large parts of

---

[27] Kingsmore's sample consists of twenty-six informants. At least four are present for each gender and age group (Kingsmore 1995: 37–52).

Scotland and traditionally in the north and north-west of England (Kolb 1966: 197ff.). The quality of this vowel (Ball and Rahilly 1996) is a prominent characteristic of both Irish and English in Ulster: *book* [bʉk] (U), [bʊk] (SS), *soon* [sʉn] (U), [suːn] (SS); Donegal Irish: *cúl* [kuːł] 'back, rear', *fiú* [fʲuː] 'even'. The geographical distribution of the high central vowel is quite considerable: in the recordings of the *Tape-Recorded Survey of Hiberno-English* it is clearly attested for Co. Louth, Co. Westmeath and Co. Longford, all of which are well within the Republic. *A Sound Atlas of Irish English* offers attestations far down the east coast, to Co. Dublin, e.g. *book* [buːk].

In rural Ulster English the /ʉ/ vowel is to be found in more words than the corresponding vowel in southern Irish English. This can be traced to the fact that many words exhibit a raising of Middle English /oː/ before /r/. The resulting high back vowel has a high central realisation in keeping with Ulster in general: *door* [dʉːɹ] (U), [doːɹ] (SS), *floor* [flʉːɹ] (U), [floːɹ] (SS), *board* [bʉːɹd] (U), [boːɹd] (SS). This raising of /oː/ before /r/ (Dobson 1968: 675; Harris 1984b: 124–6) is no longer found in the south but going on the evidence of Sheridan (1781: 144) it was typical of Dublin English in his day. The raised vowel was later replaced by the original mid vowel in the south to bring it into line with more standard forms of English.

The shift to a high central position for /u/ applies equally to the second element of the diphthong /au/. In Ulster English the onset of this diphthong is raised so that phonetically one has [æʉ] or [əʉ] as the equivalent of RP /au/. In the supraregional variety of the south, [aʊ] is the realisation of /au/. On the east coast (including Dublin) local varieties show a fronted onset for this diphthong, indicated in parentheses in the following: *cow* [kəʉ] (U), [kaʊ] ([kæʊ]) (SS), *down* [dəʉn] (U), [daʊn] ([dæʊn]) (SS), *owl* [əʉl] (U), [aʊl] ([æʊl]) (SS). The fronted onset of the east coast is present in new Dublin English and is thus becoming part of supraregional varieties among the younger generation (Hickey 2005: 75f.).

Lowering of high front vowels. The short high front vowel /ɪ/ is lowered considerably and reaches a value which in Ulster Scots can be close to RP /æ/ (but somewhat more centralised). In more standard varieties of English in Ulster the lowering is not as marked: *pick* [pëk] (U), [pɪk] (SS), *big* [bëg] (U), [bɪg] (SS).

Offglides. When mid vowels occur in stressed position they tend to develop offglides. This is particularly clear before a following consonant: *save* [seəv] (U), [seːv] (SS), *toes* [toəz] (U), [touz, toːz] (SS). An investigation by McCafferty (1995) offers evidence for the fact that Protestants in Derry prefer an offglide after the high vowel in the FACE lexical set (generally raised from /e/ to /i/ in the city). This separates them from the Catholics who have a short high unbroken vowel, i.e. [fiəs] as opposed to [fis]. According to McCafferty, it is mainly the Protestant adoption of innovations which results in linguistic divergence in the city (see further discussion in section 5.5.2).

The realisation of back vowels. A prominent trait of conservative southern Irish English is the open vowel quality in the THOUGHT and LOT lexical sets (/ɒː/ and /ɒ/ respectively). In the north, closer vowel values are to be found (Barry

1981: 66, 93): *horse* [hoɹ̩s] (U), [hɒːɹs] (SS), *pot* [pɔt], (U) [pɒt̪] (SS). In south Ulster English, open realisations of these vowels are found and form an important constituent of the transition between north and south. The closed realisation of /ɒ, ɒː/ in English in the north means that the equivalent of the southern diphthong /ɒi/ is [ɔi]. In south Ulster English this raising of the onset is not typical.

Fronting of Old English /aː/. This vowel was raised on a back track through /ɔː/ and /oː/ to yield present-day RP /əʊ/ as in *home*. In Scots this vowel was fronted and raised through /æ/ and /ɛ/ to /e/ (much as in German). This front realisation was transported to Ulster with the first settlers and a front vowel in the GOAT lexical set is a clear indication of Ulster Scots, e.g. *home* [hem].

Unstressed vowels. In unstressed positions southern Irish English has the high vowel /i/ without the centralisation to [ɪ] which is found in RP, i.e. it exhibits what is termed HAPPY-tensing (Wells 1982: 257f.). Ulster English tends to lower an unstressed /i/ to a value approaching /e/: *tricky* [trëke] (U), [trɪkɪ] (SS), *happy* [hɑpe] (U), [hæpɪ] (SS).

Vowel quantity. In Ulster, in contradistinction to the south, vowel quantity is not always distinctive (see section 3.3.3). High and mid vowels, which are elsewhere either long or short, can appear phonetically half-long, above all in Ulster Scots: *full* [fʉl] (US), [fʊl] (SS), *fool* [fʉl] (US), [fuːl] (SS). The situation with low vowels is somewhat different. Here one finds phonetic lengthening particularly before sonorants and voiced fricatives, often before all voiced obstruents and voiceless fricatives. The lengthening of /a/ leads to a retraction to [ɑː]: *card* /kard/ [kɑːɹd], *ban* /ban/ [bɑːn], *god* /gɒd/ [gɒːd], *bath* /baθ/ [bɑːθ].

For the transitional area of south Ulster English the normal quantity system of English is valid. Here there is a phonemic difference between long and short vowels, that is length is determined lexically and not by phonetic environment (Barry 1981a: 48; Harris 1984b: 123f.): *beat* [biːt] ~ [beːt], *bit* [bɪt] ~ [bɛt], *cot* [kɒt], *coat* [koːt].

3.4.3.3   Intonation

Marked differences can be found between Ulster and the south of the country in the suprasegmental area (Hickey 2004a: 51f.). With stressed lexical words a falling–rising intonational pattern is common. This contrasts with the mid-to-low intonation found in declarative sentences in the south and many other varieties of English. The fall–rise can be seen clearly in words of more than one syllable with a stressed high front vowel, e.g. *sticky*, as the drop in intonation correlates with the lowering of the vowel. There is also a parallel between word prosody and sentence prosody: non-topicalised statements[28] in

---

[28] Rahilly (1994) notes a general predominance of rises in intonation in northern areas of Britain which contrast explicitly with falls in the south of Britain. Indeed the high numbers of rising nuclei and level tails in tone sequences are regarded as typical of 'the Anglo-Irish group of dialects' rather

general Ulster English have a typical rising tone at the end rather than the common falling pattern of other varieties of English (Jarman and Cruttenden 1976).

Both major cities in Ulster have been examined from the point of view of intonation. McElholm (1986) is an investigation of intonation in Derry English. Rahilly (1997) and Lowry (2002) look at intonation in Belfast and offer an analysis and critical assessment. Orla Lowry in particular has looked at the sociolinguistic aspects of intonational variation. This variation has also been investigated in a general British/Irish context by Esther Grabe (together with other colleagues in project work); see Grabe (2004) as a summary of their findings.

The intonational patterns of English in Ulster can be recognised clearly in the relevant recordings to be found in *A Sound Atlas of Irish English* (Hickey 2004a).

3.4.4 GRAMMAR

The grammar of Irish English is the subject of the next chapter, so a discussion of features which are found in Ulster and in southern Irish English is not offered here. However, there are some grammatical traits which only occur in the north, such as 'positive *anymore*' or *whenever* for 'when' (see discussion above). Others which could be mentioned are (i) the use of a past participle as a verbal complement, especially after the verb *need*, e.g. *My hair needs washed*, and (ii) the use of *from* in the sense of 'since', e.g. *She's living here from she was married*, i.e. 'from the time she was married' (Harris 1984b: 132).

One feature, which is restricted to west Ulster, has been the subject of examination by James McCloskey. This is so-called 'quantifier floating' (McCloskey 2000), the appearance of a quantifier which is coreferential with a *wh*-word but which is separated from it by a tensed verb. Such floating is legal in other languages, notably German, cf. *Was habt ihr alles vor?* [what have you-PL all before] 'What have you got planned?', but it is supposed not to occur in forms of English. McCloskey maintains that sentences such as the following are legal in west Ulster (Donegal, Derry City, parts of west Co. Tyrone).

(5)   a. *What did you get all for Christmas?*
       b. *Who did you meet all when you were in Derry?*
       c. *Where did they go all for their holidays?*

Such usage would appear to be restricted to the localities mentioned. The present author, as a native speaker of eastern Irish English, does not find such sentences acceptable.

---

than the 'British group'. Rahilly concludes that the primary cue to prominence in Belfast is a high pitch, but with much less movement than with nuclei in Received Pronunciation (Rahilly 1997). Intonational variation in varieties of (British and Irish) English has been studied recently by several authors such as Alan Cruttenden (Cruttenden 1995) and more recently in detail by Orla Lowry (Lowry 2002) and Esther Grabe (Grabe 2004).

Table 3.7. *Grammatical features of both northern and southern Irish English*

1.	Resultative perfective, *He has his homework done.*
2.	Immediate perfective, *They're after robbing the shop.*
3.	Habitual (with inflected *be* in north), *The teachers bees strict with the pupils.*
4.	*Be* as auxiliary, *Are they gone yet?*
5.	Greater range of the present tense, *She is here since early this morning.*
6.	Non-standard subject concord, *The boys thinks the world of her.*
7.	Purposive infinitive with *for to*, *They went to Belfast for to buy the car.*
8.	Partial merger of preterite and past participle, e.g. *done, come.*
9.	Zero subject relatives, *There's a man in the hall wants to speak to you.*
10.	Lack of *do* in questions, *Have you the time, please?*
11.	*Never* with singular time reference, *He never locked the door last night.*
12.	*Till* in the sense of 'so that', *Come here till I see you.*
13.	Negative concord, *We didn't touch nothing.*
14.	Failure of negative attraction, *Everyone didn't believe him.*
15.	Formal marking of second-person-plural pronoun, especially as *ye(e)z* [jiz]

Despite such local differences, there is a large body of vernacular features which are shared by varieties of Irish English, north and south. These are listed in table 3.7 and will be discussed in the relevant sections of the following chapter.

4   The emergence of Irish English

4.1   Language shift in Ireland

The most remarkable fact in the linguistic history of Ireland since the seventeenth century is the abandonment of the Irish language by successive generations, to such an extent that the remaining Irish-speaking areas today are only a fraction of the size of the country and contain not much more than 1 per cent of the population. Bilingualism did not establish itself in Ireland, though it characterised the transition from Irish to English. No matter how long this bilingualism lasted, the goal of the shift was obvious and those who shifted to English ultimately abandoned Irish, even though this took many generations. The remaining bilinguals today are mostly native speakers of Irish in the Irish-speaking districts, all of whom also speak English. There was never any functional distribution of Irish and English, either in the towns or the countryside, so that stable diglossia could not have developed.

For external reasons, connected with employment opportunities and social advancement, the Irish relinquished their native language for that of the colonial power.[1] The process most likely began in earnest after the defeat of the old Gaelic order by the English (Ross 1998) at the beginning of the seventeenth century (see section 2.1.4). Before that Irish was, if anything, stronger than it had been immediately after the initial invasion in the late twelfth century. The shift also shows a clear geographical distribution. It is most obvious in the east of the country, where it actually began in the first period, i.e. before 1600. The number of Irish monolinguals has always been greatest along the western seaboard. Furthermore, there is an urban–rural split for the historical language shift (Filppula 1991). The cities of the east coast were the first to adopt English and the rural areas along the western coast were the last, if one neglects the dispersed language enthusiasts throughout Ireland who support the language where they can. The gradual retreat of the language to the western seaboard

---

[1] This type of language shift is dealt with by Romaine (1989: 38ff.) and by Hoffmann (1992: 186ff.). Hoffmann (1992: 190f.) sees the prestige of the second language as largely responsible for the shift and quotes the decline of the Celtic languages as an instance of this.

can be seen clearly in maps documenting the decline (see Ó Cuív 1969: 137–40; Hindley 1990: 21–42).

As always within the Irish context (see chapter 3 above), one must treat Ulster separately. Ulster Irish today is only found in parts of Co. Donegal on the west coast. But up to the beginning of the twentieth century, there were pockets of Irish still to be found in the province: in central Ulster (Co. Tyrone), in south Armagh, in parts of Antrim and on Rathlin Island off the north coast of this county. The linguistic situation in Ulster is further complicated by Ulster Scots (see section 3.3) which did not interact significantly with Irish. The shift from this variety, if any, has been towards more general forms of Ulster English which derive from northern forms of English brought to the province.

The shift in Ireland must have involved considerable bilingualism over several centuries. The native language for the majority of the population was initially Irish and recourse to this was always there. English would have been used in contact with English speakers (administrators, bailiffs or those few urbanites who only spoke English, Kallen 1994: 156–63). There was also considerable interaction between the planters and the native Irish, certainly in the countryside where this group of English speakers had settled.[2] Indeed there may be grounds for assuming that a proportion of the planters by the mid seventeenth century would have had at least a rudimentary knowledge of Irish. They would have been a source of bilingualism for the native Irish population, at the interface between themselves and those planters without any Irish. However, this source of bilingual interaction should not be overestimated. There would seem to be little evidence for the view that key features of Irish English arose through the interaction with bilingual people of English origin.

The importance of the contact situation and the precise nature of the speaker interaction – inasmuch as this can be reconstructed – are matters which have been given particular attention by Terence Odlin in a number of recent publications, (1994, 1997). The view that the planters were cared for by Irish nurses and had contact with the children of native Irish[3] is supported by authors like Bliss (1976: 557). The ultimate effect of this would have been to render the language of the planters more like that of the native Irish, so that no specific variety of planter English arose.

The language shift did not progress evenly through the centuries (Corrigan 1996, 1999). Major external events, chiefly famine and emigration, accelerated the pace. During such setbacks, Irish lost ground quickly which it was not to recover. Famine struck throughout the eighteenth century, especially in the 1720s,

---

[2] Thomason and Kaufman (1988: 43) assume that there was no emulation of English features of Irish speakers by the descendants of settlers, but that given that the first group was very much more numerous their 'speech habits prevailed anyway'. Thomason (2001: 78f.) repeats this point, maintaining that 'the shifters' interference features will become fixed in the target language'.

[3] This is a model postulated for the contact between whites and African Americans in the southern United States and given as an explanation for the many similarities in the speech of these two ethnic groups in that region.

and emigration from Ulster was considerable during this century, though this largely involved settlers of Scottish origin who moved to North America (see section 6.3.1).

The most significant blow to the Irish language was the Great Famine of the late 1840s which hit the poorer rural areas of Ireland hardest. The twin factors of death and emigration reduced the number of Irish speakers by anything up to two million in the course of less than a decade. The famine also brought home to the remaining Irish speakers the necessity to switch to English to survive in an increasingly English-speaking society and to prepare for possible emigration.

4.1.1 ACCESS TO ENGLISH AND ROLE OF INPUT

Before the seventeenth century, English was spoken mostly by small numbers of settlers, chiefly in the towns of the east coast. The only significant remnant of this period was to be found in the extreme south-east corner of Ireland, in the baronies of Forth and Bargy, and the area of Fingal just north of Dublin (see sections 2.2.4 and 2.4.5).

At the beginning of the early modern period, access to this older type of English would only have been available in towns and a few pockets on the east coast. For the majority of Irish living elsewhere in the countryside there was little or no contact with speakers of English. Only gradually did this situation change with informal contacts between speakers of Irish and English. The latter was used by relatively small numbers, consisting of English people, and their direct descendants, living in Ireland, as well as a limited group of Irish who had acquired English either by contact with town dwellers or through self-education. The opportunities for this were, however, minimal. Indeed, education for the native Catholics was forbidden under the Penal Laws (Lydon 1998: 218–38) which were not repealed until the end of the eighteenth century. Primary schooling for the native Irish was not introduced until the 1830s.

The scenario at the beginning of the early modern period is one in which a small number of English speakers conveyed the language to the native Irish. This would also explain why the language of the planters had apparently been so strongly influenced by Irish. The quantitative relationship was skewed in favour of the Irish, so that the English planters could not but have been influenced by the numerically superior, albeit socially inferior, Irish.[4] This kind of distribution also held in the late twelfth and thirteenth centuries vis-à-vis the Anglo-Norman overlords who, under pressure of numbers (among other reasons), yielded to Irish and adopted it as their native language in later generations (Hickey 1997b).

The situation just sketched can be taken to have applied on a broad front for the seventeenth century. But the transmission of English to following generations of

---

[4] See Thomason (2001: 79) who states that 'the shifters' variety of English was able to influence the English of Ireland as a whole because the shifters were numerous relative to the original native speakers of English in Ireland'. Similar remarks are to be found in Thomason and Kaufman (1988: 43, 129).

Irish was not always directly from the settlers. Rather the Irish of the eighteenth and nineteenth centuries must have learned English from Irish compatriots who had been exposed to English, however imperfectly. Again one must stress that there was little if any formal education. While it is true that so-called 'hedge schools' existed whereby self-educated teachers gave instruction to Irish on an informal basis (Dowling 1971), these could not have serviced any significant section of the population.

In present-day southern Ireland, there is no discernible difference in the speech of those who are of native Irish descent and those whose ancestors were English planters in the seventeenth century. This situation is markedly different from that in northern Ireland where this distinction is made, above all on ethnic–religious grounds, that is, it forms the basis for the segregation of the Protestant (English and Scottish) and Catholic (Irish) sections of northern Irish society. In the south, there is a small number of Protestants. The language of this section of the southern population does not, however, differ substantially from that of the Catholic majority.[5]

The historical picture one is left with is that of a gradual dissemination of English from east to west and from urban centres to rural districts, essentially over a period of at least two and a half centuries, from the early seventeenth century to the post-Famine period, i.e. to the second half of the nineteenth century. The use of speech habits and the transfer of grammatical structures from Irish on an individual level lasted long enough for these to spread to entire communities of speakers and to become general features of their forms of English.

When, and for how long, the Irish were exposed to English is one facet in the complex of language access. The second and equally important one is what varieties of English the Irish had as their input when acquiring the new language. Recent authors, such as Kallen, Harris and Lass (Lass 1990), have repeatedly pointed out that to ignore this question is to fail to grasp a vital strand in the genesis of Irish English.

Broadly speaking, western varieties of English predominated in the south from the beginning of the seventeenth century onwards. For the first period there is evidence of a south-western input (compare the parallels between Forth and Bargy and Dorset, as pointed out by Barnes in the preface to his glossary; see section 2.4). For the north of Ireland there was also much English input, frequently from the north-west, for instance from Lancashire (Adams 1967).

The western nature of Early Modern English input is relevant when considering the development of such grammatical categories as the habitual in Irish English. The west/south-west of England is an area which retained periphrastic *do* for longer than did the north and east (Ihalainen 1991). This supports the assumption that it was represented in the input to southern Irish English in the seventeenth century. There are other indications of western/south-western input. For instance, in vernacular forms of southern Irish English the verbs

---

[5] Indeed it is a moot point whether the two major confessions of the north can be distinguished linguistically. Todd (1984) propounds this view though her stance is not widely accepted.

have and *do* occur without inflectional *-s* in the third-person-singular present tense.

On a more general level, the role of input is important because it can account for why certain features occur in vernacular Irish English today which cannot be traced back to the shift from Irish. For instance, non-standard verbal concord (see section 4.4.1.1) is a feature which can only be accounted for by assuming that it was present in the input varieties of English to Ireland in the early modern period, both in the south and north of the country. A phonological feature of early English input is the fortition of sibilants in pre-nasal position, e.g. *wasn't* [wɑdn̩t], a south-west English feature which gained a foothold in Ireland and has continued since (see section 5.2).

The critical importance of the early period does not apply to language shift, however. Here one does not have features acting as seeds which are continued into later forms (Mufwene 1996). Rather transfer features arise during shift and then establish themselves as the shift variety stabilises. Because of this, some features which can be traced to the shift situation may be of a much later date. For instance, the habitual with *do (es) be* is not attested abundantly until after the mid nineteenth century. This would imply that this use has its origin in language shift, although the formal basis for it, periphrastic *do*, was probably present in forms of English input in the seventeenth century.

4.1.2 UNGUIDED ADULT LANGUAGE ACQUISITION

To assess the role which transfer from Irish possibly played in the genesis of Irish English, it is necessary to consider the type of situation in which the native Irish acquired English. Given that there was little if any formal education for the majority of the population, the environment for acquisition was non-prescriptive, indeed uncontrolled, in the technical sense that no external restrictions would have been placed on the use of non-standard features (Odlin 1991: 188) stemming from the influence of Irish, the native language of virtually all speakers. This situation of language shift can be regarded as a kind of collective second-language acquisition, as scholars working on language contact frequently point out. For instance, Donald Winford has a section on Irish English which he rightly embeds in a larger chapter entitled 'Group second language acquisition or language shift'. Winford says of the shift scenario in Ireland:

> The persisting of bilingualism within the shifting group is another impor-
> tant factor in language shift . . . there were large numbers of illiterate
> bilinguals in nineteenth-century Ireland, judging from the figures of the
> 1851 census. It is reasonable to assume also that childhood bilingualism
> was quite common, and that bilingual children played a role in the regular-
> ization of Irish English grammar. These factors would have favoured the
> retention of Irish features in the English of such speakers. (Winford 2003:
> 253)

During the language shift one can distinguish two groups, that of younger language learners, for whom English would have been a language acquired relatively early, and an adult group acquiring it much later. As Winford points out above, the children may well have played a role in the rise of non-standard features based on analogical levelling (his 'regularization'). Two examples can be quoted to illustrate this. The first is the rise of *youse* as a plural form for *you* (see section 4.4.2.1 for further discussion). This form is almost certainly of Irish origin;[6] its present-day distribution in the anglophone world is due to the spread of Irish English during the transportation of English in the colonial period (Hickey 2004c). In all likelihood, it arose through language learners applying a productive plural morpheme to a personal pronoun, *you*, perceived as singular. The second example involves the epistemic use of negated *must*, regarded as distinctively Irish (Trudgill 1986: 140f.).

(1)   a.   *He mustn't be Irish as he was born in France.*   Irish English
      b.   *He can't be Irish as he was born in France.*   non-Irish English

This would appear to derive from a generalisation of the positive epistemic use to the negative by language learners.

  Another scholar who has concerned herself with the characteristics of language shift varieties is Sarah Thomason. In a recent study she maintains that 'the shifters' variety of English was able to influence the English of Ireland as a whole because the shifters were numerous relative to the original native speakers of English in Ireland' and that in such situations 'the shifters' interference features will become fixed in the target language' (Thomason 2001: 78f.).

  Language shift does not always proceed in the same manner. There are cases where education plays a significant role, for instance in South Africa. Here the shift from Indian languages, mainly Bhojpuri and Tamil, for the Indian population in KwaZulu-Natal was accelerated considerably by children learning English in school, bringing this back into the home and thus exposing older family members to the language (Mesthrie 1992: 27–33, 1996; Hickey 2006b).

4.2   The case for contact

In recent years the field of contact linguistics has been served well. Individual studies and collections have been published, e.g. McWhorter (2000), Thomason (2001), Myers-Scotton (2002), Migge (2003), Winford (2003), Heine and

---

[6] If one is making a case for *youse* being a specifically Irish development, then one must exclude any English source. With the help of available text corpora this issue can be resolved with reasonable certainty. For instance, the *Corpus of Early English Correspondence Sampler* (Nevalainen and Raumolin-Brunberg 1996) does not reveal a single instance of *youse*, although *ye* and *thou* abound. *Thou* is by far the most common second-person pronoun (372 instances, with *ye* occurring 19 times). This holds for the 23 texts in the public-domain version of this corpus, covering letters from the end of the sixteenth to the end of the seventeenth century. Equally, in the 138 texts of the Early Modern English section of the *Helsinki Corpus of English Texts* there is not a single instance of *yous(e)* or *ye(e)z*. Wright (1905: 274) mentions the occurrence of *youse* and *yeez* (his *yous* and *yees*) in Ireland.

Table 4.1. *Possible sources of features in Irish English*

1.	Transfer from Irish
2a.	Dialect forms of English
b.	Archaic forms of English
3.	Features deriving from the context in which English was learned
4.	Features with no recognisable source (independent developments)

Kuteva (2004), Holm (2004), Clyne (2003), all of which consider the effect of contact between languages on their further development. These considerations have sometimes been programmatic, e.g. Heine and Kuteva (2004) which pushes the case for grammaticalisation as virtually the only valid model in contact linguistics, while other studies have had an explicit focus, e.g. Filppula, Klemola and Pitkänen (2002) which is concerned with the question of contact with Celtic in the development of English[7] and Paulasto (2006) which is a detailed examination of the effect on English of Welsh grammar.

What all these studies have in common is the goal of putting contact explanations on a firm objective footing. Within the Irish[8] context, such an aim is welcome as too many former accounts of non-standard features assumed transfer during language contact as their sole source; cf. studies by authors like P. L. Henry and A. J. Bliss. The reaction which set in against contact explanations in the 1980s, and which is most obvious in Harris (1984a), was modified somewhat in the 1990s by detailed objective reflections on the effects of contact, e.g. by Markku Filppula (2001), Mary O'Malley Madec (2002), Karen Corrigan (forthcoming) and the present author (e.g. Hickey 1995b). This type of approach also informs the present chapter. The different sources which may have played a role in the genesis of Irish English are listed in table 4.1. Sources 2a and 2b have been separated for this listing but, of course, they may well coincide with the input forms of English. The conservative nature of English in Ireland is particularly clear when one considers forms which go back to the early anglophone settlement of the island and which are found chiefly on the east coast (Hickey 2002b). In early English input, there were many dialect words which have continued to exist in Irish English, e.g. *chiseler* 'young child', *mitch* 'play truant'. On the level of syntax one could mention the variable marking of verb forms with inflectional -*s* in the present tense (see section 4.4.1.1).

---

[7] The question of very early influence of Celtic on English is outside the scope of this book, but see Braaten (1967), Dal (1952), Filppula (2003a), Isaac (2003), Keller (1925), Mittendorf and Poppe (2000), Poussa (1982, 1990), G. Visser (1955) and Hickey (1995a, 2002e, 2002f) for relevant studies in this context.

[8] Mention should be made here of the significant study by Annette Sabban on contact between Gaelic and English in Gaelic-speaking areas of Scotland (1982). Over long stretches, the book reads as if it were on Irish English. Features such as the *after*-perfective, overuse of the conditional, unbound reflexives, punctual *never*, overuse of the expanded form and the definite article, use of *on* to express relevance and inversion in embedded questions are all traits of contact English in Scotland, dealt with in detail by Sabban, which have direct equivalents in Irish English.

Table 4.2. *Features of unguided adult language acquisition*

1. Omission of the definite article
2. Omission of finite *be* (in equative sentences)
3. Reduction and/or generalisation of verbal and nominal inflections
4. Reduction of tense distinctions, e.g. use of present for present perfect
5. Avoidance of subordinating conjunctions (parataxis favoured over hypotaxis)
6. Various topicalisation strategies such as fronting

The above division of sources raises a major question, namely, whether one can assign a specific feature unambiguously to a certain source. There are really only a few traits of Irish English on which there has been general agreement among scholars with regard to their Irish origin (see Harris 1984a for a classic discussion of the issue). First and foremost, this is true of the *after*-perfective (see section 4.4.1.4.1), but even there the development of this construction over a few centuries has been quite intricate and is much more than a simple case of transfer from Irish to Irish English (see the detailed history offered in McCafferty 2004a).

Further factors in the genesis of Irish English must also be taken into account. The specific conditions of the language shift may well have led to characteristics of unguided second language acquisition coming to the fore, source 3 above. The analogical extension of epistemic *must* and the analogical plural form *youse* mentioned above are instances of this. Other instances may be gathered under the heading 'universals of language acquisition' and have been considered by a number of authors recently, notably Peter Siemund and Lukas Pietsch (see Siemund 2004; Pietsch 2004a, 2004b) for whom they have attained the status of a 'third way' alongside contact and retention. It is claimed here that adult speakers make certain assumptions about the structure of the language they are acquiring in a non-prescriptive environment. Siemund (2004) maintains that there are unmarked values for categories which are preferred in these situations, e.g. nominative over accusative. In individual cases, the validity of their analyses has been disputed, but the general assumption that certain unmarked, or default, characteristics of language are favoured in situations of unguided language acquisition is uncontested (Hickey 1997a). These traits also surface in so-called New Englishes, where English is derived from a second-language variety used in an environment of one or more indigenous languages (see the discussion in Hickey 2004i in the context of English in Africa and Asia).

Some of these characteristics are attested in Irish English, while others are not. Of those listed in table 4.2, the first is not found in Irish English, while 3–6 are. The omission of finite *be* is attested in south-eastern Irish English (see section 4.4.1), but it is not a general feature of Irish English.

Table 4.2 shows features which stem from the removal of redundancy and the reduction in structural distinctions, both processes typical of unguided adult language acquisition. It also shows, in feature 6, how pragmatic highlighting can

Table 4.3. *Types of contact*

Type	Effect
1. Indirect cultural contact, no speaker interface (German–English today). Contact, but little if any bilingualism (French in Middle English)	Only loanwords, 'cultural borrowings'. No effect on grammar of receiving language
2. Contact with approximation of one or both languages (late Old English and Old Norse). Strong speaker interaction	Koinésation or dialect levelling, some structural permeation with typologically similar languages
3. Contact with language shift (Irish → English; Bhojpuri/Tamil → English [South Africa])	'Speech habits' of outset transferred to target, grammatical interference found in non-prescriptive environments
4. Contact but restricted input, unguided acquisition (Caribbean, central and south-west Pacific), no continuity of indigenous languages	Pidginisation, grammatical restructuring; creolisation, if the pidgin is continued as the mother tongue of a later generation

be used to foreground information in discourse. By and large, these features can be taken to have occurred during the historical language shift in Ireland because they have clear counterparts in later forms of vernacular Irish English, as will be discussed below.

4.2.1 TYPES OF CONTACT

There are many possible situations of contact which yield different linguistic outputs. In the main, it is the intensity and duration of contact between speakers of different languages which determines the effects which languages have on each other. The typological distance between languages is also important: where similarities are present, structural matches may well exist and be responsible for transfer, especially in a language shift scenario such as that for Irish English during its genesis. A further factor is whether the environment of the contact is prescriptive or not. Where the individuals involved in contact do not enjoy general schooling, transfer is not inhibited by notions of correctness and the effects of contact are considerable. There have also been many cases where language contact has been indirect, i.e. there was no speaker interaction, rather the contact was through the written medium. This situation is responsible for so-called 'cultural borrowings' (Campbell 1998: 57–88) and is characteristic of the influence of English on so many other languages today (see table 4.3).

Depending on the type of contact, different linguistic levels are affected. The lexicon is the most easily influenced, as it is an open class, and can show borrowings even where there is no speaker contact (scenario 1 in table 4.3). The second type of contact is where the languages in question are similar in type and so structural borrowings can occur. The verb form *are* in the plural present tense of *be* is a well-known borrowing from Old Norse into English, illustrating this phenomenon. If the languages in question become more similar structurally, then one can speak of levelling. Should one language come to be used in the area of the other as a general means of communication one can speak of koinéisation.

Neither of these scenarios applies to the genesis of Irish English as Irish and English are typologically very different. The dialect levelling view is one which needs to be scrutinised carefully as it is often posited for contact situations. For instance, a well-known view on contact specifies that 'one of the universal constraints on change . . . [is] that in contact situations, mergers expand at the expense of distinctions' (Herzog, quoted in Labov 1972: 300). If at all, this is only true of phonology. On a grammatical level such statements do not apply or at least cannot be shown to hold for contact situations such as that between Irish and English in the early modern period. Nonetheless, on a large timescale and considering all the languages of Ireland (indeed, of Britain; see Wagner 1959; Vennemann 2000, 2001, 2002; Filppula 2004b), one can note that transfer due to shift has led to convergence, to the formation of a linguistic area (Hickey 1999b). This is, however, the outcome of the language shift from Irish to English; it was not the outset for the shift in Ireland.

The third type of contact above involves the speakers of one language shifting to another over time. The duration of bilingualism is an important factor as is the manner in which the new language is presented to those shifting to it. A further subdivision can be made with type 3 in table 4.3 where the group which shifts is in a socially superior position. This was the case in Early Modern Irish (1200–1600) where members of the French-speaking Anglo-Norman community abandoned this language and shifted to Irish in subsequent generations. Normally, superstrate speakers do not switch to a substrate language, spoken by those in a socially lower position. But if the circumstances are right, this may happen. Among the circumstances one could list as relevant here are (i) separation of superstrate speakers from the larger community from which they stem and (ii) significant numerical inferiority vis-à-vis the substrate language community. Both these factors held for the Anglo-Normans in late medieval Ireland who lived in the countryside surrounded by native Irish. The type of shift involved here has been termed 'imposition' (Guy 1990; Ross 1991) because the superstrate speakers may in time 'impose' (Stewart 2004) features of their variety of the substrate language on majority forms of this language.

When delimiting types 3 and 4 in table 4.3 the additional distinction between transfer and restructuring is essential. The first process involves structural borrowings between two languages (in one or both directions), while the second involves a reorganisation of grammar by children given a poverty of linguistic input during first-language acquisition. The latter scenario is not one which can be assumed for the early modern period in Ireland. Nonetheless, in terms of structure, Irish English does come close to many English-based creoles and the question of how close language shift and creolisation are as scenarios of language change (Hickey 1997a) is worth considering; this is addressed in section 4.5.3.

Generalisations concerning contact

There would seem to be a general principle whereby the 'deeper kernel' of grammar of a language (Thomason and Kaufman 1988: 5) is more resistant to change because it is highly structured and acquired early by native speakers. Hence it is not surprising that inflectional morphology, along with core vocabulary, is used as a defining criterion for determining genetic relationships. For any highly structured subsystem there is a standard wisdom that, if it travels, then this is most likely when it fits easily into the recipient language. Conversely, free-standing discourse elements migrate easily, e.g. Irish *bhuel* for English *well* or (former) Irish English *arrah* from Irish. The reason for this is probably that such elements are not integrated into the grammatical lattice of a language and are free to move without any structural consequences for either donor or recipient languages.

The resistance to structural influence is connected with the duration and extent of contact. Long-term substratum interference can lead to a typological reorientation of a language but within a time frame of several centuries at least (Hickey 1995a). That is definitely too long for the switch from Irish to English, which was long enough for considerable grammatical influence, but not for a major typological realignment of English in Ireland.

With language contact the various linguistic levels are affected to differing degrees. The lexicon, as an open class, enjoys a higher degree of awareness among speakers. Given the fact that Irish was the substrate language in the contact scenario, extensive transfer of lexical material was not to be expected and it did not occur. One can generalise this point and maintain that, in a language shift situation, lexical borrowing is unlikely (Thomason and Kaufman 1988: 129). Speakers orient themselves towards the target language which enjoys greater prestige for them; this is probably the reason for the shift anyway. They are not likely to take salient elements like words from the language they are shifting away from. With cultural contact, for instance, in the Middle English period with English and French, the position was quite different. Speakers were not shifting to French, so the adoption of words from the prestige code took place into English, although there may well have been a degree of imposition from the French-speaking minority who shifted to English.

In a large-scale shift scenario the phonology of the substrate language plays a significant role. When speakers are acquiring the target language in adult life, they will retain the accent of their native language. Such massive phonological influence of Irish on early Irish English is evident in the many eye dialect representations found in the early modern period. It is true that many of these are exaggerations, but the reoccurrence of so many features across different genres with different authors at different times would justify the assumption that these features were indeed characteristic of early Irish English. Once the shift variety became established, subsequent generations continued it, but there was a toning down of salient phonological features, especially as later speakers became aware of what constitutes a standard pronunciation of the target language.

What happens on contact?

Many scholars who have considered language contact, e.g. Lass and Wright (1986), emphasise that languages are self-sufficient entities with a coherent internal structure and that forces operating within are enough to explain change. Contact explanations in their view would put the burden of proof on the linguist who favours these. While this view is basically correct, if two languages are in close contact for long enough then the language-internal resistance to structural change can be overcome. Indeed if the contact scenario is one of language shift then it is not so much a question of structural permeation of one language by another, but of the transfer of features from one to the other by those individuals who speak both languages.

The language shift in Ireland lasted some centuries and in that time many sociolinguistic configurations were to be found. On the east coast, especially in the towns, there were native speakers stemming from original English settlers who came during the late Middle Ages. Elsewhere in the countryside, there were English-speaking planters, again the descendants of native speakers, but of a more recent date. When considering whether these native speakers had an influence on the emerging varieties of Irish English, one must remember that, in the centuries after the initial settlement in the late twelfth century, an increasing gaelicisation took place in Ireland. This included the original English areas of the east coast, so that the English-speaking section of Irish society was reduced numerically. The planters on the other hand lived in relative isolation in the countryside. In their localities they were probably the source for the Irish learning English. Indeed the retentionist view (see section 4.5.1 below) would see them as the bearers of non-standard features of English which have been continued in vernacular varieties of Irish English. But there does not seem to have been a distinctive planter variety of English; at least none is attested, nor has any survived. Only in the north, where large numbers of planters from lowland Scotland and the north of England settled in areas which they took over from the native Irish, did their varieties of English have a lasting effect on the profile of later Ulster English. The conclusion here is that the transfer features of the native Irish became fixed in the English of Ireland, at least in the south, because this group was numerically far greater than any other.

When does contact-induced change appear?

Contact-induced change (Winford 2005) is not confined to transfer by the generations directly involved in the language shift. The seed for later change may be planted during the shift, but the effect may only be apparent much later. For instance, low-level phonetic influence from one language can lead to far-reaching changes in the other over a longer time span. This type can be termed 'delayed effect' contact because the effect is not immediate. There is no structural upheaval in the recipient language but a gradual penetration due to prolonged exposure to another language by largely bilingual sections of a community. In such a scenario 'speech habits' migrate from one language to another. In time, this may even lead to typological change. Within the history of English, an example is provided by Celtic influence on Old English (see Hickey 1995a for details) where the speech habits of the British Celts – which included considerable phonetic lenition – may well have furthered, if not actually triggered, the phonetic reduction of unstressed syllables in Old English and thus contributed centrally to the demise of inflectional endings, the precondition for the typological shift from synthetic to analytic in the history of English. Furthermore, given that speech habits are largely unconscious for speakers, the question of the relative prestige of languages does not play an important role, i.e. they can be adopted from a language of relatively low social status.

This kind of delay in the appearance of contact-induced features may be evident in the rise of the *do(es) be* habitual in Irish English. This is only attested on a wide scale after the middle of the nineteenth century, a time when the language shift was past its peak.

4.2.2 WHAT CAN BE TRACED TO CONTACT?

It goes without saying that there is no proof in contact linguistics. If a structure in one language is suspected of having arisen through contact with another, then a case can be made for contact when there is a good structural match between both languages. Take as an example the phrases at the beginning of the following sentences which have an exact equivalent in Irish (see mention of this in Taniguchi 1956: 43f.).

(2) a. *More is the pity, I suppose.* (TRS-D, M42, M)
         Is mór an trua, is dóigh liom.
         [is big the pity, is suppose with-me]
     b. *Outside of that, I don't know.* (TRS-D, C42–2, F)
         Taobh amuigh de sin, níl a fhios agam.
         [side out of that, not-is COMP know at-me]
     c. *There's a share of jobs alright.* (TRS-D, M7, M)
         Tá roinnt jabbana ann, ceart go leor.
         [is share jobs-GEN in-it right enough]

However, the case for contact as a source, at least as the sole source, is considerably weakened if the structure in question is attested in older forms of the language which has come to show it. Many of the features of Irish English are of this type, that is they could have a source either in older forms of English taken to Ireland or in Irish through contact. An example of this is provided by doubly

Table 4.4. *Category and exponence in Irish and Irish English*

Category	Exponence in Irish English	Exponence in Irish

Habitual	1. *do(es) be* + V-*ing*
	    They do be fighting a lot.
	2. *bees* (northern)
	    The lads bees out a lot.
	3. verbal -*s* (first person)
	    I gets tired of waiting for things to change.
		bíonn + non-finite verb form
		Bíonn siad ag troid go minic.
		[is-HABITUAL they at fighting often]

marked comparatives. In Irish, comparatives are formed by placing the particle *níos* 'more' and inflecting the adjective as well. For instance, *déanach* 'late', consisting of the stem *déan-* and the stem-extending suffix -*ach* (Hickey 2003f), changes to *déanaí* in the comparative although the comparative particle *níos* is used as well.

(3)   *Beimid ag teacht níos déanaí.*
       [will-be-we at coming more later]
       'We will be coming later.'

This double marking may have been transferred in the language shift situation. But such marking is also typical of earlier forms of English (Barber 1997 [1976]: 200f.) and may well have been present in input forms of English to Ireland. It is found with writers like Carleton and O'Casey (Taniguchi 1956: 42) and is still well attested today, as in the following examples.

(4)   a. *He's working more harder with the new job.*   (WER, F50+)
       b. *We got there more later than we thought.*   (DER, M60+)

In such cases it is impossible to decide what the source is, indeed it is probably more sensible to postulate a double source, and to interpret the structure as a case of convergence.

Before broaching the details of the case for contact, it is important to consider the difference between the presence of a grammatical category in a certain language and the exponence of this category. For instance, the category 'future' exists in the verb systems of both English and Irish but the exponence is different, i.e. via an auxiliary *will/shall* in the first language, but via a suffix in the second language. This type of distinction is useful when comparing Irish English with Irish (Ó Sé 2001: 123–5), for instance when comparing habitual aspect in both languages, as can be seen from table 4.4.

4.2.3 THE SEARCH FOR CATEGORIAL EQUIVALENCE

Many scholars, who have considered the initial stages of language change, have posited that low profile sites in the syntax of a language, such as subordinate clauses or weak affirmatives, are often the loci for variables which are incoming and are being adopted by diffusion into a community (Cheshire 1996). Authors also distinguish between pronunciation, which is always available for sociolinguistic assessment, and grammar, which is linked more to situational or stylistic conditioning. These factors are mentioned because they show the major difference between change being adopted into a variety and change resulting from language contact and shift.

When switching to another language, temporarily or permanently, adults expect the same grammatical distinctions in the target which they know from their native language. To this end they search for equivalents in the target to categories they are familiar with. This process is an unconscious one and persists even with speakers who have considerable target language proficiency. If the categories of the outset language are semantically motivated then the search to find an equivalent in the target is all the more obvious. A simple example can be taken to illustrate this. In Irish there is a distinction between the second-person-singular and plural pronoun but not in standard English. In the genesis of Irish English, speakers would seem to have felt the need for this non-existent distinction in English and three solutions to this quandary arose.

(5)   a. the use of available material, yielding *you # ye*
          (*ye* was available from early English input)
       b. the analogical formation of a plural: *you # youse < you + {S}*
          (not attested before early to mid nineteenth century)
       c. a combination of both (a) and (b) as in *you # yez < ye + {S}*
          (not found before mid nineteenth century)[9]

In all these cases the search for an equivalent category of second person plural was solved in English by the manipulation of material already in this language. At no stage does the Irish *sibh* [ʃɪv] 'you-PL' seem to have been used, in contrast, for instance, to the use of West African *unu* 'you-PL' found in Caribbean English (Hickey 2003d).

Apart from restructuring elements in the target, speakers can transfer elements from their native language. This transfer of grammatical categories is favoured, if the conditions listed in table 4.5 apply. In a language-shift situation, transfer must first occur on an individual level, perhaps with several individuals at the same time. But for it to become established, it must be accepted by the community as a whole. If such transfer is to be successful, then it must adhere to the principle of economy: it must embody only as much change in the target as is necessary for other speakers in the community to recognise what native structure it is intended to reflect.

To illustrate how this process of transfer is imagined to have occurred in the historical Irish context, consider the example of the immediate perfective formed

---

[9] Analogical possessive forms, *yeer* and *yeers*, developed because the related forms *your* and *yours* came to have exclusively singular reference.

Table 4.5. *Factors favouring transfer of grammatical categories*

---

1. The target language has a formal means of expressing this category.
2. There is little variation in the expression of this category.
3. The expression of this category is not homophonous with another one.
4. The category marker in the outset language can be identified – is structurally transparent – and can be easily extracted from source contexts.

---

by the use of the prepositional phrase *tar éis* 'after', which is employed temporally in this case (see section 4.4.1.4.1 for more details).

(6)   *Tá siad tar éis an obair a dhéanamh.*
      [is they after the work COMP do]
      'They are after doing the work.'

The pivotal elements in this construction are listed below; the complementiser *a* is of no semantic significance.

(7)   a.   adverbial phrase *tar éis* 'after'
      b.   non-finite verb form *déanamh* 'doing'[10]
      c.   direct object *obair* 'work'

It would appear that the Irish constructed an equivalent to the output structure using English syntactic means. Item (a) was translated literally as 'after'; (b) was rendered by the non-finite V-*ing* form yielding sentences like *They're after doing the work*. With a translation for *tar éis* and a corresponding non-finite form the task of reaching a categorial equivalent would appear to have been completed. Importantly, the Irish word order object + verb was not carried over into English (**They're after the work doing*).

   It betrays a basic misunderstanding of the mechanism of transfer for authors to express reservations – as Harris (1991: 205) does – because the order of non-finite verb form and object is different in Irish and English in the construction being discussed here. The aim in the contact situation was to arrive at a construction which was functionally equivalent to that in the outset language. A word order such as that in *John is after the house selling* would not only unnecessarily flout the sequence of verb and object in English (unnecessary as it would not convey additional information) but would also give rise to possible confusion

---

[10] This non-finite form is called the 'verbal noun' in Irish scholarship. The reason for this is that it can be qualified by a possessive pronoun which corresponds to the object in English: *Bhí sé á déanamh* [was he at-her doing] 'He was doing it-FEM' (e.g. *obair* 'work'). In this respect it resembles the English gerund somewhat. The verbal noun can also take an object in the genitive: *Tá sé ag déanamh na hoibre* [is he at doing the work-GEN] 'He is doing the work'.

with the resultative perfective, which in Irish English is realised by means of a past participle following its object.

In the transfer of structure during language shift, it would seem both necessary and sufficient to achieve correlates to the key elements in the source structure. Another instance of this principle can be seen with the resultative perfective of Irish English.

(8)   *Tá an obair déanta acu.*
      [is the work done at-them]
      IrEng: 'They have the work done.'
      'They have finished the work.'

Essential to the semantics of the Irish construction is the order object + past participle. Consequently, it is this order which is realised in the Irish English equivalent. The prepositional pronoun *acu* 'at-them' (or any other similar form) plays no role in the formation of the resultative perfective in Irish, but is the means to express the semantic subject of the sentence. As this is incidental to the perfective aspect expressed in the sentence, it was neglected in Irish English.

The immediate perfective with *after* does not appear to have had any model in archaic or regional English (Filppula 1999: 99–107). With the resultative perfective, on the other hand, there was previously a formal equivalent, i.e. the word order object + past participle.[11] However, even if there were instances of this word order in the input varieties of English in Ireland this does not mean that these are responsible for its continuing existence in Irish English. This word order could just as well have disappeared from Irish English as it has in forms of mainland English (van der Wurff and Foster 1997). However, the retention in Irish English and the use of this word order to express a resultative perfective can in large part be accounted for by the wish of Irish learners of English to reach an equivalent to the category of resultative perfective which they had in their native language.

The additive transfer of syntactic features to a target can be captured by the notion of imposition (Guy 1990: 49f., following work done previously by Frans van Coetsem; see Coetsem 2000 for a summary of his earlier work) whereby speakers in a shift situation impose categorial equivalents to structures of the outset language onto the target language.

Another issue to consider, when the question of contact has been discussed, is whether the structures which were transferred still apply in the same sense in which they were used in previous centuries. It would be too simplistic to assume that the structures which historically derive from Irish by transfer have precisely the same meaning in present-day Irish English. For instance, the immediate perfective with *after* has continued to develop shades of meaning not necessarily found in the Irish original, as Kallen (1989) has shown in his study.

---

[11] Visser (1963–73: 2189–90) cites instances of OV word order from Shakespeare such as 'Have you the lion's part written' (*Midsummer Night's Dream* I, ii, 68).

4.2.4 THE PROSODY OF TRANSFER

The case for contact should be considered across all linguistic levels. However, those authors who have been examining this recently, Corrigan, Kallen, Filppula and McCafferty, to mention the more prominent among them, have not considered phonological factors in their investigations, despite the benefits for analyses from doing this (Hickey 1990: 219). If one looks at structures which could be traced to transfer from Irish, then one finds in many cases that there is a correspondence between the prosodic structures of both languages. To be precise, structures which appear to derive from transfer show the same number of feet and the stresses fall on the same major syntactic category in each language (Hickey 1990: 222). A simple example can illustrate this (in (9) the Irish equivalent is given which is not of course the immediate source of this actual sentence as the speaker was an English-speaking monolingual).

(9)   *A . . . don't like the new team*   *at all at all.*   (WER, M55+)
                                             [ˌ ' ˌ ']
     Ní thaitníonn an fhoireann nua le hA . . . ar chor ar bith.
                                             [ˌ ' ˌ ']
     [not like the team new with A . . . on turn on anything]

The repetition of *at all at all* creates a sentence-final negator which consists of two stressed feet with the prosodic structure WSWS (weak–strong weak–strong) as does the Irish structure *ar chor ar bith*. This feature is well established in Irish English and can already be found in the early nineteenth century, e.g. in the stories of John Banim (1798–1842) written in colloboration with his brother Michael.

   Consider now the stressed reflexives of Irish which are suspected by many authors (including Filppula 1999: 77–88) of being the source of the Irish English use of an unbound reflexive.

(10)   ˌAn 'bhfuil ˌsé 'féin ˌis 'tigh ˌin 'niu?
      [interrog is he self in today]
      IrEng: "Is ˌhim'self 'in ˌto'day?'
      'Is he himself in today?'

   The strong and weak syllables of each foot are indicated in the Irish sentence and its Irish English equivalent above. From this it can be seen that the Irish reflexive is monosyllabic and, together with the personal pronoun, forms a WS foot: ˌsé 'féin [he self]. In Irish English the equivalent to this consists of a reflexive pronoun on its own: ˌhim'self, hence the term 'unbound reflexive' (Filppula 1997c), as no personal pronoun is present. If both the personal and reflexive pronoun were used in English, one would have a mismatch in prosodic structure: WS in Irish and SWS ('he ˌhim'self) in Irish English. One can thus postulate that the WS pattern of ˌhim'self was interpreted by speakers during language shift as the prosodic equivalent of both the personal pronoun and reflexive pronoun of Irish ˌsé 'féin and thus used as an equivalent of this. Later a distinct semanticisation of this usage arose whereby the unbound reflexive came to refer to someone who is in charge, the head of a group or of the house, etc. (see section 4.4.2.3 for examples).

Another example of prosodic match can be seen with the well-known immediate perfective of Irish English which corresponds, in the number of stressed syllables, to its Irish equivalent.

(11) a. *She's*   *after breaking the glass.*
                         [ˈ ˌ ˈ ˌ ˌ ˈ]
          Tá sí   *tréis an ghloine a bhriseadh.*
                         [ˈ ˌ ˈ ˌ ˌ ˈ ˌ]
      b. *He's*   *after his dinner.*
                         [ˈ ˌ ˌ ˈ ˌ]
          Tá sé   *tréis a dhinnéir.*
                         [ˈ ˌ ˈ ˌ]

This consists in both languages of three or two feet depending on whether the verb is understood or explicitly mentioned (it is the number of stressed syllables which determines the number of feet). In both languages a stressed syllable introduces the structure and others occur for the same syntactic categories throughout the sentence.

This prosodic similarity would also have helped people during language shift to recognise the new English structure – in the speech of others – as an equivalent to the Irish structure they already knew. Thus cases of individual transfer would have spread easily, ultimately becoming established as community-wide features which were then passed on to following generations.

A similar prosodic correspondence can be recognised in a further structure, labelled 'subordinating *and*' (see section 4.4.6.2), in both Irish and Irish English.

(12) a. *He went out ˈand ˈit ˈraining.*
          'He went out although it was raining.'
      b. *Chuaigh sé amach ˈagus ˈé ag cur ˈbáistí.*
          [went he out and it at putting rain-GEN]

Again there is a correlation between stressed syllable and major syntactic category, although the total number of syllables in the Irish structure is greater (due to the number of weak syllables). The equivalence intonationally is reached by having the same number of feet, i.e. stressed syllables, irrespective of the distance between them in terms of intervening unstressed syllables. And again, it is a stressed syllable which introduces the clause.

A prominent feature in Irish is the lack of a word for 'yes' and 'no'. Questions are replied to in the affirmative or negative by using a form of the verb *be*, in the negative if required.

(13) *An bhfuil tú ag dul go dtí an cluiche amárach?*
      [INTERROG is you-SG going to the match tomorrow]
      Tá. [t̪ɑː]ˇ   *Níl.* [nʲiːlʲ]ˇ
      [is]   [not-is]

The single-word verb forms are frequently spoken with a fall–rise intonation (indicated by $^\vee$) and this was evident in the speech of the informants recorded for *A Collection of Contact English* (see section 4.4).

(14)   *Are you getting support from the EU for sheep farming?* (RH)
        I am $^\vee$ (CCE-S, M60+)

A fall pattern (without the rise in *tá* and *níl*) is found with a stressed short vowel which occurs when negating something in the past.

(15)   a.   *An raibh tú riamh i Meiriceá?*   *Ní raibh.* $^\setminus$ (CCE-S, M60+)
             [INTERROG were you ever in America] [not was]
       b.   *Did your brother work on the farm as well?* (RH)
             He did not. $^\setminus$ (CCE-W, M75+)

Yet another case, where prosodic equivalence can be assumed to have motivated a non-standard feature, concerns comparative clauses. These are normally introduced in Irish by two equally stressed words *'ná 'mar* 'than like', as in the following example.

(16)   *Tá sé i bhfad níos fearr anois 'ná 'mar   a bhí.*
        [is it further more better now not like COMP was]
        'It's now much better than it was.'

Several speakers from Irish-speaking regions, or those which were so in the recent past, show the use of *than what* to introduce comparative clauses.

(17)   a.   *It's far better than what it used to be.* (TRS-D, C42–1, F)
       b.   *To go to a dance that time was far better than what it is now.*
             (TRS-D, C42–1, F)
       c.   *Life is much easier than what it was.* (TRS-D, C42–1, F)
       d.   *They could tell you more about this country than what we could.*
             (TRS-D, M7, M)

It is true that Irish *mar* does not mean 'what', but *what* can introduce clauses in other instances and so it was probably regarded as suitable to combine with *that* in cases like those above. From the standpoint of prosody *'than 'what* provided a combination of two equally stressed words which match the similar pair in equivalent Irish clauses.

The use of *than what* for comparatives was already established in the nineteenth century and is attested in many emigrants' letters such as those written from Australia back to Ireland, e.g. the following appeared in a letter from a Clare person written in 1854: *I have more of my old Neighbours here along with me than what I thought* (Fitzpatrick 1994: 69). It is also significant that the prosodically similar structure *like what* is attested in the east of Ireland where Irish was replaced by English earliest, e.g. *There were no hand machines like what you have today* (SADIF, M85, Lusk, Co. Dublin).

4.2.5 COINCIDENTAL PARALLELS

Despite the typological differences between Irish and English there are nonetheless a number of unexpected parallels which should not be misinterpreted as the result of contact. Some cases are easy, such as the homophony between Irish *sí* /ʃiː/ 'she' and English *she* (the result of the vowel shift of /eː/ to /iː/ in Early Modern English); see remarks in section 5.6. A similar homophony exists for Irish *bí* 'be' and English *be*, though again the pronunciation of the latter with /iː/ is due to the Great Vowel Shift.

Other instances involve parallel categories, e.g. the continuous forms of verbs in both languages: *Tá mé ag caint léi* [is me at talk-NON-FINITE with-her] 'I am talking to her.' Indeed the parallels among verbal distinctions may have been a trigger historically for the development of non-standard distinctions in Irish English, i.e. speakers during the language shift who found equivalents to most of the verbal categories from Irish expected to find equivalents to all of these. An example of this is habitual aspect, which is realised in Irish by the choice of a different verb form (habitual *bíonn* versus non-habitual *tá*).

(18)   *Bíonn sé ag caint léi.*
       [is-HABITUAL he at talking with-her]
       IrEng: 'He does be talking to her.'
       'He talks to her repeatedly.'

The possible pathway by which an equivalent to this arose in Irish English is discussed in the section on the habitual in 4.4.1.4.3.

Another coincidental parallel between the two languages involves word order, despite the differences in clause alignment which both languages show. In both Irish and English prepositions may occur at the end of a clause. A prepositional pronoun is the most likely form in Irish because it incorporates a pronoun which is missing in English.

(19)   *An buachaill a raibh mé ag caint leis.*
       [the boy that was I at talk-NON-FINITE with-him]
       'The boy I was talking to.'

Further parallels may be due to contact which predates the coming of English to Ireland. For example, the use of possessive pronouns in instances of inalienable possession is common to both English and Irish.

(20)   *Ghortaigh sé a ghlúin.*
       [injured he his knee]
       'He injured his knee.'

This may well be a feature of Insular Celtic which was adopted into English (Vennemann 2000, 2001), especially given that other Germanic languages do not necessarily use possessive pronouns in such contexts, cf. German *Er hat sich am Knie verletzt*, lit. 'He has himself at-the knee injured.'

4.2.6 WHAT DOES NOT GET TRANSFERRED?

If the expectation of categories in the target language which are present in the outset language is a guiding principle in language shift, then it is not surprising to find that grammatical distinctions which are only found in the target language tend to be neglected by speakers undergoing the shift.

The reason for this neglect is that speakers tend not to be aware of grammatical distinctions which are not present in their native language; at least this is true in situations of unguided adult learning of a second language. What is termed here 'neglect of distinctions' is closely related to the phenomenon of underdifferentiation which is known from second-language teaching (Major 2001). This is the situation in which second-language learners do not engage in categorial distinctions which are present in the target language, for instance when German speakers use the verb 'swim' to cover the meanings of both 'swim' and 'float' in English (*schwimmen* is the sole verb in German) or when they do not distinguish between *when* and *if* clauses (both take *wenn* in German). This neglect can be illustrated by the use of *and* as a clause co-ordinator with a qualifying or concessive meaning in Irish English.

(21)   *Chuaigh sé amach agus é ag cur báistí.*
       [went he out and it at putting rain-GEN]
       IrEng: 'He went out and it raining.'
       'He went out although it was raining.'

To account for the neglect of distinctions in more detail, one must introduce a distinction between features which carry semantic value and those which are of a more formal character. Word order is an example of the latter type: Irish is a consistently post-specifying language with VSO as the canonical word order along with noun + adjective, noun + genitive for nominal modifiers. There is no trace of post-specification in Irish English, either historically or in present-day contact varieties of English in Ireland. The use of the specifically Irish word order would, per se, have had no informational value for Irish speakers of English in the language shift situation.

Another example, from a different level of language, would be the distinction between palatal and non-palatal consonants in Irish phonology. This difference in the articulation of consonants lies at the core of the sound structure of Irish. It has no equivalent in English and the grammatical categories in the nominal and verbal areas which it is used to indicate are realised quite differently in English (by word order, use of prepositions, suffixal inflections, etc.).

An awareness of the semantic versus formal distinction helps to account for other cases of non-transfer from Irish. For instance, phonemes which do not exist in English, such as /x/ and /ɣ/, have not been transferred to English, although there are words in Irish English, such as *taoiseach* 'prime minister', pronounced ['tiːʃək], with a final [-k] and not [-x], which could have provided an instance of such transfer. Although the /k/ versus /x/ distinction is semantically relevant in Irish, it would not be so in English and hence transfer would not have helped realise any semantic distinctions in the target language. A further conclusion from these considerations is that the source of a sound like /x/ in Ireland can only be retention from earlier varieties of English. This explains its occurrence in Ulster Scots and in some forms of mid Ulster English, but also its absence elsewhere, although it is present in all dialects of Irish.

The literature on Irish English contains remarks on the relative infrequency of the present perfect in Irish English (as early as Hume 1878; see Kallen 1990). This is a category which has no equivalent in Irish and so it is not surprising that it is underrepresented in Irish English, as seen in the following examples.

(22) a. *I'm seven years home now.* (TRS-D, C42–2, F)
      b. *She's there for six years.* (TRS-D, C42–2, F)

Several features from Irish syntax are conspicuously absent from historical documents in Irish English. That this is not an accident of the textual record was confirmed by the material in *A Collection of Contact English*, a data collection consisting of the English of good present-day speakers of Irish (see section 4.4). Table 4.6 lists the salient features of Irish grammar which were never transferred into English in this collection, even in discourse situations with considerable code-switching.

The argument from parameter setting

Irish is a post-specifying language (VSO, N+Gen, N+Adj) and the fact that English is pre-specifying (SVO, Gen+N, Adj+N) is recognised quickly by language learners, and would have been in the historical language shift as well. This recognition then blocks (and blocked in the past) the transfer of any post-specifying strategies from Irish to English. The view that the direction of specification is a parameter of language, which needs to be recognised by only one setting and which is then fixed for all others, is supported by the data in *A Collection of Contact English* and by the history of Irish English.

The question of structural match

Initial mutation in Irish (see last item in table 4.6) is a central device for indicating essential grammatical categories such as tense, number, gender, case, etc. And yet it is a structural principle which is never transferred to English. The reason probably lies in its unique phonological character. There is no way of matching it to any grammatical process in English and then transferring it, something which is possible with many syntactic structures which can be mapped reasonably well onto English syntax.

Other factors in neglect of features

The neglect of a form in the target language may in some instances be motivated not so much by its absence in the outset language, but by some other factor. Take,

Table 4.6. *Non-occurring features of Irish in* A Collection of Contact English

1. Verb-initial sentences or clauses
    Tiocfaidh mé thart ar a hocht.
    'I'll come by around eight', lit. 'come-FUTURE I . . .'
2. Pro-drop (absence of personal pronoun in present tense)
    Ní thuigim an dream óg.
    'I don't understand the young crowd', lit. 'not understand-1ST_PERS_SG . . .'
3. Post-posed adjectives
    an fear bocht
    'the poor man', lit. 'the man poor'
4. Post-posed genitives
    teach Sheáin
    'John's house', lit. 'house John-GEN'
5. Order prepositional object + pronominal object
    Chonaic mé thuas ar an trá í.
    'I saw her up on the strand', lit. 'saw I up on the strand her'
6. Split demonstratives
    an gluaisteán sin
    'that car', lit. 'the car that'
7. Autonomous verb form
    Rinneadh an obair.
    'The work was done', lit. 'done-was the work'
    Rugadh mac di.
    'She bore a son', lit. 'born-was a son to-her'
8. Zero realisation of indefinite article
    Chas sí le déagóir.
    'She met a teenager', lit. 'met she with teenager'
9. Initial mutation
    Chuir [ch x < k] mé an cheist [ch x < k] chuici.
    'I put the question to her', lit. 'put me the question to-her'
10. *wh*-word plus relative pronoun
    Cathain a tharla an timpiste?
    'When did the accident happen?', lit. 'when that happened the accident'
    Cad a dhéanfaidís leis?
    'What would they do with him?', lit. 'what that do-CONDITIONAL they with-him'
11. Possessive pronoun and 'verbal noun'[a]
    Bhí sé á bhagairt.
    'He was threatening him' / 'He was threatening (to do) it', lit. 'was he at-his threatening'
    Bhí sé á bagairt.
    'He was threatening her', lit. 'was he at-her threatening'

---

[a] The 'verbal noun' is a non-finite verb form in Irish which is similar in function to the continuous form in English. However, it has nominal properties as well, e.g. it can be governed by a pronoun and differentially inflected for gender, as in the present instance.

for example, the lack of *do* support with negated *have* in Irish English (Trudgill, Schreier, Long and Williams 2004). Here *not* is cliticised onto *have* and not onto *do* which is absent in negated sentences of this type.

(23) a. *You haven't much trouble at all with it.* (WER, M55+)
          (cf. *You don't have . . .*)
      b. *You haven't to dry it or anything.* (WER, F55+)
          (cf. *You don't have . . .*)

One explanation for this is that the use of *do* in habitual structures (as of the nineteenth century in Irish English) may well have triggered its avoidance in sentences with negated *have*. Another instance of this avoidance would be the past of *use to* which does not occur with *do* in (southern) Irish English, e.g. *He usen't to drive to work*, not *He didn't use to drive to work*.

Overrepresentation

The mirror image of the neglect of distinctions is the overrepresentation of features, that is the scope of a feature in the outset is applied to the target language where this scope is usually smaller. The Irish English use of the conditional illustrates this phenomenon. It is non-standard inasmuch as it represents an overuse compared with other forms of English, e.g. as an equivalent to the imperative or in interrogatives as with the following examples.

(24) a. *Would you hurry up with your tea!* (WER, M55+)
      b. *Would the both of youse get off out of here!* (DER, M35+)
      c. *Would you be able to cook if you had to?* (WER, M50+)

This overrepresentation also applied to the definite article (see section 4.4.4 for more details). Curiously, the indefinite article, which does not exist in Irish, is not dropped in English. This might be expected because it is known from other languages, such as Russian, that the lack of an article (here the definite article) leads to its neglect in a target language, such as English, which has one.

4.3   Structural features of Irish

In terms of structure, Irish[12] and the other Celtic languages show certain features which link them typologically (Borsley and Roberts 1996). They all have the

---

[12] Irish is a member of the Celtic languages and, along with Scottish Gaelic and Manx (now extinct), it forms the Q-branch. The complementary P-branch consists of Welsh, Cornish (partially revived) and Breton. This division is derived from the treatment of inherited Indo-European *k*/*kw* which appears as /k/ in the Q-branch and /p/ in the P-branch; compare Irish *ceann* 'head', *ceathair* 'four' with Welsh *pen, pedwar*. The proto-Celtic language appeared on the European mainland in the last centuries BC. Between roughly 500 and 300 BC Celtic speakers moved across to the British Isles. The Celts who came to Ireland were speakers of Q-Celtic and possibly came through different routes and at separate times from the P-Celtic speakers who settled in Britain.

system of initial mutation whereby such essential grammatical categories as tense, gender, case and number are indicated by altering the initial sound of a word. In grammar, all Celtic languages share the principle of post-specification (see remarks in previous section) which can be seen in the following Irish examples.

(25)   a. *Dhún an cailín an doras.*
           [closed the girl the door]
           'The girl closed the door.'
       b. *Tá hata Sheáin ar an mbord.*
           [is hat John-GEN on the table]
           'John's hat is on the table.'
       c. *Is oileán álainn Inis Meáin.*
           [is island beautiful Inishmaan]
           'Inishmaan is a beautiful island.'

The typological structure of Modern Irish was already established by the time of the first attestations in the Old Irish period (AD 600–900). What happened in the following centuries is that the nominal inflections and complex verb forms were simplified considerably, yielding a morphologically simpler system by the end of the Middle Irish period (AD 900–1200). This was the time when the first settlers from England arrived so that it is Irish of the early modern period (AD 1200–1600) which they came in contact with. Some structures, which had an apparent influence on emerging forms of English in Ireland, were not completely established by then, notably the use of *iar, tar éis* (*tréis*) or *i ndiaidh*, 'after/behind', to express an immediate perfective (Ó Corráin 2006), though the initial use in Irish probably does go back to the early modern period (Ó Sé 1992 *pace* Greene 1979).

The following sections (4.3.1–4.3.4) offer a brief description of the grammar of Irish[13] which provides the basis for the ensuing discussion of contact and language shift. Only those structures of Irish are discussed here which could possibly have influenced English in Ireland. For instance, verb forms in the past or conditional are not listed as these have never had any influence on a variety of Irish English.

---

[13] Unfortunately, there is no comprehensive reference grammar of Irish written in English. A useful introductory book to consult is the short school grammar produced by the Christian Brothers, *New Irish Grammar* (1977). Other grammars, but written in Irish, are available, notably a fuller form of the Christian Brothers' grammar: *Graiméar Gaeilge na mBráithre Críostaí* 'Grammar of the Christian Brothers' (latest edition: 1999). There is also a comprehensive academic overview of the history of the Irish language from the beginning to the present day, which again is in Irish, *Stair na Gaeilge* 'The history of Irish' (McCone et al. 1994). An envisaged English version has not been published to date (mid 2006). Some other works could be mentioned in this context. Ó Siadhail (1989) is an overview by a good speaker of Irish but which is linguistically unreliable. Good résumés are to be found by MacEoin in Ball and Fife (1993) and Ó Dochartaigh in Macaulay (1992).

The verb system of Irish has been greatly simplified since the earliest period. What is left is a system with three tense distinctions – present, past and future – and a formal distinction between indicative and subjunctive. These distinctions are made by inflectional endings and, in the past and subjunctive, by an initial mutation as well. Because of the large number of former verb forms, many suppletive forms survive, rendering the paradigms of common verbs very irregular.

Non-finite verb forms

There is no infinitive in Irish. What corresponds to that of English is a non-finite verb form, traditionally known as the 'verbal noun' (Christian Brothers 1977: 126–30), abbreviated as 'VN' in the following, which can be the equivalent of an infinitive complement or the progressive in English.

(26) a. *Ba mhaith leis dul amach.*
          [would like with-him go-VN out]
          'He wants to go out.'
      b. *Tá Brian ag foghlaim* (VN) *na Fraincise.*
          [is Brian at learn-VN French-GEN]
          'Brian is learning French.'

When this non-finite verb form occurs with sentences expressing purpose, the preposition *chun* 'in order to' is found.

(27) *Chuaigh Nóra amach chun móin a fháil.*
      [went Nora out in-order-to turf get-VN]
      'Nora went out to get turf.'

The infinitival phrase has the word order Obj + Verb-NON-FINITE with the particle *a* before the verb form much like English *to*. This applies to any such structure, irrespective of whether the sentence expresses purpose or not. For an infinitival phrase in the negative, *gan* 'without', i.e. 'not to', is used instead of *a*.

(28) a. *Mhol sé dúinn teach a cheannach.*
          [advised he to-us house to buy-VN]
          'He advised us to buy a house.'
      b. *Dúirt sí linn gan a bheith dána.*
          [told she with-us without be misbehaved]
          'She told us not to misbehave.'

Tense

The tripartite division of tense of Irish – present, past, future – corresponds on first sight to that of English. However, the future is formed synthetically in Irish and the present has a greater range as it covers that of the present perfect of English.

(29) a. *Rachaidh mé chuige níos déanaí.*
          [will-go I to-him more late]
          'I will go to him later on.'
      b. *Tá mé anseo le trí huaire anois.*
          [is I her with three hours now]
          'I have been for three hours now.'

It is nonetheless possible in Irish to express the continued relevance of an action to the present (30a) and contrast this with a structure (Ó Sé 1992) where this is not the case (30b).

(30) a. *Tá ocht bpota déanta aige.*
          [is eight pots made at-him]
          'He has made eight pots.' (and will possibly make more)
      b. *Rinne sé ocht bpota.*
          [made he eight pots]
          'He made eight pots.' (and is not making any more now)

Analytic tense structures indicating the future are available in Irish by combining the verb *tá* 'be' with the non-finite form of a further verb, much as in English.

(31) *Tá mé ag dul go Luimneach amárach.*
      [is me at go-VN to Limerick tomorrow]
      'I am going to Limerick tomorrow.'

Aspect

Irish has several aspectual categories which are expressed with particular structures. Progressive aspect can be expressed using *tá* and a non-finite verb form (the verbal noun). This can contrast with a simple present which suggests an iterative action, much as in English.

(32) a. *Tá sí ag scríobh leabhar nua.*
          [is she at write-VN book new]
          'She is writing a new book.'
      b. *Scríobhann sí leabhar nua gach bliain.*
          [writes she book new every year]
          'She writes a new book every year.'

To express habituality (Ó Sé 2001: 123), Irish makes use of a particular verb form *bí* (this verb conjugates in the present) which, like *tá*, combines with a non-finite verb form (the verbal noun).

(33) *Bíonn sí ag scríobh go luath gach maidin.*
      [is-HABITUAL she at write-VN early every morning]
      'She is always writing early in the morning.'

Perfect and perfective

In the current context, it is important to distinguish between the perfect and the perfective. The former is a temporal category and refers to an action which takes place before the time of discourse. The latter, the perfective, is an aspectual category which refers to how an action is viewed, how it has taken place and how it is used to convey information which is relevant to the current discourse structure. Obviously, there is a degree of overlap between these two categories inasmuch as a single sentence refers to a point in time and also conveys information – via the verbal phrase – about the discourse. For this reason the distinction between perfect and perfective can be seen as one which is made for the purposes of analysis, but where the two categories in question blend together in actual sentences.

Classification of perfective aspect in Irish

There is a traditional classification of aspect in Irish which distinguishes two types of perfective. The perfective aspectual types are given a numerical classification (Greene 1979) which has been carried over into studies on Irish English by such authors as Markku Filppula (see, for instance, Filppula 1997a: 946).

(34) PI   Immediate perfective: *after* + V-*ing*
     PII   Resultative perfective: Obj + Past Participle
     PI   Irish: *Tá siad tar éis teach a thógáil.*
           [is they after house build-VN]
           IrEng: 'They are after building a house'.
           'They have just built a house.'
     PII   Irish: *Tá na leabhair léite aige.*
           [is the books read at-him]
           IrEng: 'He has the books read'.
           'He has finished reading the books.'

For the present discussion the terms 'immediate perfective' for the first type and 'resultative perfective' for the second will be used as they have been by the author in previous publications. They have the advantage of being descriptively obvious, something which is not true of 'PI' and 'PII'.

In the literature on aspect, various other terms have been employed. For instance, the immediate perfective has been frequently termed the 'hot news' perfect (*sic!*) after James McCawley's characterisation in English (McCawley 1976 [1971]). This label has been used by many authors on Irish English such as John Harris and Jeffrey Kallen. The resultative perfective has been variously called the 'completive' or 'accomplishment' perfective (see Kallen 1989: 16ff., for example).

The immediate perfective can be expressed in two possible ways in Irish: either using the word for 'after' *tar éis* (also written *tréis*, reflecting the pronunciation [t^{j}r^{j}e:ʃ]) or the word for 'behind', *i ndiaidh* (especially in northern Irish), as in the following example.

(35) *Tá sí i ndiaidh dul abhaile.*
[is she behind go-VN home]
'She is after going home.'

If the verb is obvious, then elliptical constructions are common due to an optional deletion of the present participle.

(36) *Tá sé tar éis a dhinnéar (a ithe).*
[is he after his dinner (eat-VN)]
'He is after (eating) his dinner.'

The resultative perfective is found in sentences with the word order object + past participle. However, this is the only word order in Irish, i.e. past participle + object does not occur. This means that sentences with O + PP word order allow of two interpretations (Ó Sé 1992), the default one being the second.

(37) *Tá litir scríofa agam.* [is letter written at-me]
1. state reached (stative)
2. result achieved (resultative)

In order to guarantee a stative interpretation, Irish may avail itself of syntactic devices which operate on a contrast, as seen in the following sentences.

(38) a. *Tá an litir críochnaithe agam.*
[is the letter finished-PP at-me]
'I have finished the letter.'
b. *Tá an litir chríochnaithe agam.*
[is the letter finished-ADJECTIVE at-me]
'I possess the letter which has been finished.'

The contrast here is based on the fact that in the second sentence the past participle acts as an adjective post-modifying the noun 'letter' and is lenited as the adjective for a feminine noun should be, i.e. the form is *chríochnaithe* with /xʲ-/ as opposed to the non-lenited form *críochnaithe* with /kʲ-/ in the first sentence.

   Irish can also realise this contrast suffixally, again with a past participle and adjective, for those verbs which are de-adjectival in type and which have a final /-tə/ on the past participle (Ó Sé 1992).

(39) a. *Tá an t-urlár glanta agam.*   (past participle)
[is the floor cleaned at-me]
'I have cleaned the floor.'   (result)
b. *Tá an t-urlár glan agam.*   (adjective)
[is the floor clean at-me]
'I have the floor clean.'   (state)

A preferred interpretation of the two main options of result and state can be attained in Irish by the use of adverbs. Consider the following two instances (from Ó Sé 1992) where the first has an immediate/resultative and the second a stative interpretation.

(40)   a.   *Tá an obair díreach déanta agam.*
            [is the work immediately done at-me]
            'I have just finished the work.'
       b.   *Tá an obair go léir déanta agam.*
            [is the work entirely done at-me]
            'I have all the work done.'

A further contrast in Irish concerns the use of *tá* and the past participle, found with transitive verbs with the direct object in an incorporated form.

(41)   a.   *Tá scríte agam chuige.*   b.   *Tá díolta agam as.*
            [is written at-me to-him]   [is paid at-me out-of-it]
            'I have written to him.'   'I have paid for it.'

According to Ó Sé (1992, 2004), these are definitely resultative perfects and contrast with the simple past tense,[14] as in:

(42)   a.   *Scríobhas chuige.*   b.   *Dhíolas as.*
            [wrote-I to-him]   [paid-I out-of-it]
            'I wrote to him.'   'I paid for it.'

The type of resultative construction discussed above with past participle plus prepositional pronoun (*agam, chuige,* etc.) is difficult to pinpoint chronologically but Ó Sé thinks that Greene's dating of the seventeenth century and non-Irish scholars' interpretation of this, e.g. Harris (1985: 47), is too late. He proposes some date intermediate between the thirteenth and the seventeenth centuries, as suggested by Dillon (1941: 50). This time scale would mean that the structure was well established before the beginning of the early modern period of Irish English and hence available to the Irish speakers involved in language shift to English. This issue will be returned to in section 4.4.1.4.2 when considering the expression of the resultative perfective in Irish English.

The passive in Irish

In Irish, there is a semantic equivalent to the passive of English (Depraetere and Reed 2006), but it is not realised by reversing subject and object. Instead, the type of structure just discussed, with *tá* 'is' and a past participle, is used (Stenson 1981: 148–50; Ó Siadhail 1989: 299). Where an agent is to be expressed, this is done by employing an appropriate prepositional pronoun (43b).

---

[14] The forms Ó Sé quotes are southern; in western and northern Irish, analytic forms would be used, i.e. *scríobh mé* and *dhíol mé* respectively.

(43) a. *Tá an obair déanta.*
          [is the work done-PP]
          'The work has been done.'
      b. *Tá an obair déanta agam.*
          [is the work done-PP at-me]
          'The work has been done by me.'

(43b) is in fact synonymous with the resultative perfective. A passive interpretation can be placed on this in an appropriate context. When only a passive interpretation is intended and when there is no wish to express the underlying subject, a special Irish verb form, unspecified for subject, is found.

(44) a. *Goideadh an rothar.*
          [stole the bicycle]
          'The bicycle was stolen.'
      b. *Ardaíodh na praghasanna anuraidh.*
          [raised the prices last-year]
          'The prices were put up last year.'

Tags in Irish

Irish has a similar system of tags to English. The same principle holds: a statement can be turned into a question by placing a verb with reverse polarity at the end of the sentence. The details are slightly different, however. Irish uses a specific dependent form of a verb (Christian Brothers 1960: 173f.) when preceded by the interrogative particle *nach* (negative, INTER-NEG) or *an* (positive, INTER-POS). Irish does not have an equivalent to the support verb *do* in English. The pronoun in the tag is normally absent in Irish (45a and b). The tag for forms of *be* (45c) does not contain a pronoun anyway.

(45) a. *Tá tú i do chónaí i gConamara, nach bhfuil (tú)?*
          [is you in your living in Connemara INTER-NEG is-DEPENDENT (you)]
          'You are living in Connemara, aren't you?'
      b. *Rinne sé dearmad ar an leabhar, nach ndearna (sé)?*
          [did he forget on the book INTER-NEG did-DEPENDENT (he)]
          'He forgot about the book, didn't he?'
      c. *Is deacair an obair í, nach ea?*
          [is difficult the work she INTER-NEG is-DEPENDENT]
          'The work is difficult, isn't it?'

The system of tags in Irish is a clear case of a structural parallel to English. As might be expected, tags are used in English without any difficulty, both by monolingual English speakers and by those who are still bilingual with Irish as a first language. For example, no non-standard usage of tags was found in *A Collection of Contact English*. But see section 4.4.6.6 for comments on *is it?* in Irish English.

4.3.2 THE NOMINAL AND PRONOMINAL AREAS

Nouns

In Irish, nouns are distinguished by gender and case in a manner which derives ultimately from Indo-European. There are two genders and two cases (nominative and genitive), although previously there were more and a few opaque examples of earlier cases still exist, e.g. *in Éirinn* 'in Ireland', which is a former dative. These formal characteristics of Irish have had no affect on Irish English and in *A Collection of Contact English* no features from the gender or case system were transferred to English.

One aspect of the numeral system of relevance here is the occurrence of singular forms after numerals, except some common words, e.g. those denoting individuals, which have special forms.

(46) a. *Fiche bliain ag fás*
          [twenty year at grow-VN]
          'Twenty years a-growing'[15]
      b. *Bhí cúigear fear ag tarraingt ar an mbád.*
          [were five man at pull-VN on the boat]
          'Five men were pulling the boat.'

Determiners

Irish has only one article, the definite article. In an indefinite context there is no article, so that the absence of an article is equivalent to an indefinite one in English.

(47) a. *An carr nua a cheannaigh sí.*
          [the car new that bought she]
          'The new car she bought.'
      b. *Tá carr nua ag teastáil uaithi.*
          [is car new at need-VN from-her]
          'She needs a new car.'

The range of the definite article is greater than English and is comparable to languages like German where the definite article is used in statements of a general nature.

(48) a. *An teangeolaíocht* 'Linguistics'
          [the linguistics]
      b. *An fhealsúnacht* 'Philosophy'
          [the philosophy]
      c. *An bheirt agaibh* 'Both of you'
          [the both at-you]

---

[15] This is actually the title used for the translation of a novel by the Blasket Islands author Maurice O'Sullivan (Muiris Ó Súilleabháin , 1904–50) which appeared in 1933.

d. *An chuid is mó di* 'Most of it'
   [the part is most of it]
e. *Tá an tsláinte go dona leis.* 'His health is bad.'
   [is the health badly with-him]
f. *Is tusa an fear cliste.* 'You're a clever man indeed.'
   [is you-EMPHATIC the man clever]

Personal pronouns

Irish has a formal distinction between first and second-person-singular personal pronouns, *tú* 'you-SG' and *sibh* 'you-PL', although it does not use the latter for formal address (as opposed to Scottish Gaelic where such usage exists).

(49) a. *An bhfuil <u>tú</u> in ann canadh?* 'Can <u>you-SG</u> sing?'
     b. *Ar ghlac <u>sibh</u> an cuireadh?* 'Did <u>you-PL</u> get the invitation?'

Demonstrative pronouns

These are formed in Irish by using the definite article before a noun and the adverbs *sin* 'that' or *seo* 'this' immediately after the noun in question. Demonstratives are very common in Irish and, together with a prepositional pronoun, usually a form of *ag* 'at', are frequently used to express possession or relevance. There is also a third demonstrative indicating distance, *úd* 'over there', comparable to archaic *yonder* in English.

(50) a. *An teach sin* 'That house'
     [the house that]
     b. *An ceann seo* 'This one'
     [the one this]
     c. *An baile seo againne* 'Our town'
     [the town this at-us]
     d. *An cnoc úd* 'Yonder hill'
     [the hill yonder]

Stressed reflexives

In Irish a stressed reflexive pronoun can occur in a statement or question to highlight the individual who is at the centre of the discourse. The element *féin* [heːnʲ] 'self' is found after a personal pronoun to form a reflexive in such cases.

(51) a. *An bhfuil sé 'féin istigh inniu?*
     [INTERROG is he self in today]
     'Is he himself in today?'

   b. *Níl sí 'féin sa bhaile anois.*
      [is-not she self in-the home now]
      'She herself is not at home now.'

This may not appear to be very different from English at first sight. However, the fact that the Irish structure consists of two syllables, pronoun + *féin*, may have provided a source for the unbound reflexives (Filppula 1997c) found in Irish English; see section 4.4.2.3.

4.3.3 THE PREPOSITIONAL AREA

In the context of the present chapter it is appropriate to mention the much greater role which prepositions play in Irish compared to English.[16] Where one has a verb in English, one frequently finds a noun in Irish, due to the strong nominalisation tendency of the language. In such situations, syntactic relations like subject and object are frequently expressed by means of prepositions with personal pronouns (Hickey 1985). These combinations resulted in the earliest stages of Irish in synthetic forms of preposition plus pronoun, a few examples of which are given in the following. Because of the clarity of the semantic relations which are expressed by such prepositional pronouns, sentences may occur in which no verb is present.

(52)   a. *Tá dhá orlach agam air.*
          [is two inches at-me on-him]
          'I am two inches taller than him.'
       b. *Tháinig meirg orainn chuige.*
          [came anger to-him on-us]
          'We grew angry with him.'
       c. *Níl seachaint agat air.*
          [is-not avoidance at-you on-it]
          'You cannot avoid it.'
       d. *Seo chugainn í.*
          [here to-us she]
          'Here she is coming towards us.'

In the following, three prepositions have been singled out for discussion because they show idiomatic uses in Irish which parallel usages in Irish English (see section 4.4.3).

   On. Apart from the literal meaning of 'location on something', this preposition is used in Irish to express the relevance of an action to a person in the discourse. In this sense, *on* is similar to the possessive pronoun. However, as the third example below shows, association with an individual, and not necessarily possession, may be the semantic relation being expressed.

---

[16] See the discussion by Amador (2006: 154–73, 'The use of prepositions') in the context of the novels by Patrick McGill.

(53) a. *D'imigh an siúinéir orm.*
           [went the carpenter on-me]
           'The carpenter left me.'
      b. *Múchadh an tine orm.*
           [extinguished the fire on-me]
           'The fire went out on me.'
      c. *Ghoid siad an carr orm.*
           [stole they the car on-me]
           'They stole the car on me.'[17]

In. Again the literal meaning of 'location within something' is the sense which *in* shares with its English counterpart. However, there is one metaphorical usage which relies on the combination of *in* 'in' plus *é* 'it' (= *ann*) and which expresses existence.

(54) a. *Drochlá a bhí ann.*
           [bad-day that was in-it]
           'It was a bad day.'
      b. *Sin an méid atá ann.*
           [that the amount that-is in-it]
           'That's all there is.'

With. Besides the metaphorical uses just mentioned, prepositions in Irish can differ from their counterparts in English, often in the manner in which they occur in a syntactic construction, as in the following examples.

(55) a. *Bhí an t-áth leis.*
           [was the luck with-him]
           'He was lucky.'
      b. *Tá sí ar ar aon aois liom.*
           [is she on the one age with-me]
           'She is the same age as me.'

4.3.4 SENTENCE STRUCTURE

Relativisation

Relative clauses are introduced in Irish by the relative particle *a* 'that' which has a negative counterpart, *nach* 'not-that'. It is common for a resumptive pronoun to occur when the verb in the relative clause takes a prepositional object (56b) or when the structure involves a noun and prepositional pronoun (56c). This then refers back to the antecedent in the main clause.

---

[17] Compare the Pertinenzdativ of German, as in *Er ist mir abgehauen* 'He has run off on me' (Polenz 1969).

(56) a.   *Sin an t-alt a bhí mé ag scríobh.*
          [that the article that was I at write-VN]
          'That's the article I was writing.'

      b.   *Seo an fear ar bhuail mé leis inné.*
          [this the man that met I with-him yesterday]
          'This is the man I met yesterday.'

      c.   *An bhean a bhfuil faitíos uirthi.*
          [the woman that is fear on-her]
          'The woman who is afraid.'

      d.   *Sin teanga nach dtuigim.*
          [that language not-that understand-I]
          'That's a language I do not understand.'

There is no special form of the relative pronoun in the genitive, unlike English. The form *ar* in the first sentence below is the form of the relative pronoun used before vowels and /h/ (here: *th-* = [h]).

(57) a.   *An bhean ar thug a hiníon cabhair dó.*
          [the woman that gave her daughter help to-him]
          'The woman whose daughter helped him.'

      b.   *An buachaill a ndíolann a athair leabhair.*
          [that boy that sells his father books]
          'The boy whose father sells books.'

Subordination

Subordinate clauses can be expressed in Irish in a manner similar to English, for instance, with an adverb of time or manner introducing the clause. The adverb in question appears together with the relative pronoun *a* which follows it immediately.

(58) *Bhí sé sa Spáinn nuair a bhí sé ina mhac léinn.*
      [was he in-the Spain when that was he in-his student (mhac léinn)]
      'He was in Spain when he was a student.'

A peculiarity in this respect is the use of verbless concessive clauses introduced by *and* which in such instances has the meaning 'although, despite'.

(59) *Chuaigh sé amach agus é go dona tinn.*
      [went he out and he badly (go dona) ill]
      'He went out although he was very ill.'

Topicalisation

The main means of topicalising a discourse element in Irish is by fronting. Because Irish is a strictly VSO language, no element can be shifted left of the verb in the same clause. As a consequence of this, fronting is achieved by clefting (Ahlqvist

2002): the element to be highlighted is shifted into a main clause opened by a dummy *is* 'it is' and the remainder of the non-topicalised input is relegated to a subordinate clause. Various elements of a sentence can be topicalised in this manner.

(60) a. *Tá Feargal imithe go Gaillimh.*
         [is Fergal gone to Galway]
         'Fergal is gone to Galway.'
     b. *Is go Gaillimh atá Feargal imithe.*
         [is to Galway that-is Fergal gone]
         'It's to Galway that Fergal is gone.'
     c. *Is imithe go Gaillimh atá Feargal.*
         [is gone to Galway that-is Fergal]
         'It's gone to Galway that Fergal is.'
     d. *Is é Feargal atá imithe go Gaillimh.*
         [is he Fergal that-is gone to Galway]
         'It's Fergal who is gone to Galway.'

Other instances of fronting do not involve clefting, but consist of a phrase which is juxtaposed with a following sentence and not formally a part of this. The link between the two is achieved by a pronoun which has an anaphoric function (*sí* 'she', i.e. *an múinteoir* 'the teacher', in the following sentence).

(61) *An múinteoir óg san áit, is dóigh liom gurb as Corcaigh í.*
     [the teacher young in-the place, is suppose with-me that-is from Cork she]
     'The young teacher in the place, I suppose she is from Cork.'

Negation

Negative concord applies in Irish, i.e. more than one negated element can occur within a clause or sentence.

(62) *Ní dhearna sé tada Dé Luain seo caite.*
     [not did he nothing day Monday here spent]
     'He did nothing last Monday.'

Irish does not have contracted forms like *nothing* from *not something*, or *never* from *not ever*. Instead it has single lexical items, such as *tada* 'nothing' or *riamh* 'ever' which, when it occurs with a negated verb, has the meaning 'never'.

(63) *Níor labhair sé le sagart riamh.*
     [not spoke he with priest ever]
     'He has never spoken to a priest.'

Augmenting negatives

Irish is rich in intensifiers used to emphasise statements which are often found at the end of a sentence, as with the phrase *ar chor ar bith*, which has the rhythmic structure [ˌ ˈ ˌ ˈ].

(64)   *Níl aon suim aici sa teangeolaíocht ar chor ar bith.*
        [not-is one interest at-her in-the linguistics on turn on anything]
        'She has no interest in linguistics whatsoever.'

The word *deamhan/diabhal* 'devil' is also found occasionally as an intensifier.[18] This has been established in Irish from at least the early modern period: there are examples from epigrammatic verse such as the following: *deamhan dán ná amhrán* [devil a poem or a song] 'neither a poem nor a song' (Ó Siadhail 1984). In the ontogenesis of negation, lexical items with inherent negative connotations can grammaticalise as negators (Odlin 1995). In Irish this development has an internal motivation in the language as it fills the gap for *neither* (see example just given). The use of *devil* is also found in literature where vernacular Irish English is portrayed (Taniguchi 1956: 45–8).

Comparatives

Phrases used for comparison which correspond to English 'more X than Y' have two elements in Irish which both begin with / n-/ as seen in the following example. The initial nasal is relevant to a transfer structure found in Irish English; see the discussion in section 4.4.5.2.

(65)   *Tá sé níos airde ná a dheartháir.*
        [is he more taller than his brother]
        'He is taller than his brother.'

Responsives

A well-known fact about Irish is that the language has no words for *yes* and *no*. Instead, the verb of the sentence which prompts a response in a discourse is repeated in either the affirmative or the negative, depending on what is appropriate (Ó Siadhail 1989: 245–9; Greene 1972: 62).

(66)   a. *An bhfuil aon Ghearmáinis agat?*   *Tá, Níl.*
           [INTERROG is one German-GEN at-you?   Is, Not-is]
           'Do you know any German?'   'Yes, no.'
        b. *Ar bhfaca tú Nóra inné?*   *Chonaic, Ní fhaca.*
           [INTERROG saw you Nora yesterday?'   Saw, Not saw]
           'Did you see Nora yesterday?'   'Yes, No.'

---

[18] See McCafferty (2005: 346) for remarks on its use in the prose of William Carleton which obviously represents a transfer from Irish.

Table 4.7. *Responsives and tag questions in English and Irish*

---

1. Responsives with echo verb

    A: *Will you come by later?*   B: *I will.*

    A: *An dtiocfaidh tú thart níos déanaí?*   B: *Tiocfaidh.*

    [INTERROG come-FUTURE you round more later]   [come-I-FUTURE]

    A: *Can you sing this song?*   B: *I can.*

    A: *An féidir leat an t-amhrán seo a chanadh?*   B: *Is féidir.*

    [INTERROG possible with-you the song this to sing]   [is possible]

2. Tag questions with echo of anchor

    A: *You'll come by later, won't you?*

    A: *Tiocfaidh tú thart níos déanaí, nach dtiocfaidh?*

    [come-FUTURE you round more later, not come-FUTURE]

    A: *You can sing this song, can't you?*

    A: *Is féidir leat an t-amhrán seo a chanadh, nach féidir?*

    [is possible with-you the song this to sing, not possible]

The Irish responses have a characteristic intonation with a fall–rise on the echoed verb form (see section 4.2.4 for further comments on this).

In his investigation of responsives throughout the history of Irish and Welsh, Greene (1972: 59f.) notes that the practice of echoing a verb in the positive or negative as an equivalent to 'yes' and 'no' was already established in Old Irish and in medieval Welsh (Greene 1972: 65–7), although the details of origin and development are different in each case. Essentially, what one has for the Celtic languages throughout their history is a practice whereby verbs are repeated in responsives, in the positive or negative depending on what is intended.

Greene (1972: 59) surmises briefly on the possible influence of Irish responsive practice on Irish English. Indeed in a wider context there may well be a case for positing a Celtic influence on the development of the responsive in British English, at least after modals, *be* and *do*, e.g. *Must we leave? You must*; *Are you tired? I am*; *Do you take sugar? I do*. Other Germanic languages, such as German, may echo such verbs in responsives, but the practice is not so widespread as in English where *do* support with a corresponding responsive form is unique and where responsives with *will* for the future are also a special feature.

Responsives can be seen in connection with tag questions because in both cases one has the repetition of a verb after a main clause, in the former case by the addressee and in the latter by the speaker, in anticipation of an answer (with reverse polarity). The principle is the same in Irish and English, as can be seen from table 4.7.

Embedded questions

The word order of a question which is embedded in a sentence is the same as that of the direct question. This fact is of relevance to Irish English; see section 4.4.6.7.

(67) a. *An raibh sé sásta?*
          [INTERROG was he satisfied]
          'Was he satisfied?'
      b. *Chuir sé ceist air an raibh sé sásta.*
          [put he question on-him INTERROG was he satisfied]
          'He asked him if he was satisfied.'
      c. *Cén áit a bhfaca sí é?*
          [INTERROG-the place that saw she him]
          'Where did she see him?'
      d. *Chuir sé ceist uirthi cén áit a bhfaca sí é.*
          [put he question on-her INTERROG-the place that saw she him]
          'He asked her where she saw him.'

4.4   The grammar of Irish English

In this section the grammar of Irish English – its morphology and syntax – is to be considered in detail. The grammatical structures which are specific to Irish English in its various forms have been the object of scholarly examination for well over a hundred years and in the past few decades there has been a series of suggestions about the origin and nature of these structures. These proposals have led to much discussion among scholars about their validity and their applicability to the Irish English data.

The various views on Irish English which have been put forward in the literature fall into two broad groups, (i) those concerned with the origin of features – contact, retention, universals, grammaticalisation, creolisation – and (ii) those concerned with descriptive frameworks for interpreting features – speech act theory, functional grammar, prototype theory. The work of major scholars in the field, e.g. Karen Corrigan, Markku Filppula, John Harris, Jeffrey Kallen, Kevin McCafferty and the present author, has largely concentrated on the question of origin, though some studies, such as Corrigan (2003a), Hickey (2000b) and Kallen (1990), have been explicitly concerned with descriptive frameworks for handling features of present-day Irish English.

In this chapter, both the issue of origin and the models for describing Irish English will be discussed. To begin with, the sources used for the current presentation are listed and then an enumeration of non-standard features of Irish English is given. This is followed by a section which considers the case for a contact origin of the features discussed. Following on this, alternative explanations are examined. The chapter closes with a consideration of the entire island of Ireland as a linguistic area with a common core of shared features. This approach to the specific grammatical characteristics of Irish English is one which has been applied by the present author (Hickey 1999b) and by Markku Filppula (2004b) in an effort to account for the similarities in vernacular grammar between the various regions of Ireland, specifically between the north and the south of the island.

Table 4.8. *Data sources for the grammatical analysis of Irish English*

<table>
<tr><td>1.</td><td>*A Collection of Contact English*</td></tr>
<tr><td>2.</td><td>*A Survey of Irish English Usage* (included in Hickey 2004a)</td></tr>
<tr><td>3.</td><td>Dublin English Recordings (used for Hickey 2005)</td></tr>
<tr><td>4.</td><td>Waterford English Recordings (used for Hickey 2001b)</td></tr>
<tr><td>5.</td><td>*A Corpus of Irish English* (included in Hickey 2003a)</td></tr>
<tr><td>6.</td><td>*Tape-Recorded Survey of Hiberno-English Speech – Digital* (included in Hickey 2004a)</td></tr>
<tr><td>7.</td><td>Irish Emigrant Letters (available in the National Library of Ireland)</td></tr>
<tr><td>8.</td><td>Old Bailey Texts (available as XML-files on CD-ROM)</td></tr>
<tr><td>9.</td><td>Material for *A Linguistic Survey of Ireland* (notebooks in University of Galway library)</td></tr>
<tr><td>10.</td><td>Sound Archive of the Department of Irish Folkore, University College Dublin</td></tr>
</table>

Data sources

The data for Irish English used in the present chapter come from a total of ten sources, five of which are based on collections made by the author. The sources are listed in table 4.8 and commented on in the following paragraphs.

1.   *A Collection of Contact English*

During several stays in the Irish-speaking areas when the author was gathering material for the project *Samples of Spoken Irish* (Hickey in press) he also collected material on English as spoken by Irish–English bilinguals. The aim of this undertaking was to record English usage with individuals who were robust speakers of Irish and for whom English was a second language. The speakers came from the three main Irish-speaking areas in present-day Ireland: (i) the tip of the Dingle peninsula in Co. Kerry, (ii) coastal Connemara, west of Galway city out as far as Carna and (iii) the coast of north-west Donegal, from Dungloe to Falcarragh (see map A6.3 in appendix 6).

The setting for the recordings was roughly as follows: speakers were asked about a subject matter which would have involved discussing people and situations outside the Irish-speaking districts (Gaeltachtaí) and the author then changed to English, thus implicitly encouraging the speakers to do this also. Where necessary, he pretended not to quite understand the Irish of a speaker and thus induced the latter to switch to English. This situation was delicate at times as speakers sometimes spoke better Irish than English and thus were somewhat insecure in the latter. In order to put speakers at their ease, no mention of making a tape recording was ever made. Instead, the author took notes of the features of interest which occurred during the sessions.

Examinations of code-switching in different languages (Auer 1998; Poplack 1980; Clyne 1987; Myers-Scotton and Jake 2000) have shown that there are pivotal points in sentences at which the switch can take place. This also applies

Table 4.9. *Code-switching in* A Collection of Contact English

1. After existential *tá sé* 'it is' / *bhí sé* 'it was'
   Bhí sé raining cats and dogs.
   [was it]
2. For a compound verbal complement
   Bhí sé . . . [pause] out clubbing I suppose   *nuair a tharla an timpiste.*
   [was he]   [when that happened the accident]
3. Before a non-finite verbal complement
   Bhí mé ag smaoineamh ar, ar . . . [pause] the way to make more money.
   [was I at thinking on, on]
4. Before a relative clause
   Tá carr nua aici anois a . . . [pause] which runs on diesel.
   [is car new at-her now]
5. For a topicalised clause (before the other clause)
   'Twas anti-biotics *a fuair sí.*
                        [which got she]
6. For an individual lexical item
   An bhfuil a fhios agat, nuair a bhí an pneumonia *uirthi.*
   [INTERROG is know at-you when that was the pneumonia on-her]
   Mise, bhí sí an- helpful *nuair a bhí m'athair tinn.*
   [well, was she very-helpful when that was my father sick]

to a switch from Irish to English. In table 4.9 the switch–over points at which code-switching occurred are listed. A pause was not always present at the pivot, especially when the speaker was equally comfortable in Irish and English.

The reasons for intrasentential code-switching are those which one would expect from other languages which also show this: (i) an English expression which does not have an exact Irish equivalent, see 1 and 2 in table 4.9, or (ii) a context in which English is normally used, i.e. as the language of commerce and technology, see 3, 4 and 5. Lexical code-switching, as illustrated in 6, is not subject to syntactic conditioning and occurred freely in the speech of all speakers in *A Collection of Contact English*.

In the following sections examples are given for grammatical features which stem from this collection. For a discussion of the possible transfer features which, however, did not occur, see section 4.2.6. There are also some samples of Irish which are quoted below and which stem from data collected in this context.

In the following, the abbreviation CCE refers to data from *A Collection of Contact English*. There follows a hyphen with a single letter which refers to the region where the speaker came from, i.e. CCE-S = 'south', CCE-W = 'west', CCE-N = 'north'.

While collecting material in Connemara, the author visited an adjacent area in north Co. Galway and collected some data from speakers who were not native speakers of Irish but who lived in an area which had been Irish-speaking up to the early twentieth century. Quotations from this set of recordings are indicated by RL (= Ross Lake, the area investigated).

2.   *A Survey of Irish English Usage*

This survey covers the areas of morphology and syntax within Irish English and was conducted over a period of several years parallel to the collection of sound recordings (Hickey 2004a). The survey was based on a questionnaire of some fifty-seven sample sentences, each of which contained a structure which is known to occur in some form of Irish English. Informants were asked to judge the sentences in terms of acceptance in casual speech among friends. They were told that the survey was about colloquial speech, not written English. The questionnaire was only done in groups of two or more as informants tended to be much less prescriptive in groups than as individuals. There were basically three types of answer which allowed for grading of acceptability. Informants could specify that a given sentence represented 'no problem', was 'a bit strange' or indeed was 'unacceptable'. The vast majority of informants were in the eighteen–thirty age bracket. This was deliberate as the goal of the survey was to determine the acceptance of certain structures in colloquial speech with the younger generation.

Questionnaires. Approximately 80 per cent of returned questionnaires were actually used. There were over 1,000 questionnaires, collected over several years, which were acceptable (1,017 in all). The criterion for acceptance was the following: each questionnaire must have had all three categories used, e.g. any informant who ticked 'no problem' for all sentences was ignored as well as anyone who said that all sentences were 'a bit strange' or 'unacceptable', as this showed a lack of discrimination. The spread among categories must have been at least 10 per cent. Naturally, all sentences must have been evaluated and the questionnaires of those informants who inserted prescriptive comments were ignored. Informants were presented the sentences without any indication of what structures they illustrated.

Awareness of structures. Awareness of grammatical structures varied greatly among participants. Many of them asked the author what was 'strange' or 'wrong' about a certain structure. This showed that speakers' perception of non-standard features in their native English varied considerably. For instance, many participants in the survey saw nothing strange in (1) *I know her for five years now* (extended present) or (2) *She has the housework done* (resultative perfect with O+PP word order) or (3) *They're finished the work now* (*be* as an auxiliary). Other structures were obviously salient for speakers because they are so often the object of prescriptive comments. Examples of this type are (1) *I seen him yesterday* (past participle as preterite) or (2) *Them shoes are too small for me* (*them* as demonstrative pronoun).

The results of *A Survey of Irish English Usage* are of relative value as they are not attestations but represent speakers' reactions to non-standard features. Nonetheless, they may well help to confirm or refute tendencies in the regional distribution of features. For the statistics offered in the various sections below, only the response 'no problem' to the structures in question was assessed. This hopefully presents a clearer picture. When dealing with responses from individual locations in Ireland the following comments should be borne in mind.

Acceptance rates. Belfast showed a high acceptance of non-standard features, something which may well be due to the mixed nature of Belfast English (J. Milroy 1981; see section 5.5.1.1). For that reason, Belfast was treated as a separate location, although it is located in the south-east tip of Co. Antrim. This allowed the separate evaluation of Belfast vis-à-vis Co. Antrim to the north and Co. Down to the south. This type of separation was not necessary for Dublin which does not show the same kind of mixture of two distinct regional inputs.

The core Ulster Scots counties, Antrim and Down, are of relevance in the statistics discussed in the following sections because there are taken to have had the strongest influence from varieties of Scots and, conversely, the weakest influence from Irish (though the north-east corner of Antrim was probably Irish-speaking up to the end of the nineteenth century). When assessing possible Irish influence, Galway and Kerry are probably the best counties as they are far from northern regions and still contain relatively vibrant Irish-speaking areas. The latter also holds true for Donegal, but this county is not always suitable when assessing possible Irish influence on English as it had considerable Scots settlement in the Laggan area to the west/south-west of Derry city.

Wicklow is the county of Ireland which appears to have been influenced least by Irish. Filppula (1999: 40f.), quoting de Fréine (1977), remarks on the fact that it had become English-speaking by 1750 and that by *c.* 1800 Irish was limited to a few western parts of the Wicklow mountains. This fact is important for *A Survey of Irish English Usage* which, in the returns for this county, shows a low acceptance of structures normally traced to Irish influence.

For non-salient features, e.g. the resultative perfective as in *She has the housework done*, high values were generally attained. Other structures, which are stigmatised in Ireland, such as the habitual, show much lower values. However, it is the relative nature of the values which helps in recognising a tendency in the geographical spread of acceptance patterns.

In the following, the abbreviation SIEU refers to data from *A Survey of Irish English Usage*. The data from this survey can be found on the DVD accompanying Hickey (2004a).

3. Dublin English Recordings

This set of recordings stems from the investigation of Dublin English which has appeared as Hickey (2005). The grammatical samples of Dublin English were collected over a period of several years and consist in the main of vernacular forms of English in the capital. These are not available in audio form (they consist of notes made by the author) because permission to tape record was not sought from the informants.

In the following, the abbreviation DER refers to data from the Dublin English Recordings. The speakers are referred to by gender and age bracket, e.g. F40+ is a female informant between 40 and 45 years of age. All the informants in these recordings were speakers of vernacular Dublin English.

4. *Waterford English Recordings*

This body of data is similar to the above collection in that it consists of handwritten notes taken by the author during contact sessions with speakers of vernacular English in the city of Waterford which is in the east of the county of the same name and on the border with Kilkenny and Wexford. This collection was made over a long period, stretching back to the early 1980s and has been used for previous publications by the author, such as Hickey (2001b).

The reason for including samples from this material in the present chapter is that Waterford is located in the south-east of Ireland, the area which was first settled by the English in the late Middle Ages. There are many features from English in this region which link up with those in varieties in the west of England and which are not necessarily found in the rest of Ireland. Waterford English does, however, share a large number of non-standard features with other regions of Ireland and its generally archaic character and distance from the remaining Irish-speaking areas in the west suggest that these common features are of considerable vintage.

In order to check the validity of the features noted for English in Waterford city, a few recordings were made in the countryside to the south of the city. The syntactic features found in urban Waterford English were confirmed. However, the phonetics was somewhat more conservative. For instance, there was a greater incidence of /eː/ for ME /eː, ɛː/ as in *cleaning* ['kleːnɪn] which was almost categorical for one of the older informants from Waterford county. The speakers who were consulted also showed a diphthongisation and breaking of long vowels which was reminiscent of that found in the glossaries of Forth and Bargy, areas which are not too far from east Co. Waterford.

In the following, the abbreviation WER refers to data from the Waterford English Recordings while WCER refers to those from speakers in county Waterford. As with the Dublin recordings, the speakers are referred to by gender and age bracket (see previous section).

5. *A Corpus of Irish English*

This corpus consists of literary attestations of Irish from the *Kildare Poems* (early fourteenth century) to the plays of John Millington Synge and Sean O'Casey in the early twentieth century. It includes those texts from the early modern period which contain parodies of Irish English. These begin at the end of the sixteenth century and continue well into the nineteenth century. It is, of course, necessary to stress that parodies cannot be taken to reflect accurately the then contemporary speech of the Irish. But given that these texts are the only attestations for earlier

Irish English, they have been used cautiously to trace the history of non-standard features.

In the following, the abbreviation CIE refers to data from *A Corpus of Irish English*. This corpus can be found on the CD accompanying Hickey (2003a).

6. *Tape-Recorded Survey of Hiberno-English Speech – Digital*
In the late 1970s and early 1980s a project was running at the Department of English, Queen's University, Belfast, with the intention of recording both word lists and free speech from speakers in all counties of Ireland. This project has long since been discontinued and has remained incomplete, but many useful recordings were made by the research assistants engaged by the organisers. These recordings were put at the disposal of the author during the 1980s and were later digitised by him. They are to be found on the DVD accompanying Hickey (2004a). In all, some eighty recordings of about thirty minutes duration are available in the digital form of the survey. The speakers are all older rural speakers and mostly male. Thus they are good representatives of the local speech of their home counties. The stretches of free speech have been used for the analyses in the present chapter.

In the following, the abbreviation TRS-D refers to data from the *Tape-Recorded Survey of Hiberno-English Speech – Digital*. The locations where speakers came from are also indicated, e.g. TRS-D, C41, F refers to the speaker from point C41 on the grid of Ireland used for the survey (see map A6.8 in appendix 6). The single letter F at the end indicates a female speaker while M stands for a male.

7. *Irish Emigrant Letters*
The National Library of Ireland harbours several sets of letters written by Irish emigrants – mostly in the New World – back to their relatives in Ireland. Many of these sets have been put at the disposal of the library by North American historians, such as Kirby Miller. These letters have been used by several scholars investigating Irish English, e.g. by Filppula (1999) and Hickey (2005), because they can be taken to represent vernacular speech, given the non-prescriptive context of this personal correspondence (see Montgomery 1995 for a general discussion and linguistic analysis of emigrant letters).

In the following, the abbreviation IEL refers to data from the Irish Emigrant Letters.[19] Where necessary, further information is provided about the correspondents, e.g. about the part of Ireland they came from and the status of the Irish language there at the time of writing.

8. *Old Bailey Texts*
A recent project of interest for the present book is the collection of court transcripts from the Old Bailey which has been put together by researchers at the

---

[19] The author is indebted to Markku Filppula for putting a large number of these letters at his disposal in electronic form. The remainder were studied by the author in the National Library of Ireland and transcribed from there.

University of Sheffield. In many cases the individuals before the court were Irish and the verbatim transcripts offer attestations of Irish English features going back to the early eighteenth century (the beginning of the period covered by the project). It is probably the case that the court clerks standardised the speech of Irish defendants in many instances, but there are enough transcripts where speech is recorded faithfully for this collection to be of value in the current context.

In the following the abbreviation OBT refers to data from the Old Bailey Texts.

9.   *Material for* A Linguistic Survey of Ireland
The project *A Linguistic Survey of Ireland* dates back to the early 1950s when P. L. Henry of the University of Galway began collecting information using a lexical questionnaire. This was structured so as to capture rural and agricultural terms and the informants were nearly exclusively elderly males. The material gathered is of limited interest today, given the very narrow sector of the population which was questioned and the severe linguistic limitations on the information which was gathered. Nonetheless, some grammatical information was noted in the speech of informants, especially the use of BE, DO and HAVE, which was given in informal sketches added at the end of each notebook, especially those collected during the late 1970s and 1980s by Séamus Ó Maoláin. Unfortunately, the project never advanced in publication beyond the report in Henry (1958).

In the following the abbreviation MLSI refers to data from the Material for *A Linguistic Survey of Ireland*.

10.   *Sound Archive of the Department of Irish Folkore, University College Dublin*
The Department of Irish Folklore, University College Dublin, houses a considerable body of archive material collected during the twentieth century by Irish folklorists. A percentage of this material is both in English and available as audio tape, which made it particularly suitable for evaluation in the context of the current book.

In the following the abbreviation SADIF refers to data from the Sound Archive of the Department of Irish Folkore, University College Dublin.

In the above collections, a name was often contained in a sentence or phrase which illustrated a vernacular feature of Irish English. In order to preserve anonymity, a pronoun or a fictitious name has been inserted instead or in some cases only the first letter of the name has been used.

With the collections of speech (1, 3, 4 and 6 above), the letter M after the abbreviation for the collection stands for 'male' and F for 'female'. The digit after this letter is a reference to the assumed age of the speaker. In the case of the *Tape-Recorded Survey of Hiberno-English Speech – Digital* the ages of the speakers were neither recorded nor estimated by the collectors of data, though an indication was given in some instances by the speakers themselves.

What is one dealing with?

A section with the title 'The grammar of Irish English' raises at least two fundamental questions. Firstly, is there such as thing as this grammar? Secondly, is it a homogenous entity? Before proceeding, it is necessary to specify just what is being referred to in this section. The label 'grammar of Irish English' is used in an inclusive sense, i.e. it encompasses – for the present discussion – all vernacular forms of English, irrespective of whether these contain structures found in supraregional forms of English in Ireland or not. Furthermore, features of English in Ulster and the south of the country are dealt with, though those which apply specifically to the north are dealt with in sections 3.3 and 3.4. Where necessary, comments are included when a feature is regionally bound or only found in a specific variety of English in Ireland.

This inclusive stance is justified on a number of grounds. Firstly, any discussion which looks at the origins of features must consider all non-standard features which are attested. The issue of their presence or absence in non-local forms of Irish English, or the possible stigma associated with them, is a discussion for another chapter (see relevant sections of chapters 1 and 5). Secondly, a cogent case can be made for regarding the island as a linguistic area (Hickey 1999b; Filppula 2004b) which has a large body of shared features, irrespective of the special status of Ulster with its historical emigration from Scotland which provided a unique linguistic input to the province.

Another issue which requires mention here is that of older features attested for Irish English. Some of these have disappeared from Irish English entirely (see the discussion of phonology in section 5.1.5). Nonetheless, they are of relevance to the present discussion as they may be traceable to Irish influence and hence strengthen the case for contact origin, an issue of central concern in this section. To illustrate this a quotation can be given from Lady Gregory's play *The Ward* (contained in *A Corpus of Irish English*, Hickey 2003a) which shows what was then dubbed the 'Kiltartan infinitive' (see Filppula 1999: 184 for a discussion of the 'narrative infinitive'), but which is generally not found in Irish English any longer.[20]

(68)   *What luck could there be in a place and a man not to be in it?*
      Cén t-ádh a bheadh ar áit gan fear a bheith ann?
      [what luck would-be on place without man to be in-it]

This may well be a calque on Irish syntax: the equivalence established was probably between the (stressed) non-finite *bheith* and infinitive *be* on the one hand

---

[20] The features used by Gregory in her plays, and in her translations of Molière into 'Kiltartan' (Cronin 1996: 139f.), are often dismissed as imitations of rural speech by a non-native. But inasmuch as these features are documented elsewhere in both the textual and the spoken record, they can be taken as genuine. From a linguistic point of view the question is whether the features found in her writings are attested elsewhere and not whether her use of them was stylistically appropriate in the literary contexts in which they can be found.

and between the (unstressed) particle *a* [ə] and *to* on the other. This would have provided the same prosodic pattern – weak + strong – for the non-finite verb structure in English as that which existed in Irish.

What did people learn?

When considering non-standard features of Irish English, especially with a view to contact origin, it is necessary to determine as far as possible what types of English served as models for the Irish shifting from their native language. While it is true that the original settlers and the later planters were only a minority, their speech was the target variety which the Irish gravitated towards. While the target variety was itself not necessarily uniform, there are non-standard features which are broadly typical of Irish English and which speakers of Irish to this day are exposed to and which they adopt.

A good example to illustrate this is the elderly male from Kilkieran, Connemara, to be heard in *Connaught_41_Free_Speech.wav* from the *Tape-Recorded Survey of Hiberno-English Speech – Digital* in Hickey (2004a). In phonology, the English of this individual is heavily influenced by his native Irish. For instance, he has [ʃ] for [s], as in *stir* [ʃtɚː], and [gɛrəls] for *girls*, showing a front vowel, schwa epenthesis and [s] for /z/, all features traceable to Irish.

Like generations of Irish before him, this individual learned the form of English which he was exposed to. Thus his phonology also shows features which have an archaic or regional English origin.

(69) a. Unraised ME <*ea*>
      Twasn't easy [ɛːsi] *to get work.*
   b. Pre-nasal sibilant fortition
      Money wasn't [wɑdn̩t] *plenty.*
   c. Final stress on trisyllabic verbs in *-ate*
      We do cele'brate the 9th of September, the feast of Saint Ciaran.

Non-standard features of grammar also occur. The variety of English he picked up was one in which the Northern Subject Rule (Ihalainen 1994) applied and this explains instances like the following.

(70) a. *Boys goes down there . . .*
   b. *There was bad times, there was . . .*
   c. *All the people back there takes you in.*
   d. *Even the tradesmen that was building the house . . .*
   e. *The young people that's growing up there now.*

Aspectual structures are also to be found, e.g. the habitual with unstressed *do*: *They do go after them.* Less telling non-standard features such as unmarked adverbials are present as well: *'Tis awful dear, 'tis terrible dear.*

Another case, which can serve to illustrate non-standard features of English in an area which until recently was Irish-speaking, is provided by an elderly female interviewed by the author on Cape Clear Island in south-west Co. Cork.

This person showed the following features traceable to English regional input in Ireland.

(71) a. Uninflected *have*
           She *have* no time left for her children.
      b. Non-standard verbal concord
           The *years wasn't* long in passing.
      c. *Ye* as second-person-plural pronoun
           And I asked them, 'Are *ye* going to stay on the island?'
      d. *Them* as demonstrative pronoun
           Them fields are no good for sowing crops.

The above features of her speech occurred alongside other vernacular traits which can be traced to Irish influence as shown in the following.

(72) a. Habitual
           I *do have* a few spuds out in the back, but the land isn't great.
      b. Immediate perfective
           I was *after getting* married, so I thought it was time to come back.
      c. Resultative perfective
           When he *has the boat painted* now, he'll take it down to the cove.

Such cases illustrate the mixture of features in vernacular speech which consists of both transfer from Irish and features of regional and/or archaic English which were taken to Ireland and diffused by English settlers. One of the main aims of the current section is to separate out these strands and identify just what traits of non-standard Irish English stem from which or, indeed, what features can plausibly be linked to both sources.

Data collections, corpus returns and statistics

Data collected for an investigation like the current one must be as representative as possible. This was ensured by choosing informants who were speakers of local forms of English. Furthermore, fairly large amounts of data were collected. When a certain structure appeared in a recording, more recordings were made in order to obtain further attestations of the structure in question. Only then could one be certain that this was typical for the speech of a locality. For instance, deletion of *be* in south-eastern Irish English (see section 4.4.1) was detected early on in the Waterford English Recordings. Subsequently, many more recordings were made to collect attestations at different times and from different speakers.

In the case of recordings not made by the author, those were chosen which were typical of particular areas. This is true for the *Tape-Recorded Survey of Hiberno-English Speech* where a number of tapes were available from various points around Ireland. As a rule of thumb, to report a feature from a recording it had to occur at least three times. For features not recorded in previous studies of Irish English, such as *were to* as past habitual (see section 4.4.1.4.3), twice that number was required. If a feature occurred less than the required amount, this is stated explicitly below.

When dealing with literary records of Irish English, particular care is necessary. Text type is an important consideration. Obviously, drama texts are going to contain more attestations of colloquial features than novels or short stories which, by their very nature, contain much descriptive text. Certain authors represented speech which they came to know as adults. This is true of John Millington Synge in his portrayals of rural speech from the west of Ireland. Furthermore, Synge took much poetic licence in his use of language, though this probably applied more to vocabulary than to grammar. Despite these caveats, literary records can be useful. For instance, the fact that Maria Edgeworth does not have a single instance of habitual *do(es) be*, but William Carleton, Gerald Griffin as well as John and Michael Banim do, is regarded as significant. However, no claims about Irish English are made going on a difference of one or two attestations in the texts of different authors.

In the following sections, statistics are presented based on the returns of computer analyses both of text corpora and of *A Survey of Irish English Usage*. All the returns were assessed explicitly by the author, i.e. statistics which were generated automatically by language processing software[21] were also checked manually to ensure accuracy.

Using statistics involves certain pitfalls and the author has tried to avoid these. For instance, when determining acceptance rates for certain sentences, returns of 100 per cent were achieved in some cases. To treat such returns as of equal value for all counties in Ireland would be a major mistake because the numbers for the counties vary greatly. The survey contains only eight questionnaires from Carlow, indeed only four from Fermanagh (a county without any city). At the other end of the scale, there were 205 questionnaires from Dublin. The significance of a high acceptance rate for counties with few questionnaires is very different from those with a large number. Assume for argument's sake that all survey factors were equal across the entire country, then the probability of four positive returns for a test sentence would have been the same for Fermanagh and Dublin. However, four returns in Fermanagh are 100 per cent but in Dublin are only 1.95 per cent. Of course, survey factors were not the same; if they were, the survey would have been pointless. But this hypothetical case does illustrate the danger of using percentages gained from populations with greatly varying sizes. For this reason, in many of the sections below, only those counties with more than fifteen questionnaires were assessed for the discussion of a particular feature. Furthermore, only large differences were treated as significant. For instance, in Ulster the mean acceptance rate of the sentence *My hair needs washed* was 78 per cent, indeed 95 per cent for the core Ulster Scots counties of Antrim and Down,

---

[21] The software used for all retrieval tasks was *Corpus Presenter*, a software package for examining texts on computers and published as Hickey (2003a). The latest update – version 10 (January 2007) – is available on the author's dedicated website for this software at www.uni–due.de/CP.

but only 1 per cent for the twenty-three counties outside Ulster. Conversely, a major lack of variation was also deemed significant. For example, the fact that fourteen counties across Ireland had over 90 per cent acceptance rate for the test sentence *Are ye going out tonight?* would imply that *ye* is an island-wide feature of Irish English.

4.4.1 THE VERBAL AREA

The area of Irish English which is furthest from standard forms of English is that of verbs. Both the form of verbs and their syntax/semantics show many non-standard features (Filppula 2004a). Below, the formal features are presented first. There then follow discussions of verbal syntax and semantic interpretations of specifically Irish English structures.

Non-standard verb forms

The verbal area shows a great deal of variation in the early modern period, as demonstrated by Lass (1994) and, for Modern English, by Cheshire (1994). The matter is not simply that of the transition from strong to weak verb type, but concerns in particular the form and distribution of strong verb forms. For many verbs in Irish English, alternative past forms are available which are shorter than those found in standard English, e.g. *blemt* [blɛmt] 'blamed' or *lep* [lɛp] 'leaped'.

(73) Non-standard preterites and past participles
  a. *Me back would be broke with the ironing.* (WER, F85+)
  b. *The lad was bet black and blue.* (WER, M55+)
  c. *I gets blemt on it all.* 'I am blamed for everything.' (WER, F55+)
  d. *I saw him lep over the wall.* (WER, F55+)
  e. *A place where cows was kep* [kɛp] *by night.* (MLSI, M80+, Bantry, Co. Cork)
  f. *The crows riz* [rɪz] *up.* (MLSI, M75+, Gurteen, Co. Laois)
  g. *They do be et* [ɛt] *out of their jackets.* (MLSI, M70+, Crookstown, Co. Cork)

Number of verb forms

For colloquial forms of Irish English, throughout the entire island, there is a frequent reduction in the number of verb forms. The most common situation is where the past participle is found for the preterite, though occasionally the reverse is attested; see example (74i). The examples in (74) are from the south-east of Ireland, but instances from other regions can also be found; cf. the discussion of the Owen Letters from north Co. Dublin in Hickey (2005: 164–6).

(74) Past verb forms
  a. *I done it before the kids come home.* (WER, F55+)
  b. *I seen him yesterday morning.* (WER, F55+)
  c. *I've went to mass with the mother.* (WER, M50+)

    d. *She's supposed to have went.* (MLSI, M70+, Tullaroan, Co. Kilkenny)

    e. *Me brother come home last summer for the wedding.* (WER, M50+)

    f. *When John come in, he sat down to the telly.* (WER, F85+)

    g. *She done her leaving, you know, and she done an interview.* (TRS-D, C42-1, F)

    h. *He was took away on the spot.* (WER, M50+)

    i. *I could have took it.* (MLSI, M75+, Gurteen, Co. Laois)

A reduced number of forms is also found with many common verbs in Ulster, both in the eastern part of the province and in the Laggan district, west/southwest of Derry, an area of original Scottish settlement (see (75c)), and in Derry city itself (see (75d)). In this context, note that Sabban (1982: 168–73; 1985: 138f.) has recorded a very similar distribution of past participles for preterites in the contact English of Scotland investigated by her. She also concludes that these usages are not attributable to Gaelic influence (Sabban 1985: 138).

Occasionally, the reduction in the number of verb forms has resulted in the use of a preterite form for a past participle, or indeed for an infinitive. This is found commonly with the verb *go*; see (75d).

(75) Past verb forms in Ulster English

    a. *I was told what I had to do and I done it.* (TRS-D, U41, F)

    b. *And maybe if you had went to the dance . . .* (TRS-D, U18-2, F)

    c. *This lady come and asked me . . .* (TRS-D, U19, F)

    d. *And you'd went to the dance, but that wasn't every night.* (TRS-D, U41, F)

Alongside the reduction in the number of verb forms one also finds the addition of a productive past ending to verbs which do not carry such endings in more standard forms of English; consider the following instances:

(76) a. *He got hurted badly when he was working on that building site.* (WER, M50+)

    b. *I was burned* ['bɚ·nəd] *right up my legs.* (DER, M70+)

Variation with prepositional and direct objects

In the history of English there is attested variation and change in whether a verb takes a direct or a prepositional object. For instance, *scold* occurred with a prepositional object governed by *at* but now it takes a direct object (Hickey 2006a: 162f.). In Irish English similar older usage is found, for example with *happen* which is found with a direct object rather than a prepositional object governed by *to*.

(77) *So that's what happened her after going to England.* (WER, F50+)

This situation is most probably a retention of usage from early input varieties of English.

Uninflected forms of third-person-singular present tense

A widespread feature of eastern and south-eastern Irish English is the lack of inflection on verbs in the third person singular. It has also spread to the south-west and west of the country, probably due to the dissemination of early forms of English from east to west.

Uninflected auxiliary and copula verb forms have been recorded in the west of England for centuries. For instance, William Humphrey Marshall (1745–1818) in his *Rural Economy of Gloucestershire* (1789) has a section entitled 'Provincialisms of the Vale of Gloucester' in which he lists certain features of English there, including uninflected verb forms, i.e. *be* for *is*, *do* for *does* and *have* for *has*. Ihalainen (1994: 226) states that, from his own observations of south-western English, inflection applies to *do* only when it is a full verb. Given that western and south-western British English (Wagner 2005) predominated in early Irish English, this is likely to be a retained feature of this input.

P. W. Joyce (1979 [1910]: 91) also noted this lack of inflection: 'In Waterford and South Wexford people are supposed to use *do* and *have* without inflections for the present. *Has he the old white horse now? He have.*' Joyce quotes a source of his – William Burke, the author of some popular articles on Irish English (Hickey 2002a: 79) – who found the uninflected *have* for the third person singular in the Waterford Bye-Laws (pre-seventeenth century) which would make this a feature from the first period of Irish English.

(78) Uninflected *be, have, do, get*
    a. *I suppose she be lonely on her own too sometimes.* (WER, F45+)
    b. *She've a grand job at the glass.* (WER, F55+)
    c. *Her mother have a car.* (WER, F55+)
    d. *'Tis he have to be the twenty-one.* (WER, M50+)
    e. *L . . . has a new car. Have she?* (WER, F45+)
    f. *Well, she do anyway, whatever about her brother.* (WER, F45+)
    g. *The way the time flies, don't it?* (WER, F55+)
    h. *[Does the bell work? (RH)] It do.* (WER, M50+)
    i. *He do come out on his own now, don't he?* (WER, M50+)
    j. *She get her hair done and all, don't she?* (WER, F45+)
    k. *Well, like, the dry day is the best day, but it don't matter . . .* (TRS-D, M64-1, M)

The lack of inflection on the above verbs has been extended in the south-east to cover a number of other verbs. Varieties in this area also have -*s* on the third person plural in the present tense (see section on verbal concord below).

The preponderance of uninflected verb forms in the east rather than the west was confirmed by *A Survey of Irish English Usage*: the counties along the western seaboard (from north to south: Donegal, Sligo, Mayo, Galway, Clare, Limerick, Kerry, Cork) all showed acceptance values of less than 15 per cent for the sentence *I suppose he have his work done now.*

(79)   Further uninflected lexical verbs
    a. *And if he come home here I can't be going out drinking.* (WER, M55+)
    b. *That's his house until he die.* (WER, M55+)
    c. *He own the place now.* (MLSI, M65+, Crookstown, Co. Cork)
    d. *The pheasant feed on 'em.* (MLSI, M65+, Paulstown, Co. Kilkenny)
    e. *The coulter split the sod.* (MLSI, M75+, Ardattin, Co. Carlow)
    f. *And he carry the milk, don't he?* (WER, M50+)
    g. *Only A . . . comes up and bring me up to mass in the car.* (WER, F85+)
    h. *If a person like a person, well that's it.* (WER, M50+)
    i. *The minute a stranger move into where we are . . .* (SADIF, M60+, Co. Wexford)

Deletion of *be*

Forms of the verb *be*, not just in the function as a copula, are variably deleted in south-eastern Irish English. Among varieties of English, this feature is definitely unusual and has the most noticeable parallel in African American English. In the latter, the absence of a copula in equative sentences is a salient feature (see Kautzsch 2002: 89–155; Cukor-Avila 1999; Rickford 1998; Weldon 2003 for detailed discussions). Generally, it is assumed that superstrate input from the British Isles did not have such copula deletion.[22] However, this may not be true or, more so, may not have been true historically. For instance, Tagliamonte and Smith (2002: 263) noticed cases of *be* deletion after existential *there* (in their material from Ulster and south-east Scotland) but did not follow up the issue, given the context of their study (negative contraction). The evidence presented in (80) for south-eastern Irish English paints a picture of a much more widespread deletion of *be*, in various syntactic functions. This may well have been much more common in Ireland in previous centuries and so could have been transported to the New World by Irish immigrants.

(80)   Deletion of *be*
    a. *When I Ø [is] gettin' in the car, I do be kind of a bit shaky on my feet.* (WER, F85+)
    b. *She Ø [is] not too far up the road.* (WER, F55+)
    c. *She Ø [is] never lonely, there Ø [is] always someone there.* (WER, F45+)
    d. *She Ø [was] not able to get up or down.* (WER, F55+)
    e. *And J . . . 's doing a great job, yeah, he Ø [is] great now.* (WER, F80+)
    f. *She Ø [was] lonely after the husband, I suppose.* (WER, F55+)
    g. *She Ø [is] only lucky 'twasn't much worse.* (WER, M50+)
    h. *But how as ever, they Ø [is] all big now.* (WER, M50+)
    i. *What happened then was there Ø [was] a chap here in Rice Park.* (WER, M50+)

---

[22] Irish also has verbless sentences, but only in copular constructions, e.g. *Sin scéal eile* [that story other], *Seán an fear is tanaí* [John the man most thin].

j. *Some say, they* Ø [were] *after buying the ground.* (WER, M55+)
k. *So what they do* Ø [is], *they come up to me on a Saturday.* (WER, F85+)
l. *She* Ø [is] *lucky to have J . . . to look after her.* (WER, F55+)
m. *Where* Ø [is] *M . . . working now?* (WCER, M75+)
n. *Another woman, what* Ø [is] *her name?* (WER, F80+)
o. *I don't know what he* Ø [is] *going to do.* (WER, F55+)
p. *I* Ø [am] *not saying they're doing great, but they're okay.* (WER, F85+)
q. *She* Ø [is] *looking well, isn't she?* (WER, M50+)

The deletion applies above all to the third person, though isolated instances are found for other persons (see above examples). Furthermore, in some instances the context implied that it was the past form of *be* which remained unrealised (see forms in square brackets in (80)). The final sentence (80q) can be taken as particularly clear evidence for *be* deletion as the reverse polarity tag at the end echoes the unrealised verb form.

Attestations such as those above would demand that statements to the effect that copula deletion does not occur in British dialects (Rickford 1998: 187) be revised. It is true that frequency and conditioning may not be the same in each variety which has such deletion, but it shows that British dialect input cannot be rejected out of hand when considering copula deletion, especially in African American English.

Sentence (80k) is especially relevant in this context as writers on African American English have maintained that copula deletion in clause- and sentence-final positions is not possible. Green (2002: 184), in her discussion of language in the novel *Jonah's Gourd Vine* (1934) by the American writer and folklorist Zora Neale Hurston (1901–60), points to the sentence *How come dat?* and considers whether sentence-final deletion was previously possible in African American English, assuming a correct representation of black speech by the author. There is hardly a universal restriction on this, as the Irish English examples in (80) show. But what may have happened is that a restriction arose which did not apply to earlier forms of African American English.

In south-eastern Irish English the fact that *-s* is missing on many common verbs in the third person singular may have supported the deletion of *be*.

Be as auxiliary

With intransitive verbs, especially those indicating states and their opposites, i.e. motion and change, *be* is used as an auxiliary as was previously the case in English and as is still the case in German, for instance. This feature can be regarded as a retention from earlier English input (see Filppula's discussion of '*be* perfects', Filppula 1999: 90, 116–22). However, the use of *tá* 'is' in Irish to form compound tenses may have also provided support (the Irish translation of sentence (81c) would be approximately: *Tá siad críochnaithe leis na deisithe anois* [is they finished with the repairs now]).

Table 4.10. *Highest acceptance figures (over 50 per cent) in* A Survey of Irish English Usage *for the test sentence* Amn't I leaving soon anyway?

County	Score	N	Total	County	Score	N	Total
Clare	63%	10	16	Limerick	54%	14	26
Roscommon	62%	8	13	Antrim	51%	21	41
Galway	61%	33	54	Donegal	50%	21	42
Mayo	57%	21	37	Louth	50%	16	32

(81)   *Be* as auxiliary
    a. *The amusements <u>are gone</u> quite expensive.* (TRS-D, M42, M)
    b. *They're certainly <u>changed</u> for the better.* (TRS-D, U39, M)
    c. *They're <u>finished</u> with the repairs now.* (DER, M70+)

The acceptance ratings for *be* as auxiliary were very high in *A Survey of Irish English Usage*. The mean for the sentence *They're finished the work now* was over 85 per cent with counties as far apart as Derry, Kerry, Offaly and Monaghan.

Verb contractions

The contractions of forms of *be* and *not* vary greatly among varieties of English, especially for the first and third person singular. Noticeable in Irish English is the common contraction of *am not* to *amn't* ['æmˀnt] (also found in Scotland, Miller 2004: 51). Some contractions, such as *ain't*, do not appear to occur at all. The form *are* can have *not* cliticised onto it, irrespective of where this occurs, i.e. in the second person (*you aren't*) and the first and third person plural (*we/they aren't*) or after *there*.

    The contracted form of *will* and *not* for the future is *won't*. Contractions of pronoun + *will* followed by *not*, e.g. *I'll not help you any more*, used to be common and were found in Irish English up to the beginning of the twentieth century, going on attestations in the plays of Sean O'Casey.

(82)   Contractions of *be* and *not*
    a. *[Are you watching the match tomorrow? (RH)]. I <u>amn't</u>, no.* (WER, M50+)
    b. *And I'll tell you this much, I <u>amn't</u> interested in no loan from them.* (DER, M70+)
    c. *I <u>won't</u> go there no matter what the lads says.* (DER, M35+)
    d. *They <u>aren't</u> doing all they could for us.* (WER, F85+)
    e. *There <u>aren't</u> any houses left now with the turf fire.* (WER, F85+)

Variation in acceptability is found across the country. That for *aren't* appears to be greater in the north (the scores in *A Survey of Irish English Usage* were over 50 per cent for Antrim, Belfast and Down). The results for *amn't* showed a southern bias (see table 4.10).

Use of *shall* and *will*

For at least two centuries it has been observed (Tieken-Boon van Ostade 1985: 129f.) that the Irish avoid the use of *shall* when forming the future tense. Noah Webster in his *Dissertations on the English Language* notes (1789: 236f.) that the Irish and the Scots 'generally use *will* for *shall* in the first person; by which means they substitute a *promise* for an intended *prediction*'. Peter Walkdenn Fogg in his *Elementa Anglicana* also notes (1792: 129) that 'our fellow citizens of North-Britain and Ireland, find much difficulty in these auxiliaries'. The difficulties with *shall* and *will* were also recognised by native writers; see Joyce (1979 [1910]: 74f.).

For present-day varieties *shall* virtually does not exist. The full form of a future auxiliary is *will* and this is only used for emphasis. In all other cases, the future is formed by suffixing the clitic *'ll* [-l]: *I'll* [aɪl] *drop in after work. I 'will ring you when I arrive.*

Overuse of the conditional

Part of the stereotype of (southern) Irish English is the overuse of the conditional. This may well have to do with its high occurrence among native speakers of Irish and people in regions where Irish was spoken in the not too distant past, e.g. *If he would be inside* 'if he were inside' (MLSI, M80+, Bantry, Co. Cork). This may also help to explain its avoidance by many speakers today. Nonetheless, there are many attestations of the conditional in the data collections where one might expect an indicative tense: *You'd* [you would] *have to think about the day you'd* [you would] *have* (i.e. '. . .what day it is') (WER, M50+). There are also instances with the conditional where one would expect 'yes' or 'no': [*Do you have any matches?* (RH)] *I would* (RL, F55+).

4.4.1.1 *Verbal concord*

The issue of inflectional *-s* in present-tense verb paradigms has been the topic of much research in recent years (Schendl 1996). A number of factors determine the appearance of this *-s* and much of the effort of scholars has gone into determining the precise nature of these factors for individual varieties. The rules governing verbal concord tend to be variable rather than categorical, a fact which makes it difficult to be accurate in describing the conditions for its occurrence. Scholars, such as Montgomery (1989), have generally recognised two constraints, *Type of Subject* and *Proximity to Subject*. In essence, the claim is that verbal *-s* is disfavoured by an immediately preceding personal pronoun but that other types of subject can (but must not always) trigger verbal *-s* across the verbal paradigm for the present tense. In addition, the distance between subject and verb form is taken to be relevant, at least in some cases. Varieties vary according to the person and number which typically show verbal *-s*. For instance, in southern Irish English there is a strong tendency for this to appear in the third person plural (see examples in (83) below). The weight of the subject (pronoun, noun, noun phrase) and the distance between subject and verb in a sentence also influence the occurrence of verbal -s across varieties (see Hickey 2004d: 48f. for more details).

Filppula (1999: 150–9) discusses the agreement between subject and verb in the present tense and is careful to distinguish the north from the south of Ireland, pointing out that the north would have inherited the distribution of verbal concord which is known from northern Middle English and Middle Scots (Mustanoja 1960). Scholars who have concerned themselves with the origin of non-standard verbal -s trace it to the early English change (in Northumbrian) from -eð/-að/-iað to a generalised -es (Pietsch 2005b: 173). Pietsch rejects the suggestion by Klemola (2000) that the rule resulted from contact with Brythonic Celtic. Klemola assumes that the concord system of Welsh with 'non-agreement with full NP subjects but agreement with accompanying personal pronouns' was transferred to English dialects in the north of England where forms of P-Celtic, related to present-day Welsh, were spoken. Pietsch, for his part, points out that the non-standard occurrences of verbal -s, i.e. outside the third person singular, are not innovations but retentions. The use of verbal -s on the plural was a genuine reflex of the original agreement marker (northern OE plural -að > -as > -s), just as the third person singular was a reflex of northern OE -eð > -es > s. He thus sees the spread of the suffixless forms, in the environment with adjacent pronoun subjects, as the main innovation. This he views (Pietsch 2005b: 174) as part of a general Germanic drift towards analytic structures with the loss of suffixes. He also considers the view, proposed by Börjars and Chapman (1998), that the lack of inflection with pronoun subjects is a kind of redundancy avoidance or 'anti-agreement' (a term used by Roberts 1997: 109).

The traditional label 'Northern Subject Rule' implies that in provenance, if not in present-day distribution, this feature is predominantly characteristic of the north of England. But recent studies, e.g. Godfrey and Tagliamonte (1999), have demonstrated clearly that non-standard verbal -s is a conservative feature of southern dialect regions in Britain (in this case of Devon). The south-west of Britain is particularly relevant in the Irish context as it provided a major input to Ireland during the early centuries of English settlement. The conclusion from this consideration is that the occurrence of non-standard verbal -s in southern Irish English does not imply an influence spreading from the north but rather that this was a feature of early input varieties to the east and south-east which were then generalised to the whole of the south, most likely by the spread of earlier eastern varieties to other parts of the country, especially the south-west and west.

Attestations of non-standard verbal -s in Irish English from previous centuries confirm the present-day distribution. The Mahon Letters from the mid eighteenth century (Hickey 2005: 160–2) have many instances: *The same day your wines was sent you by the carman* . . . (Chris Harrison); *such papers as is necessary for securing you and your heirs* . . . (Cecily Byrne). Later documents also show these patterns, e.g. the plays of Sean O'Casey (portraying early twentieth-century local Dublin English). It may be that the frequency of formally marked plurals followed by a verb with non-standard -s is in part due to a priming effect (Loebell and Bock 2003) where the occurrence of -s on a noun favours the occurrence of -s on a following verb (in non-prescriptive language usage).

Robinson (1997: 125–7) discusses it in the Ulster Scots context and confirms the frequency of verbal -s with the third person plural under similar conditions as apply to other varieties with non-standard verbal concord. For more discussion of this feature in southern Irish English in general, see McCafferty (2004b).

In the following, examples of non-standard verbal concord from throughout Ireland are listed, showing that from Ulster down to the south-east and across to the west the phenomenon is well attested. Note that speaker TRS-D, U18-2, F is from the Laggan area of Co. Donegal which was an area of Scots settlement. Speaker TRS-D, U19, F is from Derry city which experienced Scots settlement in the early seventeenth century. For details on the situation in Belfast, see A. Henry (1995); for information on English in South Armagh, see Corrigan (1997a).

(83) Verbal concord
  1. Single noun subject
     a. *But Ray, the years flies, don't they?* (WER, F85+)
     b. *The shops has changed hands several times, you see.* (TRS-D, M19, M)
     c. *Although the times is good now* . . . (TRS-D, M19, M)
     d. *Funerals is a big thing for travelling people.* (SADIF, M60+, Co. Wicklow)
     e. *The clothes was the same, you'd get your jumpers* . . . (TRS-D, L4-1, F)
     f. *. . . the full-timers gets the potatoes and the vegetables* . . . (TRS-D, U19, F)
     g. *The Maloneys was always playing music.* (TRS-D, M7, M)
  2. Noun phrase subject
     a. *Lots of the girls works, goes into Letterkenny to work.* (TRS-D, U18-2, F)
     b. *Some of them works in Oatfield in the sweet factory.* (TRS-D, U18-2, F)
     c. *A few of them goes to England, but very little.* (TRS-D, U18-2, F)
     d. *There's not many of the girls goes away either.* (TRS-D, U18-2, F)
     e. *Me other sisters goes up in the night to her.* (WER, F55+)
     f. *The women in our street has their children all reared.* (WER, F85+)
     g. *Me worrying days about me figure is over.* (WER, F80+)
     h. *As I rite this there has being another fire where seven girls and a boy is Burned . . . when the Alarm was given the most of them is Disabled in trying to escape.* (IEL, New York, 1872)
  3. Deleted coreferential subject in second verb phrase
     After I do me work, I go out and rickles me turf. (TRS-D, U41, F)

4. Third-person-plural pronoun
   a. *And they calls them small, sure what can you do?* (WER, F45+)
   b. *I think they haves them all painted now.* (WER, F55+)
   c. *They owns here and they own the back of it.* (WER, F55+)
5. Series of verbs
   a. *People keeps and sells them.* (MLSI, M70+, Templemore, Co. Tipperary)
   b. *Glory be to God, that's when children grows up and leaves home and goes off.* (WER, F85+)
6. In relative clauses
   a. *The most of them are all living out that was at school.* (TRS-D, U39, M)
   b. *There're big people now that has a lot of money.* (TRS-D, C41, M)
   c. *Lodgers that comes around, that goes out fishing . . .* (TRS-D, C41, M)

Verbal -*s* is very rare in the first and second person plural because the pronouns, which are used here, tend to block verbal -*s* anyway. Among the pronouns, it is mostly the third person plural which allows non-standard marking, but even here it is not anything like as common as with non-pronominal subjects. The rarity of verbal -*s* on the first person may well have had an influence on its development as an habitual: *I gets up early in the morning* (WER, M50+), *We goes to bingo every second Saturday of the month* (WER, F85+). It is not possible to determine here which feature came first, i.e. the historical situation may have been the reverse: habitual -*s* in the first person singular may have blocked the use of -*s* as a verbal concord marker.

The use of habitual -*s* in south-eastern Irish English can be of interest when considering other varieties of English. For instance, it could throw light on the occurrence of non-standard verbal -*s* in habitual contexts in early African American English (Poplack and Tagliamonte 2004: 206–8) and Liberian Settler English (Singler 1997). It could also have a bearing on discussions in the relevant literature about whether this is a trace of a previous creole stage for the varieties mentioned.

In *A Survey of Irish English Usage* three sentences were included to test acceptance levels for non-standard verbal concord. The first contained a plural nominal subject, the second a compound nominal subject and the third showed existential *there* with a plural reference (see table 4.11).

4.4.1.1.1   Forms of *be*

Non-standard patterns in the paradigms for *be* are found throughout the anglo-phone world from cases of extreme isolation (Schreier 2003: 111–42) to those of contact with realignment in core areas of England (Britain 2002). Ireland is no exception in this respect with the major varieties of English on the island showing distinctive patterning of *be*. Usage here is variable, not categorical, and it varies

Table 4.11. *Acceptance figures for non-standard verbal concord in* A Survey of Irish English Usage

---

1. *Some farmers has little or no cattle.*
   Mean acceptance rate: 16%. Belfast and the Ulster counties Antrim,
   Donegal, Derry and Louth (in north Leinster) showed rates of over 30%.

2. *John and his wife plays bingo at the weekend.*
   Mean acceptance rate: 39%. This is probably due to the fact that there is a
   single noun immediately before the inflected verb (despite the fact that it is
   a compound subject).

3. *There was two men on the road.*
   Mean acceptance rate: 51%. The much higher acceptance rates confirm the
   widespread use of *there* with a singular verb form.

---

between parts of Ireland.[23] For example, the patterning in Ulster is somewhat different from that in the south-east. In the latter area three patterns are attested as shown in (84).

(84) Options for *be* in the first person plural (south-eastern Irish English)
   a. Non-standard inflected *be*
       We's up to our eyes in work. (WER, F50+)
   b. Standard inflected *be*
       We're not fond of the Euro 'cause it pushed up all the prices. (WER, M55+)
   c. Invariant *be*
       We be there for the 11.20 bus, I'm telling you. (WER, F50+)

(84c) shows an habitual usage where one might expect to have *do* between *we* and *be*. This may have been deleted but it is more likely that this is the invariant *be* which is common in both the south-east and the north of Ireland, e.g. *I be grumpy myself at times* (WER, F85+), *Even when you be young, you wouldn't think of asking him* (WER, F85+); *I be there every day* (MLSI, M50, Bellaghy, Co. Derry), *People don't know who they be half the time* (MLSI, M75+, Drumlee, Co. Tyrone). There is a long tradition of this invariant *be* in Irish English, especially in generic/stative contents (see instances in (132) below), so that the usage here may represent an extension to habitual contexts.

Regularisation of *be* paradigms

In recent literature on English dialects (Tagliamonte and Smith 1998: 152f.) there has been much discussion of non-standard forms of *be*. This concerns the regularisation of these forms, especially in the past. Anderwald (2001) in

---

[23] The variation in the present tense is between *is* and *are*. Despite the occurrence of *am* and *amn't* in Irish English, neither of these forms is extended beyond the first person singular.

her study of *was/were* variation recognises three generalisation strategies: (i) *was*-generalisation, (ii) *were*-generalisation and (iii) a mixed type in which the standard number distinction has been replaced by a distinction according to clause polarity (see Schilling-Estes and Wolfram 1994 for data from dialect English in the Outer Banks, North Carolina). Such regularisation can be absolute or context-dependent. The latter applies particularly to the environment after existential *there* where patterning may be found which is independent of verbal *-s* in other contexts (see previous section).

In Irish English regularisation to *was* has been the dominant pattern with *was* extending into the plural, especially for the third person in east coast dialects, irrespective of the type of noun phrase governing the verb in question, e.g. *Sure they was only trying to help, that's all* (DER, M60+). This pattern is attested in the textual record for Dublin English as well, e.g. . . . *and they was doing Him a good turn* (Behan, *The Quare Fellow*, 1954); . . .*that they wasn't a mile from where he was livin'* (Sean O'Casey, *The Shadow of a Gunman*, 1923); *D'ye mean to tell me that the pair of yous wasn't collogin' together here* (Sean O'Casey, *Juno and the Paycock*, 1924).

Verb forms after *there*

Table 4.11 shows a mean acceptance rate of 51 per cent for *was* after *there* with plural reference (for the sentence *There was two men on the road*), reflecting a widespread usage across Ireland. A greater acceptance of the usage was apparent in the north: the ten counties with a rate of over 60 per cent were all in the north of Ireland, with the exception of Wexford which had 62 per cent. The six counties with values below 40 per cent were all in the south. The usage is already attested at the beginning of the nineteenth century in the prose of the northern writer William Carleton, e.g. . . . *and indeed there was them that could have seen me . . .*; *Sure there was three ships of it lost last week* (*Ned M'Keown*).

The somewhat higher acceptance rates of regularised *was* after *there* in the east and north along with the general prominence of *was* in plural contexts on the east coast may not be coincidental. The north and the east are regions where English settlement is oldest (east) and/or most extensive (north). This would suggest that this regularisation was a feature of English input to the east (the oldest in Ireland) and in the north, frequently with a Scottish provenance. The south-west and west of the country, on the other hand, is that part which was Irish-speaking longest. This area was exposed to varieties of English at a later date and these may have shown a degree of supraregionalisation with the distribution of *is/are*, *was/were* as in standard English. If the results of *A Survey of Irish English Usage* are a true reflection of language use throughout the country, then the difference between the north/east/south-east and the south/south-west is perceptible but not major by any means.

The data collections of the author confirm a broad acceptance of singular *was* and *is* after *there* both north and south. What is unclear is whether there is a significant levelling of *was/were* variation according to clause polarity. It is true that *was* in positive clauses is very widespread, but the distribution of *was/were* in negative clauses is uneven. Only one speaker had anything like a truly regularised system, an individual from the Laggan in north-east Donegal (TRS-D, U18-2, F), a region of original Scots settlement.

(85) Regularisation of inflected *be* after existential *there*
  1. *Is* (positive and negative) with plural reference (north and south)
     a. *Well there's lots of farmers around here, but then there's lots works in factories.* (TRS-D, U18-2, F)
     b. *Well, there's lots of them works around here in the bacon factory.* (WER, M50+)
     c. *There's different names on them now.* (TRS-D, U72–2, M)
     d. *There's not much girls around where I live anyhow.* (TRS-D, C41, M)
     e. *There's not many people with that kind of money here.* (WER, M50+)
     f. *There's lumps grows on the neck.* (MLSI, M65, Cootehill, Co. Cavan)
     g. *There's people addicted to them.* (MLSI, M77, Adamstown, Co. Wexford)
     h. *Their is* [sic!] *lots of big sheep farms here.* (IEL, New Zealand)
  2. *Was* (positive and negative) with plural reference in non-northern varieties
     a. *There was bad times, there was.* (TRS-D, C41, M)
     b. *You see, and there was buses going down that road all the time.* (WER, F50+)
     c. *There was three acres of hay.* (MLSI, M78, Ballyneety, Co. Limerick)
     d. *There was forks in it for the gentry and knives.* (MLSI, M70, Crisheen, Co. Clare)
        Sure there wasn't any cheap flights then. (DER, M60+)
  3. *Were* (positive and negative) with singular reference in northern varieties
     a. *There weren't very much for girls working then.* (TRS-D, U18-2, F)
     b. *There were no compulsion on you to learn Irish.* (TRS-D, U18-2, F)
     c. *And there were a dance hall in this village.* (TRS-D, U18-2, F)
     d. *There were a man the name of . . .* (TRS D, U72–2, M)

Discussion of *was/were* variation in the literature has centred around the question of clause polarity (Anderwald 2001; Schilling-Estes and Wolfram 1994). But Irish English, in the south-east at least, shows a preference for plural forms in two specific and related contexts which render *is/are*, *was/were* variation more predictable as shown in the following.

(86) Preference for *r*-forms – *are/were* – in south-eastern Irish English
1. Echo forms
   a. [*There's something on tonight about him, a documentary, I think.*(RH)]
   b. *You're right, there are.* (WER, F55+)
   c. [*Keeping up with the Joneses. There's an awful lot of that these days.* (RH)]
   d. *Oh God, there are!* (WER, F55+)
2. Negative tags
   a. *I was right not to go along with that carry on, weren't I?* (WER, F50+)
   b. *I was supposed to slice it up before serving, weren't I?* (WER, F55+)

4.4.1.2   Infinitives

The appearance of *for to* as a marker of the infinitive is dated by scholars to the Middle English period (see the review of literature in Corrigan 2003a: 321f.). However, it declined shortly afterwards in the south of England but was retained in the north and is still found there in traditional dialects (see Beal 1993: 200 on Tyneside and Shorrocks 1999: 248 on Lancashire). Important for the interpretation of later occurrences is that *for to* infinitives lost their connotation of purpose, so that *for* in *for to* did not then have to be understood prepositionally. In non-purposive clauses it came to be reinterpreted as a compound infinitival marker (Corrigan 2003a: 329). In the early modern period, examples can be found of both purposive and non-purposive uses of *for to*, as can be seen from the following.

(87) *For to*-infinitives in Early Modern English
1. Purposive
   a. *Then from that day foorth, they tooke counsell together for to put him to death.* (King James' Bible, 1611)
   b. *... he wente to Oxford for to get more lerninge.* (Simon Forman, *The Autobiography and Personal Diary ... from 1552 to 1602*)
   c. *And for to shewe my thankfulnesse to Master (^William Arnet^) and his wife.* (John Taylor, *The Pennyless Pilgrimage*, 1630)
2. Non-purposive
   a. *... thynkynge ther for to have had some reste* (*The Autobiography of Thomas Mowntayne*, c. 1555)
   b. *men and women for to have [seen] the execussyon of the duke of Northumberland* (*The Diary of Henry Machyn ... 1550 to 1563*)
   c. *That ys for to sey ther Chirche or Chapell.* (Richard Torkington, *The Oldest Diarie of Englysshe Travell*, 1517)

In Irish English non-standard infinitive complements have a long history. Studies in a retentionist vein, e.g. Harris (1993), point to the precursors in archaic forms of English. This would include medieval varieties in Ireland (though Harris does not mention these). The following examples are from the poem *Pride of*

Life, the manuscript of which dates from the early fifteenth century (Dolan 1991: 146).

(88)   Non-purposive *for to*-infinitives in medieval Irish English
   a. *He dredith no deth for to deye.* 'He dreaded no death for to die.'
   b. *Fonde his werkis for to wirch.* 'Eager his works for to do.'
   c. *þat ge haue for to done.* 'That ye have for to do.'
   d. *My banis for to crye By dayis and bi nigte.* 'My bones for to cry by day and by night.' (*Pride of Life*, early fifteenth century)

But if varieties of English within Ireland, and those brought there by later settlers, were the source of *for to*-infinitives in Irish English, then one would expect it to occur as a compound infinitival marker, i.e. without the suggestion of purpose. However, later attestations in Irish English, e.g. in nineteenth-century emigrant letters, can be interpreted as indicating purpose, i.e. *I will arrive for to emigrate* can be viewed as parallel to *I will arrive for my ticket*, so that the sentence can be analysed as [*I will arrive for* (PREP)] + [*to* (INFINITIVAL MARKER) *emigrate*] rather than as [*I will arrive*] + [*for to* (INFINITIVAL MARKER) *emigrate*].

(89)   *For to*-infinitives in emigrant letters
   a. *Dear frind Mr Charles Grimshaw and Co. of you Place let me know the serten [sirten?] day in July I will arive in Livirpool for to emigrate to America.* (IEL, 1864, Co. Donegal)
   b. *I hope if you Place you wont Dispoint me without writing to me and for to let me know the Sirten day in July next that meself and my Children will get Bearth for to Emigrate to America.* (IEL, 1864, Co. Donegal)
   c. *and for to let me know the sixteen day in July next that meself and my children will get bearth for to emigrate to America.* (IEL, Patrick Lavelle 1864 – location unknown)

To distinguish uses where *for to* in Irish English suggests purpose, A. Henry (1992), in her discussion of the structure in Belfast English, introduced the distinction between 'strong' instances where purpose is not suggested and 'weak' instances where this is the case, i.e. where *for to* is semantically equivalent to *in order to*. This distinction is useful when examining attestations either from native speakers of Irish or from speakers in areas which were Irish-speaking up to the modern period, such as the Ross Lake region of north Galway where the author collected data. These attestations are all of the 'weak' type, at least suggesting that *for to* received support from Irish where *chun* 'in order to' appears before a non-finite verb form, as an equivalent of the English infinitival clause.

(90)   *Cheannaigh sé adhmad chun bord a dhéanamh.*
   [bought he wood in-order-to table COMP make-VN]
   'He bought wood to make a table.'

Of course, the vernacular forms of English which Irish speakers were exposed to provided the formal means of constructing a clause of purpose in English, i.e. *for to* + infinitive. But the semantic interpretation is one which is congruent with that of the *chun* clause in Irish. It may also be that speakers during language shift were confronted with varieties of English of the 'weak' types, i.e. in which *for to* + infinitive was only used to express purpose. In this case the structure in the language shift variety would be the result of convergence.

(91)   *For to*-infinitives
    1. 'Weak' instances, purposive
        a. *You had to make the metal casting for to make the part of the plough* . . . (TRS-D, M19, M)
        b. *Well, A . . . needed a new car for to do the rounds in the new job, you know.* (WER, M50+)
        c. *You had to put down your money for to go to be learning to be a nurse.* (TRS-D, U41, F)
        d. *'Nois, caithfidh tú dul go dtí an Daingean* [a-a-a] *for to* buy the supplies. (CCE-W, M70+)
        [now, must you go to Dingle . . .]
        e. *It had to be coal for to melt down the metal. He'd go and do a journey for to see him.* (SADIF, M60+, Co. Wicklow)
    2. 'Strong' instances, non-purposive
        a. *'Twould hardly pay me now for to do any casting.* (TRS-D, M19, M)
        b. *They'll always ask a neighbour for to stay there.* (TRS-D, M42, M)
        c. *Maybe I had something new for to tell you.* (TRS-D, U18-2, F)

The distribution of *for to*-infinitives across Ireland is difficult to determine exactly. In *A Survey of Irish English Usage* more than 30 per cent (the mean) of the respondents for the counties of the west (south and north), i.e. Cork, Kerry, Clare, Galway, Mayo, Sligo and Donegal, assessed the sentence *He went to Dublin for to buy a car* (a 'weak' purposive type sentence) as constituting 'no problem' or being just 'a bit strange' (see table 4.12). But the same was also true along the east coast, with the counties of Kilkenny and Kildare, among the first to be settled by English, scoring 40 per cent and more. The highest score was in fact for Belfast with 72 per cent (23 of 32 respondents) while Antrim, the county in which the city is located, scored 61 per cent (25 of 41 respondents). Co. Down just south of Belfast had a score of 55 per cent (21 of 38 respondents) while Armagh scored 63 per cent (12 of 19 respondents). It may also be significant that Galway and Mayo, two counties which were Irish-speaking longest, had the lowest score and that Kerry, also a county with Irish-speaking districts, scored below 30 per cent.

    The question of an east–west distribution in the south is somewhat inconclusive, with the east (see values for Leinster counties in table 4.12) scoring as high if not higher than the south-west and west (see values for Munster and Connaught counties in table 4.12). But it is the north-east of Ireland which has by far the

Table 4.12. *Acceptance figures in* A Survey of Irish English Usage *for the test sentence* He went to Dublin for to buy a car

Ulster	Score	N	Total	Leinster	Score	N	Total
Armagh	63%	12	19	Kilkenny	42%	10	24
Antrim	61%	25	41	Kildare	40%	10	25
Belfast	72%	23	32	Louth	50%	16	32
Down	55%	21	38	Dublin	29%	60	205
Derry	44%	8	18	Wexford	31%	9	29
Donegal	45%	19	42				

Munster	Score	N	Total	Connaught	Score	N	Total
Cork	37%	31	84	Galway	22%	12	54
Kerry	29%	7	24	Mayo	22%	8	27
Limerick	42%	11	26	Sligo	41%	9	22
Clare	38%	6	16				
Waterford	24%	12	51				

highest scores. In fact, the figures drop off below 50 per cent in west Ulster (see Derry and Donegal in table 4.12).

If *for to*-infinitives (even in their weak purposive form) were originally, and still are, a feature of northern dialects of Britain, then this is confirmed by the above distribution: the counties of the north-east of Ulster are those in Ireland which had the highest input of northern British settlers. The relatively high scores along the east may well be due to the presence of *for to*-infinitives in very early forms of Irish English in the east.

The low scores for counties which were Irish-speaking longest would suggest that although the equivalence of *chun* 'in order to' = *for to* may have been valid for speakers during language shift, it is English in the north and east which has maintained this feature to the highest degree.

Unmarked infinitives

The mirror image, so to speak, of the situation with *for to* is where the infinitive does not take any marker preceding it. This usage is known from modal verbs which are not followed by *to* before an infinitive, e.g. *She can speak well.* In southern Irish English, the infinitive marker *to* before other verbs is sometimes dropped, e.g. with *help, allow, come.*

(92)   Lack of *to* with certain verbs
   a. *M . . . helped him wash the car after all.* (DER, M35+)
   b. *She was allowed keep the bonus although she left the job.* (WER, M50+)
   c. *They used take the barrels on the lorries themselves.* (WER, M50+)
   d. *He decided to come see the mother that winter.* (RL, M55+)

Table 4.13. *Acceptance figures in* A Survey of Irish English Usage *for the test sentence* She allowed him drive the car

Low scores (all below 45%)

County	Score	N	Total	County	Score	N	Total
Derry	44%	8	18	Down	42%	16	38
Tyrone	43%	3	7	Antrim	34%	14	41
Armagh	42%	8	19	Donegal	29%	12	42

Highest scores (all above 60%)

County	Score	N	Total	County	Score	N	Total
Limerick	92%	24	26	Laois	73%	8	11
Carlow	88%	7	8	Louth	69%	22	32
Cork	79%	66	84	Sligo	68%	15	22
Tipperary	76%	32	42	Kilkenny	67%	16	24
Kerry	75%	18	24	Clare	63%	10	16
Waterford	75%	38	51	Galway	61%	33	54

Bare infinitives show a clear geographical distribution in Ireland. In *A Survey of Irish English Usage* the seven most northerly counties showed low acceptance rates as can be seen from the values for *allow* without *to* (see table 4.13).

Past participle as verbal complement

An even clearer geographical spread could be seen in the use of a past participle as verbal complement after *need*. This feature is of uniquely Ulster provenance, a fact confirmed by the mean of 95 per cent for the six counties of northern Ireland which it showed in *A Survey of Irish English Usage* with the test sentence *My hair needs washed*. By sharp contrast, the mean was only 3 per cent for the counties of the southern provinces of Leinster, Munster and Connaught. Donegal, as so often a bridge between the counties of central and east Ulster and the rest of Ireland to the south, had an acceptance rate of 62 per cent.

Infinitival complements

A remnant of transfer from Irish can be seen in a certain type of infinitival complement found recessively with elderly rural speakers, e.g. *You'd say you're sorry they to be sick* [Irish: . . . *iad a bheith tinn* 'they to be sick'] (MLSI, M65+, Boherlahan, Co. Tipperary); *'Tis a poor thing anything to be wrong with you* [Irish: . . . *rud a bheith mícheart leat* 'something to be not-right with-you'] (MLSI, M85+, Clonmacnoise, Co. Offaly). This type of complement was previously dubbed the 'Kiltartan infinitive'; see discussion of sample sentence in (68) above.

Table 4.14. *Acceptance figures from Ulster counties in* A Survey of Irish English Usage *for the test sentence* He might could come after all

County	Score	N	Total	County	Score	N	Total
Belfast	13%	4	32	Donegal	7%	3	42
Armagh	11%	2	19	Derry	6%	1	18
Antrim	10%	4	41	Cavan	6%	1	17
Down	8%	3	38				

4.4.1.3   Modals

Double modals

The use of two modals within a verb phrase, especially the sequence *might could*, is regarded as a Scottish and northern English feature and so could be expected in Ulster Scots in the north of Ireland. There was no instance of this, or any other combination of modals, in any of the recordings made by the author in the south of Ireland. In *A Survey of Irish English Usage* the following test sentence was included: *He might could come after all.* The mean acceptance was 7 per cent with a distinctive bias towards the north where double-digit figures were reached (see table 4.14). Nonetheless, double modals cannot be regarded as a productive feature of northern varieties of Irish English today.

Perfective use of *can*

Standard varieties of English use *can* in the present tense to indicate ability or possibility and make use of the phrase *be able to* in order to express similar options in the past, e.g. *He can get a loan if he wants to* versus *He wasn't able to get a loan for years.* Varieties of Irish English often show a use of *cannot* with past reference, a feature which is paralleled by similar usage in Tyneside English (Beal 2004b).

(93)   *A . . . cannot get a loan from the corporation for more than six year now.* (WER, F85+)

Epistemic negative *must*

In standard forms of English, epistemic *must* is negated by using *can't / cannot*, e.g. *He can't be from France if he doesn't speak French.* A prominent feature of Irish English, which it incidentally shares with forms of Scottish English, is the use of epistemic *must* in the negative. In *A Survey of Irish English Usage* the test sentence *He was born here so he mustn't be Scottish* was included to test the acceptance of negative epistemic *must.* There were twenty-four counties with over fifteen responses. The mean was 70 per cent with Kerry having the highest value of 83 per cent. Core Ulster Scots counties Down and Antrim both had values of over 70 per cent, viz. 74 per cent and 76 per cent respectively, which supports the contention that this is a feature shared with Scottish English.

4.4.1.4   Tense and aspect

The area of tense and aspect in Irish English is that which has received most attention from scholars in the field. It is also the area in which the interplay of (i) input varieties of English, (ii) transfer from the Irish language and (iii) the nature of the language shift situation is at its most intricate. These three factors will be considered in the discussions below and an attempt will be made to offer a relative weighting of their influence in the genesis of aspectual distinctions in Irish English.

To begin with, it is necessary to distinguish two components of verbal expressions in Irish English. Tense refers to the point in time relative to a discourse while aspect conveys information beyond tense, typically about the manner in which an action took or takes place or about whether it has been completed or whether it is repeated at regular intervals. These latter facets can be expressed periphrastically, usually by adverbs, but in the present section the concern is with established verbal structures which do not depend on the presence of particular adverbs for their specific semantics. For instance, the well-known *after*-perfective conveys not just that something has happened recently (temporal component) but also that it was unexpected, unwanted or simply that the sentence has high informational value, e.g. *They're after catching the criminal*. The resultative perfective informs the hearer that a planned action has been completed, e.g. *Sheila has the article written*, and contrasts with sentences where this semantic element is not present, e.g. *Sheila has written an article*. This aspectual type is telic in nature, i.e. goal-oriented (Dahl 1984), hence the use of the definite article with the resultative perfective just quoted, but the indefinite article in the other sentence. An important feature of aspect is in evidence here: it is realised by contrast with another structure. This is also true of standard varieties of English where the simple present has an iterative sense and contrasts with a continuous form which does not show this element; contrast *Sheila teaches the second year students (on Thursday morning)* and *Sheila is teaching (at the moment)*.

Similar aspectual distinctions may be found in other languages (Bybee and Dahl 1989), but realised by different means, for example by lexicalised verb forms. The Slavic languages are well known for the perfective/imperfective distinction and there are normally pairs of verbs where one member is perfective and the other imperfective in meaning (Cubberley 2002: 150–3). Both verbs of such pairs refer to the past (temporal component), but one indicates that an action was completed and the other that it simply took place (no reference to completion).

In the discussion below, aspect is seen as a component of verbal expressions which goes beyond tense and conveys some 'extra information'. Two basic types

Table 4.15. *Information in verb phrases and aspectual distinctions*

1. Information: repetition	Aspect: habitual
Subdivision of habitual	*Types*
progressive	durative
punctual	iterative
2. Information: completion	Aspect: perfective
Subdivision of perfective	*Types*
very recent completion	immediate perfective
completion of planned action	resultative perfective

of such information are particularly common cross-linguistically (Dahl 1985); the first concerns repetition and the second completion. Each component can be further subdivided into two types. In vernacular varieties of Irish English these four distinctions can be formally encoded as will be shown presently (see table 4.15).

The two labels 'durative' and 'iterative' refer to whether an habitual action is characterised as lasting a certain length of time (durative) or as being more punctual in nature (iterative). The durative-habitual and the iterative-habitual are clearly distinguished in many varieties of Irish English, frequently by using *do(es) be* for the former and a non-standard *-s* inflection, typically in the first person singular, for the latter as in *I gets* [iterative-habitual] *grumpy with them all sometimes when they do be tormentin' me* [durative-habitual] (WER, F55+).

The other two labels 'immediate perfective' and 'resultative perfective' make explicit reference to the additional aspectual components of these structures and reflect a usage found in previous treatments by the present author (e.g. Hickey 1995b, 1997a). There are other terms which can be found in the relevant literature. David Greene (Greene 1979) has two labels PI and PII for the immediate perfective and the resultative perfective respectively (see section 4.3.1). Because these are not self-explanatory they have not been adopted in the literature, despite support from Markku Filppula.

In his classification, James McCawley (1976 [1971]) introduced the term 'hot news' to refer to the use of the English present perfect to convey new and unexpected information as in *They've stolen my bicycle!* McCawley labels this a perfect but inasmuch as it conveys additional information beyond tense it can be regarded as a perfective. While discussing his study, McCawley's labelling will be used, but for reasons of consistency, the term 'perfective' will be employed by the present author when treating the same grammatical distinctions in this book.

McCawley's terminology has been taken up by authors on Irish English and applied to the perfective with *after*, first by Harris (1984a: 308; 1993: 160), later by Kallen (1989: 7–9) who follows McCawley's divisions and discusses the subtypes he distinguishes in detail (see also Kallen 1990: 122–7). McCawley recognised four kinds of perfect as follows.

(94)   *McCawley's distinctions for the perfect*
   a.   'universal' perfect   b.   'existential' perfect
   c.   'hot news' perfect   d.   'stative' perfect

Kallen (1989: 7) speaks of 'a single Present Perfect TMA category' in English and found attestations in his corpus of Dublin English for each of the subtypes above (Kallen 1989: 13f.). McCawley's 'hot-news perfect' is regarded, e.g. by Kallen and Harris, as a semantic equivalent of the 'immediate perfective' of Irish English, the term used here and which is intended to cover both recency and high informational value (Hickey 2000b). Other authors call this simply the '*after*-perfect' (Ronan 2005), referring to the adverb which is central to this aspectual structure.

For the completion of planned action, the term 'resultative perfective' is employed here. It is also used by Harris (1993: 160) and Trudgill (1986: 149f.), though Kallen (1989: 17) uses the term 'accomplishment perfect'. For this type the label 'medial object perfect' is found, especially in the work of Markku Filppula (see Filppula 1999: 90). This stresses the word order used to realise the aspectual type, instead of giving a classification of semantics which is what is intended by 'resultative perfective'.

In discussions of the verbal system of Irish English the terms 'perfect' and 'perfective' are found, not always with a clear explanation of what they are supposed to mean. In the present book the label 'perfect' is taken to refer to tense and 'perfective' to aspect. It is true that the distinction is often blurred and authors tend to vary in their definitions of these terms; contrast the treatments in Comrie (1976) and Dahl (1985). Nonetheless, 'perfect' and 'perfective' can be used to characterise two different vantage points. In a sentence like *Sheila has the article written* one can talk of it embodying a 'perfect' in that it refers to an action which is located in the past and finished. But one can also classify it as a 'perfective' in that it contains the additional aspectual information of being a planned action with an explicit goal, i.e. it is telic in nature. It contributes to a greater understanding of verbal structures to distinguish as a matter of procedure between tense and aspect, at least as a starting point, even if the two categories are merged in actual examples.

The necessity to distinguish between 'perfect' and 'perfective' is seen by other authors as well, e.g. Dahl (1985: 138f.). Because the perfective focuses on completion of an action and, in the Irish English context, conveys information on whether this was intentional (resultative) or very recent and new to the hearer (immediate), it tends to occur with a definite time reference, e.g. *He's after crashing the car this morning*. The perfect on the other hand can occur in the progressive, e.g. *I have been sleeping well lately*, something which is not true of perfectives (in Irish English), e.g. **She's been after breaking the glass*. Furthermore, if the syntax of the resultative perfective is used with the progressive in Irish English, then the interpretation is automatically causative; contrast *We were having the work done* *(by a firm of decorators)* [causative] with *We had the work done (before lunchtime)* [resultative].

The 'indefinite anterior'

Filppula (1999: 91–8) discusses the use of the 'indefinite anterior perfect' (his terminology) as exemplified in *Were you ever in Kenmare?* The terminology used by Filppula may not be appropriate to Irish English, certainly when viewed from the language shift perspective. It is perhaps inaccurate to say that the Irish overrepresented the 'indefinite anterior' of English in their speech. For this to happen a choice between a verb construction with *have* and one without *have* would have been necessary. To use Filppula's example, the Irish would have had to have both *Were you ever in Kenmare?* and *Have you ever been in Kenmare?* to realise the contrast between the two forms. But if this choice was not available, then it is not justified to speak of an 'indefinite anterior' in Irish English. There is just one means of expressing the past, as there is in Irish.

(95)   *An raibh tú riamh sa Neidín?*
       [INTERROG were you ever in Kenmare]
       'Were you ever in Kenmare?'

Filppula (1999: 98) does, however, accept 'that Irish has exercised a considerable amount of reinforcing influence on this feature of HE (= 'Hiberno-English')'.

A different issue concerns the subjective element conveyed by the use of *have* in English with what is termed the 'experiential perfect' (Comrie 1976: 58f.). This can be expressed in both Irish and Irish English by emphasising the pronoun, in the first case via a special emphatic form and in the second via a reflexive pronoun used in this function.

(96)   *An raibh tusa riamh sa Neidín?*
       [INTERROG was you-EMPHATIC ever in Kenmare]
       Were you yourself ever in Kenmare?

That English *have* was probably not an option for tense formation during the historical language shift is confirmed by the fact that in *A Collection of Contact English*, *have* was only found in a possessive sense and not in present perfect constructions. This would imply that the later use of *have* in supraregional forms of Irish English represents an influence from more standard forms of English.

For Irish speakers in the language-shift situation, English *have* would have presented them with a form which was without an equivalent in their native language. The possessive meaning of *have* is expressed quite differently in Irish, which uses the form *tá* 'is' with a compound form based on the preposition *ag* 'at'.

(97)   *Tá culaith bhán agam.*
       [is suit white at-me]
       'I have a white suit.'

Extended *now*

The structure being referred to by this label (Filppula 1999: 90, 122–8; 1997b) can be seen in a sentence like *I know M . . . and A . . . for many years now* (WER, F75+). Essentially, the present tense is used in contexts where the time span is from some point in the past to the present. In these situations, standard English uses the present perfect, i.e. the sentence just quoted would be *I have known M . . . and A . . . for many years*. The use of the simple present in contexts which conceptually stretch back into the past is a widespread features of English in the entire island of Ireland.

The question of origin is difficult to answer conclusively as Filppula (1999: 123f.) rightly notes. The use of the present in English has a long vintage and is probably the older Germanic type, still seen in present-day German, e.g. *Ich kenne ihn seit mehreren Jahren*, lit. 'I know him since many years.' This type may have continued well into the early modern period and so been presented in the input varieties of English during the language shift in Ireland. On the other hand, as shown in the discussion of the 'indefinite anterior', auxiliary *have* did not, and does not, have a formal equivalent in Irish and so it is more than likely that native speakers of Irish in the language-shift situation would have ignored this form. The Irish equivalent to the present perfect is expressed quite differently as seen below.

(98)   *Tá aithne agam ar M . . . agus ar Á . . . le blianta anuas anois.*
       [is knowledge at-me on M . . . and on A . . . with years down now]

The acceptance of extended *now* in present-day Irish English was tested in *A Survey of Irish English Usage* and the rates were consistently high, as shown in table 4.16. There was a bias towards the south of Ireland with Wexford in the south-east scoring the highest value, considerably higher than the Ulster Scots core areas of Antrim and Down in the north-east of the country. This may be due to the very early settlement of the east coast and before the present perfect had become established in English.

Be perfects

This is the fourth type discussed by Filppula (1999: 90, 116–22). Again in the type of interpretation offered here the occurrence of *be* as an auxiliary in sentences like the following can in part be accounted for by the absence of *have* in language shift varieties of Irish English.

(99)   a.   *The kids <u>are gone</u> to the strand today.* (WER, F55+)
       b.   *<u>They're finished</u> the school exams now.* (RL, F55+)

The second source, which Filppula identifies correctly is, of course, the English input which Irish speakers were exposed to. The auxiliary *be* was usual with verbs of state and motion, and is still so in modern German, e.g. *Er ist mit der Arbeit fertig*, lit. 'He is with the work finished', *Sie ist zum Laden gegangen*, lit. 'She is to the shop gone.'

Table 4.16. *Acceptance figures in* A Survey of Irish English Usage *for the test sentence* I know her for five years now *(mean: 76% with 18 counties over 80%)*

County	Score	N	Total	County	Score	N	Total
Wexford	97%	28	29	Clare	81%	13	16
Tipperary	90%	38	42	Sligo	77%	17	22
Westmeath	88%	22	25	Donegal	76%	32	42
Limerick	88%	23	26	Dublin	75%	154	205
Louth	88%	28	32	Galway	74%	40	54
Mayo	86%	32	37	Meath	73%	27	37
Waterford	84%	43	51	Wicklow	71%	15	21
Derry	83%	15	18	Antrim	71%	29	41
Kerry	83%	20	24	Belfast	66%	21	32
Kilkenny	83%	20	24	Kildare	64%	16	25
Cavan	82%	14	17	Armagh	58%	11	19
Cork	82%	69	84	Down	53%	20	38

Filppula (1999: 188f.), quoting Kytö (1994), states that for the last subperiod of the *Helsinki Corpus of English Texts* (1640–1710) *be* is the preferential auxiliary with intransitive verbs, accounting for some 63 per cent of instances. When quoting Rydén and Brorström (1987) he furthermore states that *be* auxiliaries in this context were in a ratio to *have* of 3:1 for the eighteenth century, but that this situation was quickly reversed in the nineteenth century. The preference for *be* as auxiliary was confirmed by an examination of personal letters from Dublin in the eighteenth century (Hickey 2005: 163), e.g. *I am just come . . .* (1763). For verbs of motion this preference was carried through into the nineteenth century. In documents such as the personal journal of one Thomas Henry Edwards (National Library of Ireland, Ms. 16136) there are sentences like *I am arrived safe at the close of another week . . .* (23 Sept. 1843).

4.4.1.4.1   Immediate perfective

The structure which is the topic of the present section has been discussed repeatedly by scholars investigating Irish English.[24] In present-day varieties, it consists of a compound verb phrase comprising *be* + *after* + continuous verb form. In contemporary Irish English it only has past reference, though it can occur in the future perfect on occasions (see example (100f) below). Attestations from the

---

[24] Filppula (1999: 90ff.) speaks of 'Hiberno-English perfects', but two of the six types he discusses, viz. the *after* + V-*ing* and the medial object structure, are clearly aspectual types as they convey information beyond the temporal component. Thus to treat these constructions on the same level as the 'indefinite anterior' perfect as in *Were you ever in Kenmare?* Filppula (1999: 90) is to conflate structures which have aspectual meanings with those which do not.

Table 4.17. *Stages in the development of the immediate perfective in Irish*

---

1. In Old Irish, *iar* 'after'+ verbal noun introduced non-finite adverbial clauses of time.
2. This structure had retrospective and prospective uses (past and future reference) in Early Modern Irish.
3. The *after* perfective of Irish was a feature of spoken Early Modern Irish (Ó Sé and Ó Corráin contra Greene).
4. *Iar* 'after' was phonetically reduced to *ar* which was then homophonous with the preposition *ar* 'on'. Later (as of the eighteenth century) *ar* 'after' was replaced in the perfective construction by *tar éis* or *i ndiaidh* both meaning 'after'.

---

author's data collections include the following:

(100) Immediate perfective in present-day Irish English
   a. *I don't know how many pairs of shoes her mammy is <u>after buying</u> her.* (WER, F55+)
   b. *He's <u>after having</u> a lot of setbacks.* (DER, F40+)
   c. *They're <u>after finishing</u> the M50 motorway recently.* (DER, M60+)
   d. *They're <u>after building</u> lots and lots of new houses.* (WER, M50+)
   e. *Some of the boys working with A . . . are <u>after getting</u> the loan.* (DER, M35+)
   f. *By the time you get there he'll be <u>after drinking</u> the beer.* (WER, M30+)

Origin of the immediate perfective in Irish

Any consideration of origin for this structure must start with the situation in Irish. This has been the subject of much debate by Irish scholars such as David Greene, Diarmuid Ó Sé and Ailbhe Ó Corráin. Essentially, the steps recognised are as listed in table 4.17.

Ó Corráin (2006: 154–6) concurs with the view that in earlier Irish English, the *after*-perfective had future reference. His contribution is innovative inasmuch as he adduces textual evidence from Irish to show that substrate structure, which is assumed to have been the trigger for the *after*-perfective in Irish English, already had future reference in Irish. He admits that there are few texts of colloquial Early Modern Irish but cites excerpts from translations intended for the general public. His attestations range from the late fifteenth century to the first half of the nineteenth century and include both future and conditional uses (see (101b)).

(101) a. *bíaidh an ghrían arna dorchughadh*
      [be-FUTURE the sun after-its darkening]
      'the sun will be darkened'
      (*Tiomna Nuadh* 'The New Testament', Ó Domhnaill, 1603)
   b. *Go mbéimís air ar sáoradh ó láimh ar námhad*
      [that would-we after our saving from hands our enemies-GENITIVE]
      'that we would be rescued from the hand of our enemies'
      (*Tiomna Nuadh* 'The New Testament', Ó Domhnaill, 1603)

c. *beidh tú ar do fhliuchadh le drúcht nimhe*
[be-FUTURE you after your wetting with dew heaven-GENITIVE]
'you will be made moist by the dew of heaven'
(*Stair an Bhíobla III* 'History of the Bible, III', Uáitéar Ua
Ceallaigh, *c.* 1726)

d. *Beidh mé iar do bhualadh*
[be-FUTURE I after your beating]
'I will have beaten you'
(Neilson, *An Introduction to the Irish Language*, 1990 [1808])

e. *biad iar nglanadh*
[be-FUTURE after (their) cleaning]
'I will be after cleaning (them)'
(J. O'Donovan, *A Grammar of the Irish Language*, 1845)

Ó Sé in his study (see section 'The emergence of the "after" perfect', Ó Sé 2004: 186–94) offers examples of a retrospective use of *ar* 'after' from Early Modern Irish as does Ó Corráin in his study (with the newer *tar éis* 'after').

(102) a. *na cuirp atá ar tuitim co mór*
[the bodies which-are after falling that much]
'the bodies which have declined greatly'
(*Regimen na Sláinte* 'The Regimen of Health', early fifteenth century)

b. *d'iarraidh a thréada do bhí ar ndul amugha*
[seeking his flock that was after going astray]
(Flaithrí Ó Maolchonaire, *Desiderius*, 1616) (Ó Sé 2004: 189)

c. *fear mór . . . agus é tar éis a theacht ó fhionnadh mairt*
[man big and he after COMP coming from flaying a cow]
'a big man . . .and he after coming from flaying a cow'
(Seán Ó Neachtain, *Stair Éamoinn Uí Chléire*, *c.*1700)
(Ó Corráin 2006)

A further point is that the Irish structure could indicate both state (the original reference) and action (a more recent development which was particularly common in Scottish Gaelic and in Manx, T. F. O'Rahilly 1932: 135).

To summarise: the research of the Irish scholars just quoted has shown that at the beginning of the early modern period of Irish English, i.e. from *c.* 1600 onwards, the Irish language had a structure *(i)ar* 'after'+ verbal noun which could refer to the past and future and to both state and action. But the Irish structure came to refer more and more just to an action of the recent past (immediate perfective) as can be seen in sentences like Modern Irish *Tá siad tar éis teach a cheannach* 'They are after buying a house.' It is worth asking whether Irish had an internal motivation for this restriction in range. Both Ó Sé and Ó Corráin maintain that the reduction in range of *(i)ar* + verbal noun structures is causally linked to the rise of a resultative perfective in Irish. This is the sentence type seen in *Tá an obair déanta agam* [is the work done at-me] or *Beidh an obair déanta agam ar ball* [be-FUTURE the work done at-me soon]. One Irish grammarian, Bonaventura Ó hEodhasa, writing in his *Rudimenta Grammaticae Hibernicae* 'Fundamentals of Irish Grammar' (Louvain, *c.* 1610), discusses the *(i)ar* + verbal noun structure and mentions the newer structure *tá* + NP + VA (= 'verbal adjective', roughly equivalent to the past participle in English – RH) which was emerging as a substitute. This structure was to become more and more established as a resultative perfective in Irish, indicating a state reached or to be reached. This development, as Ó Corráin (2006) rightly notes, ousted the *(i)ar* + verbal noun structure from its use as a resultative perfective with past or future reference. The remaining application of the *(i)ar* + verbal noun structure was as an immediate perfective, indicating an action which was completed recently and this narrow range has remained to this day, albeit with *tar éis* or *i ndiaidh* for 'after' because *(i)ar* had collapsed phonetically with *ar* 'on' (see table 4.17 above).

Developments in Irish English

The *after*-perfective in Irish English appears at the end of the seventeenth century and would seem to have had future reference to begin with (Bliss 1979: 300). Irish scholars (Bartley 1954: 130; Greene 1979: 126) have been dismissive of Bliss's discussion of the *after*-perfective, particularly of the instances of future reference which he quotes, e.g. Ó Sé maintains that 'Bliss's counterexamples are therefore most economically explained as due to the unfamiliarity of earlier English authors with genuine Irish speech' (Ó Sé 2004: 243). The so-called counterexamples include the following instances for the late seventeenth and eighteenth centuries.

(103) Earliest records of *after* + *V-ing* with future reference
   a. Thomas Shadwell, *The Lancashire Witches* (1681/2)
      . . . and de Caatholicks do shay, dat you vill be after being damn'd
      . . . and I vill be after absolving you for it.
   b. John Michelburne, *Ireland Preserved* (1705)
      I'll bee after telling dee de Raison, de Irish Brogue carry de ill smell
      . . . and I fill be after doing fell for my shelf.
      I fell be after keeping my Cow and my Seep, and twenty Ewe Lamb.
   c. Susanne Centlivre, *A Wife Well Managed* (1715)
      An will you be after giving me the Moidore indeed.
   d. John Durant Breval, *The Play Is a Plot* (1718)
      Well, fat will you be after Drinking good Countryman?
      . . . and he will not be after hanging his Countryman.

These cannot be dismissed out of hand as inaccurate renderings by English authors.[25] Thomas Shadwell moved to Ireland as a boy and had first-hand exposure to English there. John Michelburne was born in Sussex, moved to Ireland

---

[25] See the negative criticism of such texts, and Bliss's reliance on them, in the reviews by Canny (1980) and P. L. Henry (1981). A more positive reappraisal is offered by Kelly (2000).

and was there as a soldier during the Siege of Derry in 1689. Centlivre and Breval were also English but do not seem to have spent time in Ireland.

The issue at hand is whether the *after*-perfective always had past reference as Ó Sé (2004) claims or whether this structure went through a development from the late seventeenth/early eighteenth to the mid nineteenth century. This matter has been addressed by Filppula (1999: 103) and by Kallen (1990) and more recently, in very detailed form, by McCafferty (2004a and 2005). The textual records, examined for the present study, vindicate the position adopted by Bliss and in more carefully documented form by McCafferty, namely that *after* + V-*ing* had genuine future reference in its earliest attestations.

However, it did not have only future reference. Already at the end of the seventeenth century, there are examples of *after* + V-*ing* with past reference: *Deare Catolicks, you shee here de cause dat is after bringing you to dis plaace* . . . (John Dunton, *Report of a Sermon*, 1698). The view of the present author is that this structure began in Irish English with a much less specific temporal reference than it was later to show (after the mid nineteenth century). This is essentially the conclusion to which Kevin McCafferty also comes in his study of this phenomenon; see McCafferty (2004a and 2005: 349–54).

In the language shift situation, the Irish were confronted with English in which *after* had both prospective and retrospective meanings. There is a distinction in principle between two uses of *after* in English: the first is found in contexts which express a stative meaning and the second where the meaning is dynamic. This distinction may in fact apply to other languages as well. It is certainly the case with German, as can be seen in the following examples.

(104) a. *after* + stative meaning = past
      After the lecture we were tired.
      Nach dem Essen waren wir satt. 'After the meal we were satisfied.'
   b. *after* + dynamic meaning = future
      The police are after the criminal.
      Wir suchen nach einer Lösung. 'We are looking "after" (i.e. searching for) a solution.'

There would appear to be a valid generalisation here: *after* in English (and *nach* in German) points to the future when the context is dynamic, i.e. the subject is striving towards a goal. When the goal has been achieved, i.e. a state has been reached, then *after* refers to the past. This double use of *after* may well have resulted from the manner in which we conceptualise action (towards a goal) and state (of the goal attained). If there is a general cognitive basis for such usage then it is all the more likely that it applied to the use of *after* + V-*ing* in its early stages in Irish English, that is, that this structure had both dynamic (future) and stative (past) meaning.

In addition to the two possible uses of *after* in English, the Irish model for the later *after*-perfective – first *(i)ar* + verbal noun, then *tar éis/i ndiaidh* + verbal noun – had both past and future reference (as Ó Corráin has shown; see above). The transfer of this flexible usage (compared to Modern Irish) was facilitated by the fact that the obvious formal equivalent to *(i)ar/tar éis/i ndiaidh* – *after* in English – had and has both retrospective and prospective meanings. This would appear to have lent a fluidity of reference to the *after* + *V-ing* structure which did not resolve itself until the mid nineteenth century.[26] To illustrate this early situation, consider the following verbatim transcript of an Irishman at the Old Bailey (numerical marking mine – RH). He is describing an encounter with a woman to the court, a discourse situation in which the *after*-perfective would be likely to occur.

(105)   *After* + *V-ing* in Old Bailey Texts

I wash (i) *after asking her* which Way she wash walking . . . She told me she would be (ii) *after taking me* with her, if I would give her any Thing . . . But ash to the Preceshoner, she wash (iii) *after making me* shit upon the Bed with her, and sho tumble together; but I wash (iv) *after shitting* in the Chair, and then she was coming to shit in my Lap . . . for she wash (v) *after being concerned* with my Breeches, and got away my Watch whether I would or no . . . (OBT, 1725, James Fitzgerald)

The fluidity of temporal reference is remarkable in this text. The first instance looks like an *after*-perfective as it would be used today. Instance (ii) is definitely prospective, expressing volition. Instances (iii) and (iv) are probably retrospective, though (iv) is uncertain.

Among the Old Bailey Texts is evidence by a man named Fitzpatrick in which the *after* + *V-ing* structure is attested with formal marking of the future (as in those in (103) above): *I will be after forfeiting* both my Head and Ears to thish honourable Court . . .; I hope thish honourable Court *will be after taking* it into Conshideration, for I have got a Wife . . . (1726).

The option of past or future reference for the *after* + *V-ing* structure would seem to have lasted throughout the eighteenth century and into the early nineteenth century. There would also appear to have been a transition in which attestations with future reference receded in favour of those with past reference. Towards the end of the eighteenth century, the Old Bailey Texts show an increasing occurrence of the *after* + *V-ing* structure with past reference: *A little before eleven I was after going on duty* (1791); *He said, he was after coming from the country* and that his wife had been dead a month back (1796). It is also interesting to note in this context that acquaintance with the *after* + *V-ing* structure would seem to have spread to London: in a transcript from 1823 an English witness reports hearing someone (probably Irish): *I heard somebody say, 'that man is after stealing the carpet'*.

---

[26] Kallen (1994: 173), referring to the more restricted use of *after* nowadays, maintains that there occurred 'a sort of decreolisation in which the variable range of significance for *after* is limited in accord with the demands of the English TMA system'. This statement is not very helpful, particularly as Irish English was never a creole (see the detailed arguments in this connection in Hickey 1997a). Anyway, one can hardly use this argument to explain why Irish English ended up with a structure – *after*-perfective with past reference – which contrasts with the use of *after* in standard varieties of English.

The transition to the modern retrospective reference of the *after* + V-*ing* structure was not completed before the mid nineteenth century and instances of both types of reference can be found prior to this. Consider the examples in (106) and (107) which illustrate first prospective or conditional reference and then past reference. For reasons of space, only a selection of attestations are offered.

(106) *After* + V-*ing* with future, conditional or imperative reference with early nineteenth-century writers

    a. . . . *give it to us, or you'll be afther stroking it into a wran at last, so you will.* (John and Michael Banim, *The Nowlans*)

    b. *I'll soon be after calling up the first spelling lesson; . . . don't be after making a looking-glass out of the sleeve of your jacket; . . . What! – is it after conthradictin' me you'd be?; . . .he inquired, 'will you be afther resolving me one single proposition'; . . . 'Who'll sing, sir? for I can't be afther dancin' a step widout the music.'* (William Carleton, *The Hedge School*)

    c. *'but you won't be after passing that on us for the wake, ainy how.'* (William Carleton, *Shane Fadh's Wedding*)

    d. *It is the great battle, however, which I am after going to describe; . . . we'll soon be after seeing John O'Callaghan* (William Carleton, *The Battle of the Factions*)

    e. *an' maybe he won't be afther comin' round to me for a sack of my best oats* (William Carleton, *The Station*)

    f. *'Why, I'll show you what I'd like to be afther tastin.'* (William Carleton, *Phelim O'Toole's Courtship*)

The authors who are quoted in (106) and (107) are prominent prose writers from the first quarter of the nineteenth century. John and Michael Banim were from Kilkenny and Gerald Griffin from Limerick. William Carleton is especially interesting in this context (Kallen 1991; McCafferty 2005) as he was a native Irish speaker from rural Tyrone in Ulster (Todd 1989: 129). The Banim brothers and Griffin do not seem to have been native speakers of Irish though in that pre-Famine time they would have had much more contact with the language than people from Kilkenny or Limerick today.

(107) *After* + V-*ing* with past reference in early nineteenth-century writers

    a. *for you're after breakin' Peery's heart, Peggy Nowlan; a little bird that comes to me . . . is just after telling me another thing; 'Murther!' roared Peery; 'he's afther burnin' them . . .'* (John and Michael Banim, *The Nowlans*)

    b. *dat wouldn't be afther puttin' nothin' in your pockets* (William Carleton, *The Emigrants of Ahadarra*)

    c. *but he's jist afther tellin' me that he doesn't think he'll have any further occasion for my sarvices.* (William Carleton, *The Black Baronet or The Chronicles of Ballytrain*)

    d. *And the cursed old hypocrite is just after telling me*; . . . *'You're afther sayin',' replied Sarah*; . . . *'but indeed what could I expect afther dependin' upon a foolish dhrame?'* (William Carleton, *The Black Prophet: A Tale of Irish Famine*)

    e. *'How do you feel afther bein' sacked, gentleman?'*; *'Now, boys, I'm afther givin' yez to-day and to-morrow for a holyday . . .'* (William Carleton, *The Hedge School*)

    f. *'surely your Reverence can't be long afther bein' ordained . . .'*; *dat's as good as if I was after taking all de books in Ireland of it*; *I lay my life you're afther gettin' money from the masther.* (Gerald Griffin, *The Collegians*)

Irish scholars have frequently pointed out that the past reference of the *after* + V-*ing* structure is found as early as the beginning of the eighteenth century. T. F. O'Rahilly in his study of Irish dialects (1932: 234) notes that Hugh Mac-Curtain in his 1728 grammar of the Irish language glosses an Irish sentence, which has clear past reference, 'in the Hiberno-English style': 'Daniel is after beating John'. Ó Sé, who also quotes this (Ó Sé 2004: 242), makes the mistake of assuming that the *after* + V-*ing* structure did not have future reference in earlier Irish English just because instances with past reference are available in historical documents. It is true that the instances in the Irish grammars of Vallancey (1773) and O'Donovan (1845) document past reference for the *after* + V-*ing* structure, but this does not disprove the alternative of future reference.

The situation appears to have changed by the mid nineteenth century. All the instances of the *after* + V-*ing* structure in the Irish Emigrant Letters collection have past reference, e.g. *Dear Thomas, it is with Sorrow I answer your letter I was just after writing to your Father . . . I was just after comming from the hospital* (IEL, 1904, New York). Of course, regional factors may have been at play here: the emigrant letters show a heavy bias to the south, specifically Co. Cork. But later writers from the east coast (Boucicault) or those imitating the speech of rural inhabitants in the west (Gregory, Synge) have abundant examples of the *after* + V-*ing* structure, all of which have past reference only.

The link between Irish and English

The demise of future reference for the *after* + V-*ing* structure would seem to run approximately parallel to that of the *(i)ar* + verbal noun structure with future reference in Irish. The connection between the restriction in temporal and aspectual scope for the *(i)ar* + verbal noun structure in Irish and the rise of *tá* + NP + verbal adjective (see above) as a resultative perfective in Irish would also seem to parallel the demise of the *after* + V-*ing* structure and the rise of object + past participle to indicate a resultative perfective in Irish English. This could be coincidental but the similarity seems too obvious to be dismissed.

The question is: how could this parallelism have arisen? There are two possible ways of explaining a connection between an internal development in Irish and one in Irish English. The first is that large sections of the population were bilingual up to the mid nineteenth century and so the change which took place in Irish was immediately reflected in the English of such bilingual individuals. The other explanation is that large sections of the population before the mid nineteenth century were still Irish-speaking (this was true of the pre-Famine period, i.e. before the late 1840s) and that these individuals then transferred the features of early nineteenth century Irish to English when they switched to the latter language in the course of the nineteenth century. Such a late language shift would have meant that their variety of Irish would have shown a restricted aspectual range for *(i)ar* + verbal noun (by then *tar éis/i ndiaidh* + verbal noun), i.e. only as an immediate perfective. Irish at that late date would also have shown a fully established resultative perfective expressed via *tá* + NP + verbal adjective (cf. *Tá an t-alt scríofa agam* 'I have the article written, i.e. completed'). The issue of speaker numbers is important here. There must have been enough people still engaged in language shift for them to have imposed their variety of English, heavily influenced by Irish, on other sections of the Irish population which had already shifted to English or which had indeed always been English-speaking.

The late rise of object + past participle word order for a resultative perfective in Irish English (see the discussion of 'medial object perfects' in Filppula 1999: 90ff.) has an interesting consequence for the retentionist view of non-standard grammar in Irish English: the mid nineteenth century as an approximate date for the establishment of this structure is far too late for a retention of Middle English OV word order in target varieties of English in Ireland to have played any role.

Scottish parallels

Annette Sabban, in her study of contact English in Scotland, has a section devoted to the *after*-perfective (Sabban 1982: 155–68; see also Sabban 1985: 134). In it she explicitly compares this to the identical construction in Irish English (1982: 163f.). All her examples are of *after* + V-*ing* with past reference. She does, however, mention one or two examples of future and conditional reference which she found in literary works, but dismisses these as 'fehl am Platze' ('not appropriate' – RH). She does not broach the question of how this structure developed historically and whether it also had future reference in earlier forms of contact English in Scotland.

The position in Gaelic is considered by Sabban (1982: 162). She notes that Gaelic has the construction as in *tha e air bualadh* [is he after striking] 'he is after striking'. This shows the form *air* (Irish *iar*) 'after, behind' which used to exist in Irish (see table 4.17 above) and which was later replaced by *tar éis/i ndiaidh* (both meaning 'after'), but a long time after the transportation of Irish to Scotland. This structure is, if anything, more common in Scottish Gaelic (Watson 1994: 694) than in Irish as it is used where the latter would have the verbal adjective; compare Scottish Gaelic *tha e air briseadh* [is it after breaking] with Irish *tá sé briste* [is it broken], both meaning 'it is broken' (Maclennan 1979 [1925]: 7). Sabban regards the Gaelic structure as the source of the contact English construction which was transferred during language shift, much as in Ireland. Indeed the case for a contact origin is even stronger in Scotland, given the greater range of the *air* 'after' structure in Scottish Gaelic, i.e. the likelihood of transfer during language shift would have been greater than with Irish.

The double use of *air* 'after' for both perfective and resultative aspect in Scottish Gaelic is confirmed by authors working in Celtic. Cox (1996: 85) states explicitly that 'a perfective aspect is conveyed by *air* "after": *tha mi air òl* "I have drunk"'. Macaulay (1996: 201) confirms this and quotes two different meanings of *air* which correspond to the perfective and resultative aspect in Irish English.

(108) a. *Tha Iain air a bhith ag ithe an arain.*
       (is Iain after COMP been at eating the bread)
       'Iain is after eating the bread.'
    b. *Tha Iain air an t-aran ithe.*
       (is Iain after the bread eating)
       'Iain has the bread eaten.'

In her book Sabban also considers very briefly the question of possible influence from Ireland on contact English in Scotland. She notes (1982: 164) that many Irish immigrants settled in Scotland and that they might have brought the structure with them, leading to convergence with the transfer of the same structure from Gaelic in Scotland. However, this was probably only a very minor influence on contact English in the Outer Hebrides (the region where she did her fieldwork), as opposed to further south in the region of Glasgow.

For a more general discussion of common developments in Celtic Englishes, including Irish and Scottish English, see the overview in Filppula (2006, especially pp. 520–7).

The *after*-perfective in contemporary Irish English

The spread of language shift varieties of English to the entire population of at least the south of Ireland receives confirmation in the fact that the *after*-perfective is found more or less uniformly[27] across the Republic of Ireland today. Whatever differences may be found, these are solely quantitative. There are no discernible differences in the syntax or semantics of the *after*-perfective in different parts of present-day Ireland. The quantitative differences which do exist can be recognised along the north–south axis. In *A Survey of Irish English Usage* the mean acceptance rate of the test sentence *She's after spilling the milk* was 88 per cent in the twenty-four locations with more than fifteen respondents (see table 4.18). However, the thirteen counties which had a score of over 90 per cent were all outside Ulster. In fact the three lowest rates were to be found in east Ulster, the area of greatest Ulster Scots settlement historically.

---

[27] There are some slight variations, however. For example, in vernacular varieties one may find the *after*-perfective with a continuous tense, as in *We're after bein' removin' rocks* (MLSI, M70+, Knockananna, Co. Wicklow).

Table 4.18. *Acceptance figures in* A Survey of Irish English Usage *for the test sentence* She's after spilling the milk

County	Score	N	Total	County	Score	N	Total
Sligo	100%	22	22	Louth	91%	29	32
Kilkenny	100%	24	24	Mayo	89%	33	37
Wexford	100%	29	29	Donegal	88%	37	42
Kerry	96%	23	24	Dublin	87%	179	205
Westmeath	96%	24	25	Armagh	84%	16	19
Wicklow	95%	20	21	Derry	83%	15	18
Clare	94%	15	16	Waterford	82%	42	51
Cavan	94%	16	17	Meath	81%	30	37
Tipperary	93%	39	42	Galway	80%	43	54
Cork	93%	78	84	Antrim	78%	32	41
Kildare	92%	23	25	Belfast	66%	21	32
Limerick	92%	24	26	Down	58%	22	38

With the establishment of the *after* + V-*ing* structure as an immediate perfective in the latter half of the nineteenth century, the prospective use of *after* in English, as in *The police are after the criminal*, receded. Today, sentences like *He's after his dinner* are much more likely to be interpreted as elliptical uses of the *after*-perfective, a usage which is also found in Irish where the adverb can be used without an accompanying verb to express the immediate perfective: *Tá sé tar éis a dhinnéir* [is he after his dinner] 'He has (just) eaten his dinner.'

Interpreting scholarly standpoints

Assuming the basic reliability of the textual record and assuming that for a feature to appear in literature it must have been in speech for some years before the time of writing, then one can ask the following question. Why did Irish scholars like Greene and Ó Sé reject the contention that the *after*-perfective formerly had future reference? One indication is to be found in the statement by Greene that the instances with future reference are 'laboured Hibernicisms' and conform more to a stereotype of Irish English than to actual usage. This reaction is supported by authors from the middle of the nineteenth century onwards. For instance, there are only a few cases of the *after*-perfective in the four plays by Dion Boucicault in *A Corpus of Irish English*. The following are instances of it in the imperative and interrogative, both contexts in which it does not occur today.

(109) a. *But don't ye be after forgettin'.* Your pretty girl milking her cow
   b. *Is it afther desarvin' yer riverence I'd be?* (Dion Boucicault, *The Colleen Bawn*)
   c. *Is it afther bein' up* all night on the road . . . ? (Dion Boucicault, *Arrah na Pogue*)

The reaction of the Irish scholars, native speakers of Irish English, can be understood now: the older usage, which included future reference, imperative and interrogative contexts, disappeared during the nineteenth century, but was retained in stage Irish and stereotypical usages; and, as is so often the case, stereotypes contain usage no longer current. Their reaction was to reject such instances as not genuine – Greene's 'laboured Hibernicisms' – rather than to consider whether this could be a remnant of former general usage which had, in the course of the nineteenth century, become confined to parodies and caricatures of Irish English.

4.4.1.4.2   Resultative perfective

The structure to be discussed in this section has received various labels. Greene (1979: 133) termed it PII, using PI for the immediate perfective. Filppula (1999: 90) labels it the 'medial object perfect' with reference to the typical word order found with this structure. For the treatment here the term 'resultative perfective' is used. This matches the label 'immediate perfective' found in the previous section and the suggestion of a connection between the two is quite intentional.

The resultative perfective in Irish English is used to denote that a planned action has been completed as seen in the following examples.

(110) Resultative perfective in present-day Irish English
   a. *She had the soup made when the kids came home.* (WER, F55+)
   b. *The youngest hasn't her Leaving* (final school exam – RH) *taken yet.* (DER, M60+)
   c. *I've got the vegetable plot at the back planted now.* (RL, F55+)
   d. *Bhí sé ag iarraidh a fháil amach* – ah – *if the vet had the sheep examined.* (CCE-S, M65+) [was he at trying COMP find-VN out . . .]

The word order object + past participle is used in standard varieties of English to indicate that something was instigated by the subject, e.g. *We had the front of the house painted.* This usage is found in Irish English as well but the interpretation could be resultative depending on context, e.g. *We had the front of the house painted before the winter came.*

Get and the resultative perfective

In vernacular varieties of Irish English the verb *get* is widely used as a quasi-auxiliary in the sense of 'become', as seen in examples like *The separator came on the scene and the cream tub got finished* (SADIF, M80+, Kilmore Quay, Co. Wexford) or *They'll get lamed* (MLSI, M80+, Bantry, Co. Cork). This may have led to the extended use of *get* to express a resultative perfective, as this denotes a state which has been reached: *And when he got her gone, he looked at the parcel* (SADIF, M70, Crisheen, Co. Clare); *When he had the breakfast got* (SADIF, M70, Crisheen, Co. Clare); *So when he got him away . . .* (SADIF, M60+, Bellanagh, Co. Cavan).

Table 4.19. *Contrast between simple past and resultative perfective*

Is there a difference in meaning between the following two sentences?
1. *Have you read* Ulysses?   ☐   yes   ☐   no
2. *Have you* Ulysses *read?*

Do you think the sentence *Have you read* Ulysses? means
       ☐   I started reading this novel and am now finished.
       ☐   I read this novel sometime in the past.
       ☐   Something else, please specify:
Do you think the sentence *Have you* Ulysses *read?* means
       ☐   I started reading this novel and am now finished.
       ☐   I read this novel sometime in the past.
       ☐   Something else, please specify:
Results:

There is a difference in meaning between *Have you read* Ulysses? and *Have you* Ulysses *read?*

	yes	no	
Dublin	14	3	(total: 17)
Waterford	11	0	(total: 11)
Limerick	9	2	(total: 11)
Galway	12	1	(total: 13)
	total: 46	total: 6	

Have you read Ulysses? means 'I read this novel sometime in the past.'

	yes	no	
Dublin	14	0	(total: 14)
Waterford	11	0	(total: 11)
Limerick	9	0	(total: 9)
Galway	12	0	(total: 12)
	total: 46	total: 0	

Have you Ulysses *read?* means
(i) 'I started reading this novel and am now finished.'
(ii) 'I read this novel sometime in the past.'

	(i)	(ii)	something else	
Dublin	12	0	2	(total: 14)
Waterford	10	[1]	0	(total: 11)
Limerick	7	[1]	1	(total: 9)
Galway	11	0	1	(total: 12)
	total: 40		total: 4	

Semantic contrast and the resultative perfective

The word order used in the resultative perfective has led to a contrast in present-day Irish English. This contrast can be seen in the following two sentences.

(111) a. *Have you read* Ulysses? 'Have you ever read *Ulysses?*'
     b. *Have you* Ulysses *read?* 'Have you finished reading *Ulysses?*'

Table 4.20. *Results for contrast between* simple past *and* resultative perfective

There was a difference between the two sentences	88% of 52
Have you read Ulysses? means 'I read this novel sometime in the past.'	100% of 46
Have you Ulysses *read?* means 'I started reading this novel and am now finished.'	76% (85%) of 44 (46)

In order to determine whether this distinction was recognised by contemporary speakers of Irish English a test was carried out by the author with some fifty-two young people at four different locations: Dublin, Waterford, Limerick and Galway. They were presented with the above two sentences and asked to tick a box indicating whether they thought there was a difference in meaning and what this might be, the test is reproduced in table 4.19.

The six respondents who saw no difference between the two sentences were removed from the survey so that only forty-six respondents remained. Two respondents did not realise that in stating that sentence two meant 'I read this novel sometime in the past' they were in fact maintaining that there is no difference in meaning between the two sentences. For this reason they were also removed from the statistics which further reduced the total number of respondents for the evaluation to forty-four. In percentages, the results of the survey can be expressed as shown in table 4.20.

The second sentence provoked some comments by respondents. These turned out to largely confirm the notion of resultative perfective, for instance, in Dublin the two individuals, and the single individual in Limerick and Galway, who responded 'something else' said that the sentence meant they were told to read the novel by a teacher or lecturer. Because the four instances of 'something else' were in fact comments indicating the resultative nature of the second sentence, the 76 per cent which directly confirmed the meaning offered on the questionnaire should in fact be higher, i.e. 85 per cent, as indicated in brackets in table 4.20.

Origin of the resultative perfective

Recent word-order studies, such as van der Wurff and Foster (1997), have shown that placing the non-finite verb after the object was rare already by the late fifteenth century and had declined almost completely in formal prose by the late sixteenth century (van der Wurff and Foster 1997: 448; Moerenhout and van der Wurff 2005). Where it occurs, it is characteristic of verse (in Shakespeare for instance, Franz 1939: 577) and is used to highlight the verb by end position (see van der Wurff and Foster 1997 who quantify its frequency in verse). Furthermore, it is found most often in verb groups with a modal or auxiliary and in these constructions there are more pronominal than nominal objects.

(112) *Besyde the ymage I adowne me sette.*
    (Hawkes, *The Pastime of Pleasure*, 1505)

The occurrence of this word order in literary writing would imply archaicness so the conclusion that it was even less common in spoken language would appear to be justified.

For the genesis of the resultative perfective in Irish English this would imply that input varieties of English after the fifteenth century were unlikely to show O+PP word order and hence unlikely to have provided a model for speakers of Irish shifting to English. Certainly by the eighteenth and early nineteenth centuries, when the shift was under way for the majority of the population, there can be no question of pre-past participle objects having occurred anywhere, except in causative constructions such as *He had the wood cut (by the labourer)*. The essential difference between this type and the resultative perfective of Irish English, as Filppula (1999: 109) rightly points out, is that the causative construction involves two different subjects whereas the Irish English structure contains a single subject.

As indicated in section 4.3.1 above, the past participle in Irish always follows the object with transitive verbs. A word order which placed this before the object would have had to be explicitly learned by individuals shifting to English, and equally many of the Irish would have retained the word order of their native language. The question is how the resultative semantics[28] arose in Irish English (Harris 1983). This would appear to have its origin in Irish as well. Here the past participle is used with *tá*, a verb translatable as 'be' with stative meaning, e.g. *Tá suim aici sa Ghaeilge*, lit. 'is interest at-her in-the Irish'. When used with a past participle its meaning is stative; a non-stative or 'imperfective' meaning is realised by the simple past as in the following examples.

(113) a. *Tá an leabhar scríofa aige.*
        [is book written at-him]
        'He has the book written.'
     b. *Scríobh sé leabhar (uair).*
        [wrote he book (once)]
        'He wrote a book (once).'

The distinction between the perfective and imperfective in Irish can be confirmed by the unusualness of a non-specific temporal adverb with the perfective, i.e. it is questionable whether a sentence like the following is well-formed (at least not with a specific object preceded by a definite article).

(114) ?*Tá/bhí an leabhar scríofa aige uair.*
        [is/was the book written at-him once]

---

[28] Filppula (1999: 108) characterises these as 'stative' or 'resultative' and mentions that they frequently involve a predetermined goal, an interpretation in keeping with those of others before him (Hickey 1995b, 1997b).

With the language shift it would appear that both the syntax and semantics of the Irish structure were transferred to English. This became established along with the regular English construction, as in *Have you read the book?*, yielding the contrast in present-day Irish English which was confirmed by the survey as outlined above.

The stative meaning of *have* with transitive verbs is extended on occasions to cases where *have* is normally interpreted as possessive. This usage is recorded in the author's data collections, as in the following case where the informant is referring to the age of her children at the time of a particular event.

(115)   Stative use of *have*
    And then I had them young when he came out. (WER, F55+)
    'They [the children] were young when he came out [of hospital].'

The clearly stative/resultative semantics of Obj + PP word order furthermore means that it can stand in contrast to the immediate perfective with *after*, as seen in the following sentences.

(116)   a. *They're after putting up street lights.*
       (in the process of building the housing estate)
    b. *They've the street lights put up now.*
       (this was the work they set out to accomplish)

In *A Survey of Irish English Usage* the mean acceptance rate for the resultative perfective was 94 per cent, for twenty-four locations with more than fifteen respondents, which indicates a very low salience for this non-standard feature. The distribution according to counties can be seen in table 4.21.

The situation in contact Scottish English

Given that contact Scottish English has so many structures which are directly parallel to Irish English it is worth looking at this variety in the present context. What is immediately obvious is that contact Scottish English does not appear to have a resultative perfect which is formally similar to that in Irish English (Filppula 1997a: 947 has just one example in his Hebridean corpus). Sabban, in her careful and thorough study (Sabban 1982), does not present any data illustrating anything similar to this structure. As Filppula (1999: 111) rightly notes, the lack of a resultative perfective in contact Scottish English may well be due to the fact that Scottish Gaelic did not develop a structure similar to the Irish construction with the verbal adjective (= past participle). That is, whereas Irish has *Tá sé déanta aige* [is it done-VA at-him], Scottish Gaelic has *Tha e air déanta aige* [is it after doing at-him] for 'he has it done'. Given the absence of O+PP structures in Scottish Gaelic, there would have been no impetus during the language shift in Scotland for transfer into English. Hence the Irish O+PP resultative perfective has no equivalent in contact Scottish English. The fact that it does exist in Irish English strengthens the case for assuming that it developed in Ireland because of the formal equivalent which occurs widely in Irish and which

Table 4.21. *Acceptance figures in* A Survey of Irish English Usage *for the test sentence* She has the housework done

County	Score	N	Total	County	Score	N	Total
Sligo	100%	22	22	Cavan	94%	16	17
Westmeath	100%	25	25	Tipperary	93%	39	42
Donegal	98%	41	42	Dublin	93%	191	205
Wexford	97%	28	29	Kildare	92%	23	25
Belfast	97%	31	32	Louth	91%	29	32
Mayo	97%	36	37	Derry	89%	16	18
Kerry	96%	23	24	Armagh	89%	17	19
Kilkenny	96%	23	24	Meath	89%	33	37
Limerick	96%	25	26	Down	89%	34	38
Waterford	96%	49	51	Cork	89%	75	84
Antrim	95%	39	41	Wicklow	86%	18	21
Clare	94%	15	16	Galway	85%	46	54

was most likely transferred to emerging forms of English during the historical language shift.

4.4.1.4.3   Habitual aspect

The third aspectual distinction which is found in vernacular forms of Irish English is the habitual, a grammatical category used to express an action which occurs repeatedly. This aspectual type can be further subdivided into a durative habitual and an iterative habitual. The former characterises a repeated action which typically lasts for a certain length of time (Dahl 1985: 95–102). If the repeated nature of an action is stressed and duration is backgrounded, then one can speak of an iterative. This is found in standard varieties of English, as in *He often breaks the speed limit with his sportscar*. In vernacular varieties of Irish English an iterative habitual is also found and is formally marked by verbal -*s*, as in *When* I looks *down them stairs,* I gets *dizzy* (WER, F85+). The iterative and the durative are formally encoded within the verb phrase of standard English by the simple present and the progressive respectively. But a formally encoded habitual aspect is not found in standard varieties of English.

The situation with non-standard forms of English is different. Many of them have the habitual as a grammatical category expressed by the verb phrase, i.e. not periphrastically by means of adverbs like *always, often, frequently, continually*, etc. Most prominent among the varieties of English, apart from Irish English, which have a formally encoded habitual, are south-western British English, forms of New World English, chiefly Caribbean English and African American English. The habitual in the New World may be historically connected with that in Ireland and England (Hickey 2004b, 2004h); for a discussion of this issue, see section 6.4.1.

Table 4.22. *Exponence of the habitual (iterative and durative) in varieties of English*

Structure	Example	Comment
Suffixal -*s* on lexical verb stem	*I meets my sister on a Friday afternoon.*	Suffixal -*s* indicates an iterative habitual in Irish English and is most frequent in the first person singular.
Suffixal -*s* on *be* or uninflected *be*	*The men bees at home at the week-ends.*	
Suffixal -*s* on *be* or uninflected *be*, with the lexical verb in the progressive form	*Her husband bees out working in the fields most days.*	Uninflected *be* is typical of African American English.
Suffixal -*s* on *do* or uninflected *do* plus *be*, with the lexical verb in the progressive form	*He does/do* [də] *be buying and selling old cars.*	Uninflected *do* is found in south-eastern Irish English.
Suffixal -*s* on *do* followed by the lexical verb	*He does work in the garden a lot.*	Barbadian English has invariant *does* /dʌz/. Uninflected *do* is found in south-western British English.

Any discussion of the habitual must distinguish between the grammatical category and its exponence (Hickey 1999b).[29] The latter varies across those varieties which have the category of habitual as table 4.22 shows.

Suffixal -*s* and the iterative habitual

The first type of exponence – suffixal -*s* on lexical verb stems – is particularly common in east coast varieties of Irish English (Hickey 2001b: 14–16) and is attested in the author's data collections for Waterford and Dublin. It is also found

---

[29] With the habitual, it is particularly important to distinguish between category and exponence. The existence of the category habitual in Irish would have triggered a search for categorial equivalence among the Irish speakers during language shift. The exponence of the habitual in Irish does not have anything like a formal match in English, neither in its standard form and nor in the habitual structures which have arisen in Irish English historically. This failure to distinguish category and exponence lies behind the unsuccessful attempt by Bliss to account formally for the appearance of *do(es) be* as an expression of the habitual in Irish English after the language shift. His arguments are to be found in Bliss (1972a: 75–81) and (1979: 292f.) and are summarised neatly by Filppula (1999: 137); they will not be repeated here as they have not received support from any scholars then or since. In this context, see Tristram (1997) as well.

in varieties further to the west and south-west which historically are derived from more easterly varieties. South-eastern Irish English is particularly appropriate for examining an iterative habitual marked by verbal -*s* because present-tense verbs, especially *be*, *have* and non-lexical *do*, show no inflection here. Hence the use of inflection, as in *She haves someone come in the morning to help her* (WER, F55+) or *He only haves his birthday every four years (boy born on 29 Feb)* (MLSI, M70, Ballykelly, Co. Wexford), is a clear indication of iterative usage.

(117) Suffixal -*s* as a marker of the iterative habitual
    a. *I gets all mixed up with the buttons on the recorder.* (DER, F60+)
    b. *I don't say anything, I just leaves them off, they're all old enough now.* (DER, F60+)
    c. *I gets grumpy with them all when they're at home.* (DER, M60+)
    d. *I goes down to the Bridge [Hotel] of a Saturday evening.* (WER, F55+)
    e. *I goes every Wednesday.* (MLSI, M70+, Tullaroan, Co. Kilkenny)
    f. *I diets and then I breaks the diet.* (MLSI, M70+, Tullaroan, Co. Kilkenny)
    g. *Tea mostly I drinks.* (MLSI, F65, Kinsale, Co. Cork)
    h. *I does the downstairs rooms first, then I does upstairs, you know.* (WER, F55+)
    i. *I used to feel like . . . 'cause I gets all my things in Penneys.* (WER, F55+)
    j. *The only morning I goes out is on the Tuesday.* (WER, F80+)
    k. *They says I'm Mrs Negative, but I never sees them much now.* (WER, F55+)

Speakers would appear to exploit the contrast of an iterative and a durative habitual. Consider the sentence *And I looks after the little one for her then* (WER, F55+), which could have been *And I do be looking after the little one* to stress duration, going on parallel cases (from the same speaker) like *And I do be dying for sweets* (WER, F55+) which is definitely durative in character. Because the prototypical use of suffixal -*s* is to express an iterative habitual, generic instances like *Some people likes their own little privacy* (DER, M60+) or *Some people puts people into homes* (DER, M60+) should not be taken to invalidate the iterative interpretation offered here.

Suffixal -*s* is found most clearly with the first person, usually in the singular, but also in the plural: *That's what we calls it* (MLSI, M65+, Boherlahan, Co. Tipperary); *We gets it brought to us* (MLSI, F65, Kinsale, Co. Cork); *We pities him on account of the way things happened* (DER, M60+). In other persons, above all in the third person plural, this marking is homophonous with the suffixal -*s* used as part of non-standard verbal concord rules in east coast varieties. However, in such instances the context justifies the iterative interpretation: *They brings the food back up and chews it* (MLSI, M70, Ballykelly, Co. Wexford).

In narrative contexts suffixal -*s* is also found, again typically in the first person singular, given the structure of such discourse, e.g. *I comes back to the house and* _sees_ that the door was after being pushed in (WER, M50+). Its occurrence here may be linked historically to its frequency in south-west England as confirmed by earlier studies such as Elworthy (1877: 52f.) for west Somerset. There is also an instructional use found in the second person, e.g. _You gets a piece of rope and you dips it in tar_ (MLSI, M70, Ballykelly, Co. Wexford).

As an expression of the iterative habitual suffixal -_s_ is by no means recent. It is found in emigrant letters from the early nineteenth century. For instance, there are two letters by one Kean O'Hara, writing from St John's, Jamaica, in 1818–19, back to relatives in Ireland (National Library of Ireland, Ms. 20.298). O'Hara's uses an inflected first person singular as an iterative habitual, e.g. _I hopes the_ [ ] _family are well . . ., I hopes you will except [sic!] my thanks for the same_ . . . (Kean O'Hara, 1818–19). This usage is still to be found in east coast varieties of Irish English.

_Do_ and the durative habitual

Apart from the iterative habitual just discussed, all other cases of the habitual are durative and in the following the term 'habitual' is used without further qualification to mean 'durative habitual'. The verb prototypically associated with this durative is _do_. This is clearly seen in sentences where speakers seem to exploit the option of _do_ to mark habituality as in _He paints in houses for a few bob, you know, he does painting in the houses_ (DER, M35+).

In Irish English across the entire island one can recognise two[30] basic means of expressing a durative habitual: (i) _do(es) be_ or (ii) _be(es)_. The latter is confined to the north of Ireland and Co. Wexford (as a relic area), whereas the former is found elsewhere. These types of durative habitual will be discussed in the remainder of this section.

_Do(es) be_ + V-_ing_

For southern Irish English in general the most common exponence of the habitual is _do(es)_ + _be_ + V-_ing_. It is attested in the east, south, south-west and west in different data collections used for this study. In the south-east _do_ is always uninflected and is reduced phonetically when combined with _be_: _do be_ [də bi].

(118) _Do(es) be_ + V-_ing_ habitual aspect
    a. _They do be always lifting the gates and hiding them._ (TRS-D, L4–1, F)
    b. _It wouldn't be hard for you to be as big as me, I do be saying to her._ (WER, F55+)
    c. _I do be saying, I wonder what do G . . . do with all the designer clothes?_ (WER, F55+)

---

[30] There is also a remnant of unstressed _do_ + lexical verb which is found in the south of Ireland in vernacular rural varieties: _He does 'fish_ (non-emphatic, i.e. habitual) (MLSI, M60, Edenderry, Co. Offaly), _He does 'play hurling_ (MLSI, F60+, Fermoy, Co. Cork), _Big people do 'go around it_ (TRS-D, C41, M). There are also occasional attestations of unstressed _do_ forming a non-habitual past tense, as in _That's what we did 'say to each other_ (SADIF, M 60+, Gorey, Co. Wexford), _I did 'never hear of that at all_ (SADIF, M60+, Bruff, Co. Limerick).

d. *I do be giving out* [complaining – RH] *to him about the state of his room.*
(WER, F55+)
e. *I do be up in a heap . . . I don't be able to get out at all.* (WER, F80+)
f. *I think a lot of people when they do go into homes, some might live . . .*
thrive . . . on it – other people go down the ways. (DER, M60+)
g. *I do be lost talking to him.* 'I am frequently engrossed in conversation
with him' (DER, M60+)
h. *They do be parking at the lay-by.* (RL, F55+)

Authors dealing with the habitual in the south of Ireland assume that *do(es) be*
+ V-*ing* is the most common means of realising this category (Filppula 1999: 143)
and they contrast this with the situation in the south-west of England. However,
certain extensions are also found and were confirmed by the data collections
used here. Apart from the negative habitual, there are cases where *be* itself is in
the habitual, i.e. a following lexical verb is lacking. The extension also includes
habitual *have* and a past habitual. The latter is probably an extension of the
present habitual and would seem to be homophonous with it, i.e. [də bi] (see
last example in (119)). This past habitual is separate from the use of *would* as in
She would be eating because there is a distinct schwa after the [d] following the
personal pronoun *she*.

(119) Extensions of *do(es) be* + V-*ing* habitual aspect
  a. *Do + be*
    All the dances we have now are céilí dances. They do be very good.
    (TRS-D, C42–2, F)
    Well I do be the same now, I likes to get a little walk so I don't get stiff.
    (WER, F80+)
  b. Negative habitual with *be*
    The mother don't be able for it anymore. (WER, M50+)
    And me brother up in the F . . . , his wife don't be well with the nerves.
    (DER, M35+)
  c. *Do + have*
    I do have to go to school with him every morning. (TRS-D, L4–1, F)
    In the morning I do have to get the lads out to work . . . (TRS-D,
    C42–2, F)
    I do have calves to feed of course. (TRS-D, L4–1, F)
  d. Past habitual
    When you used be meeting her, she [də bi] *eating three or four cakes at a*
    time. (DER, M60+)

The origin of the habitual in Irish English

The general title of this section actually covers two separate but related questions.
The first is the rise of the *do(es) be* habitual in the south of Ireland and the second
is the origin of the *be(es)* habitual in the north. The latter structure will be dealt

with at the end of this section and the first will be the main topic, given the many opinions on the rise of the *do(es) be* habitual in the south; see Filppula (1999: 136–50) for a discussion of several of these.

Periphrastic *do* in input varieties of English

There has been much research on the occurrence of periphrastic *do* at the beginning of the early modern period (Ellegård 1953; Kroch 1989; Denison 1985; Ogura 1993; Tieken-Boon van Ostade, van der Wal and Leuvensteijn 1998; Klemola 2002; van der Auwera and Genee 2002; Kortmann 2004). The recent study by Nevalainen and Raumolin-Brunberg (2003: 125f.) confirms that there were two peaks in 1580–99 and 1620–39 after which the structure went into decline in south-east England. But when considering Irish English, the part of Britain which is of interest is the south-west, given its long historical connection with Ireland. Filppula (1999: 141) supports the view that periphrastic *do* was present for much longer in south-west dialects of English (Weltens 1983) and quotes the studies of Klemola (1994, 1996) to support this. With this assumption, the earlier demise of periphrastic *do* in the south-east at the beginning of the seventeenth century, as confirmed by such studies of early English correspondence as Nurmi (1999), does not argue against its presence in English input to Ireland. The latter tended to stem from the western forms of English which would have maintained periphrastic *do* longer than in the east of England.

For many authors (Filppula 1999; Guilfoyle 1983; Harris 1986; Hickey 1995b, 1997a; Kallen 1986) the outset for considering the rise of the *do(es) be* habitual is the variation between the simple present and the present with periphrastic *do* in the early modern period before the language shift began in earnest. For these authors both *I work* and *I do work* would have been possible with *do* in the second case just a 'tense carrier'.

Before proceeding, this view must be refined somewhat. The south-western English input to Ireland has been strongest in the south-east and east of the country. Various phonological and morphological features are shared between the land on both sides of St George's Channel (see section 2.4.4 on Forth and Bargy above for examples and discussion). In syntax, the lack of inflection with auxiliary verbs (Elworthy 1877: 54–7; Wakelin 1986: 36) as well as non-auxiliary *be* and *do* is a prominent common feature.[31] This lack of inflection is reflected in the habitual with *do be* [də bi] in contemporary varieties of south-eastern Irish English.

South-western English input to the south-east and east of Ireland goes back to the late Middle Ages and was sustained for several centuries. It was certainly the source of periphrastic *do* in the south of Ireland. From the east coast, varieties of English deriving from this south-western English input would have later spread

---

[31] Filppula (1999: 143) mentions that a difference between south-western British dialects and Irish English is that the former have uninflected *do* in the habitual while the latter do not. This is not true for the south-east of Ireland where non-lexical *do* is not inflected, a fact of which he was unfortunately not aware.

to the west of Ireland where a certain amount of mixing with other input forms would have taken place. Features of south-western English input are found in the west, for instance, the fortition of sibilants in post-nasal position – as in *wasn't* [wɑdn̩t] – which is attested in contact English in Connemara in west Co. Galway.

For the early modern period one can note that periphrastic *do* was present in eastern varieties of Irish English.[32] In eighteenth century Dublin English there are ample attestations. The Mahon Letters, written by various members of the Mahon family and acquaintances in Dublin during the 1730s and 1740s (Hickey 2005: 162f.), have many instances of unstressed declarative *do* which show that this was still present in the mid eighteenth century: . . . *he was of opinon [sic!] himself that that concern <u>did</u> belong to him and it was to be determined by the opinon of lawyers . . .* (Elli Mahon 1739); *I <u>do</u> assure you that I have been blamed by all my friends* (Anne Kelly 1762).

Periphrastic *do* would appear to be attested in literature reaching into the early nineteenth century. It is true that it is not very common and it is sometimes difficult to decide whether *do* + verb is intended emphatically, e.g. *'Hardress, I am satisfied, I <u>do forgive</u> you'* (Gerald Griffin, *The Collegians*, 1827). But in the works of the prose authors examined for this chapter (Carleton, Griffin and the Banim brothers) there are cases which could be interpreted as periphrastic *do*, as shown in the following examples.

(120) Periphrastic *do* in early nineteenth century literature
   a. *I think that <u>I do remember</u> – it's like a dhrame to me though . . .*
   b. *That's all I tould him I would say, an' that's all <u>I do say</u>.*
      (William Carleton, *The Black Prophet: A Tale of Irish Famine*)
   c. *Indeed and indeed, I <u>do love</u> Maggy still.*
      (John and Michael Banim, *Tales of the O'Hara Family*)
   d. *. . . so <u>do I love</u> the voice of affection and of nature . . .*
      (Gerald Griffin, *The Collegians*)

But whether these occurrences of *do* + verb are meant emphatically or periphrastically is not really a central concern. For the co-option of declarative *do* (see table 4.22 above) for the expression of an habitual by people in the language shift, the actual semantics of the English construction is not the issue, rather the presence of declarative *do* + verb would have been sufficient to prompt the redeployment of the structure for the habitual in shift varieties.

The appearance of the *do(es)* be habitual in Ireland

Given the presence of declarative *do* up to the early nineteenth century in Ireland, the genesis of the *do(es) be* habitual can now be considered. The textual record of Early Modern Irish English is very scant in this respect. There is one late seventeenth century attestation in a north Co. Dublin text (from Fingal, see section

---

[32] Filppula (1999: 143f.) notes the prominence of periphrastic *do* in his Wicklow corpus (south of Dublin) and interprets this as a persisting influence of the Early Modern English input to this region.

2.4.5 above) in which one finds: *No vonder do' it be deare, in trote* 'No wonder do(es) it be dear, in truth' (*Purgatorium Hibernicum*, 1670–5). The interpretation of this as a genuine example of a *do(es) be* habitual rests on the assumption that the word order in this sentence, without the adverbial phrase *No wonder*, would be: *it do(es) be dear, in truth.*

A clearer case is provided in a text by John Michelburne (1646–1721), dating from 1705, called *Ireland Preserved, or the Siege of Londonderry*. It abounds in cases of periphrastic *do* (Filppula 1999: 138) and has one of a *does be* habitual; consider (121a) and the first instance in (121b) below.

(121) a. *Deer Joy, I do let de Trooparr ly wid my Wife in de bad, he does ly at de one side, and my self ly at de toder side, and my wife do lye in de middle side; for fen I do go out to work in de cold Morning . . . and fen de Trooparr do get up, he does go and bring home de Seep and de Muck, and de Shucking Pigg, and we do Eat togeder, and do Sleep togeder, and no body do taake any ting from me, de Trooparr does taake care of every ting.*

b. *Why Neighbour, you do be mauke de Rauvish upon de young Womans, and when dere is a Purchas, you let others run away with it, my shelf and my Comrade do get my part amongst de rest . . .*

The semantics of the instances in (121a) implies habitual action, so that what one could be dealing with here is the same exponence of the habitual as in south-west England, namely *do* + lexical verb. The first instance in (121b) is intermediary between this and the *does be* + V-*ing* habitual of later Irish English in that it has *do be* + infinitive. The implication of instances such as (121a) above is that *do* + lexical verb had habitual uses in Early Modern Irish English. If this interpretation is correct, then the source of this *do* + lexical verb habitual would have been south-western British English input to the east of Ireland which then spread to the rest of the country.

But other scholars do not consider this option. Rather they seem to believe that habitual uses of *do* arose in Ireland. Crucial to such interpretations is the assumption that there was free variation of both bare verb and periphrastic *do* + verb, i.e. that Early Modern Irish English would have had both *I take* and *I do take* without any semantic differentiation.

Under the heading 'Universalist accounts' Filppula (1999: 144f.; 1990) discusses, in a positive light, the view put forward by Eithne Guilfoyle (1983) that adult learners of English in the language shift situation would have been confronted with both a simple present and one in which *do* acts as tense-carrier, as in *I see* and *I do see*. Her view is that this led to the reanalysis of periphrastic *do* + verb as a habitual. This is similar to Kallen's 1986 view where he speaks of reinterpretation. Essentially, this is the standpoint of Harris (1986) as well.

What is important here is to specify the reason why such reanalysis/reinterpretation should have happened. In Hickey (1995b and 1997b) the author stresses that the reason for the later use of periphrastic *do* as a marker of the habitual is that learners of English in the language shift scenario would have searched for an equivalent to their habitual category in Irish and would then have hit on the afunctional periphrastic *do* and co-opted it for the purpose of expressing an habitual in English (Hickey 1997b: 1009–13). As it can be assumed that periphrastic *do* existed in Ireland in the eighteenth century, then it would have been available for co-option to express the habitual in emerging forms of Irish English arising from large-scale language shift which had been initiated in the seventeenth century and got fully under way in the eighteenth century and into the nineteenth century. This time scale would tie up with the appearance of habitual *do* in the first half of the nineteenth century. The standpoints of the various scholars, their similarities and differences are summarised as follows:

1. Both bare verb and periphrastic *do* + verb were found in target varieties of English during the language shift period, mainly in the eighteenth century (Guilfoyle 1983; Filppula 1999; Harris 1986; Hickey 1995b, 1997a, 2000b; Kallen 1986). *Do* + verb may already have had habitual interpretations in some instances (see passage from Michelburne above).
2a. Reanalysis ('reinterpretation' in Kallen's terminology) of periphrastic *do* + verb as the exponence of an habitual occurred (Guilfoyle 1983; Filppula 1999 and Harris 1986 in part; Kallen 1986).
 b. Co-option of periphrastic *do* + verb as the exponence of the habitual in emerging shift varieties occurred under the pressure for categorial equivalence of the habitual in Irish (Hickey 1995b, 1997a, 2000b).

The essential difference between steps (2a) and (2b) in the establishment of habitual *do(es) be* in Irish English is that (2a) sees reanalysis of free variants (simple verb and periphrastic *do* + verb) as the main impetus, whereas (2b) regards the search on the part of speakers of Irish for an equivalence to the habitual, which they knew from their native language, as the essential trigger. Step (2b) offers a reason for the co-option of periphrastic *do*+ verb whereas (2a) does not appear to suggest a motivation for the reanalysis, unless it implicitly assumes that the search for categorial equivalence was also operative here. In this case, it would be necessary to make this explicit particularly as this is a key issue in language shift scenarios.

Why *do(es) be* + V-*ing?*

In his discussion of the habitual, Filppula (1999: 143) discusses differences between dialects of British and Irish English with regard to exponence. As is known from Klemola's detailed studies (Klemola 1994, 1996), *do* + lexical verb is the exponence in south-western dialects of British English and Filppula (1999: 143) highlights this as a difference between British and Irish realisations of the habitual.

(122) a.   south-western British English: *He do work hard.*
      b.   southern Irish English: *He does be working hard.*

The simple question which results from this observation is: if input varieties with periphrastic *do* are the formal source of the later habitual in Irish English why does one have *do* + lexical verb in England, but *do(es)* + *be* + expanded form in Irish English?

Furthermore if, as most authors seem to accept, there was free variation between the simple present and the present with periphrastic *do* in Early Modern Irish English and if, for slightly different reasons, this *do* was reinterpreted (Guilfoyle, Harris, Kallen) or functionalised (Filppula, Hickey) as a marker of the habitual, why did it not remain as *do* + lexical verb? This would have been the most parsimonious solution (Filppula 2003b) and would have involved least restructuring or reanalysis by speakers. The combinations of *do* + *be* (+ V-*ing*), which arose as exponents of a habitual in Irish English, represent an apparently unnecessary complication for which some principled explanation needs to be found. The answer put forward in this study is that a pattern in Irish was transferred to Irish English and spread to produce the type of habitual exponence which can be observed so abundantly from the mid nineteenth century onwards.

The role of negative imperatives

Irish is known for the existence of an habitual. This is expressed using a particular form of the verb 'be' together with an expanded form, as seen in the following example.

(123) *Bíonn sé ag obair go crua.*
      [be-HABITUAL he at working hard]
      IrEng: 'He does be working hard.'

This Irish habitual would seem to have been transferred into English, but the way may have been circuitous. To understand this, observe the fact that in the regional novel *Castle Rackrent* (1801) by Maria Edgeworth (contained in *A Corpus of Irish English*; see Hickey 2003a) there are no instances of a *do(es)* + *be* habitual but the structure *do* + *be* does indeed occur, in the negative imperative. This structure is also found in the works of other authors from the early nineteenth century. Consider the following instances.

(124) a.   *Ah, don't be being jealous of that, (says she) I didn't hear a sentence . . .*
      b.   *. . .that's a great shame, but don't be telling Jason what I say.*
      c.   *. . . (says I) don't be trusting to him, Judy*
      d.   *Don't be talking of punch yet a while . . .*
      e.   *Nay don't be denying it, Judy, for I think the better of ye for it.*
           (Maria Edgeworth, *Castle Rackrent*, 1801)
      f.   *So don't be puttin' bad constructions on things too soon.*

g.   ... *behave yourself, can't you, and* <u>*don't be vexin'*</u> *the masther.*
(William Carleton, *The Black Baronet*)

h.   <u>*don't be tormentin'*</u> *us wid yourself and your brats.*
(William Carleton, *The Black Prophet*)

i.   <u>*Don't be cryin'*</u> *so much* ... (William Carleton, *The Hedge School*)

j.   ... *don't be boasting of what you did, the way you do.*
(William Carleton, *Phelim O'Toole's Courtship*)

k.   *I'll thry to think iv id, an'* <u>*don't be lookin'*</u> *so dushmal.*
(John and Michael Banim, *Tales of the O'Hara Family*, 1825–6)

l.   *'A'* <u>*don't be talking*</u>*', returned Danny, turning his head away.*
(Gerald Griffin, *The Collegians*)

m.   *'*<u>*don't be talking*</u> *bad of any one', says he*
(Samuel Lover 1797–1868, *The Gridiron*)

The negative imperative with *don't be* + V-*ing* is particularly common in the works just cited. For instance, there are more than fifty occurrences in the 1.6 million words of Carleton's *Traits and Stories of the Irish Peasantry* (1830–3) from which the instances above are taken.

The occurrence of the continuous form with the (negative) imperative in Irish English was, and is, quite typical. Its source would seem to lie in Irish where the habitual verb form *bí* 'be' is always used in the imperative; the non-habitual *tá* 'is' only occurs in the indicative. The habitual in Irish furthermore requires a continuous form of the lexical verb it governs. There is also a prosodic equivalence: both Irish and Irish English have two stressed syllables at the beginning of such structures: *Ná bí* ... [' '] and *Don't be* ... [' ']. Examples of its use are the following:

(125) a.   *Ná bí ag déanamh imní faoi na leanaí.*
[not be-IMPERATIVE at doing worry under the children]
'Don't be worrying about the children.'

b.   *Ná bí ag labhairt mar sin.*
[not be-IMPERATIVE at speaking like that]
'Don't be talking like that.'

The suggestion being put forward here is that the negative imperative was the locus at which *do* + *be* entered Irish English. It is true that for English the *do* here is the support verb found with the negative, as in *don't be ridiculous*, but for the Irish this could have been interpreted as an equivalent of the negative imperative of Irish, something which would have been underscored by the prosodic equivalence of Irish and English in this respect.

If Maria Edgeworth, publishing in 1801, has this type of negative imperative then it is safe to assume that this had established itself in Irish English at the latest by the closing decades of the eighteenth century. The language change which lies behind the attestations of the *do(es) be* habitual in the early nineteenth century would then be an extension of the (negative) imperative habitual to the indicative as follows.

(126) a. *Don't be worrying about the children.*   negative habitual imperative →
      b. *I do be worrying about the children.*   habitual indicative

Is this type of scenario credible? Apart from the formal arguments just presented, there is more general support for such a development from literature on language change. In her discussion of syntactic variation and prominence, Jenny Cheshire proposes that it is in low-profile, non-salient contexts that change can arise in a language and spread out from there (Cheshire 1996). In her treatment of the subject, Cheshire sees sites such as pre-verbal position, main clauses, emphatic declaratives and explicit negatives as having high prominence. Others, such as subordinate clauses or weak affirmatives, have low prominence. This would also apply to negative imperatives which Cheshire, given the fact that she was not looking at Irish English, did not of course specify. In a language contact/language shift scenario the low prominence positions of the donor language (here: the negative imperative) would represent the source in the initial phase of change, similar to that of incoming variants with dialect contact. Later, with the spread of a structure within the receiving language, it may become a marker for the community using the variety with this structure, as is the case with the *do(es) be* + V-*ing* habitual in vernacular forms of southern Irish English today.

If negative imperatives were the locus where the *do(es) be* + V-*ing* habitual started in Irish English then there should be at least some textual record where just this form of the habitual is found but not the indicative declarative type which later evolved. This is indeed the case with Maria Edgeworth who precedes authors like Carleton, the Banim brothers or Griffin by at least two decades.

That the negative imperative is a syntactic context of low salience received direct confirmation in *A Survey of Irish English Usage*. Here the acceptance range for the test sentence *Don't be teasing your brother* was between 100 per cent and 76 per cent and the mean was 93 per cent. Rates of this magnitude were only attained by such syntactic structures as the *after*-perfective or the resultative perfective with object + past participle word order (see relevant sections above).

The habitual in the nineteenth century

Apart from the single text by Michelburne, the eighteenth century offers no attestations of a *do(es) be* habitual. Instead one must look to the early nineteenth century when authors portraying Irish speech in their prose suddenly begin to show this structure.

(127) *Do(es) be* habitual in early nineteenth century literature
      a.   . . . *there's another set of men – these outlaws that <u>do be robbin'</u> rich people's houses.* (William Carleton, *The Evil Eye*)
      b.   *I'll be tellin' Father Finnerty that <u>you do be spakin'</u> up to the girls!* (William Carleton, *Going to Maynooth*)

    c.   . . . *when they do be spakin' soft to one another.* (William Carleton, *The Miser*)

    d.   . . . *the lawyers do be dhrawin' up their writins . . .*
       (William Carleton, *The Poor Scholar*)

    e.   . . . *'tis out of that spancel that Mull do be milking your cows every night; . . . whenever there's does be any complaints of hard usage . . .; the gould that does be always troubling us in the ground; I do be often goen' that way of a lonesome night; Still an' all, Myles do be poor . . .*
       (Gerald Griffin, *The Collegians*, 1827)

    f.   *'They do be together in the fields at night'*
       (John and Michael Banim, *The Nowlans*, 1826)

The authors quoted above are from Tyrone in the north (Carleton), from Kilkenny in the east (the Banim brothers) and from Limerick in the lower-west (Griffin). This would imply that the *do(es) be* + V-*ing* habitual was established throughout Ireland by the first quarter of the nineteenth century. It was probably the case earlier, even before the turn of the nineteenth century, assuming that all three authors were not using, in their prose, a recent innovation in Irish English. After the middle of the nineteenth century, this habitual increases considerably and is widely attested in the works of Dion Boucicault (from Dublin) and both Lady Gregory and John Millington Synge who were attempting to represent the speech of rural inhabitants of the west.

(128) *Do(es) be* habitual in Boucicault's plays

    a.   *Sure he does be always telling me my heart is too near my mouth.*
       (*The Shaughraun*, 1875)

    b.   *Sure I do be ashamed, sir. I do be afraid to go near some girls . . .*
       (*Arrah na Pogue*, 1864)

Attestations of the habitual are not confined to literary documents. The emigrant letters, used for this study, show many instances of *do(es) be* + V-*ing*, confirming that the authors who show this in their prose were reflecting a genuine and widespread feature of Irish English by the mid nineteenth century. In (129) there is a small selection of instances from individuals writing from Rossmore, Co. Cork (north of Clonakilty, Ó Cuív 1969: 138), an area which would still have been at least 50 per cent Irish-speaking (Mac Giolla Chríost 2005: 105) in the mid nineteenth century.

(129) *Do(es) be* habitual in emigrant letters

    a.   *I do be disputing with my mother sometimes that I'll go to America and my mother gets angry with me for saying that I would go for she says she would feel too lonesome.* (IEL, 1857, Rossmore, Co. Cork)

    b.   *My Dear son when I do get your letter, all the neighbours do run to see what account does be in it, except Dick Robert.* (IEL, 1861, Rossmore, Co. Cork)

c. . . . *I do not be empty any time, I do have it from time to time always but the others do send me a little* . . . (IEL, 1859, Rossmore, Co. Cork)

d. *My Dear son I am unwell in my health this length of time if I do be one day up I do be two days lying down and I never wrote that to any of ye.* (IEL, 1861, Rossmore, Co. Cork)

e. *I do be sick every year at this time but I was not prepared any time untill now.* (IEL, 1861, Rossmore, Co. Cork)

f. *A ship getting loaded with frosen meat it would open their eyes, they do be loading meat on it from eight in the morning till ten at night.* (IEL, New Zealand)

The '*be(es)*' habitual in the north of Ireland

If the above explanation for the relatively sudden appearance of the *do(es)* + *be* habitual in nineteenth-century southern Irish English is accepted, then certain developments can be linked to it. To begin with, consider that Montgomery and Kirk (1996) are puzzled by the fact that the typical habitual of northern Irish English,[33] i.e. *be(es)* /biː(z)/, is not attested before the early nineteenth century. They note that the Irish scholar O'Donovan in his *A Grammar of the Irish Language* (1845) mentions, in passing, the attempts of the Irish to produce an equivalent to the habitual of Irish (his consuetudinal present): 'The Irish attempt to introduce this tense even into English, as "he bees", "he does be", &c.' (O'Donovan 1845: 151, also quoted in Montgomery and Kirk 1996). It is significant that O'Donovan associates the habitual with the Irish and that he had already done this by 1845. But it is also significant that O'Donovan explicitly mentions *bees* as one of two options for expressing the habitual in Irish English.

The lack of attestations for inflected *be* before the nineteenth century, which is the central theme of Montgomery and Kirk (1996), might on the other hand suggest that northern Irish English speakers began to use inflected *be* in this habitual sense on the model of the *do(es) be* habitual which had become established in other varieties of Irish English prior to this. Montgomery and Kirk (1996: 316) cite two emigrant letters where habitual *be(es)* is found in a manner typical for it at later stages (see the discussion in McCafferty 2007).

(130) a. *When I be long getting A letter I have nothing to plie to but the likness.* (*Sproule Letters*, 1860)

b. *He bes up 3 or 4 times a night With Her.* (*Sproule Letters*, 1861)

These attestations are nearly four decades later than those for the *do(es) be* habitual with Griffin and Carleton (see above). Furthermore, the relatively abundant

---

[33] The north can be understood to extend down south-west into north Connaught. Henry (1957: 169) has *bees* for north Co. Roscommon (*There bees a fret o' people at the fairs o' Boyle*) and it was recorded in the material for *A Linguistic Survey of Ireland* in north Co. Mayo (*Some of 'em bees in a ramshackle way, Dohertys (a petrol station) bes open*).

occurrence of the *do(es) be* habitual with Carleton is significant here: he was an Irish speaker from Co. Tyrone (Ulster), the same location from which Montgomery and Kirk's correspondents came. This fact supports the possibility of diffusion of the habitual as a category from Irish-influenced varieties to those based more on Scots or northern English input. Whether diffusion from Irish to English or an influence of varieties of English with *do(es) be* can be plausibly posited for Ulster is an unresolved question. There remains the remarkable fact that neither structure, *do(es) be* nor *be(s)*, is significantly attested before the nineteenth century, indeed the latter is not documented at all before the middle of that century.

Other scholars have put forward different views of the genesis of the *be(s)* habitual. Traugott, in her history of English syntax, implies that this habitual is of Scots origin (Traugott 1972: 89, 191f.) and that it continues a distinction from Old English between generic *wesan* and habitual *beon* (McCafferty 2007). Harris (1986) also considers Scots a more likely source than Irish. This view is difficult to substantiate because the attestations of *bees* are relatively sparse. There is only one instance in the *Helsinki Corpus of Older Scots* of some eighty texts totalling about 800,000 words (see (131c)). In historical texts from England, mostly northern texts from the early-to-mid Middle English period, there are instances of *bes* (= *bees*) (see (131a)). This form was later replaced by *is* in all contexts, whether habitual or not. In medieval Irish English there are inflected forms of the verb *beon* 'be', particularly in one poem (see (131b)). But there are no continuations of this verb with inflectional *-s* in later varieties of Irish English. Specifically, the many texts illustrating Irish English from the seventeenth century onwards do not have any instances of *bees*. The form is not found in Restoration drama or with nineteenth century novelists like Edgeworth, Carleton, the Banim brothers or Griffin. Later dramatists of the nineteenth century and into the twentieth century, from Boucicault through Synge to O'Casey, do not have any instances of the form either.

(131) Attestations of *be(es)* in historical texts
   a. Attestations from *Helsinki Corpus of English Texts* and *International Computer Archive of Middle English Texts* (*ICAMET*, Innsbruck)
   Mi hert bes neuer broght in rest. 'My heart <u>bees</u> never brought to rest.'
   It bes not lang þat i ne dei. 'It <u>bees</u> not long that I not die.'
   (*Cursor Mundi*, northern, *c.* 1300)
   J woth þat he bes ded ful raþe. 'I wish with anger that he <u>bees</u> dead.'
   For þis wimman bes mike wo! 'For this women <u>bees</u> much woe.'
   (*The Lay of Havelock the Dane*, Lincolnshire, thirteenth century)
   . . . hit bes forloren sone. 'It <u>bees</u> (the) forlorn son.'
   (*The Ancrene Riwle*, probably western, *c.* 1230)
   tho yt bes mor gentil of colour. 'though it <u>bees</u> more gentle of colour.'
   . . . yt bes moche dirk. '. . . it <u>bees</u> much dark.'
   (*The London Lapidary of King Philip*, early–mid fourteenth century)

In welth bees oure wakyng. 'In wealth bees our waking.'
(Richard Rolle of Hampole, Yorkshire, early fourteenth century)
Bees not to wyse in youre conseytes. 'Bees not too wise in your conceits.'
Bees not to sekyr only of feyth. 'Bees not too certain only of faith.'
(*Speculum Christiani*, fourteenth century)

b. Attestations of *beo / beoþ / beon* from early fourteenth-century Irish English

þer beo dedly sinnes seuen. 'There be seven deadly sins.'
þat letten men to com to heuen. 'Which stop men coming to heaven.'
Of angur and ire ge shol here. 'Of anger and ire you shall hear.'
þat beoþ sibbe to þese fiue. 'That be related to these five.'
Bot þei man beo of heye blod. 'But the man be of high blood.'
Nou beon foure in companye. 'Now be four in company.'
(*Iesu, þat wolde for vs dye*, from material in Heuser 1904: 185–229)

c. Attestation from *Helsinki Corpus of Older Scots*

. . . if it be agreeable to your Lordship that this young man bees called to be minister of Tarbat. (John Lord MacLeod to his father, Tarbat, 8 July 1705)

Both Traugott and Harris have pointed out that the Scots origin of *be(es)* would help to explain the continuation (in their view) of this habitual in varieties of English in North America, notably African American English which shows a similarly realised habitual (*be* but without inflection). However, as Montgomery and Kirk (1996) and Kirk and Millar (1998) insist, there are no textual records to prove a continuation of a Scots *be(s)* habitual through Ulster to North America, despite the significant historical emigration from Ulster to the New World in the eighteenth century (Bardon 1996: 141).

The statements so far have concerned the rise of the option *bees* as a realisation of *be* with habitual meaning in northern Irish English. It is true that the form *bees / bes* is not attested in Ulster before the mid-nineteenth century as Montgomery and Kirk (1996: 316–18) state.[34] But (indicative) invariant *be* is well documented in a series of texts both north and south from the beginning of the early modern period onwards. The semantics of the attestations are of a generic / stative nature as shown in the following.

(132) Generic / stative usage of invariant *be* in Irish English texts

a. *. . . and you be fules, I'le stay no lenger.* 'and you be fools, I'll stay no longer.' (Thomas Randolph, *Hey for Honesty*, c. 1630/1651)

b. *But I be mostly call'd Honest Humphry.* (Richard Brinsley Sheridan, *St Patrick's Day*, 1775)

c. *Saint Patrick blesh vs we be not betraid.* 'Saint Patrick bless us we be not betrayed.' (*Captain Thomas Stukeley*, 1596/1605)

---

[34] Corrigan (1997b) sees the interaction of the Irish substrate with input forms of English and Scots as responsible for the rise of the *be(s)* habitual in east Ulster in the mid nineteenth century.

d. . . . *you be de great Fool to put your Wife in de Priest shamber.*
e. *You be de Fool, de Quaakers be our own Peoples.*
f. *We be dose, de Rebels call Rapparees, we be de Kings gued Voluntiers.*
g. *They be de braave Franch-man.*
    (John Michelburne, *Ireland Preserved*, 1705)
h. *I be quite single Thank God, my Relations be all dead.*
    (Richard Brinsley Sheridan, *St Patrick's Day*, 1775)

It is known from the present-day habitual in the south of Ireland that it can be used to make a generic statement (see table 4.40 below) so an extension in the opposite direction, i.e. from generic to habitual, should be equally possible, given that there is no a priori reason for assuming unidirectionality in these developments as opposed to what is generally assumed for grammaticalisation clines, for instance. One can also say that not all instances of a formal habitual have the same habitual meaning: there is quite a degree of fluidity in semantics here, as Montgomery and Kirk (1996: 321) readily concede, and which can best be handled within a non-binary model like prototype theory (Hickey 2000b); see comments in section 4.5.4 below.

Not only is (indicative) invariant *be* attested in Irish English, but also in British English in the early modern period (see (133)) and in early forms of American English, as Montgomery and Kirk (1996: 318) confirm.

(133) Invariant *be* in Early Modern English texts
    a. . . . *and whan they be dry, they laye them to-gether on heapes, lyke hey-cockes.* (Anthony Fitzherbert, *The Book of Husbandry*, 1534)
    b. . . . *before they be fully digested, or made ripe.*
        (*A New Boke of the Natures and Properties of All Wines*, 1568)
    c. *Syr, we be yong ientlemen; . . . And verilie they be fewest of number.*
        (Roger Ascham, *The Scholemaster*, 1563–8)
    d. . . . *where it lies ten or twelve dayes before it be enlivened.*
    e. *Sir, they be principally three, namely, March, April, and May.*
        (Izaak Walton, *The Compleat Angler*, 1653–76)

The issue in the present section can now be formulated as follows: when did inflected *be*, i.e. *bees*, arise in northern Irish English and was this directly linked with the development of an habitual sense for *bees*? This later habitual sense is not always realised with inflection because the verb *be* is sensitive to verbal concord requirements in northern Irish English. Thus habitual use as in the sentence *They be out drinking at the weekend* would not take inflected *be* as the immediately preceding pronoun *they* would block suffixal *-s* on the grounds of verbal concord. The restrictions which operate here means that any instance of personal pronoun + *be* (except the third person singular, i.e. *I be, we be, you be, they be*) could in fact be an instance of a *be(es)* habitual where the inflection is suppressed by a preceding personal pronoun.

It is worth reconsidering attestations of possible input to Ulster in the light of inflected *be* and verbal concord. The *Helsinki Corpus of Older Scots* contains many instances of invariant *be* preceded by a personal pronoun (see (134)). These appear to be of the generic/stative type but could well be precursors to later habitual usages.

(134) Invariant *be* in the *Helsinki Corpus of Older Scots*
     a. *Bot among ws Jewis (thocht we be puire) thair ar no beggaris fund.*
        'But among us Jews (though we be poor) there are no beggars found.'
        (*The Accusatioun of Mr George Wischart Gentill*, 1562/78)
     b. *Protesting alwayis we be hard concerning the ancient Docteurs.*
        (William Fowler, *Ane Answer Vnto the Epistle*, 1590)
     c. *A boll of oates, and they be gud, will give a boll of meal.*
        (John Skene (?), *Of Husbandrie*, 1669)
     d. *And that they be scotsmen or naturalized strangers and residenters within the said Kingdome.* (*The Acts of the Parliaments of Scotland*, 1661–86)

Montgomery and Kirk (1996) are correct to point to a lack of attestations for *bees* in both post-medieval Irish English texts and those from England and Scotland (see (134) and comments above). They are also right to question any assumption of a direct line from Ulster Scots to African American English with regard to the habitual. Invariant *be* was available in varieties of Early Modern English and can be found in generic/stative contexts. These may have been extended to habitual meanings within African American English, a development which would be sufficient to explain the present-day distribution there without recourse to Ulster Scots input.

For northern Irish English one can conclude that inflected *be*, i.e. *bees*, is a nineteenth century development, assuming that the textual record, including emigrant letters, is a genuine reflection of language use in the nineteenth century and before. If the latter is accurate, then *bees* did not appear in either letters or historical texts because the form did not exist in the speech of the people before the first half of the nineteenth century.

There remains the issue of why habitual *be(es)* arose in the nineteenth century in the north of Ireland. The trigger for this could have been the rise of the *do(es) be* habitual in varieties of English deriving from contact with Irish which, as Carleton (a native Irish speaker from Co. Tyrone) shows, was to be found in central Ulster. Shift varieties of Irish English also existed in the south of Ulster, in Armagh for instance (Corrigan 1997b), so that Scots-derived English in the north/north-east would have been geographically fairly close to shift-derived varieties.

A further question, following from this, is why *be(es)* should have been used for the habitual. From early modern texts it is known that invariant *be* existed in Ireland. It is also known that invariant *be* existed in older forms of Scots and so also in the input varieties of English to Ulster from Scotland. However, regular forms of the *be* paradigm, i.e. *am, is, are*, also existed so that the ultimate

Table 4.23. *Development of invariant* be *to* be(es) *habitual in Ulster English*

Period	Form	Function	Change
pre-19th c.	invariant *be*	generic/stative	— — —
early 19th c.	invariant *be*	habitual	shift in meaning due to contact with Irish or Irish English with *do(es) be?*
early to mid 19th c.	inflected *be* (*be/bees*)	habitual	application of existing verbal concord requirements

fate of invariant *be* was probably its demise or re-functionalisation. The latter path would seem to have been chosen by using invariant *be* as the exponence of the habitual as attested from the mid nineteenth century onwards. With this re-functionalisation, invariant *be* may have become subject to the requirements of verbal concord in Ulster which would have meant a change to *bees* in those environments which required suffixal -*s*. Finally, it can be said that in semantic terms the use of invariant *be* for the habitual would have represented only a small step as it was available in generic/stative senses anyway. These morphological and semantic developments can be summarised as shown in table 4.23.

Inflected *be* as habitual in south-eastern Irish English

There is a further twist to the issue of habitual *bees* in Ireland. The form is normally taken not to occur in the south. For instance, in the author's data collections there were none for Dublin and for Waterford there was only one instance: *They bees out fishin' of a Saturday* (WER, M50+); see Hickey (2002c: 304). Because this was a single example, it was not considered overly significant; the normal expression of the habitual in Waterford is with *do be* [də bi].

However, an examination of the material for *A Linguistic Survey of Ireland*, housed at the University of Galway library, revealed that inflected habitual *be* was recorded for a number of informants (all elderly rural males) in Co. Wexford as shown in (135) (the spelling *be's* for [biz] is that of the data collectors).

(135) *Be's* in south-eastern Irish English (Co. Wexford)
  a. MLSI, M70, Ballykelly, Co Wexford
    The week-day be's a quiet day.
    The cows they be's milking in stages.
    They be's on some wheat too.
    A white bird be's up there.
    Wheat be's in blossom.
    Crickets be's around the fire.

  b. MLSI, M69, M81, M90, Blackwater, Co. Wexford
     May often be's a hard month.
     Now they be's all sowed whole (seed potatoes).
  c. MLSI, M72, M77, M82, Adamstown, Co. Wexford
     All three have *be's* for habitual: *That be's* . . . (note by data collector)

In the comments on forms and usage of *be* at locations in other counties adjacent to Co. Wexford, Wicklow to the north, Kilkenny to the west (there were no informants from east Co. Waterford), the data collectors make no references to habitual inflected *be*.

The existence of this habitual form in Co. Wexford (see the returns in *A Survey of Irish English Usage* in table 4.27 below), albeit it recessively, is significant. It can help to explain why the Irish grammarian O'Donovan in his grammar of 1845 mentions the use of *be(es)* as an option for expressing the habitual (see remarks above). O'Donovan was born in Co. Kilkenny in the east/south-east of Ireland (Boylan 1988: 288), an area where *bees* may well have been an option for the expression of the habitual, given the attestations for neighbouring Co. Wexford from the materials for *A Linguistic Survey of Ireland* (see (135) above). On this point, note that Joyce, a southerner writing at the beginning of the twentieth century, mentions this type of habitual, without specifying that it is northern, let alone exclusively so: *My father bees always at home in the morning* (Joyce 1979 [1910]: 86). The single instance in the author's Waterford English Recordings may thus be a remnant of a former, much wider usage in this area. This conclusion would also help to explain why inflected *bees* appeared as an habitual marker (alongside an habitual with *do*, Clarke 1997a) in varieties of English in Newfoundland which derive from eighteenth- and early nineteenth-century immigration from the south-east of Ireland.

Past habitual with *were to*

A realisation of the past habitual, which has not been remarked on by scholars hitherto, was found in contact regions of the west of Ireland. This is the use of *were to* as a past habitual as can be seen clearly in the following examples. It occurs repeatedly in the speech of an informant of the *Tape-Recorded Survey of Hiberno-English Speech* and with two speakers in the author's *A Collection of Contact English* (see (136)). The speakers in the latter case were both males from the Carna peninsula in west Connemara. The feature seems to be local to this area and was not found in either the Kerry or the Donegal Gaeltacht. The origin of this usage is uncertain as Irish does not provide any ready pattern which could have been the model (but see the brief remarks in Ó Máille 1980). It is conceivable that modal uses of *be to* (very common in the north, see Corrigan 2000b) were reanalysed as aspectual and extended to the past where the interpretation was habitual.

(136) *Were to* as past habitual
  a. *They were to make it in the old days* . . . (TRS-D, C41, M)
  b. *They were to cut it and burn it and make kelp of out it.* (TRS-D, C41, M)

c. *They were to take iodine and soap out of this kelp.* (TRS-D, C41, M)
d. *We were to sell it down to Kilrush.* (TRS-D, C41, M)
e. *There were to be a lot of hunting.* (TRS-D, C41, M)
f. *Well, we were to go to Galway once a month or so.* (CCE-W, M1 70+)
g. *I suppose, he* [the vet – RH] *were to check the sheep for fluke.* (CCE-W, M2 70+)

A Survey of Irish English Usage

Before discussing the results of this survey, it is necessary to point out that, as a vernacular feature of Irish English, the habitual is generally stigmatised. For this reason, the acceptance figures for various forms of this aspect (see tables 4.24–4.28) never reached the values which were achieved by the immediate and resultative perfectives, both of which showed 100 per cent acceptance rates for many counties (the averages were 86 per cent and 94 per cent respectively). This means that, in relative terms, acceptance rates of over about 20 per cent for the habitual can be regarded as significant.

In the survey a number of test sentences were included to see what the acceptability of forms of the habitual were like throughout Ireland. The first test sentence embodied the use of suffixal -s as the exponence of the habitual: *I gets awful anxious about the kids at night.* The assumption that this feature has a strong south-eastern bias in Ireland was strengthened by the survey results. Suffixal -s for the habitual had the highest acceptance rate in Wexford (45 per cent) with Waterford and Kilkenny not far behind (35 per cent and 38 per cent respectively), about twice the island-wide mean of 18 per cent.

The second sentence showed the use of *does be* for the habitual: *She does be worrying about the children.* The twenty-one counties with a value of 25 per cent and more were all outside Northern Ireland, indeed Donegal with 29 per cent is the only one within Ulster. Significantly, the two counties with the strongest Ulster Scots populations showed very low acceptance rates: Down (5 per cent) and Antrim (7 per cent) (see table 4.24).

Past habitual with *used (to)*

The past habitual with *used (to)* is a common feature of Irish English and is a formal equivalent to the *do(es)* + *be* habitual of the present. However, *used (to)* can be found in both stative and habitual contexts,[35] something which is not so common in the present (but see the extension of the habitual prototype discussed in 4.5.4). *Use* in the past can take an infinitival complement without *to* (as can *help*, *allow*, etc. in Irish English).

---

[35] Binnick (2005: 342f.) denies that habits are states and hence that the habitual is used to describe states. However, given his patchy and unsystematic data (drawn largely from internet searches), he has missed the generalisation that the methods for expressing the habitual may be used in a minority of cases to express states as well. This is an extension of the habitual prototype – a recurring action of a certain duration – to non-typical instances.

Table 4.24. *Acceptance figures in* A Survey of Irish English Usage *for the test sentence* She does be worrying about the children

County	Score	N	Total	County	Score	N	Total
Louth	53%	17	32	Mayo	27%	10	37
Sligo	41%	9	22	Tipperary	26%	11	42
Galway	41%	22	54	Belfast	25%	8	32
Westmeath	36%	9	25	Kildare	20%	5	25
Meath	35%	13	37	Clare	19%	3	16
Wexford	34%	10	29	Dublin	18%	37	205
Kilkenny	33%	8	24	Derry	17%	3	18
Armagh	32%	6	19	Kerry	13%	3	24
Cavan	29%	5	17	Antrim	7%	3	41
Donegal	29%	12	42	Cork	6%	5	84
Waterford	29%	15	51	Wicklow	5%	1	21
Limerick	27%	7	26	Down	5%	2	38

Table 4.25. *Highest acceptance figures in* A Survey of Irish English Usage *for the test sentence* Did you use to cycle to school?

County	Score	N	Total	County	Score	N	Total
Antrim	78%	32	41	Down	63%	24	38
Belfast	66%	21	32	Derry	61%	11	18

(137) a. Habitual: *We used to go to the Royal Bar of a Saturday, but we've gone off it a bit now, you know it's got very loud.* (WER, F55+)
The park used be great fun, usen't it? (DER, M60+)

b. Stative: *The parcel office used be down on the quay but they're out off the Cork road now.* (WER, M50+)

The past habitual with *used to* was also tested in this survey with the sentence *Did you use to cycle to school?* The results showed a very clear pattern between north and south. Nine counties outside Ulster have zero acceptance of *did + use to* in interrogatives: Carlow, Clare, Cork, Kildare, Leitrim, Longford, Mayo, Offaly, Sligo. At the other extreme were counties in north and north-east Ulster which showed values of over 60 per cent (see table 4.25). For the six counties of Northern Ireland plus Donegal the average was 56 per cent. This dropped off drastically along the southern border with Ulster, for instance Cavan and Louth had only 6 per cent acceptance.

A hypothesis of the author is that the use of *do* with *use to* is inversely proportional to the use of *do* to express the habitual. The results of the survey seem

Table 4.26. *Relative acceptance figures in* A Survey of Irish English Usage *for the test sentences (1)* She does be worrying about the children *and (2)* Did you use to cycle to school?

County	(1) *does be* habitual	(2) combination of *did* + *use to*
Antrim	7%	78%
Belfast	25%	66%
Down	5%	63%
Derry	17%	61%
Louth	53%	6%
Sligo	41%	0%
Galway	41%	6%
Westmeath	36%	8%

to confirm this. If one contrasts the high and low values for both the sentences embodying these structures then a clear picture emerges.

An explanation for the distribution shown in table 4.26 is probably that, in those locations where the *does be* habitual is well represented, the occurrence of *do* with *use to* is low because *use to* is interpreted as an habitual anyway and the use of *do* with it – as in *Did you use to cycle to school?* – would be seen as redundant double marking.

If the general acceptance of the *does be* habitual in the north is so low, what exponence of the habitual occurs there? The answer is inflected *be*. This was tested with a sample sentence in *A Survey of Irish English Usage* and there was a clear pattern of contrasting acceptance between the north and south, as can be seen in table 4.27. Indeed for many counties in the south of Ireland the acceptance was zero: Carlow, Cavan, Clare, Galway, Kerry, Kildare, Kilkenny, Longford, Louth, Meath, Monaghan, Roscommon all had values of 0 per cent.

What is noticeable in the set of results in table 4.27 is that Co. Wexford pairs with the counties in Ulster. This might appear anomalous and seemed so to the author when evaluating the returns. But the subsequent examination of the material for *A Linguistic Survey of Ireland* revealed that *bees* was attested in Co. Wexford, but not in other counties of the east/south-east (such as Wicklow or Waterford); see the discussion above. It was obvious that the respondents from Co. Wexford recognised habitual *bees* as a vernacular option in their area, something which was true nowhere else in the south of Ireland. This finding also vindicated the survey as a valid procedure for testing acceptance of non-standard features in different regions of the country.

However, there was one difficulty with this test for *bees*. The sentence used to test for acceptance of inflected *be* was not necessarily well-formed because *bees* would not be expected immediately after the personal pronoun *they*. In order to

Table 4.27. *Acceptance figures in* A Survey of Irish English Usage *for the test sentence* They bees up late at night

Above 10%							
County	Score	N	Total	County	Score	N	Total
Antrim	22%	9	41	Wexford	17%	5	29
Belfast	22%	7	32	Armagh	16%	3	19
Derry	17%	3	18	Down	11%	4	38
Below 10%							
County	Score	N	Total	County	Score	N	Total
Sligo	9%	2	22	Westmeath	4%	1	25
Cork	6%	5	84	Mayo	3%	1	37
Tipperary	5%	2	42	Donegal	2%	1	42
Wicklow	5%	1	21	Dublin	2%	4	205
Limerick	4%	1	26	Waterford	2%	1	51

rectify this error in the choice of sample sentence the author repeated the test in autumn 2006 using the sentence *The kids bees up late at night* which would be well-formed for speakers with *bees* in their speech. Needless to say, the same number of individuals could not be reached in this short rerun of the survey. The repeat was only done in the north of Ireland as the very low acceptance of *bees* in the south, or indeed its rejection, resulted from the non-existence of this habitual form there (except in Co. Wexford).

In all, 67 individuals were queried. The interview situation was also quite different: informants were asked just one question, rather than presented with a questionnaire as in the original survey. Another major difference was that the counties included the second time had 227 informants in the original survey, 160 more than in the rerun. The smaller number of test persons for the rerun also meant that individuals had a greater representation in the percentage scores calculated afterwards (see, for instance, the figure for Tyrone where the acceptance by one individual represented 13 per cent of the total); see table 4.28.

Despite the very different nature of the repeat it did confirm the result of the original survey, namely that *bees* is a specifically northern feature. Acceptance in the north was always in double figures whereas acceptance in the south (bar Co. Wexford), if it existed at all, was never anything like this.

A final point should be made here. The author noted that many respondents answered the survey questionnaire by considering whether a certain structure occurred in their area and remarked as much, e.g. 'Yeah, you hear that around here alright.' In such cases the question of well-formedness for a test sentence was not primary. Whether the sentence was *They bees up late at night* or *The kids bees up late at night* was irrelevant to such respondents, they simply recognised

Table 4.28. *Acceptance figures in test for the sentence* The kids bees up late at night

County	Score	N	Total	County	Score	N	Total
Antrim	37%	4	11	Down	23%	3	13
Belfast	44%	8	18	Armagh	22%	2	9
Derry	38%	3	8	Tyrone	13%	1	8

bees as a vernacular option in their part of the country and ticked the box in the questionnaire accordingly.

4.4.2 THE NOMINAL AND PRONOMINAL AREAS

Unmarked plurals

In vernacular registers of Irish English, unmarked plurals are the rule when accompanied by numerals. This zero-marking is not so common in the south-west and the west, perhaps because plural marking in Irish was, and is, obligatory, irrespective of whether a quantifier accompanies the noun in question or not. However, if the input varieties of English did not show plural marking after numerals then the shift varieties based on this input do not either.

(138) Unmarked plurals
   a. *That's five year ago now.* (DER, M35+)
   b. *I remember seeing his photo about two year ago.* (DER, M60+)
   c. *'Twas over five pound, just for a joint of meat.* (DER, M60+)

In the context of numbers, one should mention a feature of rural varieties of the east coast, and others influenced by these. This is the use of 'and' in dates after the digit representing the century, e.g. *It's nineteen and forty-eight, no, it's nineteen and forty-nine, anyway* (SADIF, M60+, Co. Wexford); *Ah, about nineteen and twelve . . .* (SADIF, M85, Lusk, Co. Dublin).

4.4.2.1   Number distinctions with personal pronouns

Vernacular forms of Irish English show a distinction between second-person singular and plural personal pronouns. The singular is the standard form *you* while the plural is realised in a number of ways, typically via the archaic *ye*, or by adding the productive plural suffix *-s*, either onto the singular form or the archaic plural, yielding *youse* and *yez* respectively (see section 4.2.3 above). Analogically, the possessive pronouns show distinct forms for the second person plural: *yeer* /jiːr/ 'your'-PL, *yeers* /jiːrz/ 'yours'-PL.

A plural personal pronoun can be observed in several situations which might otherwise call for a singular form. For example, there is a kind of institutional use of *ye* as in *Do ye sell fresh milk?* (asked in a shop even if it is run by only one person). Another instance is where the plural is used as a type of politeness

Table 4.29. *Highest acceptance figures (90%+) in* A Survey of Irish English Usage *for the test sentence* Are ye going out tonight?

County	Score	N	Total	County	Score	N	Total
Clare	100%	16	16	Kerry	96%	23	24
Limerick	100%	26	26	Kilkenny	96%	23	24
Westmeath	100%	25	25	Sligo	95%	21	22
Waterford	98%	50	51	Tipperary	95%	40	42
Mayo	97%	36	37	Galway	93%	50	54
Wexford	97%	28	29	Kildare	92%	23	25
Cork	96%	81	84	Louth	91%	29	32

strategy for actions which are only carried out by a single individual, e.g. *Will ye turn off the light when ye're finished?* (this use also applies to Appalachian English, Michael Montgomery, personal communication).

(139) Generic use of *ye*
    a. *And would ye have to wear a uniform?* (TRS-D, U41, F)
    b. *You had a black and white apron . . . and a cap on ye* . (TRS-D, U41, F)
    c. *Ye shovel off the stuff. Then ye slice the turf down the whole length of the spade. Ye put it in a barrow and ye wheel it away out.* (TRS-D, U41, F)
    d. *Yeah, ye all could go yourself if ye wanted.* (WER, F55+)

Of the various options for the second person plural, it is *ye* which occurs in supraregional forms of Irish English, particularly in the south. It is the least phonetically salient of the second-person plural pronouns and non-local speakers can move along a phonetic cline which stretches from [jɪ] through [jɪ] to [jə] which is indistinguishable from the reduced form of *you*. The non-salience of *ye* may also account for its very high acceptance values in *A Survey of Irish English Usage* (see table 4.29).

Diachronic support for the preponderance of *ye* in southern counties comes from the emigrant letters examined for this chapter. The form is especially common in the letters stemming from Co. Cork, as can be seen from the following.

(140) *Ye* in emigrant letters
    a. *I cannot be too thankful to God for his mercy to ye in sparing ye after all the sickness in America the last year of which we heard.* (IEL, 1854, Co. Cork)
    b. *Thank you sincerely for the kindness ye have all shown to us.* (IEL, 1855, Co. Cork)
    c. *I and Bridget are always praying for ye. We both unite in sending ye all our love and blessings and remain your affectionate mother.* (IEL, 1857, Co. Cork)
    d. *I never wrote that to any of ye in any of your letters.* (IEL, 1861, Co. Cork)

Table 4.30. *Highest acceptance figures (70%+)* in A Survey of Irish English Usage *for the test sentence* What are youse up to?

County	Score	N	Total	County	Score	N	Total
Antrim	98%	40	41	Dublin	78%	160	205
Down	95%	36	38	Monaghan	78%	7	9
Cavan	94%	16	17	Kildare	76%	19	25
Donegal	93%	39	42	Wicklow	76%	16	21
Meath	92%	34	37	Carlow	75%	6	8
Belfast	91%	29	32	Fermanagh	75%	3	4
Derry	89%	16	18	Louth	72%	23	32
Tyrone	86%	6	7	Wexford	72%	21	29
Armagh	79%	15	19	Longford	70%	7	10

Vernacular forms of Irish English show, to differing degrees, the regular affix-ation of plural -*s* onto a pronoun. Depending on the pronoun used, one of two forms will occur, *youse* (< *you* + *s* /z/) or *yez* (< *ye* + *s* /z/). The former is particularly common in Ulster (Harris 1993: 139f.), but also in Dublin and on the east coast in general. Table 4.30 shows the results for *youse* yielded in *A Survey of Irish English Usage*.

The acceptance figures for *ye* and those for *youse* would appear to be related. The Munster counties Clare, Limerick, Tipperary, Waterford, Cork and Kerry and the Connaught counties Galway, Mayo and Sligo all scored over 90 per cent for *ye* but under 70 per cent for *youse*. It seems that outside Ulster those counties which were Irish-speaking longest tend to favour *ye* while the others in the centre and east of the country gravitate towards *youse*. The tendency to favour plural -*s* on a pronoun was confirmed by the productive formation *yez* which had very low values in the west, for instance, Cork and Galway had the lowest figures, both 30 per cent. However, the western counties, such as Kerry, Galway, Mayo and Sligo all had values of over 90 per cent for *ye*. Figures of over 50 per cent for *yez* were only obtained in counties on the east coast and in Ulster, as seen from table 4.31.

In the light of the present-day preponderance of *youse* in colloquial registers in other parts of the anglophone world, from the United States to South Africa (Wright 1997) and to Australia and New Zealand (Bauer 1994b), the question of its origin is of interest. The form *youse*, and its less common companion *yez*, would appear to be specifically Irish developments.

To confirm this one must exclude any English source. With the help of available text corpora this issue can be resolved with reasonable certainty. For instance, the *Corpus of Early English Correspondence Sampler* (Nevalainen and Raumolin-Brunberg 1996, 2003) does not reveal a single instance of *youse/yous*, although *ye* and *thou* abound (*thou* is by far the most common second-person pronoun, 372 instances, with *ye* occurring 19 times). This holds for the 23 texts in the public-domain version of this corpus, covering letters from the end of the sixteenth to

Table 4.31. *Highest acceptance figures (50%+) in* A Survey of Irish English Usage *for the test sentence* What were yez up to?

County	Score	N	Total	County	Score	N	Total
Cavan	82%	14	17	Antrim	61%	25	41
Kildare	72%	18	25	Derry	61%	11	18
Dublin	68%	139	205	Sligo	59%	13	22
Meath	68%	25	37	Donegal	57%	24	42
Louth	66%	21	32	Kilkenny	54%	13	24
Westmeath	64%	16	25	Belfast	53%	17	32
Wexford	62%	18	29				

the end of the seventeenth century. Equally, in the 138 texts of the Early Modern English section of the *Helsinki Corpus of English Texts* there is not a single instance of *youse/yous* or *yez*.

A further fact can be cited here to underline the Irish origin of *youse*. The form is found in England in only a few areas, Liverpool (Trudgill 1986: 139–41) and Tyneside (Beal 1993). In Scotland it occurs in Glasgow and, spreading out from there, in central Scotland (Macafee 1983: 51). It is hardly a coincidence that these are the areas of greatest Irish influence in Britain. Granted, the influence has been different in each case: Newcastle experienced immigration during the early nineteenth century and Liverpool somewhat later, above all by people who were fleeing the famine in Ireland. Glasgow took in Irish immigrants from seasonal movements for work up from Ulster (whereas for England the source in Ireland was south of Ulster).

The appearance of *youse* is also a relatively recent phenomenon. For instance, Maria Edgeworth (1767–1849) in her novel *Castle Rackrent* (1801), which attempts to display the speech of the native Irish realistically, has many instances of *ye* but not a single one of *youse/yous*. In the texts of *A Corpus of Irish English* (Hickey 2003a) the pronouns with -*s(e)* /z/ do not appear until the first quarter of the nineteenth century and then are more characteristic of writers from Dublin, particularly Dion Boucicault (1820–90) and later Sean O'Casey (1884–1964).

However, William Carleton is something of an exception here in that he does have these pronouns although he was a writer with a rural background. In the 21 texts by Carleton used for the present investigation, there are 430 occurrences of non-standard second-person plurals (one of *youse/yous*, 199 of *yez* and 230 of *ye*).

(141) *Boys, I'll go down to* yous *. . . I thought* yez *would out-stay your time . . . an' a sweet honeymoon to* yez *both . . . I'll massacre* yez *if* yez *don't make less noise . . . he'll bate* yez *if ye don't take the wind of him.* (William Carleton, *The Hedge School*, 1833)

Carleton also makes liberal use of *yer* both as a plural possessive pronoun (142a) and as one with singular reference (142b), a practice which is typical of vernacular Irish English today.

(142) a. *will yez hould yer tongues there . . . boys, will yez stop yer noise there*
    b. *Masther, sir, my father bid me ax you home to yer dinner.*
    (William Carleton, *The Hedge School*, 1833)

(143) Occurrences of *yuz/yez/yer* in Boucicault's *The Colleen Bawn* (1860)
    a. *Here is a lether she bade me give yuz . . .*
    b. *Arrah! whist aroon! wouldn't I die for yez? didn't the same mother foster us?*
    c. *Ye'll niver breath a word to mortal to where yer goin', d'ye mind, now; but slip down, unbeknown, to the landin' below, where I'll have the boat waitin' for yez .*
    d. *Never fear – she'll never throuble yer agin, never, never.*
    e. *Myles, why did yer shoot Danny Mann?*

The form *yuz* may reflect a pronunciation [jəz] and cannot necessarily be interpreted as a textual instance of *youse*.

The form *yer*, which occurs twenty-one times in the same text, is interesting in that it seems to represent a personal pronoun and not always a possessive pronoun (see 143 d,e). The form *yez* (of which there are nine occurrences in *The Colleen Bawn*) would seem to represent [jiz]. This may imply that the latter arose first and *youse* afterwards. The proportion of *youse* to *yez* in the Carleton texts, 1:199, would also suggest that *yez* was established before *youse*, the latter arising as an analogical equivalent to the former.

The *yez* form also seems to have singular reference in Boucicault's plays, something also found in Carleton and which is at least an option to this day in Dublin English. Indeed the question of number is not always clear with either *yez* or *youse*. The desire for vernacularity, rather than explicit plural marking, may be the motivation behind using the form. It is also frequent today to find *the both of youse/the two of youse/the pair of youse* (already documented in *The Quare Fellow* (1954) by Brendan Behan (1923–64) with redundant plural specification).

The writers who in the late nineteenth century attempted to recreate the speech of rural western Ireland on the stage were Lady Gregory (1852–1932) and the more successful John Millington Synge (1871–1909), who admittedly employed a highly idiosyncratic literary style.

The three plays by Lady Gregory in *A Corpus of Irish English* do not contain a single instance of *yous(e)* and Synge has only three instances, one in *The Tinker's Wedding* (1904) and two in *The Playboy of the Western World* (1907). Given the fact that the Dubliner Sean O'Casey has ninety-nine instances of *yous(e)* in the four plays in *A Corpus of Irish English* (fifty of these are in *The Plough and the Stars*, 1926) and the fact that Synge was himself a Dubliner, it may be that he unconsciously inserted a specifically Dublin/east coast trait into the rural western speech which he strove to represent in his plays.

The textual record does not permit an exact dating of the rise of *youse*. It can be assumed that it was not a feature of Irish English before the nineteenth century. In terms of relative chronology, it predates the mass exodus of Irish during that century and so was transported to anglophone locations beyond Ireland where it was subsequently picked up and continued.

Yous(e) is found in the letters of emigrants, such as those to Australia, from both Ulster and the south of Ireland, which are collected in Fitzpatrick (1994). For example, one emigrant from Offaly writes in 1877: *when i hope to get to yous and live and die happey when i have yous all togeder* (Fitzpatrick 1994: 348), while the father of another emigrant from Fermanagh writes in 1860: *Both of yous mentioned that yous saw me . . . thinking I might see your in the Croud* (Fitzpatrick 1994: 440). The latter case is interesting as the author was an educated 59-year-old Protestant. This implies that *yous(e)* /juz/ must have been a feature of Fermanagh speech which had established itself at least a few generations before the time of writing (1860).

4.4.2.2   Demonstrative pronouns

Further non-standard pronominal uses are to be found in the morphology of Irish English. Conspicuous among these is the use of oblique forms in subject position, a feature which Irish English shares with many other varieties of English, above all in Britain.

(144) Oblique forms in subject function
    a. *Us farmers have a hard life.* (WCER, M75+)
    b. *Him and me are off tomorrow.* (WER, M50+)

Such usage is probably due to the nature of English input in Ireland as the Irish language does not provide a model for this. The same holds for the use of *them* as a demonstrative, a ubiquitous feature of traditional British English dialects.

(145) *Them* as demonstrative
    a. *Them things they had to do.* (TRS-D, C41, M)
    b. *I went out in a boat with them kids.* (TRS-D, C41, M)
    c. *One third of them potatoes were black.* (IEL, 1861, Co. Cork)
    d. *When I see that plane, how am I going to walk up them steps?* (WER, F85+)

Another feature involving demonstratives, and attested in rural speech of the south-west, is the use of *those* in the sense of 'these' found with elderly rural speakers, e.g. *No holly or birch in those (= these) parts* (MLSI, M75+, Ballymacoda, Co. Cork), *'Tis very hot those (= these) days* (MLSI, M70+, Allihies, Co. Cork).

English input is also responsible for phonological features such as the use of an unshifted /iː/ in the first-person-singular possessive pronoun: *Me* [mi] *little bush in the front garden is gone now* (WER, F55+).

4.4.2.3 Unbound reflexives

The use of unbound reflexives (Filppula 1997c, 1999: 77–80; Amador 2006: 73–81) has been touched on in section 4.2.4 and a view of their genesis in Irish English has been offered. The essential function of such elements is to refer to an individual who has a position of authority in the context of a particular discourse. Such a position could be that of husband or father in a family, boss in a firm, head teacher in a school, etc.

(146) Third-person unbound reflexives
   a. *It was himself that would not go and the reason he gave was he would be in dread I'd have nothing after he going.* (IEL, 1854, Co. Cork)
   b. *The following night himself went back there.* (TRS-D, M64–2, M)
   c. *'Twas himself who answered the phone that time.* (WER, F55+)

Such unbound reflexives occur most frequently in the third person singular, masculine or feminine. This restriction derives from the discourse scenarios in which an unbound reflexive is used: the focus is on a single person in a discussion between two or more other individuals.

   However, there is a related usage in the second person where a reflexive is used without an accompanying pronoun for the purpose of emphasis. This usage is also paralleled by Irish where *tú féin*, lit. 'you self' (or *sibh féin* in the plural) can be found. As with the unbound reflexives in the third person, Irish uses a pronoun + reflexive which is prosodically equivalent to the bare reflexive in English, i.e. it consists of a WS foot: *tú 'féin* (again, see section 4.2.4).

(147) Bare second-person reflexives in nineteenth-century literature
   a. *. . . but, avourneen, it's yourself that won't pay a penny when you can help it . . . let us go to where I can have a dance with yourself, Shane . . . "Tis yourself that is,' says my uncle.* (William Carleton, *Traits and Stories of the Irish Peasantry*, 1830–3)
   b. *Is it yourself, Masther Hardress? . . . Faith, it isn't yourself that's in it, Danny . . .* (Dion Boucicault, *The Colleen Bawn*, 1860)
   c. *It's yourself that'll stretch Tim Cogan like a dead fowl . . . it's yourself that's to see the sintence rightly carried out . . .* (Dion Boucicault, *Arrah na Pogue*, 1864)

In *A Survey of Irish English Usage* the sentence *Himself is not in today* was used to test acceptance of such unbound reflexives. It should be said here that these are regarded as stereotypically Irish, as a stage Irish feature which is avoided nowadays as several respondents in the survey pointed out to the author. The mean acceptance across the thirty-two counties was 22 per cent. The seven counties with a score higher than 25 per cent were Waterford, Limerick, Tipperary, Galway, Armagh, Kerry, Kilkenny. Donegal had 19 per cent acceptance and the core Ulster Scots counties of Antrim and Down showed only 5 per cent and 8 per cent respectively. The latter score lends credence to the view that the stressed reflexives of Irish (see section 4.2.4) were responsible, via transfer, for the rise of unbound reflexives in Irish English.

In her consideration of contact English, Sabban (1982: 357–79) looks at the similar use of unbound reflexives in Scotland. She also compares the situation with that in Irish English (1982: 375) and points out that in both Irish and Scottish Gaelic similar reflexive pronouns occur. However, she does not consider why the personal pronoun does not co-occur with the reflexive pronoun in either Scottish or Irish English, apart from suggesting that the pronoun is deleted so that speakers do not have to decide on whether to use *I* or *me* in the first person (Sabban 1982: 379).

Other non-standard reflexives

The pronominal base for reflexives in English varies across person and number. The first and second persons have a possessive pronoun as base, i.e. *my-*, *your-*, *our-*, but the third person has a oblique form of the personal pronoun, i.e. *him-*, *her-*, *it-*, *them-*. Because of this situation, analogical formations which use a possessive pronoun as base for the third person are common in dialects of English, i.e. *hisself* and *theirself/theirselves* are found. In Irish English, only the plural shows this analogical form (though there is one instance of *hisself* in Boucicault's *The Colleen Bawn*, 1860).

(148) *Theirself* as analogical formation
    a. *. . . after that they feed away theirself.* (TRS-D, M64–1, M)
    b. *And if they wanted to go out in the night they could go theirself.* (WER, F55+)
    c. *They carry theirselves decent.* (MLSI, M75+, Gurteen, Co. Laois)

4.4.2.4   Resumptive pronouns

A pronoun is said to be resumptive when it occurs towards the end of a sentence and points back to a noun mentioned in an earlier clause, typically the main clause of the sentence in question. Resumptive pronouns are distinct from anaphoric pronouns which are used to avoid repeating a proper noun – such as someone's name – in the same stretch of discourse. They do, however, share a function with anaphoric pronouns in that they add cohesion to a discourse, especially in cases where the grammatical structure might be ambiguous or where speakers do not have a full command of the language they are using. Some languages use resumptive pronouns regularly while others, such as English, are sparing in this respect. For that reason, resumptive pronouns represent non-standard usage in English. Some instances found in the author's data collections are given in (149).

(149) Resumptive pronouns
  a. *He was the fella that the others were trying to get him to take the offer from the brewery too.* (WER, M50+)
  b. *I told him to buy a small bike that he could put it into the house.* (WER, F55+)
  c. *And the little one, she do be measuring herself.* (WER, F85+)
  d. *It's the sort of place people would be interested in going to it.* (WER, M50+)
  e. *The house where you are in it now.* (TRS-D, C41, M)
  f. *If you had a horse that he had a touch of it . . .* (SADIF, M60+, Bruff, Co. Limerick)

In the current context the status of resumptive pronouns in Irish is of particular interest. Here they are often used to remove ambiguity regarding referents in a sentence, as in the following (author's examples).

(150) a. *An fear a mhol na buachaillí.*
       [the man (SUBJ/OBJ) that praised the boys (SUBJ/OBJ)]
       'The man that praised the boys.' /
       'The man that the boys praised.'
   b. *An fear ar mhol na buachaillí é.*
       [the man (OBJ) that praised the boys (SUBJ) him]
       'The man that the boys praised.'

In such sentences the only way of recognising subject and object (unless the context provides sufficient information) is by placing a resumptive pronoun at the end which refers back to the object.[36] Because of this disambiguating function in Irish, resumptive pronouns are found in many contexts (McCloskey 1985: 65), as in the following cases which are translations of (149 d,e) above.

(151) a. *Sin an saghas áite a mbeadh suim ag daoine dul ann.*
       [that the type place that would-be interest at people go in-it]
       'That's the sort of place people would be interested in going to.'
   b. *An teach a bhfuil tú anois ann.*
       [the house that is you now in-it]
       'The house you are in now.'

Such usage provided a clear model (Filppula 1999: 195) for speakers in the language shift situation and most likely led to the appearance of resumptive pronouns in Irish English. The transfer was probably also supported by the occurrence of sentence-final prepositions in English which semantically and prosodically link up with the prepositional pronouns of Irish as in the following instance.

(152) *An fear a raibh mé ag caint leis.*
       [the man that was I at talk-VN with -him]
       'The man I was talking to.'

---

[36] This function in Irish has been recognised by some authors, such as Filppula (1999: 188–90) who points this out in his discussion of Irish parallels to English examples in his data.

4.4.3 THE PREPOSITIONAL AREA

Non-standard uses of prepositions are common in Irish English. Of these, some
stem from fixed phrases or specific words in Irish while others are of a more general nature in that the preposition is not bound to certain lexical elements (verbs,
nouns, adjectives). These two situations are illustrated in the following examples.

(153) a. *They look too much <u>on</u> the television.* (TRS-D, C41, M)
      Breathnaíonn siad an iomarca <u>ar</u> an teilifís.
      [look they the excess on the television]
  b. *My brothers are gone <u>with</u> years now.* (CCE-W, M75+)
      Tá mo chuid deartháireacha imithe le blianta anois.
      [is my part brothers gone with years now]
  c. *D . . . is dead <u>with</u> a long time now.* (CCE-S, M60+)
      Tá D . . . marbh le tamall fada anois.
      [is D . . . dead with time long now]

The first sentence above shows *on* in English, deriving from *ar* 'on' in Irish, which
is used for the prepositional complement of *breathnaigh* 'look' (or the identical
verbs *féach/amharc* in Munster and Ulster respectively). The second sentence
illustrates the use of *le* 'with' for measurements of time. This preposition has
a much wider range in Irish than in English and this, coupled perhaps with a
greater scope in input varieties of English (see the detailed discussion in Filppula
1999: 231–38[37]), has led to many non-standard uses in present-day Irish English.

(154) a. *Your man was knocked down <u>with</u> a car last April.* (WER, M50+)
  b. *God, Ray, I'm killed <u>with</u> the heat.* (DER, M60+)
  c. *The mother has been badly this year <u>with</u> the Krohn's.* (WER, M50+)
  d. *I didn't see you <u>with</u> a long time.* (MLSI, M60+, Fanore, Co. Clare)

The meanings covered by this use of *with* include 'by' and 'because of, due to' and
are attested historically, as the following instances from mid-nineteenth-century
drama and prose illustrate.

(155) Non-standard uses of *with* in nineteenth-century literature
  a. *I'm nearly killed <u>with</u> climbin' the hill . . . Maddened <u>with</u> the miseries this
      act brought upon me.* (Dion Boucicault, *The Colleen Bawn*, 1860)
  b. *. . . that you will ever again be insulted <u>with</u> the presence of Beamish Mac
      Coul.* (Dion Boucicault, *Arrah na Pogue*, 1864)
  c. *You are mad <u>with</u> fright.* (Dion Boucicault, *The Shaughraun*, 1875)
  d. *. . . and never mind that deep larning of his – he is almost cracked <u>with</u>
      it . . . Some of them, being half blind <u>with</u> the motion and the whiskey,
      turned off the wrong way . . . This is the happy day <u>with</u> me; and the blush
      still would fly across her face . . .* (William Carleton, *Traits and Stories of
      the Irish Peasantry*, 1830–3)

---

[37] In contrast to the rest of Filppula's book, the treatment here is somewhat laboured in the opinion
of the present author. The examples which Filppula discusses, such as the seven instances on
p. 232, all have *with* in English deriving from *le* 'with' in Irish. Indeed, none of the examples which
he quotes would have any other preposition but *le* 'with' in Irish.

Use of *in it*

Irish shows an idiosyncratic use of *ann* 'in it', a prepositional pronoun in the third person singular, to indicate existence (Filppula 1999: 226–31). This is probably a metaphorical extension of the literal meaning of the locative expression, similar to German *da sein* 'to be there', which was metaphorically extended in a like manner, cf. *Dasein* (n) 'existence'. In (156) a selection of attestations is offered from speakers in Irish-speaking areas or in those which were so until recently. Translations of the English sentences are given to show what the Irish equivalent would be like. The lexicalised use of 'in-it' for existence is found throughout Ireland, as shown by the examples from Dublin and Scots-settled Ulster (Laggan area) below.

(156) Use of *in it* to denote existence
   a. *There's work in it.* (TRS-D, C41, M)
      Tá obair ann. [is work in-it]
   b. *There used to be a hotel in it.* (TRS-D, C41, M)
      Bhíodh óstán ann. [was hotel in-it]
   c. *I don't know, there's a few in it.* (TRS-D, C41, M)
      Níl a fhios agam, tá cúpla ceann ann. [is not know at-me, is couple one in-it]
   d. *There are plenty of jobs in it.* (TRS-D, M7, M)
      Tá morán jabbana ann. [is much jobs in-it]
   e. *The only thing is in it, they're new.* (DER, M35+)
      There're never no functions in it. (TRS-D, U18-2, F)

Substratum influence in this usage of *in*, especially in combination with *it*, would appear to have been operative during language shift. Authors who have dealt with the matter, such as Filppula (1999: 231), readily concede this source.

Expression of relevance with *on*

A less clear-cut case is presented by the use of *on* to express relevance. In Irish English this is found abundantly, as the following examples show.

(157) Use of preposition *on* to express relevance
   a. *Someone took three hundred pound on him.* (TRS-D, L19-2, F)
   b. *Well for you, J . . . , 'cause the deal is gone on us.* (WER, M50+)
   c. *And then, he might come home on me.* (WER, M50+)
   d. *You know, sometime they all come home together and then they take over the whole house on you.* (WER, F55+)

It is obvious from just a small sample of occurrences that *on* + personal pronoun is used to express a negative effect on the person referred to. This usage is known from varieties of English outside Ireland (see the discussion in Filppula 1999: 219–26); consider such sentences as *They stole the car on him*. Here the use of *on* is often an alternative to the possessive pronoun which might not be appropriate or accurate in every context, e.g. where the car is not the speaker's but one which he/she was responsible for. It is this option of indicating relevance, but not necessarily possession, which gives added justification to the use of *on* + personal pronoun. Other languages have similar devices to realise similar semantics. German, for instance, allows the use of the dative to indicate relevance (what is called the *Pertinenzdativ* 'the dative of relevance', von Polenz 1969), e.g. *Er ist mir abgehauen* [he is me-DATIVE run-off] 'He ran away on me.'

The use of *on* with the experiencer of an action is established in English and can be seen with such verbs as *impose on s.o.*, *have mercy on s.o.*, *inflict sth. on s.o.*, *call on s.o.* Historically, there were verbs which took *on*, like *wait on*, *do on*, *look on*, which have either changed their preposition (*look on* > *look at*), dropped it (*believe on* > *believe*) or lost their compound meaning (*wait on* = 'serve, attend to'; *do on*[38] = 'do wrong to').

Despite these and other historically attested uses of *on* with verbs, an examination of the subbranch of the *Helsinki Corpus of English Texts* (covering eighty-one texts within the time span 1500–1710) had only one instance of *on* to express negative relevance: *But the humour of that time wrought so much on him, that he broke off the Course of his Studies* (Gilbert Burnet, *Some Passages of the Life and Death of John Earl of Rochester*, 1680). Significantly, the *Corpus of Early English Correspondence Sampler* did not contain any examples.

However, there are verbs and verbal phrases which take *on* expressing negative relevance, for example *to be hard on s.o.*, *bring on s.o.*, and these are attested historically, e.g. . . . *and thairfoir hes God justly brought this on me* (*The Confessioun of John Habroun*, 1567). Such uses may well have converged with the use of *ar* 'on' in Irish, as seen in the following examples, the third of which allows for a literal and a metaphorical interpretation.

(158) Use of preposition *on* to express relevance in Irish
    a. *Múchadh an tine uirthi.* [was-extinguished the fire on-her]
    b. *Theip an scéim nua air.* [the new scheme failed on-him]
    c. *Thit an dréimire orm.* [fell the ladder on-me]

Such convergence would then favour the use of *on* in post-shift Irish English. Certainly by the late nineteenth/early twentieth century, *on* + personal pronoun had become a widespread means of expressing negative relevance, as the following attestations from literature show.

(159) Use of *on* for relevance in nineteenth-/early twentieth-century literature
    a. . . . *and called me a skinflint; they have made it a common nickname on me* . (William Carleton, *The Evil Eye or The Black Spector*)
    b. *He's after dying on me, God forgive him, and there I am now.* (John Millington Synge, *In the Shadow of the Glen*, 1903)

---

[38] This combination is still found in Irish English where more standard varieties of English would have *do to*, e.g. *What did she do on you?* 'What did she do to you?'

    c. *Maybe she'd wake up <u>on us</u>, and come in before we'd done.* (John
       Millington Synge, *Riders to the Sea*, 1904)

    d. *D'ye want to waken her again <u>on me</u>, when she's just gone asleep?* (Sean
       O'Casey, *The Plough and the Stars*, 1926)

    e. *God, I'd be afraid he might come in <u>on us</u> alone.* (Sean O'Casey, *The
       Silver Tassie*, 1928)

The transfer of *on* + personal pronoun led to usages in Irish English which are largely negative in meaning. Furthermore, there are cases where there may well have been different usage previously. For instance, 'to welcome' in present-day Irish is *fáilte a chur <u>roimh</u> dhuine* [welcome to put <u>before</u> someone]. However, Carleton has the set phrase *to put the failtah <u>on him, her, etc.</u>* 'to welcome him, her, etc.', which, given the use of *failtah* as an eye-dialect rendering of Irish *fáilte* 'welcome', would imply that the preposition used in his Irish (early nineteenth century) then may well have been *ar* 'on'.

    An important issue here is chronology. Various historical texts, such as those in *A Corpus of Irish English*, show that the use of *on* + personal pronoun to express relevance is a relatively late phenomenon, not becoming evident in the textual record until later in the nineteenth century (see examples in (159) above). Writers such as William Carleton, John and Michael Banim or Dion Boucicault have few examples and Maria Edgeworth has none. Instances of *on* + personal pronoun before the late nineteenth century are where it is necessary as an obligatory prepositional complement of the verb.

(160) Use of *on* for relevance in eighteenth-century literature

    a. *. . . my Wife Shall settle <u>on me</u> the remainder of her Fortune.* (William
       Congreve, *Way of the World*, 1700)

    b. *Now may all the Plagues of marriage be doubled <u>on me</u> if ever I try to be
       Friends with you any more.* (Richard Brinsley Sheridan, *The School for
       Scandal*, 1777)

    c. *. . . that I am reveng'd <u>on her</u> unnatural Father.* (Richard Brinsley
       Sheridan, *St Patrick's Day*, 1775)

The attestations of *on* + personal pronoun to express relevance with writers like Synge and O'Casey all show an essential feature: the prepositional phrase is optional. Consider the instances of *wake(n)* in (159c, d) above: in the sentences from both Synge and O'Casey the prepositional phrase with *on* can be deleted without rendering them ungrammatical. This is also true of the sentences in (157) from the author's data collections.

    An explanation can be given for this which has recourse to the language-shift situation. The native speakers of Irish, who were acquainted with uses like *Theip an scéim nua air* [the new scheme failed on-him], transferred this to the English they were learning by adding the prepositional phrase expressing relevance to existing sentence structures in English. This is a case of *additive transfer* where an element from the outset language is added to the target providing a further semantic feature, in this case relevance of an action to a person in the discourse.

Furthermore, this additive transfer took place to express negative or positive relevance of an action to an individual. This explains why in the nineteenth century there are instances of *on* + personal pronoun which are literal translations from Irish and possibly positive in connotation. But later the use of *on* + personal pronoun settled down to the expression of negative relevance in the twentieth century, much as the *after*-perfective had settled down to past reference some time before.

The current feature was also captured in *A Survey of Irish English Usage* by testing the acceptance of the sentence *The fire went out on him*. The rate was consistently high with a mean of 79 per cent. There was no significant geographical variation with the core Ulster Scots counties, Down and Antrim, scoring 76 per cent and 85 per cent respectively. The test sentence *He crashed the car on her* showed a mean score of 61 per cent. The somewhat lower value compared to the other sentence can probably be accounted for by its potential ambiguity.

The high acceptance of *on* when expressing negative relevance in Ulster can be linked to a similar usage of the preposition in Scottish English. Here, as elsewhere (see sections 4.4.1.4.1 and 4.4.2.3 above), a comparison with the data and analysis offered by Sabban (1982) is useful. In a section dedicated to this preposition (1982: 447–54), she considers the use of *air* 'on' in Scottish Gaelic and possible transfer to English during language shift. Her conclusion is that substrate influence is most probably the source of the wider range of uses in which *on* + personal pronoun occurs in contact English (see her table of corpus samples indicating negative relevance, 1982: 457). Sabban's claim is further supported by the fact that the preposition occurs in contexts in which other elements point to Gaelic influence, e.g. the use of a verb of motion and a definite article in a sentence like *Thàinig an t-acras orra* 'The hunger came on them' (1982: 448).

A few other instances of prepositional usage are noticeable in Irish English. As with the cases above, some of these can be traced to Irish. For instance, the common use of *outside* with *of* would seem to derive from Irish: *Taobh amuigh den teach* [side out of the house] 'Outside of the house.' Other non-standard prepositional uses are not related to Irish but would appear to stem from input varieties of English, e.g. the use of *off* rather than *from* in sentences like *She gets a lift off another woman on the way back* (WER, M50+).

Oblique pronouns and the expression of relevance

In the data collections examined here there are cases where an oblique personal pronoun is used to express the relevance of an action to the speaker. Semantically, this strategy is similar to that where *on* + pronoun is found. However, the relevance expressed is not necessarily negative as is ususaly the case with *on* + pronoun. Examples are *He did me wrong with all that talk* (RL, M55+); *I got me enough money for the weekend* (WER, F55+), *We don't sow us mangolds* (MLSI, M85+, Clonmacnoise, Co. Offaly).

4.4.4 DETERMINERS

The use of the definite article in Irish English shows considerable differences compared to other varieties of English (Sand 2003). By and large it tends to be used more than in more standard forms of English. It is possible to offer a classification of the contexts which favour its appearance (see Filppula 1999: 56–77 for a discussion as well as Amador 2006: 61–73). Generic, impersonal and abstract contexts trigger the definite article, as do references to parts of the body, bodily ailments and next of kin/relatives. Units of measurement and numeric references often trigger the use of the definite article as well. Certain fixed expressions which contain the definite article are found repeatedly, especially '*the ol'* N' where the noun can be a part of the body, e.g. *He's got a bit frail now, the ol' back is gone* (DER, M35+). In such phrases the adjective *old* is pronounced [oːl] or [aul]. The deletion of the final stop is indicated in writing by an apostrophe. Some authors spell the word *owl'* to suggest the diphthong [au].

(161) Overuse of definite article
   1. Generic and impersonal reference
      a. *You'd need the wellies when crossing them fields.* (RL, M55+)
      b. *And he gave it all up to go on the sea.* (TRS-D, L19-2, F)
      c. *Do you like sugar in the tea?* (DER, M60+)
      d. *The youth now isn't inclined to take on anything.* (TRS-D, M19, M)
      e. *I remember asking the girl to get the wheelchair for you.* (WER, M50+)
      f. *I'd iron the few shirts for him.* (WER, F85+)
      g. *Cars would be beeping the horn passing.* (DER, M60+)
      h. *S . . . has the car so he can bring the kids to the school.* (WER, F55+)
      i. *The husband said, she was getting out of the bed that night.* (WER, M50+)
      j. *They don't know the comfort up in them new houses.* (WER, F85+)
      k. *M.'s the perfect clown, he is.* (DER, M35+)
   2. Abstract nouns, including languages and objects of study
      a. *Well, I think she likes the languages.* (WER, F55+)
      b. *I always found the Irish hard going, Ray.* (DER, M60+)
      c. *If you go out in the world the Irish is no good to you.* (TRS-D, M7, M)
      d. *Now the kids have to do the biology from sixth class on.* (WER, F55+)
      e. *God, I'm parched with the thirst.* (DER, M35+)
      f. *I think the drink is a bit of a problem for your man.* (WER, M50+)
      g. *They all have the longing for Ireland.* (TRS-D, M7, M)
      h. *The youth doesn't want to work.* (MLSI, M65+, Birr, Co. Offaly)
   3. Parts of the body, diseases, afflictions
      a. *There's nothing done by the hand anymore.* (TRS-D, M64-1, M)

b. *. . . tilling and sowing the seed with the hand.* (TRS-D, M64-1, M)

c. *I was out there and I got the bladder done.* (DER, M60+)

d. *I need the cap to keep the ol' head dry.* (WER, M50+)

e. *It nearly broke the leg on me.* (DER, M60+)

f. *I always had problems with the ol' back.* (DER, M60+)

g. *I had a bout of the flu the past few weeks.* (WER, M85+)

h. *The arthritis does be bothering her a lot these days.* (WER, M50+)

i. *That was the time she had the cancer.* (WER, F50+)

j. *'Twas the heart attack which got him in the end.* (WER, M50+)

4. Relatives, spouses, in-laws

a. *Go in now to see the mother.* (WER, M50+)

b. *The husband said, she was getting out of the bed that night.* (WER, M50+)

c. *He lucky he have the wife there.* (WER, M50+)

d. *The father-in-law was over for the Christmas meal.* (DER, M35+)

5. Days of the week, months, seasons, occasions

a. *So we went into town on the Saturday.* (WER, F55+)

b. *And then they could be up late in the night playing music.* (DER, M35+)

c. *No, they take four samples in the month.* (TRS-D, M64-1, M)

d. *Well, how did the Christmas go for you?* (DER, M35+)

e. *Will you be back in the summer?* (WER, M50+)

f. *She does be out all the day.* (WER, M55+)

g. *I've given up celebrating the wedding anniversary by now.* (WER, F55+)

h. *The father-in-law was over for the Christmas meal.* (DER, M35+)

6. Units of measurement, quantifiers

a. *Would they be all the one? I suppose they would.* (DER, M60+)

b. *Listen, Ray, I'm telling you, that isn't the half of it.* (DER, M60+)

c. *'Tis he have to be the twenty-one.* (WER, M50+)

d. *He have buses and taxis here in town so he have the few bob.* (WER, M50+)

e. *Would the both of youse get off out of here!* (DER, M35+)

f. *Well, you see, the both of them have to work to do the mortgage like.* (DER, M60+)

7. Institutions, buildings

a. *It's over by the Clover Meats.* [factory] (WER, M50+)

b. *C . . . started at the college last autumn.* (WER, F55+)

c. *The young ones are going to the school already.* (WER, F55+)

In *A Survey of Irish English Usage* the acceptance of the definite article in non-standard contexts was markedly high. For instance, the test sentence *He likes the life in Galway* showed a mean score of 83 per cent with values not far from this for counties in Ulster, Antrim in fact achieving 95 per cent (see table 4.32).

Table 4.32. *Highest acceptance figures (87%+) in* A Survey of Irish English Usage *for the test sentence* He likes the life in Galway

County	Score	N	Total	County	Score	N	Total
Armagh	100%	19	19	Monaghan	89%	8	9
Antrim	95%	39	41	Belfast	88%	28	32
Cavan	94%	16	17	Donegal	88%	37	42
Derry	89%	16	18	Down	87%	33	38

With the test sentence *She has to go to the hospital for a check-up* the acceptance, at 96 per cent, was even higher. However, with the sentence *Their youngest son is good at the maths* the rate, with a mean of 43 per cent, dropped considerably. Nonetheless, Belfast and Antrim scored quite highly, with 69 per cent and 56 per cent respectively. Down, at 45 per cent, lagged somewhat behind. The sentence *I suppose the both of us should go* contained the vernacular phrase 'the both of us' and scored highly with a mean of 83 per cent. The feature showed particular acceptance in the north: the only county in Ulster which showed a value lower than 80 per cent was Monaghan.

There is a long tradition of tracing the overuse of the article to Irish. Burke (1896: 778f.) mentions the influence of Irish when discussing this feature, as do all authors since the early twentieth century. It is true that there are direct equivalents to many of the sentences with the definite article in Irish, e.g. *Taitníonn an saol i nGaillimh leis* [pleases the life in Galway with-him] would be the translation of the test sentence in the above table. Furthermore, the classification offered for Irish English would apply to Irish as well, e.g. abstract nouns: *Tá suim aici sa teangeolaíocht* [is interest at-her in-the linguistics]; time units/seasons: *Beidh sé anseo sa samhradh* [will-be he here in-the summer]; quantifiers: *Bhí an bheirt acu amuigh ar an trá* [was the both of them out on the strand].

What is significant is that the acceptance rates for Antrim, Down and Belfast are among the highest in the country. Assuming that these rates reflect definite article usage in these locations, then there are two possible explanations. The first is that the use of the definite article in the contexts listed above spread from varieties to the west and south which had this from the language shift. The second is that the wider range of possible contexts was already present in imported forms of English from Scotland and was maintained in Ulster after the initial settlement. This can be shown clearly by considering the data collected and examined by Annette Sabban. In a dedicated section of her book (Sabban 1982: 380–418), she offers a taxonomy of definite article usage in contact English in north Skye and north Uist (Outer Hebrides) which is very similar, if not identical, to that offered for Irish English above and in Filppula (1999: 56–77). The similarity in the range of contexts in which the definite article is found in contact Scottish English offers clear support for the view that this greater range

Table 4.33. *Highest acceptance figures (80%+) in* A Survey of Irish English Usage *for the test sentence* She never rang yesterday evening

County	Score	N	Total	County	Score	N	Total
Galway	91%	49	54	Sligo	86%	19	22
Antrim	90%	37	41	Kerry	83%	20	24
Derry	89%	16	18	Tipperary	83%	35	42
Belfast	88%	28	32	Cork	81%	68	84
Clare	88%	14	16	Mayo	81%	30	37
Donegal	88%	37	42	Meath	81%	30	37
Down	87%	33	38				

is the result of transfer from Irish in Ireland and Gaelic in Scotland during the language shift process in both countries.

4.4.5 THE ADVERBIAL AREA

Narrow time reference with *never*

In standard varieties of English, the temporal adverb *never* covers a fairly large span of time, e.g. *He never visited us when he was living in Dublin.* However, in many varieties *never* can also have a much narrower range (Beal 1993). This is true of Irish English as can be seen in the sentence *No, he never turned up yesterday after all his talk* (WER, M50+). Irish does not seem to be the source of this usage, especially as the adverb *riamh* 'never' is used for greater time spans. Narrower time references are usually expressed using other adverbs.

(162) a. *Ní raibh sé riamh i Sasana.* [not was he never in England]
    b. *Níor tháinig sé aréir ar chor ar bith.* [not came he last-night at turn at all]

In *A Survey of Irish English Usage* the acceptance of narrow time reference was tested with the sentence *She never rang yesterday evening.* The results show a high acceptance across the entire country with the core Ulster Scots areas, Antrim and Down, among the six counties with the highest rates (see table 4.33).

Ulster usage

Three adverbial features are specifically northern in their occurrence. The first of these is the use of *whenever* in the sense of 'when' (Montgomery 1997: 219).

(163) *Whenever I was released from prison.* (Belfast, M40+)

The second is the use of *from* in the sense of 'since' (Harris 1984b: 132) and could be derived from a longer phrase like 'from that time on'/'from the time that' through ellipsis.

(164) *She's living here from she was married.*

The third is the use of *anymore* in a positive sense, a feature which appears to have been transported to the New World (Labov 1991) with the eighteenth-century emigration from Ulster (see the discussion in section 3.2.1).

Use of *but* for *only*

Other adverbial usages may well have been transferred from Irish and continue to be so in the speech of native Irish speakers, as in the following case of *but* being used in the sense of 'only'. The Irish translation of the recorded sentence is given to show what the usage there would be like. The transfer interpretation is supported by the fact that the verb is in the negative in both languages.

(165) a. *He wasn't getting but five shillings a day.* (TRS-D, C42–1, F)
 b. *Ní raibh sé a fháil ach cúig scillinge sa lá.*
 [not was he at getting <u>but</u> five shillings in-the day]

The case of *before*

Transfer through contact is facilitated not only by low salience – consider the negative epistemic modal *mustn't* in Irish English (see section 4.4.1.4) – but also by transparent and natural semantics. Here 'natural' refers to semantic developments which are common cross-linguistically. The extension of spatial adverbs into the metaphorical sphere is an instance of such a semantic development. An example of this, triggered by transfer, is provided by the following.

In Irish the adverb *roimh* /rɪvʲ/ has a spatial and a prospective temporal sense, roughly equivalent to English 'in front of' and 'ahead of', as well as the retrospective temporal meaning of 'before'. It has also many metaphorical applications based on these literal meanings (Ó Dónaill 1977: 1007). In English 'before' refers to one time preceding another time. Spatial meanings of 'before' were previously common, as this is the inherited meaning of the Old English *beforan*, but are relatively rare nowadays, one of them being that implying responsibility, e.g. *You will have to answer before a judge.* The meaning 'earlier in time' may well have developed from contexts where both this and the locative meaning merged, e.g. *They set off on the journey before us,* i.e. 'in front of us' and/or 'earlier than us'. More neutral spatial meanings are now expressed by 'in front of', attested since the early seventeenth century, e.g. *The dog lay in front of the fire.* Temporal meanings are indicated by 'ahead of', a figurative use attested since the late sixteenth century, e.g. *We still have two tests ahead of us.* The latter two senses are indicated in Irish by the same adverb, e.g. *roimh an tine* 'in front of the fire' and *romhainn* 'before-us, ahead-of-us' (compound prepositional pronoun).

In Irish English, both the spatial meaning of 'in front of' and the prospective temporal meaning of 'ahead of' are expressed by *before*, mostly probably by transfer of the greater range of *roimh* in Irish.

(166) Use of *before* in early nineteenth-century Irish English; examples from
Carleton, *Ned M'Keown*
  1. Literal use: spatial adverb (equivalent to 'in front of')
     a. *you could hardly see your finger before you*
     b. *My uncle now drove us all out before him*
     c. *By the powers, I was miles before them*
     d. *How could he gallop across you if you were far before him?*
  2. Figurative usages deriving from literal use
     a. 'ahead of'
        there's a trial before me yet
        your mother's son never had such a match before him!
     b. 'in someone's opinion'
        for we could do no good before them

The preponderance of *before* in the above sentences can be shown quantitatively.
In the Carleton story *Ned M'Keown* there are 97 instances of *before* but not a
single one of *ahead*. In the tale *Crohoore of the Bill-Hook* by John and Michael
Banim there are 21 instances of *before* and, again, none of *ahead*. There is only
one instance of *in front of* in Carleton's story – with none in that by John and
Michael Banim – and this is in a descriptive section.

In Maria Edgeworth's novel *Castle Rackrent* there are 45 instances of *before*
and none of either *ahead* or *in front of*. Edgeworth is an interesting case as there
are instances of *before* in descriptive text which are clearly the equivalent either
of *ahead*, e.g. *for my late lady had sent all the feather-beds off before her*, or of *in front
of*, e.g. *but before the servants I put my pipe in my mouth*. This usage is found still
in Irish English and can seen in attestations like the following: *He was standing
before her when they heard that noise* (DER, M60+); *I was right before her when she
admitted it* (WER, F55+).

There are other instances of English adverbs and adjectives being used in an
unexpected sense. For instance, *near* is attested with the meaning 'anything like'
as in *They didn't last near as long* (SADIF, M70, Crisheen, Co. Clare) and *whole*
in the sense of the quantifier 'all' as in *The whole guests when they seen the person . . .*
(SADIF, M60+, Bellanagh, Co. Cavan).

4.4.5.1 Augmentatives

As with so many varieties of English, vernacular Irish English does not usually show overt marking of adverbs. To add emphasis in colloquial speech,
a series of adjectives are used in an adverbial function, e.g. *wild, pure,
fierce.*

(167) a. *The butter's wild dear here.* (TRS-D, U18–2, F)
      b. *And I swear to God, I'm pure robbed with this new meter.* (WER, F85+)
      c. *God, Ray, 'tis fierce hard to get into that club now.* (WER, F85+)

Galore

This is an adverb implying abundance. It derives directly from the adverbial phrase *go leor* 'enough, sufficient, abundant' in Irish. It has inherited the syntactic positioning of the Irish phrase, i.e. it only occurs after the element it qualifies.

(168) *There was beer galore at the party.* (DER, M35+)
    *There's galore whiskey in the bottle.

The post-positioning *go leor* is not a strict condition in present-day Irish, which allows it to precede a noun when it also means 'a lot': *Bhí go leor ama againn chun an traein a fháil* [was a lot time-GEN at-us in-order-to the train get-VN]. This pre-positioning may in fact be the result of transfer from English. Curiously, in nineteenth-century literature there are a few examples where *galore* is used in English as a synonym of 'enough', e.g. *You all know that the best of aiting and dhrinking is provided . . . and indeed there was galore of both there* (William Carleton, *Traits and Stories of the Irish Peasantry*, 1830–3).

Bare quantifiers

The bare quantifier *all* is well attested in the early modern period but has been largely replaced by either *everyone* or *everything* (depending on the animacy of the referent). Typical earlier instances would include the following taken from the *Helsinki Corpus of English Texts*.

(169) a.   *. . . and our thoughts carried so many wayes, to doe good to all.*
        (John Brinsley, *Ludus Literarius or the Grammar Schoole*, 1627)
    b.   *. . . and so it will serve in part, as a general direction for all.*
        (T. Langford, *Plain and Full Instructions to Raise all Sorts of Fruit-Trees . . .* 1699)
    c.   *. . . I can subsist no longer here; for to borrow will spoile all.*
        (*Correspondence of the Haddock Family*, 1657–1719)

In south-eastern Irish English such bare quantifiers were recorded. This may well be an archaic feature of speech in this part of Ireland, given that it was the first to be settled by English in the late medieval period.

(170) a.   *He talked to all before making his decision to go.* (WER, M50+)
    b.   *He brought all something for Christmas.* (WER, F55+)
    c.   *He done all with his hands.* (MLS1, M75+, Drumlee, Tyrone)

Post-posed quantifier

Sentence-final position for conjunctions, such as *but* or *though*, is well attested for Irish English. A further case of end-position is the extension of this position from adverbial *much* to that of *much* as a quantifier. The first use is found in *Sure there's no children around anymore on the streets much* (WER, F85+), whereas the second is seen in *I don't have time much* (WER, F55+).

4.4.5.2   *Comparatives*

A prominent non-standard feature of comparatives in Irish English has been discussed in section 4.2.4. This is the use of a two-word conjunction which prosodically matches the two stressed syllables *ná mar* 'not like/than' of Irish. This feature is represented in the data collections from across the country with a preponderance in counties containing Irish-speaking areas. Of the two possibilities of translation, 'than what' is the more common and is the only one attested in data from Connemara and Munster.

(171) Two-word conjunctions
  a. 'than what': *I can shop cheaper in Raphoe than what I can do in Letterkenny*. (TRS-D, U18-2, F)
  b. 'like what': *There were no machinery in them days like what there is now*. (TRS-D, U41, F)

Nor for 'than'

Phonetic similarity and a degree of semantic match can promote transfer; consider the expression *More is the pity, I suppose* (TRS-D, M42, M), probably from Irish *Is mór an trua, is dóigh liom* [is big the pity, is suppose with-me] where Irish *mór* is matched by English *more* (see discussion in section 4.2.2).

   In comparatives, there would seem to be a similar case of such phonetic influence. This is where *nor* is used instead of *than*. Dolan (1998: 186) mentions this feature in his dictionary as does Macafee (1996: 236 *nor²*) in the *Concise Ulster Dictionary* and Taniguchi (1956: 42f.) gives examples from literature. The basis for this usage is the Irish conjunction *ná* = [nɑː] 'than' which is phonetically similar to English 'nor' (the Irish English pronunciation of this would have been with an open vowel: [nɑːr]).

(172) *Tá sé níos láidre ná a dheartháir.*
   [is he more stronger than his brother]

Nor in the sense of 'than' is attested throughout the early modern period. The earliest case is from the late seventeenth century and the usage was common well into the nineteenth century, as attestations from the Banim brothers and William Carleton show.

(173) *Nor* for 'than'
   1. Earliest attestation
      . . . *de greatest man upon eart, and Alexander de Greate greater nor he?*
      (John Dunton, *Report of a Sermon*, 1698)
   2. Nineteenth-century examples
      a. . . . *bud you, Shamus, agra, you have your prayers better nor myself or Paudge by far* (John and Michael Banim, *Tales of the O'Hara Family*, 1825–6)

b. *. . . and what was betther <u>nor</u> all that, he was kind and tindher to his poor ould mother . . . Jack spoke finer <u>nor</u> this, to be sure, but as I can't give his tall English . . .*
(William Carleton, *Traits and Stories of the Irish Peasantry*, 1830–3)

The likely Irish provenance is supported by the fact that there are no examples of *nor* 'than' in either the *Helsinki Corpus of English Texts* or the *Corpus of Early English Correspondence Sampler*. However, the picture is very different in the *Helsinki Corpus of Older Scots*. This is divided into four subperiods, three of which were examined here: 1500–70, 1570–1640, 1640–70. In the eighty files of these subperiods there were eight finds for *rather nor* and six for *rather than*, eight finds for *better nor* and seven for *better than*, and six finds for *further/farther nor* with one for *farther than*. Representative examples are shown in the following.

(174) *Nor* for 'than' in texts from the *Helsinki Corpus of Older Scots*
a. *. . . sche was assured that I loued hir ten tymes better <u>nor</u> hym*
'she was assured that I loved her ten times better than him'
(*Memoirs of his Own Life by Sir James Melville of Halhill, 1549–1593*, ed. T. Thomson, Edinburgh, 1827)
b. *seing they are worthie of credit in a gritter matter <u>nor</u> this alreddy beleuit*
'seeing they are worthy of credit in a greater matter than this already believed'
(1590, *The Works of William Fowler. . . .* ed. H. W. Meikle, Edinburgh and London, 1936)
c. *. . . albeit I wish yiou neiuer to kenne the mater farder <u>nor</u> sall be speired at yiou*
'albeit I wish you never to know the matter farther than shall be asked of you'
(Alexander, Earl of Dunfermline, Chancellor, to Thomas, Lord Binning, Secretary of Scotland, 26 September 1613)
d. *and he (?) suld make hir far better <u>nor</u> euer sche was?*
'and he should make her far better than ever she was?'
(1576–91, *Criminal Trials in Scotland, 1488–1624*, ed. Robert Pitcairn, Edinburgh and London, 1833)

4.4.6 SENTENCE STRUCTURE

4.4.6.1 *Relativisation*

There is a general preference in Irish English for *that* as relativiser with animate antecedents. This was clearly confirmed in *A Survey of Irish English Usage* where a mean acceptance rate of 78 per cent was returned for the test sentence: *I know a farmer that rears sheep*. The range across the country was from 64 per cent (Offaly) to 94 per cent (Derry) with no bias towards the north or south.

The use of *that* as a relativiser was more widespread in early modern English than nowadays in standard forms of the language (Herrmann 2005). Joseph Addison's *Humble Petition of Who and Which* (1711) satirises the overuse of *that* and apparently corrected instances of *that* in his own work to *who* when the antecedent was human (Beal 2004a: 76). Eighteenth-century prescriptivism, above all in the person of Robert Lowth, preferred to have *that* used for inanimate antecedents and Lowth bemoans its indiscriminate use for animate and inanimate antecedents alike. It is precisely this generalised use of *that* which is characteristic of Irish English. Influence from Irish can be ruled out here as it has only one relativiser *a* [ə]. Furthermore, investigations by scholars working on conservative British dialects confirm the preference in the latter for *that* and zero relatives (Tagliamonte, Smith and Lawrence 2005b).

(175) a. *Dhíol sé an carr a cheannaigh sé anuraidh.*
           [sold he the car REL bought he last-year]
           'He sold the car he bought last year.'
      b. *Tá aithne aige ar an bhfear a tháinig isteach.*
           [is acquaintance at-him on the man REL came in]
           'He knows the man that/who came in.'

However, there is one point in which the influence of Irish may be noticeable. In existential and cleft sentences zero relatives are found in colloquial forms of English, e.g. *There's some spaghetti here needs draining* and *It was the spaghetti needed draining* (Beal 2004a: 76). In Irish English such sentences definitely tend to have an explicit relative, usually *that*. The lack of zero relative may well be due to Irish influence. The latter language uses clefting extensively and this always requires the relative *a* [ə].

(176)   *Is é an salann atá ag teastáil uaithi.*
           [is it the salt that-is at need-VN from-her]
           'It's the salt that she needs.'

What as relativiser, especially with an animate antecedent, is almost a stereotypical feature of Irish English. Many respondents for *A Survey of Irish English Usage* commented on it being 'stage Irish'. In the survey the test sentence *I know a farmer what rears sheep* had a mean acceptance rate of only 5 per cent across the entire country with seven counties returning 0 per cent. In the author's data collections *what* as relativiser was very rare. One of the few examples was *That was all what she wanted* (DER, M60+).

Zero subject relative pronoun is a common feature of British English dialects and is found in Ireland, particularly in the north. It is recorded, for instance, in the speech of older speakers from Munster, Leinster and Ulster in the following examples.

(177) a. *I can handle any job Ø would come in to me.* (TRS-D, M19, M)
      b. *There is some people Ø keeps jerseys . . .* (TRS-D, U41, F)

    c. *It's nearly all the Wards Ø is up there.* (SADIF, M60+, Co. Wicklow)

    d. *These are the lads Ø does the harm.* (MLSI, M70+, Tullaroan, Co. Kilkenny)

However, a zero subject relative pronoun is not part of the supraregional variety, north or south, and this fact may explain the relatively low mean acceptance rate of 21 per cent for twenty-four counties with more than fifteen respondents in *A Survey of Irish English Usage* (the test sentence was *I know a farmer rears sheep*). Belfast showed the highest value at 53 per cent. Wicklow had 33 per cent as opposed to Dublin at 17 per cent, perhaps confirming that this is a vintage feature of English input (Wicklow is a county with early English input and only a slight influence from the Irish language during its history).

    Among the relative pronouns, genitive *whose* (see Seppänen and Kjellmer 1995 for a comprehensive review) is not frequently attested. The most common situation is for juxtaposition to occur where more standard varieties would have *whose*. Occasionally, *where* was found in this function, but it can hardly be regarded as an established feature, indeed in the example below it may have occurred under the influence of the following prepositional complement. A further semantic equivalent to genitive *whose* is *that* introducing a clause in which a noun governed by a possessive pronoun is to be found (last sentence below).

(178) a. *That's the fella, Ray, his brother is down in the brewery.* (WER, M50+)

     b. *That's the man <u>where</u> his wife is working in the shop.* (DER, M60+)

     c. *Yeah, S . . . is the other farmer <u>that</u> I know <u>his two sons</u> as well.* (WCER, M75+) 'Yeah, S . . . is the other farmer <u>whose two sons</u> I know as well.'

4.4.6.2   Subordination

The use of paratactic constructions introduced by *and* were already noted by early scholars working on Irish English, e.g. P. W. Joyce who cites as an example *He interrupted me and I writing my letters* (Joyce 1979 [1910]: 33). This structure has come to be known as 'subordinating *and*' (see the overview in Corrigan 2000b: 77–9 and forthcoming: chapter 5); discussions have taken place about the precise nature of this structure and, more importantly, about its probable origin (Ronan 2002; Häcker 1994).

    When considering possible parallels in English dialects, scholars have pointed to the existence of absolute constructions, i.e. without a finite verb form, which are introduced by *and*. Jespersen (1909–49: III, 373f.; V, 64f.) gives examples of this type of clause. He thinks it is not as rare as other scholars would believe and mentions that there are instances from Shakespeare which apparently are used for an 'exclamation of surprise or remonstrance' (also noted by Filppula 1999: 207). This would appear to hold for instances like the following:

(179)   *Suffer us to famish, and their storehouses cramm'd with grain.*
(Shakespeare, *Coriolanus*, act I, scene i)

A search for attestations in the *Helsinki Corpus of English Texts* revealed a number of instances which could be considered in the present context.

(180) a.   . . . *and looking up to Heaven*, said, *God's holy Will be done* . . .
(Gilbert Burnet, *Some Passages of the Life and Death of the Right Honourable John, Earl of Rochester*, 1680)

b.   . . . *the Bearheard miss'd his Bear, and looking for him*, found the hole, where he had made his escape. (Samuel Pepys, *Penny Merriments*, 1687)

c.   *And rising from his seat*, he went and led her into the bath. (Aphra Behn, *Oroonoko*, c. 1688)

Each of these involves *and* followed by a non-finite verb form but without a subject NP, though an object NP may be present. These instances from Early Modern English are essentially distinct from those in later Irish English. In the latter subordinating *and* always occurs in the syntactic frame *and* + NP + X, where the following conditions hold.

(181) NP =   Subject
X   =   Non-finite Verb Phrase, Noun Phrase, Adjectival Phrase, Prepositional Phrase

Essentially, X is any element which can occur after a finite form of *be* which is implicit but not realised in these constructions (this description would account for the various examples in both Irish and Irish English which are presented by Corrigan 2000b: 85, 91). The NP is furthermore commonly realised by a pronoun in the nominative. Examples of *and* + NP + VERB (present participle) – the most common type in Irish English – where the NP is subject, are extremely rare in English outside Ireland, the following two being virtually the only examples in the *Helsinki Corpus of English Texts*.

(182) a.   . . . *to the Com~ittee of Our Privy Councill for the affaires of Ireland, and they having reported their opinion thereupon to us*, and Wee considered & approved of the same. (Charles R. to the Earl of Essex, 1674)

b.   *The Prince in good health, and our fleet prepareing for another incounter*, if the Dutch comes out. (Richard Haddock to his Wife, 1673)

The first instance of this construction by an Irish author is by Farquhar (a native of Derry) who, however, has an oblique form of the pronoun:

(183)   *Yes, Sir, I left the Priest and him disputing about Religion.*
(George Farquhar, *The Beaux Stratagem*, 1707)

This attestation is similar to those in later Irish English in that the clause introduced by *and* is the final one in the sentence. This fact may well be due to an influence from Irish where subordinating *agus* 'and' often introduces a non-finite clause at the end of a sentence.

(184) a. *Chuaigh mé amach agus é ag cur báistí.* (CCE-N, M65+)
     [went I out and it at putting-NON_FINITE rain-GEN]
     'I went out although it was raining.'

  b. *Tháinig siad abhaile agus iad barrthuirseach.* (CCE-W, F55+)
     [came they back and they very-tired]
     'They came home and they were very tired.'

  c. *Níl a fhios agam an dtiocfaidh siad ar ais agus an tír seo gan obair do na feirimeoirí óga.* (CCE-S, M65+)
     [not know at-me if come-FUTURE they back and the country here without work for the farmers young]
     'I don't know if they would come back, what with this country without work for young farmers.'

Semantically, the final clauses in the above sentences are either concessive (a–b) or causal (c). Instead of an explicit conjunction, Irish uses *agus* 'and' and in the following clause no finite verb form appears.

When considering the possible origin of this structure it should be mentioned that it may well have been favoured by the language shift situation itself. It is known from second-language acquisition studies that paratactic structures are favoured over hypotactic ones. The 'pragmatic mode' (Hickey 1997a: 1013) dominates so that clause connection via *and* would have been at a premium anyway.

The early attestation of 'subordinating *and*' from Farquhar is a single occurrence from the period before 1800. However, with the beginning of the nineteenth century, the structure appears abundantly in the works of a number of prose writers, notably Maria Edgeworth, Gerald Griffin, John Banim and William Carleton. Of these authors, only Carleton was a native speaker of Irish (from rural Tyrone) and so 'subordinating *and*' cannot have been the result of individual transfer and must have been a feature of contact English in their surroundings.[39]

(185) Attestations of '*and* + NP- Subj + present participle' in Edgeworth, Griffin, the Banim brothers and Carleton

  a. . . . *asked my master, was he fit company for her, and <u>he drinking all night</u>* .

  b. . . . *when I seed my poor master chaired, <u>and he bare-headed and it raining as hard as it could pour</u>.*

  c. . . . *says I to her, <u>and she putting on her shawl</u> to go out of the house.*
     (Maria Edgeworth, *Castle Rackrent*, 1801)

---

[39] Filppula (1999: 203) confirms that in a corpus of some 120,000 words, material from 'four conservative rural British English dialects', there was only one instance of subordinating *and* (from Somerset). He furthermore points out that Hebridean English shows a similar construction to that found in Irish (Filppula 1999: 205; 1997a), a fact which he sees as supporting the substrate hypothesis for the Irish English attestations.

d. *Poh! gammon, and so many bows in the case <u>and you knowing</u> them all so well.*

e. *Why will you be obstinate, Peggy? my friends all waiting, <u>and you keeping</u> them.*
   (John and Michael Banim, *The Nowlans* in *Tales of the O'Hara Family*, 1825–6)

f. *'tis out of that spancel that Mull do be milking your cows every night, by her own chimney corner, <u>and you breaking</u> your heart at a dry udder the same time.*

g. *Well, if they did, Masther Hardress heerd 'em, <u>and he having</u> a stout blackthorn in his hand.* (Gerald Griffin, *The Collegians*, 1829)

h. *. . . sitting at his ase beside him, <u>and he smoking</u> as sober as a judge.*

i. *. . . says the little man, drawing close to her, <u>and poor Mary smiling</u> good-naturedly at his spirit.*

j. *. . . he could not make much use of such words, <u>and he going</u> to face death.*

k. *'Indeed, it's fine behavior,' a third would say, '<u>and you afther coming</u> from the priest's knee.'*
   (William Carleton, *Traits and Stories of the Irish Peasantry*, 1830–3)

There are also many instances of *and* + NP + NP where the first NP is a pronoun and the second a noun which is coreferential with the first. Examples from Maria Edgeworth (*Castle Rackrent*) illustrate this: *. . . <u>and you a young man</u>; . . . <u>and he the best of husbands</u>; . . . <u>and he a good tenant</u>; [What can Sir Kit do with so much cash,] <u>and he a single man</u>?* These instances help to explain why pronouns are the most common realisation of the first NP is this structure: this is an anaphoric element which points back to the subject of a clause preceding 'subordinating *and*', as can be seen from the main clause in parentheses in the last example just quoted. This type of sentence is precisely the type which is found in Irish with 'subordinating *and*'; see the three Irish sample sentences in (184) above.

Throughout the nineteenth and into the twentieth century[40] 'subordinating *and*' is found abundantly, especially with authors like Gregory and Synge who attempted to represent the speech of rural speakers in the west of Ireland.

(186) Attestations for 'subordinating *and*' in early twentieth-century literature

a. *. . . a better task than was ever done by Orpheus, <u>and he playing harp</u> strings to the flocks!*

b. *. . . and greasy his coat is, with all the leavings he brings away from him <u>and he begging</u> his dinner from door to door.*

c. *There was a mermaid foretelling him to win, <u>and she racking</u> her hair in the waves.* (Lady Gregory, *Hanrahan's Oath*)

d. *there was a star up against the moon, <u>and it rising</u> in the night.*

[40] See the discussion of this feature by Amador (2006: 73–81) in her examination of novels by Patrick McGill.

e. *Why wouldn't you give him your blessing and he looking round in the door?*
f. *And what time would a man take, and he floating?*
   (John Millington Synge, *Riders to the Sea*, 1904)

The position with authors from Dublin is somewhat different. Boucicault has three instances of 'subordinating *and*', viz. . . . *and me only doing my duty;* . . . *and you so poor?;* . . . *and she as innocent as a child.* but these are contained in a single play *Arrah na Pogue* (1864). There are no instances in either *The Colleen Bawn* (1860) or *The Shaughraun* (1875). Furthermore, there is only a single instance of 'subordinating *and*' in the four plays of Sean O'Casey examined here: *We've had enough for one night, and you for a serious operation tomorrow* (*The Silver Tassie*, 1928). With Brendan Behan (mid twentieth century), only three instances can be found: . . . *and you going home;* . . . *and you getting forty fags a day;* . . . *and we trucking round* (*The Quare Fellow*, 1954). This situation would suggest that in Dublin 'subordinating *and*', deriving from Irish, was not very frequent, probably because of the slight influence of language shift varieties on the speech of the capital at least in recent centuries.

Among the data collections used by the author, 'subordinating *and*' is attested, including in data from the east coast. It would appear to be a means of supplying unexpected or contradictory information which is relevant to the current discourse.

(187) Present-day instances of 'subordinating *and*'
   a. *'Twas four or five in the morning and we going to bed.* (WER, F55+)
   b. *They got married there and the house not finished yet.* (WER, M50+)
   c. *J . . . gave up the job and he near the retiring age.* (DER, M60+)
   d. *A young girl now . . . can get ten pounds no bother and her only sixteen.*
      (TRS-D, U18-2, F)

These instances all involve a clause introduced by 'subordinating *and*' at the end of a sentence. As might be expected from the historical precursors discussed above, in such clauses the verb *be*, either as auxiliary or main verb, is not realised. For example, the final clause of the last sentence above is the equivalent of 'even if she were only sixteen', that in the penultimate sentence could be rephrased as 'although he was near retiring age'. That in the first sentence would be 'when we were going to bed', etc.

That Irish provided the primary model for 'subordinating *and*' in Irish English is incidentally supported by its occurrence in contact Scottish English; see the discussion in Filppula (1997a: 950f.) in which he discusses the attestations in his own corpus of Hebridean English. Filppula sees transfer from Scottish Gaelic as the primary source of this structure in contact Scottish English.

Till in the sense of 'so that'

Till is the single-syllable variant of *until*. As a temporal adverb it is common in Irish English, both in synchronic data and in historical records, e.g. *Wait till I*

Table 4.34. *Highest acceptance figures (80%+) in* A Survey of Irish English Usage *for the test sentence* Come here till I tell you

County	Score	N	Total	County	Score	N	Total
Cavan	94%	16	17	Derry	83%	15	18
Antrim	93%	38	41	Offaly	83%	10	12
Armagh	89%	17	19	Belfast	81%	26	32
Donegal	88%	37	42	Mayo	81%	30	37
Limerick	85%	22	26	Kildare	80%	20	25

tell you what happened at the match (WER, M50+). It would seem to have gone through a metaphorical extension to the meaning 'so that' and is particularly common in combination with the verb *come*, cf. *Lookit, come here till I tell you* (DER, M35+). This usage is found throughout Ireland as *A Survey of Irish English Usage* indicated by the high acceptance figures in both the north and south shown in table 4.34.

There is a further usage of *till* in the sense of 'to' which is less frequent, but nonetheless attetested in the data collections, e.g. *You get used till it* (MLSI, M65+, Cardonagh, Co. Donegal); *Emigration was mostly till New York. There's where you come till* (MLSI, M75+, Drumlee, Tyrone).

4.4.6.3   Focussing

Focussing is a means by which a language can highlight elements of a sentence. There are various options here, moving elements to the front of a sentence, less frequently to the back, is a common one. But prosodic devices, e.g. increase in pitch, loudness or duration for words under focus, or the use of highlighting elements in the immediate vicinity of such words are two other means which may be available. Languages which have a complex inflectional morphology, like Latin or German, can move elements easily as the grammatical function of shifted elements is still obvious, e.g. German *Diesen Lehrer kenne ich nicht*, lit. 'this teacher-ACC know I not'. Languages with more rigid word orders may develop alternative devices for shifting elements within a sentence for the purpose of highlighting. Both Irish and English have such word orders, for somewhat different reasons. Irish has a fixed VSO word order which cannot be violated, while English has little inflection and hence uses word order to indicate grammatical categories like subject and object in a sentence.

In the literature on Irish English (see Filppula 1999: 242–70), the term 'focussing' covers two basic devices, (i) clefting and (ii) topicalisation. Clefting (Filppula 1999: 243–60) involves the extraction of an element from a sentence, placing it at the front in a main clause with a dummy subject *it* and relegating the remainder of the sentence to a subordinate clause which follows this, e.g. *He is gone to Cork > It's to Cork (that) he's gone.*[41] Topicalisation (via fronting) is basically every other type of focussing, bar clefting, and is particularly common with prepositional complements, e.g. *Up on the roof he was when the lightning struck < He was up on the roof when the lightning struck.*

Topicalisation in the data collections showed some additional features. A resumptive demonstrative pronoun was used to refer back to a clausal complement which was focussed (188f). Split topicalisation was also found where only the first element of a compound phrase was fronted (188g). The deletion of existential *there + be* led to sentences occurring which falsely appeared to be instances of topicalisation, e.g. [*There are*] *Some fierce chancers over there altogether* (TRS-D, M55, M). A combination of topicalisation and clefting was also to be found (188f).

(188) Topicalisation (via fronting) as a focussing device

    a. *Over at Clover Meats, he was working the while.* (WER, M50+)

    b. *Down at The Royal Bar, I met him on Christmas Eve.* (WER, M50+)

    c. *Collins' Avenue is the name of the place, I remember now.* (WER, M50+)

    d. *Quite what happened there, people have their doubts about that.* (TRS-D, M55, M)

    e. *Hay mostly, we grow, and barley.* (TRS-D, M64-1, M)

    f. *All our family, 'tis all reared now.* (DER, M60+)

    g. *But who has it, I don't know.* (SADIF, M60+, Co. Wexford)

    h. *The brother of the bishop, he done it for a bit.* (SADIF, M50+, Jerpoint, Co. Kilkenny)

Clefting

As a focussing device, clefting is clearly attested in the textual record of Irish English.[42] Early instances are found in the seventeenth century, e.g. *'Tis fit I should: Hath not my valour oft Been try'd* (Thomas Randolph, *Hey for Honesty*, *c.* 1630/51); *tis come bourying you are de corp, de cadaver, of a verie good woman* (John Dunton, *Report of a Sermon*, 1698, Filppula 1999: 255); *Be me Shoul,'tis dat I wanted, Dear Joy* (George Farquhar, *The Twin Rivals*, 1702/03). In the course of the eighteenth and nineteenth centuries clefting becomes more apparent in available texts and can encompass different kinds of subject or object as well as adverbs. It is most common in the present tense, but is also found in the past (*'Twas his meddin' you seen passin' a minute agone*, William Carleton, *Going to Maynooth*).

---

[41] Standard varieties of English also have a further device called pseudo-clefting (or *wh*-clefting) in which the non-focussed element is put in a *wh*-clause with the focussed element following this: *What he did yesterday is go to Cork*. This also occurs in Irish English but its realisation and distribution is not markedly different from that in more standard varieties, e.g. *Where they do the racing mostly now is out our way* (WER, F55+).

[42] See the discussion of this feature, along with other focussing strategies, in Amador (2006: 112–25).

(189) Clefting as a topicalisation device in early nineteenth-century literature
   a. Subject
      'Tis Barny Brady that would never turn informer.
      (William Carleton, *The Hedge School*)
   b. Pronominal subject
      'Tis we that didn't lick them well in the last fair.
      (William Carleton, *The Hedge School*)
   c. Highlighted subject
      . . . it's yourself that won't pay a penny when you can help it.
      (William Carleton, *Ned M'Keown*)
   d. Object
      It's little respect you pay to my feelings.
      (William Carleton, *The Emigrants of Ahadarra*)
   e. Prepositional object
      It's the barrack room your honor's talking on.
      (Maria Edgeworth, *Castle Rackrent*, 1801)
   f. Verb phrase
      . . . is it thinkin' to venthur out sich a night as it's comin' on yer Reverences would be? (William Carleton, *Ned M'Keown*)
   g. Adverb
      It's often men speak the contrary just to what they think of us.
      (Maria Edgeworth *Castle Rackrent*, 1801)

In order to test acceptance of clefting in present-day Irish English the test sentence *It's to Glasgow he's going tomorrow* was included in *A Survey of Irish English Usage*. The mean acceptance rate was 20 per cent for the twenty-four locations with more than fifteen respondents (there was no bias towards the north or south). This is not high compared to other structures tested for. It may well be that clefting is a salient feature of Irish English and hence was rejected by a section of the survey respondents as too stereotypical. Nonetheless, various types of clefting are attested in the data collections.

(190) Clefting as a topicalisation device in contemporary Irish English
   a. *It's because of the new regulations that I left.* (WER, M50+)
   b. *It's farming the land behind I used to be before I got married.* (WCER, M75+)
   c. *It's in the Red Cow Hotel we'll be staying in Dublin.* (WER, M55+)
   d. *It's over in Sutton that they've bought the new flat.* (DER, M35+)
   e. *You know, 'tis the petrol prices that's ruining the business.* (DER, M35+)

Because clefting is found in many other varieties of English, scholars have been slow to attribute it solely to influence from Irish. For instance, Filppula (1999: 270) is more cautious here than elsewhere is attributing influence to a particular source. In his opinion both English input and Irish have contributed to the present-day distribution. The range of clefting options in Irish is large indeed and it may well be that it is the scope, rather than just the fact of clefting, which is attributable to Irish.

(191) Clefting options in Irish
   a. Subject
      Is é Seán atá istigh sa teach.
      [is he John who is inside in-the house]
      'John is in the house.'
   b. Object
      Is le Máiréad a bhuail sé sa chathair.
      [is with Mairead who met he in-the city]
      'He met Mairead in the city.'
   c. Verb phrase
      Is ag díol an tí atá siad.
      [is at selling the house-GEN that-are they]
      'They are selling the house.'
   d. Prepositional object
      Is le carr nua a tháinig siad abhaile.
      [is with car new that came they home]
      'They came back home with a new car.'
   e. Adverb
      Is go (han-)sciobtha a rinne sí an obair.
      [is (very) quickly that did she the work]
      'She did the work quickly.'

There is also a phonological argument in favour of assuming Irish influence in the range of clefting in the present tense in Irish English. The Irish verb *is* [ɪs] is similar to English *it's* [ɪts] and would have provided speakers in the shift scenario with a readily available equivalent to the clefting device they knew from their native language.

4.4.6.4   *Negation*

There are several respects in which negation in Irish English varies from that in standard English (Anderwald 2002, 2003). Some of these have been touched upon above, but two remain which are the topics of sections below.

Negative concord

The traditional term for the phenomenon discussed here is 'double nega-tion' but this label does not capture the generalisation that it is a concord rule between a verb and its complement. Hence cases like *Nobody wouldn't help us* are excluded because the concord does not apply to the subject of a verb. Negative concord specifies that if a verb is negated then any negatable element which is part of the verb's complement will also be negated. Such elements are quantifiers, determiners or generic pronouns such as *anybody*. For all forms of vernacular Irish English the system of negative concord would seem to apply.

(192) Negative concord
    a. *The Waterford corporation <u>can't</u> give <u>no</u> loans.* (WER, F85+)
    b. *They're <u>not</u> giving out <u>no</u> loans at the moment.* (WER, F85+)
    c. *I <u>wouldn't</u> recommend a gas heater to <u>nobody</u>.* (WER, M50+)
    d. *And still he <u>wasn't</u> giving me <u>no</u> money.* (WER, F55+)
    e. *In them days there was no motors, <u>no nothing</u>.* (TRS-D, M7, M)

It is reasonable to assume that the source varieties of Irish English shared the system of negative concord which only later was removed from less locally bound varieties (probably as of the late eighteenth-century). As Tieken-Boon van Ostade (1982: 281) notes, Swift observed negative concord in his *A Compleat Collection of Genteel and Ingenious Conversation* (1738). She concludes that the censure on negative concord applied first to written English and only later did it spread to spoken English (in support of this view she quotes Defoe who used double negation in speech situations in his novels). This is also true of Irish writers like Carleton (see (193) below). Among the dramatists of the nineteenth and twentieth centuries, negative concord is rare; in fact it is only used by O'Casey in his plays from the 1920s. One reason for this is that the writers may have internalised the prohibition on negative concord which was propagated by the late eighteenth-century prescriptivists, including the Irishman Thomas Sheridan, and later elocutionists. The assumption that the lack of negative concord in the textual record has to do with unconscious notions of prescriptivism is supported by the fact that it occurs in the drama *She Stoops to Conquer* (1773) by Oliver Goldsmith (1728–74): *I love to hear him sing, bekeays he <u>never</u> gives us <u>nothing</u> that's low.* He lived just before the grammatical censures of people like Bishop Lowth began to spread among English speakers.

(193) Negative concord in eighteenth- and nineteenth-century literature
    a. *. . . however, it <u>doesn't</u> make <u>no</u> matter.*
       (William Carleton, *The Black Baronet*)
    b. *I <u>never</u> did <u>nothin'</u> agin the laws.* (William Carleton, *Willy Reilly*)
    c. *. . . for you <u>never</u> wor <u>nothin'</u> else <u>nor</u> a civil, oblagin' neighbor yourself.*
       (William Carleton, *Phelim O'Toole's Courtship*)
    d. *I <u>don't</u> come here to raise <u>no</u> argument.*
    e. *You'll <u>not</u> shut <u>no</u> door till you've heard what I've got to say.*
       (Sean O'Casey, *The Shadow of a Gunman*, 1923)
    f. *. . . an' not be clusthered round the table, as if we <u>never</u> seen <u>nothin'</u>.*
       (Sean O'Casey, *Juno and the Paycock*, 1924)
    g. *We <u>don't</u> want <u>no</u> shoutin' here.*
       (Sean O'Casey, *The Plough and the Stars*, 1926)

In *A Survey of Irish English Usage* acceptance of negative concord was tested with the sentence *He's not interested in no cars*. The rates were quite low: the maximum was 32 per cent, the six locations in Ulster (Antrim, Derry, Belfast, Fermanagh, Monaghan, Armagh) showed the highest figures and several counties had a value of 0 per cent. This is probably because negative concord is highly salient and hence stigmatised. Support for this interpretation comes from the fact that the test sentence for the failure of negative attraction (see following section), *Everyone didn't want to hear them*, had a maximum acceptance rate of 54 per cent and no county (with more than fifteen respondents) showed a zero value. The much higher acceptance rate for the failure of negative attraction compared to negative concord can be accounted for by its low salience: with a group of over fifty respondents none of them knew what, if anything, was non-standard in the sentence *Everyone didn't want to hear them*, whereas quite a number specified that *He's not interested in no cars* was non-standard ('unacceptable', 'ungrammatical', 'wrong' in their words) because 'you can't have *not* and *no* in the same sentence', to paraphrase the most common objection.

Failure of negative attraction

This feature is not generally part of supraregional varieties, but it is found in vernacular forms of English, in the north and south. It consists of the blocking of what is termed 'negative attraction' (Filppula 1999: 179–81). By this is meant that indefinite quantifiers acting as subjects, and adverbs like *ever*, are not shifted to their negative counterparts in sentences with verbal negation as in *Nobody is coming this evening* (< *Anybody isn't coming this evening*). Instead the verbal negation remains and the quantifier is unchanged, e.g. *Anything wouldn't do him, he's so fussy* (WER, F85+), *Any house wasn't within half a mile of the river* (SADIF, M70+, Miltown Malbay, Co. Clare).

(194) Failure of negative attraction
    a. *Well, they don't anyone take any notice of him.* (TRS-D, M42, M)
    b. *Anyone don't mind about lioses.* (= ring-forts) (TRS-D, M64–2, M)
    c. *Anyone couldn't help you then, you know.* (WER, M50+)
    d. *Anyone can't build on farming land no more.* (WCER, M75+)
    e. *I don't ever see her now.* (WER, M50+)

Scholars commenting on this feature (Filppula 1999: 183; Harris 1984a: 305) point out that the failure of negative attraction is missing in British English dialects as support for a substrate interpretation. The argument for Irish influence on English in Ireland has to do with the structure of negative sentences. In Irish, negation remains with the verb and cannot be transferred to a negated subject. It does not have positive–negative pairs like English *anybody/nobody*; *anything/nothing*; *ever/never*. Instead it has a specifier with an indefinite noun, e.g. *rud/duine éigin* 'thing/person particular', *aon rud/duine* 'one thing/person', *rud/duine ar bith* 'thing/person at all', which can co-occur with a negated verb if required. There are also words for 'nothing' – *faic* and *tada* – which are formally quite different from the combinations just mentioned.

(195) a. *Níl aon duine anseo.*
        [not-is one person here]
        'There's no-one here.'
     b. *Ní thagann duine ar bith anseo.*
        [not comes person at all here]
        'No-one comes here.'
     c. *Níl aon rud mícheart déanta aici.*
        [not-is one thing not-right done at-her]
        'She has done nothing wrong.'

Contractions of *will* in the negative

In the textual record of Irish English, indeed in historical varieties of English in general, contractions of *will* with a personal pronoun in the negative are to be found copiously, e.g. *I'll not wait your private concerns* (William Congreve, *The Way of the World*, 1700); *Well I'll not debate how far Scandal may be allowable* (Richard Brinsley Sheridan, *The School for Scandal*, 1777). This type of contraction would seem to have lasted until the early twentieth century. Both Synge and O'Casey have frequent attestations of the feature.

(196) Contractions of *will* with pronoun in negative sentences
     a. *He'll not stop him . . . God spare us, and we'll not see him again.*
        (John Millington Synge, *Riders to the Sea*, 1904)
     b. *you'll not stop in this house a minute longer.*
        (Sean O'Casey, *The Shadow of a Gunman*, 1923)
     c. *. . . he'll not climb up my back as easily as he thinks.*
        (Sean O'Casey, *Juno and the Paycock*, 1924)
     d. *But yous'll not escape from th' arrow . . .*
        (Sean O'Casey, *The Plough and the Stars*, 1926)
     e. *I'll not go into that room.* (Sean O'Casey, *The Silver Tassie*, 1928)

The occurrences of contractions of *will* with a personal pronoun in the negative would appear to have been on the decline between the mid nineteenth century and the early twentieth century. Even if one disregards the values for Synge in table 4.35, the two Dubliners, Boucicault and O'Casey, show a clear tendency: the contractions of *will* and *not*, i.e. *won't*, are on the increase with a corresponding decrease in the contractions with pronouns.

The contractions with a personal pronoun would seem to have died out during the first half of the twentieth century. By the time Brendan Behan was writing in the 1950s, the feature had disappeared and there is not a single instance in his plays, the contractions always being between *will* and *not*, i.e. *won't*.

The contraction of *will* with a pronoun in a negative context was tested in *A Survey of Irish English Usage* via the sentence *I'll not wait any longer for him.*

Table 4.35. *Distribution of contractions of* will *by author*

Authors	Contraction of *will* with pronoun (*I'll not*) or zero contraction (*I will not*)	Contraction of *will* with *not* (*I won't*)
Boucicault	17	32
	73	34
Synge		
	23	76
O'Casey		

The acceptance rate was quite high at 51 per cent across all thirty-two counties, although the structure was not attested for the south of Ireland in any of the recordings made by the author (not for Dublin or Waterford and not for contact English in the Irish-speaking districts). The mean for the twenty-three counties outside Ulster was 37 per cent. The mean in Ulster was 77 per cent with Belfast, Antrim and Down showing 88 per cent, 85 per cent and 84 per cent respectively. The considerably higher rate in Ulster is probably due to the presence of this feature in Scots-derived varieties of English, at least historically.[43] In general, the feature is non-salient and was not the subject of any prescriptive comments by respondents. Furthermore, the test sentence is semantically equivalent to the present-day *I won't wait any longer for him*, so that no effort at interpretation was necessary on behalf of the respondents. This would probably have increased respondent awareness, as was the case with some other sentences in the survey such as that for testing double modals, *He might could come after all.*

4.4.6.5   *Inversion with embedded questions*

In standard English, embedded questions are usually introduced by *whether* or *if* and the question shows SV word order. However, in Irish English the clause connectors are usually left out and the embedded questions have the inverted word order of a main clause question (see discussion in Corrigan forthcoming; chapter 5). There are differences in the range of inversion for speakers of Irish English varieties. The type with the widest acceptance is that in *yes/no* questions. The second kind, that involving embedded *wh*-questions, is not as widespread.

(197) Inversion with embedded questions
   a. *She asked him was he interested.* 'She asked him whether/if he was interested.'

---

[43] See Tagliamonte and Smith (2002: 253). The authors quote an example of auxiliary contraction from their northern Irish data: *He'll not be better again Margaret, no* (Tagliamonte and Smith 2002: 258). In the table of comparative results (Tagliamonte and Smith 2002: 268) they state that 91 per cent of the 64 *will* contractions were with the auxiliary and not the negator, i.e. of the *he'll not* type. This is the highest score of the eight locations in the British Isles which Tagliamonte and Smith investigated. It is probably not coincidental that the second highest score (88 per cent) was reached for Cumnock in south-west Scotland, an area which provided many migrants into north-east Ulster in the early modern period.

Table 4.36. *Hierarchy of inversion with embedded questions*

Decreasing acceptability →
1. *yes/no* question 2. *wh*-element 3. *wh*-element + word/*wh*-phrase
1. *She asked him was he interested.*
2a.*He wondered who had she talked with.*
b. *He wondered how had she got home.*
3a.*He wondered which story did they believe.*
b. *He wondered which of the films did they prefer.*

---

    b. *They asked when would you be back.* (Bliss 1984b: 148)
    c. *She asked who had I seen.* (A. Henry 1995: 106)
    d. *They asked me was I going to the meeting.* (A. Henry 1997: 90)
    e. *Our friends asked us who had we seen.* (A. Henry 1995: 91)
    f. *I don't know where do they bring them.* (TRS-D, C41, M)
    g. *We go out and see what do that man want.* (SADIF, M60+, Co. Wexford)
    h. *I don't know is there any luck with it.* (MLSI, F65, Kinsale, Co. Cork)
    i. *I do be saying, I wonder what do she do with all the designer clothes?*
       (WER, F55+)

A. Henry (1997: 90) points out, with reference to Belfast English and other dialects of Irish English, that such sentences are not cases of direct speech as the version of (197a) in this form would be the following: *She asked him, 'Are you interested?'* The 'sequence of tenses' rule changes the present tense of the embedded question to the past and a pronoun change is made for indirect speech. The co-occurrence of *whether/if* and inversion is not permissible: **She asked him whether/if was he interested.* Inversion with embedded *wh*-questions is rarer than with embedded *yes/no* questions but is nonetheless attested (A. Henry 1995: 91): *Our friends asked us who had we seen; He wondered who had she talked with.*

    A. Henry (1997: 91f.), following McCloskey (1992), maintains that the scope of inversion is greater in Ulster, and Belfast in particular, compared with the south of Ireland. They state that the number of verbs with which inversion is possible is larger in the north, e.g. with *find out, establish*, as in the following examples.

(198) a. *The police found out had the goods been stolen.*
     b. *We couldn't establish did he meet them.* (A. Henry, 1997:91f.)

In *A Survey of Irish English Usage* the assumption of a geographical spread and of a cline of acceptability for type was tested with two sentences. The results as shown in table 4.37 are inconclusive with regard to regional acceptance patterns, though there is a slight bias towards the north, if one disregards Donegal. The lower acceptance rate for the second sentence does, however, confirm A. Henry's contention that there is a cline of acceptability for inversion with embedded questions, namely that it shows greater values for *yes/no* questions than for *wh*-questions.

Table 4.37. *Tests for inversion with embedded questions in* A Survey of Irish English Usage: *(1)* yes/no *questions, (2)* wh-*questions*

1. Inversion with embedded *yes/no* questions: *She asked him was he interested*

County	Score	N	Total	County	Score	N	Total
Derry	100%	18	18	Cork	85%	71	84
Kerry	92%	22	24	Armagh	84%	16	19
Kilkenny	92%	22	24	Down	84%	32	38
Limerick	92%	24	26	Waterford	84%	43	51
Wexford	90%	26	29	Sligo	82%	18	22
Clare	88%	14	16	Louth	81%	26	32
Cavan	88%	15	17	Mayo	81%	30	37
Westmeath	88%	22	25	Meath	81%	30	37
Belfast	88%	28	32	Tipperary	81%	34	42
Dublin	88%	181	205	Galway	81%	44	54
Wicklow	86%	18	21	Kildare	80%	20	25
Antrim	85%	35	41	Donegal	79%	33	42

Ulster average: 87%　　　　　　　　Average outside Ulster: 85%

2. Inversion with embedded *wh*-questions: *He asked who had she spoken to*

County	Score	N	Total	County	Score	N	Total
Derry	78%	14	18	Kildare	60%	15	25
Kerry	75%	18	24	Westmeath	60%	15	25
Kilkenny	75%	18	24	Sligo	59%	13	22
Belfast	75%	24	32	Cork	58%	49	84
Down	71%	27	38	Mayo	57%	21	37
Tipperary	71%	30	42	Dublin	57%	117	205
Antrim	66%	27	41	Cavan	53%	9	17
Limerick	65%	17	26	Louth	53%	17	32
Armagh	63%	12	19	Wexford	52%	15	29
Waterford	63%	32	51	Donegal	52%	22	42
Wicklow	62%	13	21	Meath	51%	19	37
Galway	61%	33	54	Clare	44%	7	16

Ulster average: 65%　　　　　　　　Average outside Ulster: 60%

Both Filppula (1999: 167–79) and Amador (2006: 126–32) deal with inversion with embedded questions in detail. Filppula points out (p. 169) that Irish has no equivalent to *if/whether* found in sentences like *She asked him if/whether he was interested.* He does not regard Early Modern English input as a source of inversion with embedded questions in Irish English, given the paucity of attestations for it in studies like Visser (1963–73) and text collections like the *Helsinki Corpus of English Texts* (Filppula 1999: 176f.)

Filppula, and McCloskey who he quotes, regards inversion with embedded questions, as an interference from Irish, given that the latter has the same word order for direct questions and for embedded questions, as can be seen in the following examples.

(199) a.   *An raibh tú tinn?*
            [INTERROG were you ill]
      b.   *D'fhiafraigh siad <u>an raibh tú tinn.</u>*
            [asked they INTERROG were you ill]
      c.   *Cén uair a tháinig tú?*
            [when hour that came you]
      d.   *D'fhiafraigh siad <u>cén uair a tháinig tú.</u>*
            [asked they when hour that came you]

Additional support for the substrate hypothesis comes from the fact that inversion with embedded questions is found in Scotland, where English has been influenced by Scottish Gaelic. Sabban (1982: 460–83) has a section devoted to this issue. She quotes common examples like, *She asked me why was he crying*; *The magician asked him how did he do that* (1982: 463). In her consideration of the possible source of this inversion with embedded questions, Sabban (1982: 480) points to the fact that Scottish Gaelic (like Irish) maintains the inversion of direct questions in embedded contexts. She concludes, as does the present author, that substrate influence has meant that speakers maintained the order of direct questions for embedded questions as well.

This feature has been documented for other regions of the anglophone world (Sabban 1982: 473–8). The occurrence in other varieties of English may be an extension of the order for direct questions to embedded contexts, for instance, in African American English (Wolfram and Fasold 1974: 169f.). However, in the case of Tyneside English (see section 6.1.2) the presence of the feature (Beal 1993: 204) may derive from Irish influence in the region during the nineteenth century.

4.4.6.6   *Tag questions*

The use of tags in Irish has been explained in section 4.3.1 where the similarity between the system in English and Irish was pointed out (see also the section on responsives in 4.3.4). Tags in English are an early modern development, with attestations beginning in earnest in the second half of the sixteenth century (though they may well date from much earlier than this; Gunnel Tottie, personal communication). They only assume anything like their modern distribution from the late eighteenth century onwards (Hoffmann, forthcoming).

Tag questions in present-day Irish English are comparable to those in more standard forms of British or American English (Tottie and Hoffmann, forthcoming). They generally keep to the practice of reverse polarity between anchor and tag, e.g. *Her mother is a great singer, isn't she?* (WER, F55+). Positive–positive

polarity is found, e.g. *He has to go to England again, has he?* (DER, M60+), though instances of negative–negative polarity do not seem to occur, unless the tag is introduced by *sure*, e.g. *It's not worth your while, sure it isn't?* (WER, F55+).

One respect in which Irish English differs from other varieties is in the use of *is it?* as a question tag, something which is attested abundantly from the eighteenth century onwards. If one considers the situation with English in England then the relative scarcity of *is it?* as a question tag is obvious. There are just two instances in Shakespeare's plays, one is in the 'Four Nations scene' of *Henry V*: *It is Captaine Makmorrice, is it not?* and one in *Twelfth Night* (act I, scene v): *From the Count Orsino, is it?* Neither the *Helsinki Corpus of English Texts* (early modern section) nor the *Corpus of Early English Correspondence Sampler* has any instances of *is it?* as a tag. This contrasts strongly with the textual record of Irish English. With the major prose writers of the early nineteenth century one finds that *is it?* occurs abundantly as a general question tag.

(200) *Is it?* as a general question tag in early nineteenth-century Irish English

   a. *Where did – I come from, is it?; How am I coming on, is it?; Will I give you the shovel, is it?* (William Carleton, *Ned M'Keown*)

   b. *So Ireland is at the bottom of his heart, is it?; So this is Lord Clonbrony's estate, is it?; So then the shooting is begun, is it?*
   (Maria Edgeworth, *The Absentee*)

   c. *Myles of the ponies, is it?* (Gerald Griffin, *The Collegians*)

   d. *. . . a regiment of friars is it?; That fools should have the mastery, is it?*
   (Samuel Lover, *Handy Andy, a Tale of Irish Life*)

Any verb phrase is possible in the anchor clause as the following examples show. *Blights me, is it?* (John Millington Synge, *The Tinker's Wedding*, 1909); *Make me, is it?* (John Millington Synge, *The Well of the Saints*, 1905); *You wouldn't, is it?* (John Millington Synge, *The Playboy of the Western World*, 1907). Indeed the anchor clause often just consists of a noun or noun phrase, e.g. *Shaun, is it?* (Dion Boucicault, *Arrah na Pogue*, 1864); *Your oath, is it? . . . Michael Feeney, is it?* (Lady Gregory, *Hanrahan's Oath*); *A salary, is it?* (Shaw, *John Bull's Other Island*, 1904); *Liar, is it?* (John Millington Synge, *The Tinker's Wedding*, 1909); *Mr Grigson, is it?* (Sean O'Casey, *The Shadow of a Gunman*, 1923).

The Irish model for such usage is the general question tag *an ea?* 'is it?' which can be placed at the end of a sentence or phrase, e.g. *Níl sé agat, an ea?* [is-not it at-you, is it] 'You don't have it, is it?' Irish *is ea* (the non-tag form) has many functions, for instance, in copulative sentences, e.g. *Múinteoir is ea é* [teacher is it he] 'He is a teacher' (Ó Dónaill 1977: 467). It is also used to open a sentence, e.g. *Is ea anois, a chairde, tosóimid* [is it now, friends-VOCATIVE, begin-we-FUTURE] 'Alright, friends, we'll start now' (Christian Brothers 1960: 213). It is even used as an opener in questions, e.g. *Is ea nach dtuigeann tú mé?* [is it that not-understand you me] 'Don't you understand me?' (Ó Dónaill 1977: 468). Such instances would seem to be the source of a similar usage in nineteenth-century Irish English as attested by many authors, especially in drama: (i) *Is it a cripple like me, that would be the shadow of an illegant gintleman . . . ?* (ii) *Is it for this I've loved ye?* (iii) *Is it down there ye've been?* (Dion Boucicault, *The Colleen Bawn*, 1860); (i) *Is it that I vexed you in any way?* (ii) *Is it that you went wild and mad, finding the place so lonesome?* (iii) (Lady Gregory, *Hanrahan's Oath*).

The use of *is it* in sentence-initial and sentence-final position has fared differently in later Irish English. Its occurrence at the beginning of a sentence is not that common, perhaps because it is felt to be stage Irish, at least typical of writers like Gregory and Synge. At the end of a sentence *is it* can be found quite commonly; consider these attestations from the author's data collections: *Ye're going to Spain for a few weeks, is it?* (WER, F50+); *They're issuing new [parking] discs, is it?* (WER, F75+); *So, he wants to sell the garage, is it?* (DER, M35+); *She wants to study in Dublin, is it?* (RL, F55+).

A peculiarity of the *is it?* tag in Irish English is that the negative, which would be *is it not?*, does not seem to occur. In the texts by Carleton which were examined in this context there were forty-two instances of the *is it?* tag with only one of the negative tag: *. . . that's an island, I think, in the Pacific– is it not?* (William Carleton, *The Black Baronet*). In present-day Irish English, the negative *is it not?* is virtually unknown. This appears strange given that in Irish the negative tag is frequent, e.g. *Tá tú ag foghlaim Gaeilge, nach bhfuil?*, lit. 'is you at learning Irish, not is-it'.

The reason is that the negative tag *nach ea?/nach bhfuil?* 'not it'/'not is-it' did not transfer to Irish English and so is not represented either in nineteenth-century writers or in present-day varieties to any significant extent. The only three instances in the twenty-three nineteenth- and twentieth-century drama texts in *A Corpus of Irish English* are all from Oscar Wilde's *The Importance of Being Earnest*, which has no features of vernacular Irish English at all.

There still remains the question of why *nach ea?/nach bhfuil?* did not transfer to *is it not?* although *an ea?* did to *is it?* The reason probably lay in the number of syllables. Both *an ea?* and *is it?* have two syllables but *nach ea?* and *is it not?* differ in that the latter has three but the former two. The syllable mismatch probably inhibited the transfer of the Irish structure to English during the language shift, another example where prosody, here the number of syllables, played a role in language contact and transfer.

4.4.7 CONCLUSION: THE SIGNIFICANCE OF THE NINETEENTH CENTURY

In the scholarship on emerging varieties of English in previous centuries (see the contributions in Hickey 2004j), the role of settler speech is always stressed as this sets the scene for later forms of the language, for instance, in North America or Australia. This is known in the literature as the 'founder principle' after the explicit discussion of this in Mufwene (1996). Later generations adopt the speech patterns which were established by early settler groups, after an initial period of mixture and sorting out (Gordon et al. 2004).

In a language shift scenario this principle does not necessarily apply. In the case of Ireland, one can identify early settlers and one can also recognise their probable influence on English for later generations of Irish, including those outside the areas of original English settlement on the east coast. However, the contemporary forms of Irish English, with the probable exception of Ulster Scots, do not reflect early settler English but the outcome of the language shift process which lasted well into the nineteenth century. Those individuals involved in language shift did not just adopt a variety of English established earlier, but forged their own based on this input and the forces operative for them in the shift from Irish to English. To emphasise the role of language shift is not to assume that it was a single monolithic movement which affected the entire population at the same time, but rather to stress that, as an ongoing process for large sections of the population well into the late modern period, it continued to influence the shape of Irish English right up to the second half of the nineteenth century. The discussion of both the *after*-perfective and the *do(es) be* habitual has shown that the present-day distribution of these features was not reached until quite late.

The language shift had for all intents and purposes been completed by the late nineteenth century, some decades after the Great Famine and the demographic upheaval which this caused in Irish society. After this a further sorting out took place. In pronunciation, certain features, such as SERVE-lowering or ASK-metathesis, were rooted out entirely, while others, like unraised long E in the MEAT lexical set or dentalisation in the TRAP lexical set (see discussion in section 5.1.5), became markers of local varieties. In grammar some features, such as the *do(es) be* habitual, were relegated to vernacular forms of Irish English, while others, such as the *after*-perfective, did not become socially stigmatised.

4.5 Models and interpretations

4.5.1 RETENTION AND CONVERGENCE

There has been much discussion of the role of English input and transfer from Irish in the genesis of Irish English, most of which has centred around suggested sources for vernacular features. Two poles can be recognised: on the one hand the writings of Alan Bliss, who favoured transfer, and on the other, those of John Harris, who assigned primary importance to English input. Later treatments of this issue, by Karen Corrigan, Markku Filppula, Jeffrey Kallen, Kevin McCafferty and the present author offer reassessments of the arguments presented by Bliss and Harris.

Some developments in English ran parallel to the structure of Irish and so appeared in Irish English, not so much by transfer, which implies a mismatch between outset and target language, but simply by equivalence. One such development of the later modern period (Beal 2004a: 77–85) is the *be* + V-*ing* construction as in *What are you reading?* This would have represented an appropriate equivalent to Irish *Ceárd atá tú a léamh?* [what that-is you COMP reading]

Table 4.38. *Convergence scenarios in the history of Irish English*

1a. *Source 1 (English) independent of source 2 (Irish)*
     English development   Irish
     What are you reading?   *Céard atá tú a léamh?*
                             [what that-are you COMP reading]
     Outcome in Irish English: continuous verb phrases maintained.

b. *Source 1 (English) independent of source 2 (Irish)*
     older English input   Irish
     Are ye ready?   *An bhfuil sibh réidh?*
                             [INTERROG are you-PLURAL ready]
     Outcome in Irish English: distinct second-person-plural pronoun maintained.

2. *Source 1 (English) provides form and source 2 (Irish) semantics*
     English input (periphrastic/emphatic) Irish
                             Bíonn sé amuigh ar an bhfarraige.
     He does live in the west.   [is-HABITUAL he out on the sea]
     Outcome in Irish English: habitual is established, *He does be out on the sea.*

3. *Failed convergence:*
     Source 1 (dialectal English) shares feature with source 2 (Irish)
     English input   Irish
     They were a-singing.   *Bhí siad ag canadh.*
                             [were they at singing]
     Outcome in Irish English: *A*-prefixing does not establish itself.

or *Ceárd atá á léamh agat?* [what that-is at-its reading at-you]. Another development is the rise of group verbs (phrasal verbs – transitive and intransitive, prepositional verbs and phrasal-prepositional verbs; Denison 1998: 221). These types of verb occur widely in Irish, e.g. *Ná bí ag cur isteach orthu* [not be at put in on-them] 'Don't be disturbing them.' Indeed calques on English phrasal and prepositional verbs are a major source of loans from English into Irish today (see section 4.7).

The cases just cited represent instances of convergence, i.e. developments in two languages which result in their becoming increasingly similar structurally. Convergence can be understood in another sense which is relevant to the genesis of specific features of Irish English. This is where both English input and transfer from Irish have contributed to the rise of a feature (see table 4.38 for convergence scenarios). This applies to the *do(es) be* habitual where English input provided periphrastic *do* and Irish the semantics of the structure and its co-occurrence with the expanded form, as discussed above.

Mention should also be made of features which exist in Irish and in non-standard varieties of English in England, but not, curiously, in Irish English. The best example of this is *a*-prefixing. This is recorded for south-western British English, e.g. *I be a-singing* (Elworthy 1877: 52f., West Somerset). Such structures look deceptively Irish: the sentence could be translated directly as *Bím ag canadh* [is-HABITUAL-I at singing]. However, *a*-prefixing does not occur in modern Irish English[44] and is not attested in the textual record of the past few centuries to any significant extent. Montgomery (2000) is rightly sceptical of a possible Celtic origin of this feature, contra Dietrich (1981) and Majewicz (1984) who view the transfer interpretation favourably. See the discussion of this feature in the context of transportation below (section 6.3.1). Table 4.39 lists features of Irish English and suggests the possible sources of these. For the purpose of comparison it also includes phonological features which are discussed in detail in the next chapter.

4.5.2 EVIDENCE FOR GRAMMATICALISATION

The literature on grammaticalisation has increased greatly in the last few decades. Summaries of positions developed in the 1980s and 1990s have become available recently and in the present section that by Heine and Kuteva (2004) is considered. It is a programmatic study written by two major authors, the first of whom has developed many of the theoretical underpinnings of modern grammaticalisation models. In their monograph the authors have much to say about language contact and many of their statements are accurate characterisations, e.g. 'In situations of intense language contact, speakers tend to develop some mechanism for equating "similar" concepts and categories across languages' (Heine and Kuteva 2004: 4). This is close to what Hickey (1995b, 1997a) has termed 'the search for categorial equivalence' (see section 4.2.3) which accounts for the origin of many of the non-standard structures of Irish English.

Heine and Kuteva (2004: 2f.) use the term 'grammatical replication' to refer to those situations of contact where a replica language (R) adopts 'grammatical meanings' from a model language (M). However, despite the fact that the authors consider this a viable scenario for the genesis of Irish English, it does not apply to language shift which is the essential event in early Irish English.[45] In this situation, speakers of M (the source language) transfer structures and meanings from this language, their native language, into R (the target language) during the process of shift, i.e. during unguided adult second-language acquisition. When

---

[44] Robinson (1997: 140) mentions its occurrence in 'current Ulster Scots', specifically in passive contexts, e.g. *A'm a-calin for ma tay* 'I'm being called for my tea', *Ye'r a-wantin for yer tay* 'You're being wanted for your tea.' However, there is no objective confirmation of such usages and Robinson does not apparently have a corpus of data representing a cross-section of the present-day Ulster Scots community (his samples are his own or from historical sources).

[45] The most serious weakness in Heine and Kuteva's treatment is the complete neglect of language shift as an historical reality in Ireland. Most importantly, the scenario of first-language speakers of Irish shifting to English as adults in a situation of non-prescriptive, unguided second-language acquisition is not mentioned. But it is this scenario which provided the language-shift framework in which speakers transferred structural principles of their first language to the second language. The small numbers of first-language speakers of English in the early modern period in Ireland can be neglected.

Table 4.39. *Suggestions for sources of key features of southern Irish English*

Features	Possible source
Phonological features	
Dental/alveolar stops for fricatives	Transfer of nearest Irish equivalent, coronal stops
Intervocalic and pre-pausal lenition of /t/	Lenition as a phonological directive from Irish
Alveolar /l/ in all positions	Use of non-velar, non-palatal [l] from Irish as well as English input
Retention of [ʍ] for <wh>	Convergence of input with Irish /f/ [ɸ]
Retention of syllable-final /r/	Convergence of English input and Irish
Distinction of short vowels before /r/, TERN # TURN	Convergence of English input and Irish
Morphological features	
Distinct pronominal forms for second person singular and plural	Convergence of English input and Irish
Epistemic negative *must*	Generalisation made by Irish based on positive use
Them as demonstrative	English input only
Syntactic features	
Habitual aspect	Convergence with English input in south, possibly with Scots and English in Ulster; otherwise transfer of category from Irish
Immediate perfective aspect with *after*	Transfer from Irish
Resultative perfective with O + PP word order	Possible convergence, primarily transfer from Irish
Subordinating *and*	Transfer from Irish
Non-standard verbal concord	English input, particularly on east coast
Clefting for topicalisation purposes	Transfer from Irish, with some possible convergence
Greater range of the present tense	Transfer from Irish, with some possible convergence
Negative concord	Convergence of English input and Irish
For to infinitives indicating purpose	Convergence of English input and Irish
Reduced number of verb forms	English input only
Be as auxiliary	English input only
Single time reference for *never*	Transfer from Irish, English input

there is (unconscious) community-wide agreement on what restructurings in the target language are accepted, these become established traits of the new, restructured variety of the contact language.

Essential weaknesses in Heine and Kuteva's grammaticalisation argument (2004: 62–5) can be shown by considering an example. When discussing

Table 4.40. *Stages of grammaticalisation (Heine and Kuteva 2004: 80)*

---

1. extension, i.e. the rise of novel grammatical meanings when linguistic expressions are extended to new contexts (contact-induced reinterpretation)
2. desemanticisation (or 'semantic bleaching'), i.e. loss (or generalisation) in meaning content
3. decategorialisation, i.e. loss in morphosyntactic properties characteristic of lexical or other less grammaticalised forms
4. erosion (or 'phonetic reduction'), i.e. loss in phonetic substance

---

clefting in Irish English they imply that under the influence of Irish (based on data presented in Filppula 1986) there was a 'restructuring of existing use patterns whereby some minor pattern [i.e. clefting, RH] . . . acquires greater text frequency, is exposed to new contexts and may be applied in new contexts' (Heine and Kuteva 2004: 63). This implies that there was a period in Irish English in which clefting had a much smaller scope which then increased through contact with Irish. But the scope of clefting found in Irish English today is derived from the behaviour of large sections of the population who applied the scope it had in Irish to English during the language shift.

Another case highlighted by Heine and Kuteva is what is termed the 'extended now' use of the present tense. The authors argue as follows: 'Assuming that, at some earlier stage, Irish English had a system of tense-aspect categorization not unlike that of Standard English, expression of the extended-now function can be assumed to have shifted in Irish English from one category (present perfect) to another (non-past or progressive) without affecting the overall structure of categorization' (Heine and Kuteva 2004: 140). There are no grounds for such an assumption. Rather what happened was that Irish native speakers used the present tense of English with the same scope which the present has in Irish, i.e. including actions which start in the past and still apply – the scenario for the present perfect of standard English. In comparison to more mainstream varieties it may now look as if Irish English extended a category, but there is no evidence that Irish English once had a more restricted use of the present tense which it then extended.

One may nonetheless ask if there are any cases of grammaticalisation in the history of Irish English. To answer this question, consider Heine and Kuteva's analysis of grammaticalisation. For them, it consists of four stages which they believe they can also recognise in contact scenarios, as listed in table 4.40. These stages would seem to apply to language-internal grammaticalisation. However, on language contact, one may just have the first and possibly fourth stage. For instance, with the co-option of *do(es) be* for the habitual in Irish English there is (1) extension beyond periphrastic *do* and (4) phonetic reduction, on the east coast, of [dʌz 'bi] / [du 'bi] to [də 'bi]. The essential step here is the first, extension. In a language shift scenario, speakers moving to a new language may extend the scope of a feature in this language to have an equivalent to a category which they know from their native language. The means for expressing this category in the new language does not have to be the same as in the first language of those engaged in language shift, and with the *do(es) be* habitual of Irish English this is not the case.

Whether there are further instances of grammaticalisation in Irish English depends on how narrowly one defines this process. If the exploitation of alternative word orders is subsumed under the heading of grammaticalisation, then the O + PP word order used for the resultative perfective is another instance. The immediate perfective with *after* + V-*ing* could be treated as grammaticalisation inasmuch as it involves the extension of *after* from future reference to past reference (see discussion in section 4.4.1.4.1) with the later restriction to just past uses. But stages 2, 3 and 4 from table 4.39 do not apply here.

4.5.3 ARGUMENTS FOR CREOLISATION

The terminological difficulties surrounding grammaticalisation and language contact/shift apply, if anything, to an ever greater extent when it comes to considering whether Irish English was a creole at any earlier stage; see Hickey (1997a) for a detailed consideration of this issue. There are many definitions of 'creole' and 'creolisation', the process which leads to a creole arising.[46] The readiness of some scholars (e.g. Kallen 1994: 173) to use this term when talking about languages which have undergone periods of contact and possible shift, but no break in linguistic continuity, is not helpful in this respect (see review in Hickey 1997a: 969–75). For the following discussion three types of definition can be considered:

1. *External definition*. By this is meant that factors outside a language determine whether it can be labelled a creole or not. External definitions are favoured by some scholars, such as John Holm, who, when examining the varieties of English in the Caribbean, states: 'no particular set of syntactic features alone will identify a language as a creole without reference to its sociolinguistic history' (Holm 1994: 372). The situation in Ireland was very different to that in the Caribbean in the early modern period with a large population of African slaves (after the 'homestead' phase). The Irish remained in their native country and did not live in isolation so that on the basis of external factors, there can be no question of a creole having developed.

2. *Acquisitional definition*. This type of definition sees a creole as a language which arises when a generation of speakers develops its language from a drastically reduced and imperfectly acquired form of a (colonial) lexifier language. This definition stresses the break with the native language(s) of previous generations. In Ireland, no such linguistic discontinuity ever obtained so that on this score, Irish English cannot have been a creole at any earlier stage.

---

[46] For reasons of space it is not possible to discuss notions such as 'semi-creolisation' or 'partially restructured languages'; see Holm (2000, 2004) for further information.

3. *Structural definition*. According to this definition, a creole is a language which has undergone considerable restructuring with respect to the lexifier language and probably with regard to the substrate native language(s) as well, if it/they provided input (Baker and Huber 2001). Restructuring involves a movement towards analytical type and a simplification of morphology (independent morphemes are used for bound morphemes in the grammar of the lexifier language, the latter may be present but afunctional). Restructured languages show SVO word order and pre-specification in dyads, i.e. adjective + noun and genitive + noun. In verb phrases markers for tense and aspect precede the verb in question.

If at all, only the third of the above definitions could be used when judging whether Irish English was once a creole. There are structural parallels between Irish English and, say, Caribbean creoles. For example, aspectual distinctions appear to be at a premium in each case: both creoles and unguided second-language acquisition scenarios share 'a propensity for treating temporal relations as less fundamental than aspectual distinctions' (Corrigan 1993a: 107).

However, scholars are divided on the question of whether there are features which apply only to creoles. For instance, Mufwene (2003: 204) and Holm (1994) have argued that there are no restructuring processes which are specific only to creoles. This means that no structural definition would be sufficient for assigning creole status to an earlier stage of Irish English. Given that the external and acquisitional definitions do not apply to the genesis of Irish English, there is no conclusive evidence that Irish English may have been a creole at some early stage. Another external factor militates against a creole interpretation: language shift is not a scenario which involves creolisation (Winford 2003: 304–58). Speakers only restructure parts of the target language in order to obtain equivalents to categories in their native language. What may happen is that simplified registers of the target language arise during the language shift process. These registers could be classified as pidgins, in the sense of grammatically restricted codes of a target language which appear in a contact situation, such as that for dealings with English officials in Ireland. If these registers did exist, they died out with the completion of the language shift and the rise of later generations of native speakers of English in former Irish-speaking areas.

4.5.4 PROTOTYPE ANALYSIS

Aspectual distinctions are not water-tight binary categories like singular or plural. Any classification, which specifies that a structure embodies one type of aspect with just one meaning, is bound to run into difficulties.[47] It is true that the

---

[47] The prototype interpretation outlined below allows for overlap in the realisations chosen. Hence the fact that Kallen (1989) found examples of *after* and V-*ing* for all four perfect types in McCawley's classification is neither surprising nor does it invalidate the central semantic component of immediacy which is prototypical for this aspectual class.

meanings of the three main aspectual types in Irish English are as given in the subsections of 4.4.1.4 on tense and aspect above, but there are attestations which do not seem to fit these meanings.[48] The appearance of apparent exceptions should not be a reason for abandoning a given classification, but rather an occasion to reflect on how such attestations relate to the basic classification. One way of handling such 'exceptions' is to conceptualise aspectual distinctions as consisting of prototypes which can be more or less matched by actual sentences (see full treatment in Hickey 2000b). They can be treated in a manner similar to that of lexical semantics in the classical expositions of prototype theory (Rosch 1977, 1978; Taylor 1989) where a particular token of, say, a bird, e.g. a robin or sparrow, can be regarded as a prototype of a class. However, other tokens, such as an ostrich or a penguin, may be lacking key characteristics (such as flight) and may be located towards the periphery of the semantic space occupied by the item in question.

In the present section a number of attestations will be examined which represent prototypical and peripheral instances of aspectual classes. The three main aspectual types of Irish English have central applications – prototypes – which are indicated by their names: (i) resultative perfective, (ii) immediate perfective and (iii) habitual.

Resultative perfective

Prototype: completion of a planned action. Different scholars have tried to give a general characterisation of this aspectual type. Greene (1979: 132), with reference to Visser (1963–73: paragraph 2001), maintains that there is an emotional interest in the result reached. It might be best to state that with this aspect there is a degree of expectancy that the action described by the verb will indeed have been carried out, hence the notion of 'interest' in Greene's characterisation. The fact that it is usually, but not always, the speaker who expresses this may have led others to see it as 'subjective' in meaning. Within a discourse, the resultative serves the function of conveying to a listener or listeners that an action which was planned has indeed been completed, e.g. *They've the car fixed now*, *She has the meal cooked already*. There are, of course, peripheral uses in which this notion of intention is not foregrounded, e.g. the example *I have it forgot* (quoted by Filppula 1999: 90), unless one can assume that the speaker planned to forget something.

The example just quoted goes to show that a peripheral instance of an aspectual class by no means invalidates the prototypical interpretation of other instances, in this case, those that suggest that an action is planned. The claim that a very few counterexamples are enough to refute a proposed interpretation of some grammatical category can be judged insufficient when such categories are viewed

---

[48] Montgomery and Kirk (1996: 321) in their interpretation of *be (es)* in northern Irish English point out that it is found in senses which are not always habitual, for example durative, punctual and conditional uses are attested in their data. The authors intuitively realise that there is a prototypical use as an habitual in more than two-thirds of the cases (although they do not use this terminology) and that the remainder are peripheral uses which do not invalidate the prototype.

as classes with prototypical and peripheral instances. At any one time, peripheral instances can be recognised because they are quantitatively less significant than prototypical ones. Of course, over time, a change in status between the two types of instances can occur; see comments on language change and prototypes below.

The immediate perfective

Prototype: recent completion of an action. The manifestations of this aspectual class show a much greater range than the resultative perfective.[49] But common to the majority of instances is the notion of immediacy. In discourse situations, the element of immediacy implies high informational value as something which has just recently happened is unlikely to be known to the listener.

(201) *They're after blocking off the street to lay down new pipes.* (DER, M35+)

The flexibility of the immediate perfective becomes obvious in attestations which show high informational value, but which no longer have immediacy in the foreground. This view helps to interpret such usages as the following (Filppula 1999: 100, emphasis his).

(202) We are *after having* two great summers here. (Wicklow, DM)

Conveying information means that this construction occurs primarily when something is being reported to the listener.[50] The event which is recounted is often viewed negatively by the reporter, which is why this perfective commonly combines with the preposition *on* to express relevance: *She's after eating the yoghurt on me.* If the subject of the action mentioned is also the interlocutor in an exchange then the tone is one of reproach, e.g. *You're after ruining the stew on me.* The element of chiding (Kallen 1991: 66) can be seen as an extension of the relevance element. It can also be interpreted as an increase in subjectification with this structure. It is known from studies of semantic-pragmatic change that meanings tend to become increasingly situated in the speaker's subjective belief-state/attitude towards a situation (Traugott and König 1991: 207–9). This would help to explain why the immediate perfective has increasingly become a vehicle for expressing speakers' attitudes and/or assessment of a situation.

The relative infrequency of the negative with the *after* construction lies in its function of reporting a matter of relevance to an interlocutor. The situations in which such a report is required in the negative are rare, but there are instances where negation occurs.

---

[49] Kallen (1991: 62f.) has shown that for his corpus of Dublin English the *after* variable as an aspectual marker occurs in different types of context, but he does not offer a classification in terms of prototypical and peripheral uses.

[50] Kallen would seem to grasp this when he offers a classification according to speech acts (1991: 64ff.) and when he points out that the *after* construction is frequent in narrative situations.

(203) (*You shouldn't have taken out the car at night with only a provisional licence.*
WER, F75+) *Don't worry, I'm not after crashing it.* (WER, M25+)

The pragmatics of perfective aspects. The resultative and the immediate perfective
contrast in one important respect: the former prototypically involves a planned
action whereas the latter does not, or at least the completion of the reported
action is, to a certain degree, unexpected. Consider the following contrasting
pairs of sentences.

(204) a. *They're after putting up street lights.*
(in the process of building the housing estate)
 b. *They've the street lights put up now.*
(this was the work they set out to accomplish)
 c. *They're after selling their house.*
(highlights this fact as new information)
 d. *They have their house sold.*
(stresses that this action is now completed)

These shades of meaning make the two perfectives of Irish English mutually
exclusive in certain situations. For instance, in contexts where an action can
hardly be regarded as planned, the resultative perfective is not possible, hence
the ungrammaticality of the first of each pair of the following sentences.

(205) a. **He's the soup bowl dropped.*
He's after dropping the soup bowl.
 b. **They've the window broken.*
They're after breaking the window.

Because the resultative perfective implies that an action was definitely intended,
the *after* perfective is used in more neutral contexts, i.e. it does not always
have to refer to an immediately completed action. Neutral reports can be
made using the *after* perfective, e.g. *They're after giving the staff a pay rise
already this year.* These cases are perhaps less central, but nonetheless genuine
instances of the aspectual class, just as much as a flightless bird is of the class of
birds.

(206) *resultative*   neutral report ← (extension) *immediate perfective*
       intention   recent/high informational
                                                 value

Habitual

Prototype: regularly repeated action. The formally different types of habitual
found in different varieties of Irish English (see section 4.4.1.4.3) have in common
that they express an action which is repeated on a regular basis. Extensions of this
prototypical use also occur. In particular, the habitual is found to express a state.
This is certainly peripheral, as it is nothing like as frequent as the prototypical

Table 4.41. *Extension of the habitual in Irish English*

Step	Meaning	Example
1.	habitual indicative >	He *do be* out clubbing on Saturday night. (WER, F55+)
2.	expressing state >	I wouldn't leave them out when they'd be young anyway. (WER, F55+)
		Still an' all, Myles *do be* poor, for he never knew how to keep a hoult o' the money. (Gerald Griffin, *The Collegians*)
3.	character trait	His uncle *do be* a hard worker. (WER, F85+)

use. A further metaphorical extension of the habitual is to express a character trait. These extensions can be put in an order as shown in table 4.41.

Language change and grammatical prototypes. Prototype analysis can be useful when considering diachronic developments because it allows for overlap and a change in status for members of a category. Language change can thus be interpreted as a case of peripheral usages becoming more central, thus triggering a shift in basic meaning. For instance, in earlier stages of Irish English the central usage of the *after* perfective was with future reference as has been discussed above in section 4.4.1.4.1. Usages with past-time reference were peripheral. However, during the nineteenth century the latter become more central and the original future-time references more peripheral, finally dying out later in this century. This change can be understood as an early increase in past-tense reference, probably in the late eighteenth century, which led during the nineteenth century to a reinterpretation of the prototypical time reference of the *after* perfective by later generations of children acquiring Irish English. The course of this change can be compared to the well-known S-curves of language change (Denison 2003), with a slow beginning, a quick central phase followed by a slower terminal phase. The quick central phase can be located in the mid nineteenth century because, going on the textual record, this is when the future-time references disappear with various authors in different genres.

4.6 Ireland as a linguistic area

The notion of linguistic area (from German *Sprachbund*, lit. 'language federation') is one which is often invoked when dealing with languages which share features and are found in a geographically contiguous area (Heine and Kuteva 2004: 172–218). Some of these areas have gained general acceptance in linguistic literature as the evidence for them is quite convincing. These include the Pacific north-west, Meso-America, the Balkans, the Baltic area, Arnhem Land in northern Australia, southern India (with Indic/Dravidian languages), to mention just some of the better-known instances. Scholars concerned with linguistic areas vary considerably in their approach. Following Campbell (1998: 300), one can distinguish at least two basic orientations in the field: (i) *circumstantialist* where authors are content with listing the various features of a putative area and (ii) *historicist* where authors attempt to show that the shared features diffused historically through the languages of an area. The second approach is necessary to avoid the pitfall of raising features, which may have arisen by chance, to the level of defining characteristics of an area. Furthermore, it is essential to accord relative weight to features under consideration. Those which are typologically unspectacular cannot be appealed to when defining an area. For instance, any set of languages or varieties which show a palatalisation of velars – and just that – could hardly be regarded as forming a linguistic area as this is a very general feature. On the other hand, languages in an enclosed area which develop phonemic tone would be good candidates for a linguistic area. These simple examples highlight one feature of the entire discussion about linguistic areas which is often not rendered explicit by scholars in the field: the discussion is about relatively unusual features. Again an example illustrates this clearly: if a voice distinction among stops was sufficient as a defining feature, then the continent of Europe (perhaps excluding Finland) would be a single linguistic area. But this is plainly not the case. On the other hand, front rounded vowels are relatively unusual and, going on their occurrence, one can recognise a loose area from France across to Hungary and northwards into Scandinavia.

Apart from the typological status of features, their quantity is also important, so that one can establish a density index for areas which helps in labelling them as strong or weak. Furthermore, the linguistic levels on which the commonalities are found are of relevance. Closed-class levels such as morphology or syntax have a high indexical value. The lexical level – as an open class – is virtually irrelevant in this context as borrowing of words to and fro across languages is so common. The only exception to this would be clearly defined structural principles of lexical organisation which are shared between languages and independent of individual words.

The diffusion of features has a reverse side to it, namely the common maintenance of features which have been inherited from different inputs. In Ireland an example of this is the retention of a distinction between short vowels before /r/ which is found in all vernacular forms of English in the north (including Ulster Scots) and the south of the island as well as in Irish.

The desire to group languages into linguistic areas arose from the insight that shared features can occur in a confined geographical area among languages which are not genetically related. This is, however, an incidental issue. There may be more than one language family represented in an area, as with Indo-European and Turkic in the Balkans or Indo-European and Dravidian in southern India. The affiliation to different language families is not a defining feature of a linguistic area. At most, the presence of two (rarely more) families serves to heighten the awareness of the structural convergence which has taken place historically. In the case of Ireland, all languages and varieties belong to Indo-European, albeit different subgroupings (Q-Celtic for Irish and West Germanic for forms of English/Scots).

Linguistic areas are by their nature fuzzy concepts. If there has been a high degree of multilateral influence within the area then isomorphism in grammatical structure is likely (Thomason and Kaufman 1988: 96). Of the features found in a linguistic area, only some will be area-wide. It is more common to find localised bilateral diffusions, i.e. regions with higher and lower density within the area in question. Equally, one does not find that isoglosses bundle at the boundaries. Rather the outer boundaries of a linguistic area are as a rule defined geographically – at least approximately, for instance in the Balkans it is the large peninsula between the Black Sea and the Adriatic.

The convergence which has given rise to an area in the first place may show periods of greater or lesser activity and the synchronic picture may be one of a dormant area, if the mutual influence has receded for whatever reason.

In addition, one must distinguish between the diffusion of a structural feature within an area and the spread of the exponence of this feature. An example of this is offered by lenition in Irish and southern Irish English. A central feature in Irish phonology is the weakening of segments (stops to fricatives usually) to indicate grammatical categories. The actual changes are not reflected in English in Ireland, e.g. there is no shift of /k/ to /x/, but there is a general weakening of alveolar stops, as with the fricativisation of /t/ in environments of high sonority (Hickey 1996a); see section 5.4.3. The contrast between category and exponence is also found with the habitual aspect which is realised by *bees* in the north and *do(es) be* in the south; see 4.4.1.4.3.

A feature may be present in adjoining languages or varieties although its realisation may not be the same in all cases. Consider the second-person-plural personal pronouns found in Ireland. While the south tends to favour the morphologically transparent form *youse* < *you* + {S}, the north shows a greater occurrence of *yez* < *ye* + {S}. In the supraregional variety of the south, the uninflected form *ye* (the historical input) is found.

Another consideration concerns the presence of a feature at different points within a putative area and where the occurrences are not related to each other. Glottalisation of stops and/or the replacement of supraglottal stops by a glottal stop is just such a case. This is found both in forms of Ulster Scots and of local Dublin English, but there is no question of there being an historical connection between the two varieties.

The absence of a category or distinction can be viewed as a defining characteristic of a linguistic area, although the indexical value of absent features is usually weak. One must also distinguish between the actual lack and the quantitative underrepresentation of a feature. An instance of this is provided from the verbal area. In all colloquial forms of English in Ireland, there is a noticeable underrepresentation of the present perfect, e.g. *I know him for years* would be more common than *I have known him for years*. In Irish there is no present perfect category and the neglect of this in English is a likely consequence of the language shift which occurred historically in Ireland.

The avoidance of a category may be due to the fact that its exponent is used for a particular function thus precluding its further use. To realise habitual aspect a finite form of *do* plus *be* or – less commonly – a lexical verb is used, especially in southern Irish English. One can also observe that *do* is not found when negating *use* or *tend* so that sentences like the following would not be found in (southern) Irish English: *She didn't use to visit them at home* (rather: *She usen't . . .*) or *He didn't tend to come late* (rather: *He tended not . . .*).

The features in table 4.42 are those found in Ireland. It is possible to consider these in the context of the British Isles and regard the latter as a large linguistic area. This approach is to be found in older literature, notably Wagner (1959), and latterly in such studies as Filppula (2004b). Unfortunately, it is beyond the scope of this book to consider the arguments put forward by these scholars.

4.7   Epilogue: the influence of English on Irish

That English has had a considerable influence on the structure of Irish is only to be expected given the dominant position of English in Ireland since at least the mid nineteenth century (Stenson 1993). But for native speakers the influence is not so much felt in phonology nor in morphology, given the considerable differences between the two languages on these levels. Furthermore, the lexis of Irish has many loans from English which go back to the late Middle Ages (Hickey 1997b) and have been adapted to Irish (de Bhaldraithe 1953). The lexical influence of English is obvious in code-switching (Stenson 1991; O'Malley Madec 2002: chapter 2 'Approaches to code-switching and borrowing'), i.e. the direct use of English words in Irish sentences (Hickey 1982). Pragmatic markers, such as *well, just, now*, are also commonly inserted into Irish sentences (O'Malley Madec 2002). Many examples occurred in the *Collection of Contact English*, two of which can be seen in the following.

(207) a. *Tá sé níos diocra, just, ná mar a cheap mé.* (CCE-W, M65+)
   [is it more difficult just than what that thought I]
   'It's more difficult, just, than I thought.'
   b. *Well, tá mé ag súil leis an earrach now.* (CCE-S, M60+)
   [well is I at looking with the spring now]
   'Well, I am looking forward to spring now.'

In syntax, the influence of English is strongest, despite the typological differences between the two languages. There are certain structural parallels between Irish and English which facilitate the transfer of English patterns into Irish. This has been registered for some time by Irish scholars. For instance, Ó Cuív (1951: 54f.) remarks on the impact of English on Irish and quotes instances of English syntax in Irish, e.g. *Cuir suas ar an rothar mé* (lit. 'put me up on the bicycle me') where Irish might previously have had *Cuir i n-áirde ar an mbicycle mé* (lit. 'put me in height on the bicycle me').

Table 4.42. *Areal features in Ireland*

I. *Phonological features*	
1. Lack of interdental fricatives	(Es+I)
2. Lenition of stops	(vEs+I)
3. Syllable-final /r/	(Ens+I)
4. Short vowel distinctions before /r/	(vEns+I)
5. *Horse # hoarse* distinction	(vEns)
6. Raised /æ/ before /r/	(vEns)
7. Retention of [ʌ] for <*wh*>	(vEns)
8. Unraised E in MEAT lexical set	(vEns)
9. Mid high rounded vowel [ʉ]	(En+In)
10. Lack of phonemic vowel length	(vEn)
11. Palatal glide after velar plosives	(vEn –r)
12. Retention of syllable-final /x/	(vEn –r)
II. *Morphological features*	
1. Separate second-person-plural pronoun	(Ens+I)
2. Epistemic negative *must*	(Ens)
3. *Them* as demonstrative pronoun	(Ens)
III. *Syntactic features*	
A. *Verbs*	
1. Greater range of the present tense	(Ens+I)
2. *Be* as auxiliary	(Ens+I)
3. Reduced number of parts of verbs	(vEns)
4. Lack of *do* in *have*-questions	(Ens)
5. Habitual aspect	(vEns+I)
a. *do(es) be* (vEs) b. *bees* (vEn)	
6. Immediate perfective aspect	(Ens+I)
7. Resultative perfective aspect	(Ens+I)
B. *Adverbials*	
1. *Never* with singular time reference	(Ens+I)
2. Use of positive *anymore*	(vEn+I)
3. *Whenever* in the sense of 'when'	(vEn)
4. *From* in the sense of 'since'	(vEn)
C. *Clause structure*	
1. *That* as preferred relative pronoun	(Ens)
2. *Till* = 'so that' (Irish: *go*)	(Ens+I)
3. Clefting for topicalisation purposes	(Ens+I)
4. *For to* plus infinitive (Irish: *chun*)	(vEns+I)
5. Subordinating *and* (Irish: *agus*)	(vEns+I)
6. Negative concord	(vEns+I)
7. Non-standard subject concord	(vEns)

The abbreviations in the right-most column are as follows: E = 'English', I = 'Irish',
v = 'vernacular', n = 'northern', s = 'southern'. These can occur in various
combinations, e.g. vEns means 'vernacular varieties on both northern and southern Irish

Table 4.42. *(cont.)*

English'. The abbreviation '-r' means that a feature is recessive, e.g. the retention of syllable-final /x/ in northern Irish English.

Features shared by general forms of English and Irish
1. Continuous verb forms
2. Tags used for questions
3. Two-case system (nominative and genitive)
4. Possessive pronouns with inalienable possession

Features of Irish with no direct equivalents in English

Phonology	Systemic distinction of palatal and non-palatal consonants
	Velar fricatives, consonant clusters such as /sr-/, /tl-/, /mr-/
Grammar	VSO word order, noun + adjective, nominative + genitive
	Inflections for person and number distinctions
	Inflected form of future and conditional
	Verbal noun and verbal adjective
	Autonomous form of the verb
	Lack of indefinite article

English phrasal verbs[51] and verbs with prepositional complements are particularly common in Irish (Stenson 1997; Veselinović 2006).[52] Often they are translated (208a) or they are integrated into Irish by having the productive verb-forming ending *-áil* attached (208b).

(208) a. *Bhí sí déanta suas mar cailleach.* (CCE-W, F55+)
   [was she done up as a-witch]
   'She was done up as a witch.'
   b. *Ná bí ag rusháil back amáireach.* (CCE-W, F55+)
   [not be at rushing back tomorrow]
   'Don't be rushing back tomorrow.'

Typical word order in Irish has changed in some cases under the influence of English. Previously, it was normal to find adverbials in phrase- and sentence-final position (indicated in parentheses in (209) below). Under the influence of English, adverbs (underlined below) are drawn closer to the elements they modify. This can be a verb (209a) or a predicative adjective (209b).

---

[51] These structures seem to have spread to Welsh in a fashion similar to Irish. See the examples with *break*, for instance, where Rottet lists seven types of phrasal verb based on English models (Rottet 2005: 70).

[52] Stenson shows that Irish has been able to accommodate such constructions into its syntax quite well, probably because the language does have compound verbs with locational adverbs as in *Bhain muid Londain amach* [gained we London out] 'We reached London.'

(209) a. *Ní fhaca mé riamh rud mar sin (riamh).*
[not saw I ever thing like that (ever)]
'I never saw anything like that.'
b. *Tá a seanathair fós beo (fós).*
[is her grandfather still alive (still)]
'Her grandfather is still alive.'

This pattern also applies to the order of verb objects. Direct objects previously occurred after prepositional objects in final position, but it is increasingly common to find the order typical of English, namely direct object + prepositional object.

(210) *Chonaic mé í thíos ar an trá (í).*
[saw I her down on the strand (her)]
'I saw her down on the strand.'

The readiness of Irish to adopt syntactic patterns of English is also seen in direct translations of English idioms. These are usually translated word for word, something which is possible in quite a number of cases.

(211) a. *Thóg sé tamall fada, ceart go leor.*
[took it time long right enough]
'It took a long time sure enough.'
b. *Bhí orm súil a choinneáil ar an am.*
[was on-me eye COMP keep on the time]
'I had to keep an eye on the time.'
c. *Caithfidh tú d'intinn a dhéanamh suas.*
[must you your mind COMP make up]
'You have to make your mind up.'

The examples just discussed show how permeable the syntax of Irish is, despite the obvious typological differences between it and English (VSO word order, post-modification). Such examples of transfer have occurred between the two languages through contact, not through shift (they are found with speakers who continue to use their native language). If such transfer is possible, then it strengthens the case for transfer having occurred in the more radical historical situation of speakers abandoning Irish and shifting to English.

5   Present-day Irish English

5.1   The early modern background

While the previous chapter is devoted to grammar, the emphasis here is largely on different forms of pronunciation, their background and current distribution across Ireland. The outset for these considerations is the beginning of the modern period, i.e. the seventeenth century. Pronunciation before that has already been dealt with in the sections on the *Kildare Poems* and the dialect of Forth and Bargy (see sections 2.3 and 2.4).

Documents illustrating Irish English from the early modern period fall into two distinct types, both of which are available from the seventeenth through to the nineteenth century.[1]

(1)   a. More or less genuine representations of Irish English by native Irish, frequently anonymous writers.
       b. Stretches of texts by English writers where the non-native perception of Irish English is portrayed.

Such texts can serve as general guidelines for the more salient features of Irish English (see Sullivan 1976, 1980, who supports this view). In essence, the difficulty is that one must rely on eye dialect. The orthography of English is not necessarily suitable for rendering the idiosyncrasies of Irish English and indeed one cannot assume that a non-native speaker's attempt to caricature Irish English will be satisfying and accurate, though it may well give indications of what features of a dialect were salient for non-native listeners.

The earliest example of the first type above is the anonymous play *Captain Thomas Stukeley*, available in a single edition from 1605. It contains one scene in Irish English, the seventh, which by some curious twist is present in two consecutive versions in the extant edition. The first version is in blank verse like the remainder of the play and the second is in prose. Bliss (1979: 32f.) supports

---

[1] See the collection of texts in Bliss (1979) which contains both types. For a reassessment of Bliss's work, see Kelly (2000). For the use of Irish English in modern writing, see Kirk (1997a). On the use of rhyming slang in written Irish English, see Lillo (2004).

the view that the Irish English scene is not by the author of the rest of the play and attributes a good knowledge of Irish affairs to its original composer. There are discussions of this play in older literature, notably Duggan (1969 [1937]: 51–7), Bartley (1954: 14–16) and Eckhardt (1910–11: 38–41) who deal with phonetic peculiarities of Irish English and mention the frequent replacement of /s/ by /ʃ/ and the use of [ɸ] for /f/ and *wh*- [ʍ]. The language of the Irish English scene in this play is clearly that of the early period, i.e. before 1600. It shows a variety in which the major shifts in English long vowels had not yet taken place, e.g. *toone* 'town', *prood* 'proud', *aboote* 'about'. These spellings suggest that ME /uː/ had not been diphthongised. *Feete* 'white', *dree* 'dry', *lee* 'lie' equally imply that ME /iː/ had not shifted either. The language represented here does not seem to have merged into later Irish English but appears to have been replaced by superimposed forms which were taken to Ireland later.

The second type of text, with English representations of Irish English, can be seen in Ben Jonson's *The Irish Masque at Court* (1616). This is a satirical piece, some six pages long, in which four Irish characters are made fun of by Jonson. Certain stock features, typical of external perceptions of Irish English, are to be found here: the (over-generalised) substitution of /s/ by /ʃ/, the use of [ɸ] (written as *ph*) for /f/ and *wh*- [ʍ], the use of [t, d] for /θ, ð/. The archaic nature of the English portrayed by Jonson is evident in those words which, as with *Captain Thomas Stukeley*, suggest that the English long vowel shift had not taken place, e.g. *chreesh* 'Christ' points to ME /iː/. However, the dangers of setting too much store by English representations of Irish English are evident here: Jonson implies in spellings such as *mout* 'mouth', *now*, *tou* 'thou' that ME /uː/ had shifted, or at least he leaves the matter undecided as he does not avail of the orthography <oo> in such words (as did the author of *Captain Thomas Stukeley*). Furthermore, the question must be asked how a writer like Ben Jonson (1572–1637) attained knowledge of Irish English. He is not known to have been in Ireland (though he did visit Scotland). Perhaps he acquired some acquaintance of Irish English from inmates during his many spells in prison in London and/or through contact with Irish vagrants of which there were many in England in his time.

5.1.1 SHAKESPEARE AND IRISH ENGLISH

In the Irish context, one must distinguish between the language of Shakespeare, with possible parallels in Irish English, and the more popular view that the conservatism of Irish English links it directly to the language of England's greatest writer. The latter stance is found in non-linguistic works on English in Ireland and goes back at least a century; consider Burke (1896) who lists features from Irish English which are also found in Shakespeare's plays, for instance, double negation, interchangeable use of *this* and *that* and the partial reduction of the deictic system to one (Burke 1896: 778f.). Other works such as that by Walsh (1926) carry an explicit title, here: 'Shakespeare's pronunciation of the Irish brogue', which suggests the parallelism. On closer inspection one finds that such works tend to confine themselves to listing some of the features which the authors consider typical of the Irish brogue, such as unshifted ME /ɛ:/, the fortition of /θ, ð/, etc. More often than not there is a cultural point made as well. Walsh in the appendix to his book tries to show how unjustified the belittling attitude of the English to the Irish is by maintaining that the Irish 'brogue' is closest to what he supposed was Shakespeare's pronunciation of English. This attempt to lend dignity to historically stigmatised varieties has parallels elsewhere in the anglophone world, e.g. in the southern United States where correspondences with Shakespeare's English are often claimed (Schneider 2003: 18).

Today the value of contributions such as those by Burke and Walsh is that they offer attestations of Irish English colloquialisms which are somewhat archaic, in the case of Walsh exactly half-way between Sheridan in the late eighteenth century and today – but certainly not from the Tudor period.

The second, more serious type of study is exemplified by Patrick J. Irwin's PhD thesis in which he documents the parallels between Irish English and the language of Shakespeare's plays (which he takes as indicative of Elizabethan linguistic usage as a whole). For example, he notes that Shakespeare has *brogue* in the sense of 'shoe' used by Arviragus in *Cymbeline* (act IV, scene ii): 'and put my clouted brogues from off my feet' (Irwin 1933a: 641), this being the original meaning which had reached England as a loanword by the sixteenth century.

Shakespeare's language also shows structures which have been regarded as exclusively Irish in provenance. A case in point is the use of the conjunction *and* in a subordinating concessive sense (also noted by Burke 1896: 787): 'Suffer us to famish, and their storehouses filled with grain' (*Coriolanus*, act I, scene i); see section 4.4.6.2 on subordination for further discussion.

The language of Shakespeare and that of the Elizabethan era (in a more diffuse sense; cf. Braidwood 1964) needs to be distinguished. As a native of the west country, Shakespeare shows a number of traits of this region, such as his conservative use of periphrastic *do* (Hope 2003: 137–41). These traits were examined in detail by Hope (1995) for determining authorship. This use can be assumed to have been present in the input to Ireland at the beginning of the early modern period; see the discussion in section 4.4.1.4.3 on habitual aspect. Many non-standard features of Irish English can be attributed to this English input. For instance, Irish speakers frequently confuse complementary verb pairs distinguished by direction such as *bring, take; rent, let; learn, teach*. With the latter pair the first is used in the sense of the second. This is also found with Shakespeare, e.g. in the words of Caliban: 'the red-plague rid you for learning me your language' (*The Tempest*, act I, scene ii).

In addition to these cases, there is the 'Four Nations' scene from *Henry V* in which Shakespeare imitates the speech of a stock Irish character, Captain Macmorris. However, apart from this portrayal and the occasional parallels mentioned above, the study of Shakespeare's language is not of relevance to the historical investigation of Irish English.

5.1.2 THE TRADITION OF CARICATURE

Literature by non-Irish writers reveals what features of Irish English were salient and thus registered by non-native speakers. These features have gone into forming the linguistic notion of the 'Stage Irishman' (Duggan 1969 [1937]; Kosok 1990: 61ff.), a stock figure in much drama from the Restoration period, i.e. after 1660. The stereotypical picture of the Irishman as excitable, eloquent and pugnacious, with a fair portion of national pride, is an image that Shakespeare fuelled in the figure of Captain Macmorris in *Henry V*. These are features which Kiberd (1980) sees as consistent with the subsequent portrayals of the stage Irishman. His function as a foil within English literature is of significance and continued into the twentieth century; see '*Stage Irishmen* and *True-Born Irishmen*: Irish dramatists in London and Dublin' in Kosok (1990: 61–70) and the various references in Morash (2002).

Given the number of Irish figures which appear in English plays from the Restoration period onwards, there has been no shortage of manuals in which prominent features of Irish English are described, e.g. Blunt (1967). Blunt has a chapter on 'Irish' (1967: 75–90) in which he gives a series of guidelines to those prospective actors unfamiliar with an Irish accent of English. Other works which contain dialect descriptions for actors are Molin (1984) and Wise (1957). In such cases phonetic transcription is rare, rather some system based on English orthography is used.

5.1.3 THE LANGUAGE OF JONATHAN SWIFT

That Swift was concerned with questions of language hardly needs to be stated. His personal interests, his position as a writer in Ireland and above all his literary concern with satire meant that reflecting on language was a common occupation of his.

The studies of Swift's language fall into two broad categories. One looks at Swift's views on standardisation and language change, the second considers evidence for eighteenth-century pronunciation in Swift works, especially in his poetry. The first type is illustrated by Strang (1967) who examines Swift's wish to influence the course of English. She offers explanations for this, chiefly the great changes in the lexicon of English of his period, and suggests that the desire to be understood by future generations was the motivation for Swift's linguistic conservatism. Furthermore, his sense of order caused him to pay inordinate attention to such matters as the placing of adverbs and verbal particles.

The second type of study is exemplified by Kniezsa (1985) who, by using Swift's rhyming poetry (various odes), attempts to trace the development of Middle English long vowels which in south-east Britain underwent the major English vowel shift. She finds confirmation for the view that in early eighteenth-century Ireland, represented by Swift, Middle English /aː/ had not been raised very far, maximally to /ɛː/, as indicated by rhymes such as *fame* :

stream. She also adduces evidence for the non-raising of /ɛ:/ in words written with *ea*, a conservative feature of Irish English still found today, albeit recessively.

5.1.4 DRAMA IN THE EIGHTEENTH AND NINETEENTH CENTURIES

At the opening of the eighteenth century two Irish dramatists were active, namely William Congreve (1670–1729) and George Farquhar (1678–1707). Congreve was born in Leeds but his father was posted on military service to Ireland which led to his being educated there, first at Kilkenny School and later at Trinity College, Dublin, where he was a fellow student of Swift. He is the author of a number of dramas, the best known of which is probably *The Way of the World* (1700). The language of his plays does not, however, betray any non-standard elements and hence is not of interest in the present context.

The other dramatist just mentioned, Farquhar, was born in Derry; he later started studying in Trinity College, Dublin, and then worked as an actor in the Smock Alley Theatre, playing major Shakespearian roles. He left for London in 1697 where he began as a playwright. His best-known comedy, *The Beaux Stratagem* (1707), was written just before he died. Farquhar is one of the last Restoration dramatists and his many plays, such as *The Twin Rivals* (1702) and *The Stage Coach* (1704), had a strong influence on subsequent writers in the eighteenth century, including novelists like Fielding, Smollett and Defoe. His plays sometimes contain Irish characters and Farquhar uses eye dialect to represent the Irish speech of his time.

The late eighteenth century (Morash 2002: 67–93) saw the novelist and dramatist Oliver Goldsmith (1728–74) produce his popular comedy *She Stoops to Conquer* (1773) as well as the Dublin playwright Richard Brinsley Sheridan (1751–1816) begin his dramatic production with *The Rivals* in 1775, which was a success at Covent Garden. Soon afterwards, Sheridan produced his own major work, *The School for Scandal* (1778), which was quickly followed by another comedy of considerable merit, *The Critic* (1779). Neither Goldsmith nor Sheridan were particularly concerned with representing Irish speech in their plays. Indeed, it was Sheridan's father, the elocutionist Thomas Sheridan (1719–88), who in his one play, *Captain O'Blunder or The Brave Irishman* (1740/1754), did portray Irish speech using conventional means of eye dialect.

The eighteenth century also saw some minor dramatists of sentimental comedies who are now more or less forgotten. Of these one could mention John O'Keefe (1747–1833), who was quite successful and devised a distinctly Irish mode for plays produced in Ireland, often in the reputable Smock Alley Theatre (Morash 2002: 71–4).

In the early nineteenth century, after Richard Brinsley Sheridan's death, drama by Irish writers went into a period of decline. Figures like Charles Maturin (1782–1824), James Sheridan Knowles (1784–1862) and Samuel Lover (1797–1868) are very definitely minor. It is not until the mid nineteenth

century that Irish playwrighting produces a prominent writer in Dion Boucicault (1820–90), who was successful in Ireland, Britain and the United States.
Boucicault was also concerned with representing Irish speech in his plays and
these were consulted for the discussion of grammar to be found in the previous
chapter.

For English authors and for Irish writers without a dialect background, there
existed a repertoire of stock features which were generally assumed to be representative of Irish English. For instance, in his *Soldiers Three* (1890), Rudyard
Kipling makes use of two orthographical devices to add Irish flavour to direct
speech, as in *Those are the Black Oirish* and *'Tis they that bring dishgrace upon
the name av Oirland*, where the spelling *dishgrace* implies the use of /ʃ/ for /s/.
The second device is seen in the spellings *Oirish* and *Oirland* where *oi* can be
taken to represent [əɪ], a traditional pronunciation in Dublin and surroundings
and something for which the playwright R. B. Sheridan was ridiculed by Fanny
Burney (1752–1840) at the beginning of the nineteenth century (although he did
not try to represent this in his own writings). George Bernard Shaw (1856–1950)
occasionally used such features in his plays. For example, in *John Bull's Other
Island* one finds raising of short vowels before nasals and dentalisation of alveolars
before /r/ as in *I'm taking the gintleman that pays the rint for a dhrive*.

5.1.5 A SUMMARY OF HISTORICAL FEATURES

As was pointed out in section 2.1 above, the history of Irish English can be
divided into two periods, an early one which began in the late Middle Ages
and continued until the sixteenth century and a second period which began
around 1600. The features of the early period have already been discussed and
in table 5.1 only those which can be attributed to forms of Irish English from the
early seventeenth century onwards are listed.

In table 5.1 the dates for the latest attestations were determined by examining
texts, usually satirical drama or realistic prose (see comments at the beginning
of this chapter). These dates just give a rough indication of how long a feature
lasted or indeed whether it is still found. Some features which still exist are highly
recessive or confined to certain varieties or regions of Ireland. Attestations in
literary documents are found in the following.

1. Long U-retention
   thoo talkest to much the English (*Captain Thomas Stukeley*, 1596/1605)
2. Long I-retention
   a paire of feete trouzes, or a feete shurt (*Captain Thomas Stukeley*, 1596/1605)
3. A-back raising
   you do be mauke de Rauvish upon de young Womans (John Michelburne,
   Ireland Preserved, 1705)
4. ER-retraction
   Worn't his sons gintlemen no less? (William Carleton, *The Tithe Proctor*, 1833)

. . . if they <u>wor</u> what Beamish Mac Coul is this day. (Dion Boucicault, *Arrah na Pogue*, 1864)

5. SERVE-lowering

. . . is this the way ye <u>sarve</u> the poor fellow? (John and Michael Banim, *Tales of the O'Hara Family*, 1825–6)

6. I-ʌ-interchange

<u>shit</u> ub strait (*The Pretender's Exercise*, ?1727)

Him that's <u>jist</u> left ye, ma'am (Dion Boucicault, *The Colleen Bawn*, 1860)

7. CATCH-raising

you haven't th' guts to <u>ketch</u> a few o' th' things (Sean O'Casey, *The Plough and the Stars*, 1926)

8. Long O-raising

. . . that will never see you more on her <u>flure</u> . . . (William Carleton, *The Hedge School*, 1833)

9. Short E-raising

. . . the shadow of an <u>illegant</u> gintleman (Dion Boucicault, *The Colleen Bawn*, 1860)

. . .'tis a <u>Profissor</u> of Humanity itself, he is (William Carleton, *The Hedge School*, 1833)

<u>divil</u>, <u>togithir</u> (Dion Boucicault, *Arragh na Pogue*, 1864)

<u>riverince</u>, <u>niver</u> (Dion Boucicault, *The Colleen Bawn*, 1860)

10. Unraised long E

Merciful <u>Jasus</u>! what is it I see before me! (Maria Edgeworth, *Castle Rackrent*, 1801)

<u>spake</u> 'speak' (Dion Boucicault, *Arragh na Pogue, The Colleen Bawn, The Shaughraun*)

<u>rade</u> 'read' (Dion Boucicault, *The Shaughraun*, 1875)

<u>kape</u> 'keep' (Dion Boucicault, *Arragh na Pogue*, 1864)

11. Final-O-fronting

'He'll be <u>folleyin'</u> you,' says he; he heard she'd gone to <u>folly</u> her husband (Sean O'Casey, *The Plough and the Stars*, 1926)

12. OL-diphthongisation

it's an <u>ould</u> thrick you have (John and Michael Banim, *Tales of the O'Hara Family*, 1825–6)

the last of the Grameses <u>sould</u> the estate (William Carleton, *Traits and Stories of the Irish Peasantry*, 1833)

13. WH/W-approximation

<u>fan</u> I get into Dundalk (*Captain Thomas Stukeley*, 1596/1605)

<u>Phaat</u> dosht dou taalk of shome things? (Thomas Shadwell, *The Lancashire Witches*, 1681/2)

<u>Ve</u> lost <u>van</u> Couple of our Min (*A Dialogue between Teigue and Dermot*, 1713)

14. ASK-metathesis

<u>Ax</u> me no questions about her (William Carleton, *Traits and Stories of the Irish Peasantry*, 1833)

if you'll only ax me, dear (Dion Boucicault, *Arragh na Pogue*, 1864)

don't ax me any questions at all (Dion Boucicault, *The Colleen Bawn*, 1860)

15. S-palatalisation

    ...for my shister's afraid of ghosts (Maria Edgeworth, *Castle Rackrent*, 1801)

16. T/D-dentalisation

    thravels, murdher (Dion Boucicault, *Arragh na Pogue*, 1864)

17. TH-fortition

    ... and what will people tink and say (Maria Edgeworth, *Castle Rackrent*, 1801)

    wid 'with' (Dion Boucicault, *Arragh na Pogue*, 1864)

    den 'then' (Dion Boucicault, *The Colleen Bawn*, 1860)

18. SOFT-lengthening

    (not indicated in writing)

19. Post-sonorant devoicing

    ... but my lady Rackrent was all kilt and smashed (Maria Edgeworth, *Castle Rackrent*, 1801)

20. Post-sonorant stop deletion

    he was bringin' twenty poun's a week into the house; his arm fell, accidental like, roun' me waist (Sean O'Casey, *Juno and the Paycock*, 1924)

21. R-Vowel-metathesis

    as purty a girl as you'd meet in a fair; a sartin purty face I'm acquainted with (William Carleton, *Traits and Stories of the Irish Peasantry*, 1833)

5.2 Vernacular Irish English

Non-standard features of pronunciation are found most commonly in rural regions and in local urban varieties. These features have been indicated in many historical documents, mostly literary, such as those used for the discussion above, and so their genuineness as historically derived features is confirmed. But not all features are attested. There are aspects of pronunciation which simply fail to appear in the historical record. For instance, although William Carleton was from rural Co. Tyrone and although the T-to-K shift, as in *fortune* ['fɒrkuːn], is attested there and in north-central Leinster,[2] he does not represent this feature anywhere in his writings. In addition to this difficulty, there are features which cannot be indicated easily in writing. While it would have been possible for Carleton to have written a word like *fortune* as *forcune*, there is no obvious means of representing a uvular /r/ rather than an alveolar /r/ in dialect spelling. In effect this means that the written records before the twentieth century do not suggest that a uvular /r/, as in *square* [skweəʁ], was present in Ireland. This is, however, the case, as many recordings in *A Sound Atlas of Irish English* (Hickey 2004a) clearly show.

---

[2] This shift would seem to occur, or at least to have occurred across into north Connaught. The material for *A Linguistic Survey of Ireland* notes [frɛɪkən] for *frighten* in north Co. Mayo.

Table 5.1. *Historical features of Irish English pronunciation*

Feature	Realisation	Representation	Attested until
Vowels			
1. Long U-retention	*town* [tuːn]	*<oo>, toone*	early 18th c.
2. Long I-retention	*dry* [driː]	*<ee>, dree*	early 18th c.
3. A-back raising	*make* [mɔːk]	*<au>, mauke*	late 18th c.
4. ER-retraction	*were* [wɔːr]	*<or>, wor*	late 19th c.
5. SERVE lowering	*serve* [saːrv]	*<ar>, sarve*	late 19th c.
6. I-ʌ-interchange	*just* [jɪst]	*<i>, jist*	early 20th c.
7. CATCH-raising	*catch* [ketʃ]	*<(k)e>, ketch*	early 20th c.
8. Long O-raising	*floor* [fluːr]	*<uCe>, flure*	today, recessive
9. Short E-raising	*yes* [jɪs]	*<i>, yis*	now only pre-nasally
10. Unraised long E	*speak* [spɛːk]	*<aCe>, spake*	today, recessive
11. Final-O-fronting	*follow* ['fɑli]	*<i>, folly*	today
12. OL-diphthongisation	*old* [auld]	*<ou>, ould*	today
Consonants			
13. WH/W-approximation	*when* [ɸɛn]	*<f, ph> fen*	mid 18th c.
14. ASK-metathesis	*ask* [æks]	*<x>, ax*	early 20th c.
15. S-palatalisation	*self* [ʃɛlf]	*<sh>, shelf*	today, recessive
16. T/D-dentalisation	*drop* [d̪rɑp]	*<dh>, dhrop*	today
17. TH-fortition	*thank* [t̪æŋk]	*<t>, tank*	today
18. SOFT-lengthening	*soft* [sɒːft]	—	today
Phonological processes			
19. Post-sonorant devoicing	*killed* [kɪlt]	*kilt*	today
20. Post-sonorant stop deletion	*poun'* [peun]	'	today
21. R-Vowel-metathesis	*pretty* [pɚːti]	*purty*	today, only in unstressed syllables

Notes:

1/2   The English long vowel shift (the 'Great Vowel Shift', Pyles and Algeo 1993 [1964]: 170–3), which began in the late Middle English period, was slow to be implemented in Ireland. /uː/ and /iː/ were recorded in the MOUTH and PRICE lexical sets respectively until the early eighteenth century. Unraised long E is also connected to the English long vowel shift: the vowel stems from Middle English /ɛː/ (and by extension from words with /eː/ in Middle English) which was not raised to /iː/ in Ireland. In the nineteenth century, non-local Irish English adopted an /iː/ pronunciation in line with mainstream British English. With the pronoun *me*, an /iː/ is still commonly found: *Me own, yes, me great-grandfather* . . . (TRS-D, M19, M).

3   This feature was censured by Thomas Sheridan in the late eighteenth century; see Sheridan (1781: 141). Its origin is uncertain.

Table 5.1. *(Notes cont.)*

4   Rounding after /w/ is probably responsible for this retraction. It is most likely a feature of the West Midland dialect of Middle English (Mossé 1952: 84) which was present in later input varieties of English in Ireland. Earlier Irish English (from the *Kildare Poems* to the eighteenth century) contains no attestations of this retraction. However, in the nineteenth century it is common, for instance with both William Carleton and Dion Boucicault.

5   This is the same feature which produced *barn, dark, Berkshire, Hertfordshire*, etc. in British English. It had a much wider range in Irish English, probably due to its quantitative representation in input varieties.

6   A shift of [ɪ] to [ʌ] is a basilectal Ulster Scots feature and found occasionally with speakers from Scots-settled parts of Ulster: *If you'd be lucky enough to win* [wʌn] *anything* (TRS-D, U18–2, F, from the Laggan, south-west of Derry city). Some words with this shift are lexicalised vernacular forms used by supraregional speakers for local flavour, e.g. *onions* [ˈɪnənz]. [ɛ] for [ʌ] is a common feature of contact Irish English, e.g. *brush* [brɛʃ], *justice* /dʒɛstɪs/, and is probably due to the automatic alternation /ʌ/ ~ /ɛ/ which is found in Irish between nominative and genitive with many nouns, e.g. *roc* /rʌk/ 'wrinkle-NOM' ~ *roic* /rɛkʲ/ 'wrinkle-GEN'. Because the front vowel is used in Irish in the environment of a palatal consonant (here: /kʲ/), contact Irish English speakers often use this vowel in English words where the consonant flanking a short vowel is interpreted as palatal.

7   This feature appears to have been continued among the Anglo-Irish land-owning class into the twentieth century (it was a prominent characteristic of conservative Received Pronunciation until the mid-twentieth century, Bauer 1994a: 120f.). For example, the novelist Elizabeth Bowen, a native of Co. Cork, had this feature in her speech. It is still recorded in vernacular varieties in Cork city and county, e.g. *Mallow* [ˈmɛlə] (SADIF, M40+, Cork city), *You'd catch* [kɛtʃ] *the churn* . . . (MLSI, M80+, Bantry, Co. Cork).

8   The pronunciation [fluːr] for *floor* was only found with one speaker for Antrim in *A Sound Atlas of Irish English* (Hickey 2004a), but it is known to occur in west Ulster as well (Kevin McCafferty, personal communication).

9   Short E-raising is common today, but only in south-western and mid-western rural Irish English and only in pre-nasal position, e.g. *when* [ʍɪn], *pen* [pɪn]. Joyce (1979 [1910]: 100) states that 'short *e* is always sounded before *n* and *m*, and sometimes in other positions, like short *i*: "How many arrived? *Tin min and five women.*"' Occasionally, some speakers have this raising outside a pre-nasal environment: *They used be skimming the well* [wɪl] *on May mornings* (TRS-D, M64–2, M), *He's very clever* [klɪvəɹ] *you know* (TRS-D, C42–4, M).

10 Unraised long E has a special status as a stereotypically Irish feature which has been lexicalised in the expletive *Jaysus!* [dʒɛːzɪz] and in set expressions like *lea'* [lɛ:] *me alone!* It is found regularly in vernacular varieties throughout Ireland, e.g. *I didn't know I'd be eatin'* [ˈɛːtn̩] *German cake* (WER, F85+), . . . *to sing in either* [ˈɛːdə] (SADIF, F60+, Gorey, Co. Wexford), . . . *a decent* [ˈdɛːsɪnt] *way of living* (SADIF, M60+, Gorey, Co. Wexford).

Table 5.1. *(Notes cont.)*

11	Final-O-fronting is common in southern rural Irish English, e.g. *We were doing it and the old people followed* [faliːd] *on* (TRS-D, M64–1, M), and also in parts of the north. It can appear as a reduction of the vowel to schwa. This leads to alternative pronunciations and lexical splits with non-local and vernacular forms of words (see section 5.3).
12	OL-diphthongisation is most common with *old* and *bold* today. Joyce (1979 [1910]: 99) mentions it with reference to these words and to *hould* where it is not found today in supraregional speech. However, in vernacular varieties, both north and south, there is a greater range of forms with OL-diphthongisation. On its occurrence in British English, see Tagliamonte and Temple (2005).
13	What appears to have happened here is that Irish non-palatal /f/ (phonetically [ɸ]) was used as an equivalent for [ʍ] and Irish non-palatal /v/ (phonetically [β]) for [w] by individuals in language shift. In eye dialect the bilabial fricative [ɸ] is rendered as *f* or *ph*, and its voiced counterpart [β] as *v*. This development would appear to be independent of developments in Britain, although a case might be made for the transportation of [ɸ] and [β] to the Caribbean by indentured Irish in the seventeenth century (see Trudgill, Schreier, Long and Williams 2004 on approximants in this context but without a consideration of the Irish situation).
14	Metathesis of /s/ + stop was already a feature of Old English (Lass 1984: 188) and the sequence /ks/ in *ask* is attested there. It was most likely a feature of input varieties to Ireland which was retained.
15	S-palatalisation is a still feature of contact Irish English and attested in the data collections used for this chapter: *Hone*[ʃ]*t, they believe in hone*[ʃ]*t people* (TRS-D, C 42–4, M). Related to this is the feature noted by Joyce (1979 [1910]: 98) that 'there is a curious tendency among us to reverse the sounds of certain letters, as for instance *sh* and *ch* "When you're coming to-morrow bring the spade and *chovel*, and a pound of butter *frech* from the *shurn*."' No confirmation of this was found when collecting data for *A Sound Atlas of Irish English* (Hickey 2004a) and it is not represented in any literary portrayals of Irish English.
16	T/D-dentalisation is a feature which is confined to vernacular varieties and found across Ireland. It occurs before /r/.
17	TH-fortition takes on two forms (i) fortition to dental stops and (ii) fortition to alveolar stops. The former is part of supraregional Irish English, e.g. *thin* [t̪ɪn], *this* [d̪ɪs], whereas the latter is stigmatised.
18	SOFT-lengthening is a regular feature of Dublin English (see section 5.4.1) which has spread outside the capital by imitation of its speech.
19/20	Post-sonorant devoicing (19) is generally a rural feature and post-sonorant stop deletion (20), in a way its mirror image, is typical of urban vernaculars of the east coast.
21	R-Vowel-metathesis is still very common in many varieties but is now confined to unstressed syllables and the metathesis of /r/ and a short vowel, e.g. *modern* ['mɒdɹən], *secretary* ['sɛkəɹtɹi]. The form *purty* 'pretty', so common in nineteenth century literature, is not found anymore.

Unraised long E. This continues in all vernacular varieties across the country. In the data collections it is attested in such areas as south Ulster: *leave* [lɛːv] (TRS-D, U72-2, border with Co. Louth), Connemara in the mid west: *'Twasn't easy* [ɛːsi] *to get work* (TRS-D, C41, M) and Waterford in the south-east: *God, you can't beat* [bɛːt̪] *the superglue for stickin' things* (WER, M50+).

Sibilant fortition. Originally a feature from the south-west of England, brought to Ireland and found in the south-east, it has travelled with the spread of English from here to the centre and west of Ireland: *They weren't* [wɚdn̩t] *able to* ... (TRS-D, M19, M). It is also found in parts of the southern United States (Schilling-Estes 1995).

Unstressed /ju/. In supraregional Irish English yod deletion in stressed syllables after alveolar sonorants is normal, e.g. *new* [nuː]. In unstressed syllables this yod tends to remain, but in vernacular varieties it too is deleted, e.g. *million* [milən], *occupy* ['ɒkəpaɪ] (TRS-D, M64-2, M). There are a few cases of yod insertion on the part of vernacular speakers, e.g. *column* ['kɒljəm], *minute* ['mɪnjut̪].

(ng) variable. The use of an alveolar [n] in *ng* [ŋ] clusters, especially in present participles and gerunds, is widespread across the anglophone world. It also goes back considerably in time: Wyld (1956 [1936]: 289) points to spelling evidence which suggests that alveolar [n] for [ŋ] occurred in England from the fourteenth century onwards. This shift to an alveolar articulation is particularly common in Ulster, e.g. *comin'*, *keepin'*, *goin'*, etc., and is somewhat more prevalent among mainstream speakers in the north than in the south.

The most detailed examination of this variable is to be found in Kingsmore (1995: 100–10) in the context of her Coleraine study. Her sample consists of twenty-six informants. At least four are present for each gender and age group (Kingsmore 1995: 37–52). Kingsmore recognises [ɪn] as an intermediary form between the syllable nasal [n̩] and the standard [ɪŋ]. She also notes that young females have the highest incidence of an alveolar nasal with the (ng) variable: 83 per cent for males and 89 per cent for females with verbal forms in final *-ing*, e.g. *talking*, *walking*. These and similar verbal forms have the highest incidence of [n] for (ng), as they do in other varieties of English.

Epenthesis. This is the first of two major phonological processes which are prominent in most varieties of Irish English. Epenthesis is a process by which an unstressed short vowel is inserted in a cluster of sonorants to resyllabify the cluster in question such that the sonorants belong to different syllables after epenthesis.

(2)   Heavy coda resolution: *film* /.tɪlm./   →   [.fɪl.əm.]

The heavy coda cluster, consisting of two sonorants, is split between two syllables by introducing a schwa between them (the dot represents a syllable boundary).

The range of epenthesis varies. It is universal in /lm/ clusters and in vernacular varieties it extends to other clusters, as seen in (3). Epenthesis tends to shorten the stressed vowel as the overall quantity of words remains more or less the same.

Furthermore, vowel distinctions may accompany epenthesis which are not found when this does not occur, contrast *girl* ['gɔːl] with *girl* ['gɛɹəl].

(3)   Supraregional   Vernacular
      /lm/   /ln/, /rl/, /rn/, /rm/
      film ['fɪləm], *helm* ['hɛləm]   *kiln* ['kɪlən], *girl* ['gɛɹəl], *earn* ['ɛɹən],
                                              farm ['faːɹəm]

Epenthesis is an areal phenomenon in Ireland (Hickey 1986b), occurring even more frequently in Irish (Hickey in press) than Irish English. As might be expected it is often found in contact Irish English: *the single-farm* ['faːɹəm] *payments*; *she's two young girls* ['gɛɹəls] *at secondary school* (CCE-W, M65+). It is also attested historically, for instance in emigrant letters such as the following: . . . *who wish to goe on the same ship with and Comreade [?]* <u>*gerrel*</u> *of hers* . . . (IEL, 1864, Co. Kilkenny).

In vernacular varieties, medial epenthesis in stop + sonorant clusters is also found, e.g. *arthritis* [ærtə'raɪtɪs], *children* ['tʃɪldərən] (WER, F80+), *petrol* ['pɛtəɹəl] (WER, M50+). One or two instances of sandhi metathesis are attested, e.g. *It's only ten* [ə] *past six* (WER, F55+). The conditions here correspond to those for epenthesis in Irish, especially in Munster where epenthesis is widespread, e.g. *dorcha* ['dʌɹəxə] 'dark', *an-mhaith* ['anəva] 'very good'.

A few examples of /t/-epenthesis after a sibilant were found in the sound archives of the Department of Folklore, University College Dublin, e.g. *he had a little box*[t] (SADIF, M85, Lusk, Co. Dublin), *He had his brush*[t] (SADIF, M85, Lusk, Co. Dublin). This type is found in (western) Irish also, e.g. *arís* [ə'riːʃt] 'again'.

Metathesis. Again an areal phenomenon, metathesis is commonly found in Irish (Hickey in press) and Irish English. Historically, it would appear to have occurred in stressed syllables (see discussion of R-Vowel-metathesis above) but is now confined to unstressed ones and to cases of /r/ and a short vowel. There are many quasi-lexicalised instances which are not stigmatised, e.g. *modern* ['mɒdɹən], *lantern* ['læntɹən]. The least stigmatised type of metathesis is that of /r/ and short vowel, and it generally goes unnoticed by speakers. In the recordings for *A Sound Atlas of Irish English*, many of the speakers did not notice that they said ['mɒdɹən] for *modern* until it was pointed out to them.

Again in vernacular varieties, more radical metathesis is found, for instance, between stops separated by a vowel as in *hospital* /'hɒspɪtl̩/ → ['hɒstɪpl̩] (WER, F80+) or that of two sonorants as in *more of these awful phe'nonemons happened* (SADIF, M50+, Lough Gur, Co. Limerick).

As with epenthesis, metathesis is a phenomenon which is widely recorded in the history of Irish and in present-day forms of the language (see Breatnach 1947: 147; Ó Cuív 1944: 127f.; de Bhaldraithe 1945: 115f. for examples from southern, south-western and western Irish respectively). This fact confirms the interpretation of both metathesis and epenthesis as areal phenomena in Ireland.

Intonation. Non-standard intonational patterns are found in vernacular speech in Co. Cork and Co. Kerry (Hickey 2004a: 33). Here there is a drop in pitch on stressed syllables with a slight rise preceding it. This can occur several times within a sentence, yielding an undulating intonational pattern. It may be spread across two syllables in disyllabic words or be contained within a single syllable in monosyllabic words. This pattern is shared by Irish in both south-west Cork and north-west Kerry. It can be heard on the English recordings for Cork/Kerry in *A Sound Atlas of Irish English* (Hickey 2004a) and in the Irish recordings for the same areas (see Hickey in press).

5.3   Supraregional Irish English

Supraregionalisation is an historical process whereby varieties of a language lose specifically local features and become less regionally bound. The upper limits of supraregionalisation depend on a number of external factors, such as the state in which the set of varieties is spoken. If this state was historically a colony of another country, then there may be an (unconscious) wish within the state to maintain some linguistic distinctiveness vis-à-vis the varieties of the former colonising country.

To discuss the matter of supraregionalisation one needs the notion of 'extra-national variety'. A variety is extranational if is has significance in a country but stems from outside its borders. For instance, German is an extranational variety to Austrians, French is to Walloons and Dutch is to Flemings. Extranational varieties may be perceived as a single type, as with the perception of British English by many Irish who often simply refer to someone speaking with 'an English accent'.

A consideration of the history of English in Ireland shows that there was not only (i) internal change within the English brought to the country as of the late twelfth century and (ii) influence from Irish during the long period of language shift from the seventeenth through to the nineteenth century, but also (iii) a large degree of superimposition or adoption of more standard forms of English due to considerable exposure to forms of British English. This superimposition has led to layering in Irish English: remnants of former distributions, such as the presence of unshifted ME /ɛː/ (see discussion of unraised long E above) or /ʊ/ (unrounded, unlowered /u/), have become confined to certain registers and/or are indicative of strongly localised varieties (such as those in Dublin).

Superimposition of more standard forms has led in turn to the process of supraregionalisation. The question which is of particular linguistic interest is whether generalisations concerning this process can be made. For instance, non-standard vowel features among earlier forms of Irish English have been largely ironed out, but consonantal peculiarities have been retained in the supraregional standard of the south.

Supraregionalisation must be carefully distinguished from dialect levelling or the formation of compromise forms. For instance, in late medieval Irish English

there is some evidence that a middle way was chosen among competing morphological forms from different dialect inputs from the British mainland: the
quantifier *euch(e)* 'each' was seen by Samuels (1972: 108) as a hybrid between
ech(e) and *uch(e)*, both of which were probably represented in the initial input
to Irish English.

Because a supraregional variety is not locally bound it can never serve the
identity function which the vernacular fulfils for members of social networks (L.
Milroy 1976; J. Milroy 1991). For that reason supraregional varieties tend not
to show the degree of phonological differentiation present in the vernaculars to
which they are related. For instance, in local forms of Irish English, both urban
and rural, there is a distinction between short vowels before historic /r/, i.e. the
vowels in *term* and *turn* are distinguished: *term* [tɛɹm] versus *turn* [tʌɹn]. In the
supraregional variety, however, a single vowel is found in both cases, namely a
rhotacised schwa [ɚ].

Another feature, which shows that supraregional varieties are less differenti-
ated than their related vernaculars, is *t*-lenition (see section 5.4.3). In supraregional Irish English *t*-lenition is nearly always realised by the apico-alveolar
fricative [ṱ]. But in local Dublin English, there is a range of realisations, from [ṱ]
through [ɹ, h, lʔ] to zero.

The triggers for supraregionalisation

In Ireland, and presumably in other European countries, the main trigger for
supraregionalisation was the introduction of general schooling and the rise of
a native middle class during the nineteenth century. The Catholic Emancipation Act of 1829 was introduced after political agitation under the leadership of
Daniel O'Connell. Shortly afterwards, in the 1830s, so-called 'National Schools',
i.e. primary schools (Dowling 1971: 116–18), were introduced and schooling for
Catholic children in Ireland became compulsory and universal (see figures for
illiteracy in section 2.1.6 above). The experience of general education for the
generation after this increased their acceptance in the higher classes of Irish
society (Daly 1990). A native middle class came into existence with all that this
meant in terms of linguistic prejudice towards vernacular varieties of English. It
is thus no coincidence that the disappearance of certain features of Irish English
is located in the nineteenth century. These features were replaced by the corresponding mainland British pronunciations. An instance is provided by unshifted
ME /aː/ which was a prominent feature up to the eighteenth century. George
Farquhar in his play *The Beaux' Stratagem* (1707) has many of the stereotypes
of Irish pronunciation, including this one: *Fat sort of plaace* (= [plaːs]) *is dat
saam* (= [saːm]) *Ireland?* 'What sort of place is that same Ireland?' Somewhat
later, Swift used end-rhymes which indicate that for him words like *placed* and
last rhymed. At the end of the century, Thomas Sheridan criticised the Irish use
of /aː/ in *matron*, *patron*, etc. But by the mid nineteenth century there are no
more references to this. Dion Boucicault, who does not shy away from showing phonetic peculiarities in his dramas, does not indicate unshifted ME /aː/

Table 5.2. *Occurrences of* serve, service, deserve, certain *with* SERVE-*lowering among nineteenth- and twentieth-century authors*

	Total	Percentage
1. John and Michael Banim (1820s), one story (6,000 words): *sarve* (2); *desarve* (2); *sart(a)in* (8)	12	0.2%
2. William Carleton (1830s), one story (20,000 words): *sarve* (13); *sarvice* (3); *desarve* (7); *sartin* (6)	29	0.15%
3. Dion Boucicault (1860s), three plays (56,500 words): *desarve* (2); *sarvice* (1); *sarched* (1); *sartin* (1)	5	0.01%
4. George Bernard Shaw (1904), *John Bull's Other Island* (33,500 words): *sarve* (1)	1	0.00%

Synge (early 1900s, 6 plays), Gregory (1890s, 4 plays), O'Casey (1920s, 4 plays) and Behan (1950s, 2 plays) have no instances of SERVE-lowering.

when writing some eighty years after Sheridan. This kind of development can be shown to have applied to a number of features. For instance, SERVE-lowering appears to have died out during the nineteenth century and by the beginning of the twentieth century the feature had all but disappeared (see table 5.2).

How supraregionalisation proceeds

Supraregionalisation is a type of language change. It too is subject to the phases of actuation, propagation and conclusion. The actuation is probably triggered by a consciousness of the provinciality of one's own language and the presence of more mainstream varieties, be these extranational or not.

For the propagation phase there are two competing views of how the process takes place. The elimination of local features may be lexically abrupt with the substitution of local feature X by supraregional feature Y in all words in which it occurs. This corresponds to the Neogrammarian view of change. But equally a scenario is conceivable in which a local feature is replaced by a supraregional feature, if not word by word, at least not across the entire lexicon at once. Lexical replacement of this kind would correspond to lexical diffusion as conceived of by scholars like Wang (1969).

An example of this would be the following. In the south of Ireland the remnants of the widespread diphthongisation of historical /oː/ before velar [ɫ] + /d/ (see OL-diphthongisation above) are *old* and *bold*. But historically, this pronunciation is recorded for many other words, like *cold, hold, sold*. The pronunciation would seem to have applied previously to all words which matched the phonetic environment and there are many attestations in older recordings of elderly speakers, e.g. *It would hold* [haul] *anything* (MLSI, M70, Crisheen, Co. Clare); *He sold* [saul] *the estate* (SADIF, M60+, Bellanagh, Co. Cavan); *Keep them from getting cold* [kaul] (SADIF, M85, Lusk, Co. Dublin). These and similar examples have been replaced by the more standard /oː/ or /oʊ/ (RP: /əʊ/) by a process of lexical diffusion (the same would seem to have applied in the north to Belfast; J. Milroy 1981: 28f.). Furthermore, the words with the /au/ pronunciation (with deleted final /-d/) have retreated into more colloquial forms of speech so that now there is a lexical split between *old* /aul/, /oːld/ and *bold* /baul/, /boːld/: the form /aul/ for *old* implies a degree of affection and /baul/ for *bold* a sneaking admiration as in *Nothing beats the* /aul/ *pint*; *The* /baul/ *Charlie is some crook* (the adjectives in these senses only occur attributively).

The conclusion of supraregionalisation is somewhat difficult to pinpoint. To establish whether a change has been completed it is necessary to recognise the goal, so to speak. But what would the goal be in the Republic of Ireland? Surely not the wholesale adoption of standard English pronunciation. Indeed, the maintenance of differential linguistic features can be equally viewed as a goal vis-à-vis extranational varieties of English. This view would see the supraregional variety of the south of Ireland as the standard of the Republic of Ireland. Such a standard does not show the classic features enumerated and discussed by Haugen (1972): it is not codified, at least not orthographically, nor does it exist as an elaborated written form. Although it is a spoken variety of English, there is a large body of unconscious consensus about what features are characteristic of this standard. An essential part of being a native speaker of Irish English lies in knowing what features are part of the supraregional variety and what are not. For instance, such speakers are aware that *t*-lenition, as in *city* ['sɪt̪i], is permissible in the supraregional variety but that the extension of lenition to a glottal stop, as in *city* ['sɪʔi], is not. A case from grammar would be the *after*-perfective (see section 4.4.1.4.1), as in *He's after breaking the glass*, which is acceptable in the supraregional variety, whereas the *do(es) be* habitual (see section 4.4.1.4.3), as in *He does be mending cars in his spare time*, is not.

The features of a supraregional variety are not immutable but at any given time speakers know what belongs to it: features may be added, such as the raised back vowels or retroflex /r/ of recent Dublin English (see section 5.5.4.3). Equally, speakers know what does not belong to the supraregional variety: *h*-dropping, or syllable-final deletion of /r/, for instance.

Paths of supraregionalisation

Apart from the question of actuation, propagation and conclusion, the paths which supraregionalisation can take are of linguistic interest. In the Irish English context the following paths are attested.

1. Entire replacement of vernacular features

A number of archaic pronunciations are still to be found in early modern documents of Irish English. For instance, the word for *gold* still had a pronunciation with /uː/ (as did *Rome*) in late eighteenth-century Ireland: *goold* /guːld/, a pronunciation criticised by Walker (1791). The word *onion* /ʌnjən/ had /ɪnjən/, an older pronunciation mentioned by Joyce at the beginning of the twentieth century (Joyce 1979 [1910]: 99). This was recorded by the lexicographer Nathan

Table 5.3. *Restriction of vernacular features as of the twentieth century*

Feature	Pre-twentieth century	twentieth century and later
1. /ɛ/ to /ɪ/ raising	unconditional *togither, yis, git*	only before nasals (south-west) *pen* [pɪn], *ten* [tɪn]
2. metathesis	in stressed syllables *purty* ['pɚːti] 'pretty'	only in unstressed syllables *modern* ['mɒdɹən]

Bailey in 1726 (*Universal Etymological English Dictionary*) but was not typical of mainstream pronunciations, as Walker notes at the end of the eighteenth century.

Vowels before /r/ provide further instances where Irish English was out of step with developments in England. *R*-lowering did not occur in words like *door* /duːr/, *floor* /fluːr/, *source* /suːrs/, *course* /kuːrs/, *court* /kuːrt/ which, according to the Appendix to Sheridan's *Grammar* (1781: 137–55), were typical Irish pronunciations. This means that the southern mainland English lowering of back high vowels before /r/ had not occurred in Ireland by the late eighteenth century but was introduced by lexically replacing those pronunciations which conflicted with mainland British usage, probably in the course of the nineteenth century.

2. *Restriction to a specific phonetic environment*

When a local feature is being removed from a supraregional variety then there may be a phase in which the feature goes from being unconditional to conditional. This is recognisable if the conditional realisation is still attested. Consider the case of short E-raising. This is recorded in many environments in historical documents but later texts show a restriction to pre-nasal environments (as found nowadays in south-western and mid-western varieties of Irish English). Another instance is the metathesis of a vowel and /r/. In the nineteenth century and earlier it is attested in stressed syllables but later only in unstressed ones (see table 5.3).

One explanation for the survival of features as conditional variants is that these are less salient (Kerswill and Williams 2002) than unconditional ones. If a feature like short E-raising is restricted to a pre-nasal position, a phonetically preferred environment for this raising, then it is automatic (for the variety which has this raising) and so less salient for speakers. Similarly, if metathesis is confined to unstressed syllables then it is less acoustically prominent and again less salient and hence less likely to be removed by supraregionalisation. The same argument could be used for the shift in occurrence of S-palatalisation from all positions to just the end of a syllable, i.e. one previously had cases like *shelf* 'self' and *shin* 'sin' but now, if at all, only instances like *best* [bɛʃt], *past* [paːʃt] occur,[3] which in fact involve the further restriction that the syllable be closed by a following stop.

---

[3] Alongside instances in syllable-codas – *He got lost* [laʃt] (MLSI, M80+, Dougher, Co. Mayo), *most* [moːʃt], *twist* [twɪʃt] (SADIF, M60+, Bruff, Co. Limerick) – older recordings show this shift in syllable-onsets, e.g. *stable* [ʃteːbl̩]] (MLSI, M70, Crisheen, Co. Clare).

3. Relegation to colloquial registers

Although the supraregional form of English is the native style of many speakers in Ireland, they may deliberately manipulate salient features and adopt a vernacular pronunciation, for example for the purpose of caricature or when style-shifting downwards (Labov 2001). Simple instances of this are the replacement of *ye* by *youse*, the use of [lɛp] for *leap* [liːp] or the high vowel in *get* as in *Get* [gi̥t] *out of here!*, all typical of colloquial registers of Irish English.

In the course of its development, Irish English has evolved a technique for attaining local flavouring. This consists of maintaining two forms of a single lexeme, one a standard British one, adopted during supraregionalisation, and another an archaic or regional pronunciation which differs in connotation from the first. This second usage is always found on a more colloquial level and plays an important role in establishing the profile of vernacular Irish English. The following are some typical examples to illustrate this phenomenon.

Eejit [ˈiːdʒət] for *idiot* (Dolan 2004: 83f.) has adopted the sense of a bungling individual rather than an imbecile.

Cratur [ˈkreːtəɹ] shows a survival of the older pronunciation and denotes an object of pity or commiseration.[4] Indeed for the supraregional variety of the south, unraised /ɛː/ automatically implies a vernacular register. Other words which, colloquially, still show the mid vowel are *Jesus*, *decent*, *tea*, *queer* (represented orthographically as *Jaysus*, *daycent*, *tay*, *quare*). This situation is quite understandable: the replacement of an older pronunciation by a more mainstream one has led to the retreat of the former into a marked style, here one of local Irishness.

Fellow has final /ou, oː/ in the supraregional standard. But a reduction of the final vowel to /ə/ is historically attested in Irish English as in *yellow* [jɛlə]. There is now a lexical split with the first word such that the pronunciation [fɛlə] means something like 'young man, potential boyfriend' in colloquial Irish English.

Mergers and supraregionalisation

Sociolinguistic research on vernacular forms of English in Belfast (see J. Milroy 1981) has shown that non-standard phonology is more complex than standard phonology and that mergers are more common in standard and koiné varieties. At first sight this might seem to hold for southern Irish English as well. For instance, there is no distinction between historically different short vowels before /r/. Hence one has a single rhotacised vowel [ɚ] in the supraregional variety but in vernacular forms /ɛ/ and /ʌ/ are kept distinct before /r/ as in *girl* [gɛɹəl] and *burn* [bʌɹən] (possibly with epenthesis).

There is an apparent contradiction here because with dental stops in the THIN (and THIS) lexical sets, a shift to an alveolar articulation, which leads

---

[4] This word also has the meaning 'whiskey, liquor' and is attested at least as far back as the early nineteenth century in the stories of William Carleton (Dolan 2004: 65f.). The meaning 'object of commiseration' applies to the Irish word *créatúr* [kreːtuːr], a borrowing from English *creature* with the unraised <ea> vowel.

to merger with the alveolar stops in the TWO lexical set (cf. *thinker* and *tinker*, both ['tɪŋkəɹ]), is stigmatised in Irish English. However, stigma or acceptance of mergers in varieties of English depends crucially on whether the merger is unconditional or not. With the single rhotacised vowel [ɚ] one is dealing with a merger in a specific phonological environment, namely before tautosyllabic /r/. With dental vs alveolar stops on the other hand one finds that it is the unconditional merger, leading to considerable homophony, which is stigmatised.

Hypercorrection

In the Ireland of the eighteenth and probably the nineteenth centuries, when many of the pronunciations discussed above were not confined to specific styles, hypercorrection was common. Both Sheridan (1781) and Walker (1791) remark on the fact that the Irish frequently say *greet, beer, sweer,* unaware of the fact that these words had /eː/ rather than /iː/, the normal realisation of the vowel in words like *tea, sea, please,* in more standard varieties of English.

Sheridan also has /ʌ/ in the words *pudding* and *cushion.* This could be explained not only as hypercorrection, vis-à-vis mainstream English, but also with regard to local Dublin English which now, and certainly then, had /ʊ/ in these and all words with Early Modern English /ʊ/. Indeed, according to Sheridan, /ʌ/ was found in *foot, bull, bush, push, pull, pulpit,* all but the last of which have /ʊ/ in (southern) Irish English today.

Hypercorrection would appear to die away with supraregionalisation. This stands to reason: if local features are replaced by more standard ones then later generations master the correct distribution of sounds immediately.

Unaffected features

Supraregionalisation does not appear to be something which speakers are aware of, e.g. no comments on how it was occurring in Irish English are recorded. There is no question of it being a planned process and so some features, which might have been affected, are not involved. An example of non-participation in the process is provided by the shortening of Late Modern English /uː/, seen in words like *took* and *look,* which now have short /ʊ/, despite the spelling which suggests a former /uː/. In supraregional Irish English, a long /uː/ before /k/ has been retained in some words where this was shortened in British English, e.g. *cook* [kuːk] and sometimes *book* [buːk].

The shift from long to short vowel probably took place in England by lexical diffusion and in Ireland not as many words have been affected by this process. It is most likely that Irish English speakers did not proceed with the shift to the same extent as those in England because the long /uː/ was not stigmatised, i.e. a pronunciation like *cook* [kuːk] was, and is, not used in Ireland to assess a speaker socially.

5.4   The sound system

In the following the sound system of supraregional southern Irish English is described with remarks on possible variants both within this form and in more vernacular varieties. Many of the statements made here will probably be superseded when the recent forms of Dublin English (Hickey 1999a, 2005) have spread completely throughout the south of Ireland and have ousted the older supraregional variety permanently. Realisations which refer to advanced Dublin English are indicated by ADE in brackets below. For information on specifically northern Irish English features, see sections 3.3 and 3.4.

5.4.1   VOWELS

In many respects the vowel system of Irish English is different from that of more mainstream varieties of British English. The differences are almost exclusively due to the conservative character of Irish English. There is a greater resemblance to the vowel system of Early Modern English, as has been noted by many authors (see Bliss 1972a, 1979), than to that of mainstream British English. For the purposes of comparison the reference values for English are those of RP, as described, for instance, in Cruttenden (2001).

(4)   a. Long vowels
  /iː/   /uː/
      /eː/   /oː/   (ADE: /əu/)
          /aː/   /ɒː/   (ADE: /ɔː/)
  b. Diphthongs
      /aɪ/   /au/   (ADE:/æu/)   /ɒɪ/ (ADE: /ɔɪ/)
  c. Short vowels
  /ɪ/   /u/
      /ɛ/   /ə/   /ʌ/
          /æ/   /ɒ/   (ADE: /ɔ/)

Long vowels. Almost all vowels which occur independently are also to be found before /r/. As Irish English is rhotic there are no diphthongs corresponding to /ɪə, ɛə, uə/ in RP. Short vowels normally merge with /r/ to yield a long rhoticised vowel [ɚː]. The original distinction between a front and back short vowel before /r/, as in *term* [tɛɹm] and *turn* [tʌɹn] (Hogan 1927: 65, 77), does not apply to supraregional Irish English.

For many speakers word pairs such as *morning* and *mourning* are not homophonous, that is, the first word has /-ɒːr-/ and the second word /-oːr-/ (Wells' NORTH/FORCE distinction). For those speakers who observe this distinction, it is lexically determined. Nonetheless, one can say that the majority of words with /oːr/ derive from French loanwords in Middle English. The higher vowel would seem to occur preferentially before /-rt, -rs/ or just /-r/. In pre-nasal position, i.e. before /-rn/, the lower vowel predominates.

(5)   a. /oːr/   court, sport, force, forge, fort, port, source, fore, lore, pore, score;
           hoarse
      b. /ɒːr/   horse, gorse, Morse, Norse, born, corn, scorn but: forlorn (of
           Dutch origin)

Diphthongs /aɪ/ and /aʊ/. These have realisations with a common starting point,
[a]. Here the supraregional variety differs from other varieties: both local and
advanced Dublin English show a front onset for /aʊ/, i.e. [æʊ]. Local Dublin
English has a centralised onset for /aɪ/, i.e. [əɪ].

The diphthong /ɒɪ/ has the same lowered and unrounded onset as the short
vowel /ɒ/. Here advanced Dublin English differs, showing raised realisations
for both these segments.

Short vowels. The distinction between /æ/ and /aː/ is weak as there is a
tendency to retract /æ/ and lengthen it somewhat, especially before voiced
consonants: man /mæn/ [mæːn] ~ [maːn], staff [staːf], pass [paːs], past [paːst].
Conservative speakers may have [æ] for [ɛ] in many and any.

The low back vowel /ɒ/ is typical of supraregional Irish English, e.g. wash
[wɒʃ], want [wɒnt], wasp [wɒsp]. The non-retraction of early modern /a/, as
in want [want], is stigmatised supraregionally. This vowel is raised in advanced
Dublin English. Word pairs like cot/caught are distinguished on the basis of
quantity, i.e. one has [kɒt̪] vs [kɒːt̪].

The mid back unrounded vowel /ʌ/ has a realisation which is further
back than that found in RP, i.e. bun is [bʌ̈n] and not [bän] (RP). In vernacular varieties there can be a degree of rounding for this vowel which is
why many Irish scholars have transcribed it as [ɔ].[5] In general, one can say
that this realisation is similar to that in most forms of Irish (certainly outside
the north of the country): fliuch [fʲlʲʌ̈x] 'wet', moch [mʌ̈x] 'early', rud [rʌ̈d]
'thing'.

Vowel reduction. Schwa is found as a pretonic short vowel, as in about [əˈbaʊt̪].
It is rhotacised before /r/: butter [ˈbʌt̪ɚ] and occurs in unstressed -ed, as in
naked [ˈneːkəd], a feature which distinguishes it from RP and links it to overseas
varieties like Australian English; see section 6.6. Schwa also occurs outside the
supraregional variety as a reduced form of unstressed high back vowels, e.g.
windows [ˈwɪndəz].

HAPPY-tensing (Wells 1982: 257f.; Fabricius 2002a), a high vowel [i] in final,
open position, e.g. pity [pɪt̪i], applies across the board in Ireland. However, for
Irish (outside the north) there appears to have been a reduction of long vowels
when borrowing English words. Thus the English first name Bartley appears in
Irish as Beartla with a final schwa.

---

[5] There may be areas where this vowel is close to [ʊ], e.g. in the transition from the south-west to the
west: brush [bruʃ], stuff [ʃtʊf] (SADIF, M60+, Bruff, Co. Limerick), tongue [tʊŋ] (MLSI, M70,
Crisheen, Co. Clare).

5.4.2 CONSONANTS

Dentals and alveolars

The area of coronal obstruents, those in front of the palate and behind the lips, is the most complex in Irish English phonology (Hickey 1984a). In most varieties of English the segments of this area look like the following.

(6) a. ambidental fricatives   /θ/   :   /ð/
     b. alveolar stops   /t/   :   /d/
     c. alveolar fricatives   /s/   :   /z/

In supraregional Irish English the situation is complicated by the fortition of the ambidental fricatives. This means that there is a systemic distinction between dental and alveolar stop articulations: *thank* [t̪æŋk] versus *tank* [tæŋk]. The fortition of ambidental fricatives to dental stops can be interpreted as a result of language contact: the Irish used the nearest phonetic equivalent to the English sounds, i.e. the dental stops of Irish as in *tuí* [t̪iː] 'straw' and *daor* [d̪iːr] 'expensive'. However, an additional factor could have been the non-prescriptive language acquisition scenario for the majority of the population during the historical language shift. In such situations 'natural sound change' (Blevins 2006: 10–12) would be favoured. Given that ambidental fricatives are 'highly marked sounds' and 'are rare in the languages of the world and learned late by children' (Dubois and Horvath 2004: 111), it is not surprising that fortition of these to corresponding stops should have taken place during the unguided second-language acquisition of the language shift, irrespective of the phonology of the background language, Irish.

A further complication in the coronal area is due to the allophony of /t/ and /d/. These stops only have a stop realisation when they are in one of the following positions.[6]

(7) a. immediately before a stressed vowel, word-initially: *tea* [tiː],
         word-medially: *titanic* [taɪˈtænɪk]
     b. immediately before or after a non-vocalic segment: *lightning* [laɪtnɪŋ],
         bent [bɛnt]

In all other positions alveolar stops are realised as apico-alveolar fricatives. According to a transcription introduced in Hickey (1984a: 235), this fricative is indicated by placing a subscript caret below the relevant voiced or voiceless stop, i.e. [t̬] or [d̬]. Instances of these fricatives can be seen in the following.

(8) a. *but*   [bʌt̬]   b. *butter*   [ˈbʌt̬ɚ]
     c. *educate*   [ˈɛdʒukeːt̬]   d. *wood*   [wud̬]

---

[6] The phonotactic position for this lenition (Hickey 1996a) excludes syllable-initial and immediately pre-stress positions, despite the statements by Wells (1982: 430) and Bertz (1975: 278).

The fricative realisation of alveolar stops is particularly audible with /t/, given the fortis nature of this consonant. Because of the sensitivity of frication to stress, lenited and non-lenited realisations may be found within a pair of morphologically related words, e.g. *Italy* ['ɪt̞ɪli] vs *Italian* [ɪ'tæljən].

As [t̞] and [d̞] are apical fricatives they are kept clearly apart from the corresponding laminal-fricatives /s/ and /z/ and from the alveolo-palatal fricatives /ʃ/ and /ʒ/. The sets of forms in the following are thus not homophones.

(9) a. *puss* [pʌs]   b. *putt* [pʌt̞]
     c. *push* [pʊʃ]   d. *put*   [pʊt̞]

The distinction between the final sounds in the first set is between a laminal and an apical articulation and in the second set between a broad-grooved fricative and an apical articulation. In addition, the lip-rounding accompanying /ʃ/ is lacking with [t̞]. The realisations of /s/ and /z/ and of /ʃ/ and /ʒ/ in Irish English are essentially the same as in other varieties of English, as are the realisations of the affricates /tʃ/ and /dʒ/.

The apico-alveolar fricatives of Irish English are the result of lenition which is discussed in more detail in section 5.4.3.

Labio-velars

A conservative feature of Irish English is the distinction between voiced and voiceless labio-velar glides. The voiceless glide is to be found in all instances where there is *wh-* in the orthography, cf. *witch* [wɪtʃ] versus *which* [ʍɪtʃ]. In the phonological analysis of the sound [ʍ], it is interesting to review the arguments for assuming two segments /h/ + /w/ or just one /ʍ/. There is strong system-based evidence for analysing [ʍ] in Irish English as consisting of /h/ + /w/. One might think to begin with that /w – ʍ/ form a voiced – voiceless pair in English like /s – z, t – d, p – b/, etc. However, the arguments for regarding [ʍ] as /h/ + /w/ are more compelling.

The first segment in /hw/ correlates with /h/ word initially, that is, to postulate /h/ + /w/ has additional justification in the fact that initial /h-/ occurs anyway (in all varieties with [ʍ]). Conversely, no variety of English which has /h/-dropping also has [ʍ], i.e. lack of /h-/ precludes the cluster /hw-/, [ʍ]. There is a further argument from syllable position. Standard wisdom on syllable structure sees an increase of sonority from edge to centre. Analysing [ʍ] as /hw/ means that one has a fricative /h/, then a glide /w/ (a continuant with open articulation) and a following vowel, which is in keeping with the sonority cline for sound segments. There are also other considerations. Cross-linguistic observations in phonology have led to many valid statements concerning markedness, here understood in a statistical sense. Thus voice is unmarked for vowels, glides and sonorants just as voicelessness is for obstruents, i.e. there are more languages with voiced sonorants than with voiceless ones and more languages with voiceless obstruents than with voiced ones. English does not have voiceless sonorants or glides, so that to posit /ʍ/ would mean that there would be an unevenness in the distribution of sonority going from syllable edge to centre as can be seen from the following two phonological interpretations of [ʍ].

(10)   [ʍ] = /hw/

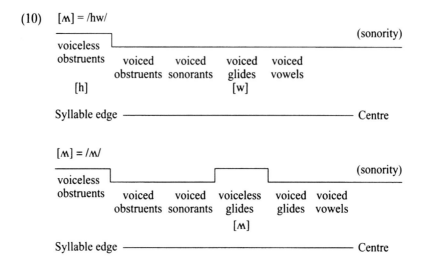

Types of /r/

In Irish English /r/ appears in all instances where it is etymologically justified, i.e. it occurs both syllable-initially and syllable-finally. Neither the 'linking-*r*' nor the 'intrusive-*r*' of RP (Wells 1982: 222– 7) is to be found. There are, however, three main realisations of /r/ discussed in the following.

1.   Velarised alveolar continuant
Conservative mainstream varieties of southern Irish English have a velarised alve-olar continuant which can be indicated, in narrow transcription, by the normal symbol for a frictionless continuant together with the diacritic for velarisation, [ɹˠ], e.g. *core* [koːɹˠ], *barn* [bɑːɹˠ]. An offglide from a front vowel to this velarised [ɹˠ] can be heard, e.g. *tear* [teːᵊɹˠ].

2.   Uvular /r/
In north-east Leinster (in Co. Meath and Co. Louth) a uvular /r/ – [ʁ] – is found in local varieties of English. This is clearly documented in the recordings for *A Sound Atlas of Irish English* (see Hickey 2004a: 79), e.g. *square* [skwɛəʁ], *beer* [biəʁ]. This uvular [ʁ] is recessive and now only found in syllable-final position. However, it is obviously the remnant of a much wider distribution. Further westwards, along the counties of southern Ulster (Co. Monaghan, Co. Cavan) and north Leinster (Co. Westmeath, Co. Longford), a retraction of vow-els before syllable-final /r/ with attendant lip-rounding is found, indicating that these localities previously had uvular /r/ before it was replaced by a more

mainstream alveolar [ɹ] (this pronunciation is clearly documented in the sound atlas recordings for this region).

Support for the assumption that uvular /r/ was previously much more widespread in Ireland comes from recordings of Irish. In areas as far apart as west Connemara (Co. Galway) and Dingle Peninsula (Co. Kerry), older Irish speakers with uvular /r/ have been found (Hickey in press).

In the material for *A Linguistic Survey of Ireland* (see section 4.4) references abound to uvular /r/ occurring in a broad band from the south-east through the mid south to the south-west (in terms of counties: Wexford, Kilkenny, Waterford, Tipperary, Cork and Kerry). For instance, when reporting on a group of speakers from Tullaroan, Co. Kilkenny, the data collector notes 'All informants have a uvular quality to their /r/ but it is most consistent with one, a 77-year-old male, e.g. *farm* [faʁəm], *right* [ʁəɪt], *there're a* [deːʁə].' Because the informants for the survey, when the recordings were being made twenty-five to thirty years ago, were mostly elderly rural males, it may well be that the localities with uvular /r/ then no longer show this feature today (2006). The recessive nature of uvular /r/ was recognised by one specific data collector for the survey (Séamus Ó Maoláin, University College Galway) who noted that often only a retraction of the tongue, with 'uvular coloration', is perceptible with younger speakers in localities where older speakers clearly had uvular /r/.

3. Retroflex /r/
The changes in Dublin English, which mainly took place in the 1990s, led to the rise of a retroflex [ɻ], in all likelihood as a reaction to the low rhoticity of local Dublin English (Hickey 2005: 76f.). This realisation has become ubiquitous with younger female speakers and has spread very rapidly outside the Dublin area. With time, it will most probably become the dominant realisation of /r/ for all mainstream varieties of Irish English in the south. Retroflex [ɻ] is also found in Ulster, both in Ulster Scots and Ulster English. This is not a new realisation and it is very unlikely that the recent Dublin pronunciation is related to it.

Types of /l/

Traditionally, /l/ in Irish English has been alveolar in all syllable positions. Conservative varieties, both mainstream and local ones, still show this realisation. The only exception to this is contact Irish English where Irish speakers tend to use the velarised [ɫ] they have in Irish in positions in which it would occur in their first language, e.g. word-initially before /aɪ/ as in *like* [ɫaɪk], cf. Irish *(ar a) laghad* [ɫaɪd] '(at) least'.

However, the recent changes in Dublin English include a velarised realisation of /l/ in syllable-final position (Hickey 2005: 77), e.g. *field* [fiːˀɫd], *meal* [miːˀɫ], *deal* [diːˀɫ]. Again, because of the spread of the new Dublin pronunciation, velarised [ɫ] has become a characteristic of younger non-local speakers in the south of Ireland, especially females.

The position of /h/

Etymological /h/ is to be found in all positions in Irish English. *H*-dropping, so characteristic of present-day urban English in Britain, is unknown in Ireland and so not part of any sociolinguistic assessment of speakers (Mugglestone 2003: 107–59). Due to the influence of Irish, /h/ also occurs word-medially and word-finally, above all in names of Irish origins, e.g. *Fahy* ['fæhi], *Haughey* ['hɒːhi], *MacGrath* /mə'graːh/.

The /h/ of Irish English involves a particular distribution of forms of the indefinite article. Where /h-/ is the onset of a stressed syllable, the simple form *a* is used, where the syllable of which it is a part is unstressed the longer form *an* is found (Schlüter 2003: 83–8), contrast *a history of drama* but *an historical drama*.

5.4.3 LENITION IN IRISH ENGLISH

The term 'lenition' refers to phonetic weakening, that is an increase in sonority with a given segment, e.g. when a stop changes to a fricative as in /k/ to /x/. This is a common diachronic development and in some cases such changes have become part of the inflectional morphology of a language, for instance, in Irish and the other Celtic languages. Lenition is a phenomenon which usually manifests itself as a shift from stop to fricative or a shift from voiceless to voiced sound with fricatives. It normally consists of several steps and diachronically a language may exhibit a shift from stop to zero via a number of intermediary stages. Attested cases of lenition are represented by the Germanic sound shift (stop to fricative), West Romance consonantal developments (Martinet 1952) such as lenition in Spanish or more dialectal phenomena such as the *gorgia toscana* in Tuscan Italian (Rohlfs 1949; Ternes 1977) or lenition in Canary Spanish (Oftedal 1986).

If one looks at English in this light one can recognise that the alveolar point of articulation represents a favoured site for phonetic lenition (Hickey 1996a). Alveolars in English can involve different types of alternation, three of which are summarised below, the labels on the left indicating sets of varieties in which these realisations are frequently found.

(11)	*Variety or group*	*Lenited form of stop*	*Example*
a.	American English	tap	*water* ['wɑːɾɚ]
b.	urban British English	glottal stop	*water* ['wɔːʔə]
c.	southern Irish English	fricative	*water* ['wɒːt̞ɚ]

Glottalling involves the removal of the oral gesture from a segment. Tapping is also lenition as it is a reduction in the duration of a segment. However, there are differences between tapping, glottalling and frication.

Tapping can only occur with alveolars (labials and velars are excluded). Furthermore, it is only found in word-internal position and only in immediately

post-stress environments. As tapping is phonetically an uncontrolled articulation, it cannot occur word-finally (except for sandhi situations) and cannot initiate
a stressed syllable. For some younger non-local speakers in Ireland, it is fashionable to use tapping as an alternative to frication, e.g. *Waterford* ['wɔːɾɚfɚd],
better ['bɛɾɚ] (Hickey 2005: 77f.).

Glottalling can in principle apply to labials, alveolars and velars but for those
varieties of English best known for it, e.g. popular London English, it is characteristic of alveolars as in *bottle* [bɒʔl̩], *butter* [bʌʔə]. It can also occur medially
and finally, e.g. *but* [bʌʔ]. Varieties with glottalling may vary in the environments
which allow this.

Frication is a type of lenition which is in fact a cline, with a stop at one end
and zero at the other. For the supraregional variety of southern Irish English
it encompasses only one sound [t̞].[7] This fricative is maintained through different style levels and functions as an indicator of Irish English. However, in
more colloquial urban varieties of the east coast (including Dublin) there are
other attested points on a scale of lenition. These other realisations are sociolinguistically sensitive markers which disappear with an increase of formality in
speech.

(12) t   >   t̞   >   h   ~   ʔ   >   Ø
      button   *but*   *water*   *water*   *what*

The removal of the oral gesture, as seen in glottal realisations of /t/, can result
in either a glottal fricative [h] or glottal stop [ʔ]. The latter is less frequent and
practically confined to local Dublin speech. An alveolar [ɹ], as a further reduction
of [t̞], also occurs in local Dublin English, especially as a sandhi phenomenon
across word boundaries, e.g. *Get off, will you!* [gɛɹ ɒf wɪl jə] (DER, M35+). This
can be interpreted as a stage before the complete loss of the oral gesture, i.e. it
is less than [t̞], as it involves a frictionless continuant, but more than [h] or [ʔ]
which have no oral component.

In one or two words, a lenition stage is lexicalised. Thus the colloquial pronunciation of *Saturday*, even with speakers who do not lenite beyond [t̞], is
commonly ['sæhɚde], perhaps influenced by the Irish pronunciation of the word
Sathairn ['sahɚnʲ] 'Saturday'. This is true of non-local forms of Irish English,
which generally do not permit lenition beyond [t̞].

From the above discussion it is obvious that Irish English lenition is found
in syllable codas. But to account for attestations exhaustively, the nature of the
coda must be taken into account.[8] The fricative realisations of lenition are found

---

[7] The fricative *t* of Irish English is sometimes referred to as 'slit-*t*'. Some of the descriptions of this
sound have unfortunately been inaccurate. The sound is not an affricate and it is always distinct
from [s]. On the question of transcription, see the discussion in Pandeli, Eska, Ball and Rahilly
(1997).

[8] Despite his detailed treatment of lenition in various languages and varieties of English, Kallen
(2005b: 61–70) fails to grasp this essential condition on lenition, specified in Hickey (1996a), which
is absent from his study.

Table 5.4. *Syllable position and lenition in Irish English*

Position	Example	Permitted realisations of lenition
1. intervocalic	*pity*	ṯ, h, ʔ, Ø
2. word-final	*pit*	ṯ, h, ʔ, Ø
3. pre-consonantal	*little*	ʔ, h, Ø
	[-tl̩]	
4. post-consonantal	*spent*	ʔ, Ø ([-tˢ])

Table 5.5. *Classification of lenition alternatives in Irish English*

	Type of change	Segment	Example	Environment
lenition 1	reduction of effort	ɾ	*sitter* ['sɪɾɚ]	only intervocalic
lenition 2	stop to fricative	ṯ	*sit* [sɪṯ]	(default)
lenition 3	stop to continuant	ɹ	*sit* [sɪɹ ʊp]	mainly sandhi
lenition 4	removal of oral gesture	h, ʔ	*sit* [sɪh, sɪʔ]	(default)
lenition 5	segment deletion	Ø	*sit* [sɪ]	(default)
default: (i) intervocalic or (ii) post-vocalic and pre-pausal				

where the input /t/ comes after a vowel and immediately before a further vowel or is word-final (1 and 2 in table 5.4). If the /t/ is followed by a consonant, in effect by a syllabic /l/ or /n/, then a glottal stop or /h/ is permitted (in local varieties of Dublin English, but not usually any continuant realisation of lenition like [ṯ]) (3). The same is true in post-consonantal position (4), although here a slow release may lead to slight affrication (this is phonetically a prolongation of articulation and hence does not have to be classified as lenition). In the position after /r/, e.g. *cart*, *port*, fricative realisations are often to be found because of the continuant nature of /r/. It is true that lenition, of the type discussed above, does not occur in syllable-initial position. However, what one does find, especially among younger female speakers in Dublin, is a slight affrication of /t/ in pre-vocalic initial position, e.g. *two* [tˢuː], *town* [tˢæʊn]. This is independent of the realisations of lenition in syllable codas and may well be an age-grading phenomenon as it is not represented among middle-aged or older female speakers.

Lenition in Irish English is of interest as a general phenomenon which shows several stages with specifiable conditions for their occurrence. In table 5.5 the different types of lenition are classified according to the type of change made to underlying stops which provide the input. There are two default environments for lenition, (i) intervocalic, (ii) post-vocalic and pre-pausal. These can in fact be collapsed to a single environment: open or no articulation on both flanks of the input segment, here /t/. This will allow lenition in *putty*, *putt*, but block lenition which retains an oral gesture in words like *belt*, *bent*, *fact*, *cupped*, *button*, *little*. However, lenition which involves the removal of the oral gesture, i.e. types 4 and 5 in table 5.5, can occur post-consonantally and pre-consonantally (before syllabic [l̩] or [n̩]), e.g. *fact* [fæk?], *little* [lɪhl̩]. Lenition 3 is largely a sandhi phenomenon and occurs across word boundaries. The overriding condition on lenition in Irish English, i.e. that it only occurs in syllable codas, holds for all the above types. This condition assumes that /t/ between two vowels belongs to the coda of the first syllable when this is stressed, e.g. *pretty* ['pɹɪt̬.i], but to the onset of the second syllable if this carries the stress, e.g. *pretence* [pɹɪ.'tɛns].

Lenition of stops at other points of articulation is not taken to occur in present-day Irish English. However, /k/ can be lenited to /x/ locally in Co. Limerick, an observation of the author confirmd by recordings in the sound archives of the Department of Folklore, University College Dublin, e.g. *They had a live wake* [weːˀx] (SADIF, M60+, Bruff, Co. Limerick), *a bar of chocolate* ['tʃɒxlət̬] (SADIF, M50+, Lough Gur, Co. Limerick). Whether this is an independent development in the English of this area or a remnant of lenition with a wider scope is difficult to say. The matter could well be of relevance in the context of lenition in Liverpool and Middlesbrough (see sections 6.2.1 and 6.2.2).

5.4.4 YOD DROPPING

The sequence /juː/ arose of out the Middle English diphthongs /ɛʊ/ and /ɪʊ/; consider *beauty* from Anglo-Norman *beuté* and *suit* from Anglo-Norman *siute* respectively. In many dialects of English the sequence has been simplified to /uː/, a process commonly known as 'yod-dropping' (Wells 1982: 247). In Irish English there are clearly definable conditions for the deletion of yod as outlined below.

(13)   a. Deletion assumes that /j/ is not in absolute initial position, i.e. it must be preceded by another segment, hence *year* /jiːr/.
       b. The segment before /j/, in the onset in which it is deleted, is regularly a sonorant, in effect /n/ or /l/ as /j/ does not occur after /r/ in an onset, hence *lute* /luːt/, *news* /nuːz/. After /s/ yod is also deleted, hence *suit* /suːt/.
       c. The sonorant in question is alveolar, hence *news* /nuːz/ but *mews* /mjuːz/ (and *cute* /kjuːt/ with a non-sonorant velar stop).
       d. The syllable to which the onset in question belongs is stressed, hence *numerous* /'nuːmərəs/ but *numerical* /njʊ'mɛrɪkl̩/, *Italian* /ɪ'tæljən/

For comments on epenthesis and metathesis, see section 5.2.

5.4.5 STRESS PATTERNING

Non-standard stress patterns are a common feature of Irish English (Ó Sé 1986) and typically involve the placement of stress on the last syllable of a trisyllabic form, usually a verb: *edu'cate, adver'tise, rea'lise, investi'gate, distri'bute, concen'trate*. Various reasons for this phenomenon have been put forward. One common view, propounded by Bliss, is that the Irish learned their English from hedge schoolmasters who did not know the standard pronunciation of English and the non-standard pronunciation perpetuated itself (Bliss 1977a).

Another reason could well have been the variable stress patterns among input sources of English. In the early modern period, initial stress on trisyllabic verbs was by no means universally established (Lass 1994).

However, there is another possible cause, a language-internal reason that does not require recourse to external factors such as teachers or insufficient knowledge of English. In southern Irish (Munster Irish) the prosodic pattern which arose in the late medieval period required that long syllables towards the end of a word be stressed, as the equation of length with stress position had taken place (Hickey 1997b). The Munster stress rule demands that the stress placement be worked out by moving backwards from the end of a word, the stress resting on the first heavy syllable or the first syllable, if there is no non-initial heavy syllable in a word. Significantly, this stress placement rule will account for the non-standard stress patterning with verbs of three or more syllables in Irish English because the long vowel of the final syllables of such words makes these phonologically heavy.

5.4.6 LEXICAL SETS FOR IRISH ENGLISH

A lexical set consists of a group of words all of which have the same pronunciation for a certain sound in a given variety. For instance, the lexical set TRAP is used to refer to the pronunciation which speakers of a variety have for the sound which is /æ/ in RP. So if speakers use [a] or [ɛ] in TRAP it is taken that they will use [a] or [ɛ] in all other words which contain this vowel, e.g. *bad*, *latter*, *shall*, that is in the words which comprise the lexical set. The advantage of this is that instead of talking about the realisation of the /æ/ vowel in variety X, which phonetically can be quite far removed from [æ], one can simply refer to the vowel in the lexical set TRAP.

Lexical sets were first presented in an explicit form in John C. Wells' three-volume work *Accents of English* (Wells 1982). These were intended to cover the vowels of RP and their realisations in accents of English throughout the world. However, it became increasingly apparent that the group was not sufficient to deal with the phonetic distinctions present in many forms of English outside RP. For instance, there may also be historical distinctions present in varieties of English which have been lost elsewhere. Indeed, innovations outside RP may demand different lexical sets for their descriptions via this technique. For instance, in local Dublin English short high vowels before tautosyllabic /r/, and back vowels after /w/ in the same position, have developed into a vowel which is phonetically something like [ʊː], e.g. *first* [fʊː(ɹ)st], *work* [wʊː(ɹ)k]. Mid front vowels in this position, however, are realised by [ɛː], e.g. *germ* [gɛː(ɹ)m], thus merging with the vowel realisation in the SQUARE lexical set. Because of this, Wells' NURSE

Table 5.6. *Lexical sets for supraregional Irish English*

Short vowels		Long vowels		Rising diphthongs	
KIT	/ɪ/	FLEECE	/iː/	PRICE/PRIDE	/aɪ/
DRESS	/ɛ/	FACE	/eː/	MOUTH	/aʊ/
TRAP	/æ/	BATH	/aː/	CHOICE	/ɒɪ/
LOT	/ɒ/	THOUGHT	/ɒː/	GOAT	/oʊ/
STRUT	/ʌ/	SOFT	/ɒ(ː)/		
FOOT	/ʊ/	GOOSE	/uː/		

Centring diphthongs / rhotacised vowels; unstressed vowels

NEAR	/iɚ/	SQUARE	/eɚ/	CURE	/uɚ/
START	/aːr/	NORTH	/ɒːr/	FORCE	/oːr/
NURSE	/ɚː/	TERM	/ɚː/	LETTER	/-ɚ/
COMMA	/-ə/	HAPPY	/-i/		

Low vowel before nasal + obstruent   DANCE   /aː/

Consonantal lexical sets for Irish English

Dental stops/fricatives   *Alveolar stops*

THIN	/t̪(θ)/	TWO	/t-/	WATER	/-t-/	GET	/-t/
THIS	/d̪(ð)/	DIP	/d-/	READY	/-d-/	SAID	/-d/

L-sounds   *R-sounds*

RAIL	/-l/	RUN	/r-/
LOOK	/l-/	SORE	/-r/

Velar stops   *Velar nasal*

GAP	/g-/	TALKING	/-ŋ/
CAP	/k-/		

Alveolar and alveolo-palatal sibilants

SEE	/s/	SHOE	/ʃ/
BUZZ	/z/	VISION	/ʒ/

Labio-velar glide, voiced and voiceless

WET	/w-/	WHICH	/hw-/

lexical set is represented by two such sets in the present book, NURSE illustrating the [ʊː] pronunciation and TERM showing the [ɛː] realisation (in local Dublin English).

The original lexical sets devised by Wells only refer to vowel values. But of course the variation among consonants across forms of English is considerable, so for this book consonantal lexical sets have been included. The relevant consonant in such sets is indicated by underlining, e.g. WHICH referring to the use of [ʍ] or [w] at the beginning of this word and all others like it. Again the usefulness of lexical sets is immediately obvious here: for varieties of English in the Republic of Ireland it makes little sense to talk of the realisation of /θ/ or /ð/ because so many speakers never have either [θ] or [ð]. Instead, the possibilities include a dental or alveolar stop, i.e. [t̪, d̪] or [t, d]. For this reason, the lexical sets THIN and THIS have been introduced to refer to sounds which in more mainstream varieties of English are [θ] and [ð] respectively.

Table 5.6 indicates the lexical sets necessary for a comprehensive treatment of Irish English. The realisations indicated after the keywords are those found in supraregional Irish English.

1. *Vowels*

   KIT /ɪ/ This is identical to present-day British English. No lowering or centralisation is found in southern Irish English, as opposed to varieties in the north, especially Ulster Scots, which do show this lowering.

   DRESS /ɛ/ This is essentially the same as in present-day British English; perhaps slightly lower, hence the use of /ɛ/ rather than /e/.

   TRAP /æ/ As in more recent forms of southern British English, this vowel is quite open. In vernacular varieties it is raised before /r/, e.g. *car* [kæːɹ].

   LOT /ɒ/ This low back vowel is traditionally an open mid to front low vowel. CLOTH words have the same realisation as THOUGHT words, i.e. a long low back vowel, which is quite open in mainstream varieties, but raised in new forms of Dublin English.

   STRUT /ʌ/ A retracted and perhaps slightly rounded short vowel is used here. This is often written as [ʌ̈] where the diaeresis indicates centralisation of the cardinal vowel. Any rounding is insignificant and *pot* is acoustically separate from *putt*. This phonetic realisation is the same as the vowel in Irish *fliuch* [fʲlʲʌ̈x] 'wet', which was probably the source for the Irish during the language shift in previous centuries and is the source for contact Irish English today. In local Dublin English the STRUT set has the same vowel as the FOOT set (similar to northern England). It is the only variety in Ireland (north or south) where this is the case. The high rounded vowel of local Dublin English is a retention of early English input to the city.

   FOOT /ʊ/ Basically, the same as present-day southern British English; a quite forward realisation is found in advanced Dublin English.

   FLEECE /iː/ The vowel used in this set is unremarkable in mainstream Irish English but it tends to break in local Dublin English, e.g. *mean* [miʲən].

   FACE /eː/ A long monophthong [eː] is the normal realisation in Irish English in the south. The rising diphthong [eɪ] is not found but the whole vowel may be lowered in vernacular varieties, i.e. one may have [fɛːs].

   BATH /aː/ Eastern dialects of Ireland (the most conservative stemming from before 1600) have a short /æ/, e.g. *bath* is [bæt] (with alveolar [t] for TH). Other varieties have a long [aː] in such words. Due to general low vowel lengthening in Dublin English, the BATH vowel is always long, i.e. one has [bæːt]. This long vowel is also present in new Dublin English.

   THOUGHT /ɒː/ In mainstream varieties the vowel in this set is rather open and unrounded, more so in colloquial varieties. In advanced Dublin

English the vowel here is raised considerably as part of the Dublin vowel shift, i.e. *thought* is [t̪ɔːt̪] or even [t̪oːt̪].

SOFT /ɒ(ː)/ This word, and others with the same vowel, e.g. *cross, frost, lost,* has a long vowel in Dublin (traditionally and in newer varieties), although other varieties of Irish English have a short vowel here.

GOOSE /uː/ The vowel in this set is not a marker of any variety of Irish English, except in local Dublin English where the vowel may be broken (parallel to the similar breaking of /iː/), e.g. *school* [skuʷəl]. In its unbroken form, the vowel is quite forward, especially in advanced Dublin English.

PRICE /aɪ/ There are basically three types of realisation of this diphthong. General Irish English varieties have [aɪ], eastern dialects (including local Dublin English) have [əɪ]. Advanced Dublin English may have a retracted starting point – seen in [ɑɪ] – as a remnant of the original retraction of 'Dublin 4' English of the 1980s, but this would appear to be recessive.

PRIDE /aɪ/ For some speakers the retraction of the starting point, as in [ɑɪ], may only be present when /aɪ/ is stressed and followed by a voiced consonant or a word boundary. Such speakers have a conditional realisation of /aɪ/ similar to that in so-called Canadian Raising (Chambers 1973). Where the phonetic environment favours a back realisation, e.g. before a velarised [ɫ], this can be found quite often, e.g. *mild* [mɑɪɫd] or *wild* [wɑɪɫd].

MOUTH /au/ In eastern dialects and in Dublin (traditionally and in newer varieties) there is a front starting point for the vowel in this set, at least [æ], colloquially [ɛ]. Because of the influence of newer varieties of Dublin English the raised starting point is spreading very quickly, especially among young females. But traditionally, Irish English has a low starting point, i.e. [aʊ] is normal.

CHOICE /ɒɪ/ The starting point here is quite open, except for newer varieties of Dublin English which have characteristic raising of the onset, e.g. *toy* [tɔɪ] or [toɪ].

GOAT /oʊ/ In traditional vernacular and rural varieties, outside Dublin, a long monophthong is found here: [goːt̪]. In local Dublin English, a diphthong with a low starting point is typical: [gʌot̪]. In mainstream Irish English there is normally slight diphthongisation with a higher end point, i.e. [gout̪]. The realisation with a centralised starting point, [əʊ], is a prominent feature of advanced Dublin English.

NEAR /iɚ/, SQUARE /eɚ/, CURE /uɚ/ These sets have a vowel followed by a rhotacised schwa which means that the three centring diphthongs of RP, consisting of vowel plus schwa, do not exist in Irish English.

START /ɑːr/ Although the TRAP vowel is central or front, there is some retraction before /r/ in mainstream varieties. Local Dublin English does not show this and has a rather fronted realisation, i.e. [stæː(ɹ)ʔ].

NORTH /ɒːr/ Traditionally, the vowel in this set is quite open. However, it has been raised considerably in advanced Dublin English and has merged with the FORCE vowel for many speakers. This means that words like *morning* and *mourning* are homophones, whereas for mainstream speakers, the first word would have a lower vowel than the second.

FORCE /oːr/ The [oː] vowel found in this set is typical of all varieties of Irish English, i.e. the open realisation, typical of the NORTH set, does not apply here.

NURSE /ɚː/ A centralised rhotacised schwa, without lip rounding, is found in this set. In local Dublin English, the vowel is raised, retracted and often non-rhotic, i.e. [nʊː(ɹ)s].

TERM /ɚː/ For mainstream varieties, this set is identical to the previous one. But local Dublin English has an [ɛː] vowel here, possibly rhotacised somewhat. The distribution of the vowels in this and the previous lexical set is as follows: after historic /u/ and after labials (irrespective of the vowel) [ʊː] is found; in all other cases [ɛː] occurs. This accounts for the following realisations: *nurse* [nʊː(ɹ)s], *turn* [tʊː(ɹ)n], *work* [wʊː(ɹ)k], *first* [fʊː(ɹ)s(t)], *bird* [bʊː(ɹ)d]; *circle* [sɛː(ɹ)k], *certain* [sɛː(ɹ)tn̩], *germ* [dʒɛː(ɹ)m]. Historic /ir/ after alveolar stops is also retracted, e.g. *dirt* [dʊː(ɹ)t], *third* [tʊː(ɹ)d], but not /er/, e.g. *term* [tɛː(ɹ)m].

LETTER /-ɚ/ A rhotacised schwa is found in this set, except in local Dublin English, which is only very weakly rhotic. In non-rhotic forms of Dublin English the vowel here is quite low, in the region of [ɐ].

COMMA /-ə/ Here a schwa is found which maybe somewhat lowered in local Dublin English.

HAPPY /-i/ A tense vowel in this position is typical of Irish English. See section 3.3 for comments on Ulster Scots.

DANCE /aː/ The vowel in this set is never retracted, as in southern British English, although it is always long. Retraction is taken as a stereotype of British English and often deliberately imitated as in *She speaks with a grand* [grɑːnd] *accent*. A conditional retraction before /r/ is found (see comments on START lexical set) and may also occur before /ð/ [d̪] as well, e.g. *father* ['fɑːd̪ɚ], *rather* ['ɹɑːd̪ɚ].

2. *Consonants*

T̪HIN /t̪ (θ)/ A dental stop is found in both mainstream Irish English and advanced Dublin English, but an alveolar stop is typical of local Dublin English. /t̪/ → [θ] is found with some speakers, but only word-finally as an approximation to standard English in careful speech or in a reading style. This is furthered by the fact that /t/ is fricativised in word-final positions anyway so there is a parallelism between the following two realisations: (i) *pat* /pæt/ → [pæt̪], (ii) *path* /pæt̪/ → [pæθ].

T̪HIS /d̪(ð)/ As with the previous lexical set, a dental stop is characteristic of supraregional varieties. Local Dublin English shows an alveolar stop. The shift to [v] (or to [f] in the T̪HIN lexical set), which occurs in other varieties of English, is unknown in Ireland. However, this shift was found in the dialect of Forth and Bargy; see section 2.4.4.

TWO /t-/ In initial position /t/ is not lenited so that one has a normal stop. In advanced Dublin English there is a tendency for very slight affrication, especially in the speech of young females, i.e. one frequently has realisations like [tˢuː] for *two*. The same remarks apply to an initial voiced alveolar stop, i.e. to the DIP lexical set.

WATER /-t-/ In mainstream varieties this intervocalic /t/ is fricativised. The resulting segment is an apico-alveolar fricative; see discussion in section 5.4.3. A tap is regarded as fashionable with some younger speakers, especially females.

READY /-d-/, SAID /-d/. In principle, the lenition which applies to /t/ also holds for /d/. However, it is not as obvious and generally has low phonetic salience.

GET /-t/ For mainstream varieties of Irish English, the realisation here is the same as that in the WATER lexical set. In local Dublin English the /t/ is frequently deleted, e.g. *foot* [fʊh] or [fʊ]. If an element of this lexical set is followed by a vowel-initial word then a tap [ɾ] may occur. This can be heard clearly with many young female speakers in *A Sound Atlas of Irish English* with the test sentence *They bought* [ɾ] *a new bath last week*.

RAIL /-l/ A velarised [ɫ] was previously only found in local Dublin English. Non-local varieties and supraregional Irish English had an alveolar [l] in all positions. However, the [ɫ] of local Dublin English has been adopted into advanced Dublin English and hence is spreading rapidly in the speech of young people throughout the Republic of Ireland.

LOOK /l-/ The lateral in word-initial position is alveolar, irrespective of the syllable-final realisation. In contact Irish English a velarised [ɫ] may occur; see comments above.

RUN /r-/ In word-initial position, /r/ is realised as an alveolar continuant, i.e. [ɹ].

SORE /-r/ In advanced Dublin English, a retroflex [ɻ] is used here. This has no precedent in varieties of southern Irish English and is a genuine innovation of the past two decades. Mainstream varieties still use a non-retroflex [ɹ] (as in word-initial position). With the spread of retroflexion, the next generation will use [ɻ] in mainstream varieties, unless the current trend is reversed. A uvular [ʁ] is found in north-east Leinster; see comments above.

GAP, CAP The realisation of the velar stops is similar to standard British English. A velar offglide to the front low vowel is indicative of northern Irish English.

TALKING /-ŋ/ As in so many varieties of English, the shift from [ŋ] to [n] in unstressed syllables is typical of vernacular modes of speech. The alveolarisation of /ŋ/ is not as widespread in southern Irish English as it is in the north.

SHOE, VISION; SEE, BUZZ /ʃ, ʒ; s, z/ The realisation of sibilants is generally the same as in mainland British English. In the context of Irish English it is important to stress that [s] and [ʈ] are clearly distinguished phonetically so that *kiss* [kɪs] and *kit* [kɪʈ] are *not* homophones.

WET /w/ is always realised as [w].

WHICH /hw-/ Mainstream Irish English generally distinguishes phonetically between *which* and *witch*, but advanced Dublin English is losing this distinction (by voicing the first segment in *which*). The use of [w] in this set is also typical of local Dublin English which is probably why the merger of *which* and *witch* in advanced Dublin English is not categorical.

5.5   Urban Irish English

5.5.1 ENGLISH IN BELFAST

The city of Belfast[9] was founded by Sir Arthur Chichester in 1603 (Bardon 1996: 71). It lies at the mouth of the River Lagan, a fact reflected in the Irish name *Béal Feirste* 'the mouth of the sandbank or ford'. Belfast was intended for English and Scots settlers. The present-day Catholic population, particularly in West Belfast, stems from those who migrated into the city from surrounding areas in search of work in the linen and cotton industries and later in ship-building which blossomed in the late nineteenth century and the first half of the twentieth century. However, throughout the eighteenth century Belfast was a small town on the west bank of the Lagan, with Ballymacarrett a separate settlement on the east bank. By 1821 the population was still only 37,000, by 1861 it had increased threefold to 121,000 and by the close of the nineteenth century it was 350,000, ten times its size at the beginning of the century (J. Milroy 1981: 22). By the middle of the twentieth century the population had risen to over 440,000 and then dropped off with people spreading into neighbouring towns such as Newtownabbey, Finaghy, Newtownbreda.

There are two main rises in population in the nineteenth century. The first is concentrated around the late 1840s: due to the Great Famine, many rural inhabitants moved into urban centres after the massive failure of the potato crop (this affected cities throughout Ireland, notably Dublin in the south). The second and more important reason was increasing industrialisation. This set in somewhat later in Ulster than in Great Britain. The mechanisation of linen production and the development of ship-building were the two main industrial developments in nineteenth-century Belfast. There was in-migration from all nine counties of Ulster. The area of contemporary Belfast is characterised by a conurbation which now stretches along the north shore of Belfast Lough at least to Newtownabbey in County Antrim and, on the south shore, at least to Holywood in County Down.

---

[9] In 1603, Chichester was granted Belfast Castle and surrounding lands and acquired escheated estates in Antrim, Down and on the Inishowen peninsula in Co. Donegal. He is also the founder of the Donegall family (note the spelling with two *ll*; not to be confused with the name of the county with a single *l*) and came from England as a professional soldier before the turn of the sixteenth century. He was made Lord Belfast in 1613.

Along the Lagan Valley, the city stretches to the south-west at least to Lisburn. The Lagan Valley is the hinterland of Belfast and is now served by a motorway which links up Belfast with the triad of towns Lurgan, Craigavon and Portadown to the south of Lough Neagh. There is a similarity between accents in the city and those in its hinterland to the south-west. The east of the city shows greater similarity with accents from rural North Down, an originally Scots area of set-tlement as opposed to the Lagan Valley which was settled largely by people from England.

5.5.1.1 Sources of Belfast English

The English spoken in Belfast is an amalgam of features which come from the two main forms of English in Ulster, along with some independent traits only found in the city. The following is a list of features which can be clearly attributed to one of the two main English-language sources in Ulster (J. Milroy 1981: 25f.). These are phonological in nature, on the syntax of Belfast English; see Finlay (1994) and A. Henry (1995, 1997).

Ulster English (Ulster Anglo-Irish) features

1. palatalisation of /k, g/ before /a/, /kjat/ for *cat*
2. dentalisation of /t, d/ before /r/, /bet̪ɚ/ for *better*
3. lowering and unrounding of /ɒ/, /pɑt/ for *pot*
4. ME /ɛ:/ realised as a mid vowel, /be:t/ for *beat*, /ʊ/ for /ʌ/ in *but*, *luck*, etc.
5. lowering of /ɛ/ to /æ/, *set* /sæt/
6. the use of /au/ before /l/ in monosyllables, /aul/ for *old*, also a feature of Lowland Scots

Ulster Scots features

1. raising of /æ/ to /ɛ/ before velars, /bɛk, bɛg/ for *back*, *bag*
2. raising of /æ/ to /ɛ/ after /k/ and residually after /g/, /kɛp, kɛs/ for *cap*, *castle*
3. short realisations of high vowels, /bit, but/ for *beet*, *boot*
4. lowering and possible centralisation of /ɪ/, /bɛt, sɛns/ or /bʌt, sʌns/ for *bit*, *sense*

Early Belfast English

When trying to determine what Belfast English was like in the formative period of the city's industrial expansion (mid nineteenth century) one is fortunate is having a book which has, as the express aim of its author, the description of non-standard features of English in and around the city along with suggestions about how to correct and avoid them. This is David Patterson's *The Provincialisms of Belfast and the Surrounding Districts Pointed out and Corrected* from 1860, which has been put to good use by linguists attempting to ascertain the profile of Belfast

English a century and a half ago (J. Milroy 1981: 26f.). In a way, Patterson is to Belfast what Sheridan is to Dublin, although the latter was writing nearly a century before.[10]

Without identifying them as such, Patterson notes a number of Ulster Scots features in Belfast such as *deaf* /diːf/, *soft* /saːft/, *pouch* /puːtʃ/. There are also pronunciations which are archaic, like *gold* /guːld/, which was also to be found in the south of the country (noted by Sheridan in the late eighteenth century). Some of Patterson's features are no longer present in Belfast English. An instance of this is the lengthening of /ɪ/ to /iː/ before velars: *brick* /briːk/, a feature almost lost today.

If not lost, then some features had a greater distribution in Patterson's day. The lowering of /ɛ/ to /a/ before /r/ is an example. This was much more widespread (as in the south of Ireland as well, see section 5.1.5): the words *serve*, *merchant*, *Derry*, for example, all had /ar/.

Patterson also notes the use of /ʌ/ for two sets of words, (i) those which quite recently have had their vowel shortened from /uː/ to /ʊ/, e.g. *took*, *shook*, *look*, *foot* and (ii) those with inherited Early Modern English /ʊ/ after labials and frequently before an historically velarised [ɫ] or /ʃ/, *put*, *pull*, *bush*. These pronunciations have persisted in Belfast despite the pressure to standardise English (J. Milroy 1981: 30).

There are traits of present-day Belfast English which are not the object of comment by Patterson, such as the use of a back [ɑ] before nasals or /d/ in words like *hand*, *man*, *bad*, *family*. This is normally taken to be an east Ulster Scots feature which spread first into east Belfast and then from there into the west of the city. Furthermore, Patterson does not comment on the merger of [ʍ] and [w] which makes word pairs like *whine* and *wine* homophones. This has led James Milroy to conclude that the merger had not taken place at the time of Patterson's study.

The characteristics of present-day Belfast vernacular speech are largely those which were the object of censure by Patterson. Some minor changes have taken place, in particular dialect input features have gained sociolinguistic significance in the city. The use of [ɑ] for /a/ before nasals or the lexical occurrence of [ʌ], usually greater for more colloquial registers, are examples.

Recessive features can nonetheless be observed. The palatalisation of /k, g/ before /a/, e.g. *car* /kjar/ and *gas* /gjas/, was fashionable in England in the

---

[10] Biggar (1897) is also a source of information, though somewhat later, and for Ulster in general. There is a section in this pamphlet entitled 'The Ulster vowels' which points out the lowering of short vowels, a prominent characteristic of Ulster speech of various types. Importantly, Biggar refers incidentally to the raising of /æ/ to /ɛ/ in the environment of velars: *ketch*, *thenk*, *plenk* are the spellings he uses for *catch*, *thank*, *plank* (p. 17). He also refers to the retraction to /ɑ/ of the same low vowel when in the environment of /m/, at least that is what seems to be implied by the spelling *mannyfest* for *manifest*. Many other features come in for mention, such as the palatal glides after /k, g/ and before /a/, the use of *ye* for the second-person-plural personal pronoun and the use of the past participle for the preterite, as in *I seen it*. Biggar also confirms the lack of *h*-dropping and the ubiquitous *r* in Ireland.

eighteenth century but died out later. The palatalisation was typical of English-derived forms of speech in Ulster and Belfast and it became stereotypical of Ulster English. With this heightened consciousness, the feature came to be avoided.

Degrees of vernacularity can be observed with variable pronunciations or variable numbers of tokens for certain segments. An instance of this is the variable use of /ɛː/ for /iː/ in words like *beat*, *weak* where the lower pronunciation is the more colloquial (Milroy and Harris 1980). This is similar to the south of Ireland where ME /ɛː/ was not raised to /iː/, the latter pronunciation being introduced to southern Irish English by supraregionalisation (see section 5.3).

James Milroy (1981: 32) notes a tendency in Belfast for speakers to reduce the distinctions made in the rural hinterland where their forefathers came from. The vowels in the words *fir*, *fur* and *fair* tend to merge for younger speakers (though only *fir* and *fur* have merged in more standard forms of English).

Equally, the distinction between /ɔː/ and /oː/ before /r/ tends to be lost so that word pairs like *horse* and *hoarse* become homophones with only the /oː/ vowel being used.

Intervocalic /ð/ before /r/ tends to be variably lost in words like *mother*, *brother*, *gather*, *northern*, increasing with informality of speech.

There is a difference in quality between the realisation of /aɪ/ before voiceless and voiced consonants respectively (J. Milroy 1981: 78). In a word like *pipe* [pɛɪp] the starting point is higher and the length of the diphthong shorter than in *five* [faˑɪv]. This is embryonically the situation which one has for mainland Canada with the phenomenon called Canadian Raising (Chambers 1973).[11]

5.5.1.2 Belfast English and social networks

Among linguists nowadays, knowledge of Belfast English is due to the pioneering work of James and Lesley Milroy who began investigating language use in the city in the mid 1970s. In the decades since, they have published a large number of articles and several books concerned with the social conditioning of language, introducing insights not hitherto formulated with their clarity and precision.

At the centre of the Milroys' work on Belfast English is the notion of social network. All speakers have a place in the network of their social environment. This network consists of ties of varying strength depending on the social bonds speakers entertain within their neighbourhood. There is a general assumption that for those on the lower end of the socio-economic scale the ties are stronger than for those further up this cline. Furthermore, networks can be defined by

---

[11] Gregg (1973) traces the development of long Middle English /iː/ through a number of stages of diphthongisation. He assumes that the underlying form is /əɪ/, which is changed into /aɪ/ by rule (before voiced segments). He links up those forms of rural Ulster Scots (his Scotch-Irish), which still have /iː/, with more standard varieties showing /əɪ/. He thus seeks to demonstrate, within a generative phonological framework, the validity of the derivation of /əɪ/ from /iː/. Because of the occurrence of /əɪ/ in Ulster Scots before voiced segments, Gregg does not favour tracing the Canadian dichotomy /əɪ/ # /aɪ/ to transfer from Ulster Scots, despite the significant numbers of Northern Irish and Scottish immigrants in Canada.

how dense and multiplex they are (L. Milroy 1987 [1980]: 20–2). For instance, if a speaker A not only knows other speakers B, C, D, E, etc. but the latter also know each other and evince similar linguistic behaviour, then the network is dense. If the individuals in a network are more isolated and not mutual acquaintances, then it shows low density. A network is multiplex if its members interact in more than one way, e.g. if members have a number of colleagues in their network with whom they spend their spare time, through communal neighbourhood activities or sports for example, then the network is multiplex because there is more than one factor uniting its members. A focussed and bound network can impose rigid linguistic norms on its members which in turn acquire a defining character, albeit an unconscious one, for the network itself. Such networks tend to be impervious to influence from outside, specifically from the prestigious norm of the society of which they are part. Speakers who engage in loose-knit networks, such as the suburban middle classes, are more exposed to the prestige norm. Because loose networks do not show clear defining features, these speakers adopt the norms of the socially prestigious standard (L. Milroy 1987 [1980]: 196). Conversely, working-class sections of society – those with strong networks – do not see middle-class speech as a model because their linguistic norms stem from within the network itself.[12]

Collecting data from close-knit networks presents certain difficulties, above all gaining acceptance from network members in order to elicit linguistic data. In order to penetrate a network, Lesley Milroy, who collected most of the Belfast data, established contact through 'a friend of a friend'. She was introduced into a network by someone who was already a member and the positive relationship with this member ensured acceptance by others in the network.

Certain generalisations about networks hold irrespective of their individual circumstances. The relative strength of a network depends on the weight accorded by speakers to two conflicting forces in society: *status* and *solidarity* (L. Milroy 1987 [1980]: 194–8). If speakers opt for status, then they are likely to have weak ties, as they try and move upwards on a social scale, striving to achieve professional status and economic success. Should speakers opt for solidarity, then they generally remain in their surroundings, maintaining ties with neighbours and participating in the life of the community. Solidarity is an aspect of social behaviour which has a linguistic dimension: speakers who demonstrate solidarity also exhibit allegiance to the vernacular norms of their community, frequently in contradistinction to those of the socially prestigious form of a language. The linguistic norms of a community are local whereas status features are diffuse and hold for a much wider area, typically for an entire country. The number of defining features of low-status, high-solidarity varieties is usually quite high.

---

[12] In J. Milroy (1991) the conclusion drawn from his examination of various phonological variables in Belfast is that, with the weakening of networks, there is a loss in phonological complexity as variation is not required to achieve high degrees of social identification. The social mobility characteristic of much of the middle classes has led to a weakening of network ties and the backgrounding of phonological variation.

The linguistic norms of such communities can be difficult, if not impossible, for outsiders to acquire. This aspect is regarded as intentional: the identity function of high-solidarity varieties implies that one can exclude those who are not native to the community within which the particular norms obtain. Dense multiplex network ties seem furthermore to hold primarily for young males. Women and middle-aged speakers in general tend to opt more for status and to tone down the linguistic signs of strong network ties.

A discussion of networks necessitates that these be put in relation to the notion of class. Two features of networks need to be highlighted in this connection. Networks are different from social classes. Class is an abstract characterisation of social status whereas a network consists of those individuals who are acquainted with each other. There is, of course, a correlation with class inasmuch as people in a network usually belong to a single socioeconomic group and those in the strongest networks tend to be lowest on this scale. Given their relatively small scale, networks form a consensus-based microlevel within society. The bonding within a class, on the other hand, is achieved through similarity in sociopolitical outlook and not by identification with a certain locale.

The Belfast investigations

The insights into sociolinguistic behaviour just sketched were gained by a close study of the following three areas of Belfast.

(14) a. Ballymacarrett   (Protestant east Belfast)
      b. The Hammer   (Lower Shankhill Road, Protestant west-central Belfast)
      c. Clonard   (Lower Falls Road, Catholic west-central Belfast)

The three areas are different in the social importance they attach to certain features. For instance, the palatalisation of /k, g/, as in *cap* /kjap/ and *gap* /gjap/, is generally regarded as a rural feature of Ulster English. In Belfast it is found mostly with older males (aged forty to fifty-five), chiefly in Catholic west Belfast. In the eastern section of the city, which has had a largely Ulster Scots input from north Co. Down and where the palatalisation is not an indigenous feature, this trait is avoided, as can be seen from its percentual representation in the data collected by the Milroys.

(15) Clonard   62% palatalisation
      Hammer   14%
      Ballymacarrett   0%   (J. Milroy 1981: 94)

This pattern would also seem to apply to the dental realisation of /t/ before /r/ in unstressed syllables, i.e. the pronunciation [bʌt̪ɚ] rather than [bʌtɚ] for *butter*, which occurred with older males more than with younger men and women in west Belfast (Clonard and Hammer).

The raising of /a/ before velars, as in *bag* /bɛg/, is quite common and is more frequent in west Belfast than in east Belfast; young males in east Belfast seem

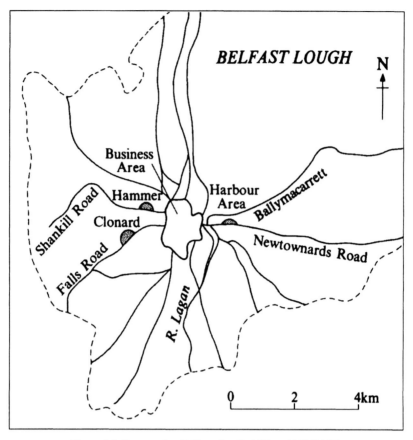

Figure 5.1 Present-day Belfast after L. Milroy 1987 [1980]

to have lost this raised vowel entirely (J. Milroy 1981: 31), perhaps as the result of peer-group pressure. With the variable (ʌ) James Milroy found that young males display vernacular loyalty and preserve this dialect feature in words such as *pull* [pʌl] (J. Milroy 1981: 95f.).

Correlates of community structure. The heading for this paragraph is taken from an early article by Lesley Milroy (1976) in which she analysed the relation between realisations of three phonological variables, (th), (ʌ) and (a) within the framework of the network model of language ties in society. With regard to (th), Lesley Milroy notes that the deletion of [ð] intervocalically, as in *brother* [brʌ ər], has been a stable marker of lower-class speech for some time and shows little change. On the other hand, (ʌ) would appear for young men, particularly in Catholic west Belfast, to have overcome its inherent stigma in the community and be used more frequently. The situation with (a) is more complex as there is a phonetically conditioned front raising after velars and back raising before nasals, as in *hand* [hɑnd]. It, too, is subject to socially determined variation within the phonotactic constraints just mentioned.

The insight here is that it is not just the use of one realisation as opposed to another that is sociolinguistically significant, but the numbers of tokens for a given realisation are relevant, i.e. both the qualitative and the quantitative aspects of a variable are important within a social network.

Beyond Belfast. Confirmation of the Milroys' insights was gained a few years later by Ellen Douglas-Cowie (see Douglas-Cowie 1978) whose work represents a deliberate departure from sociolinguistic investigations of language in large urban centres. She concentrated on the use of English in a small community – Articlave, Co. Derry – and arrived at a number of conclusions after examining variables such as (1) – short *i* as in *bit* – and the diphthong (ai) – as in *time* (these show characteristic variation in Ulster speech, typically lowering of /ɪ/ to [ɛ] or [æ] and centralisation of the starting point of /ai/ [əɪ]; see above). The major correlation, according to Douglas-Cowie, is between relative standardness and social ambition on the one hand, and between community networks and vernacular norms on the other. This well-known investigation shows that sociolinguistic patterning on a small urban scale is essentially no different from that on a much larger scale.

Diffusion of change and network markers. Not only phonological phenomena are subject to sociolinguistic conditioning, the lexicon is equally affected, as James Milroy has shown in an article concerned with the extent to which variation in lexical realisation is determined by social factors (J. Milroy 1978). He examined alternants which involve the lowering of /ɛ/, and the raising of this vowel in some cases, as well as the fluctuation between /ʉ/ and /ʌ/ in items such as *pull* and *foot*. James Milroy also compared the distribution in the 1970s with that in 1860, when Patterson's work on Belfast appeared, and noted that the environments for variation have effectively been reduced.

This reduction took place because most of the words which previously had an /ʌ/ realisation migrated to the lexical set with /ʉ/ by a process of diffusion: gradually nearly all the words shifted from the non-standard pronunciation with the low vowel /ʌ/ to that with the regionally standard high central vowel /ʉ/. By 1975, only eighteen words were still found with the alternation /ʌ/ ~ /ʉ/. It might be assumed that this was the tail end of an S curve and that with time the remaining instances with /ʌ/ would be lost. But in fact the small /ʌ/ class had become significant as a network marker for the vernacular community, especially among young males (L. Milroy 1987 [1980]: 189). On reflection, this makes linguistic sense: a small class of elements is more likely to attain sociolinguistic value than a much larger class; hence the reduction in the number of /ʌ/ realisations, for words belonging to the /ʉ/ class in the regional standard, would seem to have led to marker status being assigned to them. Here the general implication is that residual lexical sets may have not only a phonetic motivation – as with those words which have /ʊ/ in standard English in environments with phonetic rounding – but they may also have a social motivation as a clearly recognisable and easily memorised small group of words.

The converse can also be found. In Belfast English there is a class of words which show either an [ɛ] or an [æ] variant in words which have /e/ in RP.

The lower vowel was once categorical as a realisation. But now it is only found before monosyllables with a final voiced stop or fricative in conservative speech in Clonard, e.g. *dead* [dæd] and *bless* [blæs] (L. Milroy 1987 [1980]: 190). At present, women appear to be using the incoming variant [ɛ▴] more than men. A reason might be that this pronunciation does not function as a network marker (contrast this with /ʌ/ above). Instead it is becoming associated with young female speech in Ballymacarrett.

The course and nature of language change. The examination of closed networks has also posed the question of how language change occurs and spreads. James Milroy (1992a: 17) states 'linguistic change is to be understood more broadly as a change in consensus on norms of usage in a speech community'. In a study from 1985 the Milroys addressed the question of spread and maintained that innovations in a speech community may well be transferred from one group to another by persons who have weak ties in each group and hence straddle the divide between both. Furthermore, James and Lesley Milroy see evidence for the assumption that in a situation of social mobility and instability the network ties are weak and hence linguistic change is liable to be rapid. For western-style societies, the people who contract many weak ties are typically in a position to diffuse linguistic innovations.

The nature of language change is a recurrent theme in later articles by both authors. J. Milroy (1993), for instance, concerns himself with the theory of sound change from a sociolinguistic perspective. He begins by reviewing the standpoint of the Neogrammarians and challenges their notion that sound change is phonetically gradual but lexically abrupt because their approach is dichotomous, non-social, and based on written documents rather than on spoken language. Instead, he views language change as a shift in community norms. He also distinguishes, here as elsewhere, between speaker innovation on the one hand and change in the system on the other, presenting data from Belfast to support this distinction. The Neogrammarian view of sound change may appear to be the correct model if a particular instance of change is carried through to its conclusion. If all the words with a particular phonetic value shift to a new value then in the end one can say that sound A changed into sound B, for instance, if all instances of /ʊ/ shifted to /ʌ/. The phonetically recalcitrant exceptions in standard English can be accommodated within the Neogrammarian framework because it allows for phonetic blocking of a change, but the socially determined residual set of words with /ʌ/ in Belfast cannot be accounted for within the essentially non-social view of language change of the Neogrammarians.

5.5.1.3 Wider implications of the Milroy studies

The work of the Milroys on vernacular speech in Belfast has had wider implications for linguistic studies, above all for the development of phonological norms in English. James Milroy has devoted his attention to the relationship between standard and vernacular norms, stressing the uniform nature of the standard and the essentially variant structure of vernaculars, but where the rules governing the variation are understood by speakers using this form of language. He has stressed that speakers use vernaculars not standard forms and that this viewpoint is beneficial in examining English historically, e.g. in accounting for fluctuation in the realisation of *a* from Middle English onwards.

The nature of mergers. The apparent reversal of the MEAT/MATE merger is a matter which James Milroy has looked at against the background of the Belfast studies. The issue here is how the Middle English vowels in the MEAT/MATE/MEET lexical sets developed so as to produce the present-day situation where MEAT and MEET go together, although it would appear that MEAT and MATE were once homophonous. Is this a case of a reversed merger? On the basis of evidence from Belfast, James Milroy and John Harris, looking at the Early Modern English period, claim that (1) orthoepic reports on mergers may be unreliable because they are not phonetically accurate enough; (2) speakers may believe that lexical sets have merged, although their realisations are slightly different; (3) biuniqueness, the notion that one phoneme has a unique phonetic realisation which is not shared by another phoneme, may not in fact hold; (4) phonetic change may well have been gradual (by a process of lexical diffusion); and (5) the realisation of vowels may have had additional characteristics, such as a final in-glide (typical of many forms in Belfast) which in fact separated vowels with the same height level. For a further discussion of the issues dealt with here, see Hickey (2004f).

Standard versus vernacular. This is an area of investigation which James Milroy has expanded consistently in his research. In J. Milroy (1982), for instance, he focusses his attention on the notion of a 'complex' variable and the difficulties of giving a correct quantificational account of such variables. He deals with many pitfalls, on the one hand with the rounding of /a/ after /w/, which is in his view a *correctional feature*, determined by the presence of this rounding in the standard, and on the other hand with the rounding in the environment of labials or nasals, e.g. of the vowel in *man*, *hand*, *bad* in Belfast English, which is a *vernacular characteristic*. James Milroy concludes that non-standard segmental phonology is more complex than standard phonology and discusses the theoretical issues which arise from this, such as whether speakers 'know' that /a/ is a low-front vowel when they do not pronounce it as such.

What is prestige? All too often vague references to 'prestige' are made in linguistic treatments of language change. James Milroy has criticised that the notion of prestige has often been appealed to in explanations of language variation/change and that such appeals frequently lead to contradiction and confusion. Instead he suggests that explanations based on the identity function of language would appear to be more successful (J. Milroy 1992b).

The nature of the vernacular. The work of the Milroys in Belfast has heightened linguists' awareness of the vernacular. Its norms oppose standardisation and prescription because they serve the function of identity maintenance. Such norms are not codified but are transmitted orally. In this context, one must distinguish between grammaticality, typical of standards, and norms of usage, characteristic of vernaculars. Furthermore, in-group variation can be quite complicated and not necessarily accessible to outsiders. Supralocal varieties, which tend towards koinés, are simpler in structure than more local varieties (see section 5.3) because variation has no in-group function there. Lower-status varieties of language are dynamic and the locus of change.

Gender and networks. The interaction of gender and network structure on a phonological level is the concern of Lesley Milroy (1981). She defines clearly how a network score is arrived at for an individual by considering membership in a high-density, territorially based group, ties of kinship, similar place of work to others from this group and voluntary association with others from the group in leisure time. Lesley Milroy then examines three vernacular variables indicative of network strength in Belfast, (a), (th) and (ʌ). She concludes that the first two variables are important as gender markers for men but as network markers for women. The last variable is a weaker gender marker but important to men as a network marker, which shows the essential interdependence of both types of marking and the complex relationship between them.

Language attitudes. A region like Ulster, which contains a variety of accents and which relates to other regions which surround it, is a good testing ground for attitudes towards accent (Millar 1990). In L. Milroy and McClenaghan (1977) a number of accents were looked at from the point of view of attitude. These were (1) Scottish, (2) southern Irish, (3) Received Pronunciation and (4) Ulster English. The informants were asked to evaluate the speakers with these accents in terms of positive characteristics such as intelligence, ambition, confidence, etc. Both the RP and the southern Irish accents were rated highly, possibly due to the belief that these countries possess power and influence over Ulster. Scottish and Ulster accents received lower but similar ratings which would suggest that speakers perceive an affinity between the groups which use these accents.

5.5.2 ENGLISH IN DERRY

The city of Derry[13] has a population of over 95,000 (going on the 1991 census) and is ethnically over 70 per cent Catholic as opposed to Belfast which has a majority Protestant population. There is a large degree of segregation in terms of residence for the two communities: east of the River Foyle, which divides the city, the inhabitants are largely Protestants and west of the river they are almost exclusively Catholic. The segregation increased greatly during the decades of

---

[13] 'Londonderry' refers to the town and county of Derry and is used by Protestants in Northern Ireland and by the English. The prefix 'London-' goes back to a charter in 1613 given to London companies commissioned with the task of transporting English settlers there and initiating commercial activity in the city. The politically sensitive use of the longer and shorter form of the name has its roots in the confessional polarisation of Northern Ireland and is of recent date. To avoid using either one or the other form, inhabitants of the city and others in the province often refer to it as 'stroke city'. The city's name is an anglicisation of Irish *doire* 'oak-grove', a common name, or element of a name, in the north and south of the country.

Table 5.7. *Changes in Derry English (DE)*

Variable	Supraregional NIE	Older general DE	Recent local DE	Lexical set
(ʌ)	[ʉ]	[ʌ]	[ʉ]	PULL (1)
(e)	[e]	[ɪ]	[iə]	FACE (2)
(ð)	[ð]	Ø	[l]	MOTHER (3, 4)

sectarian violence which began in the late 1960s. This segregation applies to all spheres of life: occupation and leisure time activities apart from place of residence. Contact between the two communities is kept to a minimum by the members themselves to avoid hostility resulting from sectarian friction.

The only research on the English of Derry city is that by McCafferty (see various items in the references section), apart from one study of intonation (McElholm 1986). The city has a special status within Northern Ireland as it is on the one hand the second largest and on the other the only major city with a Catholic majority. It is understandable that it would receive innovations which arise in Belfast but also that the Catholic majority in the city might well show an inherent resistance to these. A number of changes are recorded for Derry as seen in the following list (see also table 5.7).

1. A gradual replacement of [ʌ] by [ʉ] (standard in Northern Ireland) which has been ongoing in Ulster and Scotland for some time.
2. A widespread vernacular innovation, originating in the east of Northern Ireland, which involves older [ɪ] being replaced by [iə] in the FACE lexical set and both of these alternating with supraregional [e].
3. A vernacular innovation by which intervocalic [ð] is being dropped. This appears to have originated in the east in the last hundred years.
4. A localised Derry English vernacular innovation which sees the same intervocalic [ð] realised as a lateral [l].

Changes according to ethnicity. Given the inverse proportion of ethnic communities in Derry compared to the rest of Northern Ireland, the question of ethnicity and change is of particular interest. This question has of course been treated before. Todd (1984) presented material, which the scholarly community regarded as inconclusive, if not to say inaccurate (see Millar 1987b). However, McCafferty's examination of Derry English (McCafferty 1998a, 1998b) is on an entirely different footing. He has carried out a statistically based sociolinguistic investigation of speech in different communities and across different generations in the city and published his results in a number of papers and a monograph.

McCafferty (1999, 2001) maintains that there is a tendency for the SQUARE and NURSE lexical sets to merge, a feature spreading from east Ulster and typical

Table 5.8. *Changes in Derry English according to ethnicity*

Ethnic group				Source
Protestants	[oːr]	>	[ɔːr]	East Ulster
	[ɛr]	>	[əːr]	— — —
	[e, ɪ]	>	[iə]	— — —
Catholics	[- ð -]	>	[- l -]	Local to Derry city

of the Protestant middle class. For this group a lack of quality distinction with the NORTH and FORCE lexical sets is also found.

The shift of older [ɪ] to [iə] in the FACE lexical set is taken to be characteristic of younger Protestants. Protestant changes are in general incoming innovations which are spreading from east Ulster, i.e. from the Belfast conurbation. In this case the changes for the Protestants in Derry have arisen through the suprare-gionalisation of Belfast innovations.

The only *leading* change among the Catholics in Derry is the shift of intervo-calic [ð] to a lateral [l], a change which is clearly attested in the recordings for *A Sound Atlas of Irish English* (Hickey 2004a: 52f.). The Protestants in Derry have no vernacular innovations of their own.

5.5.3 ENGLISH IN COLERAINE

The town of Coleraine is situated in the far north of Ireland, in a relatively rural and Protestant area of north-east Co. Derry. It is also the seat of the major campus of the University of Ulster, founded in 1964 (then called the New University of Ulster). The English of this town has been investigated by Rona Kingsmore and the results made available in the revised, published version of her PhD thesis, *Ulster Scots Speech: A Sociolinguistic Study* (1995). This is an examination of phonological variation in the speech of the urban community of Coleraine by considering a small group of variables, (ing), (t) and (l). Her book applies the methods for urban sociolinguistics developed chiefly by William Labov in the 1960s.

For her study, Kingsmore investigated the use of English within families. In section 4, 'The family model' (Kingsmore 1995: 53–63), she elaborates on the technique used to collect data. She posited the family as the basic structural unit and interviewed three generations in five working-class families interlinked by neighbourhood and/or friendship ties, the common denominator of each family being an adolescent or young adult member. Her goal was to explore evidence for sound change using this basis and in particular to look at male and female language. Her findings show that gender differences would appear to take priority over class differences. Investigating the principle non-standard variants of the (t) variable in her community, under the influence of metropolitan speech from Belfast, she established that men prefer [d] while women tend towards the glottal stop [ʔ]. Thus the latter group cannot simply be viewed as using more standard, higher-status forms. Kingsmore concludes that features of female speech, initially employed for demarcation vis-à-vis men, could become status markers in time. Kingsmore also concludes that patterns of speech are spreading from Belfast out to Coleraine and differentially affect various social groups.

5.5.4 ENGLISH IN DUBLIN

Dublin has been the political and cultural centre of Ireland from the earliest days of English settlement. The English were quick to recognise the importance of the city for the government of the country and took possession of it shortly after their arrival. As of 1171, the city stood under the control of the English. In the early years of the conquest the linguistic landscape of Ireland was more diverse than later. From the late twelfth to the fourteenth century at least four languages must be assumed for Ireland: (1) native Irish, (2) English, (3) Anglo-Norman and (4) Latin in which, beside Anglo-Norman, many documents of the cities were written (Hogan 1927: 30f.). Later both Latin and Anglo-Norman fell into disuse. Neither language survived after the fifteenth century.

Dublin was not founded by the Anglo-Normans. The oldest references to a settlement at the mouth of the Liffey date from the second century AD (Moore 1965: 9). The Vikings expanded the settlement by building fortifications and several buildings in the ninth and tenth centuries (Moore 1965: 10; Brady and Simms 2001: 18–39). The Anglo-Normans, on the other hand, did not, in the beginning, make any significant contribution to the architecture of Dublin. They formed a rural aristocracy which was interested in the land of the Irish (Mitchell 1976: 183ff.). The areas which they occupied were chiefly in the east, north-east and south east with some settlements in the west, for instance, in Limerick and Galway.

The English king entertained a legal advisor, the 'king's lieutenant', who resided in Dublin and who represented his interests in Ireland. In later centuries this position developed into that of 'viceroy' who quite naturally was posted in Dublin. Because of the centralised government of the time the city of Dublin increased in importance (Wallace 1973: 30) and the English language was able to establish itself there. There developed a permanent presence with an English or Anglo-Norman speaking clergy and ruling class. Evidence for these groups is to be found in such buildings as St Patrick's cathedral (Ossory-Fitzpatrick 1977 [1907]: 56; Brady and Simms 2001: 47) and Christ Church in Dublin.

The presence of the Anglo-Normans in Dublin is not a contradiction of their primarily rural settlement policy. The conquest of Ireland shows a typical pattern which is a mixture of the rural and the urban. The Anglo-Normans won large stretches of land from the Irish in their initial campaigns in the east, south-east and north-east. This land gain was followed by the development of bases with typical Norman castles (Moody and Martin 1967: 137). Later, these expanded to minor settlements with the arrival of craftsmen and artisans (Graham 1977: 30). The English king granted city rights to these Anglo-Normans settlements in charters. It was only in the case of Dublin, and some of the cities on the east coast, such as Wexford and Waterford, that these settlements had existed prior to the arrival of the Anglo-Normans. Nonetheless, charters were granted in these cases as well, such as that for Dublin in 1171 or 1172 by Henry II (Graham 1977: 32; Boran 2000: 23–7). Henry recognised the necessity for a centralised government in Ireland for two reasons. On the one hand, he was experiencing difficulties in restraining his own vassals from plundering the land of the Irish. On the other hand, the Norman areas were claimed by the Irish despite the 'Treaty of Windsor' of 1175 between Henry and Rory O'Connor, the Irish leader of the time. Henry retained the area around Dublin with its hinterland (Moody and Martin 1967: 135). Later John II had Dublin Castle built which served as the seat of English government in Ireland up to the twentieth century.

The area around Dublin received the name 'Pale' (Moore 1965: 14; Curtis 1939: 245; Clarke, Dent and Johnson 2002: 29f.) and was the centre of English in Ireland. It is remarkable that quite a number of decrees specifying the use of English for official purposes (Hogan 1927: 29) were issued. These decrees should be seen in connection with the re-gaelicisation of the country which set in during the fourteenth and fifteenth centuries. The area of the Pale was not untouched by the expansion of the rebellious Irish tribal leaders (Moody and Martin 1967: 159). However, a military victory over Dublin was never achieved. Rather what occurred was an ever-increasing gaelicisation of the originally English section of the population of Ireland.

This gaelicisation peaked in the fifteenth and early sixteenth centuries and was finally reversed with the destruction of the Gaelic social order in the early seventeenth century, above all in Ulster. This break is the external justification for the division of the history of Irish English into an early period from the late twelfth century until 1600 and a second, modern period from 1600 to the present day. Many authors assume that with the reversal of Gaelic fortunes in the early seventeenth century, newer varieties of English were brought to Ireland which did not represent continuity with the older varieties (P. L. Henry 1958: 58ff.). However, in Dublin there is evidence, above all in phonology (Hickey 2002b), that many features of local Dublin English go back further than the seventeenth century. Knowledge of English in the capital before this derives from the language of Dublin municipal manuscripts (Waterhouse 1909: xlvii, lxvii). These began to appear in the middle of the fifteenth century. Up to this time texts were composed in Latin or French: 1451 is the date given by Hogan (1927: 30); P. L. Henry (1958: 64) mentions the year 1447. It is not coincidental that the features listed in table 5.9 coincide with many of those ascertained for the *Kildare Poems* (see section 2.3).

The documentation of Dublin English is unfortunately quite scanty. What little material there is can be found in the city records just mentioned. These offer a glimpse of some archaic features of Dublin English which are still present in local Dublin English, such as 4 above. A few documents are available from the seventeenth century, especially for the area of Fingal to the north of the city: see the discussion in section 2.4.5.

Table 5.9. *Features of fifteenth-century Dublin English*

---

1. *t* and *d* in place of *th*
2. *u* and *v* in place of *w*
3. substitution of *t* for final *d*
4. deletion of stops after sonorants
5. raising of *a* to *o* before nasals
6. substitution of *sh* or *ss* for *s*
7. omission and erroneous insertion of *h*[a]

---

[a] This feature may be due to Anglo-Norman scribal practice and uncertainties about this.

Apart from non-fictional prose documents, one could consider the language of authors from Dublin. However, one cannot simply assume that this reflected the local speech of the capital. Authors like Jonathan Swift (1667–1745) or Richard Brinsley Sheridan (1751–1816) wrote in standard English. Nonetheless, there are glimpses of what contemporary Irish English, if not Dublin English, might have been like. For instance, Swift wrote two small pieces which purport to represent the English of the native Irish and the English planters of the early eighteenth century (*Irish Eloquence* and *Dialogue in Hybernian Stile*, Bliss 1976: 557). In this context it is worth noting that a certain amount of code-mixing (Irish and English) is also to be found among Irish writers during the eighteenth century (L. Mac Mathúna 2003), one of whom, Seán Ó Neachtain, was a contemporary of Swift (Ó Háinle 1986).

5.5.4.1 The late eighteenth and nineteenth centuries

The year 1781 saw the publication of *A Rhetorical Grammar of the English Language* by Thomas Sheridan (1719–88).[14] Sheridan was a self-appointed authority on language matters and also a well-known elocutionist who travelled widely in the British Isles. His grammar includes an appendix on the language of educated Dubliners and others, 'the gentlemen of Ireland' as he labels them. This he examines and corrects (laying out a series of rules to be observed by the Irish in order to speak English properly).

---

[14] Sheridan was born in Co. Cavan in 1719 and died in London in 1788. He enjoyed a chequered career as actor, lecturer and writer. The godson of Swift, he produced *The Works of Swift with Life* (18 volumes) in 1784. As a dramatist, Sheridan is known for one play, *Captain O'Blunder or The Brave Irishman* (1754), which he wrote as an undergraduate. He is also known as the manager of the Smock Alley Theatre in Dublin where he worked for some years. Apart from the grammar under consideration here, Sheridan is also the author of a successful *General Dictionary of the English Language* (1967 [1780], 2 volumes) and an earlier *A Course of Lectures on Elocution* (1970 [1762]). Probably on the grounds of these linguistic interests, Sheridan developed a close friendship with the lexicographer Dr Samuel Johnson. Thomas Sheridan is the father of the playwright Richard Brinsley Sheridan.

Although one can determine Sheridan's group of speakers easily, it is not so apparent just what he regarded as standard English and who is supposed to have spoken it. In the preface to his grammar he talks of 'our pronunciation' (1781: xxii) and refers to Johnson with regard to spelling (1781: xxiii). He furthermore notes that the pronunciation of English by the people in Ireland, Scotland and Wales can deviate from a standard, without offering any more specific information on what he regards this standard to be. His praising remarks on the correct pronunciation of the 'Augustan Age' in England (1781: xix) is of little help here. From this one can only conclude that Sheridan was prescriptivist and assumed a conservative variety of English as standard when assessing the English of the Irish.

Sheridan's brief treatment is nonetheless a valuable source of information on Dublin English more than two centuries ago. Among the features remarked on by him are the following.

1.   The pronunciation of *a* was /aː/ and not /eː/ in words like *patron, matron*.
2.   The pronunciation of English /ai/ from ME /iː/ was [əi] (assuming a correct interpretation of Sheridan's spellings) and this tallies with what is known from present-day Dublin English, e.g. *mine* [məin] for [main].
3.   There was an unshifted realisation of ME /ɛː/ and /eː/ as [ɛː] in words like *beat, leave, meet* which is in agreement with local Dublin English usage up to the beginning of the twentieth century at least.
4.   A realisation of /aː/ before former liquids as /ɔː/ as in *psalm* [sɔːm], *balm* [bɔːm] appears to have been current. This pronunciation is unknown nowadays though the back vowel before velarised /ɫ/ probably resulted in the pronunciations [baul] and [aul] which are still found for *bold* and *old* in colloquial registers today.

With regard to consonants, Sheridan remarks on 'the thickening (of) the sounds of *d* and *t* in certain situations'. By this one can assume that he is referring to the realisation of dental fricatives as stops, as found in Dublin English today. However, there is no hint in Sheridan of anything like a distinction between dental and alveolar stops.

Ebb and flow

Accepting Sheridan's characterisation of late eighteenth-century Dublin English implies that Dublin English showed a number of features which are unexpected, going on present-day forms of English in the city and in the south of Ireland as a whole.

(16)   a.   Raising of /æ/, *gather* > *gether*
       b.   Retraction and raising of /aː/, *psalm* > [sɔːm]

These realisations are all the more surprising as mainstream Irish English shows (1) a quite open variant of /æ/ and (2) a low central realisation corresponding to RP /ɑː/ (MacMahon 1998: 455f.), i.e. [aː]. At some stage after the eighteenth century these tendencies must have been reversed. By the early twentieth century they had disappeared as none of the authors, who began commenting on Irish English at this time, mention anything like these realisations. One can conclude that during the nineteenth century a reversal of the above raising tendencies occurred.

One possible explanation for this situation is that the raising became salient for speakers and that they then began avoiding it. Typically, this could have happened as a form of intergenerational dissociation, i.e. children, recognising that raising was a feature of their parents' speech, started avoiding it, reversing the trend and producing lowered realisations of /æ/ and /ɑː/ which is the situation in present-day Irish English.

This type of development could be termed 'ebb and flow' (Hickey 2002d) because it can lead to shifts going backwards and forwards rather than following a uniform trajectory in a single direction. Evidence for this view is found in the topical changes in Dublin English at present (outlined below) where the raising of low back vowels has become fashionable again as younger speakers avoid very open vowel realisations in words like *lot* [lɑt̪] and *thought* [t̪ɑːt̪].

The nineteenth century

Sheridan is not the only source of comments on Irish English during the past two centuries. The general study of English pronunciation by Alexander Ellis (1868–89) contains references to the pronunciation of Irish English in his time. Ellis is not, however, as valuable a source as Sheridan, not least because there is a period of nearly one hundred years between his work and that of Sheridan (vol. IV, published in 1874, contains the remarks on Irish English, Ellis 1874: 1234ff.). What is more serious, however, is the fact that Ellis mixes up various areas within Ireland in his comments. He includes remarks on the English of Belfast and Cork in the same sentence and does not always localise and identify the forms which he quotes. The reason for his choice of towns had to with his informants, above all David Patterson in Belfast, who published a description of Belfast speech in 1860; see section 5.5.1.1. Despite Ellis' somewhat confused presentation one can recognise typical features of Irish English. The most important of these can be listed as follows.

1. Dentalisation of alveolar stops before /r/ (1874: 1239, 2)[15]
2. Final devoicing with alveolars (1874: 1241, 1)
3. Exchange of sonorants (1874: 1241, 2)
4. Cluster simplification with /-ŋkθ/ (1874: 1241, 2)
5. /eː/ in the MEAT lexical set (1874: 1235, 2)
6. Vowel lowering before /r/ (1874: 1236, 2)
7. High vowel alternation (1874: 1238, 2)

Although there are no other studies dealing with English in Ireland at this time, many popular comments are found from the nineteenth century which confirm

---

[15] The numbers after the page references indicate the column on the particular page.

the features enumerated by Sheridan and Ellis. For instance, an English cartoon from 1829 (the year of Catholic emancipation, McGuire 1987: 103), ridiculing the Irish, has in one sentence the forms *ye*, *asy* and *crater*. The first shows the use of the former second-person-plural pronoun, the second and third show /eː/ for /iː/ and the third also indicates the reduction of unstressed syllables, here /-juər/ to /ər/. While such references are very general, they nonetheless confirm the genuineness of features which have long been viewed as salient traits of Irish English and, by implication, of Dublin English.

Rural input to Dublin English?

During the nineteenth century, especially in the years of the Great Famine (1845–8) and afterwards, large numbers of rural inhabitants passed through Dublin (Bertz 1975: 41f.) at the start of their journey of emigration to Britain, the New World and the southern hemisphere. A certain percentage of these people remained in Dublin and the population of the city grew at a time when the countryside was being abandoned. In all, Dublin expanded by about 10 per cent in the years during and immediately after the famine (Dudley Edwards with Hourican 2005: 219).

It is difficult to assess the linguistic contribution of this segment of the population as it clearly had only low social status and was hence not recorded. However, one possible influence of speakers from the west of Ireland could have been the introduction of a dental stop realisation in the THIN lexical set. Local Dublin English had, and still has, an alveolar realisation for the first sound in this word, but the later supraregional standard of the south, which has its origins in middle-class Dublin usage from the early twentieth century, shows a dental stop in THIN. In the west of Ireland, particularly for speakers of Irish, a dental realisation was and is also found in this lexical set (de Bhaldraithe 1945: 25ff.). The reason for this is that the non-palatal /t/ in (western) Irish is dental and, for these speakers, it was, and is, the best fit for the initial sound in THIN. The adoption of this realisation by the middle classes in Dublin, via the in-migrants from the west, would have had the advantage of 'demerging' words like *thinker* and *tinker*, which have clearly not been homophones in middle-class Dublin English since the late nineteenth century, even if they were before.

The re-emergence of a distinction between dental and alveolar stops in Dublin English raises the question of whether one is dealing with a genuine case of merger reversal. In the history of English there have been similar instances such as the distinction between *point* and *pint*, *boil* and *bile*, etc. (MacMahon 1998: 413f.) which now exists for most dialects of English but did not always do so. In the latter case, the usual assumption is that those varieties which had the merger reversed it by adopting the distinction between /ɔɪ/ and /aɪ/ from other varieties. The parallel in Dublin English would be the adoption of the distinction within the area of coronals – that between dental and alveolar stops – from the western in-migrants into Dublin.

Apart from this unsubstantiated case, there is no obvious mixture of inputs in Dublin in contradistinction to Belfast, which has an Ulster Scots and an Ulster English component both of which played a significant role in its genesis (J. Milroy 1981).

5.5.4.2 Present-day Dublin English

The city of Dublin lies at the mouth of the river Liffey in the centre of the east coast, and spreads along the shores of the horseshoe shape of Dublin bay. The suburbs, which have increased dramatically since the 1960s, reach down to Bray and beyond into Co. Wicklow in the south, to the west in the direction of Maynooth and to the north at least to Swords, the airport and beyond. The Dublin conurbation now encompasses nearly a third of the population of the Republic of Ireland, i.e. well over one million inhabitants.

Like any other modern city, Dublin shows areas of high and low social prestige. There is a clear divide between the north and the south side of the city. The latter is regarded as more residentially desirable (with the exception of Howth and its surroundings on the peninsula which forms the north side of Dublin bay). Within the south, there is a cline of prestige with the area around Ballsbridge, Donnybrook and Montrose enjoying high status. This is the area of certain key complexes like the Royal Dublin Society (an important exhibition and event centre in the capital) and the national television studios RTE (Radio Telefís Éireann, 'Irish Radio and Television') and of the national university (University College Dublin) in Belfield. This entire area is known by its area number, Dublin 4. Indeed this number has given its name to a sub-accent within Dublin English known as the 'D4 accent' which shows the major changes in pronunciation which took place in the late 1980s and 1990s. The less prestigious parts of the city are known by their district names such as the Liberties in the centre of the city, immediately north of the River Liffey (now largely gentrified) and Ballymun, the only suburb in Ireland with high-rise flats and associated with adverse social conditions.

Although English has been present in Dublin for upwards of 800 years, the degree of consciousness of the language has not led to a term for it developing. In not having a designation for its own variety of English, Dublin contrasts with many large cities in England such as London with Cockney, Liverpool with Scouse or Newcastle with Geordie.

Local Dublin English

In the area of vowels the clearest traits of local Dublin English are the centralisation of the /aɪ/ diphthong, the fronting of /aʊ/, the over-long realisation of phonemically long vowels, the realisation of historically short vowels before /r/ and that of Early Modern English short /ʊ/ (see table 5.10).

Table 5.10. *Vowel realisations in local Dublin English*

1. Centralisation of /aɪ/
    time   [təɪm] – [təʲəm]
2. Fronting of /aʊ/
    down   [dæʊn] – [dɛʊn]
3. Over-long vowels with frequent disyllabification
    school   [sku:ˑl] – [sku:əl] – [sku:ʷəl]
    mean   [mi:n] – [mi:ˑən] – [mi:ʲən]
4. Historically short vowels before /r/
    circle   [ˈsɛ:k], *first* [fʊ:(ɹ)s(t)]
5. Early Modern English short /ʊ/
    Dublin   [ˈdʊblən]

In the area of consonants there are equally clear features. Some are unique to local Dublin English and others are extensions of features found in more mainstream varieties.

1.   Alveolar stops for dental fricatives
As mentioned above (see section 5.4.6), the dental fricatives of British English correspond to dental stops in supraregional Irish English. The standard wisdom on why this is the case runs as follows. In Irish there is a systemic distinction between a palatal and non-palatal articulation for all consonants (bar /h/). The Irish who acquired English in adulthood during language shift used, for the fricatives of English, the nearest equivalents in Irish. These were the dental allophones of the non-palatal stops of Irish (Bliss 1979: 232; Hogan 1927: 71ff.).[16] The alveolar plosives of English were thus equated with the palatal stops of Irish and in the course of time, with increasing distance from Irish, these were depalatalised in English.

(17)   Irish   English
    a. /t, d/ [t̪, d̪]   →   [t̪, d̪]   (no alteration)
    b. /tʲ, dʲ/   →   [t, d]   (depalatalisation)

This equivalence led, however, to slightly different results in different regions of Ireland because of the manner in which palatal and non-palatal stops are realised in Irish. The realisation of Irish non-palatal stops as dentals holds for the west and north. In the south-west and south the situation is different as alveolar realisations are found here (Hogan 1927: 72). The alveolar allophones also occur in Deise Irish, previously found in Co. Waterford in the south-east. Information about

---

[16] They are termed 'fan' stops in the older literature because the area of contact immediately behind the teeth is relatively large (the contact is laminal rather than apical) and there is a traditional convention of transcribing them with small capitals, e.g. *thin* [TɪN] and *this* [Dɪs].

Irish on the east coast, where it died out some considerable time ago (Wagner 1958: xxvii), is very scarce (T. F. O'Rahilly 1932: 260) and not of any value in the current context. What one does have, however, is a continuous band of English dialects which stretch from Waterford in the south-east up to Dublin, an area which corresponds to the original settlement area with an unbroken tradition of English from the first period.[17]

On the east coast local urban varieties show alveolar stops in the THIN and THIS lexical sets. Rural forms of Irish English have alveolars in a geographical area which stretches across the south to Co. Kerry and perhaps up as far as Co. Clare. The upshot of these considerations is that, for local Dublin English, the alveolar stops in the THIN and THIS lexical sets represent an archaic feature which is also present in conservative varieties of English outside Dublin to the east and south (Hickey 2001b). Hogan (1927: 71f.) notes that the alveolar stops are found in seventeenth-century plays (assuming that *t, d* represented [t, d]) and also in the Dublin City Records (from the first period, i.e. before 1600) where the third-person-singular ending *-th* appears as *-t*.[18]

The acoustic sensitivity of the Irish to the shift from dental to alveolar derives not least from the merger which can result from it. To Irish ears the retraction of the dental stops to an alveolar position is immediately noticeable and stigmatised because it is typical of low-prestige speech.[19]

(18)   Mainstream Dublin English   Local Dublin English
    a. *thinker* ['tɪŋkɚ]   *thinker, tinker* ['tɪŋkɚ]
    b. *tinker* ['tɪŋkɚ]
    c. *breathe* [bɹiːd̪]   *breathe, breed* [bɹiːd]
    d. *breed* [bɹiːd]

2. Cluster reduction

The simplification of consonantal syllable codas, particularly of stops after fricatives or sonorants, is a good indicator of local Dublin English. Intermediate registers may have a glottal stop as a trace of the stop in question. This feature is typical of Dublin English. In other varieties in the Republic the tendency is

---

[17] In Irish by this stage there were no dental fricatives although these had survived as lenited forms of dental stops until the end of the Middle Irish period (thirteenth century, T. F. O'Rahilly 1932: 65).

[18] According to Hogan, alveolar realisations are common in rural varieties in the south and south-west of Ireland (an observation confirmed by Hickey 2004a). Here they are probably a contact phenomenon deriving ultimately from the realisation of non-palatal /t, d/ in Irish. Hogan also remarks on the dental stops which are found in present-day Irish English (Hogan 1927: 71f.). According to Ó Baoill (1990), the use of alveolar stops is found in a widespread area throughout Munster and South Leinster where he assumes that the pronunciation of Irish /t, d/ as [t, d] was responsible for this. He also points out that the alveolar stops are found in Dublin city (1990: 159f.). See Lunny (1981) for a consideration of this question in the context of south-west Cork Irish (Ballyvourney).

[19] Joyce (1979 [1910]: 2f.) comments on the use of alveolar for dental stops and remarks that this is an older and stigmatised pronunciation which should be avoided.

not to delete the stop in this position but to retain it and, if voiced, to devoice it, e.g. *bend* [bɛnt]. The Dublin phenomenon is noticeable after /n, l, s/: *pound* [pɛʊn(ʔ)], *belt* [bɛl(ʔ)], *last* [læːs(ʔ)].

3.   Further reduction of lenited /t/

The lenition of /t/ to [ṱ] is not continued in non-local Dublin English beyond the initial stage with one or two lexicalised exceptions (see discussion in section 5.4.3). The extension beyond the apico-alveolar fricative is characteristic of local Dublin English.

5.5.4.3   Change in Dublin English

For the discussion of Dublin English in the present section a twofold division, with a further subdivision, is necessary. The first division comprises those speakers who use the historically continuous vernacular in the capital. The term 'local' is intended to capture this and to emphasise that these speakers show strongest identification with traditional Dublin life of which the local accent is very much a part. The reverse of this is 'non-local' which refers to sections of the metropolitan population who do not identify with what they see as a narrow and restricted local culture. This group then subdivides into a larger, more general section, labelled 'mainstream', and a further group which perhaps more clearly rejects a confining association with low-prestige Dublin. This group is labelled 'new'.[20]

(19)   1. *local* Dublin English
　　　 2. *non-local* Dublin English
　　　　　 a. *Mainstream* Dublin English
　　　　　 b. *New* Dublin English

When considering change in contemporary Dublin English the group which is most dynamic is that labelled 'new'. This group uses a variety which includes many features which up to twenty-five years ago did not exist in Dublin English. Before looking at these features, it is worthwhile considering why change should have taken place at all.

Dissociation as a form of language change

Dublin provides a typical scenario for language change given the following facts. Firstly, in the last three or four decades the city has expanded greatly in population. The increase in population has been due to both internal growth and migration into the city from the rest of the country. Secondly, it has undergone an economic boom in the last fifteen years or so, reflected in its position as an important financial centre and a location for many international firms which run their European operations from Dublin.

---

[20] In previous publications, I have used the term 'fashionable' for this group. This was justified several years ago when the group was smaller and more 'avantgarde'. By now (2007), it has become much more general and much larger so that a more neutral term like 'new' is preferable.

The increase in wealth and international position has meant that many young people aspire to an urban sophistication which is divorced from strongly local Dublin life. For this reason the developments in new Dublin English diverge from those in local Dublin English, indeed can be interpreted as a reaction to it. This type of linguistic behaviour can be termed 'dissociation' as it is motivated by the desire of speakers to hive themselves off from vernacular forms of a variety spoken in their immediate surroundings (Hickey 1998, 1999a). It is furthermore an instance of speaker-innovation leading to language change, much in the sense of James and Lesley Milroy (J. Milroy 1992a: 169–72; 1999; J. and L. Milroy 1997).

If people in Dublin do not wish to use the local vernacular then it might be thought that they would just adopt more a standard pronunciation of English, e.g. RP from Britain. But in the Irish context the adoption of an English accent is not acceptable. RP is not a pronunciation norm for the Irish, north or south. This makes the situation in Dublin different from that in Britain where dialect levelling and approximation to southern pronunciation models can be observed (Kerswill 2003). The situation is also different from instances like St John's, Newfoundland, which is a local capital and where younger speakers are adopting features of mainland Canadian English (D'Arcy 2005).

The changes in Dublin English involve both vowels and consonants. While the consonantal changes seem to be individual changes, those in the area of vowels represent a coordinated shift which has affected several elements. In keeping with previous publications (Hickey 1999a), these changes are labelled here the 'Dublin Vowel Shift'. To all appearances this started about twenty years ago (mid 1980s) and has continued to move along a recognisable trajectory. In essence, the change involves a retraction of diphthongs with a low or back starting point and a raising of low back vowels. Specifically, it affects the diphthongs in the PRICE/PRIDE and CHOICE lexical sets and the monophthongs in the LOT and THOUGHT lexical sets. The vowel in the GOAT lexical set has also shifted, probably as a result of the other vowel movements. See table 5.11 for a summary of the principal movements.

For reasons of space the exact origins of this change cannot be discussed here (see the detailed discussion in Hickey 2005: 45–72). Suffice it to say that the original shift was to be seen in the 'Dublin 4' accent of the 1980s which involved the movements shown in table 5.11, though not with quite the same degree of vowel raising. This accent provided the impetus for movement, but in the course of time it became old-fashioned. A more widespread variant developed in the 1990s which did not have the retraction and rounding of /a/ before /r/ in the START lexical set. The older pronunciation was often ridiculed as 'Dortspeak' (from 'Dartspeak', itself from 'Dart' = Dublin suburban railway line + 'speak') with [ɒr] for <ar> which in mainstream Dublin English is [ɑr] as in *start* [stɑrt]. In fact, the new pronunciation has a front realisation of /a/ before /r/, again probably as a reaction to the retraction and rounding of the stuffy 'Dublin 4' accent: *Dart* [dæːɹt]. The realisation of /a/ when not followed by /r/, i.e. in

Table 5.11. *Dublin Vowel Shift, principal movements*

1.	retraction of diphthongs with a low or back starting point					
	time [taɪm]	→	[tɑɪm]			
	toy [tɒɪ]	→	[tɔɪ], [toɪ]			
2.	a raising of low back vowels					
	cot	[kɒt̪]	→	[kɔt̪]		
	caught	[kɒːt̪]	→	[kɔːt̪]		[koːt̪]
				oɪ		oː
				↑		↑
	Raising			ɔɪ	ɔ	ɔː
				↑	↑	
				ɒɪ	ɒ	
	Retraction aɪ	→	ɑɪ			

the BATH lexical set, is [aː] in southern Irish English and remains so in both mainstream Dublin English and the new pronunciation. The older 'Dublin 4' accent had a retracted vowel in this set, i.e. [ɑː], which made it sound 'English' and 'snobbish'.

Another feature which has had a precarious continuation from the 1980s is the retracted onset for the /aɪ/ diphthong. In the recordings published in Hickey (2004a), the vast majority of female speakers under twenty-five had [aɪ] for this diphthong, even before voiced segments where [ɑɪ] was found in the 1990s (see Hickey 1999a for discussion). It would seem that pronunciations like *five* [fɑɪv], *time* [tɑɪm], *side* [sɑɪd] also became increasingly undesirable among young speakers, although they are still to be found with slightly older individuals.

In order to test these assumptions, a small survey with twenty-six persons (nine male and fifteen female) was done in 2005 (after the publication of Hickey 2005) to determine attitudes to features found in the older 'Dublin 4' accent. For the test two sentences were recorded, one with the older accent (Recording 1) and one with the vowel values of new Dublin English (Recording 2). Both recordings were done by the author and no attempt to emphasise or exaggerate the features of either accent was made. The results were as shown in table 5.12.

The test shows that the older 'Dublin 4' accent was generally perceived as 'affected' (85 per cent) and the new pronunciation was seen as 'not affected' by 92 per cent. There was no major difference in the assessment of the new pronunciation as 'quite normal' (38 per cent) or 'colloquial and relaxed' (54 per cent). The reason for this might well be that the test sentences did not contain the raised and shortened vowels of the new pronunciation, e.g. *fork* [foˈɹk], which might have provoked a different reaction especially from the test persons outside Dublin.

The conclusion to be drawn from these considerations is that new Dublin English has its origins in the older 'Dublin 4' accent inasmuch as speakers in

Table 5.12. *Reactions to vowel retraction and rounding*

Recording 1:	*She asked him to start the car.*	[ʃi ɑːskt hɪm tə stɒːɹt d̪ə kɒːɹ]
	She said 'Time is on his side.'	[ʃi sɛd tɑɪm ɪz ɒn hɪz sɑɪd]
Recording 2:	*She asked him to start the car.*	[ʃi aːskt hɪm tə staːɹt d̪ə kaːɹ]
	She said 'Time is on his side.'	[ʃi sɛd taɪm ɪz ɒn hɪz saɪd]

Do you think the speech in Recording 1 is:
• quite normal
• colloquial and relaxed
• somewhat affected

Do you think the speech in Recording 2 is:
• quite normal
• colloquial and relaxed
• somewhat affected

Results:

Recording 1	quite normal	colloquial/relaxed	somewhat affected	
Dublin	2	1	8	(total: 11)
Waterford	1	0	6	(total: 7)
Limerick	0	0	8	(total: 8)
Recording 2	quite normal	colloquial/relaxed	somewhat affected	
Dublin	5	5	1	(total: 11)
Waterford	3	4	0	(total: 7)
Limerick	2	5	1	(total: 8)

Table 5.13. *Comparative vowel values of local, mainstream and new Dublin English*

Lexical set	Local DE	Mainstream DE	New DE
PRICE	[əɪ]	[aɪ]	[aɪ]
CHOICE	[aɪ]	[ɒɪ]	[ɔɪ], [oɪ]
THOUGHT	[ɑː]	[ɒː]	[ɔː], [oː]
GOAT	[ʌɔ]	[ou]	[əu]

the 1990s adopted features of this accent which were opposed to those in local Dublin English but rejected others which were regarded as affected. The primary motivation remains dissociation as the classification of vowel values in new and local Dublin English in table 5.13 and figure 5.1 shows.

New Dublin English: how to avoid local features

The raising of back vowels is an acoustically salient feature of new Dublin English but it is by no means the only one. There are other new features, among consonants and among vowels, other than those discussed above, which can be interpreted

Table 5.14. *Further features of new Dublin English*

1. A retroflex realisation of /r/ occurs, e.g. *north* [noˈɻʈ]. This has the advantage of clearly delimiting the /r/ vis-à-vis local Dublin English which, if at all, only has a weak syllable-final /r/.
2. Phonemically long vowels are shorter in new Dublin English than their local Dublin English counterparts, e.g. *caught* new: [koˈt̂], local: [kɑːh].
3. There is strict avoidance of retraction of /ə/ before /r/ in *third, first*, i.e. new Dublin English [t̪əːɻd], [fəːɻst] which contrasts with local [tʊ:(ɹ)d], [fʊ:(ɹ)s(t)].
4. The back rounded /ʊ/ is replaced by an unrounded front vowel, which is almost /ɪ/, as in *Sunday* [ˈsɪ⁔nde].
5. Local Dublin English has a distinction between historic back and front short vowels before /r/, [ɛː] and [ʊ:]. But because the open front realisation is typical of local Dublin English, there is a migration in new Dublin English of historic front *long* vowels to the central rhotic type as seen in *care* [kɚ:], *pear* [pɚ:], etc. These can be somewhat rounded for some speakers, i.e. *carefully* [ˈkɶɹfəli] and *pear* [pɶɹ].

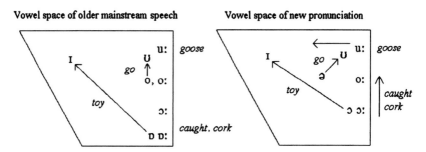

Figure 5.1   Changes in vowel constellations in Dublin English

as avoidance strategies used to differentiate new forms of speech from more local ones (see table 5.14).

A curious fact about new Dublin English is that although its salient features are opposed to those of local Dublin English, there are nonetheless some traits of the vernacular in this new variety and which it does not share with older mainstream Dublin English. Two of these can be mentioned here (see Hickey 2005: 75–8 for a discussion of others): (i) velarised [ɫ] in syllable-final position as in *meal* [miːᵊɫ], (ii) the front onset in the MOUTH lexical set as in *town* [tæun/teun]. The retention of these features in new Dublin English may in part be a reaction to the older 'Dublin 4' accent which did not have the front onset and only variably had velarisation of /l/.

A final feature which sets new Dublin English off from more conservative mainstream varieties of Irish English is the voicing of [ʍ] (see discussion in section 5.4.2). Speakers who have this do not distinguish word pairs like *which/witch* or *where/wear*, using initial [w-] in all cases. The voicing of [ʍ] is a general present-day development across many varieties in the anglophone world (see discussion in Schreier 2006). It also has low salience for speakers: during the recordings for *A Sound Atlas of Irish English* (Hickey 2004a), many of the speakers with voicing of [ʍ] had not realised that they did not distinguish words like *whale* and *wail* phonetically until it was pointed out to them. In general, local Dublin English speakers do not have [ʍ] either, but this fact would seem to be irrelevant to new Dublin English, given the widespread lack of awareness of the feature.

Arguments for the shift

It could be maintained that the developments in new Dublin English are just a gradual approximation to more standard forms of southern British English due to the strong influence of England on Ireland. This looks like the simplest and most convenient explanation. However, the imitation view can be quickly dismantled. Consider the following arguments.

(i) If (southern) British influence was making itself felt, then one would expect other features to be adopted, such as /ɑː/ for long *a* as in *bath*. But words of the BATH lexical set have [aː], i.e. [baːt̪]. Indeed the low back realisation is used by the Irish to ridicule a plummy British accent by referring to someone as having 'a [gɹɑːnd] accent' (although the RP form of the word is [grænd]). The normal Irish pronunciation is [gɹaːnd/gɹænt] with a low central or front vowel.

(ii) There is no tendency in Irish English to drop syllable-final /r/. If British English influence were operative then one would expect non-rhotacism to be spreading into new Dublin English. Instead, new Dublin English shows an increase in rhoticity by having a retroflex [ɻ], which contrasts strongly with the low rhoticity of local Dublin English.

(iii) Many Irish involved in the shift push it further than the back vowel values typical of southern British English. There are speakers who have, say, [ənɔɪ] and others who have [ənoɪ], for *annoy*. This point is of theoretical significance.

Pushing the vowel shift

Speakers of new Dublin English would seem to be aware of the trajectory on which the vowel shift is located even though their own personal realisation of key vowels may not be at the most innovative end of this track. This accounts for why young speakers are seen to push the vowel shift. The trajectory for the shift is unconsciously recognised by speakers and they can not only move within a degree of personal variation in this direction but they can also shift their range of realisations in the direction of innovation, in this case backwards and upwards.

As mentioned above, the vowel shift is moving beyond height values which are found in southern British English for corresponding vowels. This is particularly clear with the diphthong /ɔɪ/ in the CHOICE lexical set: [ɒɪ] > [ɔɪ] > [oɪ], e.g.

boys [boɪz], *noise* [noɪz], and the vowel of the THOUGHT lexical set: [ɒ:] > [ɔ:] > [o:], e.g. *bought* [boːt̚]. This continuing upward movement in the back vowel region would seem to be responsible for the shifting forward of the vowel in the GOOSE lexical set, i.e. former [guːs] has become [guː+s].

New Dublin English and Estuary English

There has been much discussion in the past decade or so about change in southeastern British English. This has been centred around the variety which, since its description by David Rosewarne in 1984, has been known somewhat vaguely as 'Estuary English'. The estuary in question is that of the River Thames and the alliteration in the label has obviously contributed much to its popularity or infamy, depending on one's point of view (Coggle 1993: 24–35).

In linguistic terms, Estuary English represents an intermediate variety between Cockney and RP, and its use by many people, who previously would have favoured RP, may well be due to the somewhat stand-offish attitude associated with the latter. There have been a number of investigations of Estuary English in recent years (Altendorf 2003; Przedlacka 1999) and information on the internet has been made available by J. C. Wells of the Department of Phonetics and Linguistics, University College London.

Comparing Estuary English with new Dublin English (Hickey 2007; see table 5.15 below), one can see that the latter is a new variety based on dissociation from local Dublin English whereas the former is a middle way between Cockney and RP. However, Estuary English may be adopted by speakers for the same reason as new Dublin English: to dissociate themselves from strongly local metropolitan speech, that is Estuary English can be used by speakers not only to move downwards from RP but upwards from Cockney.

The spread of new Dublin English

Ireland is a centrally organised country with something under one-third of the population living in the metropolitan area. In size, Dublin outweighs all other cities put together. Most prestigious organisations are located in the capital as is the government along with the national radio and television service. There are also three universities in the city and numerous other colleges. For these and other reasons, the status of Dublin English is greater than that of any other city or region in the country. In the context of the recent changes, this has meant that the new pronunciation has spread rapidly to the rest of the country. For all young people who do not identify themselves linguistically with their own locality (especially females), the new pronunciation is their phonological norm. This fact has been confirmed many times over by the recordings in *A Sound Atlas of Irish English* (Hickey 2004a). An important consequence of this is that the new pronunciation is fast becoming the mainstream, supraregional variety of Irish English. Young people outside Dublin are not aware of the dissociation which was the original driving force behind the rise of the new pronunciation in Dublin. But because young people's speech in Dublin is 'cool' (Hickey 2003c),

Table 5.15. *New Dublin English (NDE) and Estuary English (EE) / Cockney*

	NDE feature	status	EE feature	comment
1.	back vowel raising	innovation	✓	RP
2.	GOAT-diphthongisation	innovation	✓	RP
3.	HAPPY-tensing	innovation	HAPPY-tensing	not RP
4.	yod deletion	continuation	✓	not RP
5.	yod coalescence	continuation	✓	not RP
6.	velarised [ɫ]	innovation	[ɫ] vocalisation	partially RP
7.	retroflex [ɻ]	innovation	—	—
8.	T-flapping	innovation	—	—
9.	—	—	T-glottalling finally	partially RP
10.	—	—	linking-*r*	RP
11.	MOUTH-fronting	innovation	MOUTH-monophthong	Cockney
12.	—	—	FACE-lowering	Cockney
13.	—	—	H-deletion	Cockney
14.	—	—	TH-fronting	Cockney
15.	—	—	T-glottalling internally	Cockney: Cockney

Notes

1. The raising of back vowels is a feature of both RP and, in more advanced form, of Cockney (Wells 1982: 256f.). This should be seen in connection with FACE-lowering (12). Because the vowel shift in Dublin English is more restricted, it only affects back vowels. There is no shift with the vowels in the FLEECE or FACE lexical sets.

2. This is a significant parallel between new Dublin English and Estuary English. Furthermore, both local Dublin and local London show a lowering of the diphthong onset in GOAT, i.e. both have a vowel like [ʌɔ].

3. HAPPY-tensing is general in the south of Ireland and always has been, apparently.

4,5. Yod deletion (j > Ø as in *new* [nuː]) and yod coalescence ([tj] > [tʃ] as in *tutor* [tʃuːtɚ]) are uncontroversial in Irish English.

6. Velarised [ɫ] in new Dublin English is not showing any signs of vocalisation as in Estuary English.

7,8. Syllable-final /r/ is a major difference between Ireland and south-east England. On the rise of retroflex [ɻ], see comments above. T-flapping is also a feature without a counterpart in south-eastern British English.

9,15. T-glottalling is highly stigmatised in Dublin and hence avoided in new Dublin English. On its increased occurrence and acceptance in RP, see Fabricius (2002b). On the spread of glottalisation, see Milroy, Milroy and Hartley (1994).

10. Because new Dublin English is highly rhotic, there is no linking *r*.

11. There is no indication in Dublin English that the fronted realisation of MOUTH, neither [mæʊt] (new Dublin English) nor [mɛʊt] (local Dublin English), is being smoothed to a monophthong.

13. H-deletion is a feature of urban vernaculars in Britain but not found in Ireland.

14. TH-fronting is not found in Ireland although historically it is attested for Forth and Bargy (see section 2.4.4).

it is being adopted by other young people who probably unconsciously see it as a means of partaking in the urban sophistication of modern Irish life.

5.6   The lexicon of Irish English

Any treatment of the lexicon of Irish English, however brief, must begin with the distinction between lexical items which are retentions from the English brought to Ireland and those which can credibly be regarded as borrowings from Irish. Furthermore, as with other levels of language, the distinction between northern and southern Irish English is important. Much research has been carried out on the northern lexicon with a concentration on traditional rural terminology; see Adams (1966b, 1978), J. Bradley (1986), Braidwood (1965, 1969, 1972), Fenton (2000 [1995]), Macafee (1996), Marshall (1904). For lexical information on Donegal (Ulster, but outside Northern Ireland), see Traynor (1953). Recent publications, which deal largely with the south of Ireland, are Share (2003 [1997]) and Dolan (2004 [1998]).

Archaic and/or regional words in Irish English. By no means all the particular lexical items of Irish English derive from Irish. Quite a considerable number represent archaic or regional usage which has survived in Ireland. For instance, the adjectives *mad* and *bold* retain earlier meanings of 'keen on' and 'misbehaved' respectively. In some cases the words are a mixture of archaism and regionalism, e.g. *cog* 'cheat', *chisler* 'child', *mitch* 'play truant', *lock* 'quantity' (Dolan 2004: 142; e.g. *There's been none of that this lock of years*, TRS-D, U39). Yet other words are of foreign origin but entered via English, for example *hames* (from Dutch) 'curved pieces forming horse collar', but now a very general word meaning 'complete failure, mess'.

Another feature is the confusion between items which are complementary in meaning: *ditch* is used for *dyke*; *bring* and *take*, *rent* and *let*, *borrow* and *lend* are often interchanged as are *teach* and *learn* (colloquially and only the latter for the former, e.g. *And the little one's trying to learn me how to do it* (WER, F55+). There are also a few attestations of *speak* for *say*, e.g. *Didn't he speak it from the altar?* (MLSI, M80+, Baile na gCloch, Co. Cork). Phonetic similarity is often the reason for the confusion as in *They're rising (raising) up the prices all the time* (DER, M60+). In some instances, a particular pronunciation of an English word adopts connotations not found elsewhere, e.g. *eejit* /iːdʒɪt/ for *idiot* has more the sense of 'bungling person'; see section 5.3.

Irish use of English lexis. Needless to say, over the centuries in which English has been spoken in Ireland, specifically Irish uses of English words and phrases have arisen which contribute to the lexical profile of Irish English. A good example of this is the very common phrase *to give out about sth./s.o.* in the sense of 'complain', 'criticise'. Another is *leave* which can be used in the sense of 'accompany, bring', as in *Can you leave me home?*

Some words with a specific Irish English meaning are homographs with English words of quite a different meaning, e.g. *callow* means in Irish English 'low-lying land liable to be submerged' and is probably derived from Irish *caladh* 'landing place; river meadow' (Breeze 1997: 158).

One can also observe semantic extensions which have taken place in Ireland, as with *yoke* meaning thing/device or *delf* meaning any type of crockery (from delftware, formerly produced in Dublin). *Grand* has broadened its scope considerably to form a general adjective of approval: *It's a grand day*; *Sure you're grand where you are*; *Michael's a grand hurler*. The adjective has all but lost its meaning of 'displaying grandeur'. The adjective *foreign* can have the meaning 'unfaithful' as in *She went foreign on him and he after paying for the house* (WER, F55+).

Various English adverbs, which are not formally marked, have developed functions as intensifiers, e.g. *We were pure robbed by the builders* (DER, M35+); *Your man is fierce rich* (WER, M50+). The word *fierce* is also common in vernacular registers to express magnitude or severity: *The drinking at the wedding was fierce* (WER, M50+); *The weather was fierce* (WER, M35+). A particular use of adjectives and past participles in Ireland is as descriptions of drunkenness. There is a whole battery of such items, e.g. *bollixed, buckled, flootered, jarred, langered, paralytic, plastered, sozzled, sloshed, stocious, twisted, well on, well oiled*, all meaning 'drunk'.

Some words involve a degree of morphological and/or phonological manipulation of the English original. For instance, *insurrection* is clipped to *ruction* 'uproar, great trouble' (with /ɛ/ > /ʊ/ for the stressed vowel), often used in the plural: *There were ructions when she came home late from the disco* (DER, M60+).

A morphological feature is the addition of *-er* to create new words, e.g. *nixer* 'job on the side'; *killer* 'sth. that would stress you', as in *The climb up that cliff was a right killer*; *sticker* 'difficult matter', as in *The price of houses in Ireland is a real sticker*; *bogger* 'country lout', as in *Your man's some bogger*. It is also used on shortened forms of a name or nickname: *beamer* 'fast German car' < 'BMW'; *Jockser* < *Jack*. The ending *-er* may receive an *s* on adverbs used elliptically for adjectives, e.g. *japers/jakers* (especially common in Dublin English), used as a general expression of incredulity, surprise or disapproval and probably deriving from ME *jape* 'a practical joke' (from Old French, Hickey 2002b): *Japers, I wouldn't pay that much for a meal in any restaurant* (DER, M35+). The ending *-o* is similarly common in colloquial registers, again especially in Dublin English, e.g. *boyo* 'admirable rogue', as in *Trev's some boyo* (DER, M35+).

Still other cases involve quasi-lexicalised uses of phrases. For instance, *man* and *one* have particular connotations when used with possessive pronouns as in *Your man* 'The (male) person currently being referred to' or *Your one* [wan] 'disrespectful reference to a woman'.

In many instances, words in English are given a scope which is derived from that of their semantic equivalent in Irish: *I'm destroyed with the work* (WER, M55+) derives from the use of the word *millte* 'destroyed'; *I'm drowned with the rain* (WER, M35+) comes from *báite* 'drowned' in Irish. The use of the preposition *with* in each of these cases corresponds to usage in Irish. This transfer of scope may also be responsible for the Irish use of *evening* with a beginning in the late afternoon: *She came home at five in the evening* (WER, F85+), a scope also found in the north.

Irish loans in present-day Irish English. Although Irish today is spoken natively by about one per cent of the population and although the knowledge of Irish among the majority is, in general, very poor, there is a curious habit of flavouring one's speech by adding a few words from Irish, what is sometimes called using the *cúpla focal* (Irish 'couple of words'); see O'Malley Madec (2002: 222–7, 'Functions of Irish "loanwords" in English discourse'). The words used are always alternatives to English terms readily available, e.g. *ciúnas* 'silence', *piseog* 'superstition' (anglicised as *pishogue*), *sláinte* 'health' or *plámás* 'flattery'. Such incursions into the lexicon of Irish are brief and superficial and do not imply that a speaker could carry on a normal conversation in Irish. Ultimately, the phenomenon of the *cúpla focal* derives from school Irish and not from any natural knowledge of the language.

Sugaring of one's language with Irish words must be distinguished from genuine loans from Irish. Some of these are long attested such as *colleen* 'Irish girl', *leprechaun* 'garden gnome', *banshee* 'fairy woman', all part of sentimental Irish folklore. In essence, such words have to do with Irish manners and life, for instance, *planxty* 'a joyful tune played on the harp', *tilly* 'additional bit, small extra portion' (< Irish *tuilleadh*), *gab/gob* 'mouth' (< Irish *gob* 'mouth, beak'), common in English in the compound *gob-smacked*. Many of these words are parts of idioms such as *gift of the gab* 'ability to speak eloquently', *soft day* 'mild, misty weather' (< Irish *lá bog* 'day soft'), *the poor mouth* (< Irish *an béal bocht*) 'eternal complaining'.

Linguistically interesting among such loans is undoubtedly the word *crack*, here from Irish *craic*, itself a borrowing from English, with the general meaning of 'fun, good time, enjoyment on a social occasion, typically in a pub'. There are distributional restrictions on its use, so much so that the correct application cannot simply be guessed and an incorrect use can betray one as non-Irish. It can occur in various tenses, in a definite and an indefinite sense. However, it is not possible in an imperative or optative construction.

(20) a. *We had a great crack.*   'We enjoyed ourselves.'
      b. *How's the crack?*   'Are you getting much enjoyment?'
                                    (out of life, etc.)
      c. **Have a crack this evening,* **Let's have some crack.*

Instances like these show that, despite the paucity of Irish words in Irish English, its lexicon has a clear profile and it can fulfil the dual function of identification and demarcation vis-à-vis other forms of English. This 'local flavouring' is particularly common when speakers shift into colloquial registers and use words which have a specific Irish flavour to them, e.g. *bog(house)* 'toilet', *bogman/bogger* 'uncultured, coarse individual', both from *bog* 'marsh'.

In present-day Ireland, Irish words are used in officialese, by ministries, government offices and semi-state bodies when coining names for new institutions and agencies. This is a corollary of the official attitude of the government and the lip service paid to Irish (constitutionally speaking the first language in Ireland, though this is, and always has been, wishful thinking). These words are treated as opaque by the Irish, for instance the government employment agency is called *fás* but it is doubtful if the majority of people know that this word means 'growth' in Irish. Equally, names for political positions are often referred to by their Irish equivalents, for instance, there is no prime minister or deputy prime minister in Ireland but a *taoiseach* and a *tánaiste* ['ţˠɑːnˠɪʃtə]. The use of these terms should not be construed as allegiance to the Irish language, indeed most Irish pronounce them using English phonetics: ['tiːʃək] is the usual rendering of Irish *taoiseach* ['ţˠiːʃəx].

There are also a small number of terms from Irish which have a specific meaning and are not alternatives to English words. *Currach* 'a boat with a wooden frame covered with tarred canvas', *crannog* 'lake dwelling' (Irish *crannóg*) and *carrageen* 'edible seaweed' (Irish *carraigín*), are examples of such words which are generally known to most Irish.

For some words the etymology is uncertain, that is, neither an Irish, English or other source can be clearly established. Examples of this are *shenanigans* 'trickery, nonsense, dubious behaviour' (Dolan 2004: 209), *banjaxed* 'completely broken, kaput' (Dublin slang) and *hooley* 'wild and noisy party' which sounds like a borrowing from Irish but could well be a Hindi word borrowed into English (Dolan 2004: 122).

The question of currency. This is a difficult issue because the use of Irish-derived lexis is dependent on register in Irish English. In addition, there is an historical and regional dimension to the question. There are loans which are attested in the history of Irish English, such as *clamper* 'noise, hub-bub' (< Irish *clampar*, itself from English), to be found in the play *Captain Thomas Stukeley* (late sixteenth century). Equally, there are words which have a distinct regional distribution, for instance, *drisheen*, a type of blood sausage, is a typical Cork word.

Many words listed in dictionaries may be the result of spontaneous code-switching or may be attested with Irish authors using them for flavour, but they cannot always be regarded as established generally, e.g. *cooramagh* 'careful' (< Irish *cúramach*), *flahool* 'generous' (< Irish *flaithiúil*), *keen* 'wail' (from Irish *caoineadh*), *kiottogue* 'left-handed person' (< Irish *ciotóg*), *shannachee* 'story teller' (< Irish *seanchaí*), *sleeveen* 'sly fellow' (< Irish *slíbhín*).

Furthermore, the Irish-derived vocabulary available to the elderly rural population is much greater than that which the younger generation, both rural and urban, display. In the materials collected for *A Linguistic Survey of Ireland* (see section 4.4) a large number of words were recorded which are basically Irish words with an English pronunciation, e.g. *bookelawn* 'ragwort' (< Irish *buachalán*), *prashuck* 'charlock; mess' (< Irish *praiseach* 'wild cabbage; thin porridge; mess'), *mweelawn* 'hornless cow' (< Irish *maoláin*, itself the source of English *moiley*), *puckawn* 'male goat' (< Irish *pucán*). These and similar words can be regarded as vernacular survivals of the language shift, but which are not found in non-local forms of present-day Irish English. The same is true of expressions which are literal translations from Irish; consider the following examples from the data collections of older rural speech: *You'd notice it coming on him* [Irish: *ag teacht air* 'coming on him'] (SADIF, M60+, Bruff, Co. Limerick), *There was never a bit from that out* [Irish: *as sin amach* 'from that out' = 'after that'] (SADIF, M70, Crisheen, Co. Clare), *I didn't see you with a long time* [Irish: *le tamall fada* 'with time long'] (MLSI, M60+, Fanore, Co. Clare), *He put the cattle to the mountain* [Irish: *chun an tsléibhe* 'to the mountain'] (MLSI, M80+, Ballycroy, Co. Mayo), *I've no name on it* [Irish: *ainm agam air* 'name at-me on-it'] (MLSI, M60+, Ballymahon area, Co. Longford).

Irish loans in English. The quantity of borrowing from Irish into mainland or overseas English (Stalmaszczyk 1997: 81–3) has been slight indeed (in the latter case, probably because of the desire of emigrants not to associate themselves with their Irish background). Most of the words are colloquial, e.g. *smithereens* 'broken pieces' from a diminutive of *smiodar* 'fragment'; *blarney* 'flattery, sweet talk' from a town near Cork; *brogue* 'thick, country accent of Irish English' from the word for 'shoe' or 'knot in the tongue' (Murphy 1943; Bergin 1943); *gob* 'mouth'; *omadawn* 'fool' from Irish *amadán*. Some are now more or less obsolete in English like *shillelagh* 'cudgel' (Dolan 2004: 209f.). The word *tory* is from Irish *tóraidhe* 'a pursued person' and came, through various stages, to mean a member of the British Conservative Party in the 1830s (the American usage refers to a colonialist loyal to Britain). *Bother* is from Irish *bodhar* 'deaf' and is attested from the early nineteenth century, e.g. *I'm bothered to death this night* (Maria Edgeworth, *Castle Rackrent*, 1801: 78).

On less certain ground is *shanty* 'hut, run-down house' either from Irish *sean tí* (genitive of *sean teach* 'old house', here the oblique case militates against the Irish interpretation) or from Canadian French *chantier* 'lumberjack's cabin' (Bliss 1968). The word also occurred in the nineteenth century as an attributive adjective, with reference to two ethnic groups: *shanty Irish* 'poor Irish-Americans' and *shantyman* 'lumberjack' (Canadian, American).

The word *galore* is from Irish/Scottish Gaelic *go leor* 'plenty'. It is a quantifier like *enough*, and hence appears after the noun it qualifies, but cannot precede it (see section 4.4.5.1).

A *yahoo* is originally a 'brute' from a race mentioned in Swift's *Gulliver's Travels* but now has the meaning of a wild, unruly person. It also occurs as a verb, e.g. *The kids were yahooing around in the corridor.*

Closely linked to Ireland is the word *shamrock* (< Irish *seamróg*) for a species of small-leafed clover which grows in clumps and is the national symbol of Ireland, much as the thistle and the rose are for Scotland and England respectively.

Where the etymologies of English words are uncertain, some scholars have suggested an Irish source. Phonetic similarities between present-day forms can be deceptive and scepticism is called for before trying to construct an Irish etymology for an English word. A case in point is the personal pronoun *she* which, it has been suggested, derives from Irish *sí*. The contention of Todd (1999: 33f.), and echoed by Sammon (2002: 187), is that there was considerable influence from Irish scribes on English in the later Scandinavian period and that these would have donated their third-person-singular feminine pronoun to the English they were in contact with. There are two major difficulties with this view.

The first is that elements of core grammar, to which personal pronouns belong, are not transferred easily between languages. Indeed, if such elements appear later in another language, then frequently this occurs by imposition, that is the speakers of the donor language use a core grammatical element from their own language in the host language and then the speakers of the latter adopt this element from the variety of their language which the donor language speakers use. Such a language change scenario is termed 'imposition' (Guy 1990) and usually only applies when the speakers of the donor language have greater social prestige than speakers of the host language, or are at least their social equals. This scenario may be assumed to have applied between the Normans and the native Irish in the late medieval period. But it is not a likely sociolinguistic situation to have obtained between Irish scribes (possibly along with Scandinavians who had lived in Ireland) and English in the late Old English period.

The second difficulty with Todd's view concerns vowel pronunciation. *She* has only been pronunced [ʃiː] since the vowel shift which led to the raising of long vowels in late Middle English, possibly starting in the thirteenth century (Lass 1987: 226f.). Before this the pronunciation was [ʃeː] which could not have been the result of the English borrowing the Irish feminine pronoun *sí* [ʃiː] 'she'.

Irish and international usage. A few Irish words have become international terms. These are not necessarily borrowings from Irish but eponyms deriving from surnames: *to boycott* comes from one Captain Charles Boycott (1832–97), an English land agent in Co. Mayo, who resisted the demands for reform by the Irish Land League (1879–81) and who was blacked by Irish peasants and workmen. His name now stands for a policy of deliberate non-cooperation. *To lynch* may come from the name of a mayor of Galway city in the thirteenth century who acquiesced to the execution of his own son for crimes committed, though this term could also stem from Captain William Lynch (1742–1820) of Virginia who set up and presided over tribunals outside the judicial system. *Hooligan* is a term for someone who behaves violently and comes from the name of a boisterous Irish family in a song. *Limerick* is a reference to a type of doggerel verse with the rhyming pattern AABBA. All these words have spread from English to other languages, for instance, *Hooligan* (noun), *Limerick* (noun), *boykottieren* (verb) and *lynchen* (verb) are current in German with the meanings they have in English. Other terms may be known to speakers of English outside Ireland, e.g. *shebeen* 'country pub'.

Non-colloquial terms. The words given so far are often colloquial and confined to informal registers. There are, however, some words deriving from Irish which have a neutral, often technical, meaning. The following is a short list of samples.

bog   marsh or moor, frequently cultivated for the harvesting of peat. From Irish *bog* 'soft', i.e. 'soft ground'.

clan   extended family, from Old Irish *clann*, a borrowing from Latin *planta* (with loss of final vowel and cluster simplification) at an early stage when /p/ was still shifted to /k/ in Q-Celtic.

crannog   dwelling on an artificial island or stilts in a lake (< Irish *crannóg*).

drumlin   small rounded hill or island resulting from glacial drift (derives from Irish *droim* 'back').

esker   a long narow ridge of gravel deposited under a glacier (< Irish *eiscir*).

gallowglass   mercenary, particularly of Scottish origin, from Irish *gall-óglach* 'foreign warrior'.

glen   narrow or small valley (< Irish *gleann*).

lough   lake (< Irish *loch* /lʌx/).

soogawn   rope of straw used in making chairs (< Irish *súgán*).

Irish loans in American English. Because of the considerable Irish immigration to the United States since the early eighteenth century (see section 6.2) a number of words have entered English there which could be of Irish origin. Two of these which are also current in Ireland but whose etymology is uncertain are *shibang* 'entire lot' and *shenanigans* 'trickery'. Two further words/phrases, this time not found in native Irish usage, are *so long* and *phoney*. The first may derive from Irish *slán* 'goodbye', where the transition from [s] to a velarised [ł] would suggest an extra syllable to English speakers. The semantic link between 'goodbye' and 'so long' is also not too far-fetched. The word *phoney* is taken to derive from the Irish word *fáinne* 'ring', which goes back to the (Irish) vendors' practice of smuggling bogus rings among good ones when selling jewellery in north-eastern American cities where the Irish chiefly settled (Dolan 2004: 175).

An Irish source is not always clearly identifiable despite the Irish association of a word. Consider *malark(e)y* 'ridiculous talk, nonsense' which appeared in the United States in the early twentieth century. One source is the Irish sur-name *Malarkey/Mullarkey* (MacLysaght 1997 [1957]: 226f.) which is phonet-ically identical with *malark(e)y* (and stressed on the second syllable). Another source could be the related Irish words *meallaireacht* 'beguilement, deception', *meallaire* 'deceiver' (Ó Dónaill 1977: 842), but the fact that these are stressed on the first syllable is difficult to reconcile with the American English word. A combination of sources may have operated here: the form from the surname with the semantics deriving from the Irish words. In addition, the word *malark(e)y* shares a prosodic structure which may well have phonoaesthetic value and which ties up with other words of a similar meaning, such as *baloney* 'nonsense', i.e. it consists of three syllables, the first of which has schwa, the second a long stressed vowel and the third a front high vowel, i.e. [Cə. 'CV:.Ci].

Irish usage of English words may have spread to American English as a result of emigration. An example would be the use of *leave* in the sense of *let* 'allow, permit', as in *Leave me go* (Adams 2000: 295). It is difficult to be certain in such cases as both regional English input and other languages (in this instance, German, Adams 2000: 300) could equally well have been the source.

Irish names in English. Proper names from Irish enjoy a considerable popularity as firstnames, especially in the United States and Canada, and not only with the section of the population there which has an Irish background. *Patrick* is probably the most common; its diminutive *Paddy* is often derogatory and, in England, is a generic term of disrespect for the Irish. Other firstnames are *Kevin*, an Irish saint, *Desmond*, lit. 'South Munster' (Irish *deas* 'south' + *Mumhan* 'Munster' + epenthetic /d/ after the final nasal), an area controlled by a Norman family which adopted the geographical term as its name; *Moira* < *Máire* (Irish for *Maria/Marie*); *Maureen* is a diminutive from *Máirín* < *Máire* + *-ín* where the latter is a productive diminutive suffix. This is also found in *colleen* 'small girl, Irish girl' < *cailín*, morphologically *cail* + *ín*, found as a firstname. *Shawn* < *Seán* (Irish) derives from Anglo-Norman *John*, the Latin form *Johannes* having resulted in the earlier form *Eoin* in Ireland (*Ian* in Scotland and *Owen* in Wales). *Kelly* is an American firstname and a surname in Ireland and stems from the Irish surname *Ó Ceallaigh*; another such case is *Casey*. Extensions of Irish firstnames are also found in America, e.g. *Brianna* as a girl's name from *Brian* (the only Irish form). In Australia, a *sheelagh* is a generic term for a girl. This derives from the Irish girl's name *Síle* (anglicised as *Sheila*), itself ultimately from *Cecilia*.

Within Ireland, there are some names which are used as generic terms for groups. The term *Jackeen* is a somewhat dated reference to someone from Dublin (*Dubs* is also found), a *West Brit* is an Irish person with strong English leanings, *Castle Catholic* is a loose term for Catholics with class pretensions and a condescending attitude to their fellow Irish. The term *Emerald Isle* for Ireland stems from the poet William Drennan (1754–1820) and was first used about 1800.

Irish or Scottish Gaelic. In a few instances, it is not certain whether the source for a word has been Gaelic in Scotland or Irish in Ireland as the phonetic form of the words would have been more or less identical in both languages. *Dig* (usually the American form) and *twig* 'understand' are both from *tuigim* 'I understand' (Ahlqvist 1988). *Sonsy* 'agreeable in appearance, comely', from *sonas* 'good fortune', is certainly Scottish Gaelic, cf. *unsonsy* 'unlucky' as well. *Whiskey* < Irish *uisce (beatha)* 'water (of life)' has been borrowed from both forms of Gaelic (the Scottish spelling is *whisky*).

The lexicography of Irish English

The study of Irish English vocabulary from a more or less linguistic perspective can be said to begin with Joyce (1979 [1910]) and Clark (1977 [1917]). The first work is more general in its scope and rests on Joyce's considerable knowledge of Irish and local history. Clark's study is a single piece of scholarship from a writer about whom little is known. In later work on Irish English, such as Hogan (1927), there are remarks on vocabulary. It was not until the 1950s with the work of P. L. Henry, somewhat dated now, but seminal at the time, that renewed interest in the vocabulary of Irish English developed. During the 1960s, focus shifted to the north with studies by Adams and Braidwood (e.g. Adams 1958, 1966b, 1978b; Braidwood 1964, 1965, 1969). Towards the end of the decade Alan Bliss in Dublin began his series of many articles on Irish English, including lexical questions, which established his reputation in the field. The 1970s and 1980s saw a few reprints (of Barnes 1867 and Clark 1977 [1917]). The 1990s saw a considerable expansion in this field. Christensen (1996), Moylan (1996), Ó Muirithe (1996a, 1996b and 1997) and Share (1997) continue a tradition of word collecting (of these Ó Muirithe and Share are the most thorough). Görlach (1995) and Kallen (1996 and 1997) have participated in the research into the Irish English lexicon. With Dolan's dictionary (1998) another comprehensive work appeared which covers all aspects of lexical usage, dealing with both terms from Irish and survivals of regional and archaic English input to Ireland. Both Share and Dolan have gone into second editions, in 2003 and 2004 respectively.

Several studies of Ulster vocabulary also appeared during the 1990s. Starting with Todd (1990) and continuing through various articles up to the dictionary by Macafee (1996), an expansion in quality and scope of lexical studies can be observed. A specific treatment of Ulster Scots is to be found in Fenton (2000 [1995]).

Apart from the studies listed above, there are many collections of words from Irish English compiled out of an interest in the folk knowledge embodied in the vocabulary. Such studies go back at least to the middle of the nineteenth century when vocabulary of a local or specialist nature was collected and published in the form of word lists, mainly in Irish journals dedicated to matters of local interest. A fairly complete list of these can be found in the relevant sections of Hickey (2002a).

A number of vocabulary aids are available for English works by Irish authors (Wall 1995, 2001), especially for James Joyce (O'Hehir 1967), but also for Swift (P. O. Clark 1953; Scott-Thomas 1945–6) and Synge (Bliss 1972b, 1972c). There are also sections of works dedicated to vocabulary, e.g. Amador (2006: 177–263) on the lexicon of the author whose novels she investigated.

5.7   The pragmatics of Irish English

Differences in language use between varieties of English are obvious to the casual observer. But in recent years, many linguists have begun the task of establishing objectively what differences exist and how these compare among varieties of English. For Irish English, the most significant publication to date is Barron and Schneider (2005b), a collection of innovative articles on three areas: (i) the private sphere, (ii) the official sphere and (iii) the public sphere. The editors of the volume stress the need for a new orientation which they label 'variational pragmatics' (Barron and Schneider 2005a: 11–13). In the Irish English context, the data basis for this approach is provided by two major corpora, which have been completed recently: (i) the *Limerick Corpus of Irish English* and (ii) *International Corpus of English – Ireland* (Kallen and Kirk 2001; Kirk, Kallen, Lowry and Rooney 2003). Both corpora are collections of contemporary Irish English, prepared for linguistic analysis, above all from a pragmatic point of view.

There is no doubt that the structure of discourse in the Republic of Ireland is quite different from that in other anglophone countries, including Northern Ireland. The following represents an attempt to highlight some of its salient features. Given restrictions of space, the present section can only be brief and many of the statements must be taken at face value. Indeed, for many of the assertions, confirmation by substantial quantities of data is not possible, because the necessary collections are not yet available.

5.7.1 THE VERNACULAR MODE

The tone in Irish English discourse is achieved by a series of adjectives, generic references, discourse markers and fillers of various kinds. Most of these are elements of English which have been redeployed for this specific purpose. For instance, the adjective *grand* expresses approval of a person or a generally positive situation, e.g. *Mary's a grand cook, I'm grand now.*

So is used in sentence-final position to indicate consent or acquiescence: *I'm just putting on the kettle.* (RH) *I'll have a cup of tea so* (WER, F55+) and may well be an equivalent to Irish *más ea* 'if-that-is so' which is also found sentence-finally: *Beidh cupán tae agam más ea*, lit. 'will-be cup tea-GEN at-me if-that-is so'.

Not unexpectedly, the vernacular mode is characterised by its own pronunciation features, as in other varieties of English, e.g. *yeah* [jæː] for *yes*. In general there is considerable reduction of word forms, e.g. the ubiquitous use of [ˈhaəjə] for *how are you?* The phrase *hello there* [hɛˈlo dɛɹ] is common when informally addressing strangers.

Occasionally, a feature of discourse may be old-fashioned, or virtually obsolete, as with *arrah* [ˈærə], a discourse filler which can be used as a reaction to something said or an indication of inalterability or unimportance of some fact or situation.

5.7.2 CONSENSUALITY

Friends and strangers. At the risk of over-generalisation, one can state that discourse interaction in Ireland has been based on customs and practices which have their origins in the rural background out of which modern Ireland emerged in the twentieth century. As one might expect, given this context, interaction is largely consensual and much emphasis is placed on personal acquaintance. If this is not present, as in official exchanges, then patterns of interaction are favoured which would be typical of acquaintances or friends.

An offshoot of this background is a particular aspect of Irish social behaviour: when two Irish strangers meet in an unofficial context they search for a common acquaintance, or at least a common experience. On more than one occasion, the author has found that the non-Irish in a company have been startled by the attempts on his part and that of another Irish person present to find some common link on first meeting. Once this has been found, the exchange proceeds along other lines.

The pragmatics of reassurance. Because partners in conversation are expected to support each other, Irish English conversation shows a lot of backchannelling. For instance, repetition of *yeah, right, sure, of course*, while the other is speaking, is viewed positively as is interspersing one's own contributions by phrases expressing gratitude like *thanks a million!* or reassurances like *just a sec* or *I'll be with you in two minutes* while waiting. Of course, such features of conversation are in general regarded as essential to cooperation among participants. The assumption that they seem to be somewhat more common in Irish English, compared to other varieties of English, is something which is awaiting quantitative confirmation.

Contradiction is not generally welcome and must be couched in weak terms. Equally, direct criticism is avoided. The friendliness of exchanges is achieved by supporting the views of one's interlocutor. If, for whatever reason, this cannot be maintained, a cut-off point is quickly reached and the exchange can easily become acrimonious.

Consensual exchanges. The origin of consensual exchanges lies in the type of discourse used by relatives, friends and acquaintances. Here there is a large degree of agreement and the exchanges serve the important function of maintaining social ties. This immediately creates difficulties for those exchanges which involve disagreement or demands from the addressee which he/she does not wish to fulfil. There are different ways of packaging such contents without overtly threatening the face of the other (Brown and Levinson 1987).

External mitigation. Consensual exchanges are easy to realise, if the subject matter is innocuous (like the weather) or there is agreement among interlocutors (both wish to do the same thing). However, if this is not the case, then there are strategies for maintaining consensuality in exchanges. One of these is to explicitly locate the cause for disagreement at some external source. That way, no interlocutor can be held personally responsible. The following are two examples taken from service encounters the author had in Dublin.

(21)   RH: *Can I listen to some of the tapes from the archive?*
      Receptionist: *Yeah, you can.*
      RH: *Okay, I was wondering . . . Could I go along to the archive now, maybe?*
      Receptionist: *Sure, you can. But I have to . . . right, well look, I'm afraid it costs 20 pounds an hour, sorry about that now. That's the way it works, okay?*

(22)   RH: *But the case is scarcely two kilograms overweight.*
      Check-in assistant: *I know, but I have to ask you to pay the extra cost. They're the new regulations. I know it used be different, but there you are.*

The construction of consensuality. Participants in an exchange can use various means to construct consensuality in any language. They can emphasise the common ground they share (Kallen 2005a: 139), e.g. *Sure we all have to pay these fierce Euro prices, don't we now?* (WER, M50+). Speakers can also send out appeals for agreement. Tags are a well-known means of doing this in English. In Irish English, they are often reinforced by *though* which in this context does not signal a contradiction: *It's grand to have company, though, isn't it?* (WER, F55+); *He was in some pain with that though I'd say* (WER, F85+).

If a speaker is not sure how the addressee will react to what is said, then strategies for 'feeling one's way forward' can be employed. In Irish English such attempts at sounding out the situation are usually tentative and often followed by a withdrawal if the reaction of the other is perceived as unfavourable. This can be seen in the following exchange recorded by the author. The prominent use of *would* as a hedging device in such contexts has been noted (Farr and O'Keefe 2002).

(23)   A: *Would you be interested in seeing the new pub down on Mayor's Walk?*
       B: *Sure, it's a great place, I bet.*
       A: *Well, you know, if you wanted to, you could drop in on Friday.*
          There's a group of us meets up for a few drinks after about nine.
       B: *Okay, well, I'll have to see about this Friday.*
       A: *Oh yeah, well it was just an idea, you know. I was just thinking, don't worry about it.*
       B: *Right, right, sure, but it's a great idea alright. We'll definitely do it sometime soon.*

The status of interlocutors. The type of consensual exchanges favoured by the Irish imply that the interlocutors are on a comparable social level. Because of this, highlighting social differences in an exchange is generally frowned upon. Where there is an undeniable social cline between interlocutors the one with higher social status may downtone his/her parts of the exchange and background his/her social position (Farr and O'Keefe 2002: 42).

How to say 'no'. Refusing a request is one of the most common threats to the face of the other in an exchange. In a culture where exchange is based on consensuality, a refusal must be couched in a series of hedges to minimize the threat to face. An answer like the following, given to the author after a request for a drive into town, is typical: *No, no, I won't be able to drive you back now. Sorry about that, now, sorry. But there's nothing I can do now, I'm afraid, sorry.* Another means of minimizing the threat to face is to make a vague promise of future compliance to a request (see example is last paragraph but one).

What to do with 'no'. Although refusal of a request or offer is often difficult in Irish English, once refused, there is no going back. It is pointless providing factual arguments in favour of 'yes'. When doing recordings for *A Sound Atlas of Irish English* (Hickey 2004a) the author found that once a potential informant had said 'no' to a request for a recording it was futile to try and have him/her revise this decision. Factual arguments, e.g. that the recordings were anonymous and the sentences to be read out innocuous, were in vain. Fortunately, the number of refusals were very small indeed.

Rituals in exchanges: offers. Whether the Irish are as hospitable as their reputation claims, is not an issue for this book. What is certain, however, is that hospitality involves pragmatic rituals. One of these, which has been investigated in detail (Barron 2005), is that of offers. This study has shown that ritual repetition of an offer is a prominent feature of Irish English exchanges and that particular structures are used to minimize the chance of the offer being refused. Predication of future action (Barron 2005: 152f., 165f.), as in *You'll have another drink before you go*, is typical and declining an offer, without affecting the face of the offerer, is not easy. Hospitality, in a country with a rural background, requires one to press the offeree somewhat. This in its turn make refusal and the maintenance of consensuality all the more difficult.

Silence and interlocutor overlap. It has been remarked that communicative silence plays a significant role in Irish English discourse (Barron and Schneider 2005a: 7); indeed, one recent study is devoted to just this topic (Kallen 2005a). Certainly, in older male–male, rural contexts, such as that investigated by Kallen, silence is a mark of authority and position. But in urban contexts with young people, it is not silence, but continuing exchange with interlocutor overlap, which is the prominent feature. In consensual exchanges in contemporary Ireland, it is interpreted negatively if interlocutors leave pauses between turns, unless such pauses have a clear external motivation, like considering factual information. The reason for this negative view of silence at turn-taking is that it is interpreted as disinterest in the interlocutor and is very face-threatening. To avoid an unintentional pause, a speaker may take the turn in a conversation before the current speaker has actually stopped. This can convey the impression to foreigners that the Irish interrupt each other frequently, but in a consensual context such overlap is viewed positively. Indeed, the absence of exchange, in situations where it is possible, is liable to negative interpretation, e.g. in waiting rooms, at bus stops, out in the countryside, where at least a salutation and brief remark is normal.

Silence in conversation should not be confused with the avoidance of topics (a point missed by Kallen 2005a: 57). Certain issues, above all those of an emotional or intimate nature, are generally not broached by Irish people, even in discourse among friends, and flattery is viewed negatively (as Kallen rightly notes). However, this does not mean that the Irish fall into silence when a matter is not addressed, the conversation is just continued with another topic.

5.7.3 PRAGMATIC MARKERS

Pragmatic markers are words or short phrases that have a metalinguistic function in discourse (Brinton 1996). They serve several purposes, typically to express the relevance of the present contribution to what has preceded and what is likely to follow in the discourse. They can also convey an attitude to, or solicit agreement from, the hearer. Because of this, such markers are not normally part of the syntactic structure of the sentence in which they occur. A deletion test will normally show that the sentence without the pragmatic marker is still well-formed.

Given the consensual nature of Irish English discourse, it is not surprising that pragmatic markers occur frequently. They typically offer reassurance or stress mutually accepted knowledge among speakers, for example, in the case of *you know* (Östman 1981). Sentence-final *then* is also common in Irish English to signal tacit agreement after receiving information from one's interlocutor. This use of *then* does not contain a temporal reference.

(24) Typical pragmatic markers in Irish English
   a. *Grand*: reassurance, general approval
      I'm grand now, yeah. I'm fine. (after being seated) (WER, F85+)
      And the party was in the hotel. So that was grand. (DER, M35+)
   b. *Ah well*: reassurance, consolation
      Ah well then, it's not too bad. (WER, F85+)
   c. Use of sentence-final *then*
      I suppose it might be safe, then. (DER, F60+)
   d. *You know*: explanation, appeal for understanding, emphasising common attitudes, beliefs
      I have to pay a lot on the old mortgage, you know. (WER, M50+)
      It is my duty, and the reg'lation, you know.
      (Dion Boucicault, *Arrah na Pogue*, 1864)
      The softy I am, you know, I'd ha' lent him me last juice!
      (Sean O'Casey, *Juno and the Paycock*, 1924)
      Well, you know, Fine Gael aren't capable of governing the country.
      (WER, M50+)
   e. *Sure*: inevitability of situation
      Sure, that the way it is. (WER, F85+)
      Sure, we all have to go some time. (WER, F85+)
   f. *Though*: slight contradiction
      You'd be wondering where they came from, though. (WER, F55+)
   g. *Oh, stop!* Strong agreement with preceding statement
      I suppose you get stuck for income tax. (RH) *Oh, stop! Don't talk to me about tax.* (WER, M50+)
   h. Final *but*: implied contradiction
      Jimmy's the best husband in the world, but. (DER, M60+)
      It's mostly the men, but. (WER, F55+)
   i. *How as ever*: relativisation of situation
      But how as ever, he's lucky to have your mam. (WER, F55+)
   j. *An' all* ('and all') as reinforcer
      The women an' all have to drive. (WER, M50+)
      Sure he had to go to Dr O'C . . . with that an' all, hadn't he? (DER, M60+)

Stressed 'some'. The meaning of the determiner *some* can vary in Irish English depending on the degree to which it is stressed. When it carries slight stress it has the meaning one would expect from other varieties of English, i.e. 'a small quantity', as in *There are some chairs on the balcony.* But when strongly stressed *some* adopts the function of highlighting the noun it qualifies, often expressing surprise mixed with admiration, e.g. *Your man's "some chancer* (DER, M35+), *God, that's "some car he's got now* (WER, F55+); *He was in "some pain with that though I'd say* (WER, F85+). This can lead to situations in which there is a semantic contrast depending on the degree of stress placed on the determiner, e.g. *There some people* (a few individuals) *living in them houses now* and *There "some people* (important, rich people) *living in them houses now* (WER, M50+).

Focuser 'like'. The pragmatic marker *like* is frequent in Irish English. In vernacular varieties the indigenous use is as a focuser. Quotative *like* is also found, particularly in young people's speech and has probably been imported from American English (Ferrara and Bell 1995; Dailey-O'Cain 2000), e.g. *I'm, like, 'No way will my parents pay for that!'* (F16, Limerick). Focuser *like* is found in all age groups and is particularly common in explanatory contexts as the following selection shows.

(25)   Focuser *like* in recordings of Irish English

  a. *They'd go into the houses, like, to play the cards.* (TRS-D, M42)
  b. *'Tis quality now, like, and all this milk and everything. You're getting paid on the quality of your milk, like, and you could lose, like, you know . . .* (TRS-D, M64–1)
  c. *He's producing, like, we'll say, at a lesser expense.* (TRS-D, M64–1)
  d. *I'm just telling you what I heard, like.* (TRS-D, M64–2)
  e. *Nowadays, like, the kids have new suits now for every week.* (TRS-D, L4–1)
  f. *If they don't do their sums they're not slapped, like, they try to explain.* (TRS-D, L4–1)
  g. *I think, like, the full-timers doesn't work half as much as the part-timers, like.* (TRS-D, U19)
  h. *And she was looking for someone, like, to do some housework for her.* (TRS-D, U19)
  i. *Do they look like you?* (RH) *Well, kinda, like.* (WER, F55+)

Epilogue 1: Irish English as a second language

The great increase in immigration into Ireland which occurred in the 1990s and which has continued to the present (2007) has meant that there are ever greater numbers of people for whom English in Ireland is a second language. Among the immigrants certain countries are particularly well represented. These include Nigeria and certain east European countries. For the present book a short study was made by the author to determine how specific features of Irish English were

Table 5.16. *Group of non-native speakers of Irish English*

Country	Years in Ireland	Number	Gender spread	Native language
Nigeria	4	5	3m, 2f	Yoruba
Poland	$2^1/_2 - 3$	7	5m, 2f	Polish
Latvia	2	2	2m	Latvian
Russia	2	3	2m, 1f	Russian

acquired by those who are not native speakers of Irish English. In the study only those individuals were investigated who had not any significant amounts of instruction in English to ensure that Irish English was their model in acquiring the language.

The test group consisted of seventeen individuals, five from Nigeria and twelve from eastern Europe (see table 5.16). The Nigerians claim to have had exposure to English in their home country, probably forms of West African Pidgin English (Huber 1999: 75–134). They did not have formal training in English. This also applied to the Poles, but both the Latvians and Russians did have English at school. However, they claimed that this instruction was of little if any use to them in Ireland. For all the test persons involved, except perhaps for those from Nigeria, their exposure to colloquial spoken English occurred in Ireland.

The immigrants also showed typical labour patterns. The women worked in supermarkets, at cash desks or stocking shelves, or in the case of the Poles and Russians in the catering industry. Not all the males had employment. Those who did, worked manually, typically in the construction industry, but some of the east Europeans worked in the agricultural sector.

The place of residence in Ireland is relevant in any study of non-native Irish English as second-language speakers tend to pick up the variety of English spoken in their environment. The Nigerians in this study lived in Waterford, in the south-east, as did four of the Poles. The remaining Poles, as well as the Latvians and the Russians, lived in Limerick in the lower west. This meant that none of them were exposed to varieties of Dublin English or forms of English spoken in the north of Ireland.

Pronunciation. None of the speakers had interdental fricatives, /θ/ or /ð/, in the THIN and THIS lexical sets; sometimes the stops were dental, with the Slavic speakers (Poles and Russians). The Yoruba speakers used alveolar stops all the time. This meant that they had not picked up the occasional variant [θ], to be found with some Irish people in a more formal style in post-vocalic, pre-pausal position, e.g. *path* [pɑːθ], *truth* [truːθ]. In a question and response session, the difference between dental and alveolar stops, as in *tank* and *thank*, was not grasped by any of the speakers. In this respect, these individuals were no different from native speakers from outside Ireland who do not normally grasp the distinction in these sets of stops for the Irish.

All speakers variably had a fricative [t̪] in positions where it would be expected in Irish English, i.e. intervocalically and in post-vocalic, pre-pausal position. Of the two positions, the intervocalic one was preferred and seemed to be that in which [t̪] appeared first, both for the Slavic and the Baltic speakers. For the Yoruba speakers, final /t/ was frequently unreleased, which precluded a realisation as [t̪].

The Yoruba speakers kept largely to their five-vowel system, and one of them reported that this had caused difficulties for the Irish in understanding them. Furthermore, when asked by the author, the Yoruba speakers all claimed that the Irish spoke indistinctly, a claim which is likely to stem from the very different prosodic character of Irish English and of forms of West African Pidgin English, which they were probably exposed to in Nigeria. The former is stressed-timed and the latter is syllable-timed.

The Slavic and Latvian speakers tended to maintain non-distinctive vowel length, though in a question and response test most of them could distinguish word pairs like *bit* and *beat*, *pull* and *pool*, probably because of the additional vowel quality difference between members of these word pairs in (Irish) English.

Syllable-final /r/ was present for all the east Europeans as one would expect, given the phonologies of their native languages. With the Yoruba speakers, syllable-final /r/ was present to a slight extent and then only variably. In certain common words, especially when stressed in sentence- or phrase-final position, /r/ was present, e.g. with *more*, *car*, *beer*. Grammatical words, such as *for*, *or*, *are*, *our*, never showed /r/. Where /r/ was present, it was not strongly retroflex as in the new pronunciation of Irish English (see section 5.4). Instead an alveolar continuant, like that typical of conservative mainstream Irish English, was employed. The realisation used by the Yoruba speakers should not be interpreted as an unconscious rejection of retroflex [ɻ]. It probably just reflects the type of realisation found in their immediate social environment.

Grammar. The focus of the survey of non-native Irish English was on vernacular features and how these were picked up by second-language learners in an unguided acquisition environment. Non-standard features in English which clearly derive from the native languages of the test persons were ignored. The underrepresentation of the definite article by the Slavic speakers was just such a feature.

Certain Irish English features were grasped quickly by the test group. Above all, the immediate perfective seems to be have been understood intuitively, e.g. *But K . . . is after selling that car because he wants to buy a bigger one soon* (male Nigerian). The word order O + PP was found with all the east European speakers in nearly all cases and variably with the Nigerians, e.g. *Now we have that building finished. I have my loan paid off.* However, none of the test persons had grasped the distinction between O + PP and PP + O word order embodied in contrastive sentences like *She has read the book* ('She read this book sometime in the past') and *She has the book read* ('She has finished reading the book'); see section 4.4.1.4.

In a question and response session, the Nigerians recognised that the sentence *He does be talking about his children* was habitual in meaning. A few of the Slavic and Baltic speakers did, but this was probably guesswork. For the Nigerians, exposure to West African Pidgin English may be responsible for their recognition of the habitual. They also used a few other constructions which existed in Irish English and which the east Europeans never used, e.g. *on* to express relevance as in *You know J . . ., his girlfriend went off on him not too long ago*. The Nigerians also had variable *-s* marking on third-person-singular verb forms, whereas the Poles, Russians and Latvians showed a much firmer grasp of English morphology. This may be connected with the inflectional nature of their native languages which would have caused them to pay attention to this level of language in English.

This very brief survey shows that second-language varieties of Irish English can offer insights both into the manner in which second-language acquisition proceeds, depending on the first-language background, and into the order in which non-standard features of Irish English are picked up by foreigners. Such varieties also provide insights into structural transparency and permeability of languages in contact situations. This latter aspect can in turn throw light on the question of historical transfer of such features from Irish to English, a matter which has been discussed in detail in chapter 4.

Epilogue 2: The language of Irish Travellers

A notable segment of Irish society consists of people who are not settled in one place. This group has received various designations, some of which, such as 'gypsies' and 'tinkers', are unacceptable today. The designation 'Travellers' – with a capital *T* – replaced 'itinerants', which was used for some time as an alternative to the first two labels. It is intended as a neutral reference to their nomadic lifestyle.

Estimates for the number of Travellers in Ireland vary, ranging between 20,000 and 25,000. Most of them are in the south of Ireland and tend to congregate on the edges of towns or on wider verges of major roads where they often sell their wares, usually used goods, such as furniture or electrical appliances. The former practice of going around to houses offering to do odd jobs and repairs has all but disappeared. The notion of them as living in horse-drawn carriages is not borne out by their present-day lifestyle which relies on motor cars, caravans and trailers, although the attachment of Travellers to horses does remain as does their skill in metal-working. Despite changes in means of transportation and living quarters, the internal organisation would seem to have remained constant: Travellers form groups based on extended patriarchal families, frequently with dozens of members, which tend to move around and camp together.

Reliable, objective information about Travellers is difficult to obtain, not least because they form a social group which is closed to outsiders. They interface with the settled population through their commercial activities and often resist the attempts of authorities to make them take up permanent residence, e.g. on housing estates where they would have access to health care and their children to regular schooling. In the 1960s, the government of Ireland made several official attempts at weaning the Travellers away from their nomadic lifestyle; indeed, there was a body, the Itinerant Settlement Commission, whose declared aim was to integrate them into the settled community. In the following decades newer approaches evolved which stressed the status of the Travellers as an ethnic group with their own cultural norms, based on mobility and self-employment. Various public bodies arose, such as the National Council for Travelling People (set up in the early 1980s and later disbanded), the Federation of Irish Travelling People and the Irish Travellers Movement. Despite agitation for recognition of their legitimate lifestyle, the popular view of the Travellers as a social problem has persisted.

Some Travellers have abandoned their nomadic lifestyle and there are no indications that members of settled communities are joining them, so that in absolute terms their numbers are declining. Indeed, with the great increase in prosperity in Ireland during the 1990s and the early 2000s, their position in Irish society has become even more marginal. This reality is unaffected by the increase in academic interest in Travellers which arose during the 1980s and 1990s and which is evident in such volumes as McCann, Ó Síocháin and Ruane (1994). Interest in questions of language culminated in the volume by Kirk and Ó Baoill (2002).

It is difficult to find accurate information on the origins of Irish Travellers. The view that they are of Romani stock is not borne out by history. There is no record of any sizeable movement of Roma to Ireland in previous centuries,[21] as opposed to England and Wales where groups have been recorded and where remnants of their languages, Anglo-Romani and Welsh Romani, are documented. Scholars who have worked on Romani, such as Yaron Matras (see Matras 1995, 2002), do not assume an Irish segment for the Roma. Outwardly, in dress and/or physical appearance, there is nothing to suggest that the Travellers are anything but Irish.

Whatever about previous generations, present-day Travellers are all speakers of English. They do not seem to camp in the Irish-speaking areas and the author has never seen any in the Gaeltachtaí (Irish-speaking districts) during fieldwork there. Given that they speak English, one can ask if this is a focussed variety which is only used by them. Furthermore, one can ask if their speech is separate from local forms of Irish English.

It is not easy to give answers to these questions because research on language among the Travellers has not been done and what exists from earlier scholars is replete with speculation and unsubstantiated assertions. A work such as Macalister (1937) – *The Secret Languages of Ireland* – betrays in its title the approach

---

[21] There have been, however, a number of Roma from south-east Europe who have come to Ireland in recent years, usually seeking asylum. Up to a few thousand Roma may be currently living in Ireland; they are quite separate from the Travellers.

taken by previous scholars. This research has concentrated on the question of whether the Travellers have their own language, called Shelta.

What is Shelta? There is much mystery surrounding Shelta. Partly because of the closed nature of the communities which are reputed to use it and partly because of the lack of information about it. Awareness of Shelta arose in the 1880s as a result of Charles Leland's *The Gypsies* (1882) in which he mentioned a language, older than Romani, and spoken by Irish travellers (Binchy 1994: 134f.). This sparked off interest,[22] particularly with the English scholar John Sampson and the German Celtologist Kuno Meyer, who were among the first to attempt a description (see Sampson 1890 and Meyer 1891). Both of these relied on the speech of one individual, John Barlow (born in 1811), to describe Shelta (Ní Shuinéar 2002: 37). Macalister (see above) even admitted that he had never heard Shelta spoken. Nonetheless, the glossary which Macalister has in his book (1937: 174–224) is the main source for all the forms of Shelta quoted since (see Ní Shuinéar 2002 for a good overview of scholarship on Shelta).

The uncertainty about Shelta is reflected in its name (Hancock 1984: 385). It is also referred to as Sheldru, a related form which, however, poses certain difficulties in terms of interpretation. The labels *Gammon* and *(Tinkers')* Cant (< Irish *caint* 'talk')[23] are also found.[24] The term *Shelta* may well be connected with Irish *siúl* [ʃuːɫ] 'walk', especially in the phrase *lucht siúil* 'the walking people'. The verbal adjective *siúlta* ['ʃuːɫtə] is phonetically quite close to *Shelta*, but this form does not occur in the phrase just quoted so there is a grammatical difficulty with this interpretation.

The numbers for Shelta speakers in Ireland vary, but the figure of 6,000 is quoted frequently, above all in the various websites concerned with Shelta. Given the fact that demographic research is lacking, it can be assumed that what sources there are have all copied from one another, hence the general agreement on the numbers of speakers. The suggested number of 6,000 is at most a quarter of the 20,000–25,000 Travellers in Ireland (north and south) which means that on any interpretation only a fraction of these use Shelta. Furthermore, even if the figures were based on actual surveys, the question of just what constitutes a speaker of Shelta would still have to be addressed (see Ó Baoill 1994: 156f. for a discussion of these issues).

Shelta can hardly be described as a language, but is more a jargon. It consists of a grammatical base, here Irish English, with words, phrases and idioms of

---

[22] There was also at this time a certain fascination in Britain with gypsies (Nord 2006), as evidenced in the interest in the novels *Lavengro* (1851) and *The Romany Rye* (1857) by George Burrow (1803–81), in which language has a highly symbolic value (Nord 2006: 86–97).

[23] In this context *cant* is probably from Irish. The general use of cant is more likely to derive from Old French (deriving ultimately from Latin *cantare* 'to sing') and not from Irish *caint* 'talk' (although both derive from the same Indo-European root).

[24] One of the informants on an archive tape of the Department of Irish Folklore, University College Dublin, claimed when asked that *Nackers' Gammon* or *Nackers' Cant* are terms used by the Travellers themselves rather than *Shelta*.

Table 5.17. *Selected lexical items supposedly typical of Shelta (from recordings of Travellers in the sound archives of the Department of Irish Folklore, University College Dublin)*

I *Items with an identifiable Irish source*

	Shelta	Irish	gloss		Shelta	Irish	gloss
1	garéad	airgead	'money'	2	rodas	doras	'door'
3	grookra	siúcra	'sugar'	4	lackeen	cailín	'girl'
5	srochar	eochair	'key'	6	cam	mac	'son'
7	camra	madra (?)	'dog'	8	skiock	uisce	'water'
9	mogue	muc	'pig'	10	soorck	gruaig (?)	'hair'

II *Items without an identifiable Irish source*

	Shelta	gloss		Shelta	gloss
1	feenathah	'man'	2	bjore	'woman'
3	nishkeen	'father'	4	nadrum	'mother'
5	njuck	'head'	6	grug	'nose'
7	gushig	'kettle'	8	gillymucks	'shoes'
9	tugs	'clothes'	10	nacker	'tinker'

its own which derive from Irish. This fact supports the assumption that Shelta has existed for a few centuries at least, because there must have been sufficient exposure to Irish, or bilingualism on the part of Travellers, for the Irish words to have been integrated. Indeed, it is conceivable that Shelta started out as a form of Irish, before the historical language shift in Ireland, and that later generations, who had switched to English, retained the Irish lexis to ensure that Shelta was not easily comprehensible to outsiders. Unfortunately, there are no means of ascertaining how much of its special lexis is presently in use among Travellers who speak the jargon and none of the scholars working in this area have addressed the question of currency. Ó Baoill (1994: 161–4) is aware of this and shares the suspicion of the author that active Shelta vocabulary among Travellers is considerably less than is commonly assumed. Certainly, it is very doubtful whether the several hundred items contained in Macalister (1937) are in everyday use among speakers of Shelta today. In the sound archives of the Department of Irish Folklore, University College Dublin, there are a few recordings, made in the 1960s, of travellers talking about Shelta. These speakers had difficulties recalling words of their jargon (one of them could not remember the word for 'son', 'brother' or 'sister'), though given time they did manage to recollect a certain amount.

The basic principle of Shelta lexis is transposition, the deliberate switching around of consonants from syllable onset to syllable coda, what is also called 'back slang', a type of metathesis. There are also other kinds of rearrangement, including insertion and deletion.[25] Certain sound patterns are typical, such as final /-g/ or /-k/, frequently preceded by /ʌ/ or /ɪ/. The general sound shape of words, even those demonstrably from Irish, led to them becoming unrecognisable to the uninitiated, hence the view that it is a secret language. Because of the limited numbers of basic terms available, certain compounds were formed as equivalents to single lexical items in English, e.g. *fay* 'bacon' + *bleeter* 'sheep' = *bleetersfay* 'mutton'.

Mention should be made here of diaspora Travellers. There are groups in Britain and North America who both seem to have maintained Shelta lexis for internal communication (Binchy 1994: 139 confirms that the lexical items are more or less the same as in Ireland). The American branch stems from emigrants to the United States in the mid nineteenth century, as a result of the Great Famine, and who settled in the south. Exact numbers are difficult to come by, but scholars who have studied these groups maintain that there are many thousands of them, in fact more outside Ireland than within. The speech of Irish–American Travellers has been studied in the past few decades; see Harper and Hudson (1971, 1973). The speech of both American and British Shelta speakers has become increasingly anglicised. The latter group are responsible for the well-known Shelta word in English: *bloke* 'man', a borrowing comparable to *pal* 'friend' from Romani.

---

[25] There are parallel cases from other languages. Jahr (2003) reports on the language game found in *Smoi* from the Mandal dialect of Norwegian. It consists of rearrangements such as the following: *kom* → *mok* 'come'; *bil* → *lib* 'car'; *krem* → *mekr* 'cream'; *blod* → *dobl* 'blood' (Jahr 2003: 283).

6   Transportation overseas

6.1   Emigration from Ireland

The story of emigration from Ireland begins with a brief period of territorial expansion on the part of the Gaels in Ireland (then called *Scoti*). By the end of the third century AD they had established footholds in western Scotland and in south Wales. The settlement in Scotland was considerable (Dudley Edwards with Hourican 2005: 126f.): the kingdom of Dalriada included the transfer of Q-Celtic to Scotland and its establishment as the native language of the population of the western and northern parts of the country, later developing as a separate branch which still survives, albeit with greatly diminished numbers, as Scottish Gaelic. With the advent of Christianity the zeal of the Irish switched from being military to religious and the Irish Church in Scotland became an institution which in many respects stood on opposite ground to Rome. Once Gaelic expansion subsided, Irish colonial settlement faded and was never to be revived. After this the Irish no longer came to any foreign country as conquerors but as more or less welcome guests and many of their leaders left their mark on their host countries.

For at least the last 1,500 years the Irish have left Ireland to settle abroad more or less permanently. There have been two chief reasons for this. The first applied in the earliest period, between about 500 and 800 (Dudley Edwards with Hourican 2005: 128). This was to establish religious centres on the continent (Fowkes 1997) and thus strengthen the fledgling church there. The second type of emigration applies much later, to escape unfavourable circumstances in Ireland. The latter can in turn be broken down into at least four subtypes.

The first is where Irish military leaders were defeated and forced to submit to the English crown. The most famous instance of this type of emigration was the so-called Flight of the Earls in 1607 from Lough Swilly in the north of the

The information provided in this chapter is in summary form. For more details, in both data and analysis, see the various contributions in Hickey (2004j). For annotated bibliographical information, see the dedicated sections of Hickey (2002a). I am grateful to a number of colleagues, chiefly Lisa Green (African American English), Joan Beal (Tyneside), Carmen Llamas (Teesside) and Kevin McCafferty (Ulster Scots), who checked the sections on their areas of expertise. Needless to say, any inadequacies are my own responsibility.

country, after the defeat of the Irish by the English in 1601 and the subsequent subjugation of Gaelic lords in Ulster. This type of exodus peaked at key periods in Irish history, hence there is another rise after 1690 when the Jacobite rebellion was finally quelled in Ireland. Emigration for essentially military reasons was quite common with the Irish frequently earning their living as mercenaries abroad. The military readiness of the Irish was known on the continent at least since the sixteenth century; witness the famous picture of Irish soldiers and peasants (1521) by the German artist Albrecht Dürer (1471–1528).

The second subtype has to do with deportation by the English authorities. There are two occasions when significant groups of Irish were deported to overseas locations. The first was in the south-east Caribbean, to Barbados (and from there to Montserrat), where Irish were deported in the early 1650s by Oliver Cromwell. The second was to Australia where deportations of Irish took place in the early days of the country, i.e. in the decades immediately following the initial settlement of the Sydney area in 1788.

A third subtype of emigration has to do with religious intolerance, whether perceived or actual. During the eighteenth century the tension between Presbyterians of Scottish origin in Ulster and the mainstream Anglican Church over the demands of the latter that the former take an oath and sacramental test resulted in an increasing desire to emigrate (along with economic pressure), in this case to North America (see below).

The fourth subtype is that which one might most readily imagine to be the primary cause of emigration, economic necessity. This kind of emigration is what later came to characterise the movement of very large numbers of Irish to Britain, Canada and above all to the United States in the nineteenth century, but it was also a significant factor with the Ulster Scots in the eighteenth century.

Emigration from Ireland must have started quite early, long before the beginning of the early modern period around 1600. In the fifteenth and sixteenth centuries there was seasonal migration to England during harvest time and Irish vagrants were common (Dudley Edwards with Hourican 2005: 131f.). Their speech must have been known in rough outline before the second period of English in Ireland, i.e. before 1600. After all, Shakespeare was in a position to characterise some of the more prominent features of Irish English in the figure of Captain Macmorris in the 'Four Nations' scene of *Henry V* (Blank 1996: 136–9). Ben Jonson was able to write a short satirical piece, *The Irish Masque at Court* (1613/16), at the beginning of the seventeenth century which is replete with salient features of Irish English.

6.1.1 ASSESSING FEATURES IN OVERSEAS VARIETIES

Before examining the histories of overseas locations with input from Irish English, one can consider what would constitute evidence of Irish influence at such locations. There are at least three sources for the features in an overseas variety (see

Table 6.1. *Possible sources for features in overseas varieties*

Source 1:	Irish English input only
Source 2:	Irish English input and/or other input (dialects of English or substrate languages)
Source 3:	Independent developments

the general discussion in Tagliamonte 2006), as shown in table 6.1. Naturally combinations of these three are also to be found.

The essential difficulty lies in deciding which of the sources in table 6.1 is the most likely for a given feature. In general, one can say that source 1 is only likely where (i) the feature in question is unique to the variety in question and to Irish English and (ii) the location of the overseas variety has been isolated from outside influences throughout its history. There are not many features which fulfil these conditions, but one example would be the *after*-perfective of Irish English also found in Newfoundland (Clarke 1997b). A similar case (with an English source) would be initial voicing attested in traditional dialects in England from Kent across to Devon (Trudgill 1990: 29) and in Newfoundland among the English-based community there (Clarke 2004: 248).

A further problem with parallels between an overseas and an input variety is that source 3 could constitute the origin. An instance of this is so-called 'diph-thong flattening' (Wells 1982: 614), a term used to refer to the lack of an upward glide with the /ai/ and /au/ diphthongs in particular, i.e. *wife* when realised as [waːf, wɑːf]. Such 'flattening' is found today in areas as far apart as the southern United States and South Africa (Lass 1987: 305f.), quite apart from its occurrence in parts of England such as Yorkshire and Merseyside.

In such cases additional evidence might help in deciding a matter. For instance, it is known from diaspora varieties of African American English that this flatten-ing is a fairly recent phenomenon (Bailey and Ross 1992) and not characteristic of African American speech before the twentieth century. This fact would support the view that the 'flattening' in both the locations referred to is an independent development.

Another factor of importance when considering possible sources is the relative unusualness of features. Two different examples of this are special forms of the second person plural and the feature known as 'positive *anymore*'.

English is virtually unique among European languages in not having a dis-tinction between singular and plural forms of personal pronouns (see section 4.4.2.1). This situation arose due to the demise of the special second-person-singular form *thou* in the early modern period which is now found with only a very restricted distribution in parts of England and in ritualised language such as religious services. Non-standard varieties of English largely compensated for this by developing specific plural forms of their own, retaining the form *you* as a singular personal pronoun. There are various forms used in the plural, e.g. *ye*, *yez*, *youse*, *y'all*, *you'uns* (see Hickey 2003d for a detailed discussion). This means that the mere existence of a special plural form for the second-person pronoun is not sufficient to posit an historical connection between varieties. What one needs is a clear formal parallel. It is known that the form *youse* is of Irish English origin (see section 4.4.2.1 for details) so that its occurrence in forms of southern hemisphere English,[1] such as Australian and New Zealand English, clearly points to an Irish origin.

Some formal parallels are of a very general nature, such as the contraction of *you* and *all* to *y'all*. This makes it unlikely that varieties as far apart geographically as southern American English and South African Indian English could be historically related in this respect. Other features of such generality would be (i) unmarked adverbs, i.e. where the ending *-ly* is not present, as in *He's awful busy these days*, and (ii) *them* as a demonstrative pronoun, e.g. *Them boys out on the street*. The ubiquity of such usages (Trudgill 1990: 79; Wakelin 1984: 82) greatly reduces their value as diagnostics.

The feature known as 'positive *anymore*' (Labov 1991) is quite unusual. However, it may occur in the Midland area of the United States (and further into the west, Wolfram and Schilling-Estes 1998: 142; Eitner 1991), as in *They go to Florida on their holidays anymore*. It may well derive from the speech of eighteenth-century Ulster Scots settlers whose predecessors had in turn picked this up from native speakers of Irish (see above) before emigration, though see Butters (2001: 331f.) for a dissenting opinion.

In table 6.1 above what is labelled source 2 has also been a matter of dispute among scholars. Essentially, one is dealing here with features which have more than one possible source. For instance, the occurrence of a habitual aspect in forms of English in the eastern Caribbean, above all in the English of Barbados, is something which could be traced back to input forms of English from either England or Ireland or to the substrate influence of the African languages which form the linguistic background of early slaves in the region. It may be that the Irish and the English inputs came together in this region; this would be a case of convergence. The contact account on the other hand would favour African substrate languages as the most likely source for the habitual aspect (for detailed discussions, see the contributions in Hickey 2004j).

6.1.2 FEATURES NOT FOUND OVERSEAS

Considerations of dialect transportation will invariably touch on those features which have not appeared at overseas locations. The features themselves may be of interest, but the larger question is why transportation did not take place. Before considering specifically Irish English features, one can mention a prominent feature of northern England which did not survive anywhere overseas, namely [ʊ]

---

[1] On such structures in American English, see Wolfram and Schilling-Estes (1998: 343).

in the STRUT lexical set. This realisation is a clear indicator of northern dialects of English to this day and represents a continuation of the historical /u/ in this lexical set. It is also known that sizeable numbers of northern English emigrated to overseas locations without this feature having survived in the speech of their offspring. Furthermore, it is known that appreciable numbers of Dubliners were also among emigrant groups, above all to Australia and New Zealand. They would also have had [ʊ] in the STRUT class and nonetheless this realisation has not asserted itself anywhere in these countries.

The explanation for the disappearance of features after transportation would seem to lie in the social position of the speakers with these traits and in the relative salience of the features involved. The high back vowel [ʊ] is a very obvious feature of northern English and one which would have rendered this speech immediately recognisable at an overseas location. Given the fact that northern English did not in general become dominant, despite significant emigration (South Africa; see Lass 2004), its prominent features were discontinued. The more salient the features of a non-dominant group were (Hickey 2000a), the more likely these were to be avoided by later generations in the formative period of any new overseas variety.

However difficult it may be to define acoustic salience definitively, there are certain aspects which one can highlight. One aspect is the unusualness of a putatively salient feature in the sound system of the language in question. The high central [ʉ] vowel, found in Ulster and Scottish English (Harris 1984b: 118f.), is just such a case. Any non-back rounded vowel is unusual in English, so the [ʉ] vowel is, and would have been, acoustically salient at any overseas location. As the group with this variant did not become dominant at any new location, such clearly perceptible features would have not been continued by subsequent generations, i.e. they would have been disfavoured in the 'new dialect formation' process (Hickey 2003e). This process is probably responsible for the disappearance of non-standard dialect features in cases where speakers from different regional backgrounds came together and a new variety arose (Trudgill 2004). For example, it is known from studies like that of Matthews (1935) and of Bailey and Ross (1988) that many non-standard features were taken to the New World which did not survive there to any appreciable extent. Matthews examined ships' logs which were deposited at the Navy Office and in the Public Records Office, mostly after 1660 and a few before that date. He found evidence for such features as the substitution of /ʌ/ for /ɪ/ (e.g. *bushop*, *druselling* 'drizzling'), the raising of /ɛ/ to /ɪ/ before nasals (e.g. *inemy*, *wint*, *frinds*), the retraction and raising of /æ/ to /ɔ/ (e.g. *tollow* 'tallow', *for* 'far'), the lowering of /e/ to /a/ before historic /r/ (e.g. *marcy*, *sarvant*), the use of *th* [ð] for *d* as in *orther* 'order', *ruther* 'rudder' (all these pronunciations have parallels in Irish English).

Another salient feature which has been lost from most varieties is the velar fricative, typical of Scots (McClure 1994: 65) and Ulster Scots (Adams 1981b), and seen in a word like *enough* [ɪ'nʌx]. There are no fricatives in the velar area in English so that [x] is definitely phonetically salient. This fact goes a long way towards explaining why, despite the significant Ulster emigration to the United States in the eighteenth century, there do not seem to be any traces of this sound overseas.

Phonetic salience can be due not just to the unusualness of a sound in a specific language, but to the difference between an expected and a realised value. This can be seen with the lowering of /e/ to /a/ before /r/, previously widely attested in many varieties of English and established in standard English in words like *bark*(< *berke*), *dark* (< *derke*), *clerk* /klɑːk/ (Lass 1987: 277) and the names of some British counties (Ekwall 1980: 27) such as *Berkshire* and *Hertfordshire*. Further instances of this lowering, such as *serve* /sɑːrv/, are attested historically but have been abandoned by supraregional speakers and, if at all, are only maintained by rural speakers, notably in East Anglia (Trudgill 2002: 37). Historically, there is evidence of a much wider distribution of the lowering before /r/, e.g. in the south-west of England (Wakelin 1988: 628).

Morphological parallels to the type of phonetic salience just discussed are also to be found, a good example being the singular forms of the second-person pronoun – *thou, thee* – which disappeared from early forms of American English or were relegated to religious usage.

6.1.3 SURVIVAL OF NON-STANDARD FEATURES IN OVERSEAS VARIETIES

The reverse of features which have not survived are those which are attested at overseas locations but no longer found in the input varieties. The reason for this is invariably that the latter lost the feature in question, leaving the overseas varieties with the sole attestation of the trait in question. An example of this would be initial /h-/ in pronominal forms. This is still found as *hit* 'it' in Appalachian English and Outer Banks English (Wolfram and Schilling-Estes 1998: 326) and is attested in Ulster.

A further example concerns the diphthong in the CHOICE lexical set which is now /ɔi/ in standard varieties of English. But up to the eighteenth century the pronunciation was often /ai/, i.e. *boil* and *bile* were homophones (Barber 1997 [1976]: 304), and this realisation was transported to many locations, including Ireland and the United States. In the latter there are dialectal survivals of the older /ai/ pronunciation (Montgomery 2001: 139).

Another case involves the coalescence of /w/ and /v/, historically a stereotypical feature of Cockney. It can be found in other varieties of English in the New World (in the Caribbean) and may have been present in the initial English input to Australia and New Zealand. The merger may have been to a bilabial approximant [β] which was later de-merged through contact with varieties without the merger (Trudgill, Schreier, Long and Williams 2004). Here the situation in some minor overseas varieties can throw light on the former situation in south-eastern British English.

The transmission of English at overseas locations may be responsible for the survival of some dialect features. For example, in the context of South Africa,

Mesthrie (1992: 21) notes that in the second half of the nineteenth century missionaries in charge of education came from diverse backgrounds, including a few from Ireland (and Scotland), and could conceivably have transferred the following features: (i) *but* as tag marker: *He has gone to the races, but?* (i.e. *hasn't he?*), (ii) *like* as a clause-final focus marker: *She's hard-working, like* (i.e. *you know*); see section 5.7. Bobda (2006) offers a discussion of this topic in the context of Cameroon.

6.1.4 FURTHER DEVELOPMENTS OVERSEAS

Even if a link between features at overseas anglophone locations and those in putative source varieties in Britain or Ireland can be established, this does not account exhaustively for the manifestation and distribution of such features. Varieties continue to develop and will take parts of the historical input and in some cases background them, but in some instances foreground and expand them. Not only that, but the source varieties themselves develop further, often shifting or indeed losing features which they had at the time of emigration so that the pattern overseas does not correspond to that in contemporary forms of the British or Irish source. This is probably true of double modals. These are regarded as characteristic of northern English, Scottish and Ulster English. However, their present-day distribution is extremely limited and the author has not found a single instance in any of the corpora for Ulster English which he used for this book. Reports for Appalachian English, however, speak of clear attestations there (Montgomery and Nagle 1994; see Mishoe and Montgomery 1994 for a discussion of their use and means of elicitation). This could be due to the retention, or indeed expansion, of double modals at this overseas location while they receded in the source varieties in Britain and Ireland.

6.2   The Irish in Britain

There is a long history of Irish emigrants in Britain, reaching back many centuries (Fitzgerald 1992). But mass emigration only set in during the nineteenth century (Hickman 2005) and was considerable to various parts of north-central and northern Britain and to the London area. In recent years there has been much research into this emigration, especially by historians. Various contributions in the six-volume edited work by O'Sullivan (1992) deal with the movement of Irish to Britain. Monographs on the subject include G. Davis (1991), R-A. Harris (1994) and Swift (2002), along with the edited volumes by Swift and Gilley (1985 and 1999). There are also contemporary accounts of the Irish in Britain which stem from the late nineteenth century; see Denvir (1892) and Heinrick (1990 [1872]).

Similar to the pattern of emigration to the United States (see below), the Irish congregated in areas where labour for industries like mining was required (O'Connor 1972; MacRaild 1999). It is estimated that by 1841 nearly 2 per cent of the population of England was born in Ireland (Dudley Edwards with Hourican 2005: 137f.). In Wales the percentage was much less, but there was a concentration in Swansea and Cardiff, cities which have always had connections with cities on the south coast of Ireland like Cork (O'Leary 2000). In Scotland the figures were much higher: 4.8 per cent of the population there was Irish-born (in 1841) and again these lived chiefly in the large cities, Glasgow and Edinburgh, which have a tradition of accepting migrant labour from Ireland, especially from nearby Ulster (Devine 1991; Handley 1943, 1947).

As with the United States, the key period for the rise in the Irish sector of the population lies after the late 1840s. This was largely as a result of the Great Famine, which triggered a wave of immigration to both Britain (Crawford 1997; Neal 1997) and the New World (see section 6.3). The censuses of 1841 and 1861 returned 415,000 and 806,000 Irish-born in Britain respectively (G. Davis 2000: 20). This increase led to much friction between the English and Irish, especially as the Irish were frequently under-nourished and diseased, and in 1852, for instance, there were anti-Catholic, i.e. anti-Irish, riots in Stockport (Dudley Edwards with Hourican 2005: 140).

The linguistic effect of the Irish on the areas in which they settled depended on at least three main factors: their numbers, the structure of the English communities they were in contact with and whether they displayed focussed or diffuse settlement patterns. For instance, the city of Sheffield experienced immigration during the nineteenth century from Irish who came to work in the steel industry and who largely congregated in the north-western part of the city (Hey 1998: 148). Sheffield had a dense system of networks based on the families traditionally employed in the cutlery industry, a precursor to steel production. The numbers of Irish were relatively low: between 3 and 4 per cent was the figure returned by the 1851 census (Hey 1998), perhaps below the threshold to have penetrated the established networks in the city (Beal, personal communication) and so have had an effect on speech there.

The density of settlement is a significant factor as well. In many cases the Irish were to be found in certain well-defined areas which would have maintained Irish features, possibly transferring these in the course of time to the English communities surrounding them, as was probably the case in Liverpool (see following section). More diffuse settlement was found in Lancashire to the north, often associated with work in the agricultural sector (O'Dowd 1991). Such diffuse settlement probably had no influence on varieties of English in the areas where it occurred.

6.2.1 MERSEYSIDE

The areas of England which absorbed most Irish were Merseyside and its hinterland of Cheshire to the south and Lancashire to the north. The reason for this is obvious: the port of Liverpool is directly opposite Dublin and there was, and still is, a constant ship service between the two cities. Liverpool was an important port for emigration to North America and many Irish who had travelled there with this intention ended up staying in Merseyside, usually because they lacked the money for transportation (G. Davis 2000: 23). This group would have provided an input to vernacular speech in this region in the second half of the nineteenth century.

The local dialect of Liverpool is Scouse and it is characteristic of its speakers to show a degree of fricativisation with /p, t, k/ in environments where they are flanked by vowels or before a pause, i.e. in intervocalic and word-final position (Honeybone 2001: 234–42; Sangster 2001: 402; Knowles 1978). Scholars such as Wells (1982) generally ascribe this to an independent development in Scouse. In more detailed treatments, the origin and predominance of Liverpool lenition[2] in working-class speech is highlighted (Sangster 2001: 411). This section of society is of course that which has the strongest historical links with Ireland, given that many of its members are both Catholic and descendants of poor Irish emigrants. Another feature associated with working-class Catholics in Liverpool is the fortition of /θ, ð/ as in *month* [mʌnt̪] and *that* [d̪at] (Wells 1982: 371).

In the nineteenth century the Irish language in Ireland was relatively strong. Furthermore, the Irish who were forced to emigrate were the economically disadvantaged, which is tantamount to saying that they were Irish speakers or poor bilinguals. This fact is evident in the faulty English, used when communicating with English officials and shipping firms (many in Liverpool), to be found in the corpus of Irish emigrant letters used for this book. Indeed, in many cases the English of the emigrants was poorer still and it was often an individual in the neighbourhood, with slightly better English, who wrote any letters which were necessary. The emigrants would thus have spoken a variety of English which was strongly affected by their native Irish and would thus have been likely to show lenition as a transfer phenomenon. In Irish, the stops /p, t, k/ lenite to /f, h, x/[3] respectively. When considering Liverpool and Irish English lenition, the lenited form of /t/ is uncontroversial as it is the same is both cases, i.e. an apico-alveolar fricative. What remains is the lenition of /p/ and /k/ to their corresponding fricatives, /f/ and /x/, in local Liverpool English.

One possible explanation for the situation in Liverpool is that it represents a continuation of an original type of lenition in Irish English which affected /p, t, k/. If this was the case, then why is lenition of all these stops not a characteristic of modern Irish English? Recall that in the supraregional variety of present-day Irish English lenition only applies to alveolars. The explanation could be as follows. In the course of the nineteenth century the position of English strengthened as that of Irish was weakened. With this increased influence, lenition would have been reduced to alveolar stops, i.e. it ceased to occur with labials and velars (with the former it would have caused considerable homophony in word pairs like *cup* and

---

[2] Sangster (2001: 410f.) furthermore confirms that the lenition of /t/ in Liverpool English does not lead to a neutralisation in the realisation of /t/ and /s/, contrary to external perceptions of this variety.

[3] The lenition of /t/ to [h] is a special historical development stemming from the original output of lenition, [θ], which was lost by the end of the Middle Irish period (T. F. O'Rahilly 1926).

cuff). The alveolar point of articulation would then have survived with lenition as this is a preferred site for such reduction across varieties of English.

One could now account for *t*-lenition in modern Irish English. There was generalised lenition of labials, alveolars and velars. Supraregionalisation masked the lenition of labials and velars leaving that of alveolars. The generalised lenition in Scouse may thus be a remnant of a wider and more regular distribution of lenition from Irish English which has been maintained, albeit recessively, in this location outside Ireland (see Hickey 1996a for a fuller discussion). Although this scenario cannot be proven for Irish English there is evidence from a further area in Britain, which had considerable Irish immigration in the nineteenth century and which shows lenition similar to that in Liverpool. This is Middlesbrough on the east coast, roughly half way between Newcastle and York, which is the topic of the following section.

6.2.2 TEESSIDE

The city of Middlesbrough, since 1996 a unitary authority located in the former county of Cleveland, lies between county Durham to the north and north Yorkshire to the south (Llamas 2006: 96f.). The city is on the south bank of the Tees estuary. It was founded in 1830 when a railway was built in order provide transportation for coal mined in the area, making Middlesbrough the first railway town. Iron works were established in 1841 and iron ore was discovered in the region. Within a few decades Middlesbrough had become the largest producer of pig-iron in the world. This led to a phenomenal growth in the labour force and hence in the population so that within forty years, by the 1870s, it had become a major town. By 1901 the population had increased to 91,000 from a mere 154 in 1831 (Llamas 2001).

The dramatic increase in population for Middlesbrough was fed from a number of sources, one of which was immigrant Irish. Due to the heterogeneous composition of the population it can be seen that by the census year of 1851 there were no specifically Irish quarters in Middlesbrough. In addition no aversion to the Irish by the non-Irish was discernible at this time (Willis 2003: 20–4). The Irish section of the population had grown rapidly as seen in the increase from 6.3 per cent in 1851 to 15.6 per cent by 1861. By the 1870s one in five adult males was Irish, putting Middlesbrough second only to Liverpool in terms of the size of its Irish population.

Given the significant portion of Irish and the looser nature of its structure as a new town, as opposed to the much more established city of Sheffield, for instance, it is not surprising that an Irish influence is discernible in Middlesbrough speech, a legacy of nineteenth-century demographics. The similarity between Liverpool and Middlesbrough accents has been remarked upon repeatedly, including in the scholarly literature (see Kerswill and Williams 2000), with the Middlesbrough speakers being mistaken for Liverpool speakers. Jones and Llamas (2003) have also commented on this in the context of fricated /t/ in both areas.

Among the Middlesbrough features which can be seen as indicative of Irish influence are alveolar /l/, second-person-plural from *youse* and vowel epenthesis in words like *film* ['fɪləm]. To these can be added fricated /t/ and, importantly, a less common tendency to fricate word-final, pre-pausal /-k/,[4] as in *back* [bax] (Llamas, personal communication). The lenition of labials, e.g. *cup* [kʌ f], does not appear to occur. This fact matches the cline in Liverpool English where the preferential sites for lenition are (i) alveolar (*slit* [slɪt̪]), (ii) velar (*slack* [slax]) and (iii) labial (*slap* [slaf]).

It is no coincidence that both Merseyside and Teesside are dialect areas of Britain which show consonant lenition and that it is these areas which had the greatest input from (southern) Irish English. Add to this the folk perception experiments in Kerswill and Williams (2000), which linked the speech of the two areas, and the conclusion seems justified that the shared speech characteristics can be traced to nineteenth-century Irish migrants into these areas. The greater scope of stop lenition in both Liverpool and Merseyside would furthermore support the view that this is a kind of 'colonial lag', i.e. a remnant of wider lenition which was later narrowed in Ireland to alveolars due to the effects of supraregionalisation in the late nineteenth and early twentieth century (see section 5.3).

6.2.3 TYNESIDE

Another area of England with considerable Irish immigration in the nineteenth century is Tyneside. House (1954: 47) in Beal (1993: 189) notes: 'In 1851 [the year of a census – RH], Newcastle, the most cosmopolitan of the north-eastern towns, had one person in every ten born in Ireland.'

When considering possible influence of Irish English in Tyneside one must take the history of features within England into account. For instance, it is true that Tyneside English shows *ye* as the second-person-plural pronoun (Upton and Widdowson 1996: 66f.), an obvious parallel with Irish English. But this is a survival from older forms of English and is present in Scotland as well. So at best one could argue for a certain convergence of Irish English and Tyneside English in this respect, but even this should not be exaggerated. The same caution should be exercised when considering non-standard syntactic features, such as the use of *what* as relative pronoun. This is found in Tyneside, but in their study of Newcastle and Sheffield (Beal and Corrigan 2005) the authors found that *what* as a relative pronoun was much more common in the latter location, the one with a considerably smaller Irish influx in the nineteenth century. The situation is somewhat different with features which are known to be specifically Irish, such as the use of epistemic *must* in the negative (Beal 1993: 197; 2004b: 126) or the second-person-plural form *yous* (see relevant section of table 6.2) which is most likely to be of Irish origin (see discussion in section 4.4.2.1 above).

---

[4] The lenition of /k/ to /x/ is only found in Ireland in rural vernacular varieties in Co. Limerick (see section 5.4.3).

Table 6.2. *Features of Tyneside English attested in the Newcastle Electronic Corpus of Tyneside English (NECTE)*

1. Negative epistemic *must*
    You mustn't have had a sink then if you, if you screamed when it disappeared right down the sink; We mustn't have had what ever it is, claustrophobia or anything, must we? (F 51–60, secretary, lower middle class)
2. Second-person-plural *ye* and *yous*
    I'm telling ye – well – what's the age group you – you eh knock about with; . . . eleven driving lessons ye should need . . . (M 16–20, car mechanic, working class); *yous are cocky 'yous are cocky like' we goes . . .* (M 16–20, student, lower middle class); *that's the way yous were when yous went* (M 51–60, retired plumber, lower middle class)
3. *What* for relative pronoun *which*
    I don't mind the uniform what we have; that's right, it's difficult with money what surprises me (M 41–50, local government officer, middle class)

The use of singular inflection with third-person-plural verbs, e.g. *Her sisters is quite near* (Beal 1993: 194), is both a feature of northern English in general and of vernacular Irish English. Like *ye* this could be a continuation of an older situation here and in Ireland. Failure of negative attraction is also attested for Tyneside English, e.g. *Everyone didn't want to hear them*, for *Nobody wanted to hear them*, as is *never* as a negative with singular time reference, e.g. *I never done the work* 'I didn't do the work' (Beal 1993: 198). In Tyneside English the use of *whether* is less common (Beal 1993: 204), the indirect question maintaining the word order of the direct question, as in: *She asked her son did he clean up*. This type of inversion is typical of Irish English, both northern and southern forms. Furthermore, relative clauses may be introduced by *that* in restrictive contexts, e.g. *The man that you know is outside*, and *what* may also occur as a relative pronoun with an animate referent, e.g. *The man what was interested in linguistics*, as can *which*, e.g. *The ladies which accompanied him had curly hair* (Beal 1993: 207; 2004b: 131–4).

Some of the features are reminiscent of northern Irish English, e.g. the use of double modals (not found in the south of Ireland and only very rarely in the north nowadays), especially in the negative in urban Tyneside, e.g. *they mustn't could have made any today* (Beal 1993: 195; 2004b: 127f.). This is also true of the use of a past participle after *need*, e.g. *My hair needs washed* for *My hair needs washing* (Beal 1993: 200). With these features one may be dealing with a geographical continuum including Tyneside and Scotland north of it. Indeed, the use of a past participle after *need* would seem to have been taken to northern Ireland by Scots settlers. This feature is also found in western Pennsylvania, probably as a relic of Ulster Scots speech from the eighteenth century (Montgomery 2001: 149).

Not all the specific features of Tyneside speech point to possible Irish influence, e.g. the use of *for to* + infinitive is a common dialectal feature in the British Isles, as is the use of *them* as a demonstrative pronoun (*I like them books*, Beal 1993: 207) and of course the use of singular nouns after numerals (*I lived there for ten year*, Beal 1993: 209). Items from phonology, where convergence with Irish English input may have been operative, include the retention of word-initial /h-/ and the retention of /hw/, [ʍ], e.g. *which* [ʍɪtʃ] (initial /h-/ is a characteristic of the far north of England, Upton and Widdowson 1996: 46f.). The adverb *geet* [giː?] in the sense of 'really', e.g. *This is geet hard*, is not known in Ireland. Verb contractions like *divvent* 'do not' (Beal 2004b: 124) do not occur in Ireland either.

Further parallels between Tyneside English and Irish English

1. Preference for *will* over *shall* (Beal 1993: 194f.): <u>*Will*</u> *I put the kettle on?*
2. *For to* + infinitive (Beal 2004b: 134): . . . *it just didn't enter me head <u>for to</u> say I wonder what if it'll be different.*
3. Sentence-final *but* in the sense of 'though': *I'll manage, <u>but</u>.*
4. *Can* or *could* are found in perfective constructions where more standard forms of English have *be able to*: *He <u>cannot</u> get a job since he's left school.*
5. The use of *can*, rather than *may*, to express permission. Connected with this is the use of *might* to express possibility rather than *may* (Beal 1993: 194): *Mind, it looks as if it <u>might</u> rain, doesn't it?*
6. Extended use of the definite article, for instance with reference to age: *So I never really started work 'till I was about <u>the fifteen</u>* (Beal 2004b: 129).

6.2.4 SCOTLAND

The present chapter is concerned with identifying features of Irish English which might have been transported to locations outside Ireland. In the case of Scotland this endeavour must consider whether parallels between forms of Irish English and Scottish English are (i) historical continuations of earlier varieties of English or (ii) both due to transfer from Q-Celtic (Irish in Ireland and Scottish Gaelic in Scotland) during the language shift which affected both Ireland and Scotland. Furthermore, when considering possible parallels, it is sensible to examine forms of English in Ulster (Ulster Scots and Ulster English), rather than forms further south, given the geographical proximity of Ulster to Scotland and the historically attested emigration which was often seasonal and driven by the search for work in Glasgow and west-central Scotland and which has been typical of Ulster for the last two centuries. This latter situation, together with the seventeenth-century planting of Ulster by Scots, means that many features of English in Ulster may be imports from Scotland, i.e. that transportation was into, and not out of, Ireland. For a discussion of features of Older Scots which have survived in Ulster, see section 3.3.3.

For the following discussion vernacular Glasgow English has been examined. This has been investigated thoroughly by Caroline Macafee (see Macafee 1983 and 1994), and it is furthermore an urban vernacular which shows influence from

Ulster English (from Co. Donegal across to Co. Down) due to emigration from the north of Ireland to the Glasgow region.

Parallels between Glasgow English and northern Irish English

1. In general vowel length tends to be determined by the Scottish Vowel Length Rule. Here the phonetic environment following the vowel determines its length (Stuart-Smith 2004: 56f.; McClure 1994: 51); see section 3.3.3 above for details. Basically, this also applies to Ulster Scots, as an imported feature, and has affected Ulster English to a certain extent. There is no trace of the rule further south in Ireland.
2. The fronted [ʉ] sound is shared with English in Ulster (and Ulster Irish). The sound can be fronted as far as [ɪ] in Glasgow which gives pronunciations like *boot* [bɪt], *good* [gɪd], traditionally written as *buit, guid*, etc. These realisations are also typical of conservative Ulster Scots.
3. The non-retraction of /a/ after /w/, found in Glasgow, is also a conservative feature of Irish English in the north and south (mentioned by Sheridan 1781: 145).
4. The merger of the SQUARE and NURSE lexical sets in Glasgow is also found in northern Irish English, but not in southern forms. Macafee (1994: 225) considers this the result of Irish influence on Glasgow English.
5. The Glaswegian shift of /ð/ to /r/ (Stuart-Smith 2004: 62) is not a feature of Irish English, though the deletion of intervocalic /ð/ is a common northern feature, e.g. *northern* [nɔːɹn]. The use of [f] (TH-fronting) by younger speakers (Stuart-Smith 2004: 62) is probably an adopted feature from southern British urban vernaculars.
6. Vowel epenthesis in final clusters of /-lm/, e.g. *film* [fɪləm], and often extended to /-rl/ clusters, e.g. *girl* [gɛrəl], is an areal feature of both Ulster English and Irish as well as vernacular Scottish English and Scottish Gaelic.
7. L-vocalisation (McClure 1994: 48) is an established feature of Scots and continued in Ulster Scots. However, elsewhere in Ireland it is unknown (but see comments on l-velarisation in new Dublin English in section 5.5.4.3 above).
8. Post-stop sonorant deletion, *col', ol'*, etc., is also shared with Irish English in the north and south.
9. The reduction of final, unstressed /o/ in *follow, yellow*, etc. is shared with both the north and south of Ireland.
10. The enclitic negative /-ne, nɪ/, common in vernacular forms of Scottish English, is shared with Ulster Scots, but not with southern Irish English, though it can be found sometimes in general forms of Ulster English.
11. /t/ epenthesis with *once* /wʌnst/ maybe an Irish feature (McArthur 1992: 441).
12. *Youse, yiz* are probably imports from Ulster to Glasgow and western Scotland, but *you'ns, yins* (< *you ones*) are Scottish in origin.

13. *See* as an opener highlighting a topic, e.g. *See football, I hate the stuff*, is not common in Ireland.
14. The form *ken*, equivalent to the pragmatic marker *you know*, is not found in Ireland.

There are a number of grammatical parallels between Scottish English and forms of Irish English. Some are very general, such as the past-tense forms of verbs, e.g. *come* 'came', *done* 'did' (J. Miller 2004: 48) or the use of inflected verb forms with plural subjects, e.g. with the third person plural. However, verbal *-s* with the first person plural is not a common Irish feature (there is only one occurrence of *we was* in *A Corpus of Irish English* (Hickey 2003a), namely in Shaw's play *John Bull's Other Island*). Other features, like negative epistemic *must*, e.g. *This mustn't be the place* (J. Miller 2004: 53) are clear parallels with Irish and northern British English.

Another grammatical parallel is the resultative O + PP word order, as in *That's the letters written and posted* (J. Miller 2004: 56); see section 4.4.1.4.2. Other features one could mention in this context are the overuse of the definite article (see section 4.4.4 above), compared to more standard forms of English (J. Miller 2004: 59f.), the use of *than what* in comparatives (see section 4.4.5.2), unbound *myself* (see section 4.4.2.3). These last three features have clear parallels in Scottish Gaelic, as their equivalents in Ireland have in Irish, and can probably be regarded as transfer features originating in the historical language shift in Scotland. The widespread use of cleft sentences for topicalisation purposes (J. Miller 2004: 66f.) is similar to the situation in Ireland, as is the preference for *that* as a relative pronoun with an animate antecedent.

6.3   The United States

Irish emigration to the United States can be divided into two phases. The first is that of Protestant emigration from Ulster in the eighteenth century, largely to Pennsylvania and from there further down to the inland south-east.[5] The second phase is that of the nineteenth century, especially the second half, which was largely characterised by Catholic emigrants from the south of Ireland. Both phases are dealt with below in sections 6.3.1 and 6.3.2 respectively. There are, however, general features of American English which cannot conclusively be traced to either phase and which may have diffused into general varieties of English during the long period from the beginning of the eighteenth to the end of the nineteenth century.

Such features are not necessarily salient; indeed, it is their low profile which probably accounts for their survival in more standard varieties of American English. The following three features may serve to illustrate this point. (i) The

---

[5] The importance of settlement history for patterns of geographical variation is a given in American dialectology (see the discussion of Kurath's work in Kretzschmar 1996) although this has not received the same degree of attention in the study of Irish English. See also Montgomery (2004).

first concerns the use of the definite article. In varieties of English which historically have been in contact with Celtic languages the definite article is found in generic senses (Harris 1993: 144f.): *The life there is hard, He asked the both of them* (see section 4.4.4). A certain consensus exists that the greater application of the definite article in forms of American English is a legacy of Irish influence (Montgomery 2001: 133; Butters 2001: 337). It is especially common in generic statements, e.g. *She has gone to the hospital, The child has got the measles, They go to Florida in the spring.* (ii) The second feature involves a semanticisation of post-sonorant stop variation. There are a large number of verbs in English which end in a sonorant, i.e. /l, n, r/. The past participle of such verbs may vary between a voiced and a voiceless stop with the former being used to indicate a process and the latter to indicate a state (and used attributively), e.g. *The milk spilled onto the floor,* but *spilt milk; The house burned for hours,* but *burnt wood* (Lass 1987: 278). Such distinctions exist for Irish English and also for American English (Hamp 1997) and there may be a causal connection between them. (iii) The third feature is negative epistemic must, as in *She mustn't be very old,* which has been mentioned in the context of Tyneside and Scottish English above. In an investigation with several informants (undergraduates, pupils and some others), Tottie (1985: 110) found that *must* occurred in 23 per cent of the sentences in her control group, with a negative epistemic sense for the Americans.[6] This contrasts with a single instance in the British group. Again the existence of this feature in American English could be traced to its presence in Irish English input.

6.3.1 ULSTER SCOTS IN THE UNITED STATES

Emigration from Ulster. The eighteenth century is a period during which considerable emigration from Ulster (and Scotland) took place to North America with many people leaving the province. Estimates for the numbers vary. At the one end, historians like Kerby Miller suggest that anywhere between 250,000 and 400,000 emigrated between 1700 and the American Revolution and that only between one-fifth and a quarter of these were Catholics (K. Miller 1985: 137). Duffy (1997: 90f.) maintains that throughout the eighteenth-century emigration ran at about 4,000 a year and totalled over a quarter of a million. At the other end one has estimates for the Ulster Scots migration in the eighteenth-century which favour lower numbers. Louis Cullen suggests 40,000 in the period 1701–75 (Cullen 1994: 139f.). Bernard Bailyn suggests that 55,000 Protestant Irish (from the north and the south) left for North America in the years 1700–60 (Bailyn 1986: 24–7). While Miller's figures apply to Ulster and Scotland together, those of Cullen and Bailyn apply to Ulster alone. Nonetheless, there is a considerable discrepancy between the estimates, something which is no doubt due to the lack

---

[6] Tottie (1985: 92) contains one mention of negative epistemic *must* in a quote from a novel by Edna O'Brien. But the author does not grasp that this is a general Irish feature.

of exact figures, e.g. in census returns, for the period in question. Notwithstanding these differences, one can still recognise that a sizeable proportion of settlers to eighteenth-century North America were of Ulster or Scots provenance and that these must have had a significant influence on speech in the emerging society in the New World.

The situation in Ulster, which at the beginning of the eighteenth century triggered this emigration, was characterised by a combination of economic and religious grievances. The religious motivation was rooted in such demands as the sacramental test which, according to an *Address of Protestant Dissenting Ministers to the King* (1729), was found by Ulster Presbyterians to be 'so very grievous that they have in great numbers transported themselves to the American Plantations for the sake of that liberty and ease which they are denied in their native country' (Bardon 1996: 94). The desire of the Ulster Scots Presbyterians, who left in the eighteenth century, to seek more freedom to practise their variety of Protestantism in America has been underlined frequently (K. Miller 1985: 137–68). But there is consensus among historians today (K. Miller 1985; Foster 1988: 215f.; Bardon 1996) that economic reasons were probably more important: the increase in rents and tithes along with the prospect of paying little rent and no tithes or taxes in America. Added to this were food shortages due to failures of crops, resulting in famine in 1728/9 and most severely in 1741. Foster (1988: 216) stresses that the nature of Ulster trade facilitated emigration: the ships which carried flax seed from America were able to carry emigrants on the outward journey. Up to 1720, the prime destination was New England and this then shifted somewhat southwards, to Pennsylvania (from where the Irish frequently pushed further south, Algeo 2001: 13f.; Montgomery 2001: 126) and later to South Carolina. The rate of emigration depended on the situation in Ireland. In the late 1720s, in the 1760s and in the early 1770s there were peaks of emigration which coincided with economic difficulties triggered by crop failure or destruction in Ireland (Montgomery 2000: 244f.).

The option of emigration in the eighteenth century was open more to Protestants than to Catholics. The latter would equally have had substantial motivation for emigrating, after all the Penal Laws, which discriminated against Catholics in public life, were in force from at least the late seventeenth to the end of the eighteenth century. But emigration did not take place to the same extent with Catholics (the overwhelming majority for the eighteenth century were Protestants). It could be postulated that the Catholics lacked the financial means for a move to the New World. However, the Protestants who left were not necessarily in a financially better position; indeed, many were indentured labourers who thus obtained a free passage. Foster (1988: 216) assumes that the Protestants were more ready to move and subdue new land (as their forefathers from Scotland had done in Ulster in the previous century). The Protestant communities were separate from the Catholics and more closely knit. Furthermore, they were involved in linen production, so that the cargo boats used for emigration would have been in Protestant hands anyway.

The Ulster Scots emigration (Wood and Blethen 1997) is not only important because of its early date but because it established a pattern of exodus to North America which, apart from Merseyside and to a much lesser extent Tyneside and some other locations in the north of England, became the chief destination of Irish emigration in the northern hemisphere (Miller and Wagner 1994).

The features of regional forms of American English which are suspected of deriving from Ulster Scots input in the eighteenth century cover phonology, morphology and lexis (Crozier 1984). In the following a few features of pronunciation and grammar are discussed. For a detailed consideration of lexis, see Montgomery (2004).

The vowels in *cot* and *caught* are not always distinguished, either in length and/or quality. The lowering /ɔ/ to /ɒ/ and then unrounding and centralisation to /a/ (Wolfram and Schilling-Estes 1998: 68f.) may have been influenced by Irish English speakers. Traditionally, it is a feature of western Pennsylvania which had considerable Ulster Scots settlement (Montgomery 2001: 141f.); though as Lass (1987: 286) notes, the shift is to the back vowel in Lowland Scots/Ulster Scots but to the central vowel in American English. The unrounding of /ɒ/ is common in the far north of England as well (Trudgill 1990: 19), e.g. *lang* for *long*.

In Appalachian English (Christian 1991), the position of a reflexive is occupied by a simple personal pronoun, as in *I washed me quickly*. This may well be a transported Ulster Scots feature, also found in Pittsburgh, western Pennsylvania (Montgomery 2001: 125).

In varieties which historically have had an Ulster Scots and/or Scots input, notably Appalachian English, sequences of two modals can be found, e.g. *She might could come tomorrow* (Montgomery 2001: 148; Feagin 1979; Bernstein 2003). Here it might be more the mechanism than the actual form which was inherited. Such constructions are also found in African American English (see Martin and Wolfram 1998: 32–5). On the occurrence in Scottish English, see J. Miller (1993: 120f.); for Scots, see McClure (1994: 72f.). There are also attestations from Tyneside; see Beal (1993: 191).

According to Mishoe and Montgomery (1994: 20), the most common multiple modals in both Northern Ireland and the *Linguistic Atlas of the Gulf States Concordance* are *might could*, *used to could* and *might can*. Multiple modals are quite scarce in both documentary records and dialect fiction on both sides of the Atlantic. A reason for this is offered by the two authors: multiple modals (Fennell and Butters 1996) are not neutral lexical items or idioms but bound to well-defined pragmatic restrictions which have to do with face-saving, negotiation among interlocutors and interactional 'give and take'. They conclude (Mishoe and Montgomery 1994: 22) that 'the documents that we have access to lack the types of contexts in which they most often were employed'.

So-called 'positive *anymore*' (see introduction to this chapter) may occur in the Midland area of the United States (and further west, Wolfram and Schilling-Estes 1998: 142; Eitner 1991), as in *They go to Florida on their holidays anymore*. It may well derive from the speech of eighteenth-century Ulster Scots settlers whose predecessors had in turn picked this up from native speakers of Irish before emigration. Butters (2001: 331f.) views positive *anymore* as an extension of the negative use and is doubtful of the proposed Ulster Scots/Irish antecedent. However, he does not specify why this should have occurred in American English and not in other parts of the anglophone world.

A feature of northern Irish English is the use of *whenever* in the sense of 'when', e.g. *Whenever George VI was King* (Milroy and Milroy 1999: 70). This is also attested for the American Midland region (Montgomery 2001: 150).

A-prefixing has a source in English where the *a* is a reduced form of *on*, much as in adverbs like *alive, asleep* (< *on life, on slæpe*): *She was a-singing*. In Irish a similar construction exists: the preposition *ag* 'at' is used with the so-called verbal noun (a non-finite verb form with nominal characteristics) *Bhí sí ag canadh* lit.: 'was she at singing'; *Fiche bliain ag fás* lit.: 'twenty years at growing'. However, the structure is not found in contemporary Irish English and its attestation historically is meagre, so that British English input is likely to be the source of the construction in Appalachian English (Montgomery 2001: 148); see Wolfram (1991) and Wolfram and Schilling-Estes (1998: 334) as well as Dietrich (1981).

6.3.2 NINETEENTH-CENTURY EMIGRATION

Introduction. Although the reasons for Irish people leaving the country became purely economic after the eighteenth century, the role of the church in the Irish diaspora should not be underestimated (Gilley 1984). The Catholic Church had a definite stance vis-à-vis emigration and used to send clergy to cater for Irish emigrants and also attempted to regulate such essential social services as schooling. This was frequently interpreted as meddling in the internal affairs of the host country: the matter of Catholic education for emigrants was of central importance for Irish, Italian and Polish emigrants in the United States and the clash of interest, which this concern of the church evoked, was not resolved until the twentieth century in some instances, for example in New Zealand.

Parallel to economically motivated emigration, there was missionary activity overseas. This began in Africa in 1842 – in Liberia at the behest of Pope Gregory XVI – along with missionaries from the major European colonising nations in the scramble for Africa: France, Belgium, Holland and Germany. Despite the obvious Irish presence in this phase of African settlement there is no discernible influence of Irish speech on any form of English in Africa. In South Africa the numbers of immigrants from Ireland was under 1 per cent (mainly in the area of Grahamstown, north-east of Port Elizabeth) and was thus insignificant for the development of English there,[7] although the level of education, and hence the social position, of these immigrants was generally high (Akenson 1996: 127–39).

---

[7] However, Wright (1997: 180) maintains that the use of *youse* in 'extreme' South African English may have been influenced by the presence of Irish English speakers. She also claims that the use of *youse* in Irish (and Scottish) English is a nineteenth-century innovation which resulted from the increasing split between rural and urban varieties in Ireland and Scotland.

Table 6.3. *Irish-born in the United States*
after the mid nineteenth century

Year	Number	Year	Number
1851	962,000	1871	1,856,000
1891	1,615,000	1911	1,352,000

The deportation of Irish convicts to Australia began in 1791 (Dudley Edwards with Hourican 2005: 134–6) and within a decade there were over 2,000 of them in the young colony. By 1836 there were over 21,000 Catholics and only half of them were convicts by this stage. In 1835 a Catholic bishop was appointed. During the rest of the nineteenth century the orientation of the Catholic Church in Australia towards a homeland, of which the descendants of immigrants had no direct experience, diminished.

Catholic emigration to North America began in earnest after the Napoleonic wars, i.e. after 1815. During this period Ireland had benefited from heightened economic activity (Dudley Edwards with Hourican 2005: 131f.) but the agricultural depression which followed struck the country severely. An estimated 20,000 left the country in 1818 alone. Economic factors were significant here. The North Atlantic timber trade meant that ships plying across the ocean could take immigrants on the six- to eight-week outward journey at a reasonable price (with wood as cargo on the return trip). Again an estimate gives an approximate picture: between 1831 and 1841 some 200,000 Irish left for America (via Britain), as is known from the figures kept at British ports. By this time – the early nineteenth century – immigration was also taking place to destinations in the southern hemisphere as well, i.e. to Australia. Figures from the colonial administration for 1861 show that in Australia just under 20 per cent of the population was Irish.

Emigration to the United States. Of all countries which absorbed Irish immigrants it was the United States which bore the lion's share. The figure for the entire period of emigration to America is likely to be in the region of 6–7 million (Montgomery 2001: 90) with two peaks, one in the eighteenth century with Ulster Scots settlers (see above) and the second in the mid nineteenth century, the latter continuing at least until to the end of that century. The greatest numbers of Irish emigrants went in the years of the Great Famine (Kinealy 1994; Ó Gráda 1989) during the peak of 1848–9 and immediately afterwards, with more than 100,000 per year leaving between 1847 and 1854. The increase in the Irish-derived sector of the population can be recognised by viewing the figures for the numbers of Irish-born living in the United States after the mid nineteenth century (from Dudley Edwards with Hourican 2005: 144), the greatest increase being in the two decades from 1851 to 1871 (an increase of almost one million); see table 6.3.

The nineteenth-century Irish emigrants show a markedly different settlement pattern compared to their northern compatriots who left in the previous century. Whereas the Ulster Scots settled in Pennsylvania and South Carolina, the Catholic Irish, from the mid nineteenth century onwards, stayed in the urban centres of the eastern United Status accounting for the sizeable Irish populations in cities like New York and Boston (Algeo 2001a: 27; Montgomery 2000: 245). The reason for this switch from a rural way of life in the homeland to an urban one abroad is obvious: the memories of rural poverty and deprivation, the fear of a repetition of famine, were so strong as to deter the Irish from pushing further into the rural mid west, unlike, say, the Scandinavian or Ukrainian immigrants.

The desire to break with a background of poverty explains why the Irish abandoned their native language (Corrigan 1996). It was associated with backwardness and distress; even in Ireland, leaders of the Catholics, such as Daniel O'Connell, were advocating by the beginning of the nineteenth century that the Irish switch to English as only with this language was there any hope of social betterment (Corrigan 2003b).

It should be emphasised that there was a major difference between the medium numbers of able-bodied Ulster Protestants in the eighteenth century on the one hand and the enormous numbers of weak, poverty-stricken Catholics fleeing from famine-ridden Ireland in the mid nineteenth century on the other. The Ulster Scots were welcome on the then frontier in order to keep the native Americans in check (it is estimated that by the close of the eighteenth century over half the settlers on the trans-Appalachian frontier were of Ulster lineage, K. Miller 1985: 161). In southern states like South Carolina they additionally served to dilute the high proportion of African Americans with whom they initially competed for lower-paid jobs (Dudley Edwards with Hourican 2005: 144). Their relative numbers were also significant: by the eve of the War of Independence (1775–83), the Scots-Irish represented about a quarter of the population of the Thirteen Colonies. In addition to this relatively large proportion of the entire population, the fact that they were early immigrants meant that they had an influence on American English during its formative years.

Neither of these factors applied to the nineteenth-century immigrants. Furthermore, diminished tolerance and their own desire to assimilate rapidly meant that virtually no trace of nineteenth-century Irish English was left in the English spoken in the eastern United States where the later Irish immigrants settled. According to Nilsen (2002 [1997]: 63), Irish was used in New York up to c. 1880 and the notion that all the emigrants were monoglot English speakers would seem to be false. There was a Gaelic movement in the United States (Ní Bhroiméil 2003: 32–57) with missions of the Gaelic League continuing up until the beginning of the twentieth century (Ní Bhroiméil 2003: 105–21). But despite the efforts of small groups and individuals (see the contributions in Ihde 1994), there was no significant continuation of the language in any part of the United States. Reasons for this can be recognised by considering the position in New York which, of all American cities, had a considerable Irish population.

Attempts to establish Irish in education in New York were not successful and the language was never able to gain a foothold with the Irish population of the city. Nilsen (2002 [1997]: 67) notes that the majority of Irish-speakers in New York did not in fact engage with any organisations which were devoted to the language. Given this attitude to language maintenance it is not surprising that it was not transmitted to subsequent generations.

There is perhaps one feature in the English of Boston which could be traced to Irish English. Laferriere (1986) maintains that the latter could be the source of the /ɒ/-pronunciation in words like *short, forty*. See section 5.6 for possible lexical borrowings from Irish in American English.

6.3.3 AFRICAN AMERICAN ENGLISH

There is no doubt that there was contact between Irish people and Africans in both the Caribbean and the later United States in the early part of the colonial period, i.e. from the beginning of the seventeenth century onwards. For instance, by the middle of this century the white population of Barbados, England's first colony in the Caribbean, was about one-fifth Irish (K. Miller 1985: 139) and this increased in the second half of the seventeenth century with the Irish settling on other Leeward Islands, notably Montserrat (see discussion of Caribbean English below). Somewhat earlier than this, during the 1620s, ships from southern Irish ports like Cork and Kinsale carried on a brisk trade in sugar and tobacco with the colonies on the east coast of America (K. Miller 1985). The connections established then were maintained and during the eighteenth century many Catholic immigrants from the south of Ireland settled in Virginia, Maryland and the Carolinas.[8]

For reasons of space, the treatment of possible parallels between Irish English and African American English in this section will be restricted to a consideration of the habitual. However, one other feature of African American English should be mentioned. This is copula deletion as in *How long Ø your paper* (Green 2002: 184) and auxiliary deletion *They Ø walking too fast* (Green 2002: 40f.). Such deletion is often regarded as a sole feature of pidgins and creoles and their derivatives, but it does occur in Ireland, in south-eastern Irish English (see section 4.4.1). For discussions of further parallels, see the chapters of Hickey (2004j) and the 'Checklist of features' (Hickey 2004e: 586–621).

Although most forms of mesolectal creole English in the Caribbean (except Jamaican English) have *does* /dʌz/ as the expression of habitual aspect, a notable

---

[8] S. Davis (2003: 286), in his discussion of the German-American writer Francis Lieber (1798–1872), 'the originator and first editor of the *Encyclopedia Americana* (1829–32)', notes that the latter discusses *biant* (= [biyant]) and assumes an Irish origin for this (S. Davis 2003: 291), a view which Davis supports. The use of a final /-t/ for /-d/ would agree with the practice of devoicing alveolar stops after nasals in Irish English, something which is still found to this day.

feature of African American English is that it does not, although it is found in Gullah as *duh* (Rickford 1986: 260). This fact is a major difference between the latter variety and the speech of other African Americans and may offer support for the view that Gullah is an imported creole from the Caribbean which developed independently of African American English in the southern United States. Pargman (2004: 17–19), in her consideration of the possible origin of Gullah *duh*, is sceptical of an Irish influence on its development.

The concern in this section is with the use of uninflected *be* in African American English (Myhill 1988) and its possible historical source. Sentences illustrating its current use would be: *I think those buses be blue*, *The children be at school when I get home*, *They be done left when I get there* (Green 1998: 39; 2002: 47–54; Feagin 1991). There are essentially three views on the rise of uninflected *be* to express habituality in African American English.

Views on the origin of the habitual in African American English

1. It arose in Caribbean English and was carried to the south of the later United States. Unstressed *do* (Rickford 1986: 265) was deleted, which left the bare *be* to express habituality (Rickford 1980). In Bahamian English this intermediary stage is attested (Holm 1994: 375). An essential difficulty with this interpretation is that it requires that uninflected *do* was dropped and inflection introduced for those varieties which use *bees*, i.e. an inflected form of *be*.

2. It is an inherited habitual marker from Ulster Scots which was passed on to African American English in its early stages due to the large number of northern Irish immigrants in the eighteenth century, especially with those in South Carolina. There may be evidence for a continuation of *beon* 'to be' with habitual meaning from the Northumbrian variety of Old English. In Scotland this was the predecessor of Scots which was transported to the United States via Ulster (Traugott 1972: 177ff., 190f.). Rickford (1986) further maintains that the use of *be* in African American English and *does be* in Caribbean creoles may well reflect a differential influence of northern Irish English on the former and southern Irish English on the latter. However, the question of contact between Irish and African Americans in the later United States is unresolved, particularly as the former settled further inland whereas the African Americans were to be found on the Atlantic seaboard.

3. The use of uninflected *be* is an innovation in nineteenth-century African American English as it is not attested in the documents for Ulster English which are extant before this date (Montgomery and Kirk 1996: 318f.). This view assumes that if habitual *be* did in fact already exist in early Ulster English then it would be attested somewhere. This leaves one with a shared nineteenth-century innovation – habitual *be* (uninflected in America, inflected in Ulster) – between two varieties which showed some contact historically, but little if any settlement overlap. This innovation is incidentally not found anywhere else between two varieties of English. The argument

of Montgomery and Kirk is reinforced by the fact that habitual *be* does not occur in present-day or historical forms of Appalachian English where influence from Ulster was considerable (Montgomery 2001: 136). A minor but not irrelevant point is that the investigation by Montgomery and Kirk (1996) is of emigrant letters in Ulster English and of present-day material outside the core areas of Ulster Scots settlement in northern Ireland. Montgomery (personal communication) is of the opinion that habitual *be* was borrowed from Ulster English into Ulster Scots.

The last view is the most recent and it throws doubt on many of the postulations concerning the historical continuity of habitual forms in New World English.[9] If Montgomery and Kirk (1996: 331) are right in their rejection of a link between African American English *be* and regional British/Irish English, then a similar question must be asked about the link between the *do/does* + *be* habitual, derivatives of which are found in the Caribbean, and southern Irish English (see section 6.5).

6.4   Canada

Irish emigration to Canada can be divided into two sections. The first involves those Irish who settled in Newfoundland and the second those who moved to mainland Canada, chiefly to the province of Ontario, the southern part of which is contained in what was previously called Upper Canada.

The oldest emigration is that to Newfoundland which goes back to seasonal migration for fishing, with later settlement in the eighteenth and early nineteenth-centuries (Clarke 2004). The second group is that of nineteenth-century immigrants who travelled up the St Lawrence river to reach inland Canada. There was further diffusion from there into the northern United States. Far fewer Irish emigrants settled in Canada, only somewhat more than 300,000 for the entire nineteenth century. But relative to the population of Canada throughout this century, this is still significant and some scholars maintain that elements of Irish speech are still discernible in the English of the Ottawa Valley (Pringle and Padolsky 1981, 1983; Carroll 1983).

6.4.1   NEWFOUNDLAND

Newfoundland is unique in the history of overseas English colonies. The initial impetus for involvement with the island in eastern Canada was the discovery of abundant fishing grounds off its shores on the continental shelf known as the Grand Banks. Irish and West Country English fisherman began plying across

---

[9] Dillard (1976: 95f.) makes the valid point, when dealing with the possible source of features of Black English in Irish English, that none of the putatively Irish features are present in the English of the community of white speakers of Irish descent in the United States. He is also sceptical about the possible Irish provenance of invariant *be* in Black English (1976: 116).

the Atlantic in the seventeenth century in a pattern of seasonal migration which took them to Newfoundland to fish in the summer months, just like French and Basque fisherman, returning home for the winter months. This meant that there was continual contact with the varieties of English in the British and Irish regions from which the seasonal migrants came. Added to this is the fact that, well into the twentieth century, Newfoundland was isolated from the rest of Canada, so that no influence of central Canadian English was felt then, a situation which has of course changed since (D'Arcy 2005).

The English ships traditionally put in at southern Irish ports such as Waterford, Dungarvan, Youghal and Cork to collect supplies for the transatlantic journey. Knowledge of this movement by the Irish led to their participation in seasonal migration (consider the Irish name for Newfoundland: *Talamh an Éisc*, lit. 'ground of fish'). Later in the eighteenth century, and up to the third decade of the nineteenth century, several thousand Irish, chiefly from the city and county of Waterford (Mannion 1977), settled permanently in Newfoundland and thus founded the Irish community there (Clarke 1997b) which together with the West Country community forms the two main anglophone sections of Newfoundland to this day (there was also a small Scottish input to the extreme south-west of the island). These two groups are still distinguishable linguistically; see Clarke (2004) for a detailed discussion. Newfoundland became a largely self-governing colony in 1855 and only as late as 1949 did it join Canada as its tenth province.

Vernacular Newfoundland Irish English. Among the features found in the English of this area, which can probably be traced to Ireland, is the use of *ye* (which could be a case of convergence with dialectal English) and/or *youse* for 'you'-PL, the perfective construction with *after* and present participle, as in *He's after spilling the beer*, and the use of a habitual with an uninflected form of *do* plus *be*. Although Clarke (1997a: 287) notes that the use of this is unusual in general Newfoundland English today – her example is *That place do be really busy* – it is found in areas settled by south-eastern Irish. This observation correlates with usage in conservative vernacular forms of south-eastern Irish English today (Hickey 2001b: 13) and is clearly suggestive of an historical link. Furthermore, Newfoundland English can have zero inflection on auxiliary forms of verbs. A distinction is found here between an auxiliary *do* with no inflection and a lexical verb *do* with inflection. This feature is typical of both historical inputs to Newfoundland, i.e. of both south-west England (Ihalainen 1991) and south-east Ireland (Hickey 2001b).

There are also phonological items from Irish-based Newfoundland English which parallel features in south-eastern Irish English. Examples are the use of stops for dental fricatives, syllable-final /r/, the lenition of word-final, postvocalic *t*, the low degree of distinctiveness with /ai/ and /ɒi/ (cf. *bile* vs *boil*), if present at all, and the use of an epenthetic vowel to break a cluster of liquid and nasal as in *film* [fɪləm]. There are also lexical items of Irish origin such as *sleeveen* 'rascal' (Irish *slíbhín*), *pishogue* 'superstition' (Irish *piseog*), *crubeen* 'cooked pig's foot' (Irish *crúibín*) (Kirwin 1993: 76f.; 2001). An interesting case of folk etymology can be seen in *hangashore* from Irish *ainniseoir* 'good-for-nothing' with a hypercorrect initial /h-/. For a detailed discussion of these and similar features of Newfoundland English, see Clarke (2004) and Hickey (2002c).

6.4.2 MAINLAND CANADA

The Irish in mainland Canada were among the earliest immigrants and enjoyed a relatively privileged status in early Canadian society. By the 1860s they formed a large section of the English-speaking population in Canada and constituted some 40 per cent of the British Isles immigrants in the newly founded Canadian Confederation. These Irish came both from the north and south of the country, but there was a preponderance of Protestants (some two-thirds in the nineteenth and twentieth centuries) as opposed to the situation in Newfoundland where the Irish community was almost entirely Catholic.

The Protestants in Canada had a considerable impact on public life. They bolstered the loyalist tradition which formed the basis for anglophone Canada. In the Canadian context, the term 'loyalist' refers to that section of the American population which left the Thirteen Colonies after the American Revolution of 1776, moving northwards to Canadian territory where they were free to demonstrate their loyalty to the English crown. As these Irish Protestants were of Ulster origin, they later maintained their tradition of the Orange Order which was an important voluntary organisation in Canada.

In Ontario there were sizeable numbers of Catholics and they in turn mounted pressure on the government to grant them separate Catholic schools and funding to support these, much as the Catholics in New Zealand had campaigned for the same goal in that country.

In mainland Canada the Irish dispersed fairly evenly throughout the country, even if there is a preponderance in Ontario and in the Ottawa Valley. But there is nothing like the heavy concentration of Scots-Irish in Appalachia (Montgomery 1989) or that of later, post-Famine Irish in the urban centres of the north-eastern United States such as New York and Boston.

The drive west through Manitoba, Saskatchewan, Alberta across to British Columbia followed a pattern of internal migration westwards in the late eighteenth and nineteenth centuries. In this newer period of population growth, Canada, like the United States, was fed by a continuous stream of English-speaking immigrants via Grosse Île at the entrance to the St Lawrence river estuary, the Ellis Island of Canada so to speak. The influence of this later wave of immigration on Canadian English is not as evident as in Newfoundland. Nonetheless, one should mention one feature which Canadian English has in common with the English in the north of Ireland (Gregg 1973; Scargill 1977: 12), what is known in linguistic literature as 'Canadian Raising' (Chambers 1973). The essence of this phenomenon is a more central starting point for the diphthongs /ai/ and /au/ before a voiceless consonant than before the corresponding voiced one: *house, lout* [həʊs, ləʊt] but *houses, loud* [haʊzɪz, laʊd].

6.5   The Caribbean

Although the Caribbean is an area which is not immediately associated with Irish influence, the initial anglophone settlement of the area, during the so-called 'homestead phase', i.e. before the importation of African slaves, did involve considerable Irish input. The island of Barbados was the earliest to be settled by the British (Holm 1994), as of 1627. Cromwell in the early 1650s had a sizeable number of Irish deported as indentured labourers in order to rid Ireland of those he considered politically undesirable. This input to Barbados is important to Caribbean English for two reasons. The first is that it was very early and so there was Irish input during the formative years of English there (before slaves from West Africa arrived in large numbers in the latter half of the seventeenth century). The second reason is that the island of Barbados quickly became overpopulated and speakers of Barbadian English moved from there to other locations in the Caribbean and indeed to coastal South Carolina and Georgia, i.e. to the region where Gullah was later spoken (Hancock 1980; Littlefield 1981).

The views of linguists concerning possible Irish influence on the genesis of English varieties in the Caribbean vary considerably (Bailey 1982). Wells (1980) is doubtful about Irish influence on the pronunciation of English on Montserrat. Rickford (1986) is a well-known article in which he postulates that southern Irish input to the Caribbean had an influence on the expression of the habitual aspect in varieties of English there, especially because *do(es)* + *be* is the preferred form of the habitual in the south of Ireland. This matter is actually quite complex and Rickford's view has been challenged recently by Montgomery and Kirk (1996); see discussion of the habitual in African American English in section 6.3.3.

It should also be stressed that for many phenomena in varieties of Caribbean English, a convergence scenario may be closest to historical reality, difficult as it is to determine just what this was probably like. For instance, the presence of aspectual categories in regional forms of British and Irish English is paralleled by similar categories, albeit with very different exponence, in the West African languages which represented the substrate for slaves in the early anglophone Caribbean and on the mainland of the later United States. Convergence may also have been operative on the phonological level. The occurrence of stops in Caribbean English as equivalents to ambidental fricatives in standard English (in such words as *thin* and *this*) is paralleled both by stops in Irish English and by the non-existence of ambidental fricatives in West African languages.

Recent reorientation has apportioned a much greater role to superstrate models in the early stages of English in the Caribbean and also in the American south (Schneider 1993, 2004), an area it is closely associated with. The view of scholars such as Winford (1997–8: 123) is that creolisation is a development which occurred somewhat after the initial settlement of the Caribbean and the American south and which was triggered by the establishment of a widespread plantation rural economy, something which was not present at the outset in either region. Supportive evidence for this stance is to be found in areas of the Caribbean where plantations were not established, e.g. on the Cayman Islands, which retain distinctive traces of English regional input (Holm 1994: 332). Among the many views in this field are those which claim that the African slaves taken to the Caribbean had already learned a pidgin (Cassidy 1980) or possibly a creole (Hancock 1980) before their transportation. However, if this was true, then it was not so for the period in which the earliest slaves were taken to the Caribbean, i.e. not for the seventeenth century.

The scenario in which approximation to English regional input precedes possible creolisation has wide-ranging implications for the interpretation of key structures in both present-day Caribbean creoles and African American English. It suggests that the first few generations – the founder generations during the formative years – were exposed sufficiently to regional British and Irish English input for structural features of the latter to be transferred to incipient varieties of Caribbean English due to an unguided second-language acquisition process among adults. In this respect the earliest years of English in the Caribbean for African slaves show distinct parallels with English in Ireland (Hickey 1997a) in the early modern period (from the early seventeenth century onwards). In both cases, speakers shifted to English as adults, learning the language in an unguided fashion with obvious imperfect results. Such a scenario is one where both syntactic transfer from the substrate languages and the adoption of salient grammatical features of the superstrate language are at a premium. In the present context, the concern is with discerning the latter features and considering whether these were adopted into early forms of non-native English in the Caribbean.

6.5.1 THE CASE OF BARBADOS

In the history of anglophone settlement in the Caribbean the island of Barbados in the south-east (along with St Kitts somewhat to the north) plays a central role. There were various reasons for the exploitation of Barbados by the English. Initially, the island functioned as a bridgehead for the English in the Caribbean which, by the beginning of the seventeenth century, was dominated by the Spanish. It was later to become important with the development of the cane sugar trade (B. Taylor 2001: 205–17; Dunn 1972), something which also came to be true of Jamaica after it was wrenched from Spanish control in the mid seventeenth century (B. Taylor 2001: 217–21; Le Page 1960). Before the large-scale importation of African slaves got under way in the later seventeenth century, the English had a system of indenture whereby settlers from the British Isles went to the Caribbean to work for a period, typically five to eight years, after which they were free to move at will, their circumstances permitting.

The settlement of Barbados is also linked to the deportation of Irish dissidents by Oliver Cromwell, as mentioned above, this element forming a significant proportion of early white settlers from the late 1640s onwards (O'Callaghan 2000: 65–76; Aubrey 1930–1). These would have been in contact with African slaves in a work context (Rickford 1986: 251). There was also a later deportation to

Table 6.4. *Development of English on Barbados*

1627–50	Pre-plantation period with predominance of white settler speech
1650–80	Early plantation period with a great increase in African population
1680–1800	Core plantation period
1800–1900	Late and post-plantation period

Jamaica (O'Callaghan 2000: 77–88). The vicissitudes of the Civil War in England (1642–51) were responsible for the emigration of English as well.

Given the size of Barbados and the relatively low social position of the Irish in the white community on the island, there would have been fairly intensive contact between Africans and the Irish. P. Campbell (1993: 148) mentions the late 1640s as the beginning of the sugar revolution with the switch from tobacco. This period also saw the switch from white indentured servants to black slaves (Harlowe 1969 [1926]: 292–330) and the exodus of the former from Barbados. From 1650–80 upwards of 10,000 people left Barbados (a conservative estimate). Settlers from other parts of the Caribbean left for the south-east of the North American mainland, chiefly to South Carolina, a movement which began in 1670 and which was largely completed by 1700 (Holm 1994: 342). It should also be mentioned that, with the later concentration of African slaves on Barbados, settlement patterns arose which were conducive to creolisation: Rickford and Handler (1994: 230) point out that 'these slaves lived in compact village settlements located next to the plantation yard' and that 'these are just the kinds of demographic and settlement patterns which would have produced and/or maintained creole-speaking communities'.

Tense and aspect systems. The area of syntax in Caribbean English which has received most attention from scholars working in variety studies is the tense and aspect system. Creoles tend to show formal marking of certain aspectual distinctions, notably the perfective and the habitual. What is remarkable here is that in general creoles are sparing in the explicit expression of grammatical categories, so it is all the more remarkable that they should do so in the area of aspect. Furthermore, the means for marking aspect stem as a rule from superstrate sources, usually with semantic motivation for the choice of markers (Schneider 1990). An example of this is completive *don* in Caribbean English. It is consistent with the meaning of *do* to use it to express a completed action. Many dialects of English, e.g. virtually all vernacular forms of Irish English, have only one form *do* in the past, namely *done*, e.g. *He done all the work for her.* The verb *do* was also co-opted to serve as a marker of the habitual, at least in most forms of creole English in the Caribbean, e.g. the pre-verbal *does* of Barbadian speech (Burrowes and Allsopp 1983: 42).

The tense distinctions of creole verbal systems are based on a binary or tertiary system: (i) time in focus, (ii) time anterior to this and (iii) time beyond that in focus, this being a future or conditional. Aspectual distinctions are also either binary or tertiary: (i) an imperfective, non-punctual mode, (ii) a perfective, e.g. with completive *done*, (iii) a habitual, e.g. with *does/do* + *be*.

Habitual marking in Caribbean English. The major study of possible connections between English in Britain and Ireland and in the Caribbean is Rickford (1986). Among other things, Rickford is concerned with the possible diffusion of (*does*) *be* as an aspectual marker from Irish English to African American English in the United States. He devotes a large portion of the article to determining how extensive, and of what nature, the contact between the Irish and African American population of America was. He begins, however, with the Caribbean (Barbados, Montserrat and to a lesser extent St Kitts). Rickford also points out that there was considerable contact between Irish indentured servants and African slaves. He looks at periphrastic *do*, a common feature of south-western varieties of English, and suggests that this too could have diffused from the speech of the many immigrants from this part of England into the Caribbean area.

A similar study is Winford (2000) which takes a close look at superstrate antecedents of aspectual marking in Caribbean English, specifically in Barbadian English. Winford (2000: 228f.) initially favours south-western British English as the source of Barbadian *does* for the habitual, *did* for the imperfective and *done* for the perfective (completive) aspect. However, later in the same article he maintains that the Irish English input was significant on Barbados. The reason for considering the latter is that Barbadian English favours the use of invariant *does*, rather than uninflected *do*, as well as the co-occurrence of *does* with *be*. Both these features are not characteristic of present-day south-western British English, nor do they seem to have been, at least for the nineteenth century, as attested in the study by Elworthy (1877).

Another author to consider this question is Mufwene. He sees the [dəz] of Gullah and the [dɔz] of Guyanese Creole as causally linked to immigrants to the Caribbean from Ireland and south-west England, where a *do* habitual would have existed (Mufwene 2001: 31f.). However, his assumption that the habitual *does* was brought directly from south-west England and Ireland is unsubstantiated. The contention (Mufwene 2001: 32) that the habitual was established by 1700 is unproven.

Unfortunately, the picture which emerges from the textual attestation of Irish English is not as conclusive as supporters of historical connections would like it to be (see Hickey 2004a for a fuller discussion). In historical texts, the habitual *do(es)* + *be* in Irish English does not go back much before the nineteenth century (see discussion in section 4.4.1.4.3), although there is one text from 1705 with instances of it. For the seventeenth century, when the Irish immigration into the Caribbean was taking place, no instances of the habitual in the textual record can be found.

There is no simple answer to the question of possible influence by the Irish on early Caribbean English. It is true that many Irish were deported from Ireland or from England, from where many Irish vagrants were sent to the Caribbean as indentured servants (Beier 1985). It is also possible that refunctionalisation of periphrastic *do* by speakers of Irish and/or non-fluent speakers of Irish English occurred during the contact with English dialect speakers and African slaves in early anglophone Barbados (during the seventeenth century). This view would crucially depend on establishing objectively what percentage of Irish settlers on Barbados were Irish-speaking (Rickford 1986: 253). As the records are not sufficient to allow definite conclusions, one is left with the formal parallels between Irish English and Caribbean English in the expression of the habitual, but without the clinching evidence to prove a historical connection.

6.6   Australia

White settlement in Australia began in 1788 and from its early years it consisted of both British and Irish (Baker 1966). The latter arrived early and in relatively large numbers (Akenson 1996: 92). The Irish emigration to Australia (Fitzpatrick 1994) had been established well before the Great Famine of 1845–8 and was thus different in kind from the wave of emigration triggered by that traumatic event to other parts of the anglophone world. The view of these early immigrants as mostly convicts, a potent image in the Irish collective imagination, is not borne out by the facts, as Akenson points out (1996: 94). The Irish comprised only about 25 per cent of the criminals sent to the penal colonies. Furthermore, as was true of New Zealand, the Irish were a 'charter group' which ensured them certain privileges. From the beginning, the free emigrants merged into a society in which both the free and the convicts intertwined. Those who were excluded were the non-whites (here as in the United States). By the mid nineteenth century the difference between the free emigrants and the convicts had been lost and in 1853 the transportation of prisoners to the eastern Australian colonies was abandoned (Akenson 1996).

The Irish section of the population in nineteenth-century Australia ranged somewhere between 20 and 30 per cent.[10] Given the sizeable number of Irish among the original settlers of Australia, one might expect an influence on the formation of Australian English commensurate with their numbers. Before considering this issue, it is worth pointing out that the Irish in Australia, as opposed to the immigrants to the United States after the Great Famine, did indeed settle in the countryside. This meant that there were fewer Irish in Australian towns than other immigrants (Akenson 1996: 109). Another point is that the Irish assimilated well to early Australian society and were noted for their 'ordinariness' (Fitzpatrick in Akenson 1996: 108). These two facts may well have meant that their influence on early Australian English was slighter than the simple numbers of immigrants might imply.

---

[10] Demographically, Australia today is *c.* 75 per cent Anglo-Celtic, by which is meant of English, Scottish or Irish extraction (the remaining 25 per cent consists of more recent immigrant groups and a very small number of aborigines).

The features traceable to Irish input are few and tenuous (see lists below). It is furthermore difficult to determine just what constitutes Irish influence. For instance, initial /h/, e.g. *hat, humour, home* all with [h-], is retained in Australian English. This sound has disappeared in urban vernaculars in Britain and its continuing existence in Australian English could be due to Irish influence, though this just remains a matter of opinion and no conclusive evidence can be adduced, for instance of loss in the British sector of Australian society and reinstatement through contact with the Irish.

As a representative examination of Australian English with historical information, one can consider Horvath's study from the early 1980s. She points out several features which she believes Australian English shares with Irish English (Horvath 1985: 39):

1. *Youse* [juz] for second person plural (Hickey 2003d)
2. Adverbial *but*, 'I went to the store, but'
3. The expression *good on ya*
4. Epenthetic schwa in *film* [fɪləm] (Hickey 1986b)

To this list could be added the following features which Australian English quite definitely shares with Irish English:

5. The realisation of unstressed short vowels in checked syllables as [ə] and not [ɪ], e.g. *trusted* [trʌstəd] (Trudgill 1986: 139ff.).
6. A low central to front vowel in words of the DANCE lexical set, i.e. [daːns/ dæːns] for *dance* (in traditional pronunciations; see D. Bradley 1991: 227f.). B. Taylor (2001: 335) reports that A. G. Mitchell believed the Australian realisation could have been influenced by Irish English, but it is more likely to have resulted from convergence with the /aː/ of south-eastern British English which in the late eighteenth / early nineteenth century had not yet been retracted to /ɑː/.
7. Epistemic negative *must*, e.g. *She mustn't be here today* (Newbrook 1992: 4). This could possibly be due to Scottish influence as well; see J. Miller (1993: 119).

Primary linguistic data for Australian English before the mid nineteenth century are not available so that there is no way of quantifying the amount of Irish English input to incipient forms of Australian English in the first few generations after initial settlement. The situation improves somewhat in the second half of the nineteenth century, for instance, with the publication of humorous pieces by Charles Adam Corbyn in which he has stretches of verbatim speech in different British dialects, the majority of which are Irish and south-eastern English. Some of the features of Irish characters in the reports by Corbyn (1970 [1854]) are taken from extracts in B. Taylor (2001) and presented below. None of the following features are present in any variety of Australian English; see B. Taylor (2001: 320f.) and Troy (1992) for a discussion of the early relationship between Irish English and Australian English. For examples of first-generation Irish English in Australia, in the context of emigrant letters and Irish-Australian history, see Fitzpatrick (1994).

Features of Irish English in Australia from Corbyn (1970[1854])

1. Unshifted ME /ɛ:, e:/, e.g. *taytotaler* 'teetotaller'
2. Dentalisation of /t/ [t̪] before /r/, e.g. *Pathrick*
3. Low and fronted realisation of /ɔ:/, e.g. *darter* 'daughter'
4. Occurrence of /ɪ/ in place of /ʌ/, e.g. *jist* 'just'

It is obvious that these features disappeared quickly from the speech of later generations in Australia. Furthermore, the features listed above, which are possibly still found in Australian English, are slight indeed, so the comparative lack of influence of Irish English on Australian English is something which requires explanation. The low prestige of the Irish sector of the early Australian community is probably the chief reason. It can be assumed that rural immigrants from Ireland in the early days of Australian society used an identifiable contact variety of Irish English (see above list of features from Corbyn 1970 [1854]) and so its features would have been avoided by the remainder of the English-speaking Australian population and, importantly, by following generations assimilating to emerging Australian society. This is also true for speakers from the Dublin area who would have had a distinct accent as the supraregionalisation which affected Irish English considerably did not set in until the mid to late nineteenth century (Hickey 2003b). The view that salient Irish features were rejected – consciously or unconsciously by other English speakers – is in fact supported when one considers what features may be of Irish origin in Australian English. Consider the use of negative epistemic *must* again. Prescriptive consciousness of modals in English is slight, most probably because of the irregularity in the system: all of them lack an infinitive and a regular past form. It would have been easiest for a form from Irish English to enter the speech of those the Irish were in contact with in an area of English usage which displays little or no paradigmatic regularity. Another fact which may be indicative of the status of early Irish settlers in Australia is that the inflected form of *you* for the plural, *youse*, is found in vernacular usage in Australia. This form is definitely of Irish origin (see Hickey 2003d for a detailed discussion) and was probably adopted by the English in Australia through contact with the Irish, but on a level outside formal usage.

In the history of transported English a situation where a minority variety is maintained from one generation to the next has only obtained where its speakers have been in relative isolation and where language learners were not under peer pressure to adopt the variety of the group with greater social status. There are cases where this isolation has held, e.g. in Otago in the south of the south island of New Zealand, where varieties of English reminiscent of Scottish English have been maintained. Another instance is Newfoundland in eastern Canada (see section 6.4.1) where the English and Irish communities maintained their specific varieties of English unaffected by mainland Canadian English until well into the twentieth century.

Summarising, one can say that the early development of Australian society was probably similar to that in New Zealand where the social standing of the Irish was lower than that of the British (Hickey 2003e). Later generations descending from early Irish settlers would have avoided salient features in their speech and gravitated towards that of the more prestigious group whose speech was based on south-eastern English.

6.7   New Zealand

The remarks just made about possible Irish influence on Australian English apply in equal measure to New Zealand English. The formative period for this variety post-dates that for Australian English somewhat. It was not until after the Treaty of Waitangi in 1840 that the anglophone settlement of New Zealand began in earnest. In the latter half of the nineteenth century many people from England, Scotland and Ireland moved to New Zealand (often via Australia) to settle there permanently. Certain parts of the country had concentrations of settlers from distinct regions of the British Isles. The Scottish settled largely in Otago in the far south. The Irish were found in large concentrations in Hawke's Bay on the south-east coast of the north island and in the Auckland region. But as opposed to the Scots they did not maintain a separate identity, let alone a separate variety of English in the new country. One reason for this may be that the Irish who emigrated to New Zealand were often young unmarried men (Akenson 1996: 61) who would have married in New Zealand, possibly non-Irish women. Irish women who emigrated would also have been unmarried (Akenson 1996: 83) and typically unskilled. This would have meant that Irish influence – linguistic and otherwise – on the formation of later New Zealand society would have been slight despite the fact that more than 20 per cent of the initial anglophone population of New Zealand was Irish. Parental origin was a significant fact for the descendents of settlers (Gordon et al. 2004: 263). Furthermore, most of the Irish emigrants were Catholics and the emerging New Zealand government in the late nineteenth century was tacitly Protestant, so that any linguistic features which might have been associated with a Catholic family background would not have enjoyed prestige in the community.

Irish linguistic input does not seem to have had a significant influence on later New Zealand English. The raising of short vowels, a prominent feature of English in New Zealand, would only have had a late nineteenth-century counterpart in E-raising in Ireland (see section 5.1.5). The situation may have been different where adoption of a feature would have led to mergers. H-dropping is a feature which was not viewed favourably, if the retention of the initial fricative, despite deletion in some cases of early New Zealand English, is any indication. Furthermore, some mergers were not pushed through from the start: /hw/ [ʍ] and /w/ [w] seemed to merge, to later diverge and still later to come close to merger once more

(Gordon et al. 2004: 274). Early New Zealand English, in particular that collected for the *Origins of New Zealand English* project at the University of Canterbury in Christchurch, offers much data for and against vowel shifts, mergers and the relative sociolinguistic position of different emigrant groups. For a detailed discussion of these issues and how they combined to yield modern New Zealand English, see Gordon et al. (2004) and Hickey (2003e).

Appendix 1   An outline of Irish history

8,000 BC	First settlers appear in the north of Ireland, probably coming from Scotland.
3,000 BC	Arrival of Neolithic people in Ireland.
500–300 BC	Probable arrival of Celts in Ireland; assimilation of previous non-Indo-European population.
c. 130–80	Ptolemy gives a geographical sketch of Ireland.
c. 400	Ireland has strong footholds in western Scotland (the kingdom of Dalriada) and south Wales; the Irish language is brought to Scotland.
432	St Patrick arrives and officially christianises Ireland (date is contested).
795	Viking raids in Ireland begin from the north.
c. 800	Book of Kells, the most famous illuminated manuscript, is completed.
c. 840	Dublin is founded by the Vikings as a base on the estuary of the Liffey.
c. 900	Beginning of Middle Irish period.
1014	Battle of Clontarf signals the final decline of Scandinavian power in Ireland.
1169	Anglo-Norman invasion in the south-east of the country (Wexford and Waterford) by Normans from Pembrokeshire, south-west Wales.
1172	Charter of Dublin issued; Anglo-Normans strengthen their presence in the city.
c. 1200	Beginning of Early Modern Irish period (until c. 1600).
1235	Anglo-Norman invasion of Connaught (western province).
1315–18	Bruce invasion from Scotland with resistance to Anglo-Norman rule.
1366	Statutes of Kilkenny, proscribing the Irish language and Irish customs, attempt to curb the rapid gaelicisation of the Anglo-Norman settlers.

15c	Gaelic revival continues.
1509	Accession of Henry VIII as King of England.
1541	Henry VIII accepted by Irish parliament as King of Ireland.
1549–57	Plantation of Laois and Offaly (centre of country).
1558	Elizabeth I, last of the Tudors, ascends the throne.
1586–93	Plantation of Munster.
1592	Foundation of Trinity College, Dublin.
1595–1603	Rebellion of Hugh O'Neill, Earl of Tyrone.
c. 1600	Beginning of Modern Irish period.
1601	Irish and Spanish forces defeated by the English at Kinsale, Co. Cork.
1603	Death of Elizabeth I. Accession of James I (James VI of Scotland).
1607	On 14 September many Ulster leaders leave for the continent ('Flight of the Earls'), depriving Ulster of native leadership.
1641	Beginning of the Ulster rising against Protestant settlers.
1642	Outbreak of civil war in England.
1649–50	Oliver Cromwell's campaigns in Ireland.
1652–3	Cromwellian confiscation of lands. Act of Settlement regulates this.
1660	Restoration of the monarchy (with Charles II as king). The Cromwellian conquest is maintained.
1685	Death of Charles II and accession of James II (Catholic).
1690	Arrival of William III (of Orange) in Ireland. Battle of the Boyne (1 July).
1691–1703	Land confiscation follows.
1695	Beginning of a series of legislative measures against the Irish Catholics known as the 'Penal Laws' which were to last up to the beginning of the nineteenth century.
1713	Jonathan Swift becomes Dean of St Patrick's in Dublin.
1740–1	Famine breaks out in large parts of the country.
1796–8	Rebellion by the United Irishmen.
1801	Act of Union of Great Britain and Ireland comes into force (1 Jan).
1823	Catholic Association founded, led by Daniel O'Connell.
1829	Catholic Emancipation Act.
1837	Reign of Queen Victoria begins.
1845	Potato blight starts in some counties and begins to spread. Beginning of the Great Famine (1845–9).
1850	Queen's University of Belfast founded.
1854	Catholic University of Ireland founded with John H. Newman first rector.
1867	Fenian rising takes place in five counties including Dublin.
1870	Home Rule movement launched by Isaac Butt. Gladstone's first Land Act recognises the rights of tenants.

1875	Parnell returned to parliament as member for Co. Meath.
1879–82	'Land War' is waged.
1881	Parnell imprisoned; Gladstone's second Land Act.
1893	Second Home Rule Bill is introduced. The Gaelic League is founded.
1899–	Literary revival gets well under way; Irish Literary Theatre founded.
1904	Abbey Theatre opened.
1908	Irish Universities Act establishes the National University of Ireland.
1916	Rising of rebels on Easter Monday in Dublin with an Irish Republic proclaimed on 24 April. In the Battle of the Somme the Ulster Division of the English army suffers severe losses.
1918	General election leads to success for the republicans.
1919–21	Anglo-Irish War begins consisting of sporadic resistance to British presence.
1920	Government of Ireland Act provides for separate parliaments for the north and south of the island of Ireland.
1922	The Irish Free State established, Northern Ireland excluded. The majority of the population is for the treaty in the ensuing election. Civil war begins.
1923	End of civil war. The Irish Free State admitted to League of Nations.
1937	New constitution introduced by Eamonn de Valera. The country is now officially called 'Éire' (this replaces 'Irish Free State', the former name).
1949	Ireland is declared a republic (18 April).
1955	Ireland becomes a member of the United Nations.
1964	Talks on reconciliation between Seán Lemass (Éire) and Terence O'Neill (Northern Ireland). Anglo-Irish free trade agreement is introduced.
1966	New University of Ulster at Coleraine, Co. Derry opened.
1968	Civil rights marches begin. Clashes in Derry.
1970	Provisional IRA begins a campaign of violence against British troops.
1972	Direct rule follows the suspension of the parliament of Northern Ireland.
1974	Power sharing executive set up, but defeated by the Protestants in an all-out strike (May).
1985	Hillsborough Anglo-Irish Agreement is rejected by Protestants.
1990	Ireland electorate vote for Mary Robinson as seventh president of Ireland, the first woman to hold this office.
1994	Both the IRA and the loyalist paramilitaries announce cease-fires.

1996	IRA ceasefire terminated.
1997	New Labour are victorious in British general elections.
1997	IRA declare a resumption of the 1994 ceasefire.
1998	Loyalist paramilitaries announce a ceasefire. 'Good Friday' agreement reached.
1999–2006	Stalemate in the peace process. Generally, the ceasefire still holds.

Appendix 2   The history of Irish English studies

early 14th c.   *Kildare Poems* were probably composed somewhere in the east of Ireland, between Dublin and Waterford. A number of other smaller pieces from this period also survive.

1366   Statutes of Kilkenny. A set of laws which, among other things, proscribed the use of Irish by the Normans in Ireland and insisted that they use English. In order to be understood, the statutes were written in French and were largely ineffectual.

15th c.   Municipal records from Dublin and Waterford document early features of English along the east coast of Ireland.

1577   Richard Stanihurst, *Treatise Containing a Plaine and Perfect Description of Ireland* appears in *Holinshed's Chronicles* (1577). It contains the first references to the dialect of Forth and Bargy.

1589   *Captain Thomas Stukeley*, the earliest dramatic piece satirising the use of English by the Irish, appears anonymously.

1735   Jonathan Swift, *Dialogue in Hybernian Stile between A & B* appears, a parody of the speech of a rural planter and an urban dweller.

1781   Thomas Sheridan, *A Rhetorical Grammar of the English Language* is published in Dublin. A prescriptive work which contains an appendix suggesting corrections to Irish 'mispronunciations of English'.

1788   Charles Vallancey publishes a glossary of some twenty-eight pages containing words in the dialect of Forth and Bargy, Co. Wexford.

1801   *Castle Rackrent* by Maria Edgeworth, considered the first regional novel in English, is published. Many Irish English features are to be found in stretches of direct speech.

1807   Jacob Poole published a glossary of words from Forth and Bargy. This is more comprehensive than that of Vallancey.

1845   John Donovan, *Grammar of Irish*, the first modern description of the language, appears. This contains some references to the Irish use of English.

1860	David Patterson, *The Provincialisms of Belfast and the Surrounding Districts Pointed out and Corrected . . .* appears. This is an important source of features of Belfast English in the nineteenth century.
1867	William Barnes publishes an edition of Poole's glossary with some introductory notes.
1910	Patrick Weston Joyce, *English as we Speak it in Ireland*, the first full-length monograph on Irish English, appears.
1927	James Jeremiah Hogan, *The English Language in Ireland*, a philological work on the development of Irish English since the Middle Ages, appears.
1932	Thomas Francis O'Rahilly, *Irish Dialects Past and Present* is published. It contains references to English in the south-east of the country.
1934	James Jeremiah Hogan, *An Outline of English Philology, Chiefly for Irish Students.*
1958	Patrick Leo Henry, *An Anglo-Irish Dialect of North Roscommon.*
1958	Patrick Leo Henry, 'A linguistic survey of Ireland. Preliminary report'.
1964	George Brendan Adams (ed.), *Ulster Dialects.*
1977	Diarmuid Ó Muirithe (ed.),*The English Language in Ireland.*
1979	Alan J. Bliss, *Spoken English in Ireland 1600–1740.*
1980	Lesley Milroy, *Language and Social Networks* (2nd edition 1987).
1981	James Milroy, *Regional Accents of English: Belfast.*
1981	Michael V. Barry (ed.), *Aspects of English Dialects in Ireland*, vol. 1: *Papers Arising from the Tape-Recorded Survey of Hiberno-English Speech.*
1985	John Harris, *Phonological Variation and Change.*
1985	Dónall Ó Baoill (ed.), *Papers on Irish English.*
1986	John Harris, David Little and David Singleton (eds.), *Perspectives on the English Language in Ireland: Proceedings of the First Symposium on Hiberno-English, Dublin 1985.*
1990	Terence P. Dolan (ed.), *The English of the Irish.*
1996	Alison Henry, *Belfast English and Standard English: Dialect Variation and Parameter Setting.*
1996	Caroline Macafee (ed.), *A Concise Ulster Dictionary.*
1997	Bernard Share, *Slanguage – a Dictionary of Slang and Colloquial English in Ireland* (2nd edition 2003).
1997	Jeffrey Kallen (ed.), *Focus on Ireland.*
1997	Hildegard Tristram (ed.), *Celtic Englishes. Proceedings of the Potsdam Colloquium on Celtic Englishes, 28–30 September 1995.*
1998	Terence P. Dolan, *A Dictionary of Hiberno-English* (2nd edition 2004).
1999	James P. Mallory (ed.), *Language in Ulster.*

1999	Markku Filppula, *The Grammar of Irish English: Language in Hibernian Style.*
2000	Tony Crowley, *The Politics of Language in Ireland, 1366–1922.*
2000	Hildegard Tristram (ed.), *Celtic Englishes II: Proceedings of the Second Potsdam Colloquium on Celtic Englishes.*
2000	John Kirk and Dónall Ó Baoill (eds.), *Language and Politics: Northern Ireland, the Republic of Ireland, and Scotland.*
2001	Kevin McCafferty, *Ethnicity and Language Change: English in (London)Derry, Northern Ireland.*
2001	John Kirk and Dónall Ó Baoill (eds.), *Language Links: The Languages of Scotland and Ireland.*
2002	Raymond Hickey, *A Source Book for Irish English.*
2002	John Kirk and Dónall Ó Baoill (eds.), *Travellers and their Language.*
2002	Markku Filppula, Juhani Klemola and Heli Pitkänen (eds.), *The Celtic Roots of English.*
2003	Hildegard Tristram (ed.), *Celtic Englishes III: Proceedings of the Third Potsdam Colloquium on Celtic Englishes.*
2004	Raymond Hickey, *A Sound Atlas of Irish English.*
2005	Anne Barron and Klaus Schneider (eds.), *The Pragmatics of Irish English.*
2005	Raymond Hickey, *Dublin English: Evolution and Change.*
2005	John Kirk and Jeffrey Kallen: completion of *ICE-Ireland.*
2006	Hildegard Tristram (ed.), *Celtic Englishes IV: Proceedings of the Fourth Potsdam Colloquium on Celtic Englishes.*

Appendix 3 Extracts from the *Kildare Poems*

IV *Christ on the cross*
(commentary in Heuser 1904: 125–8)

1 Behold to þi lord, man, whare he hangiþ on rode,
And weep, if þou migt, teris al of blode,
And loke to is heued wiþ þornis al bewonde
And to is felle so bispette and to þe sper is wnde.
5 Bihold to is brest is nakid and is blodi side;
Stiuiiþ is armis, þat sprad beþ so wide;
His fair lere falowiþ and dimmiþ is sigte;
Þer to is hendi bodi on rode so is ytigte.
His lendin so hangiþ as cold as marbre stone,
10 For luste of lechuri nas þer neuer none.
Behold to is nailes in hond and ek in fote,
And how þe stremis erniþ of is swet blode.
Beginne at is heued and loke to is to:
Þou ne findest in is bodi bot anguis and wo;
15 Turne him uppe, turne him doune, þi swete lemman:
Ouer al þou findist him blodi oþer wan.

1 Behold thy lord, man, where he hangs on the cross
And weep, if thou might, tears of blood
And look to his head wreathed with thorns
And to his skin so spoiled and to the wound of the spear.
5 Behold his breast that is naked and his bloody side
Stiff his arms that are spread so wide
His fair face grows pale and his sight dim
And his noble body is taught on the cross.
His loins hang as cold as marble stone:
10 Lust of lechery, none was ever there.
Behold his nails on his hands and his feet
And how the streams of his sweet blood flow.

Begin at his head and look to his toes:
Thou willst not find in his body but anguish and woe
15 Turn him up, turn him down, thy sweet beloved one
Over all his body thou willst find him bloody or wan.

(translation: RH)

VII *The land of Cockaigne*
(commentary in Heuser 1904: 139–45)

1 Fur in see bi west Spayngne
Is a lond ihote Cokaygne,
þer nis lond vnder heuen riche
Of wel, of godnis hit iliche.
5 Þog paradis be miri and brigt,
Cokaygne is of fairir sigt,
What is þer in paradis
Bot grasse and flure and grene ris?
Þog þer be ioi and gret dute,
10 Þer nis met bote frute;
Þer nis halle, bure no benche,
Bot watir man is þursto quenche.
Beþ þer no men bot two,
Hely and Enok also;
15 Elinglich mai hi go,
Whar þer woniþ men no mo.

1 Far in the sea by west Spain
Is a land called Cockaigne
There is no land under heaven's realm
In wellness and goodness its like.
5 Though paradise be merry and bright
Cockaigne is of fairer sight
What is there in paradise
But grass and flowers and green twigs?
Though there be joy and great pleasure
10 There is no food but fruit;
There is no hall, nor bower nor bench,
But water to quench the thirst of man.
There are only two men there,
Elijah and Enoch also;
15 Drearily may they go,
Where men no longer live.

(translation: RH)

VIII *Satire on the people of Kildare*
(commentary in Heuser 1904: 150–4)

1   Hail seint Michael wiþ þe lange sper!
Fair beþ þi winges vp þi scholder,
Þou hast a rede kirtil anon to þi fote,
Þou ert best angle þat euer god makid.
5   Þis uers is ful wel iwrogt,
Hit is of wel furre ybrogt.

Hail seint Cristofre wiþ þi lang stake!
Þou ber ur louerd Iesus Crist ouer þe brod lake,
Mani grete kunger swimmeþ abute þi fete.
10   Hou mani hering to peni at West Chep in London?
Þis uers is of holi writte,
Hit com of noble witte.

Seint Mari bastard, þe Maudlein is sone,
To be wel icloþid wel was þi wone!
15   Þou berrist a box on þi hond ipeintid al of gold,
Woned þou wer to be hend, giue us sum of þi spicis.
Þis uers is imakid wel
Of consonans and wowel.

1   Hail St Michael with the long spear!
Fair be the wings upon thy shoulders
Thou hast a red tunic down to thy foot,
Thou art the best angel God ever made.
5   This verse is very well made,
It is brought from far away.

Hail St Cristopher with thy long stake!
Thou borst Our Lord Jesus Christ over the broad lake,
Many a great conger swims around thy feet.
10   How many herrings for a penny at West Cheap in London?
This verse is from the Holy Scripture,
It comes from a noble mind.

St Mary's bastard, the son of Magdalen,
To be well clothed was always thy custom!
15   Thou bearst a box in thy hand all painted in gold
Thou wert accustomed to be kind, give us some of thy spices.
This verse is made well
Of consonants and vowels.

(translation: RH)

Appendix 4 Forth and Bargy

The following item is the first in the section *Songs, Metrical Pieces, etc. in the Old English Speech of Forth and Bargy* which is to be found after the glossary of Poole in Dolan and Ó Muirithe (1996: 76f.). It is available in two versions, one in 'Forth' and the other in 'English', both of which were supplied in the original edition.

A Yola Song (Forth)

1
Fade teil thee zo lournagh, co Joane, zo knaggee?
Th' weithest all curcagh wafur, an cornee.
Lidge w'ouse an a milagh, tis gaay an louthee:
Huck nigher; y'art scuddeen; fartoo zo hachee?

2
Well, gosp, c'hull be zeid; mot thee fartoo, an fade;
Ha deight ouse var gabble, tell ee zin go t'glade.
Ch'am a stouk, an a donel; wou'll leigh out ee dey.
Th'valler w'speen here, th'lass ee chourch-hey.

3
Yerstey w'had a baree, gist ing oor hoane,
Aar gentrize ware bibbern, aamzil cou no stoane.
Yith Muzleare had ba hole, t'was mee Tommeen,
At by mizluck was ee-pit t'drive in.

4
Joud an moud vrem earchee ete was ee Lough.
Zitch vaperreen, an shimmereen, fan ee-daff ee aar scoth!
Zitch blakeen, an blayeen, fan ee ball was ee-drowe!
Chote well aar aim was t'yie ouz n'eer a blowe.

5

Mot w'all aar boust, hi soon was ee-teight
At aar errone was var ameing 'ar 'ngish ee-height.
Zitch vezzeen, tarvizzeen, 'tell than w'ne'er zey.
Nore zichel ne'er well, nowe, nore ne'er mey.

An Old Song (English)

1

What ails you so melancholy, quoth John, so cross?
You seem all snappish, uneasy, and fretful.
Lie with us on the clover, 'tis fair and sheltered:
Come nearer; you're rubbing your back; why so ill tempered?

2

Well, gossip, it shall be told; you ask what ails me, and for what;
You have put us in talk, 'till the sun goes to set.
I am a fool and a dunce; we'll idle out the day.
The more we spend here, the less in the churchyard.

3

Yesterday we had a goal just in our hand.
Their gentry were quaking, themselves could not stand.
If Good-for-little had been buried, it had been my Tommy,
Who by misluck was placed to drive in.

4

Throngs and crowds from each quarter were at the Lough;
Such vapouring and glittering when stript in their shirts!
Such bawling and shouting, when the ball was thrown!
I saw their intent was to give us ne'er a stroke.

5

But with all their bravado they were soon taught
That their errand was aiming to bring anguish upon them.
Such driving, and struggling, 'till then we ne'er saw
Nor such never will, no, nor never may.

Appendix 5 Glossary

This glossary only contains items specific to issues discussed in this book. For reasons of space, general terms found in books on varieties of English have not been included.

ascendancy Originally a reference to the Protestant ruling class in eighteenth-century Ireland. It later came to refer, as a rather vague term, to a putative Protestant elite in Ireland, usually on country estates.

Belfast The capital of Ulster at the estuary of the river Lagan in the north-east of the country. It was founded in the seventeenth century and expanded greatly with the development of such industries as ship-building in the nineteenth century. Linguistically, it is an amalgam of Ulster Scots and mid Ulster English inputs along with independent developments of its own, especially in the last century. It is largely Protestant, though west Belfast has a Catholic majority.

blarney An impressionistic term for flattering, cloying speech which is supposed to be typical of the Irish. It has been known in this sense since the time of Elizabeth I who is reputed to have used the term. The term derives from a stone on a rampart of Blarney Castle near Cork city which is supposed to give anyone who kisses it 'the gift of the gab'.

brogue A term stemming from the Irish word either for 'shoe' (*bróg*) or 'a knot in the tongue' (*barróg teangan*). The label has been used in the past four centuries for any strongly local accent of Irish English. Occasionally, the term is used outside Ireland as in 'Ocracoke Brogue' to refer to the local accent of offshore islands in North Carolina.

cant A term which has been used for the speech of Irish Travellers. It is taken by Irish scholars to stem from Irish *caint* 'talk' but the use in the New World can in fact be derived from French.

Celtic A branch of the Indo-European family which spread from the European continent to the British Isles during the first millennium BC. The split into two branches, a Q-branch, maintaining inherited /kw/, and a P-Celtic branch, in which this sound shifted to /p/, took place on the continent. Today there are six surviving languages (strictly speaking, four with native speakers):

Q-Celtic with Irish, Scottish Gaelic and Manx (extinct) and P-Celtic with Welsh, Cornish (extinct, but with attempts at revival) and Breton.

Connaught   The western-most of the four provinces of Ireland. 'Connacht' is the spelling in Irish.

Connemara   An area of flat land immediately west of the city of Galway extending out to the mountains on the west coast. It contains one of the few remaining Irish-speaking areas. 'Conamara' is the spelling in Irish.

convergence   A linguistic scenario in which two or more languages become increasingly similar in their structures, usually because of prolonged contact in a geographically delimited area. This convergence is realised by speakers adopting features of other languages they are in contact with and passing these features on to later generations. See *language contact, language shift* and *transfer*.

Cork   The second largest city in the south of Ireland. It has an easily recognisable accent with an undulating intonational pattern which is found in the south-west in general (in counties Cork and Kerry).

Derry   The second largest city in Ulster on the banks of the river Foyle near where it enters the sea. It has always had a special status in west Ulster and, in the context of Northern Ireland, it is remarkable in having a Catholic majority. The label 'Londonderry' stems from the seventeenth century when London undertaker companies were commissioned to plant the city with English settlers.

Dublin   The capital of the Republic of Ireland at the mouth of the river Liffey on the east coast. It is by far the largest city in the entire island, with nearly one-third of the Republic's population (over 1 million people) living in its metropolitan area.

east coast dialect area   A reference to the east coast of Ireland, roughly from Dublin down to Waterford, where vernacular forms of speech show features which go back to the earliest days of English settlement, well before 1600. See *Pale*.

First period (1200–1600)   One of the two main divisions in the history of Irish English. It begins with the Anglo-Norman invasion in the south-east in 1169. By 1600, Gaelic resurgence, and with it that of the Irish language, had come to an end. The seventeenth century saw the importation of newer varieties of English on a wide scale in both the north and south of the country. See *Second period*.

Forth and Bargy   Two baronies in the extreme south-east of Ireland, in Co. Wexford, where a particularly archaic form of English, stemming from the late medieval period of settlement in Ireland, was spoken up to the beginning of the nineteenth century.

Gaelic   A generic term for the Q-Celtic branch of the Insular Celtic languages consisting of Irish, Scottish Gaelic and Manx. In a Scottish context, the bare term 'Gaelic' or 'Gallick' (reflecting the local pronunciation) is taken to refer to Scottish Gaelic.

Gaeltacht   An Irish term meaning 'Irish-speaking area'. Two types are recognised officially, *Fíor-Ghaeltacht*, the 'true' Gaeltacht with a high density of Irish speakers, and *Breac-Ghaeltacht*, adjoining areas in which the number of native speakers is considerably less.

Hibernia   The Latin word for Ireland, possibly deriving from the word for 'winter', but more likely from the name of an ancient tribe, the *Everni*, mentioned by Ptolemy (O'Rahilly 1946) as the *Iverni*, and associated with Ireland.

Irish   The name for (i) the people of Ireland and (ii) the Celtic language still spoken by a small minority, chiefly on the western seaboard.

language contact   A situation where speakers of one language come into contact with speakers of another. Such contact can lead to speakers abandoning their language and switching to that of the other group in which case one is dealing with language shift. This is what happened in the past few centuries in Ireland. See *language shift, convergence* and *transfer*.

language shift   A situation in which speakers of a language abandon this and move to another language with which they are in contact, usually over a prolonged period. This shift happened historically in Ireland with the move from Irish to English for the great majority of the population. See *language contact, convergence* and *transfer*.

Leinster   One of the four provinces of Ireland in the east, south-east of the island.

mid Ulster English   A linguistic term referring to the speech of that section of the population of Ulster which is derived from English settlers of the seventeenth century. It is one of the two major linguistic groupings in Northern Ireland, the other being Ulster Scots. It has also been referred to as *Ulster Anglo-Irish*. It is also spoken by the native Irish who switched to English during the historical language shift.

Munster   One of the four provinces of Ireland in the south, south-west of the island.

Northern Ireland   Since 1921, a part of the United Kingdom. It consists of six of the nine counties of the province of Ulster and was created as an option for the Protestant majority in the north-east of Ireland, descended from original Scottish and English settlers, who wished to remain within the British union.

New English   A label sometimes used for English settlers who arrived in Ireland in the sixteenth and seventeenth centuries and who were Protestants. These settlers were different from the older Catholic English who had come to Ireland in the late Middle Ages. See *Old English*.

Old English   A reference to the English (and Anglo-Norman) settlers in pre-Reformation Ireland, i.e. the descendants of the late medieval settlers who came at the end of the twelfth century. This group assimilated largely to the native Irish.

Pale   A term for the area of Dublin, its immediate hinterland and a stretch of the east coast down to the south-east corner which was first settled by the English and fairly successful in resisting increasing gaelicisation up to the sixteenth century. The varieties of English in this area still show features which stem from late medieval Irish English whereas those further west in the country show greater influence from Irish. See *east coast dialect area*.

Presbyterians   Non-conformist Protestants who are particularly strong in Scotland and who came from there to Ulster in the seventeenth century.

Republic of Ireland   Since 1949, the official name for the south of Ireland (excluding Northern Ireland). With the declaration of a republic, Ireland left the Commonwealth.

retentionist view   A standpoint in Irish English studies where considerable weight is accorded to regional English input to Ireland. This stance implies that Irish did not play a central role in the genesis of Irish English.

Scouse   The city dialect of Liverpool which, due to heavy Irish immigration to the Merseyside region in the nineteenth century, shows not insignificant traces of Irish English, especially in the lenition of stops.

Second period (1600 to the present)   The second main division in the history of Irish English. In the early seventeenth century the widespread settlement of Ulster by people from Scotland took place. By the middle of this century, newer varieties of English were also being imported in the south. These newer varieties fed directly into modern forms of Irish English. See *First period*.

Shelta   The assumed language, or jargon, of Irish Travellers about which only a little is known (mainly vocabulary). Reliable information is not available today.

stage Irish   A stereotype which began to appear in English drama in the seventeenth century. The term is popularly used to denote anyone who displays supposedly Irish traits, such as flattering, flowery language and melodramatic behaviour.

substratist view   A standpoint in Irish English studies where considerable weight is accorded to structural transfer from Irish into English. This stance implies that regional English input was correspondingly less important in the genesis of Irish English.

supraregionalisation   A process which is assumed to have taken place in late nineteenth- and early twentieth-century Ireland and to have been triggered by the rise of general school education for the native Catholic Irish. It consisted of the replacement of salient dialect features by more standard ones. Because of this, vernacular forms of speech (for middle-class speakers) lost their local identity and became 'supraregional'.

transfer   A process whereby speakers of a language adopt and incorporate features of a further language into their own. Transfer presupposes language contact and is at a premium in scenarios of *language shift*.

Ullans   A term for (written) Ulster Scots which has been formed on analogy with Lallans, the Lowland Scots term for itself. It is also the name of a journal.

Ulster   A province in the north of Ireland. It consists of nine counties, six of which now form Northern Ireland. Co. Donegal in the extreme north-west is part of the Republic of Ireland but has more features in common with speech in Northern Ireland, both Ulster Scots and mid Ulster English.

Ulster Scots   The language of the Scottish settlers and their descendants in the coastal regions in the north and north-east of Ulster. Much assimilation and mixing has taken place in the past few centuries, especially in Belfast. Ulster Scots has undergone a considerable revival in recent years.

universalist view   A kind of 'third way' in Irish English studies seen as complementing both the substratist and retentionist views (see relevant entries). In essence, it assumes that there are universals of unguided adult second-language acquisition which are similar in many ways, but not identical to creolisation. These are assumed to be responsible for many of the specific structures, such as aspectual distinctions, which arose during the language shift from Irish to English.

Yola   The form of the word 'old' in the dialect of Forth and Bargy which came to be used as a reference to the dialect itself.

Appendix 6 Maps

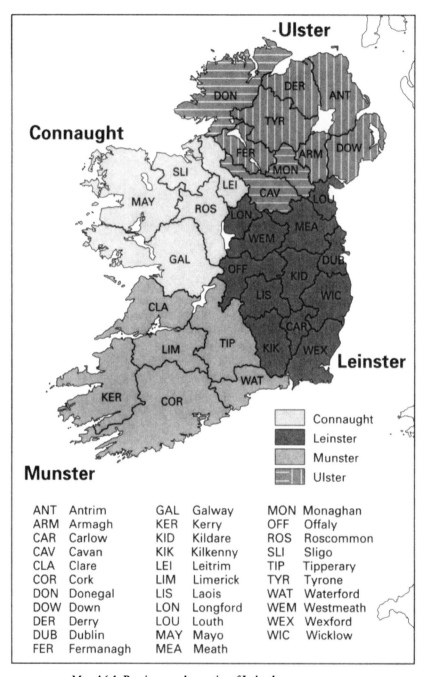

Map A6.1 Provinces and counties of Ireland

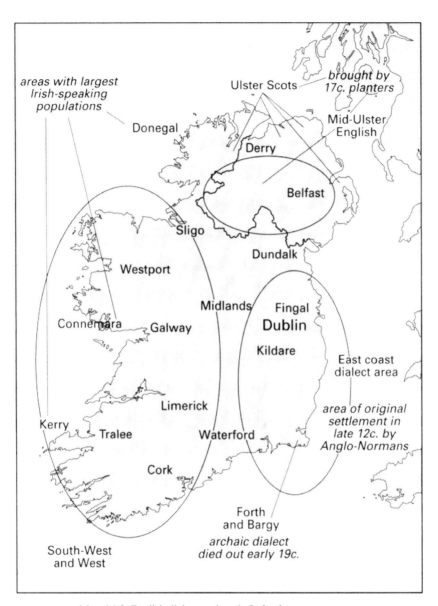

areas with largest
Irish-speaking
populations

Ulster Scots

brought by
17c. planters

Donegal

Mid-Ulster
English

Derry

Belfast

Sligo

Dundalk

Westport

Midlands

Fingal

Dublin

Connemara

Galway

Kildare

East coast
dialect area

Limerick

area of original
settlement in
late 12c. by
Anglo-Normans

Kerry

Tralee

Waterford

Cork

Forth
and Bargy

*archaic dialect
died out early 19c.*

South-West
and West

Map A6.2 English dialect regions in Ireland

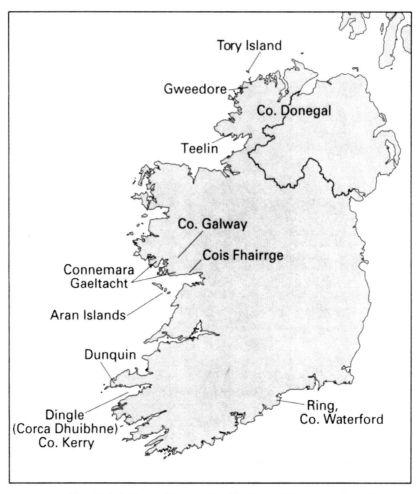

Map A6.3 Irish-speaking districts (Gaeltachtaí) in present-day Ireland

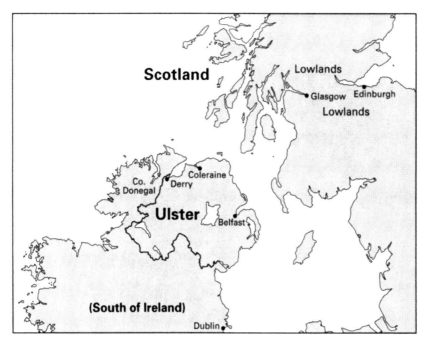

Map A6.4 Source areas in Scotland for seventeenth-century emigration to
Ulster

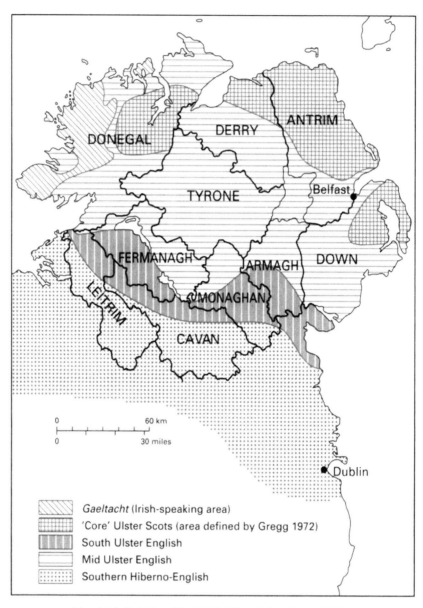

Map A6.5 Varieties of English in Ulster (after Harris 1985)

Map A6.6 The present-day greater Dublin area

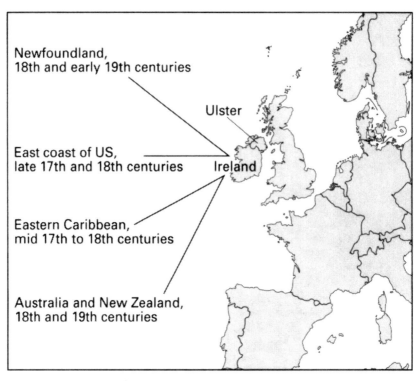

Map A6.7 The spread of English from Ireland

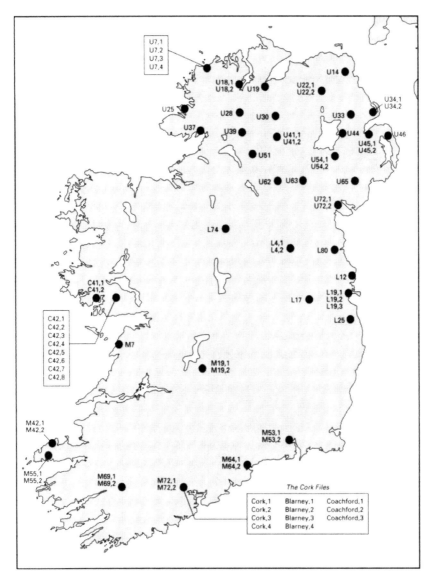

Map A6.8 Locations of informants from the *Tape-Recorded Survey of Hiberno-English Speech*

References

Aarts, Bas and April McMahon (eds.) 2006. *The Handbook of English Linguistics*. Oxford: Blackwell.

Adams, George Brendan 1958. 'The emergence of Ulster as a distinct dialect area', *Ulster Folklife* 4: 61–73.

1964a. 'A register of phonological research on Ulster dialects', in Adams (ed.), pp. 193–201.

(ed.) 1964b. *Ulster Dialects: an Introductory Symposium*. Holywood, Co. Down: Ulster Folk and Transport Museum.

1965. 'Materials for a language map of 17th century Ireland', *Ulster Dialect Archive Bulletin* 4: 15–30.

1966a. 'Phonemic systems in collision in Ulster English', in Schmitt (ed.), pp. 1–6.

1966b. 'Glossary of household terms', *Ulster Folklife* 12: 31–4.

1967. 'Northern England as a source of Ulster dialects', *Ulster Folklife* 13: 69–74.

1977. 'The dialects of Ulster', in Ó Muirithe (ed.), pp. 56–70.

1978a. 'Prolegomena to the study of Irish place-names', *Nomina* 2: 45–60.

1978b. 'Some Ulster words describing persons and animals', *Ulster Folklife* 24: 69–82.

1980. 'Common features in Ulster Irish and Ulster English', in Thelwall (ed.), pp. 85–104.

1981a. 'Dialect work in Ulster: an historical account of research in the area', in Barry (ed.), pp. 5–17.

1981b. 'The voiceless velar fricative in Northern Hiberno-English', in Barry (ed.), pp. 106–17.

Adams, Michael 2000. 'Lexical Doppelgängers', *Journal of English Linguistics* 28. 3: 295–310.

Adamson, Ian 1994. 'The Ulster-Scottish connection', in Wood (ed.), pp. 1–21.

Adamson, Sylvia et al. (eds.) 1990. *Papers from the 5th International Conference on English Historical Linguistics*. Amsterdam: John Benjamins.

Ahlqvist, Anders 1988. 'Of unknown [?] origin', *Studia Anglica Posnaniensia* 21: 69–73.

2002. 'Cleft sentences in Irish and other languages', in Filppula, Klemola and Pitkänen (eds.), pp. 271–81.

Ahlqvist, Anders and Vera Čapková (eds.) 1997. *Dán do oide* [A poem for a mentor]: *Essays in Memory of Conn R. Ó Cléirigh*. Dublin: Linguistics Institute of Ireland.

Aitken, Adam J. 1977. 'How to pronounce Older Scots', in Aitken, McDiarmid and Thomson (eds.), pp. 1–21.

1981. 'The Scottish vowel length rule', in Benskin and Samuels (eds.), pp. 131–57.

Atiken, Adam J., Matthew P. McDiarmid and Derick S. Thomson (eds.) 1977. *Bards and Makars. Scottish Language and Literature: Medieval and Renaissance.* Glasgow: Glasgow University Press.

Akenson, Donald 1996. *The Irish Diaspora: a Primer.* Toronto: Meaney Company.

Aldus, Judith Butler 1976. 'Anglo-Irish dialects: a bibliography', *Regional Language Studies Newfoundland* 7: 7–28.

1997. *Irish English: a Bibliography.* Memorial University Newfoundland, Mimeograph.

Algeo, John 2001a. 'External history', in Algeo (ed.), pp. 1–58.

(ed.) 2001b. *Cambridge History of the English Language*, vol. 6. *English in North America.* Cambridge: Cambridge University Press.

Allen, Harold B. and Michael D. Linn (eds.) 1986. *Dialect and Language Variation.* Orlando: Academic Press.

Altendorf, Ulrike 2003. *Estuary English: Levelling at the Interface of RP and South-Eastern British English.* Tübingen: Narr.

Amador Moreno, Carolina P. 2006. *An Analysis of Hiberno-English in the Early Novels of Patrick MacGill: Bilingualism and Language Shift from Irish to English in County Donegal.* New York: Edwin Mellen Press.

Andersen, Henning (ed.) 1986. *Sandhi Phenomena in the Languages of Europe.* Berlin: Mouton de Gryuter.

Anderson, Malcolm and Eberhard Bort (eds.) 1999. *The Irish Border: History, Politics, Culture.* Liverpool: Liverpool University Press.

Anderwald, Lieselotte 2001. '*Was/were*-variation in non-standard British English today', *English World-Wide* 22.1: 1–21.

2002. *Negation in Non-Standard British English: Gaps, Regularizations and Asymmetrics.* London: Routledge.

2003. 'Non-standard English and typological principles: the case of negation', in Rohdenburg and Mondorf (eds.), pp. 507–29.

Andrews, John 2000. 'Plantation Ireland: a review of settlement history', in Barry (ed.), pp. 140–57.

Aubrey, Gwynn 1930–1. 'Cromwell's policy of transportation', *Studies* 19: 76.

Auer, Peter 1998. *Code-Switching in Conversation.* London: Routledge.

Auer, Peter, Frans Hinskens and Paul E. Kerswill (eds.) 2005. *Dialect Change: Convergence and Divergence in European Languages.* Cambridge: Cambridge University Press.

Auwera, Johan van der and Inge Genee 2002. 'English *do*: on the convergence of languages and linguists', *English Language and Linguistics* 6.2: 283–307.

Bailey, Charles-James N. 1982. 'Irish English and Caribbean Black English: another rejoinder', *American Speech* 57: 237–9.

Bailey, Guy and Gary Ross 1988. 'The shape of the superstrate: morphosyntactic features of ship English', *English World-Wide* 9: 193–212.

1992. 'The evolution of a vernacular', in Rissanen, Ihalainen, Nevalainen and Taavitsainen (eds.), pp. 519–31.

Bailey, Richard W. and Manfred Görlach (eds.) 1982. *English as a World Language.* Ann Arbor: University of Michigan Press.

Bailyn, Bernard 1986. *The Peopling of British North America: an Introduction*. New York: Knopf.

Baker, Sidney John 1966 [1945]. *The Australian Language*. 2nd edition. Sydney: Currawong Press.

Baker, Philip and Magnus Huber 2001. 'Atlantic, Pacific, and world-wide features in English-lexicon contact languages', *English World-Wide* 22: 157–208.

Ball, Martin J. and James Fife (eds.) 1993. *The Celtic Languages*. London: Routledge.

Ball, Martin J. and Joan Rahilly 1996. 'Spectrographic analysis of /u/ in Northern Irish English', in Henry, Ball and MacAliskey (eds.), pp. 1–18.

Barber, Charles 1997 [1976]. *Early Modern English*. Edinburgh: Edinburgh University Press.

Bardon, Jonathan 1996. *A Shorter Illustrated History of Ulster*. Belfast: Blackstaff Press.

Barnard, Toby C. 2000 [1975]. *Cromwellian Ireland: English Government and Reform in Ireland 1649–1660*. Oxford: Clarendon Press.

Barnes, William (ed.) 1867. *A Glossary, with Some Pieces of Verse, of the Old Dialect of the English Colony in the Baronies of Forth and Bargy, County of Wexford, Ireland, Formerly Collected by Jacob Poole*. London: J. R. Smith.

    1970 [1886]. *A Glossary of the Dorset Dialect with a Grammar of its Word Shapening and Wording*. St Peter Port, Guernsey: Toucan Press.

    1878. *An Outline of English Speech-Craft*. London: Kegan Paul.

Barron, Anne 2005. 'Offering in Ireland and England', Barron and Schneider (eds.), pp. 141–76.

Barron, Anne and Klaus Schneider 2005a. 'Irish English: a focus on language in action', Barron and Schneider (eds.), pp. 3–15.

    (eds.) 2005b. *The Pragmatics of Irish English*. Berlin: Mouton de Gruyter.

Barry, Michael V. 1981a. 'The southern boundaries of northern Hiberno-English speech', in Barry (ed.), pp. 52–95.

    (ed.) 1981b. *Aspects of English Dialects in Ireland*, vol 1: *Papers Arising from the Tape-Recorded Survey of Hiberno-English Speech*. Belfast: Institute for Irish Studies.

    1982. 'The English language in Ireland', in Bailey and Görlach (eds.), pp. 84–133.

Barry, Michael and Philip Tilling (eds.) 1986. *The English Dialects of Ulster: an Anthology of Articles on Ulster Speech by G. B. Adams*. Belfast: Ulster Folk and Transport Museum.

Barry, Terry 2000a. 'Rural settlement in medieval Ireland', in Barry (ed.), pp. 110–23.

    (ed.) 2000b. *A Settlement History of Ireland*. London: Routledge.

Bartley, John Oliver 1954. *Teague, Shenkin and Sawney: Being an Historical Study of the Earliest Irish, Welsh and Scottish Characters in English Plays*. Cork: Cork University Press.

Bauer, Laurie 1994a. *Watching English Change: an Introduction to the Study of Linguistic Change in Standard Englishes in the Twentieth Century*. London: Longman.

    1994b. 'English in New Zealand', in Burchfield (ed.), pp. 382–429.

Beal, Joan C. 1993. 'The grammar of Tyneside and Northumbrian English', in Milroy and Milroy (eds.), pp. 187–213.

    1996. 'The Jocks and the Geordies: modified standards in eighteenth-century pronouncing dictionaries', in Britton (ed.), pp. 363–82.

    2004a. *English in Modern Times 1700–1945*. London: Arnold.

2004b. 'English dialects in the North of England: morphology and syntax', in Kortmann et al. (eds.), vol. 2, pp. 114–41.

Beal, Joan C. and Karen Corrigan 2005. 'A tale of two dialects: relativization in Newcastle and Sheffield', in Filppula, Klemola, Palander and Penttilä (eds.), pp. 211–29.

Beecher, Seán 1991. *A Dictionary of Cork Slang*. Cork: Collins Press.

Beier, A. Lee 1985. *Masterless Men: the Vagrancy Problem in England 1560–1640*. London: Methuen.

Bernstein, Cynthia 2003. 'Grammatical features of southern speech: *yall*, *might could*, and *fixin to*', in Nagle and Sanders (eds.), pp. 106–18.

Benskin, Michael 1980. 'The English Language in Medieval Ireland'. Unpublished PhD thesis, University of Glasgow.

1989. 'The style and authorship of the Kildare Poems – (i) *Pers of Bermingham*', in Mackenzie and Todd (eds.), pp. 57–75.

1990. 'The hands of the *Kildare Poems* manuscript', in Dolan (ed.), pp. 163–93.

Benskin, Michael and Michael Samuels (eds.) 1981. *So Meny People Longages and Tonges: Philological Essays in Scots and Mediæval English Presented to Angus McIntosh*. Edinburgh: The Editors.

Bergin, Osborn 1943. '*Bróg* "shoe"', *Éigse* 3: 237–9.

Berndt, Rolf 1960. *Einführung in das Studium des Mittelenglischen*. [An introduction to the study of Middle English] Halle: Niemeyer.

Bertz, Siegfried 1975. 'Der Dubliner Stadtdialekt', Teil I: 'Phonologie'. [The dialect of Dublin city. Part 1: Phonology] Unpublished PhD thesis, University of Freiburg.

Bhaldraithe, Tomás de 1945. *The Irish of Cois Fhairrge, Co. Galway*. Dublin: Institute for Advanced Studies.

1953. 'Nua-iasachtaí in nGaeilge Chois Fhairrge' [New borrowings in the Irish of Cois Fhairrge (Co. Galway)], *Éigse* 7: 1–34.

Bielenberg, Andy (ed.) 2000. *The Irish Diaspora*. Harlow: Longman.

Biggar, J. J. 1897. *Our Ulster Accent and Ulster Provincialisms*. Belfast: The Religious Tract and Book Depot. Appeared under the pseudonym of 'One Who Listens'.

Binchy, Alice 1994. 'Travellers' language: a sociolinguistic perspective', in McCann, Ó Síocháin and Ruane (eds.), pp. 134–54.

Binnick, Robert I. 2005. 'The markers of habitual aspect in English', *Journal of English Linguistics* 33.4: 339–69.

Blackshire-Belay, Carol Aisha (ed.) 1994. *The Germanic Mosaic: Cultural and Linguistic Diversity in Society*. Westport, CT: Greenwood Press.

Blair, David and Peter Collins (eds.) 2001. *English in Australia*. Amsterdam: John Benjamins.

Blake, Norman 2002. *A Grammar of Shakespeare's Language*. London: Palgrave.

Blank, Paula 1996. *Broken English: Dialects and the Politics of Language in Renaissance Writings*. London: Routledge.

Blevins, Juliette 2006. 'New perspectives on English sound patterns: "natural" and "unnatural" in evolutionary phonology', *Journal of English Linguistics* 34.1: 6–25.

Bliss, Alan J. 1965. 'The inscribed slates at Smarmore', *Proceedings of the Royal Irish Academy, Section C*, 64: 33–60.

1968. '*Shanty* and *bother*', *Notes and Queries* 213: 283–6.

1972a. 'Languages in contact: some problems of Hiberno-English', *Proceedings of the Royal Irish Academy, Section C*, 72: 63–82.

1972b. 'The language of Synge', in Harmon (ed.), pp. 35–62.

1972c. 'A Synge glossary', in Bushrui (ed.), pp. 297–316.

1976. 'The English language in early modern Ireland', in Moody, Martin and Byrne (eds.), pp. 546–60.

1977a. 'The emergence of modern English dialects in Ireland', in Ó Muirithe (ed.), pp. 7–19.

1977b. *A Dialogue in Hybernian Style between A and B' and 'Irish Eloquence' by Jonathan Swift*. Dublin: Cadenus Press.

1979. *Spoken English in Ireland 1600–1740. Twenty-Seven Representative Texts Assembled and Analysed*. Dublin: Cadenus Press.

1984a. 'Language and literature', in Lydon (ed.), pp. 27–45.

1984b. 'English in the South of Ireland', in Trudgill (ed.), pp. 135–51.

Bliss, Alan J. and Joseph Long 1987. 'Literature in Norman French and English to 1534', in Moody, Martin and Byrne (eds.), pp. 708–36.

Blunt, Jerry 1967. *Stage Dialects*. San Francisco: Chandler.

Bobda, Augustin Simo 2006. 'Irish presence in colonial Cameroon and its linguistic legacy', in Tristram (ed.), pp. 217–33.

Bolton, Kingsley and Helen Kwok (eds.) 1991. *Sociolinguistics Today: International Perspectives*. London: Routledge.

Boorde, Andrew 1552. *The Breviary of Healthe*. London.

Boran, Pat 2000. *A Short History of Dublin*. Cork: Mercier.

Börjars, Kersti and Carol Chapman 1998. 'Agreement and pro-drop in some dialects of English', *Linguistics* 36: 71–98.

Borsley, Robert D. and Ian Roberts (eds.) 1996. *The Syntax of the Celtic Languages: a Comparative Perspective*. Cambridge: Cambridge University Press.

Boylan, Henry 1988. *A Dictionary of Irish Biography*. 2nd edition. Dublin: Gill and Macmillan.

Braaten, Björn 1967. 'Notes on continuous tenses in English', *Norsk Tidskrift for Sprogvidenskap* 21: 167–80.

Bradley, James 1986. 'A glossary of words from South Armagh and North Louth', *Ulster Folklife* 32: 91–4.

Bradley, David 1991. '/æ/ and /a:/ in Australian English', in Cheshire (ed.), pp. 227–34.

Brady, Joseph and Anngret Simms 2001. *Dublin through Space and Time (c. 900–1900)*. Dublin: Four Courts Press.

Braidwood, John 1964. 'Ulster and Elizabethan English', in Adams (ed.), pp. 5–109.

1965. 'Local bird names in Ulster – a glossary', *Ulster Folklife* 11: 98–135.

1969. *The Ulster Dialect Lexicon*. Belfast: Queens University of Belfast.

1972. 'Terms for "left-handed" in the Ulster dialects', *Ulster Folklife* 18: 98–110.

Breatnach, Risteard B. 1947. *The Irish of Ring, Co. Waterford*. Dublin: Institute for Advanced Studies.

Breeze, Andrew 1997. 'A Celtic etymology for Hiberno-English *callow* "river meadow"', *Éigse* 30: 158–60.

Brinton, Laurel 1988. *The Development of English Aspectual Systems: Aspectualizers and Post-Verbal Particles*. Cambridge: Cambridge University Press.

1996. *Pragmatic Markers in English: Grammaticalization and Discourse Functions*. Berlin: Mouton de Gruyter.

(ed.) 2001. *Historical Linguistics 1999*. Amsterdam: John Benjamins.

Britain, David 2002. 'Diffusion, levelling, simplification and reallocation in past tense BE in the English Fens', *Journal of Sociolinguistics* 6: 16–43.

(ed.) in press. *Language in the British Isles*. 2nd edition. Cambridge: Cambridge University Press.

Britain, David and Jenny Cheshire (eds.) 2003. *Social Dialectology: in Honour of Peter Trudgill*. Amsterdam: John Benjamins.

Britton, Derek (ed.) 1996. *English Historical Linguistics 1994*. Amsterdam: John Benjamins.

Britton, Derek and Alan J. Fletcher 1990. 'Medieval Hiberno-English inscriptions on the inscribed slates of Smarmore: some reconsiderations and additions', in Dolan (ed.), pp. 55–72.

Brown, Penelope and Stephen C. Levinson 1987. *Politeness: Some Universals in Language Usage*. Cambridge: Cambridge University Press.

Browne, Kathleen A. 1927. 'The ancient dialect of the baronies of Forth and Bargy, County Wexford. With a number of songs in that dialect, together with translations', *Journal of the Royal Society of Antiquaries of Ireland* 57: 127–37.

Burchfield, Robert (ed.) 1994. *The Cambridge History of the English Language*; vol. 5: *English in Britain and Overseas: Origins and Development*. Cambridge: Cambridge University Press.

Burke, William 1896. 'The Anglo-Irish dialect', *Irish Ecclesiastical Record*, 3rd series 17: 694–704, 777–89.

Burrowes, Audrey and Richard Allsopp 1983. 'Barbadian Creole: a note on its social history and structure', in Carrington et al. (eds.), pp. 38–45.

Bushrui, Suheil Badi (ed.) 1972. *Sunshine and the Moon's Delight: a Centenary Tribute to J. M. Synge 1871–1909*. Gerrards Cross: Colin Smythe.

Butlin, Robin A. (ed.) 1977. *The Development of the Irish Town*. London.

Butters, Ronald R. 2001. 'Grammatical structure', in Algeo (ed.), pp. 325–39.

Butterworth, Brian, Bernard Comrie and Östen Dahl (eds.) 1984. *Explanations for Language Universals*. Berlin: Mouton.

Bybee, Joan and Östen Dahl 1989. 'The creation of tense and aspect systems in the languages of the world', *Studies in Language* 13: 51–103.

Byrne, Joseph 2004. *Byrne's Dictionary of Irish Local History from Earliest Times to c. 1900*. Cork: Mercier Press.

Cahill, Edward 1938. 'Norman French and English languages in Ireland, 1170–1540', *Irish Ecclesiastical Record*, 5th series 51: 160–73.

Caie, Graham et al. (eds.) 1990. *Proceedings of the Fourth Scandinavian Conference on English Studies*. Copenhagen: Department of English.

Cairns, Edward and B. Duriez 1976. 'The influence of speaker's accent on recall by Catholic and Protestant school children in Northern Ireland', *British Journal of Social and Clinical Psychology* 15: 441–2.

Campbell, Alastair 1959. *Old English Grammar*. Oxford: Clarendon Press.

Campbell, Lyle 1998. *Historical Linguistics*. Edinburgh: Edinburgh University Press.

Campbell, Peter F. 1993. *Some Early Barbadian History*. Barbados: Caribbean Graphics.

Canny, Nicholas 1980. Review of Alan J. Bliss (1979) *Spoken English in Ireland 1600– 1740. Twenty-Seven Representative Texts Assembled and Analysed*, *Studia Hibernica* 20: 167–72.

(ed.) 1994. *Europeans on the Move: Studies on European Migration, 1500–1800*. Oxford: Oxford University Press.

2001. *Making Ireland British 1580–1650*. Oxford: Oxford University Press.

Carrington, Lawrence D. et al. (eds.) 1983. *Studies in Caribbean Language*. St Augustine: Society for Caribbean Linguistics.

Carroll, Susan 1983. 'Remarks on FOR-TO infinitives', *Linguistic Analysis* 12: 415–51.

Cassidy, Frederic G. 1980. 'The place of Gullah', *American Speech* 55: 3–16.

Chambers, J. K. 1973. 'Canadian raising', *Canadian Journal of Linguistics* 18: 113–35.

Chambers, J. K., Peter Trudgill and Natalie Schilling-Estes (eds.) 2002. *The Handbook of Language Variation and Change*. Oxford: Blackwell.

Chase, Malcolm 1995. 'The Teesside Irish in the nineteenth century', *Cleveland History: the Bulletin of the Cleveland and Teesside Local History Society* 69: 3–23.

Cheshire, Jenny L. 1982. *Variation in an English Dialect: a Sociolinguistic Study*. Cambridge: Cambridge University Press.

(ed.) 1991. *English around the World: Sociolinguistic Perspectives*. Cambridge: Cambridge University Press.

1994. 'Standardization and the English irregular verbs', in Stein and Tieken-Boon van Ostade (eds.), pp. 115–34.

1996. 'Syntactic variation and the concept of prominence', in Klemola, Kytö and Rissanen (eds.), pp. 1–17.

Cheshire, Jenny L. and Dieter Stein (eds.) 1997. *Taming the Vernacular: from Dialect to Written Standard Language*. London: Longman.

Christensen, Lis 1996. *A First Glossary of Hiberno-English*. Odense: Odense University Press.

Christian, Donna 1991. 'The personal dative in Appalachian speech', in Trudgill and Chambers (eds.), pp. 11–19.

Christian Brothers, The 1960. *Graiméar Gaeilge na mBráithre Críostaí* [Christian Brothers' Irish Grammar]. Dublin: Gill and Son.

1977. *New Irish Grammar*. Dublin: Fallons.

Clark, James M. 1977 [1917]. *The Vocabulary of Anglo-Irish*. Philadelphia: R. West.

Clark, Paul Odell 1953. 'A Gulliver dictionary', *Studies in Philology* 50: 592–624.

Clarke, Aidan 1994 [1967]. 'The colonisation of Ulster and the rebellion of 1641', in Moody and Martin (eds.), pp. 152–64.

Clarke, Howard, Sarah Dent and Ruth Johnson 2002. *Dublinia: the Story of Medieval Dublin*. Dublin: O'Brien Press.

Clarke, Sandra 1986. 'Sociolinguistic patterning in a New World dialect of Hiberno-English: the speech of St John's, Newfoundland', in Harris, Little and Singleton (eds.), pp. 67–82.

(ed.) 1993. *Focus on Canada*. Varieties of English around the World, General series, vol. 11. Amsterdam: John Benjamins.

1997a. 'On establishing historical relationships between New and Old World varieties: habitual aspect and Newfoundland Vernacular English', in Schneider (ed.), pp. 277–93.

1997b. 'The role of Irish English in the formation of New World Englishes: the case from Newfoundland', in Kallen (ed.), pp. 207–25.

2004. 'The legacy of British and Irish English in Newfoundland', in Hickey (ed.), pp. 242–61.

Cleary, Joe and Claire Connolly (eds.) 2005. *The Cambridge Companion to Irish Culture*. Cambridge: Cambridge University Press.

Clyne, Michael 1987. 'Constraints on code-switching: how universal are they?', *Linguistics* 25: 739–64.

2003. *The Dynamics of Language Contact*. 2nd edition. Cambridge: Cambridge University Press.

Coetsem, Frans van 2000. *A General and Unified Theory of the Transmission Process in Language Contact*. Heidelberg: Carl Winter.

Coggle, Paul 1993. *Do You Speak Estuary? The New Standard English – How to Spot it and Speak it*. London: Bloomsbury.

Comrie, Bernard 1976. *Aspect*. Cambridge: Cambridge University Press.

Connolly, Sean J. 1998. *The Oxford Companion to Irish History*. Oxford: Oxford University Press.

Corbyn, Charles Adam 1970 [1854]. *Sydney Revels of Bacchus, Cupid and Momus; Being Choice and Humorous Scenes at the Sydney Police Office, and Other Public Places, During the Last Three Years*. London: Ure Smith [Sydney: Hawksley and Williamson].

Corkery, Daniel 1967 [1924]. *The Hidden Ireland: a Study of Gaelic Munster in the Eighteenth Century*. Dublin: Gill and Macmillan.

Corpas na Gaeilge, 1600–1882 [A Corpus of Irish, 1600–1882]. 705 texts on CD-ROM. Dublin: Royal Irish Academy.

Corrigan, Karen P. 1990. 'Northern Hiberno-English: the state of the art', in Dolan (ed.), pp. 91–119.

1993a. 'Hiberno-English syntax: nature versus nurture in a creole context', *Newcastle and Durham Working Papers in Linguistics* 1: 95–131.

1993b. 'Gaelic and early English influences on South Armagh English', *Ulster Folklife* 39: 15–28.

1996. 'Language attrition in nineteenth century Ireland: emigration as "murder machine"', in Henry, Ball and MacAliskey (eds.), pp. 43–84.

1997a. 'The Syntax of South Armagh English in its Socio-Historical Perspective'. Unpublished PhD thesis, University College Dublin.

1997b. 'The acquisition and properties of a contact vernacular grammar', in Ahlqvist and Čapková (eds.), pp. 75–93.

1999. 'Language contact and language shift in County Armagh 1178–1659', in Mallory (ed.), pp. 54–69.

2000a. '"What bees to be maun be": aspects of deontic and epistemic modality in a northern dialect of Irish English', *English World-Wide* 21.1: 25–62.

2000b. 'What are "small clauses" doing in South Armagh English, Irish and Planter English?', in Tristram (ed.), pp. 75–96.

2003a. '*For-to* infinitives and beyond: interdisciplinary approaches to non-finite complementation in a rural Celtic English', in Tristram (ed.), pp. 318–38.

2003b. 'The ideology of nationalism and its impact on accounts of language shift in nineteenth century Ireland', in Mair (ed.), pp. 201–30.

forthcoming. *Parametric Variation within a Socially Realistic Linguistics: Syntactic Variation and Change in South Armagh English*. Transactions of the Philological Society. Oxford: Basil Blackwell [revised and expanded version of Corrigan 1997a].

Cosgrove, Art 1967. 'The Gaelic resurgence and the Geraldine supremacy (c. 1400–1534)', in Moody and Martin (eds.), pp. 158–73.

Cowie, Roddy et al. 1984. 'Northern Irish listeners' assessments of accents', *Northern Ireland Speech and Language Forum* 10: 77–88.

Cox, Richard A. V. 1996. 'Tense and aspect in the Scottish Gaelic verbal system: a working paper on definitions and presentation', *Scottish Gaelic Studies* 27: 82–6.

Crawford, E. Margaret (ed.) 1997. *The Hungry Stream: Essays on Emigration and Famine*. Belfast: Institute of Irish Studies.

Cronin, Michael 1996. *Translating Ireland: Translation, Languages, Cultures*. Cork: Cork University Press.

2006. 'Contemporary translation of Irish poetry', *Irish English: Varieties and Variations*. Special issue of *Etudes Irlandaises*.

Cronin, Michael and Cormac Ó Cuilleanáin (eds.) 2003. *The Languages of Ireland*. Dublin: Four Courts Press.

Crozier, Alan 1984. 'The Scotch-Irish influence on American English', *American Speech* 60: 310–31.

Crowley, Tony 2000. *The Politics of Language in Ireland 1366–1922: a Sourcebook*. London: Routledge.

Cruttenden, Alan 1995. 'Rises in English', in Windsor-Lewis (ed.), pp. 155–73.

2001. *Gimson's Pronunciation of English*. 6th edition. London: Arnold.

Cubberley, Paul 2002. *Russian: a Linguistic Introduction*. Cambridge: Cambridge University Press.

Cukor-Avila, Patricia 1999. 'Stativity and copula absence in AAVE: grammatical constraints at the subcategorical level', *Journal of English Linguistics* 27.4: 341–55.

Cullen, Louis 1994. 'The Irish diaspora and the seventeenth and eighteenth centuries', in Canny (ed.), pp. 113–49.

Curtis, Edmund 1919. 'The spoken languages of medieval Ireland', *Studies* 8: 234–54.

Dahl, Östen 1984. 'Temporal distance: remoteness distinctions in tense-aspect systems', in Butterworth, Comrie and Dahl (eds.), pp. 105–22.

1985. *Tense and Aspect Systems*. Oxford: Blackwell.

Dailey-O'Cain, Jennifer 2000. 'The sociolinguistic distribution and attitudes towards focuser *like* and quotative *like*', *Journal of Sociolinguistics* 4.1: 60–80.

Dal, Ingerid 1952. 'Zur Entstehung des englischen Participium Praesentis auf -*ing*' [On the origin of the English past participle in -*ing*], *Norsk Tidskrift for Sprogvidenskap* 16: 5–116.

Daly, Mary 1990. 'Literacy and language change in the late nineteenth and early twentieth centuries', in Daly and Dickson (eds.), pp. 153–66.

Daly, Mary and David Dickson (eds.) 1990. *The Origins of Popular Literacy in Ireland: Language Change and Educational Development 1700–1920*. Dublin: Anna Livia.

D'Arcy, Alex 2005. 'The development of linguistic constraints: phonological innovations in St John's English', *Language Variation and Change* 17: 327–55.

Davis, Graham 1991. *The Irish in Britain 1815–1914*. Dublin: Gill and Macmillan.

2000. 'The Irish in Britain, 1815–1939', in Bielenberg (ed.), pp. 19–36.

Davis, Stuart 2003. '"Is this Negroish or Irish?" African American English, the antebellum writings of Francis Lieber, and the origins controversy', *American Speech* 78.3: 285–306.

Day, Richard R. (ed.) 1980. *Issues in English Creoles: Papers from the 1975 Hawaii Conference*. Varieties of English around the World, G2. Heidelberg: Groos.

Deane, Seamus (ed.) 1991. *The Field Day Anthology of Irish Literature*. 3 vols. Derry: Field Day Publications.

de Fréine, Séamus 1965. *The Great Silence*. Cork: Mercier.

1977. 'The dominance of the English language in the 19th century', in Ó Muirithe (ed.), pp. 127–49.

de Klerk, Vivian (ed.) 1996. *Focus on South Africa*. Amsterdam: John Benjamins.

Denison, David 1985. 'The origins of periphrastic *do*: Ellegård and Visser reconsidered', in Eaton et al. (eds.), pp. 44–60.

1998. 'Syntax', in Romaine (ed.), pp. 92–326.

2003. 'Log(ist)ic and simplistic S-curves', in Hickey (ed.), pp. 54–70.

Denvir, John 1892. *The Irish in Britain from the Earliest Times to the Fall and Death of Parnell*. London: Kegan Paul, Trench, Trubner.

Depraetere, Ilse and Susan Reed 2006. 'Mood and modality in English', in Aarts and McMahon (eds.), pp. 269–90.

Devine, Thomas M. (ed.) 1991. *Irish Immigration and Scottish Society in the Nineteenth and Twentieth Centuries*. Edinburgh: John Donald.

Dietrich, Julia C. 1981. 'The Gaelic roots of *a*-prefixing in Appalachian English', *American Speech* 56: 314.

Dillard, Joey Lee 1976. *American Talk: Where Our Words Come from*. New York: Random House.

Dillon, Myles 1941. 'Modern Irish *atá déanta agam*' [Modern Irish 'what I have done'], *Language* 17: 49–50.

Doane, Nick, Joan Hall and Dick Ringler (eds.) 1992. *Words of Honor: Essays Presented to Frederic G. Cassidy*. New York: Garland Press.

Dobson, Eric J. 1968. *English Pronunciation 1500–1700*. 2nd edition. Oxford: Clarendon Press.

Dolan, Terence P. (ed.) 1990. *The English of the Irish*. Special issue of *Irish University Review* 20.1.

1991. 'The literature of Norman Ireland', in Deane (ed.), pp. 141–70.

2004 [1998]. *A Dictionary of Hiberno-English: the Irish Use of English*. 2nd edition. Dublin: Gill and Macmillan.

Dolan, Terence P. and Diarmuid Ó Muirithe (eds.) 1996 [1979]. *The Dialect of Forth and Bargy*. 2nd edition. Dublin: Four Courts Press.

Dolley, Michael 1972. *Anglo-Norman Ireland c. 100–1318*. The Gill History of Ireland, vol. 3. Dublin: Gill and Macmillan.

Dollinger, Stefan and Ute Smit (eds.) 2007. *Varieties of English throughout their History: Festschrift for Herbert Schendl*. Vienna: Braumüller.

Dossena, Marina and Charles Jones (eds.) 2003. *Insights into Late Modern English*. Frankfurt: Peter Lang.

Dossena, Marina and Roger Lass (eds.) 2004. *Methods and Data in English Historical Dialectology*. Frankfurt am Main: Peter Lang.

Douglas-Cowie, Ellen 1978. 'Linguistic code-switching in a Northern Irish village, social interaction and social ambition', in Trudgill (ed.), pp. 37–51.

Dowling, Patrick J. 1968 [1935]. *The Hedge Schools of Ireland*. Revised edition. London: Longmans.

1971. *A History of Irish Education*. Cork: Mercier.

Dubois, Sylvie and Barbara M. Horvath 2004. 'Cajun Vernacular English: phonology', in Kortmann et al. (eds.), pp. 407–16.

Dudley Edwards, Ruth 1977. *Ireland in the Age of the Tudors: the Destruction of Hiberno-Norman Civilization*. London: Croom Helm; New York: Barnes and Noble.

Dudley Edwards, Ruth with Bridget Hourican 2005 [1973]. *An Atlas of Irish History*. London: Routledge.

Duffy, Sean 2000. *The Concise History of Ireland*. Dublin: Gill and Macmillan.

Duffy, Sean et al. (eds.) 1997. *An Atlas of Irish History*. Dublin: Gill and Macmillan.

Duggan, G. C. 1969 [1937]. *The Stage Irishman: a History of the Irish Play and Stage Characters from Earliest Times*. Dublin, Cork and London: Talbot Press.

Dunn, Richard S. 1972. *Sugar and Slaves: the Rise of the Planter Class in the English West Indies, 1624–1713*. Chapel Hill, NC: University of North Carolina Press.

Dutton, Thomas E., Malcolm Ross and Darrell Tryon (eds.) 1992. *The Language Game: Papers in Memory of Donald C. Laycock*. Pacific Linguistics. Canberra: Australian National University Press.

Eagleton, Terry 1995. *Heathcliff and the Great Hunger*. London: Verso.

Eaton, Roger et al. (eds.) 1985. *Papers from the 4th International Conference of English Historical Linguistics*. Amsterdam: John Benjamins.

Eckert, Penelope and John R. Rickford (eds.) 2001. *Style and Sociolinguistic Variation*. Cambridge: Cambridge University Press.

Eckhardt, Eduard 1910–11. *Die Dialekt- und Ausländertypen des älteren englischen Dramas* [The dialectal and foreigner figures in older English drama]. 2 vols. Louvain: Uystpruyst.

Edmondson, Jerold A., Crawford Feagin and Peter Mühlhäusler (eds.) 1990. *Development and Diversity: Linguistic Variation across Time and Space. A Festschrift for Charles-James N. Bailey*. Publications in Linguistics 93. University of Texas at Arlington: The Summer Institute of Linguistics.

Edwards, Viv 1993. 'The grammar of Southern British English', in Milroy and Milroy (eds.), pp. 214–38.

Eitner, Walter H. 1991. 'Affirmative "any more" in present-day American English', in Trudgill and Chambers (eds.), pp. 267–72.

Ekwall, Eilert 1980. *A History of Modern English Sounds and Morphology*. Translated by A. Ward. Oxford: Blackwell.

Eliasson, Stig and Ernst Håkon Jahr (eds.) 1997. *Language and its Ecology: Essays in Memory of Einar Haugen*. Berlin: Mouton de Gruyter.

Ellis, Alexander J. 1868–89. *On Early English Pronunciation*. 5 vols. London: Philological Society.

Ellegård, Alvar 1953. *The Auxiliary Do: the Establishment and Regulation of its Use in English*. Gothenburg Studies in English 2. Stockholm: Almqvist and Wiksell.

Elworthy, Frederic T. 1877. 'The grammar of the dialect of West Somerset', *Transactions of the Philological Society* 79: 143–257.

Engel, Ulrich et al. (eds.) 1969. *Festschrift für Hugo Moser zum 60. Geburtstag* [Festschrift for Hugo Moser on his 60th birthday]. Düsseldorf: Schwann.

Erskine, John and Gordon Lucy (eds.) 1999. *Varieties of Scottishness: Exploring the Ulster Scottish Connection*. Belfast: The Institute of Irish Studies, Queen's University of Belfast.

Fabricius, Anne 2002a. 'Weak vowels in modern RP: an acoustic study of HAPPY-tensing and KIT/schwa shift', *Language Variation and Change* 14: 211–37.

    2002b. 'Ongoing change in modern RP: evidence for the disappearing stigma of t-glottalling', *English World-Wide* 23: 115–36.

Fallows, Deborah 1981. 'Experimental evidence for English syllabification and syllable structure', *Journal of Linguistics* 17: 309–17.

Fanego, Teresa, Belén Mendez-Naya and Elena Seoane (eds.) 2002. *Sounds, Words, Texts, Change. Selected Papers from the Eleventh International Conference on English Historical Linguistics (11 ICEHL)*. Amsterdam: John Benjamins.

Farr, Fiona and Anne O'Keefe 2002. '"Would" as a hedging device in an Irish context: an intra-varietal comparison of institutionalised spoken interaction', in Reppen, Fitzmaurice and Biber (eds.), pp. 25–48.

Fasold, Ralph and Deborah Schiffrin (eds.) 1989. *Language Change and Variation*. Amsterdam: John Benjamins.

Feagin, Crawford 1979. *Variation and Change in Alabama English: a Sociolinguistic Study of the White Community*. Washington, DC: Georgetown University Press.

1991. 'Preverbal *done* in Southern States English', in Trudgill and Chambers (eds.), pp. 161–90.

Fennell, Barbara A. and Ronald R. Butters 1996. 'Historical and contemporary distribution of double modals in English', in Schneider (ed.), pp. 265–88.

Fenton, James 2000 [1995]. *The Hamely Tongue: a Personal Record of Ulster-Scots in County Antrim*. 2nd edition. Newtownards: Ulster-Scots Academic Press.

Fenton, Alexander and Donald A. McDonald (eds.) 1994. *Studies in Scots and Gaelic: Proceedings of the Third International Conference on the Languages of Scotland*. Edinburgh: Canongate Press.

Fernández, Francisco , Miguel Fuster and Juan José Calvo (eds.) 1994. *English Historical Linguistics 1992*. Amsterdam: John Benjamins.

Ferrara, Kathleen and Barbara Bell 1995. 'Sociolinguistic variation and discourse function of constructed dialogue introducers: the case of *be + like*', *American Speech* 70.3: 265–90.

Filppula, Markku 1986. *Some Aspects of Hiberno-English in a Functional Sentence Perspective*. Joensuu: Joensuu University Press.

1990. 'Substratum, superstratum and universals in the genesis of Hiberno-English', in Dolan (ed.), pp. 41–54.

1991. 'Urban and rural varieties of Hiberno-English', in Cheshire (ed.), pp. 51–60.

1993. 'Changing paradigms in the study of Hiberno-English', *Irish University Review* 23.2: 202–23.

1997a. 'Cross-dialectal parallels and language contacts: evidence from Celtic Englishes', in Hickey and Puppel (eds.), pp. 943–57.

1997b. 'The influence of Irish on perfect marking in Hiberno-English: the case of the "extended-now" perfect', in Kallen (ed.), pp. 51–71.

1997c. 'Unbound reflexives in Hiberno-English', in Ahlqvist and Čapková (eds.), pp. 149–55.

1999. *The Grammar of Irish English: Language in Hibernian Style*. London: Routledge.

2001. 'Irish influence in Hiberno-English: some problems of argumentation', in Kirk and Ó Baoill (eds.), pp. 23–42.

2003a. 'More on the English progressive and the Celtic connection', in Tristram (ed.), pp. 150–68.

2003b. 'The quest for the most "parsimonious" explanations: endogeny vs. contact revisited', in Hickey (ed.), pp. 161–73.

2004a. 'Irish English: morphology and syntax', in Kortmann et al. (eds.), vol. 2, pp. 73–101.

2004b. 'Dialect convergence areas or "Dialektbünde" in the British Isles', in Lenz, Radtke and Zwickl (eds.), pp. 177–88.

2006. 'The making of Hiberno-English and other "Celtic Englishes"', in van Kemenade and Los (eds.), pp. 507–36.

Filppula, Markku, Juhani Klemola and Heli Pitkänen (eds.) 2002. *The Celtic Roots of English*. Studies in Language, vol. 37. University of Joensuu: Faculty of Humanities.

Filppula, Markku, Juhani Klemola, Marjatta Palander and Esa Penttilä (eds.) 2005. *Dialects Across Borders: Selected Papers from the 11th International Conference on Methods in Dialectology (Methods XI), Joensuu, August 2002*. Amsterdam: John Benjamins.

Finlay, Catherine 1994. 'Syntactic variation in Belfast English', *Belfast Working Papers in Language and Linguistics* 12: 69–97.

Fisiak, Jacek 1968. *A Short Grammar of Middle English*, part I: *Graphemics, Phonemics and Morphemics*. Oxford: University Press.

(ed.) 1988. *Historical Dialectology*. Berlin: Mouton de Gruyter.

(ed.) 1990. *Further Insights into Contrastive Linguistics*. Amsterdam: John Benjamins.

(ed.) 1995. *Language Change under Contact Conditions*. Berlin: Mouton de Gruyter.

(ed.) 1997. *Studies in Middle English*. Berlin: Mouton de Gruyter.

Fisiak, Jacek and Marcin Krygier (eds.) 1998. *English Historical Linguistics 1996*. Berlin: Mouton de Gruyter.

Fisiak, Jacek and Peter Trudgill (eds.) 2001. *East Anglian English*. Cambridge: D. S. Brewer.

Fitzgerald, Garret 1984. 'Estimates for baronies of minimum level of Irish-speaking among successive decennial cohorts: 1771–1781 to 1861–1871', *Proceedings of the Royal Irish Academy* 84, C.3: 117–55.

Fitzgerald, Patrick 1992. '"Like Crickets to the crevice of a Brew-house": poor Irish migrants in England, 1560–1640', in O'Sullivan (ed.), pp. 13–35.

Fitzpatrick, David 1994. *Oceans of Consolation: Personal Accounts of Irish Migration to Australia*. Cork: Cork University Press.

Flanagan, Marie Therese 1989. *Irish Society, Anglo-Norman Settlers, Angevin Kingship: Interactions in Ireland in the Late Twelfth Century*. Oxford: Clarendon Press.

Flanagan, Deirdre and Lawrence Flanagan 1994. *Irish Place Names*. Dublin: Gill and Macmillan.

Fogg, Peter Walkden 1792. *Elementa Anglicana*. Stockport.

Foster, Roy F. 1988. *Modern Ireland 1600–1972*. Harmondsworth: Penguin.

Foulkes, Paul and Gerry Docherty (eds.) 1999. *Urban Voices*. London: Edward Arnold.

Fowkes, Robert A. 1997. 'Irish and Germans on the continent in the Middle Ages', *Zeitschrift für celtische Philologie* 49–50: 204–12.

Franz, Wilhelm 1939. *Die Sprache Shakespeares in Vers und Prosa* [The language of Shakespeare in verse and prose]. Halle: Niemeyer.

García, Ofelia and Joshua A. Fishman (eds.) 2002 [1997]. *The Multilingual Apple: Languages in New York City*. 2nd edition. Berlin: Mouton de Gruyter.

Geipel, John 1971. *The Viking Legacy: the Scandinavian Influence on the English and Gaelic Languages*. New Abbot: David and Charles.

Genet, Jacqueline (ed.) 1991. *The Big House in Ireland: Reality and Representation*. Dingle: Brandon Books.

Genet, Jacqueline and Elisabeth Hellegouarc'h (eds.) 1991. *Studies on Joyce's* Ulysses. Caen: G.D.R. d'Etudes Anglo-Irlandaises du C.N.R.S.

Gerald of Wales 1982 [1189]. *The History and Topography of Ireland.* Trans. John J. O'Meara. Harmondsworth: Penguin.

Gilbert, Glenn G. (ed.) 1987. *Pidgin and Creole Languages: Essays in Memory of John E. Reinecke.* Honolulu: University of Hawai'i Press.

Gilles, Peter and Jörg Peters (eds.) 2004. *Regional Variation in Intonation.* Tübingen: Niemeyer.

Gillespie, Raymond 1985. *Colonial Ulster: the Settlement of East Ulster, 1600–1641.* Cork: Cork University Press.

Gilley, Sheridan 1984. 'The Roman Catholic Church and the nineteenth-century Irish Diaspora', *Journal of Ecclesiastical History* 35.2: 188–207.

Godfrey, Elizabeth and Sali Tagliamonte 1999. 'Another piece for the verbal -s story: evidence from Devon in southwest England', *Language Variation and Change* 11: 87–121.

Goebl, Hans, Peter H. Nelde, Zdenek Stary and Wolfgang Wölck (eds.) 1996. *Kontaktlinguistik / Contact Linguistics / Linguistique de Contact.* 2 vols. Berlin: Mouton de Gruyter.

Gordon, Elizabeth, Lyle Campbell, Jennifer Hay, Margaret MacLagan, Andrea Sudbury and Peter Trudgill 2004. *New Zealand English: its Origins and Evolution.* Cambridge: Cambridge University Press.

Görlach, Manfred 1995. 'Irish English and Irish culture in dictionaries of English', *English World-Wide* 16: 164–91.

2000. 'Ulster Scots: a language?', in Kirk and Ó Baoill (eds.), pp. 13–31.

Grabe, Esther 2004. 'Intonational variation in urban dialects of English spoken in the British Isles', in Gilles and Peters (eds.), pp. 9–31.

Graham, Brian J. 1977. 'The towns of medieval Ireland', in Butlin (ed.), pp. 28–60.

Graham, Brian J. and Lindsay J. Proudfoot (eds.) 1993. *An Historical Geography of Ireland.* London: Academic Press.

Gray, Peter 1999. *Famine, Land and Politics: British Government and Irish Society, 1843–50.* Dublin: Irish Academic Press.

Green, Lisa J. 1998. 'Aspect and predicate phrases in African American vernacular English', in Mufwene, Rickford, Bailey and Baugh (eds.), pp. 37–68.

2002. *African American English: a Linguistic Introduction.* Cambridge: Cambridge University Press.

Greene, David 1972. 'The responsive in Irish and Welsh', in Pilch and Thurow (eds.), pp. 59–72.

1973. 'The growth of palatalization in Irish', *Transactions of the Philological Society*: 127–36.

1979. 'Perfects and perfectives in modern Irish', *Ériu* 30: 122–41.

Gregg, Robert J. 1959. 'Notes on the phonology of the Antrim dialect. II. Historical phonology', *Orbis* 8: 400–24.

1964. 'Scotch-Irish urban speech in Ulster', in Adams (ed.), pp. 163–92.

1972. 'The Scotch-Irish dialect boundaries in Ulster', in Wakelin (ed.), pp. 109–39.

1973. 'The diphthongs əi and ɑi in Scottish, Scotch-Irish and Canadian English', *Canadian Journal of Linguistics* 18: 136–45.

1985. *The Scotch-Irish Dialect Boundary in the Province of Ulster.* Ottawa: Canadian Federation for the Humanities.

Guilfoyle, Eithne 1983. 'Habitual aspect in Hiberno-English', *McGill Working Papers in Linguistics* 1: 22–32.

Guinnane, Timothy W. 1996. *The Vanishing Irish: Households, Migration and the Rural Economy in Ireland, 1850–1914*. Princeton: Princeton University Press.

Gunn, Brendan 1994. '"No surrender": existentialist sociolinguistics and politics in Northern Ireland', *Belfast Working Papers in Language and Linguistics* 12: 98–131.

Guy, Gregory R. 1990. 'The sociolinguistic types of language change', *Diachronica* 7: 47–67.

Häcker, Martina 1994. 'Subordinate *and*-clauses in Scots and Hiberno-English: origins and development', *Scottish Language* 23: 34–50.

Hamel, August van 1912. 'On Anglo-Irish syntax', *Englische Studien* 45: 272–92.

Hamp, Eric 1997. 'One speaker's verbs', in Hickey and Puppel (eds.), pp. 1453–5.

Hancock, Ian 1980. 'Gullah and Barbadian: origins and relationships', *American Speech* 55: 17–35.

1984. 'Shelta and Polari', in Trudgill (ed.), pp. 384–403.

Handley, James Edmund 1943. *The Irish in Scotland, 1789–1845*. Cork: Cork University Press.

1947. *The Irish in Modern Scotland*. Cork: Cork University Press.

Harkness, David and Mary O'Dowd (eds.) 1981. *The Town in Ireland*. Belfast.

Harlowe, Thomas V. 1969 [1926]. *A History of Barbados 1625–1685*. New York: Negro University Press.

Harmon, Maurice (ed.) 1972. *J. M. Synge Centenary Papers 1971*. Dublin.

Harper, Jared and Charles Hudson 1971. 'Irish Traveler Cant', *Journal of English Linguistics* 15: 78–86.

1973. 'Irish Traveler Cant in its social setting', *Southern Folklore Quarterly* 37: 101–14.

Harris, John 1983. 'The Hiberno-English "I've it eaten" construction: what is it and where does it come from?', *Teanga* 3: 30–43.

1984a. 'Syntactic variation and dialect divergence', *Journal of Linguistics* 20: 303–27.

1984b. 'English in the North of Ireland', in Trudgill (ed.), pp. 115–34.

1985. *Phonological Variation and Change: Studies in Hiberno-English*. Cambridge: Cambridge University Press.

1986. 'Expanding the superstrate: habitual aspect markers in Atlantic Englishes', *English World-Wide* 7: 171–99.

1987. 'On doing comparative reconstruction with genetically unrelated languages', in Ramat et al. (eds.), pp. 267–82.

1991. 'Conservatism versus substratal transfer in Irish English', in Trudgill and Chambers (eds.), pp. 191–212.

1993. 'The grammar of Irish English', in Milroy and Milroy (eds.), pp. 139–86.

Harris, John, David Little and David Singleton (eds.) 1986. *Perspectives on the English language in Ireland: Proceedings of the First Symposium on Hiberno-English, Dublin 1985*. Dublin: Centre for Language and Communication Studies, Trinity College.

Harris, Ruth-Ann 1994. *The Nearest Place that Wasn't Ireland: Early Nineteenth-Century Labor Migration*. Ames, IO: Iowa State University Press.

Hartmann, Hans 1974. 'Distribution und Funktion der Expanded Form in einigen Dialekten von Co. Galway' [Distribution and function of the expanded form in some dialects of Co. Galway], *Zeitschrift für Celtische Philologie* 33: 140–284.

Haugen, Einar 1972. *The Ecology of Language*. Stanford: Stanford University Press.
    2003 [1964]. 'Dialect, language, nation', in Paulston and Tucker (eds.), pp. 411–22.
Hayden, Mary and Marcus Hartog. 1909. 'The Irish dialect of English: syntax and idioms', *Fortnightly Review*, old series 91 / new series 85: 775–85, 933–47.
Hayes-McCoy, Gerard A. 1967. 'The Tudor conquest', in Moody and Martin (eds.), pp. 174–88.
Heine, Bernd, Ulrike Claudi and Friederike Hünnemeyer 1991. *Grammaticalization: a Conceptual Framework*. Chicago: University of Chicago Press.
Heine, Bernd and Tania Kuteva 2004. *Language Contact and Grammatical Change*. Cambridge: Cambridge University Press.
Heinrick, Hugh 1990 [1872]. *A Survey of the Irish in England*. Reprint edited by Alan O'Day. London: Hambledon Press.
Hendrick, Randall (ed.) 1990. *The Syntax of the Modern Celtic Languages*. Syntax and Semantics, vol. 23. San Diego: Academic Press.
Henry, Alison 1992. 'Infinitives in a *for-to* dialect', *Natural Language and Linguistic Theory* 10: 279–301.
    1995. *Belfast English and Standard English: Dialect Variation and Parameter Setting*. Oxford: Oxford University Press.
    1997. 'The syntax of Belfast English', in Kallen (ed.), pp. 89–108.
    2002. 'Variation and syntactic theory', in Chambers, Trudgill and Schilling-Estes (eds.), pp. 267–82.
Henry, Alison, Martin Ball and Margaret MacAliskey (eds.) 1996. *Papers from the International Conference on Language in Ireland. Belfast Working Papers in Language and Linguistics*. Belfast: University of Ulster.
Henry, Patrick Leo 1957. *An Anglo-Irish Dialect of North Roscommon*. Zurich: Aschmann and Scheller.
    1958. 'A linguistic survey of Ireland. Preliminary report', *Norsk Tidsskrift for Sprogvidenskap [Lochlann, A Review of Celtic Studies]* Supplement 5: 49–208.
    1977. 'Anglo-Irish and its Irish background', in Ó Muirithe (ed.), pp. 20–36.
    1981. Review of Alan J. Bliss (1979) *Spoken English in Ireland 1600–1740: Twenty-seven Representative Texts Assembled and Analysed, Éigse* 18: 319–26.
Hermkens, Hendrikus 1969. *Fonetiek en fonologie* [Phonetics and phonology]. 2nd edition. The Hague: Malmberg.
Herrmann, Tanja 2005. 'Relative clauses in English dialects of the British Isles', in Kortmann et al. (eds.), pp. 21–124.
Heslinga, Marcus W. 1962. *The Irish Border as a Cultural Divide*. Leiden: Leiden University Press. (Reprint: Assen, Netherlands, 1979).
Heuser, Wilhelm 1904. *Die Kildare-Gedichte: die ältesten mittelenglischen Denkmäler in anglo-irischer Überlieferung* [The Kildare Poems: the oldest Middle English documents attested in Anglo-Irish]. Bonner Beiträge zur Anglistik [Bonn Contributions to English Studies] vol. 14. Bonn: Hanstein.
Hewitt, John Harold 1974. *Rhyming Weavers and Other Country Poets of Antrim and Down*. Belfast: Blackstaff Press.
Hey, David 1998. *A History of Sheffield*. Lancaster: Carnegie Publishing.
Hickey, Leo and Miranda Stewart (eds.) 2005. *Politeness in Europe*. Clevedon: Multilingual Matters.

Hickey, Raymond 1982. 'The phonology of English loan-words in Inis Meáin Irish', *Ériu* 33: 137–56.

    1983a. 'Remarks on pronominal usage in Hiberno-English', *Studia Anglica Posnaniensia* 15: 47–53.

    1983b. 'Syntactic ambiguity in Hiberno-English', *Studia Anglica Posnaniensia* 15: 39–45.

    1984a. 'Coronal segments in Irish English', *Journal of Linguistics* 20: 233–51.

    1984b. 'Syllable onsets in Irish English', *Word* 35: 67–74.

    1985. 'Salient features of Irish syntax', *Lingua Posnaniensia*, 15–25.

    1986a. 'Possible phonological parallels between Irish and Irish English', *English World-Wide* 7: 1–21.

    1986b. 'The interrelationship of epenthesis and syncope, evidence from Irish and Dutch', *Lingua* 65: 239–59.

    1986c. 'Issues in the vowel phoneme inventory of Cois Fhairrge Irish', *Éigse* 31: 214–26.

    1987. 'The realization of dental obstruents adjacent to /r/ in the history of English', *Neuphilologische Mitteilungen* 88: 167–72.

    1988. 'A lost Middle English dialect: the case of Forth and Bargy', in Fisiak (ed.), pp. 235–72.

    1990. 'Suprasegmental transfer: on prosodic traces of Irish in Irish English', in Fisiak (ed.), pp. 219–29.

    1993. 'The beginnings of Irish English', *Folia Linguistica Historica* 14: 213–38.

    1995a. 'Early contact and parallels between English and Celtic', *Vienna English Working Papers* 4.2: 87–119.

    1995b. 'An assessment of language contact in the development of Irish English', in Fisiak (ed.), pp. 109–30.

    1996a. 'Lenition in Irish English', in Henry, Ball and MacAliskey (eds.), pp. 173–93.

    1996b. 'Identifying dialect speakers: the case of Irish English', in Kniffka (ed.), pp. 217–37.

    1997a. 'Arguments for creolisation in Irish English', in Hickey and Puppel (eds.), pp. 969–1038.

    1997b. 'Assessing the relative status of languages in medieval Ireland', in Fisiak (ed.), pp. 181–205.

    1998. 'The Dublin vowel shift and the historical perspective', in Fisiak and Krygier (eds.), pp. 79–106.

    1999a. 'Dublin English: current changes and their motivation', in Foulkes and Docherty (eds.), pp. 265–81.

    1999b. 'Ireland as a linguistic area', in Mallory (ed.), pp. 36–53.

    2000a. 'Salience, stigma and standard', in Wright (ed.), pp. 57–72.

    2000b. 'Models for describing aspect in Irish English', in Tristram (ed.), pp. 97–116.

    2001a. 'Language contact and typological difference: transfer between Irish and Irish English', in Kastovsky and Mettinger (eds.), pp. 131–69.

    2001b. 'The South-East of Ireland: a neglected region of dialect study', in Kirk and Ó Baoill (eds.), pp. 1–22.

    2002a. *A Source Book for Irish English*. Amsterdam: John Benjamins.

    2002b. 'Dublin and Middle English', in Lucas and Lucas (eds.), pp. 187–200.

    2002c. 'The Atlantic Edge: the relationship between Irish English and Newfoundland English', *English World-Wide* 23.2: 281–314.

2002d. 'Ebb and flow: a cautionary tale of language change', in Fanego, Mendez-Naya and Seoane (eds.), pp. 105–28.

2002e. 'Language change in early Britain: the convergence account', in Restle and Zaefferer (eds.), pp. 185–203.

2002f. 'Internal and external factors again: word order change in Old English and Old Irish', in Hickey (ed.), pp. 261–83.

(ed.) 2002g. *Collecting Views on Language Change*. Special issue of *Language Sciences* 24. 3–4.

2003a. *Corpus Presenter: Processing Software for Language Analysis. Including A Corpus of Irish English*. Amsterdam: John Benjamins.

2003b. 'How and why supraregional varieties arise', in Dossena and Jones (eds.), pp. 351–73.

2003c. 'What's cool in Irish English? Linguistic change in contemporary Ireland', in Tristram (ed.), pp. 357–73.

2003d. 'Rectifying a standard deficiency: pronominal distinctions in varieties of English', in Taavitsainen and Jucker (eds.), pp. 345–74.

2003e. 'How do dialects get the features they have? On the process of new dialect formation', in Hickey (ed.), pp. 213–39.

2003f. 'Reanalysis and typological change', in Hickey (ed.), pp. 258–78.

(ed.) 2003g. *Motives for Language Change*. Cambridge: Cambridge University Press.

2004a. *A Sound Atlas of Irish English*. Berlin and New York: Mouton de Gruyter.

2004b. 'English dialect input to the Caribbean', in Hickey (ed.), pp. 326–59.

2004c. 'Development and diffusion of Irish English', in Hickey (ed.), pp. 82–117.

2004d. 'Dialects of English and their transportation', in Hickey (ed.), pp. 33–58.

2004e. 'Checklist of nonstandard features', in Hickey (ed.), pp. 586–620.

2004f. 'Mergers, near-mergers and phonological interpretation', in Kay, Hough and Wotherspoon (eds.), pp. 125–37.

2004g. 'The phonology of Irish English', in Kortmann et al. (eds.), vol. 1, pp. 68–97.

2004h. 'Standard wisdoms and historical dialectology: the discrete use of historical regional corpora', in Dossena and Lass (eds.), pp. 199–216.

2004i. 'Englishes in Asia and Africa. Origin and structure', in Hickey (ed.), pp. 503–35.

(ed.) 2004j. *Legacies of Colonial English*. Cambridge: Cambridge University Press.

2005. *Dublin English: Evolution and Change*. Amsterdam: John Benjamins.

2006a. 'Productive lexical processes in present-day English', in Mair and Heuberger (eds.), pp.153–68.

2006b. 'Contact, shift and language change: Irish English and South African Indian English', in Tristram (ed.), pp. 234–58.

2007. 'Dartspeak and Estuary English: advanced metropolitan speech in Ireland and England', in Ute Smit, Stefan Dollinger, Julia Hüttner, Ursula Lutzky and Gunther Kaltenböck (eds.), *Tracing English through Time: Explorations in Language Variation*. Vienna: Braumüller, pp. 179–90.

in press. *The Sound Structure of Modern Irish*. Berlin: Mouton de Gruyter.

Hickey, Raymond and Stanisław Puppel (eds.) 1997. *Language History and Linguistic Modelling: a Festschrift for Jacek Fisiak on his 60th Birthday*. Berlin: Mouton de Gruyter.

Hickman, Mary J. 2005. 'Migration and diaspora', in Cleary and Connolly (eds.), pp. 117–36.

Hindley, Reg 1990. *The Death of the Irish Language: a Qualified Obituary*. London: Routledge.

Hoffmann, Charlotte 1992. *An Introduction to Bilingualism*. London: Longman.

Hoffmann, Sebastian forthcoming. 'Tag questions in Early and Late Modern English: historical description and theoretical implications', *Anglistik* 17.2.

Hogan, James Jeremiah 1927. *The English Language in Ireland*. Dublin: Educational Company of Ireland.

1934. *An Outline of English Philology, Chiefly for Irish Students*. Dublin: Educational Company of Ireland.

Hogan-Brun, Gabrielle and Stefan Wolff (eds.) 2003. *Minority Languages in Europe: Frameworks, Status, Prospects*. London: Palgrave/Macmillan.

Holm, John 1994. 'English in the Caribbean', in Burchfield (ed.), pp. 328–81.

2000. 'Semi-creolization: problems in the development of theory', in Neumann-Holzschuh and Schneider (eds.), pp. 19–40.

2004. *Languages in Contact: the Partial Restructuring of Vernaculars*. Cambridge: Cambridge University Press.

Holthausen, Friedrich 1916. 'Zu den Kildare-Gedichten' [On the Kildare Poems], *Anglia* 40: 358–64.

Honeybone, Patrick 2001. 'Lenition inhibition in Liverpool English', *English Language and Linguistics* 5.2: 213–49.

Hope, Jonathan 1995. *The Authorship of Shakespeare's Plays*. Cambridge: Cambridge University Press.

2003. *Shakespeare's Grammar*. London: Thomson Learning.

Hore, Herbert 1862–3. 'An account of the Barony of Forth, in the County of Wexford', *Journal of the Kilkenny and South-East of Ireland Archaeological Society* 4: 53–84.

Horvath, Barbara M. 1985. *Variation in Australian English: the Sociolects of Sydney*. Cambridge: Cambridge University Press.

House, John W. 1954. *North Eastern England: Population Movements and the Landscape since the Early Nineteenth Century*. Newcastle: Department of Geography, King's College.

Howell, Wilbur Samuel 1971a. 'Sheridan: minor actor as major elocutionist', in Howell (ed.), pp. 214–43.

(ed.) 1971b. *Eighteenth Century British Logic and Rhetoric*. Princeton, NJ: Princeton University Press.

Huber, Magnus 1999. *Ghanaian Pidgin English in its West African Context*. Amsterdam: John Benjamins.

Huber, Magnus and Philip Baker 2001. 'Atlantic, Pacific, and world-wide features in English-lexicon contact languages', *English World-Wide* 22.2: 157–208.

Hume, Abraham 1878. *Remarks on the Irish Dialect of the English Language*. Liverpool: T. Brakell.

Hutson, Arthur E. 1947. 'Gaelic loan-words in American', *American Speech* 22: 18–23.

Ihalainen, Ossi 1991. 'Periphrastic *do* in affirmative sentences in the dialect of East Somerset', in Trudgill and Chambers (eds.), pp. 148–60.

1994. 'The dialects of England since 1776', in Burchfield (ed.), pp. 197–274.

Ihde, Thomas W. (ed.) 1994. *The Irish Language in the United States: a Historical, Sociolinguistic, and Applied Linguistic Survey*. Westport, CT: Bergin and Garvey.

Irwin, Patrick J. 1933a. 'Ireland's contribution to the English language', *Studies* 22: 637–52.

1933b. 'The lost Loscombe manuscript: a transcript', *Anglia* 57: 397–400.

1935. 'A Study of the English Dialects of Ireland, 1172–1800'. Unpublished PhD thesis, University College London.

Isaac, Graham 2003. 'Diagnosing the symptoms of contact: some Celtic-English case histories', in Tristram (ed.), pp. 46–64.

Jackson, Kenneth 1962. 'The Celtic languages during the Viking period', in Ó Cuív (ed.), pp. 3–11.

Jahr, Ernst Håkon 2003. 'A Norwegian adult language game, anti-language or secret code: the *Smoi* of Mandal', in Britain and Cheshire (eds.), pp. 275–86.

Jarman, E. and Alan Cruttenden 1976. 'Belfast intonation and the myth of the fall', *Journal of the International Phonetics Association* 6: 4–12.

Jespersen, Otto 1909–49. *A Modern English Grammar on Historical Principles,* part I: *Sounds and Spellings*; part III: *Syntax,* vol. 2; part V: *Syntax,* vol. 4. London: Allen Unwin.

Jones, Charles (ed.) 1993. *Historical Linguistics. Problems and Perspectives.* London: Longman.

(ed.) 1997. *The Edinburgh History of the Scots Language.* Edinburgh: Edinburgh University Press.

Jones, Mari and Edith Esch (ed.) 2002. *Language Change: the Interplay of Internal, External and Extra-Linguistic Factors.* Berlin and New York: Mouton de Gruyter.

Jones, Mark J. and Carmen Llamas 2003. 'Fricated pre-aspirated /t/ in Middlesbrough English: an acoustic study', *Proceedings of the 15th International Congress of Phonetic Sciences,* pp. 123–35.

Jonson, Ben 1969. *The Complete Masques.* Edited by Stephen Orgel. New Haven and London: Yale University Press.

Jordan, Richard 1974. *Handbook of Middle English Grammar: Phonology.* Translated and revised by E. J. Crook. The Hague: Mouton.

Joseph, Brian D. and Richard D. Janda (eds.) 1999. *The Handbook of Historical Linguistics.* Oxford: Blackwell.

Joyce, Patrick Weston 1979 [1910]. *English as we Speak it in Ireland.* Dublin: Wolfhound Press.

Kallen, Jeffrey L. 1986. 'The co-occurrence of *do* and *be* in Hiberno-English', in Harris, Little and Singleton (eds.), pp. 133–47.

1989. 'Tense and aspect categories in Irish English', *English World-Wide* 10: 1–39.

1990. 'The Hiberno-English perfect: grammaticalisation revisited', in Dolan (ed.), pp. 120–36.

1991. 'Sociolinguistic variation and methodology: *after* as a Dublin variable', in Cheshire (ed.), pp. 61–74.

1994. 'English in Ireland', in Burchfield (ed.), pp. 148–96.

1996. 'Entering lexical fields in Irish English', in Klemola, Kytö and Rissanen (eds.), pp. 101–29.

1997a. 'Irish English and World English: lexical perspectives', in Schneider (ed.), pp. 139–57.

(ed.) 1997b. *Focus on Ireland.* Amsterdam: John Benjamins.

1999. 'Irish English and the Ulster Scots controversy', Mallory (ed.), pp. 70–85.

2000. 'One island, two borders, two languages: a look at linguistic and political borders in Ireland', *International Journal of the Sociology of Language* 145: 29–63.

2005a. 'Politeness in modern Ireland: "You know the way in Ireland, it's done without being said"', in Hickey and Stewart (eds.), pp. 130–44.

2005b. 'Internal and external factors in phonological convergence: the case of English /t/ lenition', in Auer, Hinskens and Kerswill (eds.), pp. 51–80.

Kallen, Jeffrey L. and John M. Kirk 2001. 'Aspects of the verb phrase in Standard Irish English: a corpus-based approach', in Kirk and Ó Baoill (eds.), pp. 59–79.

Kastovsky, Dieter and Arthur Mettinger (eds.) 2001. *Language Contact in the History of English*. Berlin: Mouton de Gruyter.

Kautzsch, Alexander 2002. *The Historical Evolution of Earlier African American English: an Empirical Comparison of Early Sources*. Berlin: Mouton de Gruyter.

Kay, Christian J., Carole Hough and Irené Wotherspoon (eds.) 2004. *New Perspectives on English Historical Linguistics*. Amsterdam: John Benjamins.

Kaye, Jonathan, Hilda Koopman, Dominique Sportiche and André Dugas (eds.) 1983. *Current Approaches to African Linguistics*, vol. 2. Dordrecht: Foris.

Keller, Wolfgang 1925. 'Keltisches im englischen Verbum' [Celtic elements in the English verb], in *Anglica: Untersuchungen zur englischen Philologie (Alois Brandl zum siebzigsten Geburtstage überreicht)* [Anglica: Investigations into English philology, presented to Alois Brandl on his 70th birthday], 55–66.

Kelly, Linda 1997. *Richard Brinsley Sheridan: a Life*. London: Pimlico.

Kelly, Patricia 2000. 'A seventeenth-century variety of Irish English: *Spoken English in Ireland 1600–1740* revisited', in Tristram (ed.), pp. 265–79.

Kemenade, Ans van and Bettelou Los (eds.) 2006. *The Handbook of the History of English*. Oxford: Blackwell.

Kennedy, Liam and Leslie A. Clarkson 1993. 'Birth, death and exile: Irish population history, 1700–1921', in Graham and Proudfoot (eds.), pp. 158–86.

Kerswill, Paul 2003. 'Dialect levelling and geographical diffusion in British English', in Britain and Cheshire (eds.), pp. 223–44.

Kerswill, Paul and Ann Williams 2000. 'Dialect recognition and speech community focusing in new and old towns in England: the effects of dialect levelling, demography and social networks', in Long and Preston (eds.), pp. 178–207.

2002. '"Salience" as an explanatory factor in language change: evidence from dialect levelling in urban England', in Jones and Esch (eds.), pp. 81–110.

Kiberd, Declan 1980. 'The fall of the stage Irishman', in Schleifer (ed.), pp. 39–60.

Kinealy, Christine 1994. *This Great Calamity: the Irish Famine, 1845–52*. Dublin: Gill and Macmillan.

Kingsmore, Rona 1995. *Ulster Scots Speech: a Sociolinguistic Study*. Tuscaloosa: University of Alabama Press.

Kirk, John M. 1997a. 'Irish English and contemporary literary writing', in Kallen (ed.), pp. 189–206.

1997b. 'Ulster English: the state of the art', in Tristram (ed.), pp. 135–79.

1997c. 'Ethnolinguistic differences in Northern Ireland', in Thomas (ed.), pp. 55–68.

1998. 'Ulster Scots: realities and myths', *Ulster Folklife* 44: 69–93.

2000. 'Two Ullans texts', in Kirk and Ó Baoill (eds.), pp. 33–44.

Kirk, John M. and Jeffrey L. Kallen 2006. 'Irish Standard English: how Celticised? How standardised?', in Tristram (ed.), pp. 88–113.

Kirk, John M., Jeffrey L. Kallen, Orla Lowry and Anne Rooney 2003. 'Issues arising from the compilation of ICE-Ireland', *Belfast Working Papers in Language and Linguistics* 16: 23–41.

Kirk, John M. and Georgina Millar 1998. 'Verbal aspect in the Scots and English of Ulster', *Scottish Language* 17: 82–107.

Kirk, John M. and Dónall Ó Baoill (eds.) 2000. *Language and Politics: Northern Ireland, the Republic of Ireland, and Scotland*. Belfast Studies in Language, Culture and Politics 1. Belfast: Queen's University.

    (eds.) 2001. *Language Links: the Languages of Scotland and Ireland*. Belfast Studies in Language, Culture and Politics 2. Belfast: Queen's University.

    (eds.) 2002. *Travellers and their Language*. Belfast Studies in Language, Culture and Politics 4. Belfast: Queen's University.

Kirkwood, Harry (ed.) 1986. *Studies in Intonation: Occasional Papers in Linguistics and Language Learning*. Coleraine: New University of Ulster.

Kirwin, William J. 1993. 'The planting of Anglo-Irish in Newfoundland', in Clarke (ed.), pp. 65–84.

    2001. 'Newfoundland English', in Algeo (ed.), pp. 441–55.

Klemola, Juhani 1994. 'Periphrastic DO in South-Western dialects of British English: a reassessment', *Dialectologia et Geolinguistica* 2: 33–51.

    1996. 'Non-Standard Periphrastic DO: a Study in Variation and Change'. Unpublished PhD thesis, University of Essex.

    2000. 'The origins of the Northern Subject Rule: a case of early contact?', in Tristram (ed.), pp. 329–46.

    2002. 'Periphrastic DO: dialect distribution and origins', in Filppula, Klemola and Pitkänen (eds.), pp. 199–210.

Klemola, Juhani and Markku Filppula 1992. 'Subordinating uses of "and" in the history of English', in Rissanen et al. (eds.), pp. 310–18.

Klemola, Juhani, Merja Kytö and Matti Rissanen (eds.) 1996. *Speech Past and Present: Studies in English Dialectology in Memory of Ossi Ihalainen*. University of Bamberg Studies in English Linguistics 38. Frankfurt am Main: Peter Lang.

Kniezsa, Veronika 1985. 'Jonathan Swift's English', in Siegmund-Schulze (ed.), pp. 116–24.

Kniffka, Hannes (ed.) 1996. *Recent Developments in Forensic Linguistics*. Frankfurt: Lang.

Knowles, Gerald O. 1978. 'The nature of phonological variables in Scouse', in Trudgill (ed.), pp. 80–90.

Kolb, Eduard 1966. *Phonological Atlas of the Northern Region: the Six Northern Counties, North Lincolnshire and the Isle of Man*. Bern: Francke.

Kortmann, Bernd 2004a. '*Do* as a tense and aspect marker in varieties of English', in Kortmann (ed.), pp. 245–76.

    (ed.) 2004b. *Dialectology Meets Typology: Dialect Grammar from a Cross-Linguistic Perspective*. Berlin: Mouton de Gruyter.

Kortmann, Bernd, Kate Burridge, Rajend Mesthrie, Edgar W. Schneider and Clive Upton (eds.) 2004. *A Handbook of Varieties of English*, vol 1: *Phonology*; vol. 2: *Morphology and Syntax*. Berlin and New York: Mouton de Gruyter.

Kortmann, Bernd, Tanja Herrmann, Lukas Pietsch and Susanne Wagner 2005. *A Comparative Grammar of British English Dialects: Agreement, Gender, Relative Clauses*. Berlin and New York: Mouton de Gruyter.

Kosok, Heinz 1990. *Geschichte der anglo-irischen Literatur* [A history of Anglo-Irish literature]. Berlin: Erich Schmidt.

Kretzschmar, William A. 1996. 'Foundations of American English', in Schneider (ed.), pp. 25–50.

Kroch, Anthony S. 1989. 'Function and grammar in the history of English: periphrastic *do*', in Fasold and Schiffrin (eds.), pp. 133–72.

Kurath, Hans 1956. 'The loss of long consonants and the rise of voiced fricatives in Middle English', *Language* 32: 435–45.

Kytö, Merja 1994. '*Be* and *have* with intransitives in Early Modern English', in Fernandez, Foster and Calvo (eds.), pp. 170–90.

Labov, William 1972. *Sociolinguistic Patterns*. Philadelphia: University of Pennsylvania Press.

   1991. 'The boundaries of a grammar: Inter-dialectal reactions to positive *anymore*', in Trudgill and Chambers (eds.), pp. 273–88.

   2001. 'The anatomy of style-shifting', in Eckert and Rickford (eds.), pp. 85–108.

Laferriere, Martha 1986. 'Ethnicity in phonological variation and change', in Allen and Linn (eds.), pp. 428–45.

Lalor, Brian (ed.) 2003. *The Encyclopaedia of Ireland*. Dublin: Gill and Macmillan.

Lass, Roger 1984. *Phonology*. Cambridge: Cambridge University Press.

   1987. *The Shape of English. Structure and History*. London: Dent.

   1990. 'Early mainland residues in Southern Hiberno-English', in Dolan (ed.), pp. 137–48.

   1994. 'Proliferation and option-cutting: the strong verb in the fifteenth to eighteenth centuries', in Stein and Tieken-Boon van Ostade (eds.), pp. 81–114.

   2004. 'South African English', in Hickey (ed.), pp. 363–86.

Lass, Roger and Susan Wright 1986. 'Endogeny vs. contact: Afrikaans influence on South African English', *English World-Wide* 7: 201–23.

Legge, M. Dominica 1963. *Anglo-Norman Literature and its Background*. Oxford: Clarendon Press.

Leitner, Gerhard (ed.) 1992. *New Directions in English Language Corpora*. Berlin: Mouton de Gruyter.

Lennon, Colm 1981. *Richard Stanihurst the Dubliner 1547–1618*. Dublin: Irish Academic Press.

Lenz, Alexandra, Edgar Radtke and Simone Zwickel (eds.) 2004. *Variation im Raum – Variation in Space*. Frankfurt: Peter Lang.

Le Page, Robert B. 1960. 'An historical introduction to Jamaican creole', in Le Page and DeCamp (eds.), pp. 1–24.

Le Page, Robert B. and David DeCamp (eds.) 1960. *Jamaican Creole*. London: Macmillan.

Lillo, Antonio 2004. 'Exploring rhyming slang in Ireland', *English World-Wide* 25.2: 273–85.

Littlefield, Daniel C. 1981. *Rice and Slaves: Ethnicity and the Slave Trade in Colonial South Carolina*. Baton Rouge: Louisiana State University Press.

Llamas, Carmen 2001. 'Language Variation and Innovation in Teesside English'. Unpublished PhD thesis, University of Leeds.

   2006. 'Shifting identities and orientations in a border town', in Omoniyi and White (eds.), pp. 92–112.

Loebell, Helga and Kathryn Bock 2003. 'Structural priming across languages', *Linguistics* 41.5: 791–824.

Long, Daniel and Dennis Preston (eds.) 2000. *A Handbook of Perceptual Dialectology*, vol. 2. Amsterdam: Benjamins.

Long, Joseph 1975. 'Dermot and the Earl: who wrote "The Song"?', *Proceedings of the Royal Irish Academy* 75, C: 263–72.

Lowry, Orla 2002. 'The stylistic variation of nuclear patterns in Belfast English', *Journal of the International Phonetic Association* 32.1: 33–42.

Lucas, Angela (ed.) 1995. *Anglo-Irish Poems of the Middle Ages*. Dublin: Columba Press.

Lucas, Angela and Peter Lucas 1990. 'Reconstructing a disarranged manuscript: the case of MS Harley 913, a medieval Hiberno-English miscellany', *Scriptorium* 44.2: 286–99.

Lucas, Peter J. and Angela M. Lucas (eds.) 2002. *Middle English: from Tongue to Text. Selected Papers from the Third International Conference on Middle English: Language and Text Held at Dublin, Ireland, 1–4 July 1999*. Frankfurt: Lang.

Luick, Karl 1940 [1914]. *Historische Grammatik der englischen Sprache* [Historical grammar of the English language] Stuttgart: Tauchnitz.

Lunney, Linde 1994. 'Ulster attitudes to Scottishness: the eighteenth century and after', in Wood (ed.), pp. 56–70.

   1999. 'The nature of the Ulster-Scots language community', in Erskine and Lucy (eds.), pp. 113–28.

Lunny, Patrick Anthony 1981. 'Belleek and Ballyvourney: notes on the retention of Irish consonant qualities in two modern Hiberno-English dialects', in Barry (ed.), pp. 48–53.

Lydon, James 1967. 'The medieval English colony', in Moody and Martin (eds.), pp. 144–57.

   1973. *Ireland in the Later Middle Ages*. The Gill History of Ireland, vol. 6. Dublin: Gill and Macmillan.

   (ed.) 1984. *The English in Medieval Ireland*. Dublin: Royal Irish Academy.

   1998. *The Making of Ireland: from Ancient Times to the Present*. London: Routledge.

Macafee, Caroline 1983. *Glasgow*. Varieties of English Around the World, Text Series, vol. 3. Amsterdam: John Benjamins.

   1994. *Traditional Dialect in the Modern World. Some Studies in the Glasgow Vernacular*. Frankfurt/Main: Lang.

   (ed.) 1996. *A Concise Ulster Dictionary*. Oxford: Oxford University Press.

Macalister, R. A. Stewart 1937. *The Secret Languages of Ireland: with Special Reference to the Origins and Nature of the Shelta Language, Partly Based upon the Collections and Manuscripts of the Late John Sampson*. Cambridge: Cambridge University Press.

Macaulay, Donald (ed.) 1992. *The Celtic Languages*. Cambridge: Cambridge University Press.

   1996. 'Some thoughts on time, tense and mode, and on aspect in Scottish Gaelic', *Scottish Gaelic Studies* 27: 193–204.

MacCurtain, Hugh 1728. *The Elements of the Irish Language*. Louvain.

MacCurtain, Margaret 1972. *Tudor and Stuart Ireland*. The Gill History of Ireland, vol. 7. Dublin: Gill and Macmillan.

MacEoin, Gearóid 1993. 'Irish', in Ball and Fife (eds.), pp. 101–44.

Mac Giolla Chríost, Diarmait 2005. *The Irish Language in Ireland: from Goídel to Globalisation*. London: Routledge.

Mackenzie, J. L. and R. Todd (eds.) 1989. *In Other Words: Transcultural Studies in Philology, Translation, and Lexicology Presented to Hans Heinrich Meier on the Occasion of his Sixty-Fifth Birthday*. Dordrecht: Foris.

Maclennan, Malcolm 1979 [1925]. *A Pronouncing and Etymological Dictionary of the Gaelic Language*. Aberdeen: Aberdeen University Press.

MacLysaght, Edward 1997 [1957]. *The Surnames of Ireland*. 6th edition. Dublin: Irish Academic Press.

MacMahon, Michael K. C. 1998. 'Phonology', in Romaine (ed.), pp. 373–535.

Mac Mathúna, Liam 2003. 'Irish shakes its head? Code-mixing as a textual response to the rise of English as a societal language in Ireland', in Tristram (ed.), pp. 276–97.

Mac Mathúna, Séamus 2006. 'Remarks on standardisation in Irish English, Irish and Welsh', in Tristram (ed.), pp. 114–29.

Mac Mathúna, Séamus and Ailbhe Ó Corráin (eds.) 1997. *Miscellania Celtica in Memoriam Heinrich Wagner*. Uppsala: Uppsala University Press.

MacRaild, Donald H. 1999. *Irish Migrants in Modern Britain 1750–1922*. Basingstoke: Macmillan Press.

Mair, Christian (ed.) 2003. *Acts of Identity*. Special issue of *Arbeiten aus Anglistik und Amerikanistik* [Research from English and American Studies] 28.2.

Majewicz, Elżbieta 1984. 'Celtic influences upon English and English influences upon Celtic languages', *Studia Anglica Posnaniensia* 27: 45–50.

Major, Roy Coleman 2001. *Foreign Accent: the Ontogeny and Phylogeny of Second Language Phonology*. Mahwah, NJ: Lawrence Erlbaum Associates.

Mallory, James P. (ed.) 1999. *Language in Ulster*, special issue of *Ulster Folklife* 45.

Mannion, John J. (ed.) 1977. *The Peopling of Newfoundland: Essays in Historical Geography*. St John's: Memorial University of Newfoundland.

Marshall, John J. 1904. 'The dialect of Ulster', *Ulster Journal of Archaeology* 10: 121–30.

Martin, Francis Xavier 1967. 'The Anglo-Norman invasion (1169–1300)', in Moody and Martin (eds.), pp. 123–43.

Martin, Stefan and Walt Wolfram 1998. 'The sentence in African-American vernacular English', in Mufwene, Rickford, Bailey and Baugh (eds.), pp. 11–36.

Martinet, André 1952. 'Celtic lenition and Western Romance consonants', *Language* 28: 192–217.

Matras, Yaron (ed.) 1995. *Romani in Contact: the History, Structure and Sociology of a Language*. Amsterdam: John Benjamins.

  2002. *Romani: a Linguistic Introduction*. Cambridge: Cambridge University Press.

Matthews, William 1935. 'Sailors' pronunciation in the second half of the seventeenth century', *Anglia* 59: 193–251.

McArthur, Tom (ed.) 1992. *The Oxford Companion to the English Language*. Oxford: Oxford University Press.

McCafferty, Kevin 1995. 'Runagates revisited, or "Even English in these airts took a lawless turn"', *Causeway* 2: 9–15.

  1998a. 'Shared accents, divided speech community? Change in Northern Ireland English', *Language Variation and Change* 10: 97–121.

  1998b. 'Barriers to change: ethnic division and phonological innovation in Northern Hiberno-English', *English World-Wide* 19: 7–35.

1999. '(London)Derry: between Ulster and local speech – class, ethnicity and language change', in Foulkes and Docherty (eds.), pp. 246–64.

2001. *Ethnicity and Language Change: English in (London)Derry, Northern Ireland*. Amsterdam: John Benjamins.

2003. 'The Northern Subject Rule in Ulster: how Scots, how English?', *Language Variation and Change* 15: 105–39.

2004a. 'Innovation in language contact: *be after V-ing* as a future gram in Irish English, 1670 to the present', *Diachronica* 21.1: 113–60.

2004b. '"[T]hunder storms is verry dangese in this courtrey they come in less than a minnits notice . . ." The Northern Subject Rule in Southern Irish English', *English World-Wide* 25.1: 51–79.

2005. 'William Carleton between Irish and English: using literary dialect to study language contact and change', *Language and Literature* 14.4: 339–62.

in press. 'Northern Irish English', in Britain (ed.).

McCann, May, Séamas Ó Síocháin and Joseph Ruane (eds.) 1994. *Irish Travellers: Culture and Ethnicity*. Belfast: Institute of Irish Studies, Queen's University.

McCarthy-Morrogh, Michael 1986. *The Munster Plantation: English Migration to Southern Ireland 1583–1641*. Oxford: Oxford University Press.

McCawley, James 1976 [1971]. 'Tense and time reference in English', in *Grammar and Meaning: Papers on Syntactic and Semantic Topics*. London: Academic Press, pp. 257–72.

McCloskey, James 1985. 'The modern Irish double relative and syntactic binding', *Ériu* 36: 43–84.

1992. 'Adjunction, selection and embedded verb second'. Unpublished manuscript, University of California at Santa Cruz.

2000. 'Quantifier Float and *Wh*-Movement in an Irish English', *Linguistic Inquiry* 31.1: 57–84.

McClure, J. Derrick 1994. 'English in Scotland', in Burchfield (ed.), pp. 23–93.

McCone, Kim, Damian McManus, Cathal Ó Háinle, Nicholas Williams and Liam Breatnach (eds.) 1994. *Stair na Gaeilge: in ómós de Pádraig Ó Fiannachta* [The History of Irish: in honour of Pádraig Ó Fiannachta]. Maynooth: Department of Irish.

McElholm, Dermot D. 1986. 'Intonation in Derry English', in Kirkwood (ed.), pp. 1–58.

McGuire, Desmond 1987. *History of Ireland*. Twickenham: Hamlyn Publishing.

McIntosh, Agnus and Michael Samuels 1968. 'Prolegomena to a study of medieval Anglo-Irish', *Medium Ævum* 37: 1–11.

McWhorter, John H. (ed.) 2000. *Language Change and Language Contact in Pidgins and Creoles*. Amsterdam: John Benjamins.

Mencken, Henry L. 1963. *The American Language: an Inquiry into the Development of English in the United States*. New York.

Mesthrie, Rajend 1992. *English in Language Shift: the History, Structure and Sociolinguistics of South African Indian English*. Cambridge: Cambridge University Press.

1996. 'Language contact, transmission, shift: South African Indian English', in de Klerk (ed.), pp. 79–98.

Meyer, Kuno 1891. 'On the Irish origin and age of Shelta', *Journal of the Gypsy Lore Society* 2.5: 257–66.

Migge, Bettina 2003. *Creole Formation as Language Contact: the Case of the Suriname Creoles*. Amsterdam: John Benjamins.

Millar, Sharon 1987a. 'Accents in the Classroom: Sociolinguistic Perspectives on the Teaching of Elocution in Belfast Secondary-Level Schools'. Unpublished PhD thesis, Queen's University, Belfast.
  1987b. 'The question of ethno-linguistic differences in Northern Ireland', *English World-Wide* 8: 201–13.
  1990. 'The role of ethnic identity in accent evaluation in Northern Ireland', in Caie et al. (eds.), pp. 243–53.
Miller, Jim 1993. 'The grammar of Scottish English', in Milroy and Milroy (eds.), pp. 99–138.
  2004. 'Scottish English: morphology and syntax', in Kortmann et al. (eds.), vol. 2, pp. 47–72.
Miller, Kerby 1985. *Emigrants and Exiles: Ireland and the Irish Exodus to North America.* Oxford: Oxford University Press.
Miller, Kerby and Paul Wagner 1994. *Out of Ireland: the Story of Irish Emigration to America.* London: Aurum Press.
Milroy, James 1978. 'Stability and change in non-standard English in Belfast', *Northern Ireland Speech and Language Forum Journal* 4: 72–82.
  1981. *Regional Accents of English: Belfast.* Belfast: Blackstaff.
  1982. 'Some connections between Galloway and Ulster speech', *Scottish Language* 1: 23–9.
  1991. 'Social network and prestige arguments in sociolinguistics', in Bolton and Kwok (eds.), pp. 146–62.
  1992a. *Linguistic Variation and Change: on the Historical Sociolinguistics of English.* Language in Society 19. Oxford: Blackwell.
  1992b. 'A social model for the interpretation of language change', in Rissanen et al. (eds.), pp. 72–91.
  1993. 'On the social origins of language change', in Jones (ed.), pp. 215–36.
  1994. 'The notion of "standard language" and its applicability to the study of Early Modern English pronunciation', in Stein and Tieken-Boon van Ostade (eds.), pp. 19–29.
Milroy, James and John Harris 1980. 'When is a merger not a merger? The *meat/mate* problem in Belfast vernacular', *English World-Wide* 1: 199–210.
Milroy, James and Lesley Milroy (eds.) 1993. *Real English: the Grammar of the English Dialects in the British Isles.* Real Language Series. London: Longman.
  1999. *Authority in Language.* 3rd edition. London: Routledge.
Milroy, James, Lesley Milroy and Sue Hartley 1994. 'Local and supra-local change in British English: the case of glottalisation', *English World-Wide* 15: 1–33.
Milroy, Lesley 1976. 'Phonological correlates to community structure in Belfast', *Belfast Working Papers in Language and Linguistics* 1: 1–44.
  1981. 'The effect of two interacting extralinguistic variables on urban vernacular speech', in Sankoff and Cedergren (eds.), pp. 161–8.
  1987 [1980]. *Language and Social Networks.* 2nd edition. Oxford: Blackwell.
Milroy, Lesley and Paul McClenaghan 1977. 'Stereotyped reactions to four educated accents in Ulster', *Belfast Working Papers in Language and Linguistics* 2.4: 1–11.
Milroy, Lesley and James Milroy 1997. 'Exploring the social constraints on language change', in Eliasson and Jahr (eds.), pp. 75–101.

Minkova, Donka 1982. 'The environment for Open Syllable Lengthening in Middle English', *Folia Linguistica Historica* 3: 29–58.

Mishoe, Margaret and Michael Montgomery 1994. 'The pragmatics of multiple modal variation in North and South Carolina', *American Speech* 69.1: 3–29.

Mitchell, Frank 1976. *The Irish Landscape*. London: Collins.

Mittendorf, Ingo and Erich Poppe 2000. 'Celtic contacts of the English progressive?', in Tristram (ed.), pp. 117–45.

Molin, Donald H. 1984. *Actor's Encyclopedia of Dialects*. New York: Sterling Publishing.

Moerenhout, Mike and Wim van der Wurff 2005. 'Object-verb order in early sixteenth-century English prose: an exploratory study', *English Language and Linguistics* 9.1: 83–114.

Montgomery, Michael 1989. 'Exploring the roots of Appalachian English', *English World-Wide* 10: 227–78.

   1991. 'The Anglicization of Scots in early seventeenth century Ulster', in Ross, Scott and Roy (eds.), pp. 50–63.

   1994. 'The evolution of verbal concord in Scots', in Fenton and MacDonald (eds.), pp. 81–95.

   1995. 'The linguistic value of Ulster emigrant letters', *Ulster Folklife* 41: 1–15.

   1997. 'The rediscovery of the Ulster Scots language', in Schneider (ed.), pp. 211–26.

   1999. 'The position of Ulster Scots', in Mallory (ed.), pp. 89–105.

   2000. 'The Celtic element in American English', in Tristram (ed.), pp. 231–64.

   2001. 'British and Irish antecedents', in Algeo (ed.), pp. 86–153.

   2004. 'Solving Kurath's puzzle: establishing the antecedents of the American Midland dialect region', in Hickey (ed.), pp. 310–25.

   2007. *Ulster-Scots Language Yesterday and Today*. Dublin: Four Courts Press.

Montgomery, Michael and Robert Gregg 1997. 'The Scots language in Ulster', in Jones (ed.), pp. 569–622.

Montgomery, Michael and John M. Kirk 1996. 'The origin of the habitual verb *be* in American Black English: Irish, English or what', in Henry, Ball and MacAliskey (eds.), pp. 308–34.

   2001. '"My mother, whenever she passed away, she had pneumonia": the history and functions of *whenever*', *Journal of English Linguistics* 29.3: 234–49.

Montgomery, Michael and Stephen J. Nagle 1994. 'Double modals in Scotland and the Southern United States: trans-Atlantic inheritance or independent development?', *Folia Linguistica Historica* 14: 91–107.

Moody, Theodore W. 1939. *The Londonderry Plantation 1609–41*. Belfast: Mullan.

Moody, Theodore W. and Francis X. Martin (eds.) 1967. *The Course of Irish History*. Second imprint 1994. Cork: Mercier Press.

Moody, Theodore W., Francis X. Martin and Francis J. Byrne 1976. *A New History of Ireland*, vol 3: *Early Modern Ireland (1534–1691)*. Oxford: Clarendon Press.

Moore, Desmond F. 1965. *Dublin*. Dublin. Three Candles.

Morash, Christopher 2002. *A History of Irish Theatre, 1601–2000*. Dublin: Four Courts Press.

Mossé, Ferdinand 1952. *A Handbook of Middle English*. Baltimore: John Hopkins University Press.

Moylan, Séamus 1996. *The Language of Kilkenny*. Dublin: Geography Publications. Published version of Ó Maoláin (1973).

Mufwene, Salikoko (ed.) 1993. *Africanisms in Afro-American Language Varieties*. Athens, GA, and London: University of Georgia Press.

1996. 'The founder principle and creole genesis', *Diachronica* 13: 83–134.

2001. 'African-American English', in Algeo (ed.), pp. 291–324.

2003. 'Contact languages in the Bantu area', in Nurse and Phillipson (eds.), pp. 195–208.

Mufwene, Salikoko, John R. Rickford, Guy Bailey and John Baugh (eds.) 1998. *African-American English: Structure, History and Use*. London: Routledge.

Mugglestone, Lynda 2003. *'Talking Proper': the Rise of Accent as Social Symbol*. 2nd edition. Oxford: Oxford University Press.

Murphy, Colin and Donal O'Dea 2004. *The Book of Feckin' Irish Slang that's Great Craic for Cute Hoors and Bowsies*. Dublin: O'Brien Press.

Murphy, Gerard 1943. 'English "brogue" meaning "Irish accent"', *Éigse* 3: 231–6.

Mustanoja, Tauno F. 1960. *A Middle English Syntax*. Helsinki: Société Néophilologique.

Myers-Scotton, Carol 2002. *Contact Linguistics. Bilingual Encounters and Grammatical Outcomes*. Oxford: Oxford University Press.

Myers-Scotton, Carol and Janice L. Jake 2000. 'Matching lemmas in a bilingual language competence and production model: evidence from intrasentential code-switching', *Linguistics* 33: 981–1024.

Myhill, John 1988. 'The rise of *be* as an aspect marker in Black English Vernacular', *American Speech* 63: 304–25.

Nagle, Stephen and Sara Sanders (eds.) 2003. *English in the Southern United States*. Cambridge: Cambridge University Press.

Neal, Frank 1997. *Black 47: Britain and the Famine Irish*. Basingstoke: Macmillan Press.

Neilson, William 1990 [1808]. *An Introduction to the Irish Language*. Iontaobhas Ultach/ Ultach Trust, Belfast.

Nevalainen, Terttu 2004. *An Introduction to Early Modern English*. Edinburgh: Edinburgh University Press.

Nevalainen, Terttu and Helena Raumolin-Brunberg (eds.) 1996. *Sociolinguistics and Language History: Studies Based on The Corpus of Early English Correspondence*. Language and Computers 15. Amsterdam and Atlanta: Rodopi.

2003. *Historical Sociolinguistics: Language Change in Tudor and Stuart England*. Longman Linguistics Library. London: Longman.

Neumann-Holzschuh, Ingrid and Edgar W. Schneider (eds.) 2000. *Degrees of Restructuring in Creole Languages*. Amsterdam: John Benjamins.

Newbrook, Mark 1992. 'Unrecognised grammatical and semantic features typical of Australian English: a checklist with commentary', *English World-Wide* 13: 1–32.

Ní Bhroiméil, Úna 2003. *Building Irish Identity in America, 1870–1915*. Dublin: Four Courts Press.

Ní Chasaide, Ailbhe 1979. 'Laterals in Gaoth-Dobhair Irish and Hiberno-English', in Ó Baoill (ed.), pp. 54–78.

Nic Craith, Mairéad 1999. 'Linguistic policy in Ireland and the creation of a border', in Anderson and Bort (eds.), pp. 175–200.

2003. 'Facilitating or generating linguistic diversity: Ulster-Scots and the *European Charter for Regional or Minority Languages*', in Hogan-Brun and Wolff (eds.), pp. 59–72.

Nilsen, Kenneth E. 2002 [1997]. 'Irish in nineteenth century New York', in García and Fishman (eds.), pp. 53–69.

Ní Shiunéar, Sinéad 2002. 'The curious case of *Shelta*', in Kirk and Ó Baoill (eds.), pp. 21–41.

Nord, Deborah Epstein 2006. *Gypsies and the British Imagination, 1807–1930*. New York: Columbia University Press.

Nurmi, Arja 1999. *A Social History of Periphrastic DO*. Mémoires de la Société Néophilologique de Helsinki 56. Helsinki: Société Néophilologique.

Nurse, Derek and Gérard Philippson (eds.) 2003. *The Bantu Languages*. London: Routledge.

Ó Baoill, Dónall 1979a. 'Vowel lengthening before certain non-obstruents in Q-Celtic', in Ó Baoill (ed.), pp. 79–107.

(ed.) 1979b. *Papers in Celtic Phonology*. Coleraine: New University of Ulster.

(ed.) 1985. *Papers on Irish English*. Dublin: Irish Association of Applied Linguistics.

1990. 'Language contact in Ireland: the Irish phonological substratum in Irish English', in Edmondson, Feagin and Mühlhäusler (eds.), pp. 147–72.

1991. 'Contact phenomena in the phonology of Irish and English in Ireland', in Ureland and Broderick (eds.), pp. 581–95.

1994. 'Travellers' cant: language or register', in McCann, Ó Síocháin and Ruane (eds.), pp. 155–69.

O'Callaghan, Sean 2000. *To Hell or Barbados: the Ethnic Cleansing of Ireland*. Dingle, Co. Kerry: Brandon Books.

Ó Catháin, Brian and Ruairí Ó hUiginn (eds.) 2001. *Béalra: Aistí ar Theangeolaíocht na Gaeilge* [Speech: essays on the linguistics of Irish]. Maynooth: An Sagart.

O'Connor, Kevin 1972. *The Irish in Britain*. London: Sidgwick and Jackson.

Ó Corráin, Ailbhe 2006. 'On the "After Perfect" in Irish and Hiberno-English', in Tristram (ed.), pp. 153–73.

Ó Cuiv, Brian 1944. *The Irish of West Muskerry, Co. Cork*. Dublin: Institute for Advanced Studies.

1951. *Irish Dialects and Irish-Speaking Districts*. Dublin: Institute for Advanced Studies.

(ed.) 1962. *Proceedings of The First International Congress of Celtic Studies*. Dublin: Institute for Advanced Studies.

(ed.) 1969. *A View of the Irish Language*. Dublin: Stationary Office.

(ed.) 1975. *The Impact of the Scandinavian Invasions on the Celtic-Speaking Peoples c. 800–1100 AD*. Dublin: Institute for Advanced Studies.

1986. 'Sandhi phenomena in Irish', in Andersen (ed.), pp. 395–414.

Odlin, Terence 1991. 'Irish English idioms and language transfer', *English World-Wide* 12.2: 175–93.

1994. 'A demographic perspective on the shift from Irish to English', in Blackshire-Belay (ed.), pp. 137–45.

1995. *Causation in Language Contact: a Devilish Problem*. Dublin: Centre for Language and Communication Studies, Trinity College. Occasional Paper, 41.

1997. 'Bilingualism and substrate influence: a look at clefts and reflexives', in Kallen (ed.), pp. 35–50.

Ó Dochartaigh, Cathair 1987. *Dialects of Ulster Irish*. Belfast: Institute of Irish Studies, Queen's University.

1992. 'The Irish language', in Macaulay (ed.), pp. 11–99.

Ó Dónaill, Niall 1977. *Foclóir Gaeilge-Béarla* [Irish-English dictionary]. Dublin: Stationary Office.

O'Donovan, John 1845. *A Grammar of the Irish Language*. Dublin: Hodges and Smith.

O'Dowd, Anne 1991. *Spalpeens and Tattie Hokers. History and Folklore of the Irish Migratory Agricultural Worker in Ireland and Britain*. Dublin: Irish Academic Press.

O'Farrell, Padraic 1993 [1980]. *How the Irish Speak English*. Cork: Mercier.

Oftedal, Magne 1986. *Lenition in Celtic and in Insular Spanish: the Secondary Voicing of Stops in Gran Canaria*. Oslo: Oslo University Press.

Ó Gráda, Cormac 1989. *The Great Irish Famine*. Cambridge: Cambridge University Press.

Ogura, Mieko 1993. 'The development of periphrastic *do* in English: a case of lexical diffusion in syntax', *Diachronica* 10: 51–85.

Ó Háinle, Cathal 1986. 'Neighbours in eighteenth century Dublin: Jonathan Swift and Seán Ó Neachtain', *Éire – Ireland* 21: 106–21.

O'Hehir, Brendan 1967. *A Gaelic Lexicon for 'Finnegans Wake' and Glossary for Joyce's Other Works*. Berkeley and Los Angeles: University of California Press.

O'Leary, Paul 2000. *Immigration and Integration: the Irish in Wales, 1798–1922*. Cardiff: University of Wales Press.

Ó Máille, Tomás 1980. 'Úsáid ar "le" den aimsir ghnáthcaite' [On the use of 'with' for the past habitual], *Éigse* 18: 24.

O'Malley Madec, Mary 2002. 'From the Centre to the Edge: the Social Contours and Linguistic Outcomes of Contact with English in an Irish Core Community and Peripheral Community'. Unpublished PhD thesis, University of Pennsylvania.

Ó Maoláin, Séamus 1973. 'An Anglo-Irish Lexicon of Kilkenny'. Unpublished PhD thesis, University College Galway. See Moylan (1996).

Omoniyi, Tope and Goodith White (eds.) 2006. *Sociolinguistics of Identity*. London: Continuum.

Ó Muirithe, Diarmuid 1977a. 'The Anglo-Normans and their English dialect of South-East Wexford', in Ó Muirithe (ed.), pp. 37–55.

(ed.) 1977b. *The English Language in Ireland*. Cork: Mercier.

1990. 'A modern glossary of the dialect of Forth and Bargy', in Dolan (ed.), pp. 149–62.

1996a. *Dictionary of Anglo-Irish: Words and Phrases from Irish*. Dublin: Four Courts Press.

1996b. *The Words We Use*. Dublin: Four Courts Press.

1997. *A Word in Your Ear*. Dublin: Four Courts Press.

2004. *A Glossary of Irish Slang and Unconventional Language*. Dublin: Gill and Macmillan.

Onions, Charles T. 1966. *Oxford Dictionary of English Etymology*. Oxford: Clarendon Press.

O'Rahilly, Cecile 1924. *Ireland and Wales: their Historical and Literary Relations*. London: Longmans, Green and Co.

O'Rahilly, Thomas Francis 1926. 'Notes on Middle-Irish pronunciation', *Hermathena* 44: 152–95.

1932. *Irish Dialects Past and Present*. Dublin: Browne and Nolan.

1946. 'On the origin of the names Érainn and Ériu', *Ériu* 14: 7–28.

Orpen, Goddard Henry 1892. *The Song of Dermot and the Earl*. Oxford: Clarendon Press.

Ó Riagáin, Pádraig 1997. *Language Policy and Social Reproduction: Ireland 1893–1993*. Oxford: Oxford University Press.

Ó Sé, Diarmuid 1986. 'Word-stress in Hiberno-English', in Harris, Little and Singleton (eds.), pp. 97–110.
  1992. 'The perfect in Modern Irish', *Ériu* 43: 39–67.
  2001. 'Gnáthach agus leanúnach i mbriathar na Gaeilge' [The habitual and continuous in the Irish verb], in Ó Catháin and Ó hUiginn (eds.), pp. 123–45.
  2004. 'The "after" perfect and related constructions in Gaelic dialects', *Ériu* 54: 179–248.
Ó Siadhail, Mícheál 1984. '*Agus(Is)* / *And*: a shared syntactic feature', *Celtica* 16: 125–37.
  1989. *Modern Irish: Grammatical Structure and Dialectal Variation*. Cambridge: Cambridge University Press.
Ossory-Fitzpatrick, Samuel A. 1977 [1907]. *Dublin, a Historical and Topographical Account of the City*. Cork: Tower Books.
O'Sullivan, Patrick (ed.) 1992. *The Irish World Wide: History, Heritage, Identity*, vol. 1: *Patterns of Migration*. Leicester: Leicester University Press.
Östman, Jan-Ola 1981. *You Know: a Discourse-Functional Study*. Amsterdam: John Benjamins.
Ó Tuama, Seán and Thomas Kinsella (eds.) 1981. *An Duanaire 1600–1900: Poems of the Dispossessed*. Dublin: Dolmen Press.
Ó Tuathaigh, Gearóid 1972. *Ireland before the Famine 1798–1848*. The Gill History of Ireland, vol. 9. Dublin: Gill and Macmillan.
  2005. 'Language, ideology and national identity', in Cleary and Connolly (eds.), pp. 42–58.
Otway-Ruthven, Annette Jocelyn 1968. *A History of Medieval Ireland*. London: Ernest Benn.
Owens, Elizabeth 1977. 'The Distribution of /l/ in Belfast Vernacular English'. MA thesis, Queen's University, Belfast.
Oxford English Dictionary on CD-ROM. Version 3.0. Oxford: Oxford University Press, 2002.
Palmer, Patricia 2000. *Language and Conquest in Early Modern Ireland: English Renaissance Literature and Elizabethan Imperial Expansion*. Cambridge: Cambridge University Press.
Pandeli, Helen, Joseph Eska, Martin Ball and Joan Rahilly 1997. 'Problems of phonetic transcription: the case of the Hiberno-English slit-*t*', *Journal of the International Phonetics Association* 27: 65–75.
Pargman, Sheri 2004. 'Gullah *duh* and periphrastic *do* in English dialects: another look at the evidence', *American Speech* 79.1: 3–32.
Patterson, David 1860. *The Provincialisms of Belfast and the Surrounding Districts Pointed Out and Corrected; to which is Added an Essay on Mutual Improvement Societies*. Belfast: Alexander Mayne.
Paulasto, Heli 2006. *Welsh English Syntax: Contact and Variation*. Publications in the Humanities 43. Joensuu: University of Joensuu Press.
Paulston, Christina Bratt and G. Richard Tucker (ed.) 2003. *Sociolinguistics: the Essential Readings*. Oxford: Blackwell.
Pedersen, Holger 1897. *Aspirationen i Irsk* [Lenition in Irish]. Copenhagen: M. Spirgatis' Boghandel.
Penhallurick, Robert 2004a. 'Welsh English: phonology', in Kortmann et al. (eds.), vol. 1, pp. 98–111.

2004b. 'Welsh English: morphology and syntax', in Kortmann et al. (eds.), vol. 2, pp. 102–13.

Phillipson, Robert 2003. *English-only Europe? Challenging Language Policy*. London: Routledge.

Picton, J. A. 1867. 'An inquiry into the origin and philological relations of the antique dialect formerly spoken in the baronies of Forth and Bargy', *Proceedings of the Literary and Philological Society of Liverpool* 21: 118–43.

Pietsch, Lucas 2004a. 'Argument omission in Irish English', *Arbeiten zur Mehrsprachigkeit*. Universität Hamburg.

2004b. 'Nominative subjects in nonfinite clause constructions in Irish English', *Arbeiten zur Mehrsprachigkeit*. Universität Hamburg.

2005a. *Variable Grammars: Verbal Agreement in Northern Dialects of English*. Tübingen: Max Niemeyer.

2005b. '"Some do and some doesn't": verbal concord variation in the north of the British Isles', in Kortmann et al. (eds.), pp. 125–210.

Pilch, Herbert and Joachim Thurow (eds.) 1972. *Indo-Celtica: Gedächtnisschrift für Alf Sommerfelt*. Munich: Max Hueber.

Polenz, Peter von 1969. 'Der Pertinenzdativ und seine Satzbaupläne' [The pertinence dative and its sentence structures], in Engel et al. (eds.), pp. 146–71.

Poplack, Shana 1980. 'Sometimes I'll start a sentence in English y termino en espanol: towards a typology of code-switching', *Linguistics* 18: 581–616.

Poplack, Shana and Sali Tagliamonte 2004. 'Back to the present: verbal -s in the (African American) English diaspora', in Hickey (ed.), pp. 203–23.

Poussa, Patricia 1982. 'The evolution of early Standard English: the creolisation hypothesis', *Studia Anglica Posnaniensia* 14: 69–85.

1990. 'A contact-universal origin for periphrastic *do* with special consideration of Old English-Celtic contact', in Adamson et al. (eds.), pp. 407–34.

Power, Patrick C. 1977. *Cúirt an Mheán-Oíche – The Midnight Court by Brian Merriman*. Cork: Mercier Press.

Pringle, Ian and Enoch Padolsky 1981. 'The Irish heritage of the English of the Ottawa Valley', *English Studies in Canada* 7: 338–52.

1983. 'The linguistic survey of the Ottawa Valley', *American Speech* 58: 325–44.

Prins, Anton 1974. *A History of English Phonemes*. Leiden: Leiden University Press.

Przedlacka, Joanna 1999. *Estuary English? A Sociophonetic Study of Teenage Speech in the Home Counties*. Frankfurt/Main: Lang.

Pyles, Thomas and John Algeo 1993 [1964]. *The Origins and Development of the English Language*. 4th edition. Harbourt, Brace, Jovanovich.

Rahilly, Joan 1994. 'Phonetic characteristics of prominence in Belfast intonation', *Belfast Working Papers in Language and Linguistics* 12: 225–45.

1997. 'Aspects of prosody in Hiberno-English: the case of Belfast', in Kallen (ed.), pp. 109–32.

Ramat, Anna Giacalone et al. (eds.) 1987. *Papers from the 7th International Conference on Historical Linguistics, Pavia, Italy*. Amsterdam: John Benjamins.

Ramisch, Heinrich and Kenneth Wynne (eds.) 1997. *Language in Time and Space: Festschrift für Wolfgang Viereck*. Stuttgart: Franz Steiner.

Rankin, Deana 2005. *Between Spenser and Swift: English Writing in Seventeenth-Century Ireland*. Cambridge: Cambridge University Press.

Ray, John 1674. *A Collection of English Words not Generally Used*. London.

Restle, David and Dietmar Zaefferer (eds.) 2002. *Sounds and Systems: Studies in Structure and Change. A Festschrift for Theo Vennemann*. Berlin: Mouton-de Gruyter.

Rickford, John R. 1980. 'How does *doz* disappear?', in Day (ed.), pp. 77–96.

1986. 'Social contact and linguistic diffusion: Hiberno-English and New World Black English', *Language* 62: 245–90.

1998. 'The creole origins of African-American vernacular English: evidence from copula absence', in Mufwene, Rickford, Bailey and Baugh (eds.), pp. 154–200.

Rickford, John R. and Jerome S. Handler 1994. 'Textual evidence on the nature of early Barbadian speech, 1676–1835', *Journal of Pidgin and Creole Languages* 9.2: 221–55.

Risk, Henry 1971. 'French loan-words in Irish (i)', *Etudes Celtiques* 12: 585–655.

1974. 'French loan-words in Irish (ii)', *Etudes Celtiques* 14: 67–98.

Rissanen, Matti, Ossi Ihalainen, Terttu Nevalainen and Irma Taavitsainen (eds.) 1992. *History of Englishes: New Methods and Interpretations in Historical Linguistics*. Berlin: Mouton de Gruyter.

Ritt, Nikolaus 1994. *Quantity Adjustment: Vowel Lengthening and Shortening in Early Middle English*. Cambridge: Cambridge University Press.

Roberts, Ian 1997. *Comparative Syntax*. London: Arnold.

Robinson, Philip 1989a. 'The Ulster plantation', *Ulster Local Studies* 11.2: 20–30.

1989b. 'The Scots language in seventeenth-century Ulster', *Ulster Folklife* 35: 86–99.

1994 [1984]. *The Plantation of Ulster: British Settlement in an Irish Landscape, 1600–1670*. Belfast: Ulster Historical Foundation.

1997. *Ulster Scots: a Grammar of the Traditional Written and Spoken Language*. Belfast: Ullans Press.

2003. 'The historical presence of Ulster-Scots in Ireland', in Cronin and Ó Cuilleanáin (eds.), pp. 112–26.

Rohdenburg, Günter and Britta Mondorf (eds.) 2003. *Determinants of Grammatical Variation in English*. Berlin: Mouton de Gruyter.

Rohlfs, Gerhard 1949. *Historische Grammatik der italienischen Sprache und ihrer Mundarten* [An historical grammar of the Italian language and its dialects]. 3 vols. Bern: Francke.

Romaine, Suzanne 1989. *Bilingualism*. Oxford: Basil Blackwell.

(ed.) 1998. *The Cambridge History of the English Language*, vol. 4: *1776–1997*. Cambridge: Cambridge University Press.

Ronan, Patricia 2002. 'Subordinating *ocus* "and" in Old Irish', in Filppula, Klemola and Pitkänen (eds.), pp. 213–36.

2005. 'The *after*-perfect in Irish English', in Filppula et al. (eds.), pp. 253–70.

Rosch, Eleanor H. 1977. 'Human categorization', in Warren (ed.), pp. 1–49.

1978. 'Principles of categorization', in Rosch and Lloyd (eds.), pp. 27–48.

Rosch, Eleanor H. and B. B. Lloyd (eds.) 1978. *Cognition and Categorization*. Hillsdale, NJ: Erlbaum Associates.

Ross, Bianca 1998. *Britannia et Hibernia: nationale und kulturelle Identitäten im Irland des 17. Jahrhunderts* [Britannia et Hibernia: national and cultural identities in seventeenth-century Ireland]. Heidelberg: Carl Winter.

Ross, G., Patrick Scott and Lucie Roy (eds.) 1991. *Studies in Scottish Literature: the Language and Literature of Early Scotland*. Columbia, SC: University of South Carolina.

Ross, Malcolm 1991. 'Refining Guy's sociolinguistic types of language change', *Diachronica* 8: 119–29.

Rothwell, William et al. 1975–6. 'The role of French in thirteenth century England', *Bulletin of the John Rylands University Library* 58: 445–66.

1992. *Anglo-Norman Dictionary*. London: The Modern Humanities Research Association.

Rottet, Kevin J. 2005. 'Phrasal verbs and English in Welsh', *Word* 56.1: 39–70.

Russell, Charles W. 1892 [1857]. 'The dialect of the barony of Forth, Co. Wexford', *Irish Monthly* 20: 580–92.

Rydén, Mats and Sverker Brorström 1987. *The Be/Have Variation with Intransitives in English with Special Reference to the Late Modern Period*. Stockholm: Almqvist and Wiksell.

Sabban, Annette 1982. *Gälisch-Englischer Sprachkontakt: zur Variabilität des Englischen im gälischsprachigen Gebiet Schottlands. Eine empirische Studie* [Gaelic-English language contact: on the variability of English in the Gaelic-speaking areas of Scotland. An empirical study]. Heidelberg: Groos.

1984. 'Investigations into the syntax of Hebridean English', *Scottish Language* 3: 5–32.

1985. 'On the variability of Hebridean English syntax: the verbal group', in Görlach (ed.), pp. 125–44.

Sammon, Paddy 2002. *Greenspeak: Ireland in her own Words*. Dublin: Town House.

Sampson, John 1890. 'Tinkers and their talk', *Journal of the Gypsy Lore Society* 2.4: 204–21.

Samuels, Michael 1972. *Linguistic Evolution*. Cambridge: Cambridge University Press.

Sand, Andrea 2003. 'The definite article in Irish English and other contact varieties of English', in Tristram (ed.), pp. 413–30.

Sangster, Catherine M. 2001. 'Lenition of alveolar stops in Liverpool English', *Journal of Sociolinguistics* 5.3: 401–12.

Sankoff, David and H. Cedergren (eds.) 1981. *Variation Omnibus*. Edmonton: Linguistic Research Inc.

Scargill, Matthew Henry 1977. *A Short History of Canadian English*. Victoria, British Columbia: Sono Nis Press.

Schendl, Herbert 1996. 'The 3rd plural present indicative in Early Modern English: variation and linguistic contact', in Britton (ed.), pp. 143–60.

Schilling-Estes, Natalie 1995. 'Extending our understanding of the /z/ – [d] rule', *American Speech* 70: 291–302.

Schilling-Estes, Natalie and Walt Wolfram 1994. 'Convergent explanation and alternative regularization patterns: *were/weren't* leveling in a vernacular English variety', *Language Variation and Change* 6.3: 273–302.

Schleifer, Ronald (ed.) 1980. *The Genres of the Irish Literary Revival*. Dublin.

Schlüter, Julia 2003. 'Phonological determinants of grammatical variation in English: Chomsky's worst possible case', in Rohdenburg and Mondorf (eds.), pp. 69–118.

Schmitt, Ludwig Erich (ed.) 1966. *Verhandlungen des zweiten internationalen Dialektologen kongresses, Marburg 1965* [Proceedings of the Second International Congress of Dialectologists, Marburg 1965]. *Zeitschrift für Mundartforschung*, new series, supplementary volume no. 3. Wiesbaden: Steiner.

Schneider, Edgar W. 1990. 'The cline of creoleness in English-oriented creoles and semi-creoles of the Caribbean', *English World-Wide* 11.1: 79–113.

1993. 'Africanisms in the grammar of Afro-American English: Weighing the evidence', in Mufwene (ed.), pp. 209–21.

(ed.) 1996. *Focus on the USA*. Varieties of English Around the World, general series, vol. 16. Amsterdam: John Benjamins.

(ed.) 1997. *Englishes Around the World*. 2 vols. Amsterdam: John Benjamins.

2003. 'Shakespeare in the coves and hollows? Toward a history of Southern English', in Nagle and Sanders (eds.), pp. 17–35.

2004. 'Synopsis: morphological and syntactic variation in the Americas and the Caribbean', in Kortmann et al. (eds.), vol. 2, pp. 1104–15.

Schneider, Klaus and Anne Barron (eds.) 2005. *The Pragmatics of Irish English*. Berlin and New York: Mouton de Gruyter.

Schreier, Daniel 2003. *Isolation and Language Change: Contemporary and Sociohistorical Evidence from Tristan da Cunha English*. London: Palgrave Macmillan.

2006. *Consonant Change in English Worldwide: Synchrony Meets Diachrony*. London: Palgrave Macmillan.

Scott-Thomas, Lois M. 1945–6. 'The vocabulary of Jonathan Swift', *Dalhousie Review* 25: 442–7.

Scragg, Donald L. 1974. *A History of English Spelling*. Manchester: Manchester University Press.

Seppänen, Aimo and Göran Kjellmer 1995. '*The dog that's leg was run over*: on the genitive of the relative pronoun', *English Studies* 26: 389–400.

Seymour, St John D. 1970 [1929]. *Anglo-Irish Literature 1200–1582*. Cambridge: Cambridge University Press.

Shakespeare, William 1995. *King Henry V*, ed. T. W. Craik (*The Arden Shakespeare*). Routledge: London and New York.

Share, Bernard 2003 [1997]. *Slanguage – a Dictionary of Slang and Colloquial English in Ireland*. Dublin: Gill and Macmillan.

2006. *Dublinese: Know what I mean?* Cork: Collins Press.

Sheridan, Thomas 1781. *A Rhetorical Grammar of the English Language Calculated Solely for the Purpose of Teaching Propriety of Pronunciation and Justness of Delivery, in that Tongue*. Dublin: Price.

1967 [1780]. *A General Dictionary of the English Language*. 2 vols. Menston: Scolar Press.

1970 [1762]. *A Course of Lectures on Elocution*. Hildesheim: Georg Olms.

Shields, Hugh 1975–6. 'The Walling of New Ross', *Long Room* 12–13: 24–33.

Shorrocks, Graham 1999. *A Grammar of the Dialect of the Bolton Area*, part II: *Morphology and Syntax*. Frankfurt/Main: Peter Lang.

Siegmund-Schultze, Dorothea (ed.) 1985. *Irland: Gesellschaft und Kultur* [Ireland: society and culture], vol. 4. Halle: Halle University Press.

Siemund, Peter 2004. 'Independent developments in the genesis of Irish English', in Tristram (ed.), pp. 283–305.

Singler, John V. (ed.) 1990. *Pidgin and Creole Tense–Mood–Aspect Systems*. Amsterdam: John Benjamins.

1997. 'The configuration of Liberia's Englishes', *World Englishes* 16: 205–31.

Skea, Margaret 1982. 'Change and Variation in the Lexicon of a Non-Standard Dialect: a Sociolinguistic Study of Dialect Semantics in North Down'. Unpublished PhD thesis, Ulster Polytechnic, Jordanstown.

Smart, Benjamin H. 1836. *Walker Remodelled: a New Critical Pronouncing Dictionary of the English Language*. London: T. Cadell.

Sommerfelt, Alf 1962. *Diachronic and Synchronic Aspects of Language*. The Hague: Mouton.

1975. 'The Norse influence on Irish and Scottish Gaelic', in Ó Cuív (ed.), pp. 73–7.

Spears, Arthur K. and Donald Winford (eds.) 1997. *Pidgins and Creoles: Structure and Status*, Amsterdam: John Benjamins.

Stalmaszczyk, Piotr 1997. 'Celtic elements in English vocabulary – a critical assessment', *Studia Anglica Posnaniensia* 32: 77–87.

Stanihurst, Richard 1965 [1577]. 'The description of Ireland', *Chronicles of England, Scotlande and Irelande*, ed. R. Holinshed. London. Reprinted by Ams Press.

Stapleton, Karyn and John Wilson 2003. 'A discursive approach to cultural identity: the case of Ulster Scots', *Belfast Working Papers in Language and Linguistics* 16: 57–71.

Steele, Robert 1898. *Three Prose Versions of the Secreta Secretorum*, vol. 1: *Text and Glossary*. Early English Text Society, extra series no. 74, 1. London: Trübner.

Stein, Dieter and Ingrid Tieken-Boon van Ostade (eds.) 1994. *Towards a Standard English 1600–1800*. Berlin: Mouton de Gruyter.

Stenson, Nancy 1981. *Studies in Irish Syntax*. Tübingen: Narr.

1990. 'Phrase structure congruence, government, and Irish-English code-switching', in Hendrick (ed.), pp. 167–97.

1991. 'Code-switching vs. borrowing in Modern Irish', in Ureland and Broderick (eds.), pp. 559–79.

1993. 'English influence on Irish: the last 100 years', *Journal of Celtic Linguistics* 2: 107–28.

1997. 'Language contact and the development of Irish directional phrase idioms', in Ahlqvist and Čapková (eds.), pp. 559–78.

Stewart, Thomas W. 2004. 'Lexical imposition: Old Norse vocabulary in Scottish Gaelic', *Diachronica* 21.2: 393–420.

Strang, Barbara 1967. 'Swift and the English language', *To Honor Roman Jakobson: Essays on the Occasion of his Seventieth Birthday*. The Hague: Mouton, vol. 3, pp. 1947–59.

Stuart-Smith, Jane 2004. 'Scottish English: phonology', in Kortmann et al. (eds.), vol. 1, pp. 47–67.

Sullivan, James 1976. 'The Genesis of Hiberno-English: a Socio-Historical Account'. Unpublished PhD thesis, Yeshiva University, New York.

1980. 'The validity of literary dialect: evidence from the theatrical portrayal of Hiberno-English', *Language and Society* 9: 195–219.

Swift, Roger 2002. *Irish Migrants in Britain, 1815–1914: a Documentary History*. Cork: Cork University Press.

Swift, Roger and Sheridan Gilley (eds.) 1985. *Irish in the Victorian City*. London: Croom Helm.

1999. *The Irish in Victorian Britain: the Local Dimension*. Dublin: Four Court Press.

Taavitsainen, Irma and Andreas H. Jucker (eds.) 2003. *Diachronic Perspectives on Address Term Systems*. Pragmatics and Beyond, new series, vol. 107. Amsterdam: Benjamins.

Tagliamonte, Sali 2006. 'Historical change in synchronic perspective: the legacy of British dialects', in van Kemenade and Los (eds.), pp. 477–506.

Tagliamonte, Sali and Jennifer Smith 1998. 'Roots of English in the African American diaspora', *Links and Letters* 5: 147–65.

2002. 'Either it isn't or it's not: NEG/AUX contraction in British dialects', *English World-Wide* 23.2: 251–81.

Tagliamonte, Sali A., Jennifer Smith and Helen Lawrence 2005a. 'English dialects in the British Isles in cross-variety perspective: a base-line for future research', in Filppula et al. (eds.), pp. 87–117.

2005b. 'No taming the vernacular! Insights from the relatives in northern Britain', *Language Variation and Change* 17: 75–112.

Tagliamonte, Sali and Rosalind Temple 2005. 'New perspectives on an ol' variable: (t, d) in British English', *Language Variation and Change* 17: 281–302.

Taniguchi, Jiro 1956. *A Grammatical Analysis of Artistic Representation of Irish English with a Brief Discussion of Sounds and Spelling*. Tokyo: Shinozaki Shorin.

Taylor, John R. 1989. *Linguistic Categorization: Prototypes in Linguistic Theory*. Oxford: Clarendon Press.

Taylor, Brian 2001. 'Australian English in interaction with other Englishes', in Blair and Collins (eds.), pp. 317–40.

Ternes, Elmar 1977. 'Konsonantische Anlautveränderungen in den keltischen und romanischen Sprachen' [Consonantal initial mutation in the Celtic and Romance languages], *Romanistisches Jahrbuch* 28: 19–53.

Thelwall, Robin (ed.) 1980. *Linguistic Studies in Honour of Paul Christophersen*. Occasional Papers in Linguistics and Language Learning, vol. 7. Coleraine: New University of Ulster.

Thomas, Alan R. 1994. 'English in Wales', in Burchfield (ed.), pp. 94–147.

Thomas, Alan R. (ed.) 1997. *Issues and Methods in Dialectology*. Bangor: Department of Linguistics, University of Wales.

Thomason, Sarah G. 1997a. 'A typology of contact languages', in Spears and Winford (eds.), pp. 71–88.

1997b. 'On mechanisms of interference', in Eliasson and Jahr (eds.), pp. 181–207.

2000. 'Contact as a source of language change', in Joseph and Janda (eds.), pp. 687–712.

2001. *Language Contact*. Edinburgh: Edinburgh University Press.

Thomason, Sarah G. and Terence Kaufman 1988. *Language Contact, Creolization, and Genetic Linguistics*. Berkeley, Los Angeles and London: University of California Press.

Thomson, Robert L. 1977. 'The emergence of Scottish Gaelic', in Aitken, McDiarmid and Thomson (eds.), pp. 127–35.

Thurneysen, Rudolf 1946. *A Grammar of Old Irish*. Dublin: Institute for Advanced Studies.

Tieken-Boon van Ostade, Ingrid 1982. 'Double negation in eighteenth century English grammars', *Neophilologus* 66: 278–85.

1985. '"I will be drowned and no man shall save me": the conventional rules for *shall* and *will* in eighteenth-century English grammars', *English Studies* 66: 123–42.

1990. 'Exemplification in eighteenth-century English grammars', in Adamson et al. (eds.), pp. 481–96.

Tieken-Boon van Ostade, Ingrid, Marijke van der Wal and Arjan van Leuvensteijn (eds.) 1998. *'Do' in English, Dutch and German: History and Present-Day Variation*. Amsterdam: Stichting Neerlandistik; Münster: Nodus Publikationen.

Todd, Loreto 1971. 'Tyrone English: the influence of Gaelic on Tyrone English', *Transactions of the Yorkshire Dialect Society* 13: 29–40.

1984. 'By their tongue divided: towards an analysis of speech communities in Northern Ireland', *English World-Wide* 5: 159–80.

1989. *The Language of Irish Literature*. London: Macmillan.

1990. *Words Apart: a Dictionary of Northern Irish English*. Gerrards Cross: Colin Smythe.

1992. 'Irish English', in McArthur (ed.), pp. 529–30.

1999. *Green English*. Dublin: O'Brien Press.

Tottie, Gunnel 1985. 'The negation of epistemic necessity in present-day British and American English', *English World-Wide* 6: 87–116.

Tottie, Gunnel and Sebastian Hoffmann forthcoming. 'Tag questions in British and American English', *Journal of English Linguistics*.

Traugott, Elizabeth 1972. *A History of English Syntax: a Transformational Approach to the History of English Sentence Structure*. New York: Holt, Rinehart and Winston.

Traugott, Elizabeth and Bernd Heine (eds.) 1991. *Approaches to Grammaticalization*. 2 vols. Amsterdam: Benjamins.

Traugott, Elizabeth and Ekkehard König 1991. 'The semantics-pragmatics of grammaticalization revisited', in Traugott and Heine (eds.), pp. 189–214.

Traynor, Michael 1953. *The English Dialect of Donegal: a Glossary, Incorporating the Collections of H. C. Hart, etc.* Dublin: Royal Irish Academy.

Tristram, Hildegard L. C. 1997a. 'DO in contact?', in Ramisch and Wynne (eds.), pp. 401–17.

(ed.) 1997b. *The Celtic Englishes*. Heidelberg: Carl Winter.

(ed.) 2000. *The Celtic Englishes II*. Heidelberg: Carl Winter.

(ed.) 2003. *The Celtic Englishes III*. Heidelberg: Carl Winter.

(ed.) 2006. *The Celtic Englishes IV*. Potsdam: Potsdam University Press.

Trotter, David A. 1994. 'L'anglo-français au pays de galles: une enquête préliminaire' [Anglo-Norman in Wales, a preliminary investigation], *Revue de Linguistique Romane* 58: 461–87.

Troy, Jakelin 1992. '"Der mary this is fine cuntry is there is in the wourld": Irish-English and Irish in late eighteenth and nineteenth century Australia', in Dutton, Ross and Tryon (eds.), pp. 459–77.

Trudgill, Peter (ed.) 1978. *Sociolinguistic Patterns in British English*. London: Edward Arnold.

(ed.) 1984. *Language in the British Isles*. Cambridge: Cambridge University Press.

1986. *Dialects in Contact*. Oxford: Blackwell.

1990. *The Dialects of England*. Oxford: Basil Blackwell.

2001. 'Modern East Anglia as dialect area', Fisiak and Trudgill (eds.), pp. 1–12.

2002. *Sociolinguistic Variation and Change*. Edinburgh: Edinburgh University Press.

2004. *New Dialect Formation: the Inevitability of Colonial Englishes*. Edinburgh: Edinburgh University Press.

Trudgill, Peter and J. K. Chambers (eds.) 1991. *Dialects of English: Studies in Grammatical Variation*. London: Longman.

Trudgill, Peter, Daniel Schreier, Daniel Long and Jeffrey P. Williams 2004. 'On the reversibility of mergers: /w/, /v/ and evidence from lesser-known Englishes', *Folia Linguistica Historica* 24.1–2: 23–45.

Upton, Clive and Katie Wales (eds.) 1999. *Dialect Variation in English: Proceedings of the Harold Orton Centenary Conference 1998*. Leeds Studies in English. Leeds: Leeds University Press.

Upton, Clive and John D. Widdowson 1996. *An Atlas of English Dialects*. Oxford: Oxford University Press.

Ureland, P. Sture and George Broderick (eds.) 1991. *Language Contact in the British Isles: Proceedings of the Eighth International Symposium on Language Contact in Europe.* Tübingen: Niemeyer.

Vallancey, Charles 1773. *A Grammar of the Iberno-Celtic or Irish language.* London.

1788. 'Memoir of the language, manners, and customs of an Anglo-Saxon colony settled in the baronies of Forth and Bargie, in the County of Wexford, Ireland, in 1167, 1168, 1169', *Transactions of the Royal Irish Academy* 2: 19–41.

Vennemann gen. Nierfeld, Theo 2000. 'English as a "Celtic" language', in Tristram (ed.), pp. 399–406.

2001. 'Atlantis Semitica: structural contact features in Celtic and English', in Brinton (ed.), pp. 351–69.

2002. 'Semitic → Celtic → English: the transitivity of language contact', in Filppula, Klemola and Pitkänen (eds.), pp. 295–330.

Veselinović, Elvira 2006. 'How *to put up* with *cur suas le rud* and the bidirectionality of contact', in Tristram (ed.), pp. 173–90.

Vising, Johann 1923. *Anglo-Norman Language and Literature.* Oxford: Oxford University Press.

Visser, Fredericus Th. 1963–73. *An Historical Syntax of the English Language*, Parts I–III. Leiden: Brill.

Visser, Gerard J. 1955. 'Celtic influence in English', *Neophilologus* 39.1: 276–93.

Wagner, Heinrich 1958. *Linguistic Atlas and Survey of Irish Dialects*, 4 vols. Dublin: Institute for Advanced Studies.

1959. *Das Verbum in der Sprachen der britischen Inseln* [The verb in the languages of the British Isles]. Tübingen: Niemeyer.

1979. *Gaeilge Theilinn* [The Irish of Teelin, Co. Donegal]. 2nd edition. Dublin: Institute for Advanced Studies.

Wagner, Susanne 2005. 'English dialects in the Southwest: morphology and syntax', in Kortmann et al. (eds.), pp. 154–95.

Wakelin, Martyn F. (ed.) 1972. *Patterns in the Folk Speech of the British Isles.* London: Athlone Press.

1977 [1972]. *English Dialects: an Introduction.* 2nd edition. London: Athlone Press.

1984. 'Rural dialects in England', in Trudgill (ed.), pp. 70–93.

1986. *The Southwest of England.* Amsterdam: John Benjamins.

1988. 'The phonology of South-Western English 1500–1700', in Fisiak (ed.), pp. 609–44.

Walker, James A. and Miriam Meyerhoff 2006. 'Zero copula in the Eastern Caribbean: evidence from Bequia', *American Speech* 81.2: 146–63.

Walker, John 1791. *A Critical Pronouncing Dictionary of the English Language.* Menston: Scolar Press.

Wall, Richard 1995. *A Dictionary and Glossary for the Irish Literary Revival.* Gerrards Cross: Colin Smythe.

2001. *An Irish Literary Dictionary and Glossary.* Gerrards Cross: Colin Smythe.

Wallace, Martin 1973. *A Short History of Ireland.* Newton Abbot: David and Charles.

Walsh, James J. 1926. 'Shakespeare's pronunciation of the Irish brogue', in *The World's Debt to the Irish.* Boston: The Stratford Company, pp. 297–327.

Wang, William 1969. 'Competing changes as a cause of residue', *Language* 45: 9–25.

Warren, Neil (ed.) 1977. *Advances in Cross-Cultural Psychology*, vol. 1. London: Academic Press.

Waterhouse, Osborn (ed.) 1909. *The Non-Cycle Mystery Plays together with the Croxton 'Play of the Sacrament' and the 'Pride of Life'*. Early English Text Society, extra series, no. 104. London: Paul, Trench and Trübner.

Watson, Seosamh 1994. 'Gaeilge na hAlban' [Scottish Gaelic], in McCone et al. (eds.), pp. 661–702.

Watt, John 1972. *The Church in Medieval Ireland*. The Gill History of Ireland, vol. 5. Dublin: Gill and Macmillan.

Webster, Noah 1789. *Dissertations on the English Language*. Boston.

Weldon, Tracey L. 2003. 'Revisiting the creolist hypothesis: copula variability in Gullah and southern rural AAVE', *American Speech* 78.2: 171–91.

Wells, John C. 1980. 'The brogue that isn't', *Journal of the International Phonetic Association* 10: 74–9.

1982. *Accents of English*. 3 vols. Cambridge: Cambridge University Press.

Wełna, Jerzy 1978. *A Diachronic Grammar of English*, part 1: *Phonology*. Warsaw: Panstwowe Wydawnictwo Naukowe.

Weltens, Bert 1983. 'Non-standard periphrastic *do* in the dialects of south west Britain', *Lore and Language* 3.8: 56–64.

Widén, Bertil 1949. *Studies in the Dorset Dialect*. Lund: Lund University Press.

Wijk, Nicolaus van 1949 [1912]. *Franck's Etymologisch Woordenboek der Nederlandsche Taal* [Franck's etymological dictionary of the Dutch language]. The Hague: Nijhoff.

Willis, J. T. 2003. 'Integration or Segregation? The Irish in Middlesbrough in the 1850s and 1860s'. Unpublished MA thesis, Open University.

Winford, Donald 1997–8. 'On the origins of African American Vernacular English – a creolist perspective', *Diachronica* 14.2: 305–44; 15.1: 99–154.

2000. '"Intermediate" creoles and degrees of change in creole formation: the case of Bajan', in Neumann-Holzschuh and Schneider (eds.), pp. 215–45.

2003. *An Introduction to Contact Linguistics*. Oxford and Malden, MA: Blackwell.

2005. 'Contact-induced changes: classification and processes', *Diachronica* 22.2: 373–427.

Windsor-Lewis, Jack (ed.) 1995. *Studies in General and English Phonetics*. London: Routledge.

Wise, Claude Merton 1957. *Applied Phonetics*. Englewood Cliffs: Prentice-Hall.

Wolfram, Walt 1991. 'Towards a description of *a*-prefixing in Appalachian English', in Trudgill and Chambers (eds.), pp. 229–40.

Wolfram, Walt and Ralph W. Fasold 1974. *The Study of Social Dialects in American English*. Englewood Cliffs, NJ: Prentice-Hall.

Wolfram, Walt and Natalie Schilling-Estes 1997. *Hoi Toide on the Outer Banks: the Story of the Ocracoke Brogue*. Chapel Hill: University of North Carolina Press.

1998. *American English: Dialects and Variation*. Oxford: Blackwell.

Wood, Curtis and Tyler Blethen (eds.) 1997. *Ulster and North America: Transatlantic Perspectives on the Scotch-Irish*. Tuscaloosa, AL: University of Alabama Press.

Wood, Ian S. (ed.) 1994. *Scotland and Ulster*. Edinburgh: The Mercat Press.

Woodham-Smith, Cecil 1991 [1962]. *The Great Hunger*. London: Hamish Hamilton.

Wright, Joseph 1905. *English Dialect Dictionary*. Oxford: Henry Frowde.

1906. *The English Dialect Grammar*. Oxford: Henry Frowde.

Wright, Laura (ed.) 2000. *The Development of Standard English 1300–1800: Theories, Descriptions, Conflicts.* Cambridge: Cambridge University Press.

Wright, Susan 1997. '"Ah'm going for to give youse a story today": remarks on second person plural pronouns in Englishes', in Cheshire and Stein (eds.), pp. 170–84.

Wurff, Wim van der and Tony Foster 1997. 'Object-verb word order in 16th century English: a study of its frequency and status', in Hickey and Puppel (eds.), pp. 439–53.

Wyld, Henry Cecil 1956 [1936]. *A History of Modern Colloquial English.* 3rd edition. Oxford: Basil Blackwell.

Zettersten, Arne 1967. *The Virtues of Herbs in the Loscombe Manuscript: a Contribution to Anglo-Irish Language and Literature.* Lund: Gleerup.

Zwickl, Simone 2002. *Language Attitudes, Ethnic Identity and Dialect Use across the Northern Ireland Border: Armagh and Monaghan.* Belfast Studies in Language, Culture and Politics, 5. Belfast: Queen's University Press.

Subject index

African American English, 214, 276, 386, 401,
    405, 406, 411, 413
  Gullah, 406, 410, 413
  parallels with Irish English, 14, 77, 176, 177,
    182, 213, 228, 230, 405
Anglo-Celtic, 4, 414
Anglo-Irish, 3, 4, 305
Anglo-Norman, 31, 32, 33, 49, 50, 51, 58, 60,
    80, 86, 123, 130, 325, 345, 369

Basque, 408
Britain, the Irish in, 390
  1840s, 390
  contact with communities, 391
  Merseyside, 391; lenition, 392; range of
    lenition, 392; Middlesbrough, 393;
    nineteenth-century population, 393;
    comparison with Liverpool, 394;
    lenition, 394
  patterns of emigration, 390
  Scotland, 396
    Glasgow, 396; comparison with northern
      Irish English, 397; grammatical
      parallels with Irish English, 398
  Tyneside, 394
    comparison with Irish English,
      396
    double modals, 395
    for to-infinitives, 395
    NECTE corpus, 394
    relative clauses, 395
    second-person-plural forms, 394
    syntactic features, 394

Canadian English, 409, 417
  Canadian Raising, 329, 335, 409
  Newfoundland English, 355, 408

Celtic, 9
  Breton, 10, 432
  Cornish, 10, 97, 432
  Gaelic, 9, 11, 32, 41, 42
  P-Celtic, 10, 180, 431
  Q-Celtic, 10, 86, 290, 368, 384, 396, 432
  Scottish Gaelic (Gallick), 9, 10, 51, 86, 97,
    98, 114, 154, 205, 212, 244, 250, 265,
    276, 366, 369, 384, 396, 397, 398, 432
  Welsh, 10, 30, 31, 48, 97, 127, 160, 180, 380,
    432
Celtic Englishes, 5, 206

Dutch, 61, 69, 309, 317, 362

English
  Cockney, 23, 351, 360, 361, 389
  Estuary English, 360, 361
  Liverpool/Scouse, 23, 351, 392, 393, 434
  Middle English, 10, 49, 56, 57, 58, 59, 61, 62,
    63, 66, 69, 72, 73, 74, 75, 104, 105, 106,
    110, 116, 117, 129, 180, 186, 205, 227,
    299, 304, 316, 325, 341, 367
  Newcastle/Geordie, 23, 351
  Old English, 64, 65, 75, 81, 103, 104, 107,
    129, 133, 227, 255, 306, 367, 406
  Received Pronunciation, 119, 305, 342
  Shakespearean English, 110

Fingal dialect, 82
  extant texts, 83
  linguistic features, 84
Flemish, 30, 31, 48, 68, 69, 79
Forth and Bargy, 31, 52, 56, 66
  twentieth-century comments, 67
  comparison with *Kildare Poems*, 67, 71
  conservative character, 61, 71

Irish language (*cont.*)
  determiners, 153
  nouns, 153
  personal pronouns, 154
  stressed reflexives, 154
  prepositional area, 155
  sentence structure
    augmenting negatives, 159
    comparatives, 159
    embedded questions, 160
    negation, 158
    relativisation, 156
    responsives, 159
    subordination, 157
    topicalisation, 157
  verbal area, 147
    aspect, 148
    non-finite verb forms, 147
    passive, 151
    perfect and perfective, 149
    question tags, 152
    tense, 147
Irish English (early modern)
  printing in Ireland, 35
  Tudor period, 34
Irish society
  Catholics, 10, 11, 16, 19, 20, 26, 32, 33, 34,
    39, 42, 43, 45, 46, 89, 90, 92, 93, 100,
    112, 113, 115, 123, 310, 332, 338, 344,
    350, 391, 392, 398, 399, 400, 402, 404,
    409, 417
  middle class, 4, 9, 13, 21, 23, 26, 43, 113, 310,
    336, 344, 350, 369, 394
  Presbyterians, 11, 42, 92, 93, 434
  working class, 392
Irish traveller language, 379
  diaspora varieties, 383
  linguistic status, 381
  organisational principle, 382
  origins, 380
  relationship to Romani, 380
  research, 380
  selected lexical items, 383
  Shelta, 381, 434
    numbers of speakers, 381
  social position, 379
Italian, 402
  Tuscan, 322

Latin, 31, 50, 54, 60, 86, 266, 345, 346, 368,
    369, 433
Latvian, 377, 379

New Englishes, 128
Nigerian, 376, 377
  Yoruba, 377, 378

Ocracoke Brogue, 7, 431

Poles, 29, 377, 379
Polish, 377, 402

Russian, 102, 145, 377, 379

Scandinavian
  Old Norse, 7, 33, 51, 129, 130
Scottish English and Scots
  Lowland Scots, 97, 103, 107, 108, 109, 333,
    401, 434
  Scottish Standard English, 103
  Scottish Vowel Length Rule, 105, 397
Slavic, 192, 377, 378
Swedish, 102

Ulster English, 1, 2, 12, 77, 99, 105, 108, 132,
    143, 174, 231, 321, 333, 335, 337, 342,
    351, 390, 396, 397, 406
  Anglo-English, 6
  contact varieties, 5, 94
  denominational differences, 112
    recall in speech, 113
  general, 95, 110, 114, 122
  grammar, 119
    'quantifier floating', 119
  intonation, 118
  mid Ulster English, 6, 93
  north–south transition, 113
  phonology, 114
    consonants, 114
    vowels, 116
  relationship to other varieties of English,
    111
  shared features with southern Irish English,
    120
  south Ulster English, 93
  types of English in Ulster, 94
Ulster Scots, xiii,xix, 1, 2, 4, 6, 12, 15, 16, 23,
    38, 40, 43, 77, 92, 93, 94, 95, 96, 98, 111,
    122, 143, 165, 172, 181, 191, 196, 206,
    230, 233, 244, 250, 254, 279, 290, 291,
    305, 321, 328, 330, 333, 334, 337, 344,
    351, 370, 385, 387, 388, 395, 396, 397,
    399, 401, 403, 404, 406, 407, 431, 433
  'Cultural Zone', 103
  areas of settlement, 97

Name index

Lightning Source UK Ltd.
Milton Keynes UK
UKOW04f0853130315

247828UK00001B/66/P